Smart Technologies for Sustainable Urban and Regional Development

Smart Technologies for Sustainable Urban and Regional Development

Editors

Rashid Mehmood
Tan Yigitcanlar
Juan M. Corchado

 Basel • Beijing • Wuhan • Barcelona • Belgrade • Novi Sad • Cluj • Manchester

Editors

Rashid Mehmood
Faculty of Computer and
Information Systems
Islamic University of
Madinah
Madinah
Saudi Arabia

Tan Yigitcanlar
School of Architecture and
Built Environment
Queensland University of
Technology
Brisbane
Australia

Juan M. Corchado
BISITE Research Group
Universidad de Salamanca
Salamanca
Spain

Editorial Office
MDPI
St. Alban-Anlage 66
4052 Basel, Switzerland

This is a reprint of articles from the Special Issue published online in the open access journal *Sustainability* (ISSN 2071-1050) (available at: www.mdpi.com/journal/sustainability/special_issues/ Smart_Technologies_Sustainable_Urban_Regional_Development).

For citation purposes, cite each article independently as indicated on the article page online and as indicated below:

Lastname, A.A.; Lastname, B.B. Article Title. *Journal Name* **Year**, *Volume Number*, Page Range.

ISBN 978-3-7258-0352-1 (Hbk)
ISBN 978-3-7258-0351-4 (PDF)
doi.org/10.3390/books978-3-7258-0351-4

© 2024 by the authors. Articles in this book are Open Access and distributed under the Creative Commons Attribution (CC BY) license. The book as a whole is distributed by MDPI under the terms and conditions of the Creative Commons Attribution-NonCommercial-NoDerivs (CC BY-NC-ND) license.

Contents

About the Editors vii

Preface ix

Rashid Mehmood, Tan Yigitcanlar and Juan M. Corchado
Smart Technologies for Sustainable Urban and Regional Development
Reprinted from: *Sustainability* **2024**, *16*, 1171, doi:10.3390/su16031171 1

Hala Alshamlan, Ghala Alghofaili, Nourah ALFulayj, Shatha Aldawsari, Yara Alrubaiya and Reham Alabduljabbar
Promoting Sustainable Travel Experiences: A Weighted Parallel Hybrid Approach for Personalized Tourism Recommendations and Enhanced User Satisfaction
Reprinted from: *Sustainability* **2023**, *15*, 14447, doi:10.3390/su151914447 9

Lolwah Binsaedan, Habib M. Alshuwaikhat and Yusuf A. Aina
Developing an Urban Computing Framework for Smart and Sustainable Neighborhoods: A Case Study of Alkhaledia in Jizan City, Saudi Arabia
Reprinted from: *Sustainability* **2023**, *15*, 4057, doi:10.3390/su15054057 28

Fanding Xiang, Haomiao Cheng and Yi Wang
Exploring the Smart Street Management and Control Platform from the Perspective of Sustainability: A Study of Five Typical Chinese Cities
Reprinted from: *Sustainability* **2023**, *15*, 3438, doi:10.3390/su15043438 46

Leon Goldsmith, Abdul Khalique Shaikh, Hacer Yildiz Tan and Kaamran Raahemifar
A Review of Contemporary Governance Challenges in Oman: Can Blockchain Technology Be Part of Sustainable Solutions?
Reprinted from: *Sustainability* **2022**, *14*, 11819, doi:10.3390/su141911819 61

Tao Li, Junlin Zhu, Jianqiang Luo, Chaonan Yi and Baoqing Zhu
Breaking Triopoly to Achieve Sustainable Smart Digital Infrastructure Based on Open-Source Diffusion Using Government–Platform–User Evolutionary Game
Reprinted from: *Sustainability* **2023**, *15*, 14412, doi:10.3390/su151914412 82

Fahimeh Golbabaei, Tan Yigitcanlar, Alexander Paz and Jonathan Bunker
Perceived Opportunities and Challenges of Autonomous Demand-Responsive Transit Use: What Are the Socio-Demographic Predictors?
Reprinted from: *Sustainability* **2023**, *15*, 11839, doi:10.3390/su151511839 106

Hloniphani Maluleke, Antoine Bagula, Olasupo Ajayi and Luca Chiaraviglio
An Economic Feasibility Model for Sustainable 5G Networks in Rural Dwellings of South Africa
Reprinted from: *Sustainability* **2022**, *14*, 12153, doi:10.3390/su141912153 124

Abood Khaled Alamoudi, Rotimi Boluwatife Abidoye and Terence Y. M. Lam
Implementing Smart Sustainable Cities in Saudi Arabia: A Framework for Citizens' Participation towards SAUDI VISION 2030
Reprinted from: *Sustainability* **2023**, *15*, 6648, doi:10.3390/su15086648 148

Anne David, Tan Yigitcanlar, Rita Yi Man Li, Juan M. Corchado, Pauline Hope Cheong, Karen Mossberger and Rashid Mehmood
Understanding Local Government Digital Technology Adoption Strategies: A PRISMA Review
Reprinted from: *Sustainability* **2023**, *15*, 9645, doi:10.3390/su15129645 169

Aleksandra Kuzior, Dariusz Krawczyk, Kateryna Onopriienko, Yuriy Petrushenko, Iryna Onopriienko and Volodymyr Onopriienko
Lifelong Learning as a Factor in the Country's Competitiveness and Innovative Potential within the Framework of Sustainable Development
Reprinted from: *Sustainability* **2023**, *15*, 9968, doi:10.3390/su15139968 . . . . **211**

Rui Ding, Jun Fu, Yiling Zhang, Ting Zhang, Jian Yin, Yiming Du, et al.
Research on the Evolution of the Economic Spatial Pattern of Urban Agglomeration and Its Influencing Factors, Evidence from the Chengdu-Chongqing Urban Agglomeration of China
Reprinted from: *Sustainability* **2022**, *14*, 10969, doi:10.3390/su141710969 . . . . **223**

Viet-Cuong Trieu and Fu-Ren Lin
The Development of a Service System for Facilitating Food Resource Allocation and Service Exchange
Reprinted from: *Sustainability* **2022**, *14*, 11987, doi:10.3390/su141911987 . . . . **242**

Jason Hung
Smart Elderly Care Services in China: Challenges, Progress, and Policy Development
Reprinted from: *Sustainability* **2023**, *15*, 178, doi:10.3390/su15010178 . . . . **271**

About the Editors

Rashid Mehmood

Rashid Mehmood is a Professor of Big Data Systems at the Faculty of Computer and Information Systems and the Director of the Centre for Technology Governance at the Islamic University of Madinah, Saudi Arabia. He has obtained qualifications and work experience from a number of universities in the UK, including Cambridge and Oxford University. Rashid has 28 years of experience in computational modeling, simulations, and design using artificial intelligence, big data, high-performance computing, and distributed systems. His broad research goal is to develop multi-disciplinary science and technology to enhance the quality of life and foster a smart economy, with a focus on real-time intelligence and autonomous system management. He has authored over 200 research papers, including nine edited books, and has organized and chaired international conferences and workshops in areas including computer networks, vehicular communication, healthcare, transportation, smart cities and societies, high performance computing, distributed systems, and artificial intelligence. Rashid has led and contributed to academia-industry collaborative projects funded by EPSRC, the EU, UK regional funds, the Technology Strategy Board UK, and KSA, with a total value exceeding GBP 50 million. He is a founding member of the Future Cities and Community Resilience (FCCR) Network, a member of ACM, OSA, Senior Member IEEE, and a former Vice-Chairman of the IET Wales SW Network.

Tan Yigitcanlar

Tan Yigitcanlar is an eminent Australian researcher with international recognition and impact in the field of urban studies and planning. He is a professor of Urban Studies and Planning at the School of Architecture and Built Environment, Queensland University of Technology, Brisbane, Australia. Along with this post, he carries out the following positions: Honorary Professor at the School of Technology, Federal University of Santa Catarina, Florianopolis, Brazil; Director of the Australia–Brazil Smart City Research and Practice Network; Lead of the QUT Smart City Research Group; and Co-Director of the QUT City 4.0 Lab. He is a member of the Australian Research Council's College of Experts.

Juan M. Corchado

Juan Manuel Corchado (15 May 1971, Salamanca, Spain) is a professor at the University of Salamanca, Director of the BISITE Research Group (Bioinformatics, Intelligent Systems, and Educational Technology), and President of the AIR Institute. He is also the director of the IoT Digital Innovation Hub, president of the AIR Institute, and principal investigator of the project funded by DIGIS3 (the Digital Innovation Hub of Castilla y León). He is also a visiting professor at the Osaka Institute of Technology and a visiting professor at Universiti Malaysia Kelantan.

Juan M. Corchado has been Vice-Rector for Research from 2013 to 2017 and Director of the Science Park of the University of Salamanca. He was elected twice as Dean of the Faculty of Science, and his research activities are significantly focused on the application of artificial intelligence (AI) and the Internet of Things (IoT) towards the development of sustainable, intelligent cities.

Preface

This reprint unfolds an essential dialogue on the transformative power of smart technologies in shaping our urban futures. It is a narrative that threads together the United Nations' Sustainable Development Goals with ground-breaking research, a narrative that weaves the urgency for sustainability into the fabric of urban living.

As you navigate through these chapters, you will encounter the pioneering work of dedicated researchers whose studies serve as beacons, guiding us through the complexities of modern cities. From the utilization of big data and AI to the intricacies of citizen engagement and participatory governance, each chapter contributes a critical piece to the puzzle of sustainable development. The diversity of approaches and depth of analysis presented here are testaments to the vibrant scholarly community's commitment to advancing our urban environments.

In drafting this preface, we recognize the collective endeavor that has brought this reprint to fruition—the insightful contributions of the authors, the meticulous evaluations of the peer reviewers, and the support from the MDPI *Sustainability* team, particularly Crystal Cheng. Together, they have curated a compendium that not only reflects the state of the art but also charts a course for future innovations.

This reprint is intended for a broad audience, ranging from academic researchers and students to urban planners, policymakers, and community leaders. It aims to inspire, inform, and instigate change, fostering a global dialogue on how smart technologies can be harmonized with sustainable practices to create resilient, liveable, and equitable urban spaces.

As we turn towards the challenges and opportunities that lie ahead, this preface serves as an invitation to explore, to question, and to act. It is a prelude to the indispensable conversations and actions needed to ensure that our shared urban future is not only smart but sustainable, inclusive, and thriving for all.

Welcome to a journey of discovery and transformation. Welcome to the future of our cities.

Rashid Mehmood, Tan Yigitcanlar, and Juan M. Corchado
Editors

Editorial

Smart Technologies for Sustainable Urban and Regional Development

Rashid Mehmood [1,*], Tan Yigitcanlar [2,3] and Juan M. Corchado [4,5,6]

1. Faculty of Computer and Information Systems, Islamic University of Madinah, Madinah 42351, Saudi Arabia
2. School of Architecture and Built Environment, Queensland University of Technology, 2 George Street, Brisbane, QLD 4000, Australia; tan.yigitcanlar@qut.edu.au
3. School of Technology, Federal University of Santa Catarina, Campus Universitario, Trindade, Florianópolis 88040-900, SC, Brazil
4. BISITE Research Group, University of Salamanca, 37007 Salamanca, Spain; corchado@usal.es
5. Air Institute, IoT Digital Innovation Hub, 37188 Salamanca, Spain
6. Department of Electronics, Information and Communication, Faculty of Engineering, Osaka Institute of Technology, Osaka 535-8585, Japan
* Correspondence: r.mehmood@gmail.com

Citation: Mehmood, R.; Yigitcanlar, T.; Corchado, J.M. Smart Technologies for Sustainable Urban and Regional Development. *Sustainability* **2024**, *16*, 1171. https://doi.org/10.3390/su16031171

Received: 23 January 2024
Accepted: 25 January 2024
Published: 30 January 2024

Copyright: © 2024 by the authors. Licensee MDPI, Basel, Switzerland. This article is an open access article distributed under the terms and conditions of the Creative Commons Attribution (CC BY) license (https://creativecommons.org/licenses/by/4.0/).

1. Introduction

In the dynamic landscape of contemporary living spaces, cities, and societies, the call for sustainable urban and regional development resonates with increasing urgency. This Special Issue addresses this urgency head-on. It is dedicated to exploring the multifaceted challenges and burgeoning opportunities in the domain of sustainable development, leveraging the immense potential of advanced technologies.

As the complexities of our urban and societal environments escalate, manifesting in various forms such as natural pandemics, disasters, civil unrest, and economic disparities, this Special Issue aims to provide a critical platform for discourse and innovation. Anchored by the United Nations' Sustainable Development Goals (SDGs), this Special Issue underscores the imperative for urgent, comprehensive, and collaborative action towards achieving the triple bottom line of sustainability—encompassing social, environmental, and economic dimensions. This Special Issue transcends the conventional boundaries of technological exploration. It explores the strategic application of a plethora of advanced technologies—from the miniaturization and digitization of sensors and actuators to AI and big data-driven insights and optimizations; digital twins; and cloud, fog, and edge computing. These technological advancements are not merely tools for efficiency but are envisioned as catalysts for sustainable urban futures, guided by ethical, responsible, and long-term sustainable practices [1–3].

Bringing together a diverse range of research articles and literature reviews, this Special Issue serves as a melting pot of ideas and innovations. It fosters a much-needed dialogue among various communities engaged in policy and infrastructure research, aiming to understand the interplay of cross-disciplinary issues and collaboratively forge holistic, sustainable, and globally optimized solutions. As we navigate through the pages of this Special Issue, we the Guest Editors invite our readers to immerse themselves in the rich tapestry of insights and perspectives. Each contribution is a piece of the puzzle in understanding and shaping sustainable urban and regional development in our intricately connected and rapidly evolving world. Within this editorial, the 13 published papers are primarily organized into five themes for simplicity and clarity, though it is important to note that many of these papers intersect with multiple themes.

Figure 1 depicts the top keywords from the articles published in this Special Issue. The word cloud visually encapsulates the thematic essence of the Special Issue. Dominant terms like "urban", "smart", "technology", "sustainable", and "development" affirm the centrality of innovative, tech-driven approaches relative to urban and regional development. Supporting keywords such as "economic", "digital", "system", "data", and "policy" reflect the multifaceted discourse spanning economic considerations, digital infrastructures, systematic planning, data utilization, and policy making. The inclusion of "citizens", "public", "education", and "environmental" underscores a commitment to inclusivity, educational outreach, and environmental stewardship. This graphic synthesis illustrates the interconnectivity of concepts that are pivotal to advancing sustainable urban futures.

Figure 1. Word cloud depicting the top keywords from the articles published in this Special Issue.

Next, we discuss each of these themes, exploring how they collectively and individually contribute to the broader narrative of sustainable urban and regional development.

1.1. Technological Innovation for Sustainable Urban Development

This theme explores how technological innovation, particularly in the realms of AI, IoT, big data analytics, and blockchain, serves as a cornerstone for sustainable urban development. It encompasses the development and application of advanced technologies to create smarter, more efficient, and sustainable urban environments. Alshamlan et al. (Contribution 1) introduce a novel weighted parallel hybrid recommendation system to enhance the tourism experience. By providing personalized travel recommendations, it addresses the limitations of existing tourism mobile applications. This system signifies the application of AI and data analytics in improving user experiences in urban tourism, showcasing how technology can personalize and elevate sustainable urban interactions. Binsaedan et al. (Contribution 6) explore the development of an urban computing framework for smart neighbourhoods in Jizan City, Saudi Arabia. Their work underscores the pivotal role of digital technologies in urban development. This study aligns with the theme by showcasing how urban computing can improve quality of life, environmental protection, and economic growth in urban neighbourhoods.

Xiang et al. (Contribution 7) focus their research on the application of smart technologies in street renewal, emphasizing sustainable urban development in China. They investigate smart street management and control in five Chinese cities, categorizing applications into areas such as smart transportation and environmental monitoring. This study exemplifies the integration of IoT and smart technologies in urban planning, enhancing the sustainability of street spaces. Goldsmith et al. (Contribution 13) investigate the potential of blockchain technology in addressing governance challenges in Oman. Their paper examines how blockchain can enhance, supplement, or reform existing governance systems. This exploration emphasizes the role of technological innovation in facilitating more transparent, efficient, and accountable governance in urban settings, showcasing its potential impact on modern urban development.

Each of these contributions underscores the vital role of technological innovation in shaping sustainable urban environments. They reflect the diverse applications of advanced technologies, from enhancing tourism experiences to improving street management and governance systems. These studies collectively illustrate the transformative impact of technology on urban sustainability.

Future research in the realm of technological innovation for sustainable urban development, drawing upon the studies of Alshamlan et al. (Contribution 1), Xiang et al. (Contribution 7), Goldsmith et al. (Contribution 13), and Binsaedan et al. (Contribution 6) could focus on expanding the scope and scalability of urban computing applications. This involves exploring sophisticated AI and IoT integrations for diverse city functions, from traffic and environmental management to public safety and utility services. The potential of blockchain technology, as investigated by Goldsmith et al., can be extended to broader urban contexts, providing efficient, transparent, and secure solutions for urban governance and service delivery. Future studies should also emphasize user-centric design in urban technology innovations, ensuring solutions are tailored to the diverse needs and preferences of urban populations. Additionally, there is a significant opportunity for interdisciplinary research that merges urban planning, information technology, and social sciences, aiming to develop holistic and sustainable urban solutions. This comprehensive approach will contribute to the advancement of smart urban environments, aligning technological sophistication with social welfare and environmental sustainability. Moreover, the insights from Binsaedan et al.'s urban computing framework (Contribution 6) highlight the importance of incorporating digital infrastructure in a way that enhances the quality of life and economic growth in urban neighbourhoods. By focusing on these areas, future research can ensure that technological advancements in urban development are not only innovative but also inclusive, adaptable, and aligned with the broader goals of sustainable urban living.

1.2. Smart and Sustainable Mobility and Infrastructure

This theme focuses on the advancements and challenges in developing smart, sustainable mobility solutions and infrastructure. It encompasses the use of innovative technologies to enhance transportation systems, improve digital infrastructure, and ensure efficient, eco-friendly urban mobility. Li et al. (Contribution 2) discuss the impact of open-source platforms in challenging the digital infrastructure triopoly of major operating systems. It emphasizes the role of government incentives and stakeholder collaboration in fostering sustainable, open-source digital ecosystems, highlighting a shift towards more equitable and accessible digital infrastructures. Golbabaei et al. (Contribution 3) explore the socio-demographic factors influencing perceptions and attitudes towards autonomous demand-responsive transit (ADRT), particularly autonomous shuttle buses. This study aligns with sustainable mobility, examining how various social groups perceive and interact with emerging transportation technologies. Maluleke et al. (Contribution 8) focus on the economic feasibility of deploying 5G networks in rural South Africa and contribute to the infrastructure aspect of sustainable mobility. They examine the integration of terrestrial and aerial networks for 5G coverage, addressing the digital divide and enhancing connectivity in rural areas. This research is pivotal in understanding how advanced telecommunication networks can support sustainable development in less urbanized regions.

Future research in the realm of smart and sustainable mobility and infrastructure, drawing from the works of Li et al. (Contribution 2), Golbabaei et al. (Contribution 3), and Maluleke et al. (Contribution 8), could explore the seamless integration of autonomous transportation systems into existing urban fabrics, emphasizing both efficiency and public acceptance. Investigating the expansion of advanced telecommunication networks, such as 6G, is crucial for supporting smarter infrastructure across diverse landscapes, from bustling urban centres to rural areas. Future studies should also focus on ensuring equitable access to digital resources, a challenge highlighted by Li et al., to bridge the digital divide and foster inclusive urban development. Additionally, the environmental impact of new mobility solutions, particularly their role in promoting green transportation and reducing urban carbon footprints, is a pertinent area for exploration. This comprehensive approach, encompassing technological, social, and environmental aspects, is key to advancing sustainable urban mobility and infrastructure.

1.3. Citizen Engagement and Participatory Governance

This theme emphasizes the importance of involving citizens in the governance and development of sustainable urban environments. It explores how participatory approaches and digital governance can enhance decision-making processes, ensuring that urban development aligns with the needs and aspirations of the community. Alamoudi et al. (Contribution 5) present a framework for citizen participation in the development of smart sustainable cities in Saudi Arabia. They underscore the significance of engaging citizens in urban planning and decision-making processes, highlighting the crucial role of human involvement alongside technological advancements in creating equitable and sustainable urban environments. David et al. (Contribution 11) focus on the adoption strategies of digital technologies by local governments and investigate the challenges and opportunities of digital governance. They stress the need for a balanced approach that includes public participation, skill development among employees, and a clear understanding of the technology's impact, advocating for a more inclusive and transparent governance model.

Building on the insights from Alamoudi et al. (Contribution 5) and David et al. (Contribution 11), future research on this theme could explore the development of more interactive and user-friendly digital platforms for civic engagement, enhancing the accessibility and inclusivity of governance processes. Studies could also investigate the impact of digital governance tools on enhancing transparency and accountability in urban management, drawing from the advancements in digital technologies discussed by David et al. Investigating strategies for effectively integrating citizen feedback into urban planning and policy making, as suggested by Alamoudi et al., is another critical area for future research. This approach should focus on understanding the diverse needs of urban populations, ensuring that governance models are adaptable and responsive to the changing dynamics of urban societies. Additionally, the exploration of novel participatory models that leverage emerging technologies like blockchain, as mentioned by Goldsmith et al. (Contribution 13), could further enhance the efficacy and trustworthiness of participatory governance systems.

1.4. Socio-Economic Aspects of Sustainability

This theme reveals the socio-economic dimensions of sustainability, showing how urban development initiatives impact and are influenced by social and economic factors. It encompasses studies on education, healthcare, quality of life, and economic patterns and how these elements interplay with sustainable development goals. Golbabaei et al. (Contribution 3) investigate the socio-demographic predictors influencing public perception and attitudes towards autonomous demand-responsive transit use. Their research offers critical insights into how different societal segments respond to new transportation technologies. This study underscores the necessity of addressing diverse societal needs and perspectives in urban development initiatives, emphasizing the importance of inclusivity in the evolution of urban transportation. Kuzior et al. (Contribution 4) investigate the relationship between adult education and a country's economic competitiveness and innovative potential, highlighting the significant role of lifelong learning in sustainable development. Their study reveals the profound socio-economic impact of education on national progress, drawing attention to the crucial interplay between educational initiatives and a nation's developmental trajectory. Ding et al. (Contribution 10) offer an analysis of the economic spatial patterns within the Chengdu–Chongqing urban agglomeration, focusing on the factors that influence economic development in these urban clusters. Their study sheds light on the uneven spatial distribution of economic development and underscores the importance of policy interventions that aim to address regional disparities. This research provides essential insights into achieving balanced economic growth, highlighting a key aspect of sustainable urban development.

Future research in this area, inspired by the works of Golbabaei et al. (Contribution 3), Kuzior et al. (Contribution 4), and Ding et al. (Contribution 10), could further investigate the intricate relationship between urban development and socio-economic factors. Studies could explore more comprehensive strategies to integrate education, particularly lifelong learning, into urban development policies to foster economic growth and innovation, as discussed by Kuzior et al. Research could also explore the social implications of emerging urban technologies, assessing their accessibility and impact across different demographic groups, building on the insights provided by Golbabaei et al. Additionally, there is a need to examine the economic disparities within urban regions, as highlighted by Ding et al., to develop more equitable and inclusive urban development strategies. This future work should aim to create a sustainable urban environment that not only advances technologically but also nurtures social well-being and economic equity.

1.5. Green AI and Sustainable Systems

This theme addresses the intersection of artificial intelligence, sustainability, and environmental consciousness. It focuses on how green AI and other sustainable technologies can be used to create systems that are not only efficient and innovative but also responsible and ecologically sound. This theme explores the development and application of technologies that prioritize long-term sustainability over short-term gains, aligning with the broader goals of sustainable urban futures.

Trieu and Lin (Contribution 9) present an important study on developing a service system for optimizing food resource allocation and service exchange, employing multi-agent systems and AI. Their work showcases the potential of advanced technology in enhancing the sustainability and efficiency of food networks. This research is a notable example of how technology can be adeptly used to bridge urban–rural sustainability gaps, offering innovative solutions to complex logistical challenges. Hung's paper (Contribution 12) offers an insightful exploration of smart elderly care services in China, addressing both the challenges and advancements in this evolving field. The integration of smart technologies in elderly care is a testament to a broader commitment to improving the quality of life for the aging population, while simultaneously promoting sustainability within healthcare systems. This study highlights the vital role of technology in transforming healthcare services to meet the needs of an aging urban society.

Future research, drawing from the findings of Trieu and Lin (Contribution 9) and Hung (Contribution 12), could explore the development of AI-driven systems that prioritize ecological and social sustainability. This includes advancing AI technologies in urban agriculture and food systems, optimizing resource use, and reducing waste. Research should also focus on creating smart healthcare systems that are not only technologically advanced but also sustainable and accessible to all segments of society, as highlighted in Hung's study. Additionally, there is scope for investigating how green AI can be integrated into various urban systems, such as waste management and energy consumption, to promote sustainable living practices. This research direction would align with the overarching goal of developing urban environments that are technologically advanced, socially inclusive, and environmentally responsible.

2. Discussion

The array of contributions in this Special Issue not only illuminates the multifaceted nature of sustainable urban and regional development but also weaves a narrative that underscores the critical interplay between technology and sustainability. As we navigate through the insights offered by each paper, a mosaic of innovative approaches and thought-provoking perspectives emerges, collectively advancing our understanding of smart technologies in the urban and regional context.

Notably, the thematic categorization of the contributions reveals an intricate tapestry of research directions. From the detailed exploration of technological innovation for urban development, as observed in the works of Alshamlan et al. (Contribution 1) and Binsaedan et al. (Contribution 6), to the profound considerations of socio-economic aspects of sustainability, highlighted by Golbabaei et al. (Contribution 3) and Kuzior et al. (Contribution 4), each theme contributes a unique hue to our understanding of sustainable development.

A critical observation across these themes is the harmonious balance between technological advancements and the human element—be it through citizen engagement, as emphasized by Alamoudi et al. (Contribution 5), or the socio-economic implications underscored by Ding et al. (Contribution 10). This balance is pivotal, ensuring that while we march forward with technological prowess, we remain grounded in the realities and subtleties of human experiences and societal needs. Furthermore, the contributions collectively underscore the importance of adaptable and resilient systems, as delineated in the discussions on green AI and sustainable systems. The innovative approaches of Trieu and Lin (Contribution 9) and Hung (Contribution 12) not only advocate for technological efficiency but also stress the need for sustainability and ethical consideration in our pursuit of urban development.

The findings and insights presented in this Special Issue have significant implications for practice and policy in the realm of sustainable urban and regional development. They highlight the integration of urban computing and AI in improving urban planning and management efficiency and the transformative role of blockchain in enhancing governance transparency. The emphasis on citizen engagement and inclusive governance underlines the importance of participatory urban development. Additionally, the focus on green AI and sustainable systems emphasizes the need to balance technological advancements with environmental sustainability. This compendium serves as a crucial guide for stakeholders in fostering innovative and sustainable urban development.

This Special Issue acknowledges the challenges and limitations in current research, offering a realistic perspective for future development. Key challenges include integrating advanced technologies like AI and IoT into urban infrastructures, revealing a gap between theoretical models and real-world applications. The scope of research also faces limitations in addressing diverse socio-economic and cultural contexts, underscoring the need for more comprehensive studies. Additionally, issues with data availability and scalability of solutions highlight the need for research that is universally applicable. Future work should focus on collaborative, interdisciplinary research, developing adaptable solutions, and bridging the gap between innovation and practical implementation. These efforts are crucial for evolving the field and creating more robust, inclusive urban solutions.

As we synthesize the insights from this Special Issue, it becomes evident that the journey towards sustainable urban and regional development is not linear but a multifaceted endeavour. It demands a collaborative approach, integrating diverse perspectives and expertise and a willingness to adapt and evolve with the changing dynamics of our urban landscapes.

3. Conclusions

As we draw to a close on this Special Issue, it is clear that the journey towards sustainable urban and regional development is multifaceted and continuously evolving. The diverse array of research presented here not only contributes to a deeper understanding of smart technologies in urban settings but also highlights the importance of integrating these technologies with social, economic, and environmental considerations.

The contributions in this Special Issue, from the implementation of innovative urban computing frameworks to the exploration of green AI and sustainable systems, collectively paint a picture of a future where technology and sustainability go hand in hand. However, as we have seen, this journey is not without its challenges. The limitations and obstacles faced by researchers remind us of the complex reality of urban development and the need for adaptable, inclusive solutions.

Looking ahead, the consolidated future work directions offer a roadmap for addressing these challenges. Building upon the insights and findings from this Special Issue, future research can explore sophisticated AI and IoT integrations for diverse city functions, expand the application of blockchain technology in urban governance, and emphasize user-centric design in technological innovations. It should also aim to develop holistic solutions that balance technological advancement with ethical, social, and environmental considerations.

Finally, this Special Issue stands as a beacon, guiding us towards innovative, sustainable, and globally optimized solutions for urban and regional development. The path forward calls for collaboration, adaptability, and a commitment to not just envision but actively construct sustainable cities and regions of the future.

Conflicts of Interest: The authors declare no conflicts of interest.

List of Contributions:

1. Alshamlan, H.; Alghofaili, G.; ALFulayj, N.; Aldawsari, S.; Alrubaiya, Y.; Alabduljabbar, R. Promoting Sustainable Travel Experiences: A Weighted Parallel Hybrid Approach for Personalized Tourism Recommendations and Enhanced User Satisfaction. *Sustainability* **2023**, *15*, 14447. https://doi.org/10.3390/su151914447.
2. Li, T.; Zhu, J.; Luo, J.; Yi, C.; Zhu, B. Breaking Triopoly to Achieve Sustainable Smart Digital Infrastructure Based on Open-Source Diffusion Using Government-Platform-User Evolutionary Game. *Sustainability* **2023**, *15*, 14412. https://doi.org/10.3390/su151914412.
3. Golbabaei, F.; Yigitcanlar, T.; Paz, A.; Bunker, J. Perceived Opportunities and Challenges of Autonomous Demand-Responsive Transit Use: What Are the Socio-Demographic Predictors? *Sustainability* **2023**, *15*, 11839. https://doi.org/10.3390/su151511839.
4. Kuzior, A.; Krawczyk, D.; Onopriienko, K.; Petrushenko, Y.; Onopriienko, I.; Onopriienko, V. Lifelong Learning as a Factor in the Country's Competitiveness and Innovative Potential within the Framework of Sustainable Development. *Sustainability* **2023**, *15*, 9968. https://doi.org/10.3390/su15139968.
5. Alamoudi, A.; Abidoye, R.; Lam, T. Implementing Smart Sustainable Cities in Saudi Arabia: A Framework for Citizens' Participation towards SAUDI VISION 2030. *Sustainability* **2023**, *15*, 6648. https://doi.org/10.3390/su15086648.
6. Binsaedan, L.; Alshuwaikhat, H.; Aina, Y. Developing an Urban Computing Framework for Smart and Sustainable Neighborhoods: A Case Study of Alkhaledia in Jizan City, Saudi Arabia. *Sustainability* **2023**, *15*, 4057. https://doi.org/10.3390/su15054057.
7. Xiang, F.; Cheng, H.; Wang, Y. Exploring the Smart Street Management and Control Platform from the Perspective of Sustainability: A Study of Five Typical Chinese Cities. *Sustainability* **2023**, *15*, 3438. https://doi.org/10.3390/su15043438.
8. Maluleke, H.; Bagula, A.; Ajayi, O.; Chiaraviglio, L. An Economic Feasibility Model for Sustainable 5G Networks in Rural Dwellings of South Africa. *Sustainability* **2022**, *14*, 12153. https://doi.org/10.3390/su141912153.
9. Trieu, V.; Lin, F. The Development of a Service System for Facilitating Food Resource Allocation and Service Exchange. *Sustainability* **2022**, *14*, 11987. https://doi.org/10.3390/su141911987.
10. Ding, R.; Fu, J.; Zhang, Y.; Zhang, T.; Yin, J.; Du, Y.; Zhou, T.; Du, L. Research on the Evolution of the Economic Spatial Pattern of Urban Agglomeration and Its Influencing Factors, Evidence from the Chengdu-Chongqing Urban Agglomeration of China. *Sustainability* **2022**, *14*, 10969. https://doi.org/10.3390/su141710969.
11. David, A.; Yigitcanlar, T.; Li, R.; Corchado, J.; Cheong, P.; Mossberger, K.; Mehmood, R. Understanding Local Government Digital Technology Adoption Strategies: A PRISMA Review. *Sustainability* **2023**, *15*, 9645. https://doi.org/10.3390/su15129645.
12. Hung, J. Smart Elderly Care Services in China: Challenges, Progress, and Policy Development. *Sustainability* **2023**, *15*, 178. https://doi.org/10.3390/su15010178.
13. Goldsmith, L.; Shaikh, A.; Tan, H.; Raahemifar, K. A Review of Contemporary Governance Challenges in Oman: Can Blockchain Technology Be Part of Sustainable Solutions? *Sustainability* **2022**, *14*, 11819. https://doi.org/10.3390/su141911819.

References

1. Alotaibi, S.; Mehmood, R.; Katib, I.; Rana, O.; Albeshri, A. Sehaa: A Big Data Analytics Tool for Healthcare Symptoms and Diseases Detection Using Twitter, Apache Spark, and Machine Learning. *Appl. Sci.* **2020**, *10*, 1398. [CrossRef]
2. Yigitcanlar, T.; Mehmood, R.; Corchado, J.M. Green Artificial Intelligence: Towards an Efficient, Sustainable and Equitable Technology for Smart Cities and Futures. *Sustainability* **2021**, *13*, 8952. [CrossRef]
3. Schwartz, R.; Dodge, J.; Smith, N.A.; Etzioni, O. Green AI. *Commun. ACM* **2020**, *63*, 54–63. [CrossRef]

Disclaimer/Publisher's Note: The statements, opinions and data contained in all publications are solely those of the individual author(s) and contributor(s) and not of MDPI and/or the editor(s). MDPI and/or the editor(s) disclaim responsibility for any injury to people or property resulting from any ideas, methods, instructions or products referred to in the content.

Article

Promoting Sustainable Travel Experiences: A Weighted Parallel Hybrid Approach for Personalized Tourism Recommendations and Enhanced User Satisfaction

Hala Alshamlan *, Ghala Alghofaili, Nourah ALFulayj, Shatha Aldawsari, Yara Alrubaiya and Reham Alabduljabbar

Department of Information Technology, College of Computer and Information Sciences, King Saud University, P.O. Box 145111, Riyadh 4545, Saudi Arabia; ghalakg.x@gmail.com (G.A.); nourahalfulaij8@gmail.com (N.A.); shathaaldawsari01@gmail.com (S.A.); yaraalrubaiya@gmail.com (Y.A.); rabduljabbar@ksu.edu.sa (R.A.)
* Correspondence: halshamlan@ksu.edu.sa

Citation: Alshamlan, H.; Alghofaili, G.; ALFulayj, N.; Aldawsari, S.; Alrubaiya, Y.; Alabduljabbar, R. Promoting Sustainable Travel Experiences: A Weighted Parallel Hybrid Approach for Personalized Tourism Recommendations and Enhanced User Satisfaction. *Sustainability* **2023**, *15*, 14447. https://doi.org/10.3390/su151914447

Academic Editors: Rashid Mehmood, Tan Yigitcanlar and Juan M. Corchado

Received: 5 September 2023
Revised: 29 September 2023
Accepted: 30 September 2023
Published: 3 October 2023

Copyright: © 2023 by the authors. Licensee MDPI, Basel, Switzerland. This article is an open access article distributed under the terms and conditions of the Creative Commons Attribution (CC BY) license (https://creativecommons.org/licenses/by/4.0/).

Abstract: With the growing significance of the tourism industry and the increasing desire among travelers to discover new destinations, there is a need for effective recommender systems that cater to individual interests. Existing tourism mobile applications incorporate recommendation systems to alleviate information overload. However, these systems often overlook the varying importance of different items, resulting in suboptimal recommendations. In this research paper, a novel approach is proposed: a weighted parallel hybrid recommendation system. By considering item weights and leveraging parallel processing techniques, this method significantly enhances the accuracy of the similarity between items, leading to improved recommendation quality and precision. With this approach, users can efficiently and effectively explore new destinations that align with their unique preferences and interests, thereby enhancing their overall tourism experience and satisfaction. To evaluate the effectiveness of the proposed weighted parallel hybrid recommendation system, we conducted experiments using a dataset consisting of 20 users. The results demonstrated that the proposed approach achieved an impressive classification accuracy of 80%. A comparative analysis revealed that the proposed approach outperformed that of existing systems and achieved the best results in terms of classification accuracy. This finding highlights the effectiveness and efficiency of the proposed method in generating and promoting sustainable travel experiences by developing a personalized recommendations system for the unique preferences and interests of individual users.

Keywords: social recommender system; mobile application; recommendation system; weighted similarity; cosine similarity; travelers; place reviews; agent-based model; tourism recommendation allocation

1. Introduction

A social network recommender system can provide personalized recommendations, based on a user's preferences, past travel experiences, and behavior, within the application. This can help travelers discover new destinations and activities that match their interests. The main focus of this study is to improve the effectiveness of hybrid recommender systems in the tourism industry by incorporating weights with cosine similarity. The motivation for developing such systems stems from the fact that planning a trip can substantially boost one's happiness. However, many travelers face the challenge of deciding where to go and may miss out on new places that match their preferences [1]. To address this issue, this study aims to improve the current methods of obtaining travel recommendations. In this study, a new method that utilizes a weighted parallel hybrid recommendation system is proposed. This approach improves the accuracy of the similarity between items and enhances the recommendation quality by exploiting the differences between items. In comparison to existing methods, the proposed approach provides more efficient and accurate results for a recommender system. Typically, travelers rely on friends, family, celebrities, or social media to find destinations. However, these sources have limitations, and it would be beneficial to have a social network mobile application that allows travelers to share their experiences with others.

The proposed method offers various features that enhance user experience, including the ability to access detailed posts and recommendations from other users, share personal experiences, and easily create trip lists. To facilitate list creation, the proposed method incorporates a hybrid recommender system that combines content-based and collaborative filtering techniques. This system suggests lists created by other users based on similarities in their profiles and behavioral patterns within the application.

The tremendous growth in digital information and Internet users has led to the problem of information overload, impeding users' ability to efficiently find relevant content. While search engines like Google have partially addressed this issue, prioritizing, and personalizing available information based on user interests and preferences remains a challenge. Consequently, the demand for recommender systems has surged. Recommender systems aim to alleviate information overload by filtering essential information from vast amounts of dynamically generated data, considering user preferences, interests, and behavior. By analyzing a user's profile, a recommendation system can predict their preferences for specific items [2]. Notably, prominent brands, such as Netflix, Amazon, and Google, have built their platforms around recommender systems.

There are three primary types of recommendation systems: collaborative filtering, content-based filtering, and hybrid systems that integrate both approaches. Collaborative filtering analyzes user behavior, activities, and preferences to predict user preferences based on similarities with other users. One advantage of collaborative filtering is that it does not require in-depth analysis or understanding of the product; the recommendation system selects items based on available user information. Content-based filtering operates on the assumption that if a user likes one item, they will likely enjoy similar items. This algorithm measures item similarity based on the user's preference profile and item de-scription. However, content-based filters have the limitation of recommending only content similar to what the user has already interacted with, potentially resulting in limited recommendations. On the other hand, hybrid recommendation systems leverage both collaborative (metadata) and content (transactional) data. This approach utilizes natural language processing tags to create item tags and employs vector equations to calculate similarity. By utilizing a collaborative filtering matrix based on user behavior and preferences, users can be recommended items. The Netflix recommendation engine serves as a classic example of a hybrid recommendation technology, considering both user interests (collaborative) and content descriptions (content-based) [3,4].

Overall, this study aims to enhance the travel planning experience by providing personalized recommendations and promoting sustainable tourism. By using this technology, travelers can make more informed decisions, discover new destinations, and share their experiences with others in the traveling community.

The rest of the paper is organized as follows: This section presents a brief background about recommender systems. Section 2 introduces the work that has been undertaken in the field of related recommender systems. Section 3 describes the dataset that has been used in this study and the proposed method. Section 4 presents the experiment stages and the results that have been obtained. Section 5 discusses the results. Finally, Section 6 concludes the study.

2. Literature Review

This section explores different applications and tools that use recommender systems to enhance their features and functionality. One such application is Google Maps [5], which allows users to search for places and to view the fastest route to a particular location by walking, car, or train. Google Maps also features a place page that displays ratings and reviews and user profiles, and offers the ability to follow other users, and make lists that can be shared with others. In Google Maps, the recommender system suggests places based on reviews, photos, and updates from people and businesses that users follow on the platform. The system uses collaborative filtering techniques to identify similarities between users' preferences and to generate personalized recommendations [5]. For example, if a user frequently searches for coffee shops and leaves positive reviews, the system may suggest similar or related places.

The RoadTrippers [6] app is designed specifically for road travelers, allowing users to plan their road trips by entering the start and end points of the trip, and to read reviews of places, view travel guides, and see recommended stops endorsed by previous travelers. In RoadTrippers, the recommender system offers recommended stops endorsed by previous travelers. The system uses content-based filtering techniques to match a user's preferences with similar places and activities. For instance, if a user frequently visits museums and historical sites, the system may suggest similar places to visit along the route.

Another popular application is TripAdvisor [7], which provides detailed information on different destinations and uses recommender system technologies to support users in their trip destination tasks. The platform's main features include creating plans, adding saved places to plans, making bookings, and leaving reviews. TripAdvisor also allows users to follow other people and to view their profiles and reviews. In TripAdvisor, the recommender system uses a combination of content-based and collaborative filtering techniques to suggest places and create personalized travel plans. The platform analyzes a user's search and browsing history to identify their preferences and suggest places that match their interests. The system also considers the ratings and reviews of other users to generate recommendations.

Wanderlog [8] is a travel application that enables travelers to create trips and post guides for other users to view and follow. Users can plan future trips on the Wanderlog app, create notes and lists of places they wish to visit, and attach reservations and add notes when building their plans. In Wanderlog, the recommender system suggests places based on a user's destination and preferences. The system uses collaborative filtering techniques to analyze a user's previous searches and activities to generate personalized recommendations. For instance, if a user frequently searches for vegan restaurants, the system may suggest similar places to visit during their trip.

As part of the related work to this research, Lin et al. [9] conducted a study that focused on developing a travel recommendation method that not only considers users' personalized needs, but also aims to maximize team satisfaction. The study was achieved through the utilization of an enhanced collaborative filtering algorithm (CFA) method, and it was grounded in key techniques for recommendation in the context of collaborative filtering algorithm (CFA) applications, encompassing fusion methods and fusion strategies. The fusion method is further classified into two categories: model fusion, where recommendation combinations are generated based on user preference models, and recommendation fusion, which involves fusing prediction scores obtained from traditional algorithms for each user and which can incorporate the list of recommended items. When it comes to fusion strategies, the mean value strategy, the least pain strategy, and the happiest strategy are widely used in recommendation key techniques. The improved CFA technique merges the similarity factor and the correlation factor, which offers a more effective solution to the issue of data sparsity in travel recommendations. The instance validation carried out on https://Qunar.com (accessed on 9 April 2023) revealed that the enhanced CFA method proposed in this study exhibited a significant decrease in both the mean absolute error (MAE) and the root-mean-square error (RMSE) when compared to the non-optimized CFA method, across different values of K. This observation highlights the efficacy of the proposed method in enhancing the accuracy and performance of the recommendation system. The utilization of the satisfaction equalization strategy is aligned with the conventional fusion strategy for varying numbers of users. The effectiveness of the improved method proposed in this study is confirmed through experimental analysis conducted on a relevant tourism dataset from the city of Chongqing, validating its ability to enhance the quality of tourism recommendations.

Jagtap and Borate [10] conducted a study that focused on a tourist destination recommendation system using cosine similarity. Since the early 1990s, for information and even recommendations, we now turn to the Internet. Finding vacation spots on the Internet is a common practice. As a result of the overwhelming number of destinations and information available, a lot of time is wasted before an appropriate tourist destination is determined. To provide cogent and fast recommendations, the destination recommendation system utilizes data analysis and machine learning. In this paper, the cosine similarity algorithm is used to provide generalized recommendations to every user. A variety of tourist locations are represented in the dataset used. The cosine similarity algorithm predicts the most relevant tourist places using some important features of the dataset, such as the tourism category, the minimum budget (per day), and the visa requirement.

Luong et al. [11] presented a novel approach to enhancing user-based collaborative filtering (UBCF) by clustering users based on cognitive similarity across different cultures. To gather feedback from cross-cultural users, the authors deployed a crowdsourcing platform that featured a simple and user-friendly feedback collection process. The experiments on the dataset showed that the proposed approach outperformed the baseline UBPS, which only considers global similarity. However, the study by Luong et al. has some limitations. Specifically, the evaluation methods used to form user clusters were not examined, and demographic and personal information that could have been collected from users were not taken into account. For this reason, this research aims to introduce a more advanced approach to splitting the user list into preferred clusters by using a priority and weighted cosine similarity measure to improve the recommendation performance. Overall, while the approach presented by Luong et al. [11] is promising, further research is needed to address the limitations of the study and to advance the field of cross-cultural recommender systems.

Abbas et al. (2022) [12] implemented new trip recommendations using the concept of serendipity. The challenges of personalized trip recommendations lie in discovering relevant, novel, and unexpected points of interest (POIs) while ensuring high user satisfaction. To address these challenges, a novel method called serendipity-oriented personalized trip recommendation (SOTR) was proposed by Abbas et al. (2022) [12]. SOTR uses serendipity to discover users' satisfaction based on relevance, novelty, and unexpectedness. The proposed recommendation algorithm aims to efficiently plan the trip and maximize the user experience.

However, one possible weakness or limitation of SOTR [12] is that it may require a significant amount of relevant and accurate user data to provide personalized and effective recommendations. Additionally, while the novelty and unexpectedness of some recommendations may be appreciated by some users, others may prefer more conventional and familiar options, which could limit the overall acceptance and adoption of the method.

Overall, these applications demonstrate the potential of recommender systems in the tourism industry, providing users with personalized recommendations, enhancing the travel planning experience, and promoting sustainable tourism. These applications use different recommender system techniques to generate personalized recommendations, enhance the travel planning experience, and promote sustainable tourism.

3. Methodology

This study outlines the data collection and preparation process, as well as the proposed hybrid recommender system that combines content-based filtering and collaborative filtering. The goal of this section is to provide a detailed explanation of the methodology employed in developing the recommendation system.

3.1. Data Collection and Preparation

Data was collected and prepared to train and test the recommendation system module. As an appropriate dataset meeting the requirements of the weighted recommender system module was not readily available, we decided to build our own dataset. The dataset was crowdsourced, allowing us to outsource questionnaires, gather data in real-time, and to obtain a larger and more diverse set of observations compared to traditional data collection methods [13].

3.2. User Characteristics and Preferences

The collected data included the following user characteristics: user ID, age (ranging from 12 to 61 years old), marital status (for users aged 18 and above), presence of children (for users aged 18 and above), gender, preferred country for travel, preferred places to visit, user-assigned tags used in created lists, and the lists that the user saved.

3.3. Proposed Hybrid Recommender System

This section presents the proposed method, which utilizes a hybrid recommender system combining content-based filtering and collaborative filtering to recommend lists of posts to users. The method involves two main components: the content side and the collaborative side.

- Content-Based Filtering: The content side of the recommender system is based on the user's characteristics. These characteristics include the user's age, gender, social state, whether they have children or not, the countries they prefer (e.g., Middle Eastern, Asian, European, American, African), and the types of places they enjoy (e.g., restaurants/cafes, shopping malls, parks, museums, sports attractions). These attributes contribute to creating a personalized recommendation for each user. To incorporate these characteristics, this study employs techniques such as the TfidfVectorizer for normalization of the tf-idf representation. This transformation converts the count matrix into a normalized or tf-idf (term frequency inverse document frequency) representation. The tf-idf algorithm provides a meaningful numerical representation for machine learning algorithms and predictions. The TfidfVectorizer produces output vectors, including Vec Places, Vec Tags, Vec Age, Vec Country, Vec Social state, Vec Children, and Vec Gender.
- Collaborative Filtering: On the collaborative side, the recommendations are based on the tags attached to the lists that the user has saved. Each tag is assigned a weight based on its importance, with higher weights given to more significant values. This weighting scheme allows us to prioritize and emphasize the most relevant tags in the recommendation process.

To combine the content-based and collaborative filtering components, this study employs a weighted recommender system based on cosine similarity. The proposed recommender system method is illustrated in Figure 1. The implementation of the method is carried out using the Python programming language. We utilize the Pandas library to manipulate the data.

The first step employs the TfidfVectorizer [14] for the normalization of the tf-idf representation. This process converts the count matrix into a normalized or tf-idf (term frequency inverse document frequency) representation. The tf-idf algorithm is commonly used to convert text into a meaningful numerical representation suitable for machine learning algorithms and predictions. The "tf" in tf-idf refers to term frequency, representing the number of times a term "t" appears in a document "d". The inverse document frequency (idf) denotes the weight of a term. The defined idf is illustrated in Figure 2.

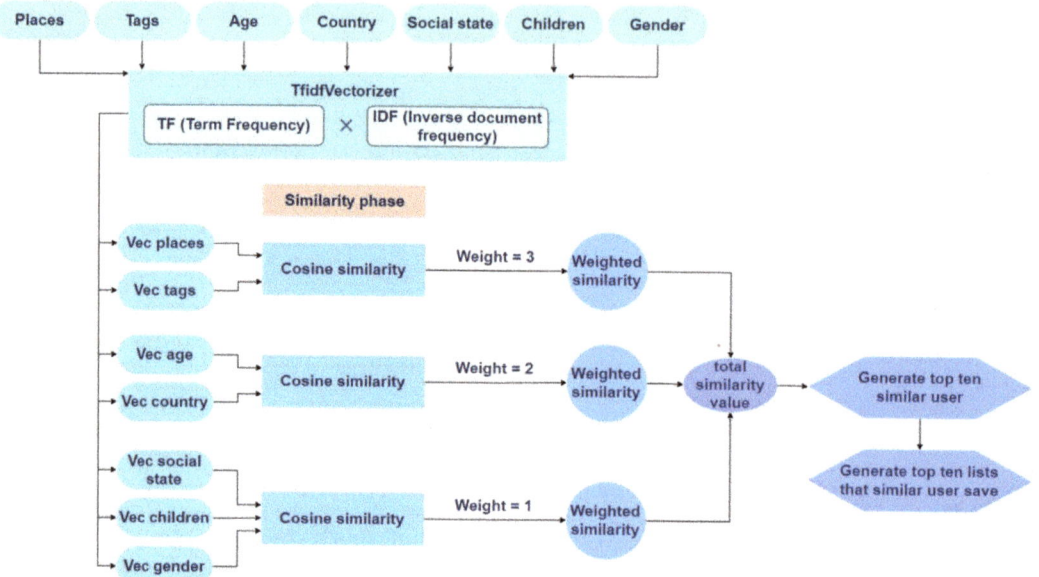

Figure 1. The proposed recommender system method.

$$idf(t) = \log \frac{|D|}{1 + |\{d : t \in d\}|}$$

Where $|\{d : t \in d\}|$ is the **number of documents** where the term t appears, when the term-frequency function satisfies $tf(t,d) \neq 0$, we're only adding 1 into the formula to avoid zero-division.

Figure 2. Idf(t) formula [13].

The TfidfVectorizer (Vec Places, Vec Tags, Vec Age, Vec Country, Vec Social state, Vec Children, and Vec Gender) produces the output. The count vectorizer provides frequency counts relative to the vocabulary index, while the tf-idf takes into account the overall document weights of words. The data is then fed into the cosine similarity calculation. The formula for the tf-idf is shown in Figure 3.

$$tf - idf(t) = tf(t,d) \times idf(t)$$

Figure 3. Tf-idf(t) formula [13].

The weights assigned to each feature category are justified based on empirical evidence and user feedback. Three categories are defined based on importance:

Category 1: Contains tags and places, assigned weight 3. This category is extremely important for generating similar lists aligned with the user's interests on the explore page.

Category 2: Contains age and country, assigned weight 2. This category is less important than Category 1 but still contributes to generating relevant lists for users on the explore page.

Category 3: Contains social state, children, and gender, assigned weight 1. This category has the lowest weight as it is less influential than Category 1 and 2 in generating similar lists for user interests on the explore page.

To determine the weight of each category, crowd-sourcing methods were utilized to gather user feedback and preferences. By analyzing the results, we identified the features that were most closely related to user choices and had the greatest impact on generating similar lists. Based on this analysis, the weights were assigned to each category according to their importance in generating recommendations aligned with the user's interests on the explore page. Cosine similarity is a metric used to measure the similarity between documents regardless of their size. It calculates the cosine of the angle between two vectors projected in a multi-dimensional space. Even if two similar documents are widely separated by Euclidean distance, they can still be considered closer together based on cosine similarity. The advantage of cosine similarity is that even if two documents are separated by a large Euclidean distance, they can still be considered similar. A smaller angle corresponds to a higher cosine similarity [15]. Figure 4 illustrates the assignment of different weights to each feature based on their importance and relationship.

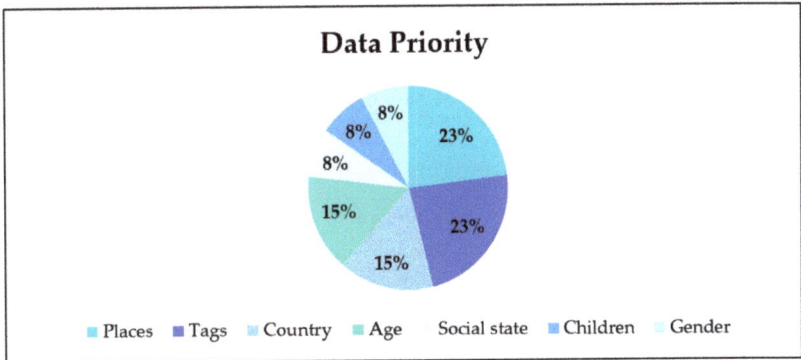

Figure 4. Data priority.

Based on this analysis, the weights were assigned to each category according to their importance in generating recommendations aligned with the user's interests on the explore page. Table 1 summarizes the weighted data, indicating the assigned weights for each item.

Table 1. Weighted data.

Item	Priority
Places	3
Tags	3
Country	2
Age	2
Social state	1
Children	1
Gender	1

Afterwards, the method displays the top 10 similar users and concludes by displaying the recommendations.

4. Analysis and Results

To investigate the performance of the recommender system by using a weighted parallel hybrid method with cosine similarity, different types of cases were tested, and the results were compared. Rather than comparing the methods to excellent state-of-the-art recommendation algorithms, the aim of this experiment was to demonstrate that weighting coefficients can be combined with cosine similarity and that the weighted cosine similarity measure improves recommendation performance.

4.1. Data

Data were collected and prepared in order to train and test the recommendation system module, which is available on the GitHub platform [16]. In order to provide academic support to the text, this section discuss the data and refers to the relevant literature.

When searching for a suitable dataset for the proposed weighted recommender system module, difficulties were encountered in finding one that fulfilled all the requirements. As a result, we made the decision to construct our own dataset. It is important to note that the minimum number of observations that a dataset should have is approximately 500 observations, as suggested in the literature [13].

To collect the data, we employed a crowdsourcing approach, which allowed us to outsource questionnaires and gather data in real-time. This method enabled us to obtain a significantly larger and more diverse set of observations compared to traditional data collection methods. By leveraging crowdsourcing, we were able to collect a rich and comprehensive dataset for the proposed recommender system [17].

Table 2 provides a detailed explanation of each item present in the dataset. The construction of our own dataset ensures that it meets the specific requirements of our weighted recommender system module and allows us to conduct thorough evaluations and experiments [18].

Table 2. Items and their characteristics.

Item Name	Characteristics
user_id	The number of the user's ID
age	Age of the user that ranges from 12 to 61 years old
married	Whether the user is married or not if he/she is 18 or above
children	Whether the user has children or not if he/she is 18 or above
gender	Whether the user is male or female
most_liked_country	The preferences of the user's most liked country to travel to
most_liked_place	Preferences of the user's most liked places to go to when traveling
user_assigned_tags	Tags that are used by users in their created lists
lists_id_save	The ID of lists that were saved by the user

4.2. Experimental Results

The recommender system will generate the top 10 similar users and then generate the lists saved by the top 10 similar users for each user for 20 users who were randomly selected to test the accuracy of the recommender system module. Table 3 shows the synthetic representation of users that contains a summary of the experimental results.

Table 3. Synthetic representation of users.

Category	Sub-Category	Number of Times Used
Gender	Female	12
	Male	8
Age	19–28	6
	30–42	7
	44–61	7
Country Preference *	European	17
	American	7
	African	4
	Middle Eastern	8
	Asian	8

Table 3. Cont.

Category	Sub-Category	Number of Times Used
Places Preference *	Restaurants/cafes	8
	Shopping malls	10
	Sports attractions	11
	Museums	9
	Parks	7
Have Children	Yes	12
	No	8
Social Status	Single	9
	Married	11
Used Tags *	#coffee	1
	#friends	1
	#waterParks	5
	#fun	5
	#america	5
	#Yummy	1
	#London	1
	#UK	1
	#food	1
	#hotel	11
	#art	3
	#swimming	6
	#History	3
	#families	3
	#flowers	5
	#fresh air	3
	#libarary	1
	#nature	1
	#castle	2
	#hiroshima	2
	#Mountain	2
	#games	1
	#mario	1
	#studio_ghibli	1
	#anime	1
	#activities	2
	#kids	3
	Did not use tags	7

* A user can have multiple values in the country and places preferences and tags.

Appendix A shows each users' characteristics and their explore page after generating lists by the 10 most similar users.

Accordingly, the proposed method produces lists of places for different countries or for the same country based on the data input. The lists contain different places related to specific categories, such as restaurants, breakfast places, and countries. We noticed the recommender system module detected (16) correct and (4) incorrect, so, the accuracy of the module by using this formula for calculating the accuracy of module is:

$$Accuracy = \frac{Number\ of\ attempts\ correct\ detected}{Number\ of\ test\ uusers} = \frac{16}{20} \times 100 = 80\%$$

In order to evaluate the proposed method, the precision and recall of the module were calculated using the following equations [8], where the true positives equal 11, the true negatives equal 5, the false positives equal 1, and the false negatives equal 3.

$$Precision = \frac{True\ Positives}{(True\ Positives + False\ Positive)} = \frac{11}{11+1} = \frac{11}{(11+1)} = 0.916 = 91.6\%$$

$$Recall = \frac{True\ Positives}{(True\ Positives + False\ Negatives)} = \frac{11}{(11+3)} = 0.785 = 78.5\%$$

To thoroughly evaluate the performance of the proposed method, a comparison was performed with two related tourism recommendation systems: user-based Pearson similarity (UBPS) [11] and a recommender system based on the cognitive similarity between cross-cultural users (CSBCC) [11]. The comparison was conducted based on accuracy, and the results are presented in Table 4. The comparison results for the proposed method and other related methods are shown in Table 4. The results indicate that the proposed method outperformed UBPS and CSBCC in terms of accuracy. Specifically, the proposed method achieved an accuracy of 80%, while SOTR [12], UBPS [11], and CSBCC [11] had accuracies of 54%, 75%, and 76%, respectively. These findings suggest that the proposed method represents a more effective approach for tourism recommendation systems.

Table 4. The performance measurement of the proposed method and comparison with more recent and related works in the literature.

RS\Performance Measurements	NO of Users	Accuracy	Precision	Recall
Proposed Method	20	80%		
SOTR [12]	11	54%	91.6%	78%
UBPS [11]	20	75%	45.1%	50.7%
CSBCC [11]	20	76%		

In conclusion, the proposed method has been shown to be a better approach for tourism recommendation systems than SOTR [12], UBPS [11] and CSBCC [11]. It has a higher accuracy rate, which indicates that it is a more effective approach for tourism recommendation.

5. Discussion

This section highlights the potential benefits of using recommendation systems in the travel industry. These systems can recommend suitable deals, such as for hotels, flights, or activities, making it easier for travelers to identify suitable places quickly and easily. The proposed solution enhances the accuracy of the recommender system by using a weighted parallel hybrid method with cosine similarity. This approach assigns a value to each item, thereby recognizing that some items are more important than others.

The experimental results presented in the previous section demonstrate that the proposed method is efficient and provides good results for a recommender system by improving the accuracy of the similarity between items, thus enhancing the recommendation quality accuracy. This approach is novel and advanced, and its application in the tourism field can benefit both local and global economies by helping people to discover the world in a way they enjoy.

Moreover, the proposed system can be useful for both travelers and local businesses. For travelers, the system helps them find suitable destinations and activities, while for businesses, it provides an opportunity to showcase their offerings to a wider audience. The use of such technology in the tourism industry can also help promote sustainable tourism by encouraging travelers to explore lesser-known destinations and reducing over-tourism in popular areas.

In conclusion, the proposed method for a recommender system in tourism is innovative and has the potential to transform the way people discover and explore the world. By using this technology, travelers can make more informed decisions, and local businesses can benefit from increased exposure. The application of such a technology in the tourism industry can also have positive economic and social impacts, making it a promising area for future research and development.

6. Conclusions

The main objective of the proposed recommender system, as described in this paper, is to enhance the accuracy of recommendations by taking into account the differences between items. The system serves as a social network for travelers, helping them plan their next trip, discover new places in a city, and save time and effort when searching for a new place by recommending lists based on the similarity between the user and other users. To achieve this goal, a novel method that utilizes a weighted parallel hybrid approach is proposed. This method assigns each item a value, recognizing that some items are more important than others, thereby improving the accuracy of the similarity between items and enhancing the quality and accuracy of recommendations.

The proposed method outperforms existing recommendation systems, providing efficient and effective results for a recommender system. It has the potential to transform the way people explore new destinations, making travel planning more efficient and enjoyable. In conclusion, the proposed recommender system method is a significant contribution to the tourism industry, providing travelers with a reliable and accurate source of information and recommendations. The use of a weighted parallel hybrid approach is a novel and advanced technique that improves the accuracy of the similarity between items and enhances the quality of recommendations. This method has the potential to promote sustainable tourism, reduce over-tourism, and to benefit local and global economies. However, the application has certain limitations, including the lack of statistics on post/list views and list additions for users. Additionally, the recommender system currently only supports Android devices and the English language, requiring improvement in accuracy, iOS device support, and language options (such as Arabic).

Future work will aim to address these limitations and to enhance the system by incorporating more statistical data on post/list views and list additions for users, improving accuracy, and expanding language support. Moreover, alternative approaches will be investigated to further improve the system's performance, such as incorporating deep learning or other advanced techniques. These enhancements aim to enable the system to provide more accurate and personalized recommendations for travelers, thereby enhancing their overall experience.

Author Contributions: Methodology, H.A.; software, G.A.; validation, H.A. and N.A.; resources, Y.A. and S.A.; data curation, H.A., S.A. and R.A.; writing—original draft, H.A., N.A., S.A. and Y.A.; writing—review and editing, H.A.; supervision, H.A. All authors have read and agreed to the published version of the manuscript.

Funding: Deputyship for Research and Innovation, Ministry of Education in Saudi Arabia funding this research (IFKSUOR3-014-2).

Institutional Review Board Statement: Not applicable.

Informed Consent Statement: Informed consent was obtained from all subjects involved in the study.

Data Availability Statement: The data used to support the findings of this study are available and can be accessed online through the GitHub platform [15].

Acknowledgments: The authors extend their appreciation to the Deputyship for Research and Innovation, Ministry of Education in Saudi Arabia for funding this research (IFKSUOR3-014-2).

Conflicts of Interest: The authors declare no conflict of interest.

Appendix A

Table A1. The experimental results of user #1.

User Number	User Details	User Explore Page
User #1	<ul><li>Female;</li><li>25 years old;</li><li>Likes the countries (European, American);</li><li>Likes the places (restaurants/cafes, shopping malls);</li><li>Single;</li><li>Does not have children;</li><li>Uses tags (#coffee #friends #waterParks #fun #america).</li></ul>	

Table A2. The experimental results of user #2.

User Number	User Details	User Explore Page
User #2	<ul><li>Female;</li><li>30 years old;</li><li>Likes the countries (European, American);</li><li>Likes the places (restaurants/cafes, shopping malls, sports attractions);</li><li>Single;</li><li>Does not have children;</li><li>Uses tags (#Yummy #London #UK #food #waterParks #fun #america).</li></ul>	

Table A3. The experimental results of user #3.

User Number	User Details	User Explore Page
User #3	<ul><li>Female;</li><li>45 years old;</li><li>Likes the countries (European, African);</li><li>Likes the places (museums, parks);</li><li>Single;</li><li>Does not have children;</li><li>Uses the tag (#hotel).</li></ul>	

Table A4. The experimental results of user #4.

User Number	User Details	User Explore Page
User #4	• Female; • 34 years old; • Likes the countries (European); • Likes the places (shopping malls, parks); • Married; • Has children; • Does not use tags.	

Table A5. The experimental results of user #5.

User Number	User Details	User Explore Page
User #5	• Female; • 36 years old; • Likes the countries (European, American, Middle Eastern); • Likes the places (restaurants/cafes, museums); • Married; • Has children; • Does not use tags.	

Table A6. The experimental results of user #6.

User Number	User Details	User Explore Page
User #6	• Female; • 20 years old; • Likes the countries (Middle Eastern, American); • Likes the places (restaurants/cafes, sports attractions); • Single; • Does not have children; • Does not use tags.	

Table A7. The experimental results of user #7.

User Number	User Details	User Explore Page
User #7	• Female; • 49 years old; • Likes the countries (African, European); • Likes the places (museums, parks, sports attractions); • Married; • Has children; • Does not use tags.	

Table A8. The experimental results of user #8.

User Number	User Details	User Explore Page
User #8	• Female; • 30 years old; • Likes the countries (Middle Eastern, European); • Likes the places (shopping malls, sports attractions); • Single; • Does not have children; • Uses tags (#art #swimming #History #families #flowers #freshair).	

Table A9. The experimental results of user #9.

User Number	User Details	User Explore Page
User #9	• Female; • 50 years old; • Likes the countries (Middle Eastern, European, African, Asian); • Likes the places (shopping malls, sports attractions, parks, museums); • Married; • Has children; • Uses tags (#libarary #nature #castle #hiroshima #flowers #Mountain).	

Table A10. The experimental results of user #10.

User Number	User Details	User Explore Page
User #10	• Female; • 42 years old; • Likes the countries (European, Asian); • Likes the places (museums, sports attractions); • Married; • Has children; • Uses tags (#games #Mountain #flowers #castle #hiroshima).	

Table A11. The experimental results of user #11.

User Number	User Details	User Explore Page
User #11	• Female; • 19 years old; • Likes the countries (European); • Likes the places (shopping malls); • Single; • Does not have children; • Uses tags (#swimming #art #History).	

Table A12. The experimental results of user #12.

User Number	User Details	User Explore Page
User #12	• Male; • 28 years old; • Likes the countries (Middle Eastern, Asian); • Likes the places (parks, restaurants/cafes); • Single; • Does not have children; • Uses tags (#families #flowers #freshair).	

Table A13. The experimental results of user #13.

User Number	User Details	User Explore Page
User #13	• Male; • 26 years old; • Likes the countries (European, American); • Likes the places (museums, shopping malls, sports attractions); • Married; • Has children; • Uses tags (#art #swimming #History).	

Table A14. The experimental results of user #14.

User Number	User Details	User Explore Page
User #14	• Male; • 61 years old; • Likes the countries (Asian, European, Middle Eastern); • Likes the places (museums, restaurants/cafes, sports attractions); • Married; • Has children; • Uses tags (#families #flowers #freshair).	

Table A15. The experimental results of user #15.

User Number	User Details	User Explore Page
User #15	• Male; • 33 years old; • Likes the countries (Asian, American); • Likes the places (restaurants/cafes, sports attractions); • Married; • Has children; • Uses tags (#activities #america #waterParks #fun #swimming #kids).	

Table A16. The experimental results of user #16.

User Number	User Details	User Explore Page
User #16	• Male; • 44 years old; • Likes the countries (Asian, Middle Eastern, European, American); • Likes the places (sports attractions, restaurants/cafes, parks, shopping malls); • Married; • Has children; • Uses tags (#america #waterParks #fun #swimming #kids).	

Table A17. The experimental results of user #17.

User Number	User Details	User Explore Page
User #17	• Male; • 49 years old; • Likes the countries (Asian, Middle Eastern, European); • Likes the places (museums, parks, shopping malls); • Married; • Has children; • Uses tags (#activities #waterParks #america #swimming #kids #fun).	

Table A18. The experimental results of user #18.

User Number	User Details	User Explore Page
User #18	• Female; • 19 years old; • Likes the countries (European); • Likes the places (shopping malls); • Single; • Does not have children; • Does not use tags.	

Table A19. The experimental results of user #19.

User Number	User Details	User Explore Page
User #19	• Male; • 60 years old; • Likes the countries (European, Asian); • Likes the places (museums); • Married; • Have children; • Do not uses tags.	

Table A20. The experimental results of user #20.

User Number	User Details	User Explore Page
User #20	• Male; • 31 years old; • Likes the countries (European, African); • Likes the places (sports attractions); • Married; • Has children; • Does not use tags.	

References

1. Kumar, A.; Killingsworth, M.A.; Gilovich, T. Waiting for Merlot: Anticipatory consumption of experiential and material purchases: Anticipatory consumption of experiential and material purchases. *Psychol. Sci.* **2014**, *25*, 1924–1931. [CrossRef] [PubMed]
2. Isinkaye, F.O.; Folajimi, Y.O.; Ojokoh, B.A. Recommendation systems: Principles, methods and evaluation. *Egypt. Inform. J.* **2015**, *16*, 261–273. [CrossRef]
3. Nick, B. What Is a Recommendation Engine and How Does It Work? Technology Network, 9 September 2020. Available online: https://www.techtarget.com/whatis/definition/recommendation-engine (accessed on 11 March 2023).
4. Ariwala, P. How Do Recommendation Engines Work? What Are the Benefits? Maruti Techlabs, 19 March 2019. Available online: https://marutitech.com/recommendation-engine-benefits (accessed on 1 March 2023).
5. Before You Continue to Google. Available online: https://www.google.com/maps (accessed on 10 March 2023).
6. Roadtrippers. Roadtrippers. 20 October 2020. Available online: https://roadtrippers.com/ (accessed on 2 March 2023).
7. Tripadvisor.com. Available online: https://www.tripadvisor.com/ (accessed on 1 March 2023).
8. Wanderlog: Best Free Travel Itinerary & Road Trip Planner App. Wanderlog. Available online: https://wanderlog.com/ (accessed on 2 March 2023).
9. Lin, K.; Yang, S.; Na, S.-G. Collaborative filtering algorithm-based destination recommendation and marketing model for tourism scenic spots. *Comput. Intell. Neurosci.* **2022**, *2022*, 7115627. [CrossRef]
10. Jagtap, S.; Borate, S. Tourist Destination Recommendation System Using Cosine Similarity. Irjet.net. Available online: https://www.irjet.net/archives/V9/i10/IRJET-V9I1020.pdf (accessed on 1 March 2023).
11. Nguyen; Vuong, L.; Nguyen, T.-H.; Jung, J.J. Tourism recommender system based on cognitive similarity between cross-cultural users. In *Intelligent Environments 2021: Workshop Proceedings of the 17th International Conference on Intelligent Environments*; IOS Press: Amsterdam, The Netherlands, 2021; Volume 29.
12. Abbas; Rizwan; Hassan, G.M.; Al-Razgan, M.; Zhang, M.; Amran, G.A.; Al Bakhrani, A.A.; Alfakih, T.; Al-Sanabani, H.; Rahman, S.M.M. A serendipity-oriented personalized trip recommendation model. *Electronics* **2022**, *11*, 1660. [CrossRef]
13. Sevey, R. How Much Data Is Needed to Train a (Good) Model? DataRobot AI Platform, 4 August 2017. Available online: https://www.datarobot.com/blog/how-much-data-is-needed-to-train-a-good-model (accessed on 10 March 2023).
14. Chaudhary, M. TF-IDF Vectorizer Scikit-Learn. Medium, 24 April 2020. Available online: https://medium.com/@cmukesh8688/tf-idf-vectorizer-scikit-learn-dbc0244a911a (accessed on 1 March 2023).

15. Khatter, H.; Goel, N.; Gupta, N.; Gulati, M. Movie recommendation system using cosine similarity with sentiment analysis. In Proceedings of the 2021 Third International Conference on Inventive Research in Computing Applications (ICIRCA), Coimbatore, India, 2–4 September 2021.
16. Nourah, A. Tourism-Recommender-System-Dataset, 11 June 2021. Available online: https://github.com/somyamakkad97/Tourist-Recommender-System/blob/master/content.py (accessed on 12 April 2023).
17. Alabduljabbar, R.; Alfulaij, N.; Aldosari, S.; Alrubaiya, Y. Odyssey: A Social Network Mobile Application Using Hybrid Recommender System. In Proceedings of the 2022 International Conference on Electrical, Computer, Communications and Mechatronics Engineering (ICECCME), Maldives, Maldives, 16–18 November 2022; pp. 1–6. [CrossRef]
18. Lenart-Gansiniec, R.; Czakon, W.; Sułkowski, Ł.; Pocek, J. Understanding crowdsourcing in science. *Rev. Manag. Sci.* **2022**, 1–34. [CrossRef]

Disclaimer/Publisher's Note: The statements, opinions and data contained in all publications are solely those of the individual author(s) and contributor(s) and not of MDPI and/or the editor(s). MDPI and/or the editor(s) disclaim responsibility for any injury to people or property resulting from any ideas, methods, instructions or products referred to in the content.

Article

Developing an Urban Computing Framework for Smart and Sustainable Neighborhoods: A Case Study of Alkhaledia in Jizan City, Saudi Arabia

Lolwah Binsaedan [1], Habib M. Alshuwaikhat [1,2] and Yusuf A. Aina [3,4,*]

[1] Department of City and Regional Planning, King Fahd University of Petroleum and Minerals, Dhahran 31261, Saudi Arabia
[2] Interdisciplinary Research Center for Smart Mobility & Logistics, King Fahd University of Petroleum and Minerals, Dhahran 31261, Saudi Arabia
[3] Department of Geomatics Engineering Technology, Yanbu Industrial College, Yanbu 41912, Saudi Arabia
[4] Geoinformatic Unit, Geography Section, School of Humanities, Universiti Sains Malaysia, Penang 11800, Malaysia
* Correspondence: ainay@rcyci.edu.sa; Tel.: +96-614-394-6226

Citation: Binsaedan, L.; Alshuwaikhat, H.M.; Aina, Y.A. Developing an Urban Computing Framework for Smart and Sustainable Neighborhoods: A Case Study of Alkhaledia in Jizan City, Saudi Arabia. *Sustainability* 2023, 15, 4057. https://doi.org/10.3390/su15054057

Academic Editors: Rashid Mehmood, Tan Yigitcanlar and Juan M. Corchado

Received: 28 December 2022
Revised: 19 February 2023
Accepted: 20 February 2023
Published: 23 February 2023

Copyright: © 2023 by the authors. Licensee MDPI, Basel, Switzerland. This article is an open access article distributed under the terms and conditions of the Creative Commons Attribution (CC BY) license (https://creativecommons.org/licenses/by/4.0/).

Abstract: Urban computing is the incorporation of computing, sensors, and actuation technology into urban life. In Saudi Arabia, the neighborhoods lack an integrated approach to social, economic, and environmental values, thereby creating consequences, such as inefficient mobility, poor environmental protection, low quality of life, and inadequate services or facilities. This article aims to develop a smart sustainable neighborhood framework (SSNF) to create districts that contribute to a healthy environment, sustain a strong community, and thrive in economic value. The framework is created by two main factors, first is identifying and analyzing the categories of urban computing. Second is choosing the appropriate indicators from sets of standards, including sustainable development goal (SDG) 11, as developed by the United Nations. These two factors shaped the proposed "smart and sustainable urban computing framework (SSUCF)" of "people", "prosperity", and "environment" dimensions, and it has been applied to the Alkhaledia district as a case study. The result indicates that urban computing can be used as the basis of support, along with smart and sustainable standards to produce an SSNF. Furthermore, with the analysis of relevant data, this framework can be used in similar neighborhoods to enhance the quality of residents' lives, environmental protection, and economic values.

Keywords: smart neighborhood; sustainable indicators; urban informatics; urban sustainability; Saudi cities

1. Introduction

Cities are currently acting as engines for economic development, providing opportunities for expansion while dealing with several internal and external challenges, such as environmental hazards, resource depletion, high energy consumption, and high production of CO_2 and greenhouse gas emissions, which results in pollution [1]. Additionally, the number of people living in cities is continually growing; by 2050, 68% of the world's population is predicted to reside in cities [2]. Rising populations increase other major concerns, such as community safety, the efficiency of mobility, and poor quality of life, especially in districts and neighborhoods.

The neighborhood or district is an important scale of development to consider since it is the core of cities. If neighborhoods suffer then cities subsequently suffer, moreover, neighborhoods need attention in order to develop livable and sustainable environments. Moreover, smart neighborhoods improve the social networking and capital of the populace [3]. Smart cities can be developed at different geographical scales, starting from the neighborhood, and should lead to the enhancement of quality of life and neighborhood livability [4]. The integration and growth of smart cities and smart neighborhoods can therefore help to alleviate the effects of urbanization and the environmental risks that most cities, especially in developing countries, are currently facing. This requires the development of new, functional, and user-friendly services and technologies, especially in the fields of energy, transportation, and information and communication technology (ICT). These solutions also need a combination of approaches in terms of advanced technology solutions, research, innovation, and deployment [5].

Several urban computing strategies can be deployed to support the systematic development of smart neighborhoods. Urban computing involves the use of smart technologies and the internet of things (IoT) as tools to reach sustainability and progressively foster resilient neighborhoods. Furthermore, it is essential to know the neighborhoods and citizens' needs to implement the right strategies and methods of smart technology to promote sustainability. Additionally, it is not only about smart technologies but also about the collection of relevant data that can guide us to solutions [6]. Moreover, the considerations should include how to manage the data and connect technology with neighborhood challenges to resolve them. Urban computing is generally understood to be a technique for acquiring, integrating, and analyzing large-scale heterogeneous data created by a range of resources inside urban environments, such as sensors, gadgets, cars, structures, and humans [7]. It is relevant to urban informatics, which involves the application of information and communication technologies in managing and understanding urban areas [8].

In the context of Saudi Arabia, it has been deduced from various literature reviews that there is a lack of a smart and sustainable framework for Saudi neighborhoods, especially in the use of smart technologies to support sustainable development. Recent studies have examined social sustainability in Saudi neighborhoods [9], greenspace usability [10], heritage management [11], the transformation of housing typology [12], and life-cycle-based strategic framework for smart sustainable cities at the city scale [13]. Thus, the focus of this article is to discuss the development of a smart and sustainable neighborhood framework by applying the concept of urban computing and various smart and sustainable standards. The development of the proposed framework goes through a process; firstly, starting by exploring multiple strategies and other frameworks from various literature reviews on the concept of urban computing. Then secondly, examining and analyzing sustainable cities or neighborhood standards in addition to smart standards. Consequently, the proposed framework is tested for its success in maintaining an economic, environmental, and social neighborhood by applying it to the Alkhaledia district in Jizan. The framework has the goal of creating an inclusive neighborhood, with a focus on having social connectivity and environmental protection. This goal, which is relevant to the current need of Saudi districts, applies to other communities. More importantly, the Saudi Arabia Vision 2030 features focus areas of "vibrant society", "thriving economy", and "ambitious nation", which establish the need for more sustainability-oriented neighborhoods that facilitate smart technologies to support sustainability and its measures.

However, the proposed framework with its context of smart technologies and dependence on data raises many challenges and limitations. Having a data-driven framework can have multiple risks, such as data security, privacy, and acquisition. Since the collection of data is restricted and confined to only what resources are available, the success of the framework depends on how much data about the neighborhood is accessible. Furthermore, having the framework depends on citizens' willingness to provide data which can cause difficulties in obtaining the data.

The analysis of this article focuses on the four elements of urban computing: urban sensing, data management, data analytics, and delivery of services. The concept of urban computing will be used as a structured procedure to implement smart aspects to transform neighborhoods into smart neighborhoods, and an assessment of sustainability by using sustainable indicators to measure social, economic, and environmental aspects of a neighborhood. This paper will also explore how to reflect this on current Saudi neighborhoods by studying literature reviews and a case study. The main objectives of this article are to:

- Investigate the sustainability standards and smart indicators to be used in smart sustainable neighborhoods;
- Develop a smart and sustainable urban computing framework for neighborhoods;
- Assess Alkhaledia district, Jizan, as a case study, using the proposed framework.

2. Review of the Literature

2.1. Smart Neighborhood

A new development paradigm combines urban sustainability with smartness, emphasizing the significance of taking both issues into account simultaneously [14]. It was developed in response to the criticism of smart urban strategies that conflict with sustainability, as well as an effort to address the needs of today's highly digitalized cities in a more comprehensive way than the conventional concept of sustainability allows, and that could be implemented on a neighborhood level [15]. The sustainable development goals (SDGs) are relevant to this research because smart city solutions are expected to play a key role in supporting cities and communities in reaching these goals by aiding stakeholders in controlling and measuring progress toward the SDGs using widely accepted indicators. Recently, attention has focused on how smart solutions can help elevate the quality of life and enhance sustainability of neighborhoods [4].

2.2. Sustainable Neighborhoods

In Saudi Arabia, specifically, achieving sustainability is a challenging task. There are many impediments to overcome to attain sustainability goals [16]. Despite these challenges, the Saudi Arabian government aspires to make the country one of the most sustainable in the region and to set it as an inspiring example for other nations. Existing conditions must be reviewed at several scales, including regions, cities, districts, neighborhoods, and buildings, to attain sustainability. The neighborhood is the city's smallest planning unit, which contains a variety of elements, such as houses, streets, people, open spaces, and so on [17]. Therefore, achieving a smart and sustainable neighborhood is a good start to attain sustainability for life quality and well-being.

To address current urbanization issues, such as population increase, urban sprawl, poverty, inequality, pollution, overcrowding, urban biodiversity, urban mobility, and energy, the UN-Habitat (the United Nations Human Settlements Program for human settlements and sustainable urban development) assists nations in developing urban planning concepts and systems. The proposed plan is based on five principles that encourage compactness, integration, and connectedness, which are three essential attributes of sustainable communities [18]. The five guiding principles are population concentration, mixed-use development, social variety, adequate street space, and limited land-use specialization. These principles are the prime focus of assessing the sustainability of the Alkhaledia district and providing possible solutions, if any, for the missing factors.

2.3. Smart and Sustainable Indicators for Neighborhoods and Communities

The International Telecommunication Union's (ITU) definition of "smart sustainable cities" is divided into two parts: the first describes a city's smart characteristics, while the second describes urban sustainability [19]. The use of information and communication technologies (ICTs) to improve quality of life, the efficiency of urban operations, and competitiveness, for instance, are examples of innovations that are associated with smart city characteristics. These innovations aim to improve the quality of life, efficiency of urban activities and services, and citizen involvement. Moreover, a city's sustainable characteristics are those that guarantee that it fulfills the economic, social, environmental, and cultural needs of both present and future generations [15]. Therefore, the proposed framework integrates smart indicators for the development of smart neighborhoods, combined with some sustainable indicators for the environmental, economic, and cultural aspects of a sustainable neighborhood with the focus on urban computing and its strategies as the inspiration for a clearer and more strategic framework for smart and sustainable neighborhoods or cities.

3. Materials and Methods

This paper focuses on connecting and integrating the smart indicators and the sustainable indicators of neighborhoods and communities, then molding them to fit urban computing strategies. Thereby, creating an urban computing framework applied to the local context of Saudi Arabia. This is mainly achieved by collecting various indicators that are smart or sustainable and fitting them into the four categories of urban computing which are urban sensing, data management, data analysis, and delivery of services. By making urban computing the overall umbrella of smart and sustainable indicators with also the ISO, ITU, and SDGs indicators, the proposed framework was constructed (Figure 1).

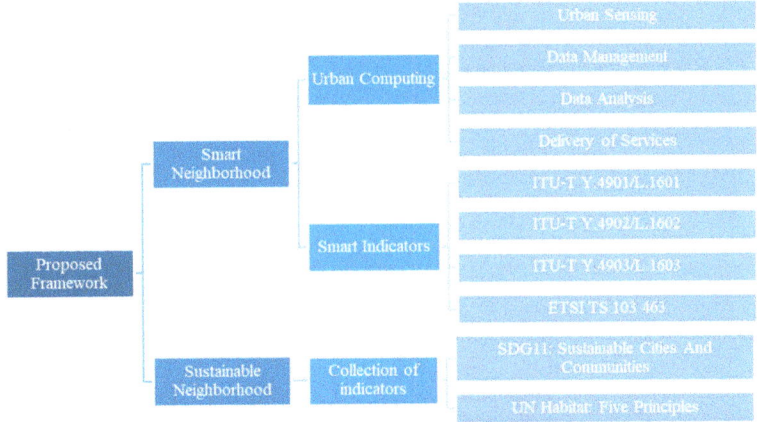

Figure 1. The chart of the proposed framework.

3.1. Developing Urban Computing Framework for the Local Context

Urban computing is a concept used in this project to develop a framework by including smart and sustainable indicators and standards, with the inspiration of urban computing strategies to create a strategic local context framework. This helps achieve smart and sustainable neighborhoods, communities, and cities. Urban computing in this context is used as an overall umbrella to support indicators to become more strategic and it shows how, with the support of urban computing strategies, we can perform successful development of smart and sustainable neighborhoods.

Urban computing is used as a base support for this framework, to formulate a strong strategy for the development of smart and sustainable neighborhoods and communities. One of the main challenges of developing smart neighborhoods is analyzing the urban data, which can be difficult due to their heterogeneity, high complexity, and vast volumes [20]. Therefore, it may cause inefficient use of these data and a lack of relevant processes for solutions. "Urban computing" is the term used to describe the method of developing, integrating, processing, analyzing, and compiling vast quantities of data from various sources to achieve a specific goal, such as addressing issues with sustainability, efficiency, adaptability, equity, and living quality. In addition, the term refers to the use of several sensors, devices, platforms, infrastructures, and networks, as well as the corresponding algorithms, strategies, processes, and protocols in the context of data-driven smart urban sustainability [21]. Urban computing is the basis for the developed framework since it is a comprehensive method of capturing and utilizing the vast amounts of big data generated in cities to improve urban forms, infrastructure, urban environments, and urban services, along with urban operational management and development planning systems.

As a result, it can produce deep insights that can be utilized to make well-informed decisions and can build feedback mechanisms between humans and their activities, as well as between humans and the urban environment [21]. Moreover, a collection of smart standards is incorporated into the developed framework to obtain quantitative and qualitative data involved in the urban computing concept. The chosen standards, including the European Telecommunications Standards Institute (ETSI) standard, are adopted to assess the standardization needs of communities and neighborhoods looking to increase their social, economic, and environmental sustainability through integrating information systems, such as ICTs into their infrastructures and processes. Therefore, the five standards used in this project (ITU-T Y.4901/L.1601, ITU-T Y.4902/L.1602, ITU-T Y.4903/L.1603, ETSI TS 103 463, SDGs) are adopted to integrate a set of indicators into the concept of urban computing and to provide a standardized basis for the framework.

3.2. Developing Indicators for Assessment

For the development of the urban computing framework, the smart indicators that were collected are (ITU-TY.4901/L.1601, 2016) [19]; (ITU-TY.4902/L.1602, 2016) [22]; (ITU-TY.4903/L.1603, 2016) [23]; and (ETSI-TS103-463, 2017) [24]. The sustainable indicators were a collection of SDG 11: sustainable cities and communities [25] and UN-Habitat: five principles [18]. Additionally, we combined all of these mentioned smart and sustainable indicators to construct an assessment tool influenced by the urban computing concept.

3.2.1. Urban Sensing Category

Urban sensing revolves around the distribution of sensors in communities and neighborhoods to reveal information and collect various data on the neighborhood to help enhance services among the neighborhoods. In this article, the urban sensing category is linked to the five standards which are shown in Figure 1. The five standards are matched to the principles of urban sensing in urban computing, which is the relevancy of sensors for serving the citizens and the environment. This applies to placing many sensors that support the IoT and machine learning analysis for the advanced development of supplying data.

3.2.2. Urban Data Management Category

Urban data are an important pillar of any smart community or city since they offer insights into environmental, economic, or social information. These data provide data-driven solutions that benefit everyone. Urban data management processes vast amounts of dynamic urban data from several areas, including traffic, meteorology, human movement, and POIs, using cloud computing platforms, data structures, and retrieval algorithms [26]. This layer is necessary since it aids in data classification and develops special indexing structures and retrieval algorithms for geographical and spatiotemporal data. Additionally, the category of urban data management is linked to the five standards listed in Figure 1. The standards are used for the efficient distribution of data management, which is for the optimal results of data gained from the distributed sensors. Figure 1 shows the linkage between the five standards and the data management of the urban computing concept.

3.2.3. Urban Data Analytics Category

Urban data analysis uses a range of data-mining techniques and machine-learning algorithms to unlock the value of information from data in a variety of fields. Using algorithms, such as clustering, classification, regression, and anomaly detection, this layer changes fundamental data mining and machine-learning approaches to handle spatiotemporal data [26], using the science of big data analytics to process big volumes of data.

Consequently, the five standards indicated in Figure 1 are linked to the category of urban data analytics. These standards are used as a platform to execute data analytics efficiently and to provide the best information. The information extracted from big data analytics can result in unexpected relations between different elements, which can be a big advantage for creating services for people, the environment, and financial prosperity.

3.2.4. Delivery of Services Category

An interface for domain systems to access knowledge from an urban computing application using cloud computing platforms is provided by the service-providing category. Due to the transdisciplinary nature of urban computing, data-driven knowledge must be incorporated into existing domain systems for them to make better judgments. For instance, air quality forecasts from an urban-computing application can be linked to current mobile apps to help people plan their trips, or they can be used by environmental protection authorities' systems to help them make pollution-control decisions [26]. This is critical to serving citizens' needs and providing efficient services. Consequently, there is a relationship between the five standards and how they can help optimize the services provided to the people, environment, and prosperity.

4. Results

4.1. Smart and Sustainable Urban Computing Framework

The five selected smart and sustainable indicators were analyzed to create relations to urban computing strategies. For instance, the smart standard (ETSI-TS103-463, 2017) [24] was selected to analyze its four dimensions and choose appropriate indicators for the concept of smart and sustainable neighborhoods. Subsequently, a checklist is created as a start to indicate the relationship of the smart indicators to the urban computing categories (urban sensing, urban data management, urban data analytics, delivery of services), this is to set a starting line on how urban computing concept can be used as a basis for the smart and sustainable neighborhood. Furthermore, the (ITU-TY.4901/L.1601, 2016) [19], (ITU-TY.4902/L.1602, 2016) [22], (ITU-TY.4903/L.1603, 2016) [23], (UN Habitat principles) [18], and (UN, SDG 11: make cities and human settlements inclusive, safe, resilient and sustainable, 2016) [25] relations to urban computing were mapped.

The next stage of the findings Is developing three new dimensions for "smart and sustainable urban computing (SSUCF)" which are people, prosperity, and environment (Figure 2). Following the analysis of those three dimensions and relating them to the urban computing concept, an extensive table was formed as a binary (yes/no) checklist for the SSUCF for neighborhoods. This checklist was developed by picking only 42 appropriate smart standards using their unit and weight. Subsequently, Figure 2 illustrates how the urban computing categories are matched for a clearer understanding of urban computing and the developed framework's dimensions. This is created by a match work diagram that shows how each category of urban computing matches the dimensions in SSUCF; for instance, the "environment" dimension requires all categories of urban computing, while, "prosperity" requires data management and delivery of services only. This is because the prosperity outlook focuses on how one can manage the data to serve citizens best. The "people" dimension requires data management and analysis to provide certain services to optimize and enhance citizens' quality of life. Nonetheless, there are some indicators in these dimensions that require all categories of urban computing. Figure 2 illustrates only what the majority of indicators fall under.

SSUCF 3 Dimensions: People, Environment, and Prosperity

The SSUCF consists of various goals, such as connecting a community, having a cleaner environment, enhancing an individual's health and well-being, building a greener economy, and finally elevating the quality of life. These goals are met by having three focus areas of the framework which are people, environment, and prosperity. Those three dimensions were derived from the standards used in the process of making this framework [(ETSI-TS103-463, 2017) [24], (ITU-TY.4901/L.1601, 2016) [19], (ITU-TY.4902/L.1602, 2016) [22], (ITU-TY.4903/L.1603, 2016) [23], (UN, SDG 11: make cities and human settlements inclusive, safe, resilient and sustainable, 2016) [25]], and these standards influenced the selection of these dimensions for the SSUCF.

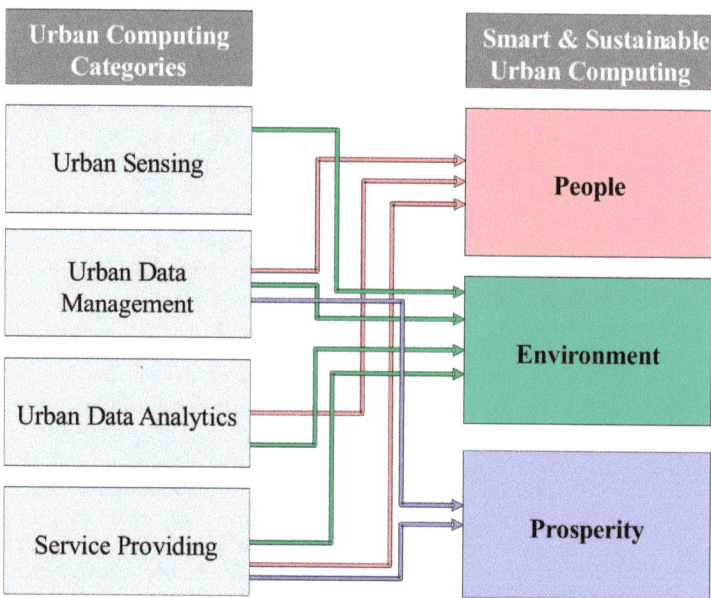

Figure 2. Framework dimensions and their relation to urban computing categories.

The first dimension is "people". This main indicator is everything related to the individual's social environment. Its focus is establishing a sense of belonging and social inclusion in neighborhoods, and most importantly the involvement of technology and smart ICTs to optimize the social environment. As seen in Table 1, there are a total of 13 indicators in SSUCF, and its area of focus is "people". Table 1 shows which urban computing categories are present or not present in each indicator. The next dimension is "environmental", which accounts for the overall good quality and efficiency of the environment in a neighborhood, in terms of air, water, and energy. As seen in Table 2, 15 indicators contribute to environmental protection in a neighborhood with also the urban computing categories to complement an efficient and smart application of the indicator. The last dimension is "prosperity", and this dimension helps build a resilient neighborhood criterion, by building a greener economic development. Table 3 shows the 14 indicators that account for the prosperity of the neighborhood. In total, the SSUCF comprises 42 indicators to have an outlook on the social, environmental, and economical areas in the neighborhood.

4.2. Application to Alkhaledia District, Jizan

The SSUCF is analyzed and altered to be tailored to the Alkhaledia district (Figure 3), which resulted in 27 indicators after filtering. This stage of the framework was fixed upon the characteristics and availability of the data in the Alkhaledia district [27]. The people, environment, and prosperity dimensions had specific indicators that are either found or not found in the Alkhaledia district, additionally, some indicators are a must-have in the context of urban computing, sustainability, and smartness, however, they were not found in the Alkhaledia neighborhood. Moreover, since Alkhaledia has some sustainable and smart objectives, some indicators are met, therefore making the urban computing framework easier to implement.

Table 1. SSUCF people dimension.

Smart & Sustainable Urban Computing Framework			Urban Computing Layers				Yes/No
			Urban Sensing	Urban Data Management	Urban Data Analytics	Delivery of Services	
Main Indicators	People	Encouraging a healthy lifestyle	✗	✗	✓	✓	
		Cybersecurity	✓	✓	✗	✗	
		Data privacy	✓	✓	✓	✓	
		Access to public transportation	✗	✓	✗	✓	
		Diversity of housing types	✗	✓	✓	✗	
		Green space	✗	✓	✗	✓	
		Use of an e-learning system	✗	✓	✓	✓	
		Sharing of medical resources and information among hospitals, pharmacies, and other healthcare providers	✗	✓	✓	✓	
		Availability of ICT-based safety systems	✓	✓	✓	✓	
		Availability of online neighborhood information and feedback mechanisms	✗	✓	✓	✓	
		Availability of parking guidance systems	✓	✓	✓	✓	
		Electricity consumption	✓	✓	✓	✓	
		Information security and privacy protection	✗	✓	✓	✗	

Table 2. SSUCF environmental dimension.

Smart & Sustainable Urban Computing Framework			Urban Computing Layers				Yes/No
			Urban Sensing	Urban Data Management	Urban Data Analytics	Delivery of Services	
Main Indicators	Environment	Domestic material consumption	✓	✓	✓	✗	
		Local food production	✗	✓	✓	✓	
		Energy consumption/demand: Annual final energy consumption	✓	✓	✓	✓	
		CO_2 emissions	✓	✓	✓	✓	
		Renewable energy generated within the neighborhood	✗	✓	✓	✓	
		Water consumption	✓	✓	✓	✓	
		Grey and rainwater use	✓	✓	✓	✓	
		Air quality index	✓	✓	✓	✓	

Table 2. Cont.

Smart & Sustainable Urban Computing Framework		Urban Computing Layers				Yes/No
		Urban Sensing	Urban Data Management	Urban Data Analytics	Delivery of Services	
	Recycling rate	✓	✓	✓	✓	
	Sewage system management using ICT	✓	✓	✓	✓	
	Street lighting management using ICT	✓	✗	✗	✓	
	Application of ICT-based noise monitoring	✓	✓	✓	✓	
	Availability of smart water meters	✓	✗	✓	✓	
	Energy saving in households	✓	✓	✓	✓	
	Solid waste collection	✓	✓	✓	✓	

Table 3. SSUCF prosperity dimension.

Smart & Sustainable Urban Computing Framework			Urban Computing Layers				Yes/No
			Urban Sensing	Urban Data Management	Urban Data Analytics	Delivery of Services	
Main Indicators	Prosperity	Innovative hubs	✓	✓	✗	✓	
		Open data	✗	✓	✗	✓	
		Accessibility of open data sets	✗	✓	✗	✓	
		Affordability of housing	✗	✓	✓	✓	
		Application of computing platforms	✗	✓	✗	✓	
		Companies providing e-services	✗	✓	✓	✓	
		Improvement of industry productivity through ICT	✓	✗	✓	✓	
		Investments in ICT innovation	✗	✓	✗	✓	
		Availability of smart water meters	✓	✓	✓	✓	
		Availability of smart electricity meters	✓	✓	✓	✓	
		Road traffic efficiency	✓	✓	✓	✓	
		Water supply ICT monitoring	✓	✓	✓	✓	
		Traffic monitoring	✓	✓	✓	✓	
		ICT Noise monitoring	✓	✓	✓	✓	

Figure 3. Rendered layout plan of Alkhaledia (Source: Salman Abdullah Bin Saedan Real Estate Group [27]).

4.2.1. The People Dimension

The "people" dimension is a set of nine indicators that were selected according to their importance to the initial framework and the availability of data. As seen in Table 4, 56% of the indicators of this dimension were not in the Alkhaledia district; this requires the urban computing contribution to enhance these indicators' existence in Alkhaledia. Moreover, 44% of the indicators were found in the Alkhaledia district, so it may need better enhancement with SSUCF. Furthermore, Figure 4 illustrates some of the indicators on the layout plan of Alkhaledia; this includes the covered indicators in Alkhaledia, such as "availability of parking guidance", which is found in mixed-use areas of the neighborhood that include stores and other facilities. Figure 4 also shows that indicators, such as "encouraging a healthy lifestyle" are not found, according to Table 4, in the neighborhood. The indicator ensures a healthier lifestyle by having a social area for people connected with green areas.

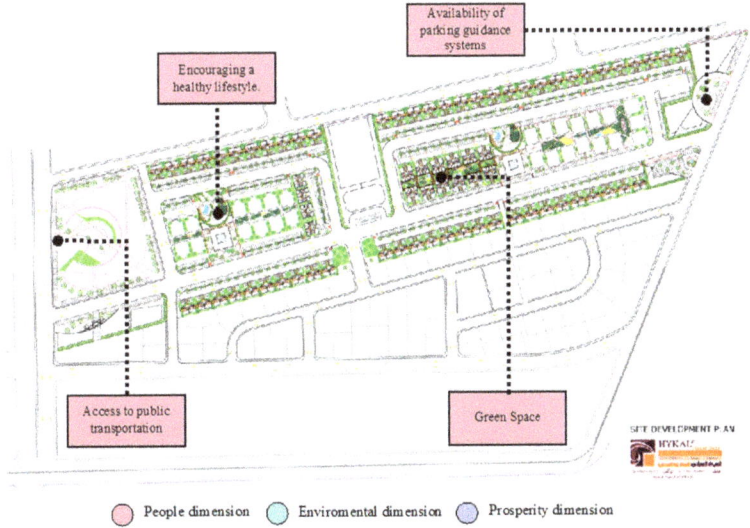

Figure 4. People dimension of the SSUCF on the layout plan (Source: Adapted from Salman Abdullah Bin Saedan Real Estate Group [27]).

Table 4. Alkhaledia—people dimension of SSUCF.

		Smart and Sustainable Urban Computing: Alkhaledia District, Jizan		
		Indicator	Coverage	Explanation
Main Indicators	People	Encouraging a healthy lifestyle	No	Although there is consideration of vegetation which conveys a healthy lifestyle, there are no other metrics to ensure a healthy lifestyle
		Cybersecurity	No	There are no technical considerations for cybersecurity
		Data privacy	No	There are no technical considerations for data privacy
		Access to public transportation	No	The design has no consideration to connect residents for public transport and there is no information on the access to public transportation either
		Diversity of housing types	Yes	Zone (3): contains three types of apartments of two or three bedrooms, penthouses, and villas
		Green space	Yes	The design of the district considered green corridors, green spaces, green plazas, and open green parks
		Availability of parking guidance systems	Yes	Connected to wi-fi networks to inform parking spot searching via smartphone
		Electricity consumption	Yes	Sensors are installed throughout the neighborhood for data collection on electricity consumption
		Information security and privacy protection	No	There is no information on how privacy is protected

4.2.2. Environment Dimension

The "environment" dimension encompasses all measures that are related to protecting the environment. Table 5 emphasizes the significance of the environmental indicators that the Alkhaledia district needs, along with indicators for environmentally sensitive matters that the region faces, such as water resources. The table has a set of nine indicators that are either "found" or "not found" in the Alkhaledia neighborhood, and it shows that to some degree, the current construction of Alkhaledia considers environmental concerns: 44% of the indicators were not found in Alkhaledia, while 56% of environmental indicators were (Table 5). This shows that Alkhaledia can easily use SSUCF to enhance the environmental aspect of the district. Moreover, Figure 5 demonstrates the contribution of SSUCF to the Alkhaledia district, illustrating how the environmental dimension provides enhancement of environmental protection.

4.2.3. Prosperity Dimension

The prosperity dimension accounts for the economic development to ensure the prosperity and longevity of the district. This dimension results in the success of building resilient neighborhoods by incorporating the nine indicators in Table 6. These indicators can be the starting point for prosperity, which can later advance to more indicators that ensure prosperity in the district. Furthermore, Table 6 shows the current state of prosperity level in Alkhaledia by having a "yes" or "no" column to indicate whether the indicators are found in the district or not. Thus, the results of the nine indicators indicate that 78% are not covered in Alkhaledia and 22% currently exist in Alkhaledia. Therefore, it highlights the need for using the SSUCF to develop the district into an enhanced neighborhood. Moreover, Figure 6 illustrates how the prosperity dimension can be incorporated into the Alkhaledia neighborhood by having some indicators shown on the layout plan of Alkhaledia.

Table 5. Alkhaledia—environmental dimension of SSUCF.

Main Indicators		Smart and Sustainable Urban Computing: Alkhaledia District, Jizan		
		Indicator	Coverage	Explanation
Main Indicators	Environmental	Domestic material consumption	No	No service acts upon domestic material consumption
		Energy consumption/demand: annual final energy consumption	Yes	Applying suitable energy conservation measures
		Carbon emissions	No	No applicable measures for the measurements of carbon emission
		Water consumption	Yes	Multiple water management strategies to measure water consumption
		Air quality index	No	There is no appropriate measure of air quality
		Recycling rate	Yes	Minimal measures of recycling waste
		Sewage system management using ICT	No	Lacks a comprehensive sewage management system by using smart technology
		Street lighting management using ICT	Yes	Available smart street lighting using sensors and ICT technology
		Solid waste collection	Yes	Available smart waste management for efficient waste collection

Figure 5. Environmental dimension of SSUCF on the residential layout plan (Source: Adapted from Salman Abdullah Bin Saedan Real Estate Group [27]).

Table 6. Alkhaledia—prosperity dimension of SSUCF.

		Smart and Sustainable Urban Computing: Alkhaledia District, Jizan		
		Indicator	Coverage	Explanation
Main Indicators	Prosperity	Open data	No	Lacks an open data platform
		Affordability of housing	Yes	Zone (3): contains affordable types of apartments of two or three bedrooms, penthouses, and villas
		Improvement of industry productivity through ICT	No	Although limited ICT technologies are used throughout the district, there is no further advancement of ICT industry productivity
		Availability of smart water meters	Yes	The district installs meters, transmitters, and sensors for the success of smart water meters
		Availability of smart electricity meters	No	There are no available meters, transmitters, and sensors for smart electricity metering
		Road traffic efficiency	No	Lacks road traffic efficiency
		Water supply ICT monitoring	No	Although limited ICT technologies are used throughout the district there is no further advancement of ICT water supply monitoring
		Traffic monitoring	No	Lacks the focus on traffic monitoring
		ICT noise monitoring	No	Lacks an ICT noise monitoring sensory system

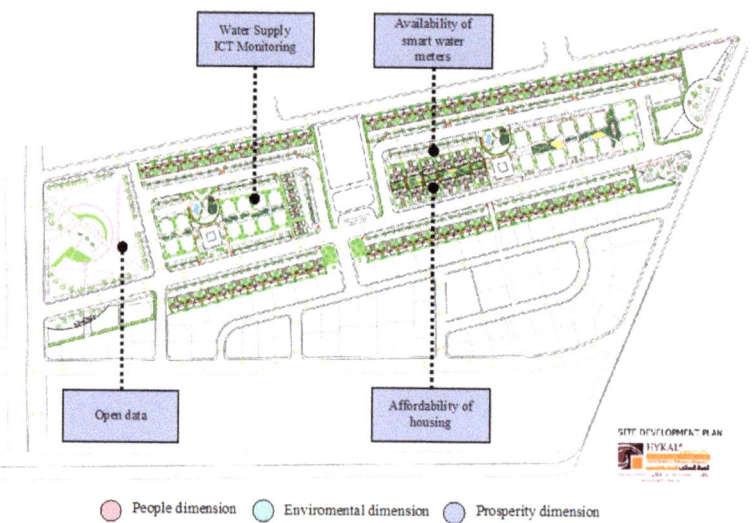

Figure 6. Prosperity dimension SSUCF on the residential layout plan (Source: Adapted from Salman Abdullah Bin Saedan Real Estate Group [27]).

5. Discussion

This article is mainly concerned with developing a framework based on the idea of urban computing, and the process of developing the framework went through multiple stages of thorough analysis to make the SSUCF. Therefore, the results of each table interpret different meanings and significance. The data on the four smart and sustainable standards, the interpretation of the urban computing concept, and their analysis support the theory that urban computing has great significance in the enhancement of neighborhood quality of life, sustainability, and smartness, as highlighted by Keshavarzi et al. [4] and Alshuwaikhat et al. [6]. A few of the chosen indicators fell under all the urban computing categories, while others had only certain urban computing categories that can relate to the indicator. Therefore, this proves that urban computing can be used as a structured format for the development of sustainability and smartness.

The initial framework for SSUCF contains the three main chosen dimensions of "people", "environment", and "prosperity", which were deduced from the filtered smart and sustainable standards while considering the local context and alignment with the Saudi 2030 vision. The table has a total of 42 indicators that relate to the environmental, social, and economic aspects that a neighborhood should focus on, to ensure the success of the framework. Furthermore, this table demonstrates the correlation between urban computing and the three chosen dimensions, which also illustrates how critical the sequence of sensors, data management, data analysis, and services are (in that order) for the indicators to be effective and efficient. Each indicator has its essential urban computing layer, which is analyzed by various literature reviews and other sustainable standards. Abusaada and Elshater [28] developed a similar framework of urban design for smart sustainable cities. However, their framework focused on two dimensions—urban economy and placemaking—which did not explicitly consider the environmental dimension.

Tables 4–6 show, as stated in Section 3.2.1, how sensors are the first detectors for data that help us attain the information to procure sustainable and efficient services [29]. This shows how important attaining data by sensors is in the urban sensing category, where 62% of the 42 indicators needed the sensory system. Moreover, the data management category showcases the importance of data being neatly organized by an indexing structure as it integrates both spatiotemporal and textual information for efficient data analytics. This finding shows that the category is critical to the achievement of the goal of the framework by having 90% of the 42 indicators including urban data management.

Urban data analytics is the use of big data analytics to analyze relations of data for the success of urban computing in neighborhoods [30–34], and 78% of the indicators may need big data analysis for the efficient use of indicators. Finally, 90% of the indicators are relevant to the delivery of services category. This shows that as part of having an inclusive and higher quality of life neighborhood, we must focus on the needs of residents and how our technology and smart gadgets can be of help for solving problems efficiently. The SSUCF has multiple limitations, some of which are how resources are limited and how ready decision-makers are for a smart-driven neighborhood. This is in terms of awareness of developers and the availability of resources for the technical success of the neighborhood projects.

Section 4.2 shows the findings of the case study, in the Alkhaledia district, Jizan. The section presents the tailored indicators for Alkhaledia from the developed framework, since the Alkhaledia project has sustainable and smart objectives, some indicators are met, however, they need some alteration to fit into the SSUCF. This was developed by analyzing indicators by the criteria of "must have", "should have", and "nice to have", and relying on the project characteristics mentioned in the literature review case study section, as to whether these indicators are found or not, and if found, it could be enhanced into the structured format of urban computing categories. If an indicator is not found and if it is a must-have for a smart sustainable neighborhood, then it will undergo the thorough process of urban computing categories to form a successful indicator that serves its residents, economy, and environment. Although this filtering of indicators yields 27 indicators, it is partly a result of the lack of data regarding the Alkhaledia districts and their policies. Therefore, the limitation of resources and data creates a constrained development of indicators for enhanced development of the SSUCF.

Another set of challenges regarding the use of data in this framework are the data-specific issues, which can fall under data acquisition, privacy, and security. Since data and computing together form the critical component of urban computing, it must be executed efficiently by considering all of its components. The most crucial factor is data privacy and security since smart applications not only gather a variety of information from people and their social networks that are sensitive to privacy [35,36], but also operate facilities and have an impact on people's lives. Furthermore, data acquisition is another challenge, as the collection of data from sensors creates a large volume of information that might be difficult to analyze with redundant data.

The SSUCF focuses on social, environmental, and economic factors. The "people" dimension relates to the socially important indicators that ensure a better quality of life. Table 4 shows the first three indicators of the people dimension in SSUCF. Furthermore, this dimension accounts for the residents' related data and what we can do when we acquire these data to better serve the people which in turn demands a security system that ensures the protection of the community's data, hence the cybersecurity indicator shown in Table 4. As mentioned in the literature review, there are precautions to ensure data security, and that is important, as a technology-based system is more prone to cyber risks, therefore, addressing these sensitive topics is critical to ensure better performance of the smart and sustainable neighborhood. These indicators are enhanced into a comprehensive indicator by plugging in the urban computing categories. The "environmental" dimension, which was missing in Abusaada and Elshater's framework [28] includes a set of indicators that promotes environmental sustainability. Though energy and water consumption and recycling indicators are covered in Alkhaledia, carbon emissions are not covered. Carbon emissions are regarded as one of the important environmental indicators since they are related to climate change [37–39].

The final dimension of this framework is "prosperity", which encompasses the economical aspect of the neighborhood that secures longevity and prosperity in the district. A neighborhood built with this framework can ensure the complete comfort of residents to live a sustainable and smart life. These objectives ensure the availability of services to enhance the quality of life in the Alkhaledia district. Table 6 shows some of the indicators that are found in the "prosperity" dimension, chosen by analyzing the report documents available from the Alkhaledia district and selecting the appropriate indicators from the selected standards to support the neighborhood's prosperity. Consequently, having urban computing layers enhances the production of this dimension, with the help of a literature review to understand how technology can elevate the prosperity of the neighborhood. For instance, affordable housing is a critical consideration when developing this framework, and since the Alkhaledia district has the design objective of constructing an affordable housing residential area, urban computing can be plugged into this neighborhood and framework.

6. Conclusions

This article aims to establish neighborhoods that support a healthy environment, a strong community, and growing economic value by having a smart and sustainable neighborhood framework, facilitated using intelligent concepts and technologies, such as urban computing. Creating smart sustainable neighborhoods is crucial to addressing the ever-changing demands of Saudi citizens who live in urban areas. A comprehensive and integrated approach to a neighborhood's social, economic, and environmental values is lacking in Saudi neighborhoods. As a result, it creates a variety of negative effects, including poor environmental protection, poor quality of life, and insufficient services and amenities. More importantly, Saudi Vision 2030 has three main areas of focus: "vibrant society", "thriving economy", and "ambitious nation", which emphasize the need for neighborhoods that are more environmentally conscious and has smart technologies to support sustainability and its measures. To build a brighter future for the country and its people, the 2030 Vision is used as the foundation for the project's proposed framework and acts as its primary goal. Furthermore, an application of this framework was created in the Alkhaledia district, for further advancement of the framework.

Two key elements are crucial to the creation of this framework: the concept of urban computing, which is the identification and analysis of the four subcategories of urban computing: urban sensing, urban data management, urban data analytics, and the delivery of services; and selecting the appropriate indications from the four sets of standards which are ITU, ETSI, and SDG 11 for sustainable cities and communities. These two elements influenced how the SSUCF is developed. Consequently, a tailored framework is developed to be implemented in the Alkhaledia district to enhance the effectiveness of this framework. This was accomplished by having filtered indicators that aim to improve the Alkhaledia district. This framework development shows that urban computing may be used as a basis for support, together with smart and sustainable standards, to establish a framework for a neighborhood that is both smart and sustainable. Additionally, this framework can be used in other Saudi neighborhoods to improve the quality of life, environmental protection, and economic values when accommodating the relevant data.

Furthermore, urban computing involves more than just smart technologies, it also considers how to gather the relevant data that will help us find solutions, manage that data, and link technology with local problems to find solutions. This serves the residents, helps the economy, and supports the environment. Since many Saudi neighborhoods do not use smart technologies to assist sustainable growth, this framework supports tackling this gap. Additionally, this analysis shows that urban computing could serve as a constructive and organized format for the use of smart technologies to serve the sustainability of the community, economy, and environment. These results were found by a matrix table checking how many smart or sustainable indicators can fall under urban computing categories.

The final finding is the application of the SSUCF in the Alkhaledia district, Jizan. This framework is tailored to the context of Jizan and its available data; therefore, to achieve these smart and sustainable goals, a variety of strategies must be used, along with advanced technology solutions, research, inventions, and deployment found in this framework. Various indicators were chosen to improve the Alkhaledia neighborhood and build a more comprehensive and inclusive district. This was achieved by first studying the current state of Alkhaledia and having indicators enhance the present elements of Alkhaledia, and constructing it if it does not yet exist.

Moreover, this framework has limitations that are related to data collection, data privacy, data security, and data analysis. Even though data collection is made easy with sensors, it could create challenges since it might collect redundant and high-volume data. Furthermore, data privacy and security are vital concerns, since all relevant data of citizens are collected to create an enhanced quality of life. Furthermore, other limitations of this article include the filtration of indicators that resulted from a lack of data regarding Jizan policies and the neighborhood's readiness for a technology-based infrastructure and development. Additionally, Alkhaledia has different sectors to focus on, and this demands integration between stakeholders and investors by involving all personal data to make decision-making more cohesive for smart and sustainable neighborhoods.

Future studies might explore enhancing the indicators concerning residents' quality of life—that is, more comprehensive indicators should be considered and extended to address more neighborhood sectors, subject to the availability of resources and data. This article is important for building a smart and sustainable neighborhood, especially in the Saudi region where it is most needed. Furthermore, despite this development of the framework being tailored to the Alkhaledia district, it can be implemented in other neighborhoods and regions since it has room for further enhancement for a more integrated, smart, and sustainable neighborhood framework. Nonetheless, with the aid of smart technology, the SSUCF can foster communities that are inclusive in all social, economic, and environmental aspects. Future studies can explore how the concepts of Kate Raworth's "doughnut economy" or "circular economy" can be integrated into the development of smart sustainable indicators [40,41]. These indicators can create not only a guideline heuristic for different cities to start to think about sustainable initiatives, but might also address sustainable macro perspectives.

Author Contributions: Conceptualization, H.M.A. and L.B.; methodology, H.M.A., Y.A.A. and L.B.; formal analysis, L.B.; writing—original draft preparation, Y.A.A. and L.B.; writing—review and editing, H.M.A., Y.A.A. and L.B.; supervision, H.M.A. All authors have read and agreed to the published version of the manuscript.

Funding: This research received no external funding.

Institutional Review Board Statement: Not applicable.

Data Availability Statement: The data presented in this study are available in the article.

Acknowledgments: The authors acknowledge the support of the Interdisciplinary Research Center for Smart Mobility & Logistics (under project number IN-ML2200), King Fahd University of Petroleum and Minerals, and Yanbu Industrial College, Saudi Arabia. The authors are also grateful to Salman Abdullah Bin Saedan Real Estate Group for providing the Jizan Master Plan Development documents.

Conflicts of Interest: The authors declare no conflict of interest.

References

1. Drobniak, A. The urban resilience–economic perspective. *J. Econ. Manag.* **2012**, *10*, 5–20.
2. United Nations. From Department of Economic and Social Affairs. Available online: https://www.un.org/development/desa/en/news/population/2018-revision-of-world-urbanization-prospects.html (accessed on 16 May 2018).
3. Nakano, S.; Washizu, A. Will smart cities enhance the social capital of residents? The importance of smart neighborhood management. *Cities* **2021**, *115*, 103244. [CrossRef]
4. Keshavarzi, G.; Yildirim, Y.; Arefi, M. Does scale matter? An overview of the "smart cities" literature. *Sustain. Cities Soc.* **2021**, *74*, 103151. [CrossRef]
5. INEA. Smart Cities & Communities. Available online: https://ec.europa.eu/inea/en/horizon-2020/smart-cities-communities (accessed on 15 December 2022).
6. Alshuwaikhat, H.M.; Aina, Y.A.; Binsaedan, L. Analysis of the implementation of urban computing in smart cities: A framework for the transformation of Saudi cities. *Heliyon* **2022**, *8*, e11138. [CrossRef] [PubMed]
7. Torres-Ruiz, M.J.; Lytras, M.D. Urban Computing and Smart Cities Applications for the Knowledge Society. *Int. J. Knowl. Soc. Res.* **2016**, *7*, 113–119. [CrossRef]
8. Shi, W.; Goodchild, M.; Batty, M.; Kwan, M.; Zhang, A. Introduction to urban informatics. In *Urban Informatics*; Shi, W., Goodchild, M., Batty, M., Kwan, M., Zhang, A., Eds.; Springer: Berlin/Heidelberg, Germany, 2021; pp. 1–7.
9. Nasser, G.M.; Alghamdi, M. Social sustainability in the built environment of Riyadh city (Case study: Al-Waha residential neighborhood). *Emir. J. Eng. Res.* **2022**, *27*, 5.
10. Ledraa, T.; Aldegheishem, A. What Matters Most for Neighborhood Greenspace Usability and Satisfaction in Riyadh: Size or Distance to Home? *Sustainability* **2022**, *14*, 6216. [CrossRef]
11. Bay, M.A.; Alnaim, M.M.; Albaqawy, G.A.; Noaime, E. The Heritage Jewel of Saudi Arabia: A Descriptive Analysis of the Heritage Management and Development Activities in the At-Turaif District in Ad-Dir'iyah, a World Heritage Site (WHS). *Sustainability* **2022**, *14*, 10718. [CrossRef]
12. Alnaim, M.M.; Noaime, E. Typological Transformation of Individual Housing in Hail City, Saudi Arabia: Between Functional Needs, Socio-Cultural, and Build Polices Concerns. *Sustainability* **2022**, *14*, 6704. [CrossRef]
13. Alshuwaikhat, H.M.; Adenle, Y.A.; Almuhaidib, T. A lifecycle-based smart sustainable city strategic framework for realizing smart and sustainability initiatives in Riyadh City. *Sustainability* **2022**, *14*, 824. [CrossRef]
14. Aina, Y.A. Achieving smart sustainable cities with GeoICT support: The Saudi evolving smart cities. *Cities* **2017**, *71*, 49–58. [CrossRef]
15. Aapo Huovilaa, P.B. Comparative analysis of standardized indicators for Smart sustainable cities: What indicators and standards to use and when. *Cities Int. J. Urban Policy Plan.* **2019**, *89*, 141–153. [CrossRef]
16. Aina, Y.A.; Wafer, A.; Ahmed, F.; Alshuwaikhat, H.M. Top-down sustainable urban development? Urban governance transformation in Saudi Arabia. *Cities* **2019**, *90*, 272–281. [CrossRef]
17. Karban, A.S. Developing a Framework for Neighborhood-Level Urban Sustainability Assessment in Saudi Arabia. Master's Thesis, Umm Al-Qura University, Mecca, Saudi Arabia, 2014.
18. UN-Habitat. A new Strategy of Sustainable Neighbourhood Planning: Five Principles. Available online: https://unhabitat.org/sites/default/files/download-manager-files/A%20New%20Strategy%20of%20Sustainable%20Neighbourhood%20Planning%20Five%20principles.pdf (accessed on 15 December 2022).
19. ITU-TY.4901/L.1601; Key Performance Indicators Related to the Use of Information and Communication Technology in Smart Sustainable Cities. International Telecommunication Union: Geneva, Switzerland, 2016.

20. Zheng, Y.; Wu, W.; Chen, Y.; Qu, H.; Ni, L.M. Visual Analytics in Urban Computing: An Overview. *IEEE Xplore* **2016**, *2*, 276–296. [CrossRef]
21. Bibri, S.E. *Data-Driven Smart Sustainable Cities of the Future: Urban Computing and Intelligence for Strategic, Short-Term, and Joined-Up Planning*; Springer: Berlin/Heidelberg, Germany, 2021.
22. *ITU-TY.4902/L.1602*; Key Performance Indicators Related to the Sustainability Impacts of Information and Communication Technology in Smart Sustainable Cities. International Telecommunications Union: Geneva, Switzerland, 2016.
23. *ITU-TY.4903/L.1603*; Key Performance Indicators for Smart Evaluation and Assessment Sustainable Cities to Assess the Achievement of Sustainable Development Goals. International Telecommunications Union: Geneva, Switzerland, 2016.
24. *ETSI-TS103-463*; Access, Terminals, Transmission and Multiplexing (ATTM); Key Performance Indicators for Sustainable Digital Multiservice Cities. ETSI TS: Sophia Antipolis, France, 2017.
25. UN. *Sustainable Development Goal 11: Make Cities and Human Settlements Inclusive, Safe, Resilient and Sustainable*; United Nations: Lake Success, NY, USA, 2016.
26. Zheng, Y. *Urban Computing*; MIT Press: Cambridge, MA, USA, 2019.
27. Salman Abdullah BinSaedan Real Estate Group. *Alkhaledia Master Plan Development*; Salman Abdullah BinSaedan Real Estate Group: Riyadh, Saudi Arabia, 2017.
28. Abusaada, H.; Elshater, A. Competitiveness, distinctiveness and singularity in urban design: A systematic review and framework for smart cities. *Sustain. Cities Soc.* **2021**, *68*, 102782. [CrossRef]
29. Behr Tech. Behr Tech Top IoT Sensor Types. Available online: https://behrtech.com/blog/top-10-iot-sensor-types/ (accessed on 5 December 2022).
30. Zheng, Y. Urban Computing: Concepts, Methodologies, and Applications. *ACM Trans. Intell. Syst. Technol.* **2014**, *11*, 55.
31. Zheng, Y. *Urban Computing: Enabling Urban Intelligence with Big Data*; The MIT Press: Cambridge, MA, USA, 2017; pp. 1–3.
32. Miltiadis, D.; Lytras, A.V.-R. IEEE Access Special Section Editorial: Urban Computing and Well-Being in Smart Cities: Services, Applications, Policymaking Considerations. *IEEE Access* **2020**, *8*, 72340–72346.
33. Pérez-Chacón, R.; Luna-Romera, J.M.; Troncoso, A.; Martínez-Álvarez, F.; Riquelme, J.C. Big Data Analytics for Discovering Electricity Consumption Patterns in Smart Cities. *Energies* **2018**, *11*, 683. [CrossRef]
34. Pettit, A.B.C. Planning support systems for smart cities. *City Cult. Soc.* **2018**, *12*, 13–24. [CrossRef]
35. Belli, A.C.L. IoT-Enabled Smart Sustainable Cities: Challenges and Approaches. *Smart Cities* **2020**, *3*, 52. [CrossRef]
36. Khatoun, S.Z.R. Cybersecurity and Privacy Solutions in Smart Cities. *IEEE Commun. Mag.* **2017**, *55*, 51–59. [CrossRef]
37. Quijano, A.; Hernández, J.L.; Nouaille, P.; Virtanen, M.; Sánchez-Sarachu, B.; Pardo-Bosch, F.; Knieilng, J. Towards sustainable and smart cities: Replicable and KPI-driven evaluation framework. *Buildings* **2022**, *12*, 233. [CrossRef]
38. Kaginalkar, A.; Kumar, S.; Gargava, P.; Niyogi, D. Review of urban computing in air quality management as smart city service: An integrated IoT, AI, and cloud technology perspective. *Urban Clim.* **2021**, *39*, 100972. [CrossRef]
39. Hancke, G.P.; de Carvalho e Silva, B.; Hancke, G.P., Jr. The Role of Advanced Sensing in Smart Cities. *Sensors* **2012**, *13*, 393–425. [CrossRef]
40. Raworth, K. A Doughnut for the Anthropocene: Humanity's compass in the 21st century. *Lancet Planet. Health* **2017**, *1*, e48–e49. [CrossRef]
41. Almulhim, A.I.; Abubakar, I.R. Understanding public environmental awareness and attitudes toward circular economy transition in Saudi Arabia. *Sustainability* **2021**, *13*, 10157. [CrossRef]

Disclaimer/Publisher's Note: The statements, opinions and data contained in all publications are solely those of the individual author(s) and contributor(s) and not of MDPI and/or the editor(s). MDPI and/or the editor(s) disclaim responsibility for any injury to people or property resulting from any ideas, methods, instructions or products referred to in the content.

Article

Exploring the Smart Street Management and Control Platform from the Perspective of Sustainability: A Study of Five Typical Chinese Cities

Fanding Xiang, Haomiao Cheng * and Yi Wang

College of Architecture and Urban Planning, Beijing University of Technology, Beijing 100021, China
* Correspondence: chenghaomiao@bjut.edu.cn

Abstract: In the context of "smart cities" and stock-based development, street renewal focuses more on quality and sustainability in China. To improve the efficiency of current smart technology applications, a comprehensive whole-life cycle system needs to be established in street space. After sorting out the application of smart technologies in the street design guidelines (SDGs) for typical cities in China, the compilation and application of smart technologies for sustainability were categorized into five areas: smart transportation, convenient living, life enrichment, the protection of vulnerable people, and environmental monitoring. Based on theoretical support and realistic needs, a smart street management and control platform (SSMCP) was built. The SSMCP is divided into four layers: the basic information layer for the background, the technology platform layer for the core processing, the institutional protection layer for the guarantee mechanism, and the scene application layer for spatial interactions. The results can provide a scientific reference for improving the sustainability of street space and implementing a "smart cities" project at the street level.

Keywords: smart city; sustainable design; stock-based renewal; street design guidelines; China

---

Citation: Xiang, F.; Cheng, H.; Wang, Y. Exploring the Smart Street Management and Control Platform from the Perspective of Sustainability: A Study of Five Typical Chinese Cities. *Sustainability* **2023**, *15*, 3438. https://doi.org/10.3390/su15043438

Academic Editors: Tan Yigitcanlar, Juan M. Corchado and Rashid Mehmood

Received: 19 January 2023
Revised: 9 February 2023
Accepted: 11 February 2023
Published: 13 February 2023

Copyright: © 2023 by the authors. Licensee MDPI, Basel, Switzerland. This article is an open access article distributed under the terms and conditions of the Creative Commons Attribution (CC BY) license (https:// creativecommons.org/licenses/by/ 4.0/).

1. Introduction

The evolution of the digital age brought about changes in smart technologies, giving rise to efficient development in many fields worldwide, such as finance, the military, ecology and environment, social and economic life, and so on [1]. In the field of urban construction, the promotion of smart cities through smart technologies has broadened its scope of application. Smart cities apply computing technology in urban planning and construction management, such as cloud computing, big data, and spatial geographic information, which make urban infrastructure more interconnected and efficient, while empowering the government with efficient operation and management mechanisms, as well as providing better living services for people [2]. As constructing a "smart city" is a significant strategic opportunity, smart construction, the smart coordination of resources, and the smart management of data has advanced rapidly in China [3]. In December 2015, the China Central Urban Work Conference noted that urban renewal should conform to the "new normal", adhere to the concepts of "smart growth" and "stock-based renewal", and promote the transformation of urban development for connotative growth [4,5]. Smart technologies should be focused on actively promoting the sustainable construction of urban public spaces in relation to the aspects of health, safety, and livability [6,7]. Therefore, the mode of enhancing the competitiveness of cities through smart technologies and sustainable development has gradually reached a consensus [8]. Applying smart technologies to the redesigning of urban space has become possible [9].

The use of smart technologies to realize stock-based development is gradually being explored in China. The city information model (CIM) has been developed to serve as the basis of smart construction [10,11]. The data-control platform elements present the characteristics of a giant system with multiple objects, departments, and levels [12]. Currently, there are several problems, such as urban data silos, single-data scenarios, a lack of information technology [13], and unsound operation and management systems [14]. In terms of street space, the application of smart technologies lacks theoretical support and overall control of the whole-life cycle, and there is insufficient consideration of the concepts of overall management and control, planning, and co-governance construction.

The city is a complex mega-system, with many sectors involved in the design of street space [15]. Street space contains many elements, and street space management involves many construction departments, as its functions are comprehensive and complex [16]. Research on developing smart street space in China began in 2016. Shanghai issued the first city-level SDGs, which answered the questions: "what kind of sustainable streets should be built?" and "what kind of smart technology should be applied?". Since then, several SDGs have been successively compiled and have continuously enriched the connotations of street space according to local circumstances (Figure 1). However, the overall coordination of the system of traffic, municipal pipelines, landscape, and urban furniture is unclear. As the SDGs provide more explicit valuable concepts and mature technical support, using smart technologies to build a comprehensive system has become an effective way to achieve sustainable development. Promoting street renewal requires a robust and comprehensive platform for the overall planning, design, and management of street space [17,18].

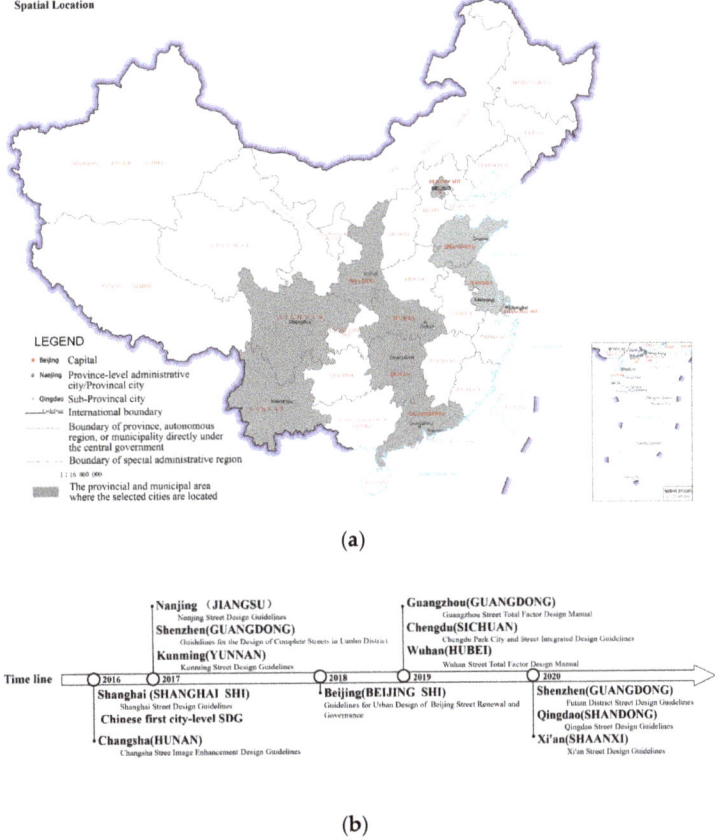

Figure 1. Spatial locations and timeline of SDGs in China ((**a**): spatial location; (**b**): timeline). Source: by author on the basis of data from [19–24].

In the context of smart cities, the use of smart technologies is becoming more widespread. Following the achievements of China's smart city construction and stock-based renewal, this study demonstrated the validity and necessity of improving sustainability and quality in street space based on analyzing SDG data. The SDG data obtained in this paper allowed us to sort out the types, ranges, and methods of application of smart technologies in each selected case. Meanwhile, in the process of analyzing data, some insightful details were highlighted as figures. After comprehensive comparison, a summary of the applications of various smart technologies, which was the theoretical basis as well, was created to present the scenarios of application and technical equipment of SDGs. Based on those details and the theoretical basis, a comprehensive platform was explored, which was the Smart Street Management and Control Platform (SSMCP) (Figure in Section 3.3). This research aimed to show an integrated real-case framework for a whole-life-cycle system based on street space, which can be of significance for smart cities research in China in the future.

2. Methods and Data

2.1. Experimental Methods

The literature review method was used in this study to analyze the SDGs of typical cities in China, and a qualitative comparative analysis method was used to build the SSMCP framework. The literature review method is a systematic way of locating and analyzing arguments. It can aid in formulating search strategies for different databases, conducting systematic studies on a particular issue, and drawing conclusions. The literature review method comprises four steps: question raising, literature determination, data extraction, and presentation of conclusions [25]. In this paper, a sustainable perspective on smart technology was proposed, and the retrieval object was determined to be the SDGs of typical cities in China. The focal points of the SDGs were summarized via text sorting. A qualitative comparative analysis method was then used to identify shared attributes in the scientific information presented in the literature. Based on the essential differences between different city development visions, the wholes and the parts that need to be compared in each city were identified, and the sustainable development and smart technology applications were summarized. This method ensured that the path of the comparative analysis could distinguish the focuses and commonalities and the underlying causal logic could be explored [26]. Based on the literature review and comparative analysis, the framework of the SSMCP was proposed.

2.2. Experimental Data

The present study analyzed the SDGs of five typical cities in China. SDGs are specialized and systematic technical manuals and methods for guiding construction and design [27]. Each of the five typical cities is endowed with unique themes and characteristics (Table 1). As China's capital city, Beijing assumes the function of a window onto city life. To optimize the elements of street space, the SDGs put forward the requirements for sustainable development as their orientation, and they highlight the value of delicate design. Value transformation emphasizes a people-oriented priority; holistic management and control; and diversified collaboration, coordination, and overall planning [28]. Shanghai is envisioned as actively responding to new urban construction and building a modern city that is harmonious, livable, vibrant, and distinctive. It also advances the construction goals of "prosperity and innovation, health and ecology, happiness and humanity", which lend a focus to transforming the mode of urban development and achieving endogenous growth through organic renewal. To further implement harmonious and livable spaces, the guidelines emphasize strengthening street design, improving service supply, and shaping the city spirit [29]. Shenzhen promotes the general theme that "the core of the city is people". There, urban development is expected to adhere to the principle of moving from "Shenzhen speed" to "Shenzhen quality". Their guidelines indicate that urban renewal and ecological restoration should be carried out on the micro-level of street space to improve urban quality. The development goal of "safety, vitality, beauty, wisdom, and green" is supported by smart facility planning and design [30]. Against the background of stock-based development, Nanjing is committed to promoting the transformation of urban development through urban design. The guidelines emphasize convenience and a sense of the scale of streets as standards for measuring the degree of perfection. Focusing on the goal of "building a modern international humanistic and green city", the guidelines highlight a "green, humanistic, smart and intensive" orientation [31]. Qingdao emphasizes that the human living environment is the intrinsic driving force of urban development. The guidelines introduce the four concepts of "people-oriented, spatial coordination, organic integration, and system coordination", which create an engine for sustainable street-level development.

Table 1. Overview of the five typical cities. Source: by author on the basis of data from [19–24].

City	Level	Location	Vision
Beijing	Capital city	Northern China	Harmonious City of Sustainability
Shanghai	Province-level administrative city	Eastern China	Prosperity, Health, and Happiness
Shenzhen		Southern China	From Speed to Quality
Nanjing	Provincial city	Eastern China	Modern International Green City of Humanities
Qingdao	Sub-provincial city		Humanization Design

3. Discussion and Results

3.1. Selected Case Studies on Smart Technology Application

The sorting of the selected cases was conducted, and all the smart technologies and application scenarios were recorded. Some especially insightful applications from selected cases were highlighted with figures.

3.1.1. Beijing

The Guidelines for the Urban Design of Beijing Street Renewal and Governance promote the development of technology applications from the perspective of efficiency and sustainability (Table 2) [19]. The guidelines propose that technologies are used for smart transportation, and they advocate that signal light poles should hold some electronic equipment (Figure 2a) and be integrated to save space. The guidelines present a vision of multifunctional combinations of urban furniture, allowing that furniture to provide a more comprehensive range of convenience services, such as newsstands (Figure 2b). In addition, from the perspective of environmental monitoring, sensors on the streetlamp shades could monitor the microclimate in real time by collecting various types of data, such as on air pollutants, light intensity, noise, heat islands, etc. The sensors could also monitor the flow of people and calculate signaling data to assess street vitality, ultimately giving feedback to managers via wireless networks. The guidelines also suggest that street-level data could be shared and first-hand information could be used for terminal analyses.

Table 2. The applications of smart technologies in the Beijing SDGs. Source: by author on the basis of data from [19].

Application Scenario	Object	Purpose	Description
Smart Transportation	Signal Light Pole	Collect traffic data	The poles carry sensors for traffic flow detection and road hazard detection
	Bus Stop	Provide bus location information	Build a bus information platform using big data to provide bus arrival information
	Vehicle Lane	Improve driving efficiency	Form a green-wave traffic zone via traffic-light signals and dynamically add reversible lanes

Table 2. Cont.

Application Scenario	Object	Purpose	Description
	Shared Bicycle	Increase utilization	Real-time control and regulation of bicycle location and use through apps
	Parking Lot	Optimize parking resources	Build a parking-fee system to realize parking-space sharing
	Comprehensive Platform	Improve urban efficiency	Use of terminal data analysis for electronic warnings
Convenient Living	Public Art Installations	Enhance interactions	Expand communications media, such as images, sounds, smells, and tactile experiences through art installations
	Urban Furniture	Provide self-service facilities	Promote the installation of interactive information systems in facilities such as newsstands, bus stops, and garbage bins to provide retail, Wi-Fi, charging piles, and other services
	Smart Device	Information sharing	Information interaction between apps, parking cloud platforms, delivery services, etc.
Environmental Monitoring	Streetlamp Shade	Collect environmental data	Monitor the local climate environment via timed and photoelectric control equipment

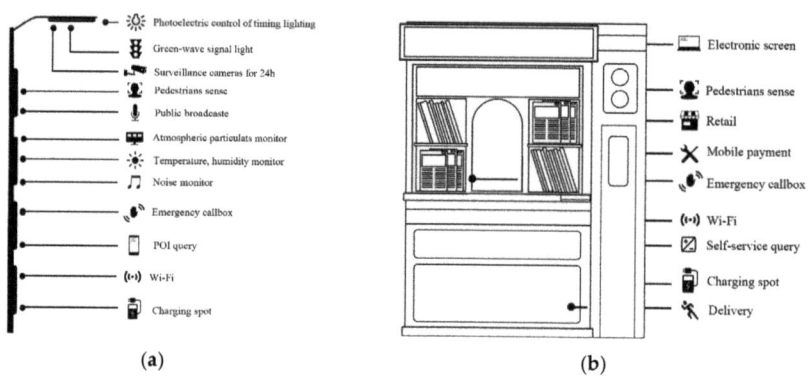

Figure 2. Urban furniture design recommended in the Beijing SDGs ((**a**): light pole; (**b**): newsstand). Source: by author on the basis of data from [19].

3.1.2. Shanghai

The Shanghai Street Design Guidelines state that new materials and technologies applied in the street space should achieve sustainable development [20]. The sustainable construction of streets according to the guidelines can be summarized as relating to five aspects: transportation, life, vitality and enrichment, safety, and the environment (Table 3). The guidelines propose that the coordination of transportation facilities is more efficient in facilitating residents' mobility. As relates to the aspect of convenient living, the installation of electronic-screen-realized multisource information dissemination and real-time release of various city information is recommended. The guidelines also state that the consolidation of municipal facilities into a facility belt should be encouraged (Figure 3). As an improvement for life enrichment, some communications media were incorporated into public art installations. The application of audio, video, and heat-sensing technologies could improve self-protection. The use of interactive media, data terminals in urban furniture, and multiple sensors achieve monitoring and management of the living environment. The guidelines also propose that data should be collected and feedback provided so as to dynamically adjust urban activities via various smart technologies. The establishment of a comprehensive smart city platform is also proposed to analyze different activities.

Table 3. The applications of smart technologies in the Shanghai SDGs. Source: by author on the basis of data from [20].

Application Scenario	Object	Purpose	Description
Smart Transportation	Signal Light	Improve traffic efficiency	Create a green-wave traffic belt and establish a bus-only signal system
	Bus Stop	Provide bus information	Make electronic station signs and provide an outlet for passenger complaints and other services
	Shared Bicycle	Combined with public transportation system	Obtain information on available bicycles through the public transportation system and make reservations for borrowing and returning bicycles
	Parking Lot	Optimize parking resources	Establish a parking guidance and parking-space-sensing system
	Traffic Information Panel	Improve information coverage	Set up information terminals that can display all kinds of traffic information and reduce dependence on mobile phones
Convenient Living	Electronic Screen	Provide handy information	Use screens to provide information for daily life, business, and medical care and to display security and disaster warning information
	Newsstand	Provide life services	Provide self-service retailing, charging piles, Wi-Fi, express delivery, mobile payment, and other services
	Garbage Can	Reduce pollution	Use solar energy to compress the volume of garbage, notify sanitation personnel of the transfer, and provide recycling information
	Municipal Facility	Intensify space	Encourage "multipurpose for one pole and box" and control the occupied proportion of facilities
Life Enrichment	Public Art Installations	Increase street vitality	Expand communications media, such as images, sounds, smells, and tactile experiences through art installations
Protection of Vulnerable People	Audio and Video Surveillance Equipment	Maintain security	Establish an analytical platform to automatically identify special situations and establish an early warning system for natural disasters via audio, video, and heat-sensing technologies
	Emergency Callbox	Focus on the needs of vulnerable people	Provide signal sound alerts at intersections and set infrared sensor alert devices at pedestrian crossings
Environmental Monitoring	Streetlamp Shade	Collect environmental data	Load with sensors for the real-time monitoring of noise, air quality, and temperature
	Green Irrigation System	Save water	Dynamic adjustment of irrigation time and volume through humidity sensing

3.1.3. Shenzhen

The application of smart technologies in Shenzhen's SDGs is reflected in smart transportation, convenient living, the protection of vulnerable people, and environmental monitoring (Table 4) [21,22]. In terms of smart transportation, the guidelines state that technologies such as radar and geomagnetic induction could be used in signal light poles to record the spatial and temporal characteristics of people and vehicles in traffic. In regard to convenient living, the guidelines propose the concept of a smart life micro-hub, which could provide customized demand services (Figure 4). Considering vulnerable people, the feasibility of providing protection could be enhanced through the application of infrared thermal imaging facilities and sound devices. Regarding environmental monitoring, the guidelines recommend comprehensive monitoring via environmental sensors, and data density in key areas should be strengthened.

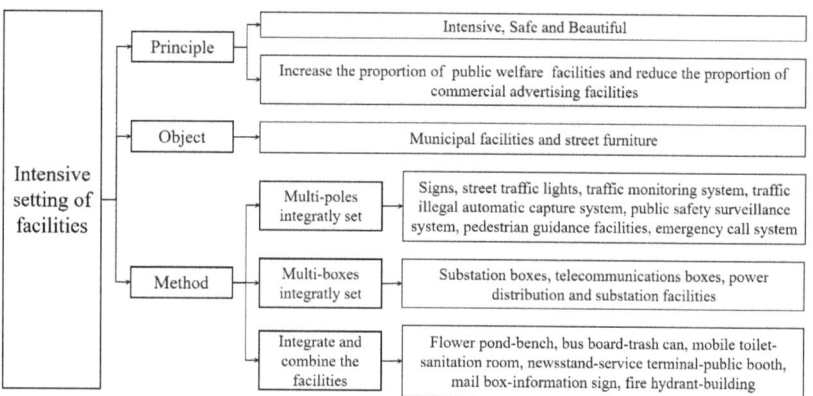

Figure 3. The integration modes of street space noted in the Shanghai SDGs. Source: by author on the basis of data from [20].

Table 4. The applications of smart technologies in the Shenzhen SDGs. Source: by author on the basis of data from [21,22].

Application Scenario	Object	Purpose	Description
Smart Transportation	Signal Light Pole	Record human and vehicle data	Use radar, geomagnetic and thermal sensing, satellite positioning, IoT, and other technologies to record information on the flow of people and the type and number of vehicles
	Composite Transportation System	Establish a barrier-free travel system	Customize travel needs for elderly, sick, disabled, and pregnant people, and implement the overall design in conjunction with barrier-free facilities
	Traffic Information Panel	Provide traffic information	Build a comprehensive traffic search panel and provide bus, subway, train, plane, and ferry information
Convenient Living	Smart Life Micro-Hub	Improve work efficiency	Use smart life micro-hubs to customize the shift-level connection of life services for office workers based on travel demands and to coordinate the connection of office, shopping, and other activities with transportation information
	Urban Furniture	Provide life services	Newsstand equipped with charging, Wi-Fi, shopping, and other functions
Protection of Vulnerable People	Underpass	Reduce crime rates	Provide a responsive space in urban underpasses with lights and sounds to improve safety
	Safety Devices	Improve safety at street crossings	Use infrared thermal imaging facilities to monitor the trajectory of pedestrians; add ground signals and intelligent road studs to ensure pedestrian safety
	Sound Devices	Protect the visually impaired	Visually impaired people can identify the signal by sound, and the volume is automatically adjusted according to the ambient noise
Environmental Monitoring	Streetlamp Shade	Collect environmental data	Monitoring of air pollutant data, noise, temperature, humidity, wind speed, and key pollution sources

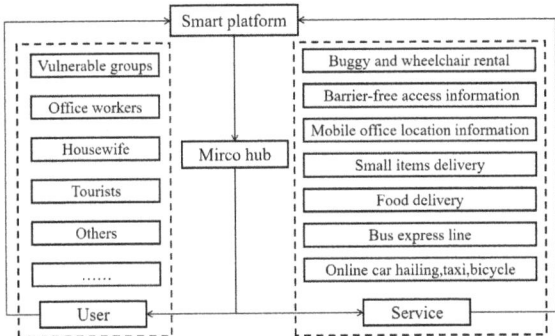

Figure 4. Smart life micro-hub system created in the Shenzhen SDGs. Source: by author on the basis of data from [21,22].

3.1.4. Nanjing

The Nanjing Street Design Guidelines apply smart technologies to the areas of smart transportation, convenient living, and the protection of vulnerable people (Table 5) [23]. They also present the idea of an information platform that could share data on these application scenarios (Figure 5). The guidelines propose transportation solutions, such as a bus corridor, green-wave transportation, a parking guidance system, and transportation hubs to improve the efficiency of urban transportation. As relates to convenient living, urban furniture should be designed to achieve sustainable development functions, such as energy saving, a low carbon output, and self-sensing using loading sensors. Furthermore, the guidelines present methods to improve safety at street crossings for vulnerable people by implementing audio and infrared induction prompters.

Table 5. The applications of smart technologies in the Nanjing SDGs. Source: by author on the basis of data from [23].

Application Scenario	Object	Purpose	Description
Smart Transportation	Bus Corridor	Improve the efficiency of public transportation	Allocate bus corridors on main traffic roads and establish bus-only signal systems
	Traffic Surveillance System	Collect traffic data	Set up traffic monitoring facilities near road intersections to achieve the comprehensive management of traffic flow
Convenient Living	Streetlamp	Save energy	Encourage the application of inductive sidewalk streetlights to provide targeted lighting
	Bus Stop	Provide weather information	Bus stops display weather forecasts and provide travel guidance
	Newsstand	Provide life services	The newsstand introduces multimedia data terminals to accept queries and provide street and surrounding information, and it is equipped with Wi-Fi, transitioning to media information terminals
Protection of Vulnerable People	Signal Light	Improve safety at street crossings	Add signal-light sound prompts, infrared induction prompting devices, and rescue facilities for vulnerable people

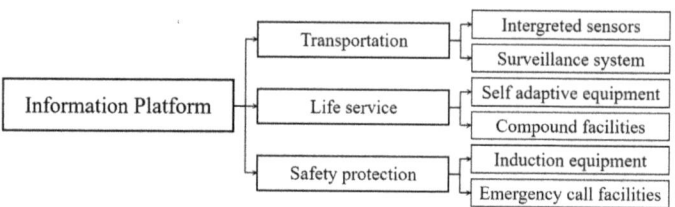

Figure 5. The framework of the information platform presented in the Nanjing SDGs. Source: by author on the basis of data from [23].

3.1.5. Qingdao

The Qingdao Street Design Guidelines propose a method for extracting urban information using smart technologies to promote street management's transformation toward a more sustainable orientation (Table 6) [24].

Table 6. The applications of smart technologies in the Qingdao SDGs. Source: by author on the basis of data from [24].

Application Scenario	Object	Purpose	Description
Smart Transportation	Intelligent Cloud Computing Platform	Improve traffic efficiency	According to the human and vehicle flow data, the dispatching of buses and taxis, online car hailing, rail transit, and static parking can be carried out by the intelligent cloud computing platform
	Signal Light	Provide green lanes for special vehicles	In the event of an emergency, the signal light uses traffic flow data to automatically allocate time to customize green lanes for ambulances and fire engines
Convenient Living	Oblique Photography Technology	Collect information on the physical spaces of streets	Oblique photography technology can be used to collect street morphology and color data for analysis of landscape corridors and city skylines to create a higher quality of life
	Portrait Technology	Improve business vitality	POI data can be used to analyze the advantages of street businesses and business models and to analyze the characteristics of the crowd for portrait technology, so as to match to commercial business and stimulate consumption
	Electronic Information Screen	Provide information for queries	Electronic information screens can provide all types of life information
	Newsstand	Provide life service	Newsstands can add self-service retail, charging piles, and express services
Protection of Vulnerable People	High-density Sensors	Optimize information dissemination channels	High-density urban data sensors can be used to perceive changes in the city's micro-environment, to predict future spatial and temporal development trends, and to establish an early warning information system to warn the city of accidents, disasters, and public health emergencies

The guidelines propose that traffic scheduling should be carried out based on the spatial–temporal characteristics of human and vehicle flows and should be supported by an intelligent cloud computing platform. As to convenient living, the guidelines point out that technologies such as oblique photography and portrait technology should be used to collect basic urban information (Figure 6). The guidelines also promote the design of smart electronic screens, and they advocate a combined functional structure for urban furniture to improve life services. In consideration of vulnerable people, high-density coverage sensors were proposed so as to optimize information dissemination channels.

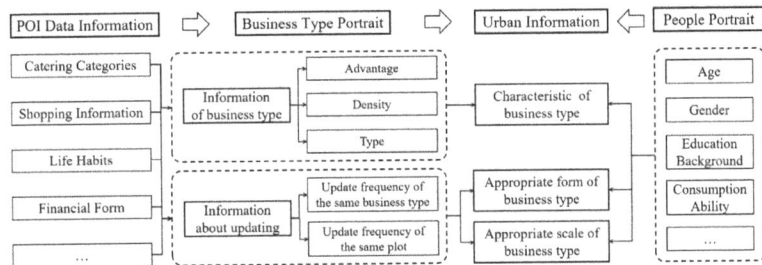

Figure 6. Business activity measurement portrait system in Qingdao. Source: by author on the basis of data from [24].

3.2. Summary of Various Smart Technologies in SDGs

In summary, the applications of smart technologies to achieve sustainable development in each of the SDGs mainly concentrate on five aspects: travel and transportation information, the convenient integration of residents' lives, improvement of the vitality of public facilities, protection of disadvantaged groups, and real-time monitoring of the living environment (Table 7). The raw data of selected cities on the application of smart technologies in the SDGs are shown in Tables S1–S5 in the Supplementary Material.

Table 7. Summary of smart technologies for sustainable development in the SDGs. Source: By author.

Application Scenario	Concept	Purpose	Technical Equipment
Smart Transportation	To create stable transportation and intermodal hubs	Creating a green-wave traffic belt for traffic-flow dispatching. Sharing static traffic space and forecasting traffic data	GPS, electromagnetic induction devices, electronic touchscreen technology, big data, app terminal, IoT
Convenient Living	To disseminate urban information	Integrating urban information and public resources	Wi-Fi, unmanned self-service system, smart space
Life Enrichment	To create sensory interactions in street spaces	Allowing people to interact with public spaces and creating enrichment value	Social network analysis, wearable technology, VR
Protection of Vulnerable People	To provide a channel to call for help in case of disasters and crimes	Improving the coverage of the surveillance system, enhancing the convenience of calling for help, and optimizing alarm analysis	Thermal sensing device, machine dialogue, cloud platform
Environmental Monitoring	To monitor the street environment and collect data	Equipping urban furniture with low-carbon and energy-saving equipment and realizing multisource information collection and environmental self-assessment	Weather probes, noise sensors, solar panels, information terminals, automatic irrigation sensors

(1) Smart transportation technology focuses on the scheduling of multiple types of vehicles via traffic flow data and feedback to the platform. Based on the collection of traffic flow data, smart technologies can create an urban green-wave transportation and transport hub and build a static traffic guidance system.

(2) In terms of convenient living, smart technology recommends the installation of multisource, interactive equipment in the urban furniture and advocates for more combined and functional furniture and facilities compatible with the necessities of everyday life, and it strives to handle daily business at the office building or home at any time.

(3) The vital improvement of street space is created via art installations that employ listening, seeing, smelling, and tactile elements. Their wireless networks could collect interactive information from more comprehensive sources and use the portrait to propose targeted strategies.
(4) For the protection of the vulnerable, smart technology can be implemented via thermal-sensing prompts and road studs at crossing facilities, and convenient urban furniture can be set up so vulnerable people can call for help, relying on real-time alarm-system monitoring and a one-button alarm device and by using tracking sensors to provide more comprehensive alarm information.
(5) The collection of environmental monitoring information is mainly based on detection and interactive sensors. Smart vehicles have been designed on the principles of low carbon emissions and convenience. These collect and upload urban environmental data to the platform for analysis and use touchscreen media to achieve timely feedback.

3.3. Smart Street Management and Control Platform

The Smart Street Management and Control Platform (SSMCP) (Figure 7) consists of four layers: the basic information layer, technology platform layer, scene application layer, and institutional protection layer. The selected cases presented valuable techniques, development trends, and space demands, which could contribute to SSMCP development. For example, Figures 2–4 are linked to the basic information layer and the scene application layer, which propose methods to acquire data, equip sensors, interact with people, and apply technologies. Figure 5 is linked to the technology platform layer, which presents the idea that a comprehensive information platform should be built to serve the whole city; the platform should be consistent, allowing some technologies to be supported and some functions to be realized. Figure 6 is linked to basic information layer, which shows some methods to record urban statistics as urban basic information.

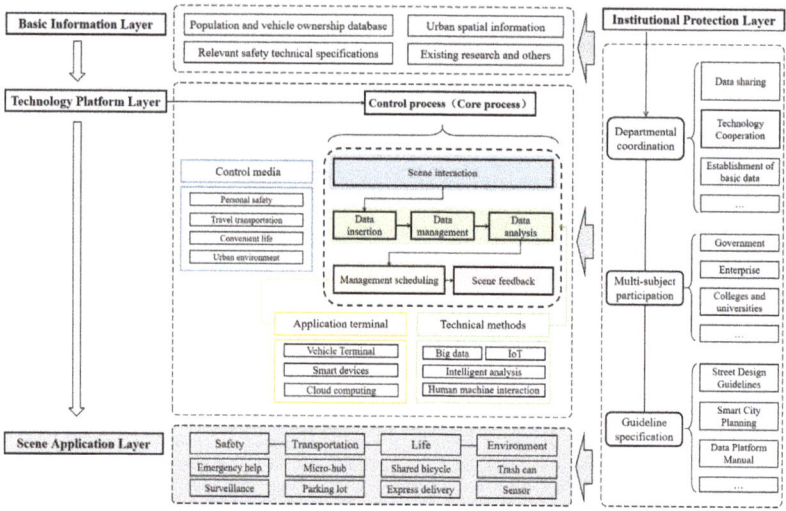

Figure 7. The SSMCP for chinese cities. Source: by author.

3.3.1. Basic Information Layer

The basic information layer collects data maps from multiple departments. The project's planning–construction–management process (whole-life cycle) must gradually promote linkages among departments, which can improve the efficiency of interdepartmental work in practice. A population database and vehicle ownership data are collected and updated based on the urban spatial information census data in this layer. Based on the relevant exceptional safety technical specifications and existing research, this layer enriches data lists and supports subsequent technical operations. The improvement of data collection provides strong support for city managers to make decisions. In practice, the collection of data can rely on various types of sensors equipped in the streets, and new methods can be applied to achieve it. As presented for previous SDGs, urban data can be captured from basic surveys, transportation statistics, and records on public services and the environment. Among these, radar, photography, and portrait technologies can contribute to measuring various types of basic information.

3.3.2. Technology Platform Layer

The technology platform layer is the core layer of the whole construction. Smart technologies in the street space are the carriers of information processing and exchange, as well as sharing and collaboration. The control media consider four scenarios: personal safety, travel transportation, life convenience, and the urban environment, which are scenarios for interactive responses and data collection in daily life. The data accessed from control media, together with the basic information from the upper layer, are sent to the scene interaction for a series of operations including data insertion, data management, and data analysis. These three operational processes are supported by big data, IoT, GPS, cloud computing, wearable technology, and other technical devices. According to the actual situation of each city, it is important to set different goals in management scheduling to achieve efficient operation on the streets. Based on the results produced by the above process, they are linked to the next layer in the scene feedback for presentation. In general, the information generated by residents' participation in street activities is calculated in the corresponding media. With the basic information layer as a reference, the data are accessed, managed, and analyzed through the smart analytic platform. This layer can conduct analysis, automatically identify abnormalities, and realize the supervision of data. It is also the pre-processing stage of the scene application layer.

3.3.3. Institutional Protection Layer

The institutional protection layer guarantees the structure of the SSMCP from the perspectives of departmental coordination and multisubject participation. This layer is promoted by compiling corresponding documents, which also clarify the authority–responsiveness relationship and define the implementation and maintenance subjects for each layer of the platform. This layer establishes a multi-departmental and whole-process guarantee mechanism and improves the protection of specification documents, which in turn realize the operation and management of the whole SSMCP, and, finally, it achieves the goals of data collection, platform processing, rapid response, and collaborative feedback. Departmental coordination enables data sharing, technological cooperation, and the establishment of data framework, converged government, enterprise, and education institutions to achieve multi-subject participation, and enriches the types of guideline manuals used in academic research.

3.3.4. Scene Application Layer

Based on scenario feedback from the upper layer, the activities occurring in the street, the needs and possibilities of the current operation, and the final effects of the feedback are all expressed in the scene application layer. Consistent with the scenario types accessed from the control media, this layer presents the results through the same scenarios: safety, transportation, life, and environment. Security is represented by safety reminders and calling facilities in all kinds of urban furniture. The efficiency of mobility is optimized through the dispatching of vehicles and the prediction of traffic information. People can improve their quality of life based on the services they need. Feedback on the environment optimizes the efficiency of sanitation, greening, and other related departments and promotes sustainable development. This layer allows various smart technologies to be demonstrated, and residents are able to experience how the scenarios of safety, transportation, life, and environment are realized in the streets. Through the residents' interactive experience, all kinds of facilities are connected to smart technologies and daily needs. Therefore, this layer can provide the most realistic picture of the SSMCP after being implemented in the street space. This layer could also visually demonstrate how the residents access a variety of smart technologies and how they fulfill their needs more sustainably.

4. Conclusions

Previous studies about smart cities have tended to be theoretical research, with less exploration of real cases. This paper studied the smart technologies of the street space. By sorting out the applications of smart technologies in several SDGs for five cities in China, the applications were categorized into five areas: smart transportation, convenient living, life enrichment, the protection of vulnerable people, and environmental monitoring. Then, to optimize the application of smart technologies, the SSMCP was explored. The SSMCP compounds the three functions of monitoring, controlling, and serving streets to create smart, efficient, vibrant, and safe streets. A response mechanism was constructed to enable data interaction, platform processing, and terminal feedback via four media, which included safety, transportation, life, and environment. Under the institutional protection of the system, the platform can improve the efficiency of data sharing and business collaboration among departments and enhance the sustainability and intelligence of the processes of "urban planning–construction–management" and holistic service. Smart technologies were used in the SSMCP to achieve street control, environmental management, and greater livability.

This conceptional and comprehensive framework for street space provides smart cities projects an actionable case and lays a foundation for future smart city advancement, which can be seen as a sample of smart city construction in practice, and can provide an original idea for a real street management platform in the future. The SSMCP could contribute to stock-based renewal and sustainable development, and the study could provide a reference for the implementation of smart cities in street space.

Because the selected cities were limited, it was not possible to summarize all the SDGs in China and all types of smart technologies according to region, and there was no section to illustrate how the SSMCP works in a certain city. Thus, in future studies, it is necessary to take more areas into account, to expand the scope of study, and to consider a practical example to explain the details.

Supplementary Materials: The following supporting information can be downloaded at: https://www.mdpi.com/article/10.3390/su15043438/s1, Table S1: The applications of smart technologies in the Beijing SDGs; Table S2: The applications of smart technologies in the Shanghai SDGs; Table S3: The applications of smart technologies in the Shenzhen SDGs; Table S4: The applications of smart technologies in the Nanjing SDGs; Table S5: The applications of smart technologies in the Qingdao SDGs.

Author Contributions: Conceptualization and methodology, F.X. and H.C.; data curation and investigation, F.X.; writing—original draft preparation, F.X.; writing—review and editing, H.C. and Y.W.; supervision and funding acquisition, H.C. All authors have read and agreed to the published version of the manuscript.

Funding: This research was funded by the National Natural Science Foundation of China, grant number 52170174.

Institutional Review Board Statement: Not applicable.

Informed Consent Statement: Not applicable.

Data Availability Statement: Not applicable.

Conflicts of Interest: The authors declare no conflict of interest.

References

1. Gharaibeh, A.; Salahuddin, M.A.; Hussini, S.J.; Khreishah, A.; Khalil, I.; Guizani, M.; Al-Fuqaha, A. Smart Cities: A Survey on Data Management, Security, and Enabling Technologies. *IEEE Commun. Surv. Tutor.* **2017**, *19*, 2456–2501. [CrossRef]
2. Zheng, Y.; Capra, L.; Wolfson, O.; Yang, H. Urban Computing: Concepts, Methodologies, and Applications. *Acm Trans. Intell. Syst. Technol.* **2014**, *5*, 1–55. [CrossRef]
3. Qiu, B. Wisely and Actively Promote the Sustainable Development of Cities and Towns in China. *Urban Dev. Stud.* **2012**, *19*, 125–128. [CrossRef]
4. Chinese Society for Urban Studies (Ed.) *China Urban Planning and Development Report 2015–2016*; China Architecture & Building Press: Beijing, China, 2016; pp. 10–25, ISBN 9787112195251.
5. Kandt, J.; Batty, M. Smart cities, big data and urban policy: Towards urban analytics for the long run. *Cities* **2021**, *109*, 102–992. [CrossRef]
6. Ismagilova, E.; Hughes, L.; Dwivedi, Y.K.; Raman, K.R. Smart cities: Advances in research—An information systems perspective. *Int. J. Inf. Manag.* **2019**, *47*, 88–100. [CrossRef]
7. Silva, B.N.; Khan, M.; Han, K. Towards sustainable smart cities: A review of trends, architectures, components, and open challenges in smart cities. *Sustain. Cities Soc.* **2018**, *38*, 697–713. [CrossRef]
8. Yigitcanlar, T.; Kamruzzaman, M.; Buys, L.; Ioppolo, G.; Sabatini-Marques, J.; da Costa, E.M.; Yun, J.J. Understanding 'smart cities': Intertwining development drivers with desired outcomes in a multidimensional framework. *Cities* **2018**, *81*, 145–160. [CrossRef]
9. Allam, Z.; Dhunny, Z.A. On big data, artificial intelligence and smart cities. *Cities* **2019**, *89*, 80–91. [CrossRef]
10. Lianfeng, W.; Gang, S.; Zhang, N.; An, X.; Liu, Z.; Jiang, X.; Zhu, H.; Wang, Z.; Mao, M.; Zhao, j.; et al. Construction of data model for smart city governance. *Urban Dev. Stud.* **2021**, *28*, 70–76+84. [CrossRef]
11. Zhen, F.; Kong, Y. An Integrated "Human-technology-space" Framework of Smart City Planning. *Urban Plan. Forum* **2021**, *6*, 45–52. [CrossRef]
12. Yang, J. A paradigm of urban big data application in planning and design: From data dimensioning to CIM platform. *Beijing Plan. Rev.* **2017**, 15–20.
13. Long, Y.; Zhang, E. Smart urban planning under the framework of data augmented design. *City Plan. Rev.* **2019**, *43*, 34–40. [CrossRef]
14. Dang, A.; Zhen, M.; Wang, D.; Liang, J. Current situation and trends of the new smart city development in China. *Sci. Technol. Rev.* **2018**, *36*, 16–29. [CrossRef]
15. de Jong, M.; Joss, S.; Schraven, D.; Zhan, C.; Weijnen, M. Sustainable–smart–resilient–low carbon–eco–knowledge cities; making sense of a multitude of concepts promoting sustainable urbanization. *J. Clean. Prod.* **2015**, *109*, 25–38. [CrossRef]
16. Boeing, G. OSMnx: New methods for acquiring, constructing, analyzing, and visualizing complex street networks. *Comput. Environ. Urban Syst.* **2017**, *65*, 126–139. [CrossRef]
17. Tao, F.; Qi, Q.; Wang, L.; Nee, A.Y.C. Digital Twins and Cyber–Physical Systems toward Smart Manufacturing and Industry 4.0: Correlation and Comparison. *Engineering* **2019**, *5*, 653–661. [CrossRef]
18. Marzouk, M.; Othman, A. Planning utility infrastructure requirements for smart cities using the integration between BIM and GIS. *Sustain. Cities Soc.* **2020**, *57*, 102120. [CrossRef]
19. Beijing Municipal People's Government Home Page. Guidelines for Urban Design of Beijing Street Renewal and Governance. Available online: http://ghzrzyw.beijing.gov.cn/biaozhunguanli/bz/cxgh/202106/t20210623_2419742.html (accessed on 23 June 2021).
20. Shanghai Municipal People's Government Home Page. Shanghai Street Design Guidelines. Available online: https://hd.ghzyj.sh.gov.cn/zcfg/zhl/201610/t20161019_696909.html (accessed on 18 October 2016).
21. Shenzhen Luohu District People's Government Home Page. Guidelines for the Design of Complete Streets in Luohu District. Available online: http://www.szlh.gov.cn/zwgk/zcjd/2018/lhqwzjdsjdzgy/ (accessed on 30 September 2018).
22. Shenzhen Futian District People's Government Home Page. Futian District Street Design Guidelines. Available online: http://www.szft.gov.cn/attachment/1/1190/1190747/4350978.docx (accessed on 26 August 2020).
23. Nanjing Municipal People's Government Home Page. Nanjing Street Design Guidelines. Available online: http://ghj.nanjing.gov.cn/ghbz/cssj/201802/t20180208_875978.html (accessed on 8 February 2018).
24. Qingdao Municipal People's Government Home Page. Qingdao Street Design Guidelines. Available online: https://www.doc88.com/p-66716030504837.html (accessed on 30 November 2021).
25. Lim, W.M.; Kumar, S.; Ali, F. Advancing knowledge through literature reviews: 'what', 'why', and 'how to contribute'. *Serv. Ind. J.* **2022**, *42*, 481–513. [CrossRef]
26. Marx, A.; Rihoux, B.; Ragin, C. The origins, development, and application of Qualitative Comparative Analysis: The first 25 years. *Eur. Political Sci. Rev.* **2014**, *6*, 115–142. [CrossRef]
27. Jiang, Y.; Wang, Y.; Xie, J. Return to Human-oriented Streets: The New Trend of Street Design Manual Development in the World Cities and Implications for Chinese cities. *Urban Plan. Forum* **2012**, *27*, 65–72.
28. Li, J.; Tang, Y.; Qi, M.; Peng, J. Street Design Guidelines Compilation For Urban Governance, Chaoyang District, Beijing. *Planners* **2018**, *34*, 42–48. [CrossRef]

29. Zhang, F.; Luo, C.; Ge, Y. Thoughts innovations of Street Design Guidelines and planning transformation. *Urban Plan. Forum* **2018**, *2*, 75–80. [CrossRef]
30. Zou, B. Practices, Effects, and Challenges of the Inventory Development Pattern: The Assessments and Extended Thoughts of Urban Renewal Implementation in Shenzhen. *City Plan. Rev.* **2017**, *41*, 89–94. [CrossRef]
31. Song, Y.; Dong, Q.; Zhang, Y. A Study on the Representation of Hierarchical Structure of Block Form in Nanjing. *Archit. J.* **2018**, *8*, 34–39. [CrossRef]

Disclaimer/Publisher's Note: The statements, opinions and data contained in all publications are solely those of the individual author(s) and contributor(s) and not of MDPI and/or the editor(s). MDPI and/or the editor(s) disclaim responsibility for any injury to people or property resulting from any ideas, methods, instructions or products referred to in the content.

Review

A Review of Contemporary Governance Challenges in Oman: Can Blockchain Technology Be Part of Sustainable Solutions?

Leon Goldsmith [1], Abdul Khalique Shaikh [2,*], Hacer Yildiz Tan [3] and Kaamran Raahemifar [4,5,6]

[1] Politics Programme, University of Otago, Dunedin 9016, New Zealand
[2] Department of Information Systems, Sultan Qaboos University, Muscat 123, Oman
[3] Institute of Social Sciences, University of Otago, Dunedin 9016, New Zealand
[4] Data Science and Artificial Intelligence Program, College of Information Sciences and Technology (IST), Penn State University, State College, PA 16801, USA
[5] School of Optometry and Vision Science, Faculty of Science, University of Waterloo, 200 University Ave. W, Waterloo, ON N2L 3G1, Canada
[6] Department of Chemical Engineering, Faculty of Engineering, University of Waterloo, 200 University Ave. W, Waterloo, ON N2L 3G1, Canada
* Correspondence: shaikh@squ.edu.om

Abstract: Oman is considering adopting the latest e-governance technology, including Blockchain-based. While much research was conducted into the benefits and risks of Blockchain-based in information systems and finance fields, fewer researchers investigated the opportunities and risks associated with adopting Blockchain-based frameworks for governance and public administration, especially in highly bureaucratic, centralized rentier states, such as Oman. As the first phase of an exploratory sequential mixed-methods study, our purpose was to identify key governance problems in contemporary Oman and analyze each problem against evidence drawn from the relevant parts of the Blockchain-based and e-governance literature to evaluate the potential utility, risks and limitations associated with adopting block-chained e-governance solutions in the Sultanate. Our initial results indicate that there are advantages for states, such as Oman, from being an early mover into block-chained e-governance systems, including greater cost efficiency, drastically improved accuracy and reliability of information systems, transparency and accountability of public services, and an upgrade in the overall level of legitimacy and public trust in the institutions of governance. However, more research into the risks related to reconciling block-chained systems with the dynamics of labor, tax reforms and centralized authority in a rentier social contract is required.

Keywords: e-government; governance; blockchain technology; social contract; development; rentier states; Oman

Citation: Goldsmith, L.; Shaikh, A.K.; Tan, H.Y.; Raahemifar, K. A Review of Contemporary Governance Challenges in Oman: Can Blockchain Technology Be Part of Sustainable Solutions?. *Sustainability* **2022**, *14*, 11819. https://doi.org/10.3390/su141911819

Academic Editors: Tan Yigitcanlar, Juan M. Corchado and Rashid Mehmood

Received: 19 June 2022
Accepted: 10 September 2022
Published: 20 September 2022

Copyright: © 2022 by the authors. Licensee MDPI, Basel, Switzerland. This article is an open access article distributed under the terms and conditions of the Creative Commons Attribution (CC BY) license (https://creativecommons.org/licenses/by/4.0/).

1. Introduction

Oman is an oil-exporting rentier state undergoing significant economic and political transformation in the early 2020s. Oman's governance model, built on a large and frequently inefficient public sector, proved increasingly problematic in the context of an urgent need to diversify its economy and mitigate its exposure to volatile global oil prices. This imperative to reform the rentier model in Oman and in other similarly positioned Gulf states, such as Bahrain, touches upon the very nature of the rentier social contract, which since the 1970s resembled the Hobbesian 'Leviathan' where the centralized state mediates all aspects of a stable bargain between the rulers and the ruled. In this vein, the technology of blockchain envisaged by Satoshi Nakamoto as a platform for a stateless and fully decentralized crypto-currency, bitcoin, seems antithetical to the rentier state. However, are the rentier 'Leviathan' and 'Nakamoto' really irreconcilable?

The main purpose of this study is to discover whether there is potential for centralized rentier states, such as Oman, to benefit from the latest blockchain technologies in terms of enhancing, supplementing, or reforming their current governance systems. Towards this end, our objectives are fourfold: (1) to identify specific areas of Oman's public administration and governance that are considered challenging or problematic from a national perspective; (2) to contextualize each of these issues in relation to Omani conditions and requirements; (3) glean from international studies whether there may be advantages to Oman from adopting blockchain solutions to the identified governance problems; and (4) gain an impression of the Oman government's outlook on blockchain solutions to governance and public administration issues. First, it is necessary to provide some brief background to the quite unusual case of Oman.

In the late 1960s, the Sultanatse of Oman, located in the southeast Arabian Peninsula, lacked any comprehensive governance systems across its territory. In fact, the ruling sultan, Saïd bin Taimūr al-Saïd, often struggled to extend effective governance beyond his palace walls [1]). Subsequently, oil wealth and stable, comprehensive governance under the next sultan, Qabūs bin Saïd al-Saïd (r.1970–2020), propelled human and infrastructural development projects forward at breakneck speed [2]. Oman came to represent a model oil-exporting rentier state with a highly centralized governance structure and a well-coopted polity [3]. Much like the other Gulf Cooperation Council (GCC) states, the nature of the social contract in Oman became based on citizens' expectations of abundant public sector employment, generous subsidies, cheap expatriate labor and zero income tax. In return, the task of governance was left to the discretion of the Sultan and his ministerial appointees. Whilst oil income remained sufficient, this social bargain between state and citizen was stable and, in fact, provided a somewhat efficient model for rapid decision-making in the development of a modern and unified state.

In the early 21st century, the Omani social contract started to buckle. In 2011 social unrest broke out over perceived uneven distribution of oil-wealth and a lack of transparency and accountability in governance. These social and political pressures were exacerbated by the collapse of global oil prices from mid-2014, which caused substantial budget deficits throughout the rest of the decade [4]. Most importantly, the long stable era under Sultan Qabūs came to an end with his death on 10 January 2020 and a transfer of power took place with Qabūs' paternal cousin, Haitham bin Tariq al-Saïd, appointed as the new sultan. Despite a smooth transition of power, the sustainability of the highly centralized rentier social contract remains in question. The main components of the old rentier bargain—public sector jobs, subsidies, and zero-taxation—are no longer viable options over the long run [5].

Oman, and similar rentier states, seek to pivot to a new post-oil social contract that can provide continuity of stable governance and development, the question is what options are available? This article explores the potential for Oman to shore up its governance systems by introducing state-of-the-art blockchain technology within new comprehensive, resilient, and efficient e-governance systems. For countries, such as Oman, that are searching for innovative solutions to pressing governance problems, a strategy involving blockchain holds significant potential in terms of efficiency, transparency, security, cost, and trust (legitimacy); however, there is also a magnitude of risk as it remains a little known and largely untested technology, especially in the context of an absolute rentier state.

The questions posed in the study are: what are the current governance issues facing Oman and what possible solutions are available within blockchain-based e-governance technologies? In addressing these questions, this paper presents an exploratory review of one critical case in an emerging broader question regarding the convergence of decentralizing digital technologies and their potential role in good governance, and the governance issues faced by highly centralized states with extensive (often inefficient) public sectors. As such, this paper seeks to highlight the types of governance issues such states face and to lay the groundwork for further targeted, quantitative enquiries into whether blockchain would, indeed, help address challenges to good governance in highly centralized states seeking reform.

The following sections will proceed as follows. Section 2 presents a review of the literature, Section 3 presents the research methodology, and Section 4 outlines the general features of blockchain technology and its application to governance. Section 5 presents the results of our survey of the current governance issues facing the Sultanate of Oman. Section 6 discusses current perspectives towards blockchain solutions based on an interview with a top policymaker in Oman. Section 7 discusses possible blockchain solutions and some risks to the identified governance issues. The conclusion sums up the overall findings of the study.

2. Review of the Literature

Scholarly literature on the various applications, implications and impacts of blockchain technology is growing. Blockchain is often defined as a distributed public ledger, which forms a secure chain of 'blocks' to store and manage data and facilitate peer-to-peer transactions [6–11]. The various benefits of managing information and transactions via blockchain were widely studied, for instance, in terms of decentralization, anonymity, auditability, persistency and security [6,8,12,13].

Researchers argued that blockchain can upgrade government authority and governance by enhancing levels of public trust in governance systems [14–16] increasing efficiency and decreasing the costs [6,17,18]. Conversely, other studies examined the risks of blockchain as a challenge to state authority and legitimacy [19–23]. This aspect is especially important to explore in terms of developing countries with shorter histories of institutional and constitutional entrenchment, such as Oman and other Gulf states.

A highly relevant trend for us in current research is the study of 'smart cities', which explores the potential for blockchain technology to support sustainable, efficient, transparent, and democratic public administration for evolving 21st-century urban conglomerations, especially in the rapidly urbanizing and developing global south [24–26]. A significant aspect of the 'smart city' literature relevant to our study was the finding that blockchain and similar technologies, while tempting for policymakers as 'temporary solutions' to governance challenges, are not necessarily 'short term' quick fixes for addressing 'deep-seated structural issues' and cannot replace genuine 'governance transformation' where it is required [25]. In addition, Praharaj, Han, and Hawken [25] make another important point regarding the persistent gap between creating digital infrastructure in the hope that it will engage people in civic deliberation and genuine promotion of active political-participant populations (2018); something that Almond and Verba (1963) described in their seminal study, *The Civic Culture* as far back as the early 1960s [27]. In fact, new data show that greater access to ICT infrastructure does not necessarily correlate to increased levels of civic culture and that ICT technology is primarily being used for other purposes, such as entertainment [24].

However, much of the evidence presented in the 'smart city' literature focuses on municipal-level governance and in democracies, including the world's largest democracy India [24,25]. Fewer studies explored the feasibility of blockchain technology implementation at national level by central governments [28]. Fewer still explore blockchain potential in highly authoritarian or rentier-state settings, such as Russia [29], Dubai [30,31], and the wider Middle East [32].

To what extent Oman's governance issues can be solved by new technologies, such as blockchain, is not shown in the existing literature. Several studies focused on the quality of e-government services being offered in Oman, including the widespread adoption of mobile applications for public interactions with government agencies [33], and the overall challenges of adopting e-government solutions in the Sultanate [34]. To our knowledge, there were no studies broadly surveying the potential benefits of blockchain for governance and public administration in Oman, which we found surprising and motivated us to address this gap.

3. Research Methodology

The method for this study constitutes the first phase of an exploratory sequential mixed-methods design [35]. This social science method involves two research phases. The first phase is an open-ended qualitative exploration to inductively identify key themes in a topic area. The second phase involves the extraction and analysis of data related to those themes in relation to a set hypothesis. In this review paper, we present results from the first exploratory phase of this method where we discovered those areas where further quantitative enquiry into blockchain solutions to Oman's public governance problems is required.

Our primary source of data for this exploratory review was taken from contemporary international, regional (Gulf) and national news media. (These included Reuters, Al Jazeera, Arab News, Haaretz, Gulf News, Oman Observer, Muscat Daily, Times of Oman.) However, given Oman's low profile in international and regional media outlets, it was necessary to derive most of our data from local Omani media in order to gain a sufficiently deep sample of specific governance issues in the Omani context. Moreover, the Omani media is reactionary; this means that while it is a 'guided media' and controlled by strict publication laws—Omani media tends to be cautious and self-censoring to ensure compliance with Royal Decree No. 49/84, which promulgated the Publications and Publishing Law (1984)—local media tends to respond to trends of public opinion to (1) test possible public reactions to upcoming policy changes (via social media), and (2) respond to those public reactions once policies are announced/implemented. This understudied media dynamic is partly due to the lack of open channels for political participation in Oman, something that the first author of this study observed over several years inside the country. As a result, Omani media, including privately owned outlets, tends to reflect the agenda and perspective of the government and reveals the policy issues important to the public, which allowed us to discover important issues from the public policy and governance points of view.

More specifically, we used local media over external international sources because the Omani media naturally provided more coverage of local affairs. We, therefore, used available regional and international news, and targeted the main private newspaper in Oman, *Times of Oman*, which publishes news in both English and Arabic, for the bulk of our data. (We also considered the Muscat Daily and Oman Observer newspapers; the latter is operated by Oman's Ministry of Information.) A dataset of 450 news articles, broadly related to the public sector and governance, was compiled from 2018 to 2020, inclusive. This dataset was then filtered down to 149 articles that directly addressed current and potential problems in the execution of public governance in the Sultanate. From this filtered sample, we quantified several discrete themes relating to issues of public governance that are deemed problematic or require solutions. The results provided us with 10 categories ranked from the most frequently reported to the least. Of the filtered sample of 149 articles, 29% focused on the general area of economic, social, and political pressures in general. The most frequent specific issues related to the following: public sector reform and e-services (15%); issues of employment (15%); and taxation (12%). Other issues included public healthcare (8%); education (7%); elections and e-participation (5%) (see also Shaikh, Ahmad, Khan, and Ali, 2021); corruption, fraud and attestation of documents (5%); and reforms to public subsidies, such as energy and utilities (4%). In addition, one article mentioned land information (Table 1).

Table 1. Frequency of references to governance-related issues in news media, 2018–2020.

Rank	Governance Issue	n	Fraction of Full Sample (n450)	Fraction Filtered Sample (n149)
1	Economic/political/social pressures	43	0.10	0.29
2	Public sector reform and e-services	22	0.05	0.15
3	Employment: expatriate labor management, Omanization, automation	22	0.05	0.15
4	Taxation reforms	18	0.04	0.12
5	COVID -19 Pandemic and Healthcare	12	0.03	0.08
6	Educational Changes- online delivery (partly caused by Covid-19)	10	0.02	0.07

Table 1. *Cont.*

Rank	Governance Issue	n	Fraction of Full Sample (n450)	Fraction Filtered Sample (n149)
7	Elections and e-participation	8	0.02	0.05
8	Corruption, fraud and attestation of documents	7	0.02	0.05
9	Government subsidy reforms	6	0.01	0.04
10	Land information	1	0.002	0.007

Source: Dataset compiled by the authors, 2018–2020.

These results determined the specific governance issues upon which we would concentrate our study. We decided, however, to omit 'economic/political/social pressures' (ranked 1) due to its generality. We also left out 'Educational changes', (ranked 6) as it was an area subject to complex and fluid changes in 2020 because of the COVID-19 pandemic and, therefore, better addressed separately by later studies. We also omitted land information due to its limited impact on the media discourse in the period under observation. (The authors note, however, that land information, despite its lack of attention in media indicated in this study, is an area of interest for potential future blockchain solutions due to issues related to the government allocation of land parcels to Omani nationals and a decline in the availability of arable land [36]. We addressed the remaining seven specific governance issues in Oman in relation to the international literature connected to each specific issue in terms of potential blockchain solutions.

Finally, we managed to obtain permission to interview the senior Omani official broadly responsible for the implementation of e-governance systems, including blockchain technology in the Sultanate: the Undersecretary for Communications and Information Technology at the Ministry of Transport, Communications, and Information Technology, Dr Ali Al-Shidhani. The resulting high-level insights give a snapshot of how Oman is positioning itself regarding new information systems technology in e-governance. The resulting data provide a useful departure point for further quantitative and mixed-methods research into blockchain-based e-governance solutions in Oman, and further targeted interviews at the relevant ministries and agencies.

It is also important to note that the political and economic system in Oman is defined as an oil-exporting rentier state, which means that the generalization of our results is perhaps limited to other similar cases in the Arab Gulf, which have similar historical experiences and similar trajectories of socio-economic and political development, as well as a need for reform. This unique regime type and its convergence with new technology are discussed in the next section.

4. Blockchain Technology and Oman's Social Contract: 'Leviathan' Meets 'Nakamoto'

The idea of a stable social contract encompassing the entire territory of a nation-state was first articulated in the works of Thomas Hobbes (1588–1679) [37]. Hobbes' pessimistic view of human nature concluded that escaping the 'brutish state of nature' required establishing an all-powerful sovereign—the *Leviathan*—which provided the bedrock for secure and stable governance [38]. Oman's modern social contract, which dates from the mid-1970s until the present, resembles Hobbes' Leviathan. Sultan Qabūs reflected the all-powerful, 'benevolent leviathan' around which political order and governance were constructed within a unitary and highly centralized national framework funded by oil revenue.

The rentier system and subsequent centralized governance structure of modern Oman would seem to be the antithesis of the ideas presented in the 2008 white paper by the mysterious figure known as 'Satoshi Nakamoto'. Nakamoto imagined a fully decentralized, de-territorialized framework for exchange, asset protection, and the upholding of contracts via blockchain technology and bitcoin [39]. This obvious polarity would logically suggest that an absolute rentier state, such as Oman, should not be able to coexist with a fully decentralized technology based within a libertarian, almost anti-statist, philosophy. Hence Nakamoto would be perplexed by the enthusiastic adoption of blockchain by an authoritarian state, such as the United Arab Emirates, for instance, who in April 2018 announced the Emirates Blockchain Strategy 2021, which involved moving fifty per cent of its government transactions onto blockchain [40].

There is an important convergence between Hobbes and Nakamoto, however. Both rested their ideas on an assumption that there is an essential lack of trust between individuals. For Hobbes, this necessitated surrendering individual autonomy to a 'social contract', that allowed individuals to escape the 'state of nature' by joining an all-powerful state (leviathan), which would serve as the intermediary between distrustful individuals, in terms of creating secure transactions in an orderly society. Nakamoto agrees with Hobbes regarding the essential lack of trust between individuals but goes a step further to also identify the flaws in the state, as it is ultimately made up of, or dominated by, self-interested individuals or the autonomous interests of the state [39]. Hence, there is a need to create an infallible technology (blockchain) that can govern peer-to-peer interactions without the need for a human third party. The lack of trust between nodes in a blockchain, which must be managed by consensus protocols, is referred to in the blockchain terminology as 'byzantine behavior,' [11], which perhaps underlines the 'realist' nature of blockchain as opposed to liberal ideals of cooperation in political terms. Essentially, 'Leviathan' and Nakamoto have different means to the same end, a socially or technologically constructed framework to create secure transactions in a world of trust scarcity. Hence, we should be less surprised by the interest of authoritarian states in blockchain, but it remains to be seen how the convergence (or divergence) of state-based and technology-based trust will develop.

5. What Is Blockchain and How Can It Be Used for Governance?

Comprehensive, up-to-date, and accessible surveys of the state of the art of blockchain technology are available [11,26], so it is unnecessary to include these details here. Instead, we provide a brief overview of the technology and how it can be used for governance. Blockchain consists of 'blocks,' or digital ledgers, that are ordered and contain the records of all transactions occurring in a blockchain network. These blocks contain a timestamp, hash, and record of transactions. The blocks are connected through the previous block's hash. The cryptographic hash ensures the integrity of data stored in these blocks. However, the verification of a transaction is performed through a consensus algorithm by parties known as 'miners'. New transactions are added to the block after verification. Every node of the blockchain network has a copy of that block. Moreover, every transaction is signed by its owner's private key, which prevents the risk of duplication, or double spending in the case of cryptocurrency [41,42].

To illustrate via the cryptocurrency Bitcoin; when user A wants to send a transaction to user B, it is signed by user A's private key and broadcast to every node in the network for verification. These nodes (miners) verify the transaction according to the rules of the consensus algorithm (proof of work). The miners provide authority to check the signatures on the transaction and account balance of user A. For this process, miners must solve the complex mathematical puzzle and create a new block. The created block is sent to each node in the network. These nodes check the validation of the created block and then add it to the chain of blocks. In the end, user B receives the transaction, as illustrated in Figure 1 [43,44]. The entire process may be complete in a matter of seconds, without being diverted through any central or mediating actor, such as a central bank, financial institution, or other regulatory body. Blockchain technology is already finding application in trading, supply chains, agriculture, real estate, health management and, increasingly, in e-government [15,16,42,45].

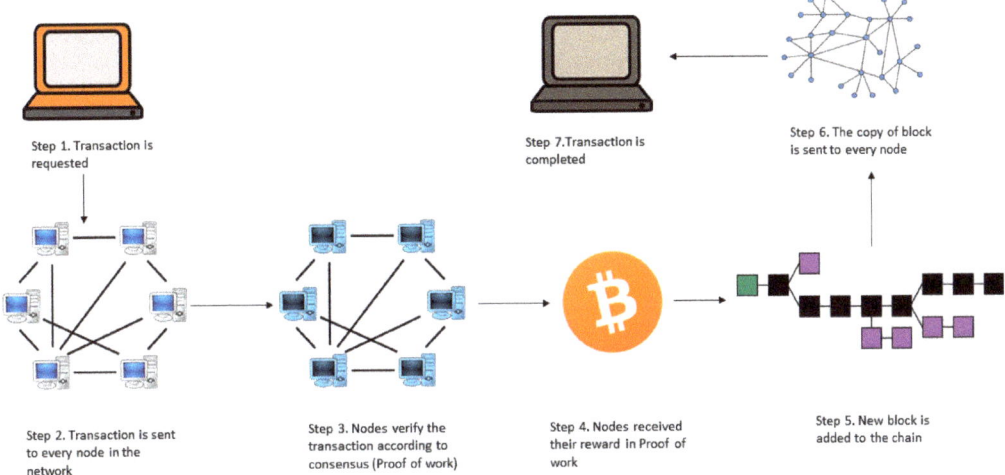

Figure 1. Blockchain Working Process.

In general, blockchain technology can be in public, private or consortium forms. The form implemented is entirely dependent on organizations and business requirements. Firstly, in a public deployment of blockchain, any participant can participate in the mining process, and transactions are validated anonymously. In other words, in public blockchains, the information is transparent to all the nodes in a network. With such transparency, this type of blockchain is secure because of the consensus algorithms. Bitcoin and Ethereum are the most famous examples of public blockchains. There are many applied examples of public blockchain in e-government. For instance, digital identities are used in e-government platforms for transaction purposes. A digital identity is a single identity assigned by the government to each citizen. Digital identity is extracted from the citizen's birth certificate, and transmitted and stored digitally. In this case, public blockchain is used to control, authenticate, and verify individuals' identity [46].

On the other hand, a private blockchain allows only specific users to enter the network. It has control over the access of keys and transaction requests. A private blockchain is more vulnerable to attack compared with a public blockchain. It requires payment for deployment and is more centralized than the public blockchain. Nevertheless, the private blockchain structure is adopted by many business and government organizations. The Dubai government, for instance, administers its house rental project through the Hyperledger private blockchain [30].

The third type of blockchain is a consortium, a hybrid of both public and private blockchain properties. The consortium blockchain is implemented in an electronic certificate-sharing system to achieve privacy and auditability over cross-border government services [47]. A privacy-preserving, consortium-based e-government infrastructure is closed and designed to share information among its stakeholders. A specific number of preselected nodes are allowed to work as users to validate the transactions. In an e-government consortium blockchain, each selected user has the right to create, access, validate, and review transactions. These types of consortia blockchains were, for example, used to overcome security and access challenges facing notarial offices in China [48].

There are several key risk factors that should be noted regarding the feasibility and suitability of blockchain governance. One is the availability of trusted hardware or IT infrastructure. Governments need a high degree of IT capacity; for example, ensuring that an endorsement key (EK) is burnt into every device to achieve a trusted network [11]. Another is the issue of privacy; blockchain was designed to protect the integrity of transactions; however, it is less focused on preserving the privacy of users. Hence, privacy issues of citizens' private data in public blockchain databases could emerge [11]. Another risk factor is the energy requirements of large scale blockchain networks, especially public blockchains. For example, the processing power required for verifying transactions, known as Proof of Work (PoW), is very energy intensive. Despite its supposed immutability, blockchain remains vulnerable to security threats, including a 51% Attack, whereby a majority of miners gain control of hash power. This risk is mitigated by the huge scale required to attack a public blockchain [11].

Governments are now presented with various decisions and options, dependent on their specific requirements, before deploying blockchain for governance functions. These relate mainly to the relative needs for security, immutability, consensus determination, privacy, the consensus process, efficiency, or read permission. From the security point of view, a public blockchain is more immutable than a private or consortium blockchain, whereas there is a higher vulnerability to tampering in private and consortium blockchains. However, private and consortium blockchains are more efficient than a public blockchain, in terms of system performance.

In determining consensus, a public-type blockchain allows all miners to participate in the consensus process, the consortium type allows a selected number of nodes, and only one organization is permitted in a private blockchain [6]. Furthermore, the consensus process is permissionless in a public blockchain, whereas it is permissioned in the consortium and private types. Read permission is accessible to anyone in a public blockchain, while in the other two blockchains, it could be public or limited. Additionally, the blockchain concept of decentralization is fully implemented in the public blockchain, is partial in the consortium, and centralized in a private blockchain. More general users and governments, such as Oman, are, therefore, attracted to the features of the public blockchain, whereas the consortium and private blockchains (Hyperledger and Ethereum) are increasingly found in the business and private sectors [49].

Blockchain technology is fast gaining a presence in governance in the oil monarchies of the Arabian Peninsula. In fact, the Gulf Cooperation countries are establishing themselves to become a global hub for pioneering the technology. As mentioned previously, in the United Arab Emirates (UAE), entire government departments are being block chained [31]. Saudi Arabia also deployed the technology to upgrade the security of its e-government systems and public data. In previous years, the Saudi Arabian government worked with a centralized system and faced many internal and external threats [50]; as a result, there is a gathering momentum to comprehend the opportunities for similar countries, such as Oman.

6. Oman's Challenges in Providing Good Governance

In recent years, decreased oil revenues and rising unemployment forced Omani policymakers to make difficult decisions to overcome challenging economic and socio-political issues, which run counter to the rentier social contract. Omani authorities stated that "tough decisions" need to be made in these areas [51–53]. Key amongst these decisions is how to accelerate economic diversification and Omanization. In other words, how to quickly promote non-oil sectors and replace expatriate labor with Omani labor. This meant tackling the nation's 'rentier mentality' through the "reduction in the public sector workforce, the expansion of the private sector, and the curtailment of [government] subsidies" [54]. These policy reforms constitute the main pillars of Oman's Vision 2040 [55], which focuses on economic diversification into non-oil industries, reforming the labor market, and changing the way that the country develops its human capital and skills base [54].

Oman's problems in converting its impressive gains in governance since the 1970s into a sustainable system are not entirely the result of recent economic problems. Government officials admit that the country's public sector have been struggling with inefficiency, unproductiveness, and inflated operational costs for at least the last decade [56]. Therefore, by the time the new sultan, Haitham bin Tariq, ascended the throne in January 2020, there was an urgent imperative to restructure the public sector, enhance efficiency in public institutions, and address the problem of rising unemployment. To his credit, and despite the unexpected calamity of the COVID-19 pandemic, measures for solving these structural problems were launched [57–59]. From our perspective, some of the most interesting steps taken in this direction involved investment in new technologies. The following sections elaborate the various issues identified above in Table 1.

6.1. e-Government and e-Services

Oman formulated an e-government strategy as early as 2003 [60]. This aimed to deliver government services in "an integrated and seamless way to foster an innovative approach" [61]. In other words, Oman's plan for e-government envisaged the collaboration of all the government organs into a 'whole-of-government' approach to achieve efficiency, transparency, and effectiveness in government services. One salient tool in this regard is the 'e-census'.

The e-census was announced in 2019 as "the first electronic [national] census without field visits" and which "requires Omanis and expats alike to update their information themselves" [62]. In this system, all information is stored on national statistical datasets, under such categories as population, housing, and establishments. Data from different ministries, government departments, electricity companies and municipalities should, in theory, be linked together in a single reference point [63]. Detailed information will be held about all Omanis and expats, based on the addresses of the properties they own or occupy. This would signify a major advance in the country's capacity for accurate planning and provision of services, especially given the previously ad hoc and vague postal address system. However, it was shown that such hyper-centralized systems, while beneficial in many ways, create serious security and privacy vulnerabilities to cyber-attacks or system failures [12].

Another example of the desire for efficient e-governance was raised when the Oman government launched e-services to regulate the funding of mosques. In January 2021, the Undersecretary of the Ministry of Endowments and Religious Affairs (MERA) announced an electronic system for managing various information about mosques, including everything from building permits to ongoing maintenance [64]. According to the government, the next stage of this system will involve regulating financial resources to cover maintenance costs and to control charitable endowments [64].

6.2. Corruption, Fraud, and Attestation of Documents

Connected to the issue of tracking public funds is the sensitive topic of corruption. In January 2021, *Times of Oman* reported the results of the 2020 Corruption Perception Index Report, which showed the Sultanate ranked 49th in the world [65,66]. A review of previous media coverage on this issue showed similar reporting, seeking to show reductions in corruption and the government's active role in this regard [67]. The establishment of institutions responsible for protecting public funds, especially, The State Audit Institute was linked with positive results in terms of fighting corruption [67].

However, a closer look at news covering fraudulent activities related to public funds reveals that the number of cases, in fact, increased in recent years. According to the Department of Public Prosecution, in 2016, the number of people accused of fraud and corruption was 112, which increased to 200 in 2018 [68]. Moreover, crimes related to public funds more than doubled from 55 reported cases in 2016 to 138 cases in 2017 [68]. Statements issued by the Public Prosecution Office, warning of long prison sentences for offenders, indicate a need for a stronger deterrent, and that embezzlement of public funds remains a serious problem in Oman [69,70].

Turning to another form of fraud, in recent years, government institutions in Oman faced problems involving fake academic certificates [71]. In 2018, the Ministry of Higher Education confirmed twenty false certification cases. In addition, Omani authorities identified thirty-nine fake universities worldwide, some of which had issued illegitimate qualifications to employees of Omani institutions (mostly educational) [72]. Besides the fraudulent activity and question marks around quality and integrity that emerge, the procedures for accreditation of certificates and degrees are time-consuming, slow, and costly for both institutions and individuals. Moreover, as the above figures show, the current system of attestation of certificates via the responsible authorities (inside and outside Oman) is clearly not working. The authors know of some cases where the procedure for accrediting the qualifications of academic staff at Sultan Qaboos University were so slow and cumbersome that genuine, qualified international faculty decided against coming to Oman.

6.3. Labor Management, Omanization, and Employment

Over recent decades Omani authorities sought solutions to the high rate of unemployment among citizens. "Omanization" policies generally aimed to increase the role of the private sector in the labor market and to shift away from an overdependence on expatriate labor. Subsequently, the number of expats gradually reduced in both the private and public sectors [73], and legal arrangements were put in place for replacing foreign workforce with Omanis [74–76].

While Omanization aims to replace expats with Omanis, it led, in many cases, to the informal employment of foreigners [77] and created labor shortages in areas lacking skilled candidates [78]. It was argued that blockchain solutions can reduce complexity in recruitment processes by identifying qualified candidates and streamlining the recruitment procedures for citizens and residents [79]. Such blockchain-based systems could be applied to both the private and public sectors in Oman. In this way, accurate block-chained information on employers and the labor force can be utilized to know the number of qualified people needed in each sector, the extent to which this need can be met by Omani nationals, and the number of foreign workers required to fill any shortfall. This could also serve to address the problem of unobserved gaps in the labor force being filled by illegal informal labor.

Another recently adopted government e-service is a register for employment contracts via an online application provided by the Labour ministry [80]. Although the Ministry cannot intervene in agreements between employer and employee, all the details about the contracts are saved in the Ministry's system to protect the parties' employment contracts. One risk of this type of centralized digital employment contract register is that the government also links its own reputation to the upholding of contracts and becomes a de facto guarantor of employment agreements within an e-government portal (as opposed to normal channels of employment relations via courts and collective bargaining, for instance). Therefore, any breach or discrediting of the contract information may cause "the loss of users' trust" and may ultimately harm citizens' trust in the government.

6.4. Subsidy Reforms

Related to a longstanding political bargain in Oman, the government attempted to roll back its model of providing heavily subsidized energy, fuel, and water to citizens and residents. To minimize the socio-economic and possible political impact of ceasing subsidies, the government sought to implement targeted subsidies to low-income families. Omani authorities stipulated that the targeted subsidy system would result in no overall economic change for households earning less than 500 Omani Rials per month, whereas households earning more than 1250 Omani Rials per month would no longer qualify for subsidies [81,82]. The system will be administered under the National Electricity and Water Subsidy System [83,84]. However, the rollout of this new system faces immense challenges of complexity, transparency, and public acceptance in the context of citizens' prior expectations around government support in a rentier state.

6.5. Tax Reforms

In the latter half of the 2010s, Oman experienced annual budget deficits due to persistently low oil prices, which were compounded by the economic shock of COVID-19. Subsequently, the Oman government was compelled to introduce major changes to its tax policy to improve its balance sheet. These included increasing the corporate tax rate, eliminating tax exemptions, the introduction of a value-added tax (VAT), and in 2019, instigating a selective 'sin-tax' on goods, such as tobacco, alcohol, energy drinks, soft drinks, and pork products [85,86]. Most crucially, in the 2020–2024 Economic Plan, it was announced that personal income tax would be introduced from 2022 [87].

The government is hesitant in initiating these tax reforms. It was initially announced that VAT would be implemented in 2019 [88] but it was delayed twice before finally being launched in April 2021 [89,90]. The official reasons given for these delays were that the taxes required new legal regulations, new IT systems for administering taxation, and specialized training for tax officials [91].

Operating a new consumption-based VAT at the same time as initiating an entire PAYE personal income tax system promises to test the administrative capacity of the Sultanate. The complexity involved in the rollout of an entirely new tax system will be challenging and could lead to vulnerability to serious error or fraud [92]. The adoption of general taxation in the formerly tax-free (for individuals) Sultanate also carries a degree of political risk, which will only be exacerbated if serious errors or fraud occur that reduce public trust in the process of deriving and disbursing public funds.

6.6. Elections and e-Participation

The Oman government consistently states that it is working towards increasing the level of political participation in the Sultanate. To maintain the legitimacy of the existing institutional structures, the government is keen for citizens to actively participate, as well as feel that they are contributing to decision-making processes. This is especially important in the context of important changes to taxation, economic diversification, and Omanization. A key existing channel of participation is the elected lower house of Oman's parliament, the Majlis Al-Shura (Consultative Council).

Elections for the 86-seat Majlis al-Shura were last held in 2019 and electronic voting was used for the first time in Oman through the 'white card' system, which involved biometric identification via fingerprints. A remote voting application was also available for citizens residing overseas [93]. To use the mobile application overseas, voters needed a mobile SIM card, issued by an Oman-based mobile service company, and a Public Key Infrastructure (PKI) number [94].

The Oman Ministry of Interior stated that 349,680 individuals out 713,335 registered voters cast ballots at 110 polling centers. A total of 52.7 per cent of those who voted were males and 47.3 per cent were women [95]. Only 25,000 voters selected candidates by using the white card option [96]. Election officials and voters reported problems in reliably and efficiently achieving biometric verification of voters' identity through fingerprint scanning [97]. Moreover, the experiment with mobile-phone voting applications led to concerns about the extent to which identity was reliably verified, as well as general security risks and system vulnerabilities. These issues served to reduce the integrity and the trust of participants in the e-voting innovations.

6.7. COVID-19 and Healthcare

Oman's struggle with the 2020–2021 global pandemic began on 24 February 2020, when two Omani citizens returned from Iran and tested positive for COVID-19 [98]. Subsequently, the government combatted the pandemic through a series of measures and restrictions, such as banning of movement around the country, closing borders to non-Omanis, banning public gatherings and Friday prayers [99], suspending public transportation [100], and closing educational institutions [101]. The economic impacts of the pandemic were severe and exacerbated the unemployment and recruitment problems outlined above.

The pandemic also highlighted issues with the governance and funding of public health services in Oman. On 24 March 2020, a public endowment fund was established to collect donations from individuals and companies to support the health sector [102]. Immediately, negative claims about the fund's transparency, legitimacy, and ultimate beneficiaries were circulated in Omani social media, which the authorities were forced to publicly denounce as false [103] It is impossible to know at this point whether there was any substance to the claims regarding the public endowment fund. The key point, however, is that lack of public trust reduced the efficacy of the collection effort.

7. Oman Government Perspectives on Blockchain Solutions

This section outlines the Oman government's attitude toward the adoption of blockchain technologies for e-governance, based on an interview via video conferencing with Dr. Ali Al Shidhani, on 7 April 2021 [51]. From the preceding review of recent and current e-governance-related issues in Oman and the academic literature regarding blockchain solutions, there is evidence of the potential of blockchain technologies. However, the question remains whether the government is open to the idea of adopting technology that promises to (1) decentralize governance in a way that is almost diametrically opposed to the centralized-governance model, established since the mid-1970s, and upon which Oman's implicit social contract rests; and (2) whether the nature of blockchain, which vastly reduces the need for human interventions in governance and administration, will only exacerbate the country's recurring problems with unemployment-related social unrest [104].

Clearly, there is significant government interest in the possible benefits of blockchain in Oman. This is increasingly evident since the first Blockchain Oman Symposium in Muscat in November 2017, which two of the authors of this study attended [105]. The government-sponsored *Blockchain Club* and a company named *Blockchain Solutions and Services* were both announced at the same Symposium. The Central Market Authority (CMA), the entity responsible for the stock market in Oman, is already using blockchain for voting in its annual general meetings (AGMs). In the private sector, Bank Dhofar [106] is already using Ripple for financial transactions and the Port of Salalah is a member of the global logistics blockchain consortium, Tradelens [107].

The government attitude to the emergence of blockchain was clear in the comments of Dr. Al-Shidhani. It was emphasized that the government is open to the benefits of blockchain. However, it was indicated that the government intends to proceed judiciously and more gradually than their neighbors in the UAE, who, as mentioned previously, stated their objective to move much of their e-governance onto blockchain. The Omani government intends to use it selectively and "in specific applications and specific situations" [51].

It was also indicated by Dr Al-Shidhani that a number of Omani government officials responsible for information and communication technologies (ICT) are well informed and aware of its potential applications. However, at the broader level of government and the general public, there is little informed awareness of blockchain, with an estimated level of awareness of informed awareness of around 25 per cent with much capacity building yet to be achieved. There is, however, an emerging awareness of the potential of blockchain, with increasing demands for tertiary education and postgraduate research into blockchain. Seminars and workshops are increasingly being offered at Sultan Qaboos University and at private universities [51].

Regarding political participation, there is openness to the idea of adopting blockchain solutions. When asked whether the Omani government might consider adopting blockchain for its elections, Al-Shidhani [51] responded:

> Yes, I think, it's an option . . . Technology must be introduced to fill gaps, to solve problems, to expedite processes and so on. If the current voting system . . . is malfunctioning or there are weaknesses in the current voting system and those weaknesses can be addressed by using blockchain, then, yes, blockchain should be the way to go. Just like what [the] Central Marketing Authority did when they introduced blockchain voting in annual general meetings of companies.

Regarding the question of the decentralizing nature of blockchain and how this could represent a complete turnaround from the centralized nature of Omani governance and state–society relations, the response of the government official is worth quoting in full.

> We have a problem of centralization, and we want to decentralize. Decentralization can be done through proper laws, regulations, delegation of authority and so on. There are some structural and regulatory frameworks that need to be put in place. If technology, like blockchain, can be used to help in this direction, it will be used. If other technologies can also be used to help this, it will also be used. I just try to be careful not to draw a direct line between what we want to do in the country in terms of decentralization with a technology known for decentralization. ... So, maybe usage of blockchain should not be [greatly] associated with [the] decentralization efforts that the government wants to [achieve]. Maybe the usage of blockchain is associated more with authenticity of information, with legitimacy of data, with tracking and immutability ... I think that is where there is more linkage to Oman than decentralization aspects [51].

Finally, we turned to the question of how blockchain might impact employment issues in Oman. It was undisputed that the adoption of blockchain as a platform for e-government would lead to the redundancy of many administrative roles within the public sector that traditionally employed large numbers of Omani nationals. In theory, however, this replacement of manual governance services with digital blockchain e-governance aligns with government priorities. Over the last quarter-of-a-century the Oman government repeatedly emphasized a desire to reduce the size of the public sector and to boost the share of the private sector in the labor market and overall economy. This was part of the country's Vision 2020 and Vision 2040 strategic plans, promoted, respectively, since 1995 [108]. Moreover, government representatives are confident that the transition to new technologies, including blockchain, should not be delayed due to fears of a negative impact on the labor force. Again, it is worth quoting, in full, the response of Dr Al-Shidhani on this issue of technology and employment.

> There is this philosophical debate about technology versus job creation, and how technology will eliminate jobs and introduction of technology will also introduce jobs but what would be the net result? Are we going to end up with more jobs than eliminated jobs? Or the opposite? Other jobs, other periphery jobs, are created because of the introduction of the technology. And, in my opinion, I don't think it is going to have a big impact because I believe that new technologies introduce new types of jobs [51].

8. Discussion

Data collected from news media between 2018 and 2020 revealed seven governance issues (excluding education, which we omitted) that can be deemed important governance issues requiring further academic attention in the Oman context. These were: public sector reform and e-services; issues of employment; taxation; public healthcare; elections and e-participation; corruption, fraud and attestation of documents; and reforms to public subsidies. This section discusses how blockchain technology may offer solutions, but also introduce risks, in each area.

8.1. Blockchain Technology, Public Sector Reform and e-Services?

Oman wants to reform its public sector and increase the efficiency, public uptake, and trust in e-services. By using blockchain technology, sensitive information and the private data of Omani citizens and residents could, in theory, be stored securely against unauthorized access, alteration, or system failure. Looking at the example of public endowments raised above, studies showed that blockchain-enabled charitable services can enhance tracking and accounting for donations, creating transparency for both beneficiaries and contributors [16]. In this way, the trust of contributors in the endowments system can be sustained, which could, in fact, attract more people to contribute to endowment funds, reducing pressure on the government to provide for the construction and maintenance of religious infrastructure for a growing population. A risk factor for block chaining e-services in government could be privacy issues of personal information within public blockchains [11].

8.2. Blockchain and Employment Issues

This is arguably the most critical risk area in terms of blockchain solutions. Potential blockchain applications include plans to establish a public block-chained employment contract register in Oman. This would be far less prone to failure and related problems. Another blockchain-based option would be for employers and employees to enter bilateral blockchain-based 'smart contracts' that do not require any government involvement. Overall, the job market in Oman will increasingly be impacted by technologies; not only blockchain, but also other automation systems, including Artificial Intelligence (AI) and robotics [109,110]. The high number of public sector jobs, mostly in administration, that underpin the redistributive model of Oman's rentier social contract will rapidly be made redundant by such technologies and could swell the ranks of the unemployed in the short to medium term. Hence, there is an urgent need for high-level technical training and re-skilling of Omani citizens to align Omanization policies with a rapidly changing work environment.

8.3. Blockchain and Taxation Reform

In the blockchain literature, it is asserted that a blockchain-based tax system can be effective in virtually eliminating tax fraud and increasing transparency in the allocation of public funds [111]. Moreover, collecting tax via blockchain-based models can eradicate double spending, reduce the potential for fraudulent tax refunds, and will "automatize a great part of the work previously conducted manually" by tax employees ([111], p. 453). This final point relates to the previous issue regarding employment—the double-edged sword of blockchain—whereby much-needed efficiencies also come at the expense of public sector jobs that formed one pillar of the rentier social contract.

8.4. Blockchain and Public Healthcare

As discussed above, regarding corruption, the immutability and transparency of a public blockchain could have prevented negative public perceptions of public health funding and could have mobilized much-needed public funds more effectively to help the government tackle the pandemic. In terms of healthcare and public health provision, especially during health crises, recent studies focused on responses to the pandemic that highlight endemic limitations of healthcare systems around the world. As a result, a consensus is emerging around the utility of adopting new technologies, such as blockchain and AI in healthcare, to fight the current pandemic and future outbreaks ([112], p. 1). This argument is based on claims that blockchain will be effective in preventing and responding to pandemics by "enabling early detection of outbreaks, [whilst] protecting user privacy, and ensuring reliable medical supply chains during the outbreak tracking [sic]" ([112], p. 1).

8.5. Blockchain, Elections and e-Participation

E-voting systems continue to be questioned in emerging studies. Issues include a lack of standards, security and reliability risks, vulnerability to attacks, fraud, malicious software programming, costly technical tools, and secure storage of transactions [13]. Blockchain-based e-voting [113] is currently being discussed as "the next generation of modern electronic voting systems", largely due to its immutable features ([13], p. 2). In theory, by applying public blockchain technology to e-voting systems, confidentiality, anonymity, and accuracy of results would be ensured. Consequently, trust in electoral processes and, therefore, participation rates, might increase, enhancing the overall legitimacy of elections and political participation [13,29].

8.6. Blockchain and Corruption, Fraud and Attestation of Documents

The literature on blockchain-based solutions shows clearly that the transparent, decentralized, and cost-effective features of blockchain technology can reduce crimes involving public funds [15]. With transparency and immutability of accounting almost guaranteed via blockchain-based technology, it could be expected that the number of crimes committed in this area could decrease. To overcome issues related to storing and managing credentials, there is evidence that blockchain-based applications may provide "a sustainable record of achievements" for users and vastly reduce administrative, reputational, and recruitment costs for universities and colleges [18]. In this area, optimum efficiency would be achieved by interfacing or integrating with global blockchains of academic achievement and qualifications to instantaneously and securely attest the qualifications of the large number of international recruits into the Omani education sector. At the time of writing, as far as we know, such a system is yet to be established.

8.7. Blockchain and Reforms to Public Subsidies

Applying blockchain to potentially complicated and politically risky subsidy reforms could have benefits. For instance, block-chained and means-tested systems for targeted subsidies could be more manageable, transaction costs would be minimized and, most importantly, the potential for corrupt exploitation of the subsidy system would be reduced [16]. In short, the application of a public blockchain to subsidy-reform measures could save money, eliminate errors and fraud, and ultimately enhance the intended effect of assisting more low-income families in need of social transfers. Similar to other e-services, privacy issues would need to be addressed in this area.

8.8. General Issues with Blockchain in the Oman Context

Early indications from the Oman government suggest that they intend to use blockchain to address technical weaknesses in existing systems, such as the verification issues described around e-voting. It would certainly help in this regard. However, there seems to be little attention given to the more intangible impacts on the legitimacy and perception of electoral processes if they were to be conducted through immutable and transparent public blockchain technology. In terms of procedures for running elections, Oman is one of the best in the Middle East, in terms of global rankings on electoral integrity [114]. Consequently, there is not an actual problem with the technical conduct of elections. There is, however, a problem around public perceptions of the elections. (This view is based on numerous private conversations with Omani citizens by the first author from 2013 to 2019.) There is not a high level of trust in the process, or the candidates themselves. Blockchain, by its very nature, cannot be manipulated easily and should in theory increase public trust and, therefore, increase public participation in elections. Nonetheless, the point raised by Praharaj et al. [24,25] that digital infrastructure is not necessarily a guarantee of improved self-participation or, for that matter, a substitute for substantive governance transformation is salient.

The notion of implementing a decentralizing technology amid a highly centralized rentier state is interesting in that there remains a government perception that decentralization of the overall government structure is a separate issue from the way that blockchain could decentralize every aspect of governance. For instance, by adopting public or even consortium blockchains in the various departments and agencies of government, it would naturally mean less capacity for centralized actors—directors, under-secretaries, ministers and so forth—to exercise discretionary authority in decision-making and in the presentation (or not) of information and policies to the public. The cumulative effect of this across different government sectors would, naturally, be decentralizing.

Moreover, the decentralizing effect would not necessarily stop at the borders of Oman. For instance, the UAE and the Kingdom of Saudi Arabia are exploring shared cryptocurrencies for cross-border payment systems [40], as well as a "Court of the Blockchain" for cross-border jurisdiction [115]. The fact that blockchain will necessarily assume cross-border dimensions was acknowledged by the government official, when he mentioned in relation to attestation of domestic and international qualifications that, the essence behind blockchain is that entrusted entities can join a network through blockchain. As a result, this ecosystem of entrusted networks is global. The networks are not within the domain, or they are not [limited to] the geographical area of one country. Indeed, for a blockchain system to be successful, it must be global. Furthermore, it must encompass most, or a majority of, stakeholders.

In terms of employment issues, the teleological perspective that technology adoption leads to new forms of labor demand does not necessarily consider: (1) the unique features of rentier systems, which operate quite differently from other types of diversified market economies and (2), the fact that Oman faces urgent pressures from unemployment at the present time.

In 2011, civil unrest occurred across Oman, largely related to the frustrations of unemployed (or underemployed) youth, who demanded more jobs and higher salaries; essentially, a larger and more transparent share in the dividends of the oil-based rentier economy [116]. The government's response to these pressures was to quickly announce the creation of up to 50,000 new jobs, mostly in the public sector, increases to the minimum wage, and jobseeker allowances to appease the protesters [117]. Ten years later, similar protests occurred in late May 2021, to which the new sultan was forced to respond in similar fashion with a promise of 32,000 additional jobs (many of which are temporary or part-time), spread across the public and private sectors [118].

Two key points are salient in this regard. First, the government faces political obstacles around implementing its Vision 2040 plan [119] to reduce the size of the public sector, due to persistent public demands for the government to uphold the main pillars of the rentier social contract jobs, subsidies, and zero taxation. This will consequently make it difficult to use blockchain solutions to shore up and enhance e-governance in the short term, as this would inevitably involve the redundancy of many administrative roles in government. Second, the demand for "side jobs" related to new technologies, such as blockchain, will require precious time to develop and will require rapid re-skilling and restructuring of the labor force, as well as raising public and governmental awareness (not to mention willingness) to move away from traditional, highly centralized public sector models.

9. Conclusions

The results of this exploratory phase of a sequential mixed-methods study suggest that there are potential advantages to be obtained for Oman from being an early mover into blockchain e-governance solutions. Data collected from news media between 2018 and 2020 revealed seven governance issues (excluding education, which we omitted) that can be deemed important governance issues requiring further attention. These were: public sector reform and e-services; issues of employment; taxation; public healthcare; elections and e-participation; corruption, fraud and attestation of documents; and reforms to public subsidies. We examined each of these areas and consulted the international literature on blockchain pertaining to each. Our results indicate that, in theory, substantive potential exists for blockchain solutions to enhance the efficiency, cost effectiveness and legitimacy (public trust) of public administration and governance functions in Oman. However, in accordance with phase two of a sequential mixed-methods design, targeted quantitative studies must be conducted into each of these issues to determine a greater degree of knowledge regarding the cost/benefit calculus. All these public governance areas need to be quantitatively examined to test potential for greater cost efficiencies, improved accuracy and reliability of information systems, transparency and accountability of public services, and an upgrade in the overall level of legitimacy and public trust in the institutions of governance.

The most critical areas highlighted as foci for future research in the Omani context are the question of employment, where blockchain could have negative impacts on an already stressed labor market, and the politically explosive question of taxation reform, both of which lie at the heart of the rentier bargain of Oman and other GCC states. The belief of the Oman government officials that new work opportunities from new technologies, such as blockchain, can offset the reduction in the traditional public sector should be tested using quantitative predictive data analysis. Moreover, while the government seems aware and open to the possible benefits of blockchain solutions, it may face political resistance to the replacement of a socially constructed system of trust—based on a centralized state and a rentier system—with a technologically constructed and decentralized mode of creating trust based on technology. This area requires further research by social scientists. In sum, while there are many good reasons why Oman should adopt blockchain solutions in the immediate future, it remains to be seen how the encounter between old social contracts based on "Leviathan" or new social contracts based on "Nakamoto" will unfold.

Author Contributions: L.G. and A.K.S. wrote this paper. H.Y.T. was engaged in data collection and literature review, also H.Y.T. wrote the first draft of Section 6. While all guidance and supervision done by K.R. All authors have read and agreed to the published version of the manuscript.

Funding: This research was funded by Sultan Qaboos University grant number [RF/EPS/POLS/19/01] to promote the academic research and to achieve the research and educational objectives of the University. The ideas and views contained in this article are from the authors and should not be interpreted as official from Sultan Qaboos University.

Institutional Review Board Statement: Not applicable.

Informed Consent Statement: Not applicable.

Data Availability Statement: The datasets used and analyzed during the current study are available from the corresponding author on reasonable request.

Conflicts of Interest: The authors declare no conflict of interest.

References

1. Townsend, J. *Oman: The Making of a Modern State*; St. Martin's Press: New York, NY, USA, 1977.
2. Phillips, S.G.; Hunt, J.S. 'Without Sultan Qaboos, We Would Be Yemen': The Renaissance Narrative and the Political Settlement in Oman. *J. Int. Dev.* **2017**, *29*, 645–660. [CrossRef]
3. Moritz, J. Reformers and the Rentier State: Re-Evaluating the Co-Optation Mechanism in Rentier State Theory. *J. Arab. Stud.* **2018**, *8*, 4664. [CrossRef]
4. Oman Plans $5.7 Billion Budget Deficit in 2021-State News Agency. 2021. Available online: https://www.reuters.com/article/oman-budget-int-idUSKBN2962AC (accessed on 18 June 2022).
5. Sultan Qaboos of Oman, Arab world's Longest-Serving Ruler, Dies Aged 79. 2020. Available online: https://www.bbc.com/news/world-middle-east-50902476 (accessed on 18 June 2022).
6. Zheng, Z.; Xie, S.; Dai, H.N.; Chen, X.; Wang, H. Blockchain challenges and opportunities: A survey. *Int. J. Web Grid Serv.* **2018**, *14*, 352–375. [CrossRef]
7. Monrat, A.A.; Schelén, O.; Andersson, K. A Survey of Blockchain from the Perspectives of Applications, Challenges, and Opportunities. *IEEE Access* **2019**, *7*, 117134–117151. [CrossRef]
8. Fenwick, M.; Vermeulen, E.P.M.; Kaal, W. Regulation tomorrow: Or, what happens when technology is faster than the law? *Am. Univ. Bus. Law Rev.* **2017**, *6*, 561–594. [CrossRef]
9. Vigna, P.; Casey, M.J. *The Truth Machine: The Blockchain and The Future of Everything*; St. Martin's Press: New York, NY, USA, 2019.
10. Filippi, P.D.; Hassan, S. Blockchain technology as a regulatory technology: From code is law to law is code. *arXiv* **2018**, arXiv:1801.02507. [CrossRef]
11. Bhushan, B.; Sinha, P.; Sagayam, K.M.; Andrew, J. Untangling Blockchain technology: A survey on state of the art, security threats, privacy services, applications and future research directions. *Comput. Electr. Eng.* **2021**, *90*, 106897. [CrossRef]
12. Manski, S. Building the blockchain world: Technological commonwealth or just more of the same? *Strateg. Change* **2017**, *26*, 511–522. [CrossRef]
13. Taş, R.; Tanrıöver, Ö.Ö. A Systematic Review of Challenges and Opportunities of Blockchain for E-Voting. *Symmetry* **2020**, *12*, 1328. [CrossRef]
14. Navadkar, V.H.; Nighot, A.; Wantmure, R. Overview of blockchain technology in government/public sectors. *Int. Res. J. Eng. Technol.* **2018**, *5*, 2287.
15. Elisa, N.; Yang, L.; Chao, F.; Cao, Y. A framework of blockchain-based secure and privacy-preserving E-government system. *Wirel. Netw.* **2018**, 1–11. [CrossRef]
16. Berg, A.; Markey-Towler, B.; Novak, M. Blockchains less government, more market. *J. Priv. Enterp.* **2018**, *35*, 1–21. [CrossRef]
17. Wolfond, G. A Blockchain Ecosystem for Digital Identity: Improving Service Delivery in Canada's Public and Private Sectors. *Technol. Innov. Manag. Rev.* **2017**, *7*, 35–40. [CrossRef]
18. Jirgensons, M.; Kapenieks, J. Blockchain and the future of digital learning credential assessment and management. *J. Teach. Educ. Sustain.* **2018**, *20*, 145–156. [CrossRef]
19. Atzori, M. Blockchain Technology and Decentralized Governance: Is the State Still Necessary? Available online: https://ssrn.com/abstract=2709713 (accessed on 1 December 2015).

20. Hsieh, Y.Y.; Vergne, J.P.J.; Wang, S. The internal and external governance of blockchain-based organizations. In *Bitcoin and Beyond*; Campbell-Verduyn, M., Ed.; Routledge: London, UK, 2017.
21. Jia, K.; Zhang, F. Between Liberalization and Prohibition. In *Bitcoin and Beyond*; Campbell-Verduyn, M., Ed.; Routledge: London, UK, 2017.
22. Miscione, G.; Kavanagh, D. Bitcoin and the Blockchain: A Coup D'État through Digital Heterotopia? Humanistic Management Network, Research Paper Series No. 23/15. Available online: https://ssrn.com/abstract=2624922 (accessed on 8 July 2015). [CrossRef]
23. Reijers, W.; O'Brolcháin, F.; Haynes, P. Governance in Blockchain Technologies & Social Contract Theories. *Ledger* **2016**, *1*, 134–151.
24. Praharaj, S.; Han, J.H.; Hawken, S. Innovative civic engagement and digital urban infrastructure: Lessons from 100 Smart Cities Mission in India. *Procedia Eng.* **2017**, *180*, 1423–1432. [CrossRef]
25. Praharaj, S.; Han, J.H.; Hawken, S. Towards the right model of smart city governance in India. *Int. J. Sus. Dev. Plann.* **2018**, *13*, 171–186. [CrossRef]
26. Bhushan, B.; Khamparia, A.; Sagayam, K.M.; Sharma, S.K.; Abdul Ahad, M.; Debnath, N.C. Blockchain for smart cities: A review of architectures, integration trends and future research directions. *Sustain. Cities Soc.* **2020**, *61*, 102360. [CrossRef]
27. Almond, G.; Verba, S. *The Civic Culture: Political Attitudes and Demcracy in Five Nations*; SAGE: Thousand Oaks, CA, USA, 1963.
28. Luthra, S.; Janssen, M.; Rana, N.P.; Yadav, G.; Dwivedi, Y.K. Categorizing and relating implementation challenges for realizing blockchain applications in government. *Inf. Technol. People*, 2022; ahead of print. [CrossRef]
29. Kshetri, N.; Voas, J. Blockchain-enabled e-voting. *IEEE Softw.* **2018**, *35*, 97. [CrossRef]
30. Alketbi, A.; Nasir, Q.; Talib, M.A. Novel blockchain reference model for government services: Dubai government case study. *Int. J. Syst. Assur. Eng. Manag.* **2020**, *11*, 1170–1191. [CrossRef]
31. Khan, S.N.; Shael, M.; Majdalawieh, M. Blockchain technology as a support infrastructure in E-Government evolution at Dubai economic department. In Proceedings of the 2019 International Electronics Communication Conference, New Tork, NY, USA, 7–9 July 2019; pp. 124–130.
32. Ghazawneh, A. Blockchain in the Middle East: Challenges and Opporttunties MCIS 2019 Proceedings 2019, 34. Available online: https://aisel.aisnet.org/mcis2019/34 (accessed on 18 June 2022).
33. Al-Azizi, L.; Al-Badi, A.H.; Al-Zrafi, T.; Sharma, S.K. Exploring the adoption of mobile applications: Case studies in government agencies in Oman. In *Proceedings of the 29th International Business Information Management Association Conference–Education Excellence and Innovation Management through Vision 2020: From Regional Development Sustainability to Global Economic Growth, Vienna, Austria, 3–4 May 2017*; International Business Information Management Association, IBIMA: Seville, Spain, 2017; pp. 1995–2022.
34. Sarrayrih, M.A.; Sriram, B. Major challenges in developing a successful e-government: A review on the Sultanate of Oman. *J. King Saud Univ.-Comput. Inf. Sci.* **2015**, *27*, 230–235. [CrossRef]
35. Creswell, J.W. *Research Design: Qualitative, Quantitative & Mixed Methods Approach*; Sage Publications: Thousand Oaks, CA, USA, 2014.
36. Government Working to Arrest Decline in Available Farmland in Oman. 2018. Available online: https://www.timesofoman.com/article/government-working-to-arrest-decline-in-available-farm-land-in-oman (accessed on 18 June 2022).
37. Bruner, J.P. Locke, Nozick and the state of nature. *Philos. Stud.* **2020**, *177*, 705–726. [CrossRef]
38. Orbell, J.; Rutherford, B. Can Leviathan Make the Life of Man Less Solitary, Poor, Nasty, Brutish and Short? *Br. J. Political Sci.* **1973**, *3*, 383–407. [CrossRef]
39. Nakamoto, S. Bitcoin: A Peer-to-Peer Electronic Cash System. 2008. Available online: https://bitcoin.org/bitcoin.pdf (accessed on 18 June 2022).
40. Papadaki, M.; Karamitsos, I. Blockchain technology in the Middle East and North Africa. *Inf. Technol. Dev.* **2021**, 1–18. [CrossRef]
41. Geneiatakis, D.; Soupionis, Y.; Steri, G.; Kounelis, I.; Neisse, R.; Nai-Fovino, I. Blockchain performance analysis for supporting cross-border E-Government services. *IEEE Trans. Eng. Manag.* **2020**, *67*, 1310–1322. [CrossRef]
42. Negara, E.S.; Hidyanto, A.N.; Andryani, R.; Erlansyah, D. A Survey Blockchain and Smart Contract Technology in Government Agencies. In *IOP Conference Series: Materials Science and Engineering*; IOP Publishing: Bristol, UK, 2021; p. 12026.
43. Alharby, M.; Aldweesh, A.; Van Moorsel, A. Blockchain-based smart contracts: A systematic mapping study of academic research. In Proceedings of the 2018 International Conference on Cloud Computing, Big Data and Blockchain (ICCBB), Fuzhou, China, 15–17 November 2018; IEEE: Manhattan, NY, USA; pp. 1–6.
44. How Blockchain Works. 2020. Available online: https://www.tutorialandexample.com/working-of-blockchain/ (accessed on 18 June 2022).
45. Andoni, M.; Robu, V.; Flynn, D.; Abram, S.; Geach, D.; Jenkins, D.; McCallum, P.; Peacock, A. Blockchain technology in the energy sector: A systematic review of challenges and opportunities. *Renew. Sustain. Energy Rev.* **2019**, *100*, 143–174. [CrossRef]
46. Sullivan, C.; Burger, E. Blockchain, Digital Identity, E-government. In *Business Transformation through Blockchain*; Treiblmaier, H., Beck, R., Eds.; Springer: Berlin/Heidelberg, Germany, 2019; pp. 233–258.
47. Gao, Y.; Pan, Q.; Liu, Y.; Lin, H.; Chen, Y.; Wen, Q. The Notarial Office in E-government: A Blockchain-Based Solution. *IEEE Access* **2021**, *9*, 44411–44425. [CrossRef]
48. Elisa, N.; Yang, L.; Li, H.; Chao, F.; Naik, N. Consortium Blockchain for Security and Privacy-Preserving in E-government Systems. *arXiv* **2020**, arXiv:2006.14234.

49. Stephen, R.; Alex, A. A review on blockchain security. In *IOP Conference Series: Materials Science and Engineering*; IOP Publishing: Bristol, UK, 2018; Volume 396, p. 012030.
50. Assiri, H.; Nanda, P.; Mohanty, M. Secure e-Governance Using Blockchain. *EasyChair*. 2020, p. 4252. Available online: https://easychair.org/publications/preprint/svXR (accessed on 18 June 2022).
51. We Took Tough Decisions for Oman: Al Sunaidy. 2019. Available online: https://timesofoman.com/article/886188/oman/we-took-tough-decisions-for-oman-al-sunaidy (accessed on 18 June 2022).
52. Oman to Have Best Growth Rate in GCC in 2020, Says World Bank. 2019. Available online: https://timesofoman.com/article/1314904/Oman/Oman-to-have-best-growth-rate-in-GCC-in-2020-says-World-Bank (accessed on 18 June 2022).
53. Public-Private Partnerships to Speed up Non-Oil Future. 2019. Available online: https://timesofoman.com/article/2032964/Oman/Government/Public-private-partnerships-to-speed-up-non-oil-future (accessed on 18 June 2022).
54. Fromson, J.; Simon, S. Visions of Omani reform. *Survival* 2019, *61*, 99–116. [CrossRef]
55. Key Non-Oil Sectors Recognised as Ripe for Growth in Oman. 2018. Available online: https://timesofoman.com/article/key-non-oil-sectors-recognised-as-ripe-for-growth-in-oman (accessed on 18 June 2022).
56. Oman's Sultan Haitham Forges on with Administrative Revolution. 2020. Available online: https://thearabweekly.com/omans-sultan-haitham-forges-administrative-revolution (accessed on 18 June 2022).
57. Abouzzohour, Y. As Oman Enters a New Era, Economic and Political Challenges Persist. 2020. Available online: https://www.brookings.edu/blog/order-from-chaos/2020/01/15/as-oman-enters-a-new-era-economic-and-political-challenges-persist/ (accessed on 18 June 2022).
58. Education, Jobs for Youth Top Priorities in HM's Royal Speech. 2020. Available online: https://timesofoman.com/article/2795805/Oman/Education-jobs-for-youth-top-priorities-in-HMs-Royal-Speech (accessed on 18 June 2022).
59. Omani Government Promises to Address Unemployment after Nationwide Protests. 2019. Available online: https://www.middleeasteye.net/news/omani-government-promises-address-unemployment-after-nationwide-protests (accessed on 18 June 2022).
60. Sultanate of Oman Ministry of Transport, Communications and Information Technology. E-Oman Main Strategic Directions. Available online: https://www.ita.gov.om/ITAPortal/eOman/Main_Strategic_Directions.aspx (accessed on 18 June 2022).
61. Oman eGovernment Services Portal. Whole of Government. Available online: https://omanuna.oman.om/en/home-page (accessed on 18 June 2022).
62. No One Will Visit Your House for E Census 2020. 2019. Available online: https://timesofoman.com/article/1546056/Oman/Government/No-one-will-visit-your-house-for-ECensus-2020 (accessed on 18 June 2022).
63. Oman Begins e-Census 2020 Data Gathering for Private Sector. 2020. Available online: https://timesofoman.com/article/3018891/oman/government/oman-begins-e-census-2020-data-gathering-for-private-sector (accessed on 18 June 2022).
64. MERA Undersecretary Issues Statement on Opening of Mosques in Oman. 2021. Available online: https://timesofoman.com/article/mera-undersecretary-issues-statement-on-opening-of-mosques-in-oman (accessed on 18 June 2022).
65. Sultanate Rank 49 in Corruption Perceptions Index. 2021. Available online: https://timesofoman.com/article/sultanate-rank-49-in-corruption-perceptions-index (accessed on 18 June 2022).
66. Transparency International. 2020. Available online: https://www.transparency.org/en/cpi/2020/index/nzl (accessed on 18 June 2022).
67. Anti-Corruption Stance of Oman Recognized Globally. 2019. Bank Dhofar to Join Hands with RippleNet. Available online: https://timesofoman.com/article/1463848/oman/anti-corruption-stance-of-oman-recognised-globally (accessed on 18 June 2022).
68. 70 Jailed for Stealing Public Funds in Oman. 2019. Available online: https://timesofoman.com/article/1167279/oman/70-jailed-for-stealing-public-funds-in-oman (accessed on 18 June 2022).
69. Embezzlement Case Accused to Be Tried in Court. 2019. Available online: https://timesofoman.com/article/embezzlement-case-accused-to-be-tried-in-court (accessed on 18 June 2022).
70. Public Servant to Face Jail Term for Embezzlement in Oman. 2019. Available online: https://timesofoman.com/article/3019195/oman/public-servant-to-face-jail-term-for-embezzlement-in-oman (accessed on 18 June 2022).
71. Government Centre Calls on Public Authorities to Address 'Fake Certificate' Claims. 2019. Available online: https://www.timesofoman.com/article/government-centre-calls-on-public-authorities-to-address-fake-certificate-claims (accessed on 18 June 2022).
72. Oman Identifies 39 Fake Universities Worldwide. 2019. Available online: https://timesofoman.com/article/1421934/Oman/Education/Oman-identifies-39-fake-universities-worldwide (accessed on 18 June 2022).
73. Omanis to Replace Expats in 19 Occupations at Health Ministry. 2018. Available online: https://www.timesofoman.com/article/omanis-to-replace-expats-in-19-occupations-at-health-ministry (accessed on 18 June 2022).
74. Ministry of Manpower Omanises Some Manager Positions. 2019. Available online: https://timesofoman.com/article/1279978/oman/ministry-of-manpower-omanises-some-manager-positions (accessed on 18 June 2022).
75. Over 50% of Omanis Earn Less than OMR500. 2018. Available online: https://www.timesofoman.com/article/over-50-per-cent-of-omanis-earn-less-than-omr500 (accessed on 18 June 2022).
76. These Visas Will Not Be Renewed for Expats Working in Oman. 2020. Available online: https://timesofoman.com/article/2688773/Oman/These-visas-will-not-be-renewed-for-expats-working-in-Oman (accessed on 18 June 2022).

77. Alsahi, H. COVID-19 and the Intensification of the GCC Workforce Nationalization Policies. 2020. Available online: https://www.arab-reform.net/publication/covid-19-and-the-intensification-of-the-gcc-workforce-nationalization-policies/ (accessed on 18 June 2022).
78. Omanisation Policies Not Helping Private Sector. 2018. Available online: https://timesofoman.com/article/136206/oman/omanisation-policies-not-helping-private-sector (accessed on 18 June 2022).
79. Vinu, S.; Sherimon, P.C.; Ismaeel, A. JobChain: An Integrated Blockchain Model for Managing Job Recruitment for Ministries in Sultanate of Oman. *Int. J. Adv. Comput. Sci. Appl.* **2020**, *11*. [CrossRef]
80. Submit Work Contracts Online, Says Oman's Ministry of Labour. 2021. Available online: https://timesofoman.com/article/100359-submit-work-contracts-online-says-omans-ministry-of-labour (accessed on 18 June 2022).
81. Oman to Start Cutting Utility Subsidies in January. 2020. Available online: https://www.reuters.com/article/oman-economy/oman-to-start-cutting-utility-subsidies-in-january-idUKL1N2J0056 (accessed on 18 June 2022).
82. Oman to Gradually Phase Out Water, Electricity Subsidies. 2020. Available online: https://www.omanobserver.om/oman-to-gradually-phase-out-water-electricity-subsidies/ (accessed on 18 June 2022).
83. Oman to Phase out Water and Electricity Subsidies in Five Years. 2020. Available online: https://timesofoman.com/article/oman-to-phase-out-water-and-electricity-subsidies-in-five-years (accessed on 18 June 2022).
84. Over 5000 Registered for Power, Water Subsidy in Oman. 2020. Available online: https://timesofoman.com/article/over-5000-registered-for-power-water-subsidy-in-oman (accessed on 18 June 2022).
85. Bertelsmann Stiftung. Bertelsmann Stiftung, BTI 2020 Country Report—Oman. 2020. Available online: https://www.bti-project.org/en/reports/country-report-OMN-2020.html (accessed on 18 June 2022).
86. New Selective Tax to Come in on June 15. 2019. Available online: https://timesofoman.com/article/1356077/Oman/Government/New-selective-tax-to-come-in-on-June-15 (accessed on 18 June 2022).
87. Oman Income Tax Expected in 2022 in Fiscal Shake-Up. 2020. Available online: https://www.reuters.com/article/oman-economy-int-idUSKBN27I0XZ (accessed on 18 June 2022).
88. No Plans to Defer Implementation of VAT: Ministry of Finance. 2019. Available online: https://timesofoman.com/article/no-plans-to-defer-implementation-of-vat-ministry-of-finance (accessed on 18 June 2022).
89. Oman to Introduce 5% VAT within Six Months. 2020. Available online: https://www.arabnews.jp/en/middle-east/article_28861/ (accessed on 18 June 2022).
90. Oman's 50th National Day: Celebrating Renewed Renaissance, Setting New Targets. 2017. Available online: https://timesofoman.com/article/omans-50th-national-day-celebrating-renewed-renaissance-setting-new-targets (accessed on 18 June 2022).
91. Bordoloi, P. How prepared is Oman to levy VAT? *2020*. Available online: https://internationalfinance.com/how-prepared-is-oman-to-levy-vat/ (accessed on 18 June 2022).
92. Applicability of VAT on Imports into Oman. 2020. Available online: https://timesofoman.com/article/applicability-of-vat-on-imports-into-oman (accessed on 18 June 2022).
93. Electronic Voting System to be Used for the First Time in Shura Elections. 2019. Available online: https://timesofoman.com/article/1576168/Oman/Science-/Electronic-voting-system-to-be-used-for-the-first-time-in-Shura-elections (accessed on 18 June 2022).
94. Majlis Elections on October 27. 2019. Available online: https://www.omanobserver.om/majlis-elections-on-october-27/ (accessed on 18 June 2022).
95. Final Results of Elections Declared in Oman. Available online: https://timesofoman.com/article/2133914/Oman/Final-results-of-elections-declared-in-Oman (accessed on 18 June 2022).
96. Over 2500 Voters Choose 'No Candidate' Option in Oman's Shura Elections. 2019. Available online: https://timesofoman.com/article/over-2500-voters-choose-no-candidate-option-in-omans-shura-elections (accessed on 18 June 2022).
97. Shura Elections: We Voted for Our Country. 2019. Available online: https://timesofoman.com/article/2131951/Oman/Government/We-voted-for-our-country (accessed on 18 June 2022).
98. The Ministry of Health Sultanate of Oman. MOH Registers First Two Novel Coronavirus (COVID-2019) in Oman. 2020. Available online: https://www.moh.gov.om/en/-/--1226 (accessed on 18 June 2022).
99. Coronavirus: Oman Bans Entry of Non-Omanis. 2020. Available online: https://timesofoman.com/article/2914190/Oman/Government/Coronavirus-Oman-bans-entry-of-non-Omanis (accessed on 18 June 2022).
100. Coronavirus: Oman Suspends All Public Transportation. 2020. Available online: https://timesofoman.com/article/2930145/Oman/Transport/Coronavirus-Oman-suspends-all-public-transportation (accessed on 18 June 2022).
101. Oman Eases COVID-19 Restrictions. 2020. Available online: https://timesofoman.com/article/3018106/oman/oman-eases-covid-19-restrictions (accessed on 18 June 2022).
102. Donations Pour in for Oman's Medical Services Support Fund. 2020. Available online: https://timesofoman.com/article/2987285/oman/government/donations-pour-in-for-omans-medical-services-support-fund (accessed on 18 June 2022).
103. Coronavirus: Oman's Ministry Quashes Rumours on Donations. 2020. Available online: https://timesofoman.com/article/2969208/oman/government/coronavirus-omans-ministry-quashes-rumours-on-donations (accessed on 18 June 2022).
104. Yaakoubi, A.; Barbuscia, D. Oman Orders Speedier Job Creation Amid Protests Over Unemployment. 2021. Available online: https://www.reuters.com/world/middle-east/job-seeking-omanis-protest-again-press-cash-strapped-government-2021-05-25/ (accessed on 18 June 2022).

105. Blockchain Oman Symposium. 2017. Available online: http://blockchainoman.om/about/ (accessed on 18 June 2022).
106. Bank Dhofar to Join Hands with RippleNet. 2018. Available online: https://timesofoman.com/article/58049-bankdhofar-to-join-hands-with-ripplenet (accessed on 18 June 2022).
107. Port of Salalah Joins Blockchain-Enabled Digital Shipping Platform. 2020. Available online: https://timesofoman.com/article/2528929/Business/Port-of-Salalah-joins-blockchain-enabled-digital-shipping-platform (accessed on 18 June 2022).
108. Oman Vision 2020. 1996. Available online: https://scp.gov.om/en/Page.aspx?I=14 (accessed on 18 June 2022).
109. Bhargava, A.; Bester, M.; Bolton, L. Employees' perceptions of the implementation of robotics, artificial intelligence, and automation (RAIA) on job satisfaction, job security, and employability. *J. Technol. Behav. Sci.* **2021**, *6*, 106–113. [CrossRef]
110. dem Moore, J.P.A.; Chandran, V.; Schubert, J. The Future of Jobs in the Middle East. World Government Summit. *Dubai*. 2018. Available online: https://www.readkong.com/page/the-future-of-jobs-in-the-middle-east-5714597 (accessed on 18 June 2022).
111. Hyvärinen, H.; Risius, M.; Friis, G. A blockchain-based approach towards overcoming financial fraud in public sector services. *Bus. Inf. Syst. Eng.* **2017**, *59*, 441–456. [CrossRef]
112. Nguyen, D.; Ding, M.; Pathirana, P.N.; Seneviratne, A. Blockchain and AI-based solutions to combat coronavirus (COVID-19)-like epidemics: A survey. *IEEE Access* **2020**, *9*, 95730–95753. [CrossRef]
113. AlAbri, R.; Shaikh, A.K.; Ali, S.; Al-Badi, A.H. Designing an E-Voting Framework Using Blockchain Technology: A Case Study of Oman. *Int. J. Electron. Gov. Res.* **2022**, *18*, 1–29. [CrossRef]
114. Norris, P.; Grömping, M. Electoral Integrity Worldwide. Available online: www.electoralintegrityproject.com (accessed on 18 June 2022).
115. Nabilah, A. Dubai's Court of the Blockchain Explained. *Zawya*. 2019. Available online: https://www.zawya.com/mena/en/story/Dubais_Court_of_the_Blockchain_explained-SNG_146941751/ (accessed on 18 June 2022).
116. Al-Rawi, A. *The 2011 Popular Protests in the Sultanate of Oman*; Springer: Berlin/Heidelberg, Germany, 2016.
117. Worrall, J. Oman: The Forgotten Corner of the Arab Spring. *Middle East Policy* **2012**, *19*, 98–115. [CrossRef]
118. His Majesty Issues Directives to Offer 32,000 Jobs. 2021. Available online: https://timesofoman.com/article/101705-his-majesty-issues-directives-to-offer-32000-jobs (accessed on 18 June 2022).
119. Oman Vision 2040. Available online: https://www.2040.om/Oman2040-En.pdf (accessed on 18 June 2022).

Article

Breaking Triopoly to Achieve Sustainable Smart Digital Infrastructure Based on Open-Source Diffusion Using Government–Platform–User Evolutionary Game

Tao Li [1,2,3], Junlin Zhu [1,2,*], Jianqiang Luo [4,*], Chaonan Yi [1,2] and Baoqing Zhu [1,2]

1. School of Intellectual Property, Nanjing University of Science and Technology, No. 200 Xiaolingwei Street, Xuanwu District, Nanjing 210094, China; taolee@njust.edu.cn (T.L.); njlgdx10095@njust.edu.cn (C.Y.); 222119010108@njust.edu.cn (B.Z.)
2. Centre for Innovation and Development, Nanjing University of Science and Technology, Nanjing 210094, China
3. School of Business, Xianda College of Economics & Humanities Shanghai International Studies University, No. 390 Dong Tiyuhui Rd., Hongkou District, Shanghai 200083, China
4. School of Management, Jiangsu University, No. 301 Xue Fu Rd., Zhenjiang 212013, China
* Correspondence: jl_zhu@njust.edu.cn (J.Z.); ljq2809@163.com (J.L.)

Abstract: Technological innovations, including the Internet of Things (IoT) and machine learning, have facilitated the emergence of autonomous systems, promoting triple bottom line (TBL) sustainability. However, the prevalent triopoly of Android, iOS, and Windows introduces substantial obstacles for smart device manufacturers in pursuit of independent innovation. This research endeavors to elucidate how open-source operating systems can counteract this triopoly and catalyze sustainable digital development. Utilizing evolutionary game theory, we scrutinize the interplay among governments, platforms, and users in championing open-source diffusion. Our analysis unveils two potent evolutionary strategies—incentivized engagement and disengagement—that notably expedite open-source diffusion and attenuate software supply chain risks affiliated with the Android–iOS–Windows triopoly (results). Consequently, this research highlights the critical role of augmenting stakeholder collaboration and bolstering platform reputation in propelling open-source diffusion, thereby providing valuable theoretical insights and practical guidance for the sustainable advancement of smart digital infrastructure.

Keywords: open-source diffusion; sustainable smart digital infrastructure; open-source operating system; evolutionary game; open innovation

Citation: Li, T.; Zhu, J.; Luo, J.; Yi, C.; Zhu, B. Breaking Triopoly to Achieve Sustainable Smart Digital Infrastructure Based on Open-Source Diffusion Using Government–Platform–User Evolutionary Game. *Sustainability* 2023, 15, 14412. https://doi.org/10.3390/su151914412

Academic Editors: Rashid Mehmood, Tan Yigitcanlar and Juan M. Corchado

Received: 29 August 2023
Revised: 27 September 2023
Accepted: 28 September 2023
Published: 1 October 2023

Copyright: © 2023 by the authors. Licensee MDPI, Basel, Switzerland. This article is an open access article distributed under the terms and conditions of the Creative Commons Attribution (CC BY) license (https://creativecommons.org/licenses/by/4.0/).

1. Introduction

With the rising complexity of contemporary smart city development and deteriorating environmental and economic sustainability, the triple bottom line (TBL), i.e., social, environmental, and economic sustainability, calls for the engagement of open innovation-style technologies [1]. Open source is an open innovation model in the digital era [2]. Open-source diffusion constitutes an information propagation paradigm, anchored on the tenets of unrestricted access, collective sharing, and amendment of source codes, knowledge, and information resources. Initially rooted in the field of computer software development, it encompasses not only the application of open-source software and open-source hardware, but also the sharing and utilization of open-source resources such as open-source data; it embodies a community-powered innovation model. The characteristics of open-source diffusion, such as openness, sharing, transparency, and customisability [3], fit with the idea of green AI aiming at efficient, sustainable and equitable development of smart cities and future technologies [4,5], and it can provide a supportive and facilitating mechanism for autonomous systems and smart digital sustainable implementations [6].

The development of open-source operating systems, as a crucial vehicle for open-source diffusion, contributes to the diversification of intelligent technologies and enables market freedom of choice [7–10]. In competition among open-source operating systems (Table 1), kernel update and optimization of an operating system is a core task of the open-source platform [11,12]. Kernel is the core of an open-source operating system, which controls the operation of computer hardware and provides services for applications. Open-source software includes the kernel of the open-source operating system, as well as other application programs, tools, and libraries, which constitute an open-source software ecosystem [13]. The source code of the operating system kernel is open for sharing [14], and people can use, modify, and disseminate it freely. Open-source operating systems have diverse brands and business models [15], and the license adopted also affects its development, distribution, and use [16].

Table 1. Open Source Operating System Competitive Landscape.

Brand	Release Version	Kernel	License	Description	Area
Linux	Ubuntu Debian CentOS Red Hat	Linux	GPL/MIT	One of the most popular open-source operating systems, widely used in servers, workstations and personal computers, with a large community of developers	Global
Kylin	NeoKylin KylinOS	Linux	GPL/MIT	Native Chinese operating system developed for China, mainly used by the Chinese government and for enterprise information construction.	China
UOS	UOS Desktop UOS Server	Linux	GPL/MIT	China's self-developed enterprise-class operating system, designed to replace foreign operating systems and improve information security and autonomous control.	China
FreeBSD	FreeBSD OpenBSD NetBSD	BSD	BSD	A Unix-like operating system, known for reliability, performance and security; it is widely used in servers, embedded, desktop systems and routers.	Global
OpenSolaris	Solaris	Solaris	CDDL	Known for being the world's most advanced file system and networking protocol, widely used in servers, desktop systems and virtualized environments, but discontinued by Oracle for maintenance.	Global
Android	Android	Linux	Apache	A mobile device operating system with cell phones and tablets as the main target; based on Linux kernel and the open-source project AOSP development.	Global
Chrome OS	Chrome OS	Linux	Chromium	Google's operating system based on Linux kernel and the Chrome browser; mainly used for cloud computing and lightweight devices.	Global
ReactOS	ReactOS	NT	GPL	Open source, Windows-compatible operating system designed to replace Windows and provide a high degree of compatibility and stability.	Global

Table 1. Cont.

Brand	Release Version	Kernel	License	Description	Area
Sailfish OS	Sailfish OS	Linux	MPL	Open-source mobile operating system from Finland, supporting Android applications; it is known for security, privacy and personalization.	Finland
Raspberry Pi OS	Raspberry Pi OS	Linux	GPL/LGPL	Debian-based operating system designed for Raspberry Pi; it is designed to provide a clean and fun environment for learning, exploration and innovation.	U.K.
Fedora	Fedora	Linux	GPL/MIT	Community-driven, free Linux operating system designed to experiment with new technologies, improve the developer experience, and deliver the latest packages as an upstream version of Red Hat Enterprise Linux.	Global
HarmonyOS	HarmonyOS	Microkernel	Apache	A distributed operating system independently developed by Huawei, it is designed to achieve cross-terminal multi-terminal collaborative operation, supporting smartphones, smart wear, car systems, etc.	China

Currently, the Android–iOS–Windows triple oligarchy of operating systems needs to be broken [17,18], which not only reduces user dependency risks and introduces more competitors, igniting greater innovation vitality, but also holds significant importance in mitigating the risk of supply chain disruptions. In parallel, the lack of resources, developers or maintainers in the open source community, or unhealthy software industry structures and trade conflicts can lead to supply chain disruption risks for open-source operating system software. Therefore, intelligent device manufacturers have started actively developing their own open-source operating systems to counter the threat of proprietary software monopolies and technology disruptions, also adopting incentive mechanisms such as software policies [19], open data [20], infrastructure [21,22], talent cultivation [23], and global collaboration [21,22] to further promote open-source diffusion [24].

To mitigate the risks associated with the supply chain of the Android–iOS–Windows triple oligarchy, open-source platforms can endeavour to expand their user communities and attract more developers to participate. Additionally, governments can enhance regulations, incentivize maintenance efforts, and allocate public resources and funding to foster the diffusion of open-source technologies and contribute to the sustainability, fairness, and efficiency of smart digital technologies. Therefore, this research is grounded in the theory of open-source diffusion and utilizes an evolutionary game approach to investigate the evolving dynamics among three key stakeholders: open-source platforms, users, and governments, within the realm of open-source diffusion. Finally, this paper proposes targeted recommendations to mitigate risk of supply chain disruptions through open-source diffusion, thereby fostering sustainable smart digital infrastructure.

This study demonstrates innovation in several aspects. Firstly, it offers a novel theoretical interpretation of how open-source diffusion becomes a pivotal factor in supporting the sustainable development of intelligent digital infrastructure. Furthermore, it presents fresh perspectives and strategies on how to disrupt the existing triopoly of the Android–iOS–Windows "Big Three" through open-source diffusion. In contrast to previous studies concentrated solely on individual stakeholders, this research adopts the evolutionary game model to encompass multiple stakeholders, such as the government, the platform, and the user. By including a diverse range of actors, this study offers a more holistic understanding of the complexities involved in open-source diffusion. It particularly focuses on the role of government in driving open-source diffusion and fostering the sustainability of smart digital infrastructure, providing effective policy recommendations in this regard.

The structure of this article is as follows: Section 1 explains the research background, raises research questions, introduces the methods, and describes the contributions. Section 2 discusses recent related work that support our study. In Section 3, we introduce the evolutionary game, solve equilibriums, perform simulations and analyse the results. In Section 4, we discuss the findings, and summarize the study in Section 5.

2. Related Works

2.1. Open Source in Smart Digital Technologies

Smart digital technologies become common solutions to urban crises associated with the climate, epidemics, natural disasters, and socio-economic factors [25,26] concerning the triple bottom line (TBL), i.e., social, environmental, and economic sustainability [1]. Artificial intelligence is rapidly becoming a key element of smart cities [27,28], helping to improve efficiency and automation [29]. Such technology poses significant risks of privacy violations and disruption through opaque decision-making processes [30]. Emerging challenges, including massive data, heterogeneities, complex dependencies, distributed storage and computing, and data [31], are open issues that need to be confronted by smart digital technologies.

The triopoly shaped by Android–iOS–Windows has brought about a technological ecological monopoly, limiting competition and innovation [17], thus leading to a lack of diversity and flexibility in the development of smart digital technologies and smart cities [18] as well as restricting consumer choice and innovation [32]. Open-source operating systems, such as Debian 12 [33], Ubuntu 23 [34], and HarmonyOS 4 [34], and open-source software, such as PyTorch 2 [35] and SciPy 1 [36], promote technology sharing and cooperation, break monopolies, establish open technology platforms [37], build collaborative ecosystems, and cultivate an open innovation culture [38]. Thus, smart digital technologies and the sustainable development of smart cities complement open source and open innovation [39], and together they promote the sustainable development of society [40].

Open innovation and open source are intricately connected. As outlined by Chesbrough [41,42], at the heart of open innovation lies the pursuit of external innovation resources from both within and outside the organization in order to generate value [43], enhance the efficiency and quality of innovation [44], spur technological transformation [45], and drive business model innovation [46]. Additionally, it promotes international collaboration and knowledge sharing [47,48], facilitates the reconfiguration and optimization of intellectual property and industrial chains [49], and fosters the overall development of industries and economies [50,51]. By adopting the paradigm of open innovation, open source is an internet-based collaborative model that pools efforts of crowd intelligence through the open sharing of knowledge and technical resources [52] to improve efficiency and quality of innovation [53]; this advocates free, shared, and co-creation [3], and it effectively addresses technological inequities and privacy violations [54]. Open-source operating systems promote technological security [55], technological pluralism [56] and smart digital infrastructure [57]. Open source as public goods expanding business models, based on its tacit knowledge [58], can be the activation engine for innovative regional development [59,60] and smart technologies [4,40,61,62]. During the evolution of open source [63], attention concerning the ecosystem radiates from hardware and software to their developers, users, communities, platforms and other relevant organizations and government departments [64], achieving fast, flexible, and secure application development through collaborations [65].

2.2. Infrastructure Risk Mitigation

With the advancement of information technology and digital transformation, an increasing number of enterprises now rely on software operating systems, and the risk of software supply chain disruption has gradually received more attention [66]. The risk of software supply chain disruption typically includes software vulnerabilities and malicious code, supplier bankruptcy, cyberattacks, and global crises, resulting in major impacts on a company's business operations and data security [67]. Enterprises need to take effective measures to manage the risks in software supply chain disruption [68], establish socio-technical frameworks [69], and reduce the impact of disruptions. Open source helps enterprises mitigate the risks of software supply chain disruption [70,71]. For instance, enterprises can use open-source software vulnerability scanners to scan for vulnerabilities in software systems and detect and repair potential issues in a timely manner [72]. Furthermore, enterprises can use open-source software supply chain security auditing tools to check source codes and assess whether security practices and processes of the suppliers comply with standards [73]. Long-term cooperation with software suppliers can also reduce the occurrence and impact of software supply chain disruption [74]. When seeking software suppliers, enterprises should focus on their reliability, technical capabilities, and security measures, establishing long-term cooperative relationships. Moreover, enterprises should work with software suppliers to explore novel security solutions, establish mutually trusted cooperative relationships, and jointly address the risk of software supply chain disruption [75].

Open source has the advantage of coping with the risk of software supply disruptions. However, open source does not reach a wide enough audience, and its low market share is major disadvantages [76,77]. Thus, the mechanism of open-source diffusion has become an urgent issue needing to be addressed.

2.3. Open-Source Diffusion

Joseph Schumpeter was the first scholar to discuss the issues of technological diffusion and product diffusion [78]. He believed technological diffusion was the process through which new technologies gradually spread from research centres to peripheral areas. In this process, the flow of technology from innovators to imitators was viewed as a kind of knowledge "penetration", which promoted productivity growth. Rapid diffusion of technology could greatly accelerate economic growth. Product diffusion was a special form of technological diffusion, referring to the process of expanding products produced originally in one country or region to other countries and regions through exportation, franchising, and other means. Product diffusion could bring wider markets and higher profits, further promoting economic growth.

The scope of technology diffusion mainly includes the domestic and global markets, intra- and inter-enterprise markets, and government markets [79]. The models for calculating technology diffusion include the innovation diffusion model, incentive model, and contagion model [80]. In practice, technology diffusion connects product diffusion. Product diffusion refers to the process of introducing and promoting new products in the market, including market demand, market segmentation, and promotion strategies [81].

Open-source software is diffused at the level of artificial artifacts [82,83]. The essence of open-source diffusion is the shared spreading of source code and technical documentation as well as asynchronous participatory innovative iterations [84]. Community-driven operation facilitates rapid software diffusion [85], and open-source software developers interact with users on community platforms to acquire user needs and proactively address relevant user issues, thus providing technical support and upgrade services to increase user retention and loyalty. Industry applications promote open-source diffusion [86] by integrating open-source software into vertical application systems; it enables vertical industries and application areas, increases software market value and demand, and achieves rapid diffusion and profit. In social network operation [87], open source software can use social media and other network platforms for community and brand promotion, actively expand user networks and increase software awareness.

In summary, open source has characteristics of openness and sharing, and is a paradigm of open innovation. Its diffusion model has unique methods. Open-source diffusion is expected to further promote smart digital infrastructure and sustainability as well as mitigate software supply chain risks.

3. Method

In open source, operating system software is fast becoming the mainstream, mainly used in industries such as the internet, cloud computing, security, and communications. Compared to traditional proprietary operating system software, open-source operating system software has the advantages of low cost, high flexibility, and good security, and its application has gradually expanded to fields such as industry, healthcare, and finance. However, the development of new releases based on various kernels is also influenced by factors such as the technical diffusion environment and policy support. Policies should not only be beneficial to users but also foster the promotion and use of open-source operating system software.

Therefore, we use the evolutionary game framework to study decision factors affecting the promotion of open-source operating system software, to find evolutionary paths, and to discuss the theoretical and practical significance of the results.

In Figure 1, a brief summary diagram of the entire analytical workflow for Section 3 is presented. This figure details the technical results of each key work node as well as the corresponding diagrams and formulas for the subsequent subsections. This figure helps the reader to quickly capture the main flow of the subsequent analysed content, and it allows the reader to locate the corresponding diagrams and related information quickly.

3.1. Premise

The underlying assumptions are as follows: the government, open-source platform and user are players (participants) in this study, conforming to limited rationality and making decisions with the goal of maximizing benefits [88]. The randomness of the strategic choices in decision making is expressed as probabilities in game theory, corresponding to the level of willingness of the players in a real situation [89,90].

The PAPI components are as follows: To present the game, we use the Players + Actions + Payoffs + Information (PAPI) framework [91], which reflects the dynamic interaction between players' decisions based on the information they observe and behaviours of others. Evolution is a long-term process with players' decisions adjusted over time, and they influence each other.

P (Players): players involved in open-source diffusion include government (denoted as G), open-source platform (denoted as P), and user (denoted as U).

A (Actions): government plays a guiding role by fostering the promotion of domestic open-source software through policies, regulations, and funding support, improving the software quality and security and facilitating the development of the domestic IT industry.

Government implements strategies: {Incentive (IC), Not Incentive (NIC)}.

As an open-source software provider, an open-source platform needs to consider the development of technology and market demand as well as promote diffusion and popularity of their software to increase the number of users and market share.

Platform has strategies: {Iterate(IR), Not Iterate(NIR)}.

User needs to balance software quality and migration costs in choosing between open source and proprietary software.

User response strategies: {Feedback(FB), Not Feedback(NFB)}.

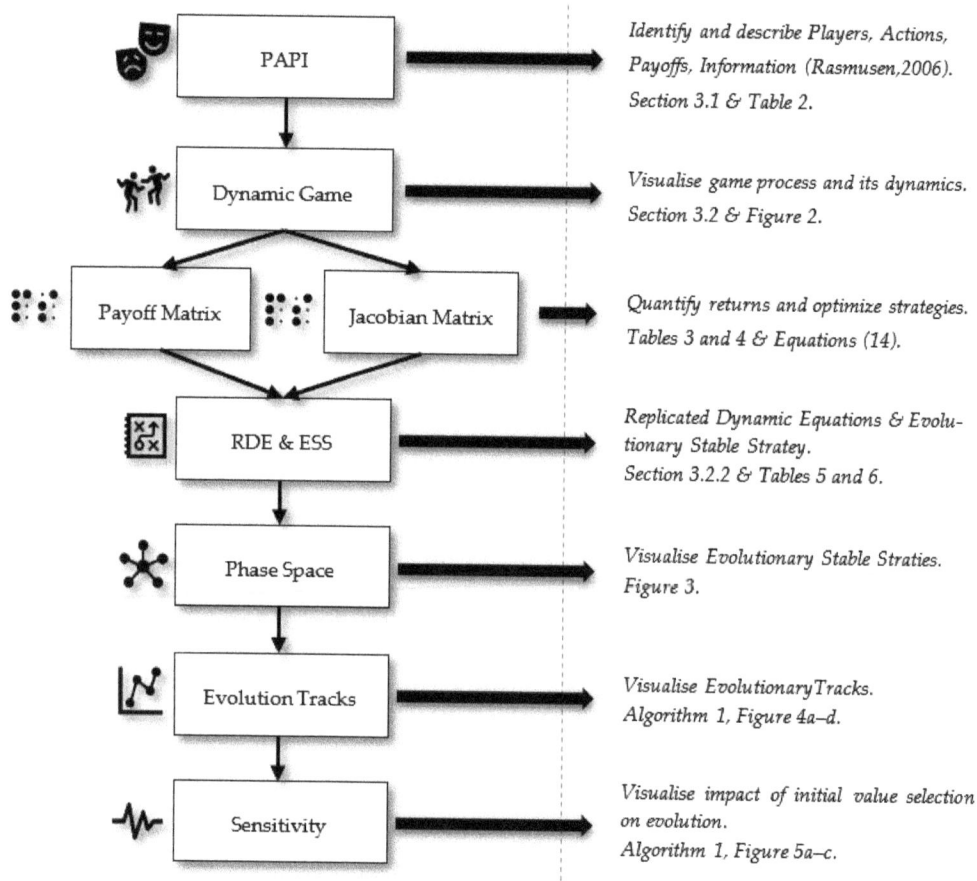

Figure 1. Analytical workflow roadmap [91].

P (Payoffs): The payoffs for players in the evolutionary game are measured in terms of their total return from the respective strategies. For simplicity, we model interactions by providing a payoffs matrix under the evolutionary game model. The process of equilibrating the ESSs based on replicated dynamic equations (RDEs) are then given sequentially in Section 3.3.

I (Information): In the evolutionary game, the government, open-source platform, and user need to balance their interests through cooperative negotiation, jointly promote the development and popularity of open-source software, and achieve a win–win situation. In short, from the government's perspective, on the platform side, the government incentives promote the diffusion behaviour of open-source platforms, prompting open-source platforms to actively seek potential user groups, actively collect user feedback, and actively innovate and optimize open-source operating system software. On the user side, government incentives guide the user to actively accept the diffusion from the open-source platform, actively submit feedback on software usage, and form a loop with the open innovation of open-source platforms to create synergy.

A list of symbols denoting the variables in the following subsections is shown in Table 2.

Table 2. List of symbols.

Symbol	Type	Descriptions
$\alpha \in [0, 1]$	probabilistic	Probability of government-imposed incentives
$\beta \in [0, 1]$	probabilistic	Probability of the open-source platform to enforce diffusion
$\gamma \in [0, 1]$	probabilistic	Probability of user-implemented feedback
$C_1 \in [0, 1]$	economic	Costs incurred by government incentives for open-source platforms
$C_2 \in [0, 1]$	economic	Costs incurred by government incentives for users
$p \in [0, 1]$	proportionate	Ratio of government non-incentives to incentive-generated benefits
$C_0 \in [0, 1]$	economic	Costs invested by open-source platforms and users for open-source diffusion in the absence of government incentives
$\Delta C \in [0, 1]$	economic	Reduction in the costs invested by open-source platforms and users for open-source diffusion in the presence of government incentives
$\theta \in [0, 1]$	proportionate	Cost-sharing ratio between open-source platforms and users
$R_1 \in [0, 1]$	economic	Benefits generated by government incentives for open-source diffusion
$R_2 \in [0, 1]$	economic	User benefits in the initial state
$R_3 \in [0, 1]$	economic	Benefits of open-source platforms in the initial state
$R \in [0, 1]$	economic	Additional benefits for open source platform and user based on open-source diffusion
$e \in [0, 1]$	proportionate	Allocation of additional benefits to open source platforms and users based on open-source diffusion
$L_1 \in [0, 1]$	economic	Benefits to users from feedback without government incentives
$L_2 \in [0, 1]$	economic	Benefits gained from proactive innovation iterations of open-source platforms without government incentives
$\tau_1 \in [0, 1]$	economic	Transfer payments for losses to open-source platforms without feedback from users under government incentives
$\tau_2 \in [0, 1]$	economic	Transfer payments for losses to users from open-source platforms without innovation iterations under government incentives

Note: The domain of definition of the above probabilistic and proportionate parameters is between 0 and 1, in line with probability theory. The remaining economic implication-type parameters can be normalized and thus converted to the [0, 1] interval.

3.2. Model

3.2.1. Dynamic Games and Payoff Matrices

Dynamic game diagrams are used to describe the decisions of players in the evolutionary game and clearly show forward-looking strategies and outcomes in different decision sequences. According to the discussion in the previous section, the dynamic process of the game between open-source platforms, users and the government is shown by following the G-P-U (Government–Platform–User) dynamic game diagram (Figure 2).

According to the above dynamic game process, the three players implement strategies successively, and the following payoff matrices (Tables 3 and 4) are obtained using the symbolic information of Table 2.

The above evolutionary game payoff matrices (Tables 3 and 4) reflect the benefits or costs corresponding to the decisions. Analysing this allows us to deduce the stable strategies in the evolutionary game. The Evolutionary Stable Strategy (ESS) refers to when all players' strategies are optimized and no alternative better strategies exist. Therefore, calculating the ESS is crucial for understanding in the G-P-U evolutionary game and predicting changes. In the following subsection, we deduce the ESS from the payoffs matrix.

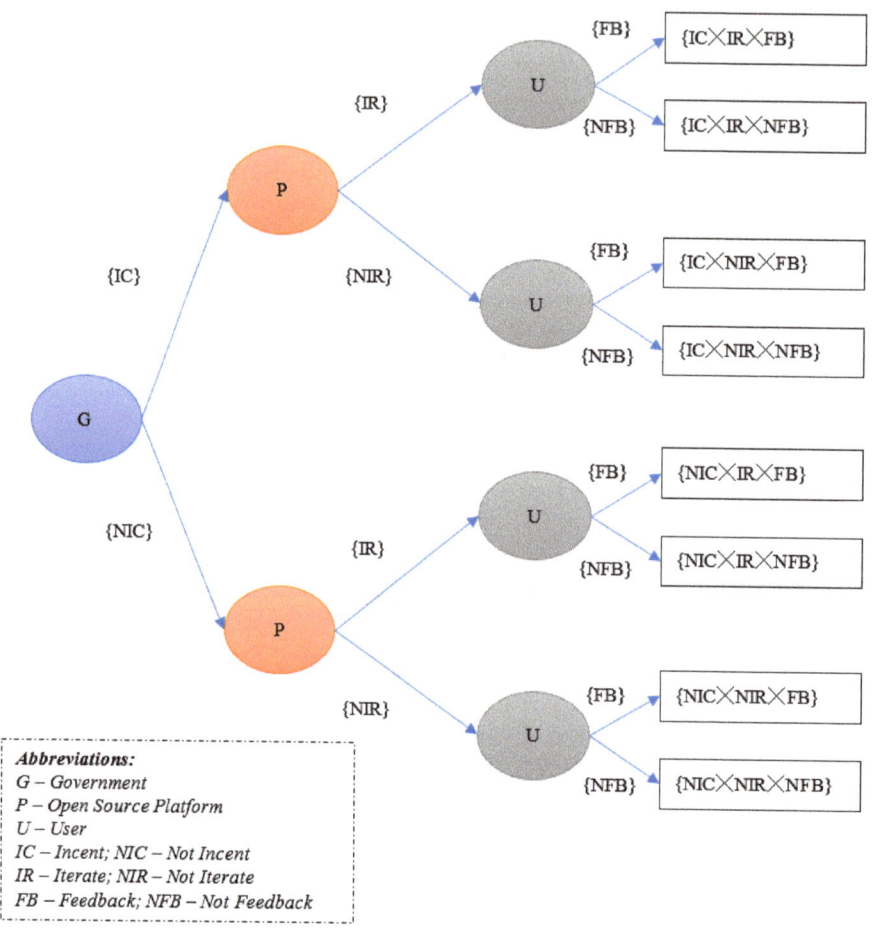

Figure 2. G-P-U dynamic game process.

Table 3. Payoff matrix for the G-P-U OSOSS proliferation evolutionary game (a).

		P {Iterate}	
		U	
		{Feedback}	{Not Feedback}
G	{Incent}	$R_1 - C_1 - C_2$;	$R_1 - C_1 - C_2$;
		$R_2 + \alpha R - \theta(C_0 - \Delta C)$;	$R_2 + L_1 - \tau_1$;
		$R_3 + (1-\alpha)R - (1-\theta)(C_0 - \Delta C) + C_2$;	$R_3 - (1-\theta)(C_0 - \Delta C) + \tau_1 + C_2$;
	{Not Incent}	pR_1;	pR_1;
		$R_2 + eR - \theta C_0$;	$R_2 - \tau_1 + L_1$;
		$R_3 + (1-e)R - (1-\theta)C_0$;	$R_3 - (1-\theta)C_0 + \tau_1$;

Note for Abbreviations: G: government; **P**: OSOSS platform; **U**: user.

Table 4. Payoff matrix for the G-P-U OSOSS proliferation evolutionary game (b).

		P {Not Iterate}	
		U	
		{Feedback}	{Not Feedback}
G	{Incent}	$R_1 - C_1$;	$R_1 - C_1$;
		$R_2 - \theta(C_0 - \Delta C) + \tau_2$;	R_2;
		$R_3 - \tau_2 + L_2$;	R_3;
	{Not Incent}	pR_1;	pR_1;
		$R_2 - sC_0 + \tau_2$;	R_2;
		$R_3 - \tau_2 + L_2$;	R_3;

Note for Abbreviations: G: government; P: OSOSS platform; U: user.

3.2.2. Evolutionary Stable Strategies

The expected return of the government {Incent} strategy is obtained in the following equation:

$$\varphi(\alpha) = \beta[\gamma(R_1 - C_1 - C_2) + (1-\gamma)(R_1 - C_1)] + (1-\beta)[\gamma(R_1 - C_1 - C_2) + (1-\gamma)(R_1 - C_1)] \quad (1)$$

The expected return of the government {Not Incent} strategy is obtained in the following equation:

$$U_{12} = \beta[\gamma pR_1 + (1-\gamma)pR_1] + (1-\beta)[\gamma pR_1 + (1-\gamma)pR_1] \quad (2)$$

The expected return to the government is obtained from Equations (1) and (2).

$$U_1 = \alpha U_{11} + (1-\alpha)U_{12} \quad (3)$$

The government's Dynamic Replication Equation is a derivative of time t.

$$\begin{aligned} H_1 = \frac{d\alpha}{dt} &= \alpha(1-\alpha)(U_{11} - U_{12}) \\ &= \alpha(1-\alpha)\{\beta\gamma[(1-p)R_1 - C_1 - C_2] + \beta(1-\gamma)[(1-p)R_1 - C_1] + (1-\beta)\gamma[(1-p)R_1 - C_1 - C_2] \\ &\quad + (1-\beta)(1-\gamma)[(1-p)R_1 - C_1]\} \\ &= \alpha(1-\alpha)[(1-p)R_1 - C_1 - \beta C_2] \end{aligned} \quad (4)$$

The expected return of the open-source platform {Iterate} strategy is obtained in the following equation:

$$U_{21} = \alpha\gamma[R_3 + (1-e)R - (1-\theta)(C_0 - \Delta C) + C_2] + \alpha(1-\gamma)[R_3 - (1-\theta)(C_0 - \Delta C) + \tau_1 + C_2] \\ + (1-\alpha)\gamma[R_3 + (1-e)R - (1-s)C_0] + (1-\alpha)(1-\gamma)[R_3 - (1-\theta)C_0 + \tau_1] \quad (5)$$

The expected return of the platform {Not Iterate} strategy is obtained in the following equation:

$$U_{22} = \alpha\gamma(R_3 - \tau_2 - L_2) + \alpha(1-\gamma)R_3 + (1-\alpha)\gamma(R_3 - \tau_2 + L_2) + (1-\alpha)(1-\gamma)R_3 \quad (6)$$

The expected return to the platform is obtained from Equations (5) and (6).

$$U_2 = \beta U_{21} + (1-\beta)U_{22} \quad (7)$$

The platform's Dynamic Replication Equation is as follows:

$$\phi(\beta) = \frac{d\beta}{dt} = \beta(1-\beta)(U_{21} - U_{22})$$
$$= \beta(1-\beta)\{\alpha[(1-\theta)\Delta C + C_2] + \gamma[(1-e)R + \tau_2 - L_2 - \tau_1] + \tau_1 - (1-\theta)C_0\} \quad (8)$$

The expected return of the user {Feedback} strategy is obtained in the following equation:

$$U_{31} = \alpha\{\beta[R_2 + eR - \theta(C_0 - \Delta C)] + (1-\beta)[R_2 - \theta(C_0 - \Delta C) + \tau_2]\} \\ + (1-\alpha)\{\beta(R_2 + eR - \theta C_0) + (1-\beta)(R_2 - \theta C_0 + \tau_2)\} \quad (9)$$

The expected return of the user {Not Feedback} strategy is obtained in the following equation:

$$U_{32} = \alpha[\beta(R_2 + L_1 - \tau_1) + (1-\beta)R_2] + (1-\alpha)[\beta(R_2 - \tau_1 + L_1) + (1-\beta)R_2] \quad (10)$$

The expected returns of the user under two strategies are as follows:

$$U_3 = \gamma U_{31} + (1-\gamma)U_{32} \quad (11)$$

As a result, the user's Replication Dynamic Equation is obtained by the following calculation:

$$\psi(\gamma) = \frac{d\gamma}{dt} = r(1-\gamma)(U_{31} - U_{32}) = \gamma(1-\gamma)[\alpha\theta\Delta C - \theta C_0 + \beta(eR + \tau_1 - L_1 - \tau_2) + \tau_2)] \quad (12)$$

The replicated dynamic system and its stabilization strategies are obtained through the joint equations of (4), (8) and (12) below.

$$\begin{cases} \varphi(\alpha) = \frac{d\alpha}{dt} \\ \phi(\beta) = \frac{d\beta}{dt} \\ \psi(\gamma) = \frac{d\gamma}{dt} \end{cases} \Longrightarrow \begin{cases} \alpha = 0, \alpha = 1 \\ \beta = 0, \beta = 1 \\ \gamma = 0, \gamma = 1 \end{cases} \quad (13)$$

A Jacobian matrix (Equation (14)) is obtained by taking the partial derivatives of Equations (4), (8) and (12).

$$J = \begin{vmatrix} \frac{\partial\varphi(\alpha)}{\partial\alpha} & \frac{\partial\varphi(\alpha)}{\partial\beta} & \frac{\partial\varphi(\alpha)}{\partial\gamma} \\ \frac{\partial\phi(\beta)}{\partial\alpha} & \frac{\partial\phi(\beta)}{\partial\beta} & \frac{\partial\phi(\beta)}{\partial\gamma} \\ \frac{\partial\psi(\gamma)}{\partial\alpha} & \frac{\partial\psi(\gamma)}{\partial\beta} & \frac{\partial\psi(\gamma)}{\partial\gamma} \end{vmatrix} \quad (14)$$

Let Equation (13) equal zero to obtain an equilibrium, and substitute it into Equation (14) to obtain the eigenvalues (Table 5). Identification of the ESS can be determined using the Friedman method, which requires determinants greater than zero $det > 0$ and a trace less than zero $tr < 0$ [92]; or using the Lyapunov method, which requires all eigenvalues of the Jacobian matrix to be less than zero [93]. Based on the eigenvalues in Table 6, we can directly apply the Lyapunov method for ESS identification.

Table 5. Eigenvalues of equilibrium points.

Equilibriums	λ_1	λ_2	λ_3
$E_1(0,0,0)$	$(1-p)R_1 - C_1$	$\tau_1 - (1-\theta)C_0$	$-\theta C_0 + \tau_2$
$E_2(0,1,0)$	$(1-p)R_1 - C_1$	$(1-e)R + \tau_2 - L_2 - (1-\theta)C_0$	$\theta C_0 - \tau_2$
$E_3(0,0,1)$	$(1-p)R_1 - C_1 - C_2$	$-\tau_1 + (1-\theta)C_0$	$-\theta C_0 + eR + \tau_1 - L_1$
$E_4(0,1,1)$	$(1-p)R_1 - C_1 - C_2$	$-(1-e)R - \tau_2 + L_2 + (1-\theta)C_0$	$\theta C_0 - eR - \tau_1 + L_1$

Table 5. Cont.

Equilibriums	λ_1	λ_2	λ_3
$E_5(1,0,0)$	$-(1-p)R_1 + C_1$	$(1-\theta)\Delta C + C_2 + \tau_1 - (1-\theta)C_0$	$\theta(\Delta C - C_0) + \tau_2$
$E_6(1,1,0)$	$-(1-p)R_1 + C_1$	$(1-\theta)\Delta C + C_2 + (1-e)R + \tau_2 - L_2 - (1-\theta)C_0$	$\theta(C_0 - \Delta C) - \tau_2$
$E_7(1,0,1)$	$C_1 + C_2 - (1-p)R_1$	$-(1-\theta)\Delta C - C_2 - \tau_1 + (1-\theta)C_0$	$\theta(\Delta C - C_0) + eR + \tau_1 - L_1$
$E_8(1,1,1)$	$C_1 + C_2 - (1-p)R_1$	$-(1-\theta)\Delta C - C_2 - (1-e)R - \tau_2 + L_2 + (1-\theta)C_0$	$\theta(C_0 - \Delta C) - eR - \tau_1 + L_1$

Table 6. Determination of ESS.

Equilibriums	Scenario1: $\begin{cases} C_2 + \tau_1 - (1-\theta)(C_0 - \Delta C) < 0 \\ \text{and,} \\ \tau_2 - \theta(C_0 - \Delta C) < 0 \end{cases}$				Scenario2: $\begin{cases} \tau_1 - (1-\theta)C_0 > 0, \\ \text{or,} \\ \tau_2 - sC_0 > 0 \end{cases}$				Scenario3 condition 1: $\begin{cases} C_2 + \tau_1 - (1-\theta)(C_0 - \Delta C) > 0, \\ \text{and,} \\ \tau_1 - (1-\theta)C < 0 \end{cases}$ or, condition 2: $\begin{cases} \tau_2 - s(C_0 - \Delta C) > 0, \\ \text{and,} \\ \tau_2 - \theta C_0 < 0 \end{cases}$			
	λ_1	λ_2	λ_3	Result	λ_1	λ_2	λ_3	Result	λ_1	λ_2	λ_3	Result
$E_1(0,0,0)$	pos	neg	pos/neg	Ns	pos	pos	pos	Sd	pos	neg	neg	Ns
$E_2(0,1,0)$	pos	pos	neg	Ns	pos	pos/neg	neg	Ns	pos	pos	pos	Sd
$E_3(0,0,1)$	pos	pos	pos	Sd	pos	neg	pos	Ns	pos/neg	neg	pos	Ns
$E_4(0,1,1)$	neg	neg	neg	ESS	neg	pos	pos	Ns	neg	pos/neg	pos	Ns
$E_5(1,0,0)$	pos	neg	neg	Ns	pos/neg	neg	neg	Ns	pos	neg	neg	Ns
$E_6(1,1,0)$	neg	pos	pos	Ns	neg	pos	neg	Ns	neg	pos	neg	Ns
$E_7(1,0,1)$	neg	pos	pos	Ns	neg	pos	pos	Ns	neg	neg	pos	Ns
$E_8(1,1,1)$	neg	neg	neg	ESS	neg	neg	neg	ESS	neg	neg	neg	ESS

Note for abbreviations: pos—positive; neg—negative; Ns—non-stable point; Sd—saddle point; ESS—Evolutionary Stable Strategy.

The underlying assumptions are as follows: assuming the government incentives have positive effects, when the government chooses to provide incentives and both open-source platforms and users actively accept the incentives, the income of all parties involved is Pareto-improved compared to other decision combinations, which is consistent with limited rationality [94]. This leads to following base constraints:

$$\text{base constraints}: \begin{cases} (1-p)R_1 - C_1 - C_2 \\ (1-e)R + \tau_2 - L_2 - (1-\theta)C_0 > 0 \\ eR + \tau_1 - L_1 - \theta C_0 \end{cases} \quad (15)$$

Through Equation (15), the evolutionary game has following ESS: $E_4(0,1,1)$ and $E_8(1,1,1)$ are two ESSs. $E_4(0,1,1)$ represents the combination of evolutionary stabilization strategies of the G-P-U as {Not Incent × Iteration × Feedback}; $E_8(1,1,1)$ represents the combination of evolutionary stabilization strategies of the G-P-U parties as {Incent × Iteration × Feedback}. These two ESSs exist under the scenarios below.

$$\text{Scenario1}: \begin{cases} C_2 + \tau_1 - (1-\theta)(C_0 - \Delta C) < 0 \\ \tau_2 - \theta(C_0 - \Delta C) \end{cases} < 0 \quad (16)$$

$E_8(1,1,1)$ is still an ESS when the following scenarios are satisfied:

$$\begin{cases} \text{Scenario2}: \tau_1 - (1-\theta)C_0 > 0, \text{ or}, \tau_2 - sC_0 > 0 \\ \text{Scenario3}: \begin{cases} \text{condition1}: C_2 + \tau_1 - (1-\theta)(C_0 - \Delta C) > 0, \text{and}, \tau_1 - (1-\theta)C < 0 \\ \text{condition2}: \tau_2 - s(C_0 - \Delta C) > 0, \text{and}, \tau_2 - \theta C_0 < 0 \end{cases} \end{cases} \quad (17)$$

All ESSs are identified by the Lyapunov method in Table 6.

The Theoretical Phase diagram (Figure 3) indicates the evolutionarily stable strategy combination $E_8(1,1,1)$ implies the formation of an open innovation system by open-source platforms and users after government incentives; ESS combination $E_4(0,1,1)$ implies the spontaneous formation of an open innovation system by open-source platforms and users in the absence of government incentives, as well as the formation of an open innovation system with the help of government incentives that is sustained even after withdrawal of such incentives.

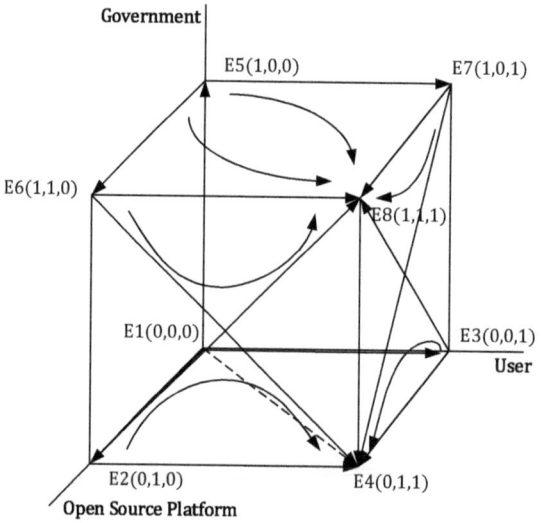

Figure 3. Theoretical Phase diagram.

3.3. Results Analysis

In this subsection, the numerical simulations are implemented. As stated above in Tables 2 and 6, the domain of definition of the above probabilistic, proportionate and economic parameters are within the [0, 1] interval, in line with probability theory or normalized and scaled, and the ESSs are determined based on the Lyapunov method [93].

Therefore, the use of Algorithm 1 below to perform random searches for parameter values can ensure the consistency of the simulation experiments and studies under the above constraints and scenarios.

Algorithm 1 Random Search for Parameter Values

1. Initialize: {parameter_i} ← random numeric sample ∈ [0, 1]
2. Define: {base constraints} in accord. with Equation (15)
3. Define: {scenario constraints} in accord. with Equations (16) and (17)
4. WHILE {base constraints} is False or {scenario constraints} is False:
5. Repeat search on random numeric sample generated
6. Until {base constraints} is True and {scenario constraints} is True
6. End WHILE
7. Output {parameter_i}
8. End Algorithm 1

A set of random samples (floating-point precision results obtained by the algorithmic program rounded to four decimal places) for parameters satisfying both base constraints and Scenario1 are as follows:

$R_1 \approx 0.9838$, $C_1 \approx 0.6952$, $C_2 \approx 0.0629$, $\Delta C \approx 0.2322$,
$p \approx 0.0268$, $C_0 \approx 0.7403$, $\theta \approx 0.6315$, $R \approx 0.9948$,
$e \approx 0.5832$, $L_1 \approx 0.0311$, $L_2 \approx 0.1708$, $\tau_1 \approx 0.0123$, $\tau_2 \approx 0.2074$

Similarly, a set of random samples for parameters satisfying both base constraints and Scenario2 are as follows:

$R_1 \approx 0.9559$, $C_1 \approx 0.4695$, $C_2 \approx 0.3267$, $\Delta_C \approx 0.2025$,
$p \approx 0.0489$, $C_0 \approx 0.9130$, $\theta \approx 0.36320$, $R \approx 0.4717$,

$e \approx 0.4797$, $L_1 \approx 0.5599$, $L_2 \approx 0.1398$, $\tau_1 \approx 0.7416$, $\tau_2 \approx 0.8507$

Likewise, two sets of random samples for parameters satisfying both base constraints and condition1 in Scenario3 are as follows:

$R_1 \approx 0.3529$, $C_1 \approx 0.0085$, $C_2 \approx 0.0754$, $\Delta C \approx 0.1823$,
$p \approx 0.6572$, $C_0 \approx 0.2280$, $\theta \approx 0.3560$, $R \approx 0.8437$,
$e \approx 0.4070$, $L_1 \approx 0.0130$, $L_2 \approx 0.4291$, $\tau_1 \approx 0.0439$, $\tau_2 \approx 0.8934$

Additionally, condition2 in Scenario3 are as follows:

$R_1 \approx 0.4486$, $C_1 \approx 0.1851$, $C_2 \approx 0.1083$, $\Delta C \approx 0.6559$,
$p \approx 0.2011$, $C_0 \approx 0.3702$, $\theta \approx 0.7539$, $R \approx 0.4617$,
$e \approx 0.4650$, $L_1 \approx 0.0876$, $L_2 \approx 0.0275$, $\tau_1 \approx 0.8159$, $\tau_2 \approx 0.0343$

Four three-dimensional evolutionary tracking diagrams (Figure 4a–d) were simulated based on the above sets of parameters. In order to analyse the evolutionary formation of the ESS more clearly, we observe the effect of the change in the initial value of the innings on the evolutionary equilibrium in the two-dimensional evolutionary perspective.

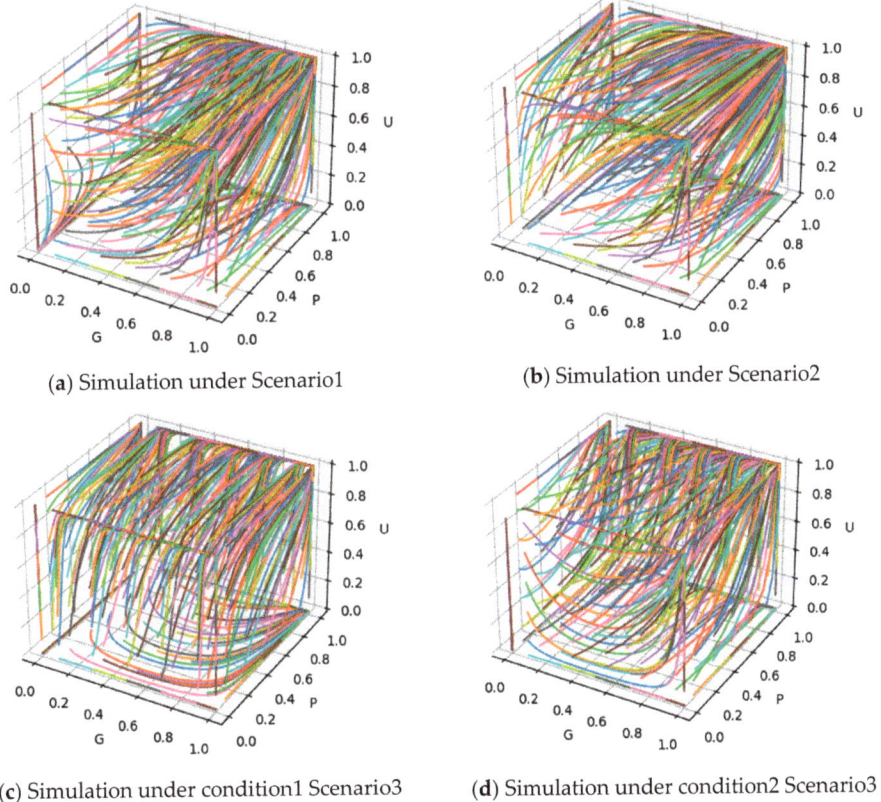

(a) Simulation under Scenario1

(b) Simulation under Scenario2

(c) Simulation under condition1 Scenario3

(d) Simulation under condition2 Scenario3

Figure 4. Simulations for the three-dimensional evolutionary tracking diagrams. Note: Axis labels G, P, and U in sub-diagrams (**a**–**d**) above represent government, open-source platform, and user, respectively. Color lines are set up for easy visual identification of tracks.

With the underlying assumptions, we note that the probability of players choosing strategies each corresponds to their respective levels of willingness [92,93]. Hence, the impact of their initial willingness value of the selection of government incentive probability on the evolution is further quantitatively simulated by controlling for the probability of open-source platform-enforced diffusion and user-implemented feedback, represented by low to medium and high willingness levels. (Figure 5a–c).

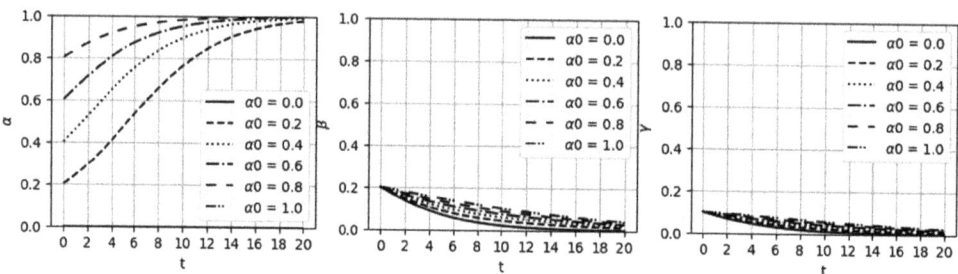

(**a**) Low initial willingness of open-source platforms ($\beta = 0.2$) and users ($\gamma = 0.1$)

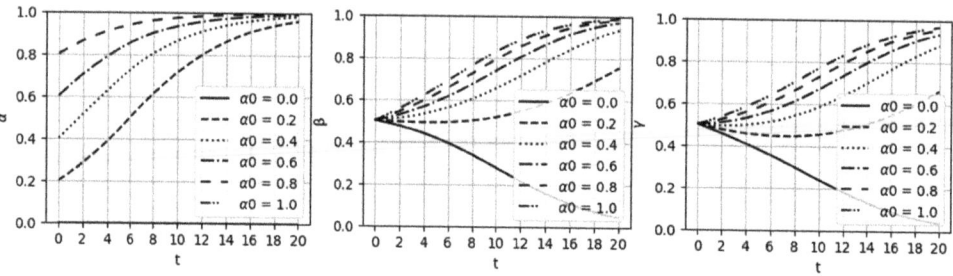

(**b**) medium initial willingness of open-source platforms ($\beta = 0.5$) and users ($\gamma = 0.5$)

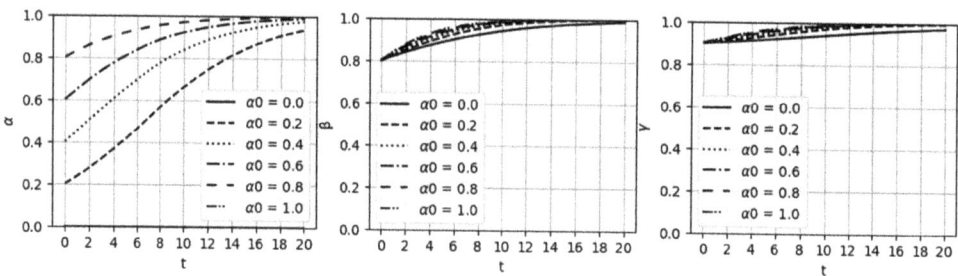

(**c**) high initial willingness of open-source platforms ($\beta = 0.8$) and users ($\gamma = 0.9$)

Figure 5. Sensitivity impact of the initial willingness selection on evolution.

Figure 5a shows that changes in the initial willingness level of government incentives are difficult to motivate platforms and users to evolve towards open-source diffusion when they are at low willingness levels, corresponding to the unstable $ESS_5(1,0,0)$. Figure 5b shows that at medium willingness levels of both platforms and users, non-zero levels of initial incentives have the opportunity to motivate both platforms and users to evolve towards open-source diffusion, corresponding to the stable $ESS_8(1,1,1)$. Figure 5c further shows that at high levels of willingness, both platforms and users are still able to spontaneously evolve towards open-source diffusion even if the government's initial willingness to incentivize is zero (probability of the government incentive strategy $\alpha 0 = 0$), corresponding to the stable $ESS_4(0,1,1)$.

3.4. Model Tradeoffs and Drawbacks

Open-source diffusion has high complexity [95], involving the ecological niche and intentions of entities in the open-source ecosystem, the technological maturity of software and hardware as objects, as well as the collaborative network formed by collective intelligence. Thus, the model has its tradeoffs and drawbacks.

The model is unable to consider every detailed variable from cultural, institutional, corporate, or user group behaviour due to technological diffusion and institutional factors. Further research in different geographical and institutional contexts is needed to enhance our understanding of open-source diffusion and its impact on enterprise strategy, R&D performance, top-level design, and institutional advantages.

Moreover, while the evolutionary game model provides valuable insights, it makes various assumptions that may filter out real-world randomness and perturbation. Participant decisions are assumed to be rationally limited [88]; however, in reality, they can be influenced by more complex factors like individual preferences and social influence.

In addition, the model conducts a sensitivity analysis to ensure the robustness and reliability of the results under controlled variables. However, the provided ESSs and diffusion path cannot cover all possible variations. In practical applications, it is recommended to combine the results with other methods and models to provide comprehensive and accurate decision support considering other factors such as economics, competition patterns, regulations, and policies.

4. Discussion

4.1. Incentive Step-In and Step-Out: From ESS_8 to ESS_4

In early stages of the diffusion of open-source operating system software, government intervention is a necessary means to propel its development. As an open-source software ecosystem has not yet been established, manufacturers and users have limited awareness and understanding of open-source software. Government intervention could help open-source software gain a market share and improve its development speed. The government could adopt various ways to encourage the development of open-source software such as providing policy support, rewards or subsidies to enterprises adopting open-source software. At this time, incentives can play a leading role. As the open-source software ecosystem gradually improves and the technology of open platform accumulates, user retention will gradually increase, which promotes stable development. During this process, open-source platforms can begin to use its sustained operating income for innovation iteration and community maintenance, thereby further enhancing software value and user experience. Government incentives for the software market gradually become weaker and withdrew from its leading position. As the ecosystem further matures, incentives gradually lose strategic value. Open-source software becomes relatively mature and stable industry, reducing government intervention and interference. The government begins to gradually withdraw from its leading position, and open-source software moves towards a more free-market track. At this point, open-source software has sufficient competitiveness and market share to autonomously participate in market competition and industrial development.

4.2. Accelerating Strategy Implementation through Incentive Platforms

The government often tends to incentivize open-source platforms more than users, in that open-source platforms, as the main subject of technological innovation, gather various economic activities and entities in the market, thus making it easier for governments to exert incentives and regulatory measures. Therefore, governments can more easily achieve their strategic goals for innovation and industrial development. For example, (1) in strategic layout goals of scientific and technological innovation and digital transformation, development of open-source platform enterprises is a key part for governments. By using open-source platforms as a point of entry, governments encourage all kinds of enterprises to use open-source platforms, promote digital transformation and enhance enterprise efficiency and innovation capabilities. (2) In promoting innovation goals, government incentives for open-source platforms help encourage companies to facilitate innovation and R&D on these platforms, improving product quality and performance, owning independent technology, intellectual property rights, and core competitiveness. (3) To drive industrial development goals, government incentives for open-source platform development can promote the development of the entire open-source ecosystem as well as related industries, markets, and ecology, thus promoting the coordinated development of industry and improving market competitiveness. Thus, from a strategic and future development perspective, governments are more willing to incentivize open-source platform development enterprises than users. This strategy of governments can also help improve the overall development level of the industry and domestic digital construction process.

4.3. Increase Willingness to Participate by Incentivizing Users

The willingness of users to participate is a gradual process as follows:

Know and Recognize → Participate and Try → Learn and Master → Contribute and Feedback → Develop and Innovate.

During the Know and Recognize stage, government incentives and promotions expand the market influence of open-source platforms and operating system software, increasing our understanding and recognition of their advantages and characteristics. Government incentives and promotions are mainly carried out through official websites, promotional materials, and promotional activities, which widely publicize information on the characteristics, usage methods, and advantages of open-source platforms and operating system software to the public. These promotional and advertising activities aim to increase users' awareness and understanding of open-source platforms and operating system software, and they make more people aware of their potential value and advantages. At the same time, government support and promotion also established a reputation for open-source platforms and operating system software among users and the market, making them competitive with other commercial software and even gaining more market share in some areas. Government incentives and promotions are an important means of promoting open-source platforms and operating system software, which can provide people with the initial knowledge and understanding of open-source platforms and lay a foundation for their subsequent use and involvement.

In the Participate and Try stage, after having a certain level of understanding of open-source platforms, some users will start to use and participate in the open-source project, contributing code, providing feedback and suggestions, and other ways to understand the open-source platform, thus improving their familiarity and trust in the open-source platform.

During the Learn and Master stage, after a period of participation and trial, some users may develop a strong interest in the open-source platform and decide to delve deeper into the relevant technologies and knowledge, thus investing more time and effort.

During the Contribute and Feedback stage, as some users become familiar with and master the relevant knowledge and technologies, they may begin to contribute code, submit bug reports and suggestions, and assist in improving and refining the open-source platform.

During the Develop and Innovate stage, some users may adopt an open-source platform as their primary technology and development platform, and actively participate in other open-source projects, gradually integrating into the developer and open source community.

As can be seen, with government encouragement and support, the willingness of these users to participate in open-source platforms is gradually increasing, and more people are willing to join in and contribute to their development and improvement. In the process of continuous innovation, iteration, and improvement of the ecosystem and reputation of open-source platform, it continues to attract more users to try it out and gradually develop user retention. The government also helps open-source platforms understand users' needs and pain points, continuously improving and optimizing products and services by encouraging users to use open-source operating system software and provide feedback. This mutual promotion and collaboration strengthen user participation and value perception, continuously driving the development and growth of open-source platforms and operating system software.

4.4. Mitigating Supply Chain Risks

The diffusion of open-source operating system software is a means of reducing risk of software supply disruption. Open source implies that the source code is made public and can be freely copied, distributed, and modified. Compared with proprietary software, open-source software is more transparent and open, allowing maintenance to be shifted to the community and developers, thereby reducing the dependence on software vendors. Therefore, with open-source operating system software as a foundation, the power of community and developers can be fully utilized to expand the scope and depth of updates and maintenance, thus reducing the risk of software supply disruption caused by supplier failure, bankruptcy, etc. Open-source operating system software can promote software interoperability and compatibility. With an open source code, developers can modify and customize software to better adapt to different hardware and software environments. This flexible feature can promote software interoperability and compatibility, avoid control of software ecosystems by a single vendor, and reduce the risk of software supply disruption. Therefore, diffusion of open-source operating system software is a prerequisite for reducing the risk of supply disruption, and active participation and cooperation of the government, open-source platforms, and users can promote the development and popularization of open-source software.

4.5. Implications

We propose the following recommendations to enhance the diffusion of open-source operating system software and address the risk of supply chain disruption.

(1) Multi-channel procurement. When procuring software, enterprise users should consider multiple channels to reduce their reliance on a single supplier and ensure the ability to switch to other suppliers at any time. For example, when purchasing operating system software, using products from multiple vendors should be considered, such as using open-source operating systems for some servers and commercial operating systems for others.

(2) Active participation in open source communities. Enterprises should actively participate in open-source platforms, trust and support software development from open-source platforms, and participate in product research and testing. By participating in open source communities, enterprises can have a better understanding of the software development and maintenance process, and make better decisions in the event of supply chain disruptions.

(3) Independent development. Enterprises should explore independent development and use open-source operating system software source code for secondary development and customization. This can avoid the reliance on suppliers, enable control over the software development and maintenance process, and reduce the risk of supply chain disruptions.

(4) Enhance and adopt virtualization and containerization technologies. Decoupling and isolating applications and operating system software using virtual machines and containerization technologies can make it easier to migrate and manage applications and operating system software, thereby reducing the risk of supply chain disruption.

(5) Actively adopt backup and recovery strategies. Enterprises should regularly backup and archive data and software to enable timely recovery in the event of a supply chain disruption. Enterprises should develop a comprehensive emergency plan, including backup strategies, backup recovery testing, and disaster recovery procedures, among others.

In summary, in order to reduce the risk of supply chain disruption, enterprises can transition to the diffusion of open-source operating system software by adopting multiple procurement channels, actively participating in open source communities, conducting independent research and development, utilizing virtualization and containerization technologies, and implementing backup and recovery strategies, among other approaches. Essentially, the recommendations to mitigate the risk of supply chain disruption involve active transformation of enterprise users into developer roles in open-source platforms. This strategy benefits enterprises by reducing the risk of supply chain disruption and promoting their own development. As supporters and contributors of open source, enterprises can participate in development and testing in open source communities to help improve and expand open-source software to meet their own needs. This approach helps to increase enterprise understanding and mastery of open-source software, reduce reliance on specific suppliers, establish their own technological advantages and competitiveness, and promote the development of the entire open source ecosystem. Additionally, active participation in open source communities can bring additional benefits to enterprises, such as being recognized as industry leaders, accelerating development speed, improve problem solving, and building a better corporate reputation, among others. Therefore, transforming from enterprise users to contributors in open source communities is not only a defensive measure to reduce the risk of supply chain disruption, but also an important avenue for technological innovation, competitive advantage, and corporate reputation.

5. Conclusions

Android–iOS–Windows has a first-mover advantage and mature market, with threats of commercial monopoly and technological supply cut-off. However, it also poses threats of commercial monopolies and technology disruptions. Adopting open-source paradigms for independent innovation and technological independence is a potential solution to these threats. Open-source diffusion is closely related to the innovation iteration of open-source platforms and the increasing size of the user base. Specifically, based on an open collaborative model, open source continuously attracts more users, contributors, and developers to improve and perfect it with collective intelligence. Its excellent performance and code quality often attract more users to join, further enhancing the reputation and influence of open-source software. As the application scenarios of open source become more extensive and deeper, its user base will continue to grow, attracting more developers and contributors to join the open source community, jointly promoting the innovation and iteration of open-source software and forming a virtuous cycle. Therefore, expansion of open source and growth of its user base are important drivers for innovation iteration in smart digital infrastructure and key factors in maintaining continuous development in the industrial ecosystem.

This study analyses open-source diffusion among the government, open-source platforms, and users as stakeholders using an evolutionary game framework. The study found two evolutionarily stable strategy combinations as follows: {Not Incent × Iteration × Feedback} and {Incent × Iteration × Feedback}. This shows that open-source platforms and users generate open-source diffusion and form an open innovation system with government incentives; or they spontaneously create an open innovation system with open-source diffusion in the absence of government incentives as well as generate open-source diffusion initially with the help of government incentives and still maintain an open innovation system after the incentives have ceased.

Further analysis indicates that the government is more inclined to incentivize open-source platforms because they can gather open-source innovation entities and various economic activities, making them more conducive to incentives and regulation. Government incentives can help achieve strategic and targeted development goals for open source. Government involvement in incentives can prompt open-source platforms and users to form an open innovation system, establish and improve the open-source operating system software ecosystem, and accelerate open-source diffusion. As open-source diffusion scales up, the software industry's ability for independent innovation based on open source increases, enhancing its competitiveness against proprietary software, gradually reducing the government's dominant role. Under the incentives, user retention increases, actively participating in open source feedback, joining open source innovation collaborations, and promoting open-source diffusion.

In conclusion, open-source diffusion is an important way to mitigate software supply chain disruption and technology supply disruption. Active participation and cooperation among the government, open-source platforms, and users can promote the development and popularization of open-source software. We suggest further strengthening of open-source diffusion to cope with supply disruption risks, such as multi-channel software procurement, encouraging participation in open source innovation, incentivizing open-source platform companies to conduct independent research and development, enhancing and applying virtualization and containerization technologies, and implementing flexible and robust disaster recovery backup strategies.

This study contributes by considering the stakeholders involved in open-source diffusion and using an evolutionary game model for analysis. Results provide theoretical value and a practical reference for the development of the open-source software engineering industry. Additionally, our study is strategically significant for sustainable technological development, especially in the context of digital transformation and data-driven economies.

The main limitation of this study is the lack of research on the software ecology of different open-source operating systems, including various kernels and distributions. Therefore, in future research, case studies on the innovation and diffusion of typical distributions of open-source operating systems, such as Linux kernel, Debian, Android, Chrome OS, etc., must be conducted using a cross-disciplinary approach towards software engineering and management science.

Author Contributions: Conceptualization, T.L. and J.Z.; Methodology, T.L.; Software, T.L.; Validation, T.L., J.Z. and J.L.; Formal analysis, T.L.; Investigation, T.L.; Resources, T.L.; Data curation, T.L.; Writing—original draft, T.L.; Writing—review & editing, T.L., J.Z., J.L., C.Y. and B.Z.; Visualization, T.L.; Supervision, J.Z., J.L. and C.Y.; Project administration, J.Z. and B.Z.; Funding acquisition, B.Z. All authors have read and agreed to the published version of the manuscript.

Funding: This research was been supported by (1) the Research Project of National Academy of Innovation Strategy (NAIS) "Research on the application of key technologies in digital economy at home and abroad" (2022-sjzx-02); (2) National Social Science Fund (NSSFC) project "Research on the Modernization of Intellectual Property Governance for Digital Innovation" (22VRC064); (3) National Social Science Fund Key Project (NSSFKP) "Research on Goals, Major Directions, and Strategies for Winning the Battle of Key Core Technology under the New Comprehensive National System" (23AZD038).

Institutional Review Board Statement: Not applicable.

Informed Consent Statement: Not applicable.

Data Availability Statement: Data sharing is not applicable to this article as no new data were created or analysed in this study.

Acknowledgments: The authors express their thanks to the Jiangsu Decision-Making and Consultation Institution of Service-Oriented Government Development fund from Nanjing University of Science and Technology.

Conflicts of Interest: The authors declare no conflict of interest.

References

1. Nogueira, E.; Gomes, S.; Lopes, J.M. Triple Bottom Line, Sustainability, and Economic Development: What Binds Them Together? A Bibliometric Approach. *Sustainability* **2023**, *15*, 6706. [CrossRef]
2. Mcgahan, A.M.; Bogers, M.L.A.M.; Chesbrough, H.; Holgersson, M. Tackling Societal Challenges with Open Innovation. *Calif. Manag. Rev.* **2021**, *63*, 49–61. [CrossRef]
3. Perens, B. The emerging economic paradigm of Open Source. *First Monday* **2005**, *10*. [CrossRef]

4. Yigitcanlar, T.; Mehmood, R.; Corchado, J.M. Green Artificial Intelligence: Towards an Efficient, Sustainable and Equitable Technology for Smart Cities and Futures. *Sustainability* **2021**, *13*, 8952. [CrossRef]
5. Alotaibi, S.; Mehmood, R.; Katib, I.; Rana, O.; Albeshri, A. Sehaa: A Big Data Analytics Tool for Healthcare Symptoms and Diseases Detection Using Twitter, Apache Spark, and Machine Learning. *Appl. Sci.* **2020**, *10*, 1398. [CrossRef]
6. Bonvoisin, J. Implications of Open Source Design for Sustainability. In *Proceedings of the International Conference on Sustainable Design and Manufacturing, Cham, Switzerland, 1 January 2016*; Setchi, R., Howlett, R.J., Liu, Y., Theobald, P., Eds.; Springer International Publishing: Cham, Switzerland, 2016; pp. 49–59.
7. Dong, X.; Jin, S.; Lu, X. Comparison of Xiaomi Smart Home and Huawei HarmonyOS Business Ecosystem. In *Proceedings of the 2022 International Conference on Business and Policy Studies, Singapore, 1 January 2022*; Li, X., Yuan, C., Ganchev, I., Eds.; Springer Nature: Singapore, 2022; pp. 640–648.
8. Kalok, S. The Analysis of Smartphones' Operating System and Customers' Purchasing Decision: Application to HarmonyOS and Other Smartphone Companies. In Proceedings of the 2022 7th International Conference on Financial Innovation and Economic Development (ICFIED 2022), Harbin, China, 1 January 2022; Atlantis Press: Dordrecht, The Netherlands, 2022; pp. 417–421.
9. Oh, S.; Seo, B.; Hahm, C.; Song, J.; Lee, J.; Lee, T. Dynamic boosting for fast user interactivity in smart devices using Tizen OS. In Proceedings of the 2016 IEEE International Conference on Consumer Electronics-Asia (ICCE-Asia), Seoul, Republic of Korea, 26–28 October 2016; pp. 1–3.
10. Liu, S.; Rong, X.; Li, S.; Dong, A. Design of harmony OS-based IOT system for wearable health monitoring. In Proceedings of the International Conference on Internet of Things and Machine Learning (IoTML 2021), Dalian, China, 17–19 December 2021.
11. Cui, P.; Liu, Z.; Bai, J. Linux Storage I/O Performance Optimization Based on Machine Learning. In Proceedings of the 2022 4th International Conference on Natural Language Processing (ICNLP), Xi'an, China, 25–27 March 2022; pp. 552–557.
12. Ugur, M.; Jiang, C.; Erf, A.; Ahmed Khan, T.; Kasikci, B. One Profile Fits All. *Acm Sigops Oper. Syst. Rev.* **2022**, *56*, 26–33. [CrossRef]
13. Haim Faridian, P.; Neubaum, D.O. Ambidexterity in the age of asset sharing: Development of dynamic capabilities in open source ecosystems. *Technovation* **2021**, *99*, 102125. [CrossRef]
14. Yu, L.; Schach, S.R.; Chen, K.; Heller, G.Z.; Offutt, J. Maintainability of the kernels of open-source operating systems: A comparison of Linux with FreeBSD, NetBSD, and OpenBSD. *J. Syst. Softw.* **2006**, *79*, 807–815. [CrossRef]
15. Lund, A.; Zukerfeld, M. (Eds.) Profiting from Free and Open Source Software. In *Corporate Capitalism's Use of Openness: Profit for Free?* Springer International Publishing: Cham, Switzerland, 2020; pp. 109–147.
16. Välimäki, M.; Oksanen, V. The impact of free and open source licensing on operating system software markets. *Telemat. Inform.* **2005**, *22*, 97–110. [CrossRef]
17. Sokol, D.D.; Zhu, F. Harming Competition and Consumers under the Guise of Protecting Privacy: An Analysis of Apple's iOS 14 Policy Updates Essay. *Cornell Law Rev. Online* **2021**, *107*, 94. [CrossRef]
18. Jenkins, G.T.; Bing, R.W. Microsofts Monopoly: Anti-Competitive Behavior, Predatory Tactics, and the Failure of Governmental Will. *J. Bus. Econ. Res.* **2007**, *5*, 1–16. [CrossRef]
19. Schmidt, K.M.; Schnizter, M. Public subsidies for open source? Some economic policy issues of the software market. *Harv. J. Law Technol.* **2003**, *16*, 473. [CrossRef]
20. Willinsky, J. The unacknowledged convergence of open source, open access, and open science. *First Monday* **2005**, *10*. [CrossRef]
21. Nørskov, S.V.; Rask, M. Observation of Online Communities: A Discussion of Online and Offline Observer Roles in Studying Development, Cooperation and Coordination in an Open Source Software Environment. *Forum Qual. Sozialforschung/Forum Qual. Soc. Res.* **2011**, *12*, 5.
22. Schweik, C.; Evans, T.; Grove, J.M. Open source and open content: A framework for global collaboration in social-ecological research. *Ecol. Soc.* **2005**, *10*, 33. Available online: http://www.ecologyandsociety.org/vol10/iss1/art33/ (accessed on 29 September 2023). [CrossRef]
23. Lerner, J.; Tirole, J. Some Simple Economics of Open Source. *J. Ind. Econ.* **2002**, *50*, 197–234. [CrossRef]
24. Lerner, J.; Tirole, J. The Economics of Technology Sharing: Open Source and Beyond. *J. Econ. Perspect.* **2005**, *19*, 99–120. [CrossRef]
25. Shin, D. Ubiquitous city: Urban technologies, urban infrastructure and urban informatics. *J. Inf. Sci.* **2009**, *35*, 515–526. [CrossRef]
26. Yigitcanlar, T.; Kamruzzaman, M. Smart Cities and Mobility: Does the Smartness of Australian Cities Lead to Sustainable Commuting Patterns? *J. Urban Technol.* **2019**, *26*, 21–46. [CrossRef]
27. Batty, M. Artificial intelligence and smart cities. *Environ. Plan. B Urban Anal. City Sci.* **2018**, *45*, 3–6. [CrossRef]
28. Zhang, Y.; Geng, P.; Sivaparthipan, C.B.; Muthu, B.A. Big data and artificial intelligence based early risk warning system of fire hazard for smart cities. *Sustain. Energy Technol.* **2021**, *45*, 100986. [CrossRef]
29. Ullah, Z.; Al-Turjman, F.; Mostarda, L.; Gagliardi, R. Applications of Artificial Intelligence and Machine learning in smart cities. *Comput. Commun.* **2020**, *154*, 313–323. [CrossRef]
30. Yigitcanlar, T.; Desouza, K.; Butler, L.; Roozkhosh, F. Contributions and Risks of Artificial Intelligence (AI) in Building Smarter Cities: Insights from a Systematic Review of the Literature. *Energies* **2020**, *13*, 1473. [CrossRef]
31. Wang, S.; Cao, J. AI and Deep Learning for Urban Computing. In *Urban Informatics*; Shi, W., Goodchild, M.F., Batty, M., Kwan, M., Zhang, A., Eds.; Springer Singapore: Singapore, 2021; pp. 815–844.
32. Etro, F.; Caffarra, C. On the economics of the Android case. *Eur. Compet. J.* **2017**, *13*, 282–313. [CrossRef]

33. Mateos-Garcia, J.; Steinmueller, W.E. The institutions of open source software: Examining the Debian community. *Inf. Econ. Policy* **2008**, *20*, 333–344. [CrossRef]
34. Tabassum, M.; Mathew, K. Software evolution analysis of linux (Ubuntu) OS. In Proceedings of the 2014 International Conference on Computational Science and Technology (ICCST), Kota Kinabalu, Malaysia, 1 January 2014; pp. 1–7.
35. Imambi, S.; Prakash, K.B.; Kanagachidambaresan, G.R. PyTorch. In *Programming with TensorFlow: Solution for Edge Computing Applications*; Prakash, K.B., Kanagachidambaresan, G.R., Eds.; Springer International Publishing: Cham, Switzerland, 2021; pp. 87–104.
36. Virtanen, P.; Gommers, R.; Oliphant, T.E.; Haberland, M.; Reddy, T.; Cournapeau, D.; Burovski, E.; Peterson, P.; Weckesser, W.; Bright, J.; et al. SciPy 1.0: Fundamental algorithms for scientific computing in Python. *Nat. Methods* **2020**, *17*, 261–272. [CrossRef] [PubMed]
37. Economides, N.; Katsamakas, E. Two-Sided Competition of Proprietary vs. Open Source Technology Platforms and the Implications for the Software Industry. *Manag. Sci.* **2006**, *52*, 1057–1071. [CrossRef]
38. Powell, A.B. Open culture and innovation: Integrating knowledge across boundaries. *Media Cult. Soc.* **2015**, *37*, 376–393. [CrossRef]
39. Yun, J.J.; Zhao, X.; Jung, K.; Yigitcanlar, T. The Culture for Open Innovation Dynamics. *Sustainability* **2020**, *12*, 5076. [CrossRef]
40. Yigitcanlar, T.; Kankanamge, N.; Regona, M.; Maldonado, A.R.; Rowan, B.; Ryu, A.; Desouza, K.C.; Corchado, J.M.; Mehmood, R.; Li, R.Y.M. Artificial Intelligence Technologies and Related Urban Planning and Development Concepts: How Are They Perceived and Utilized in Australia? *J. Open Innov. Technol. Mark. Complex.* **2020**, *6*, 187. [CrossRef]
41. Chesbrough, H. *Open Innovation: The New Imperative for Creating and Profiting from Technology*; Harvard Business School Press: Boston, MA, USA, 2003; p. 227.
42. Didenko, N.; Skripnuk, D.; Kikkas, K.; Kalinina, O.; Kosinski, E. The Impact of Digital Transformation on the Micrologistic System, and the Open Innovation in Logistics. *J. Open Innov. Technol. Mark. Complex.* **2021**, *7*, 115. [CrossRef]
43. Pedersen, K. What can open innovation be used for and how does it create value? *Gov. Inform. Q.* **2020**, *37*, 101459. [CrossRef]
44. Chesbrough, H. The Logic of Open Innovation: Managing Intellectual Property. *Calif. Manag. Rev.* **2003**, *45*, 33–58. [CrossRef]
45. Robertsone, G.; Lapina, I. Digital transformation as a catalyst for sustainability and open innovation. *J. Open Innov. Technol. Mark. Complex.* **2023**, *9*, 100017. [CrossRef]
46. Christensen, J.F.; Olesen, M.H.; Kjær, J.S. The industrial dynamics of Open Innovation—Evidence from the transformation of consumer electronics. *Res. Policy* **2005**, *34*, 1533–1549. [CrossRef]
47. Bereznoy, A.; Meissner, D.; Scuotto, V. The intertwining of knowledge sharing and creation in the digital platform based ecosystem. A conceptual study on the lens of the open innovation approach. *J. Knowl. Manag.* **2021**, *25*, 2022–2042. [CrossRef]
48. Yun, J.J.; Cooke, P.; Jung, K.; Yang, B. Theme issue: Open innovation and 'catch-up': Globalist or localist? *Eur. Plan. Stud.* **2023**, *31*, 845–861. [CrossRef]
49. Gassmann, O.; Enkel, E.; Chesbrough, H. The future of open innovation. *R&D Manag.* **2010**, *40*, 213–221.
50. Bogers, M.; Chesbrough, H.; Moedas, C. Open innovation: Research, practices, and policies. *Calif. Manag. Rev.* **2018**, *60*, 5–16. [CrossRef]
51. Yun, J.J.; Ahn, H.J.; Lee, D.S.; Park, K.B.; Zhao, X. Inter-rationality; Modeling of bounded rationality in open innovation dynamics. *Technol. Forecast. Soc.* **2022**, *184*, 122015. [CrossRef]
52. Yun, J.; Pyka, A.; Lee, C.; Won, D.; Kim, D.; Jeong, E.S.; Kodama, F.; Schiuma, G.; Park, H.; Jeon, J.; et al. *Open Innovation Dynamics; Capitalism, Socialism, and Democracy in the 21st Century*; Cambridge Scholars Publish: Newcastle upon Tyne, UK, 2023; p. 527.
53. Olson, D.L.; Rosacker, K. Crowdsourcing and open source software participation. *Serv. Bus.* **2013**, *7*, 499–511. [CrossRef]
54. Hansen, M.; Köhntopp, K.; Pfitzmann, A. The Open Source approach—Opportunities and limitations with respect to security and privacy. *Comput Secur.* **2002**, *21*, 461–471. [CrossRef]
55. Witten, B.; Landwehr, C.; Caloyannides, M. Does open source improve system security? *IEEE Softw.* **2001**, *18*, 57–61. [CrossRef]
56. Colombo, M.G.; Piva, E.; Rossi-Lamastra, C. Open innovation and within-industry diversification in small and medium enterprises: The case of open source software firms. *Res. Policy* **2014**, *43*, 891–902. [CrossRef]
57. Alpern, B.; Augart, S.; Blackburn, S.M.; Butrico, M.; Cocchi, A.; Cheng, P.; Dolby, J.; Fink, S.; Grove, D.; Hind, M.; et al. The Jikes Research Virtual Machine project: Building an open-source research community. *IBM Syst. J.* **2005**, *44*, 399–417. [CrossRef]
58. Yun, J.J.; Zhao, X. Business Model Innovation through a Rectangular Compass: From the Perspective of Open Innovation with Mechanism Design. *J. Open Innov. Technol. Mark. Complex.* **2020**, *6*, 131. [CrossRef]
59. Yun, J.J.; Zhao, X.; Park, K.; Della Corte, V.; Del Gaudio, G. The way to the 'comedy of commons' of a new business model-finding from Naples in Italy, and Jeju Island in South Korea. *Eur. Plan. Stud.* **2023**, *31*, 947–973. [CrossRef]
60. Yigitcanlar, T.; Han, H.; Kamruzzaman, M.; Ioppolo, G.; Sabatini-Marques, J. The making of smart cities: Are Songdo, Masdar, Amsterdam, San Francisco and Brisbane the best we could build? *Land Use Policy* **2019**, *88*, 104187. [CrossRef]
61. Yigitcanlar, T.; Cugurullo, F. The Sustainability of Artificial Intelligence: An Urbanistic Viewpoint from the Lens of Smart and Sustainable Cities. *Sustainability* **2020**, *12*, 8548. [CrossRef]
62. Yigitcanlar, T.; Corchado, J.M.; Mehmood, R.; Li, R.Y.M.; Mossberger, K.; Desouza, K. Responsible Urban Innovation with Local Government Artificial Intelligence (AI): A Conceptual Framework and Research Agenda. *J. Open Innov. Technol. Mark. Complex.* **2021**, *7*, 71. [CrossRef]

63. Ljungberg, J. Open source movements as a model for organising. *Eur. J. Inform. Syst.* **2017**, *9*, 208–216. [CrossRef]
64. Jullien, N.; Stol, K.; Herbsleb, J.D. A Preliminary Theory for Open-Source Ecosystem Microeconomics. In *Towards Engineering Free/Libre Open Source Software (FLOSS) Ecosystems for Impact and Sustainability: Communications of NII Shonan Meetings*; Fitzgerald, B., Mockus, A., Zhou, M., Eds.; Springer: Singapore, 2019; pp. 49–68.
65. Zhang, Y.; Zhou, M.; Stol, K.; Wu, J.; Jin, Z. How Do Companies Collaborate in Open Source Ecosystems? An Empirical Study of OpenStack. In *Proceedings of the ACM/IEEE 42nd International Conference on Software Engineering, Seoul, Republic of Korea, 27 June–19 July 2020*; Association for Computing Machinery: New York, NY, USA, 2020; pp. 1196–1208.
66. Axelrod, W. Mitigating Software Supply Chain Risk. *ISACA J.* **2013**, *4*.
67. Khojasteh, Y. *Supply Chain Risk Management*; Springer: Berlin/Heidelberg, Germany, 2018.
68. Aqlan, F. A software application for rapid risk assessment in integrated supply chains. *Expert Syst. Appl.* **2016**, *43*, 109–116. [CrossRef]
69. Sabbagh, B.A.; Kowalski, S. A Socio-technical Framework for Threat Modeling a Software Supply Chain. *IEEE Secur. Priv.* **2015**, *13*, 30–39. [CrossRef]
70. He, J.; Alavifard, F.; Ivanov, D.; Jahani, H. A real-option approach to mitigate disruption risk in the supply chain. *Omega* **2019**, *88*, 133–149. [CrossRef]
71. Lustenberger, P.; Schumacher, F.; Spada, M.; Burgherr, P.; Stojadinovic, B. Assessing the Performance of the European Natural Gas Network for Selected Supply Disruption Scenarios Using Open-Source Information. *Energies* **2019**, *12*, 4685. [CrossRef]
72. Amankwah, R.; Chen, J.; Kudjo, P.K.; Towey, D. An empirical comparison of commercial and open-source web vulnerability scanners. *Softw. Pract. Exp.* **2020**, *50*, 1842–1857. [CrossRef]
73. Erickson, J.; Brydon, M.; Vining, A.R. Adoption, Improvement, and Disruption: Predicting the Impact of Open Source Applications in Enterprise Software Markets. *J. Database Manag.* **2009**, *19*, 22.
74. Tucci, C.L.; Kaufman, A.; Wood, C.H.; Theyel, G. Collaboration and Teaming in the Software Supply Chain. *Supply Chain Forum An. Int. J.* **2005**, *6*, 16–28. [CrossRef]
75. Shekarian, M.; Mellat Parast, M. An Integrative approach to supply chain disruption risk and resilience management: A literature review. *Int. J. Logist. Res. Appl.* **2021**, *24*, 427–455. [CrossRef]
76. Blanc, M.F.H. Open Source Innovation in Physical Products: Advantages and Disadvantages, a Corporate Perspective. Doctoral Dissertation, Queensland University of Technology, Brisbane City, Australia, 2011.
77. Vukovic, V.; Raković, L. Open Source Approach in Software Development—Advantages and Disadvantages. *Int. Sci. J. Manag. Inf. Syst.* **2008**, *3*, 29–33.
78. Schumpeter, J. *The Theory of Economic Development*; Harvard Economic Studies 46; Harvard Business School Press: Boston, MA, USA, 1911.
79. Costa, Á.; Fernandes, R. Urban public transport in Europe: Technology diffusion and market organisation. *Transp. Res. Part A Policy Pract.* **2012**, *46*, 269–284. [CrossRef]
80. Nicoletti, G.; von Rueden, C.; Andrews, D. Digital technology diffusion: A matter of capabilities, incentives or both? *Eur. Econ. Rev.* **2020**, *128*, 103513. [CrossRef]
81. Mahajan, V.; Muller, E.; Bass, F.M. New Product Diffusion Models in Marketing: A Review and Directions for Research. *J. Mark.* **1990**, *54*, 1–26. [CrossRef]
82. Ma, Y.; Fakhoury, S.; Christensen, M.; Arnaoudova, V.; Zogaan, W.; Mirakhorli, M. Automatic Classification of Software Artifacts in Open-Source Applications. In *Proceedings of the 15th International Conference on Mining Software Repositories, Gothenburg, Sweden, 28–29 May 2018*; Association for Computing Machinery: New York, NY, USA, 2018; pp. 414–425.
83. Temizkan, O.; Kumar, R.L. Exploitation and Exploration Networks in Open Source Software Development: An Artifact-Level Analysis. *J. Manag. Inform. Syst.* **2015**, *32*, 116–150. [CrossRef]
84. Hellman, J.; Cheng, J.; Guo, J.L.C. Facilitating Asynchronous Participatory Design of Open Source Software: Bringing End Users into the Loop. In *Proceedings of the Extended Abstracts of the 2021 CHI Conference on Human Factors in Computing Systems, Yokohama, Japan, 8–13 May 2021*; Association for Computing Machinery: New York, NY, USA, 2021.
85. Bonaccorsi, A.; Rossi, C. Why Open Source software can succeed. *Res. Policy* **2003**, *32*, 1243–1258. [CrossRef]
86. Shanker, A. A Customer Value Creation Framework for Businesses That Generate Revenue with Open Source Software. *Technol. Innov. Manag.* **2012**, *2*, 18–22. [CrossRef]
87. Long, Y.; Siau, K. Social network structures in open source software development teams. *J. Database Manag.* **2007**, *18*, 25–40. [CrossRef]
88. Rubinstein, A. Comments on the Interpretation of Game Theory. *Econometrica* **1991**, *59*, 909–924. [CrossRef]
89. Lu, S.; Zhu, G.; Dai, J. Willingness intensity and co-evolution of decision rationality depending on aspiration enhance cooperation in the spatial public goods game. *PLoS ONE* **2023**, *18*, e0280015. [CrossRef]
90. Hurkens, S.; Schlag, K.H. Evolutionary insights on the willingness to communicate. *Int. J. Game Theory* **2003**, *31*, 511–526. [CrossRef]
91. Rasmusen, E. *Games and Information: An Introduction to Game Theory*, 4th ed.; Wiley-Blackwell: Hoboken, NJ, USA, 2006; p. 560.
92. Friedman, D. Evolutionary Games in Economics. *Econometrica* **1991**, *59*, 637–666. [CrossRef]
93. Lyapunov, A.M. The general problem of the stability of motion. *Int. J. Control* **1992**, *55*, 531–534. [CrossRef]

94. Rabin, M. Incorporating Limited Rationality into Economics. *J. Econ. Lit.* **2013**, *51*, 528–543. [CrossRef]
95. Bryant, A. Liquid uncertainty, chaos and complexity: The gig economy and the open source movement. *Thesis Elev.* **2020**, *156*, 45–66. [CrossRef]

Disclaimer/Publisher's Note: The statements, opinions and data contained in all publications are solely those of the individual author(s) and contributor(s) and not of MDPI and/or the editor(s). MDPI and/or the editor(s) disclaim responsibility for any injury to people or property resulting from any ideas, methods, instructions or products referred to in the content.

Article

Perceived Opportunities and Challenges of Autonomous Demand-Responsive Transit Use: What Are the Socio-Demographic Predictors?

Fahimeh Golbabaei [1,*], Tan Yigitcanlar [2], Alexander Paz [1] and Jonathan Bunker [1]

1 School of Civil and Environmental Engineering, Queensland University of Technology, 2 George Street, Brisbane, QLD 4000, Australia; alexander.paz@qut.edu.au (A.P.); j.bunker@qut.edu.au (J.B.)
2 School of Architecture and Built Environment, Queensland University of Technology, 2 George Street, Brisbane, QLD 4000, Australia; tan.yigitcanlar@qut.edu.au
* Correspondence: fahimeh.golbabaei@hdr.qut.edu.au

Abstract: The adoption of autonomous demand-responsive transit (ADRT) to support regular public transport has the potential to enhance sustainable mobility. There is a dearth of research on the socio-demographic characteristics associated with perceived opportunities and challenges regarding ADRT adoption in Australia. In this research, we fill this knowledge gap by determining socio-demographic predictors of perceptions and attitudes towards ADRT, specifically autonomous shuttle buses (ASBs), among adult residents of South East Queensland. This study incorporates a review of prior global studies, a stated preference survey distributed across the case study region, and descriptive and logistic regression analysis. We found that the main perceived opportunity of ASBs is reduced congestion/emissions, while the primary anticipated challenge relates to unreliable technology. Fully employed respondents are likely to be more familiar with autonomous vehicles. Females and those from lower-income households are less likely to have ridden in an autonomous vehicle. Males, those who are younger, have high employment, hail from higher-income households, and with no driver's licence are all more favourable towards ASBs. Males, those with high employment, and without driver's licence are likely to be more concerned about traffic accidents when using ASBs. Less-educated respondents and those living in peri-urban areas are likely to be more concerned about fares. Insights are drawn from the current study to inform policymakers to consider key challenges (e.g., trust issues) and target groups (particularly females) in planning public communication strategies to enhance receptiveness to ADRT.

Keywords: autonomous vehicle; autonomous demand-responsive transit; autonomous shuttle bus; user perceptions and attitudes; user adoption; technology acceptance

Citation: Golbabaei, F.; Yigitcanlar, T.; Paz, A.; Bunker, J. Perceived Opportunities and Challenges of Autonomous Demand-Responsive Transit Use: What Are the Socio-Demographic Predictors?. *Sustainability* **2023**, *15*, 11839. https://doi.org/10.3390/su151511839

Academic Editor: Nirajan Shiwakoti

Received: 14 June 2023
Revised: 17 July 2023
Accepted: 19 July 2023
Published: 1 August 2023

Copyright: © 2023 by the authors. Licensee MDPI, Basel, Switzerland. This article is an open access article distributed under the terms and conditions of the Creative Commons Attribution (CC BY) license (https://creativecommons.org/licenses/by/4.0/).

1. Introduction

Autonomous vehicles (AVs) have the potential to become a commonplace transport platform globally. However, the excessive or disorganised use of private AVs might increase traffic congestion and greenhouse gas emissions via several factors [1]. First, increased vehicle ownership and usage can result in the presence of more cars on the road, leading to overall higher vehicle miles travelled (VMT) and increased congestion. This increased traffic can lead to idling and stop-and-go driving, both of which contribute to higher emissions [2]. Second, autonomous vehicles may encourage longer trips and more single-occupancy journeys, as people may be more willing to tolerate longer commutes if they can work or relax while the vehicle drives itself. Additionally, the convenience and comfort offered by autonomous vehicles might reduce the appeal of public transportation, leading to a shift from shared mobility options to private vehicles [3]. Finally, while autonomous vehicles have the potential to improve fuel efficiency through better traffic flow and optimized driving patterns, the manufacturing and operational energy requirements, as well as the battery production and charging infrastructure, contribute to the life cycle emissions of these vehicles [4–6].

The multilevel aspect of electric vehicles (EVs) regarding sustainability and their life cycle encompass various stages from production to end-of-life management. While EVs contribute to reduced greenhouse gas emissions during operation, concerns arise from their assembly and disposal processes. At the production level, the extraction of raw materials such as lithium, cobalt, and rare-earth metals for battery production has environmental and social implications. Additionally, the energy-intensive manufacturing process and associated emissions involved during vehicle assembly need to be considered. Furthermore, the end-of-life management of EV batteries poses challenges due to their recycling, reusability, and potential environmental impacts if not properly handled. These multi-level aspects highlight the need for holistic approaches, including the sustainable sourcing of materials, efficient manufacturing processes, and effective recycling and disposal systems, to maximize the sustainability benefits of EVs while minimizing their environmental footprint [7,8].

The excessive or disorganised use of private AVs additionally has the potential to stimulate urban sprawl [9–12] by eliminating the stress of driving and enabling people to reside farther from their workplace, resulting in longer commuting distances and energy expenditure [13]. Thus, without careful planning and regulation, the unchecked proliferation and haphazard use of private autonomous vehicles can exacerbate greenhouse gas emissions. To minimise the detrimental effects, the widespread adoption of ridesharing using AVs should be publicly promoted to reduce traffic congestion by optimizing routes and minimizing empty trips towards creating a safer, more efficient, and sustainable transportation systems for the future [14,15].

Autonomous demand-responsive transit (ADRT) is a recently introduced public transit mode and is predominantly available using autonomous shuttle buses (ASBs) [14–20]. The implementation of ADRT has been stated as an applicable response to the climate change challenge [5]. ADRT has the potential to enhance mobility services and, as a result, enhance transit efficiency and reduce dependency on private vehicles [21,22]. As a feeder mode of regular public transit, ADRT could provide first-/last-mile services, supporting a transition to more sustainable mobility [11]. The use of ASBs with transport capacities of up to 15 persons enables reasonably cost-effective, flexible on-demand 24/7 operation [23]. The use of ADRT in a more dynamic, mixed-traffic environment is evolving quickly [24–26].

Attitude may be explained as "a mental state of readiness, positively or negatively associated with a particular object. It is acquired through experience and is a precursor of behaviour related to the object" ([27], p. 251). Individuals' attitudes towards ADRT are crucial as they influence "the demand for the technology, governing policies and future investments in infrastructure" ([28], p. 38). Nevertheless, if ADRT is to be deployed widely and embraced as an everyday travel mode, positive public attitudes are necessary.

In the past, many researchers have investigated public perceptions towards opportunities and challenges for AVs [20,29–35], but few have focused on the Australian context [36–43]. There is a lack of research about how Australians' socio-demographics affect their attitudes towards AVs, particularly ADRT. This study fills this research gap by fully classifying socio-demographic predictors of the publics' attitudes towards ADRT in the specific context of the South East Queensland (SEQ) region of Australia. The research method is founded on an online stated preference survey distributed across more than 250 postcodes across the region, complemented by a wide-ranging review of prior global studies, and descriptive and ordinal/binary logistic regression analysis using SPSS v.27. This study tries to address the following research question.

- How are individuals' perceptions and attitudes towards ADRT influenced by gender, age, education, employment, income, household size, residential location, and having a driver's license?

As a result, we shed more light on the social dynamics behind how potential adopters perceive different aspects of this innovative transit mode. The insights drawn from the current study may help alleviate concerns and encourage the future adoption of ASBs in this and other regions. Following this introduction, Section 2 provides an overview of relevant global studies. Section 3 explains the research method involving the questionnaire design, case study area, and the data collection process. Section 4 presents the descriptive statistics of the socio-demographic and attitudinal characteristics. Section 5 then describes the analysis method along with the detailed results. Section 6 discusses the findings and implications for the transition to ADRT. Section 7 provides concluding remarks, study limitations and suggestions for further research.

2. Literature Background

In this section, the study provides a concise review of the current literature on the association between attitudes towards ADRT, in particular ASBs, and the socio-demographic characteristics comprising gender, age, education, employment, income, household size, and residential location, adapting the reviews that were recently published in the AV context [14,27,44].

The literature on the subject of gender and attitude towards ADRT is mixed. According to Dong et al. [45] and Winter et al. [46], males have been demonstrated to be more open to using ASBs than females are, especially highly automated ASBs [47]. Other research reported that males are generally more willing to use autonomous transport services [48], preferring ASBs over traditional vehicles [49–52], and trust ASBs more than females do [53]. Similarly, males are found to be more confident to share a ride with strangers on ASBs than females are, but in terms of traffic safety or dealing with an emergency, there has been no major difference [19]. Females are less prone to believe that autonomous transit services are useful, and have more concerns about them [48]. Furthermore, females may prefer to use ASBs themselves rather than allow their partners or children to [46,54]. Nevertheless, Madigan et al. [55] and Nordhoff et al. [17,56] found no significant difference between males' and females' intention to use ASBs, and neither did Pakusch & Bossauer [57] in the autonomous transit context. No impact of gender was seen even when ASB service offerings were provided between transit hubs and parking lots or between the home and workplace [47].

Research findings on how age affects attitude and adoption are inconsistent. Some studies discovered no correlation between a person's age and willingness to use ASBs [55,58–60] or other autonomous transit services [57], or even with the likelihood of preferring ASBs over other transport modes [50,51]. Similarly, Salonen [19] reported an insignificant effect of age on concerns about safety on-board, in traffic or an emergency, as did Dekker [53] regarding trust in ASBs. Even when ASBs offered mobility services between transit hubs and parking lots, or between the home and workplace, age was shown to not influence the willingness to use transit [27]. ASBs seemed to be more popular among young individuals [47]. According to Acheampong & Cugurullo [48], there is a negative relationship between age and favourable attitudes towards technology, the perceived benefits of or intent to use autonomous transit services. Those of ages between 18–35 were more likely to use ASBs than those over 45 years old [45]. Portouli et al. [61] found that frequent customers of ASBs were younger than non-users, contrary to Nordhoff et al. [17] who reported a higher acceptance of ASBs among older participants than among younger ones, though the former considered ASBs less efficient than their present transport mode.

Level of education was discovered to affect the intention to use ASBs [47], perceived usefulness, perceived ease of use, and willingness to use autonomous transit services [48]. ASBs were preferred by those with a higher education level over their traditional counterparts in some regions where ASBs were implemented in city centres [49,50,62]. In contrast, neither concerns about safety on-board, in traffic, nor an emergency seemed to be influenced by education levels [19], nor did trust in ASBs [53]. The impact of education level between frequent users of ASBs and those who had never used such modes was insignificant [61].

Employment was found not to affect preference for ASBs over their traditional counterparts [50], or concerns regarding safety on-board, in traffic or in an emergency [19].

Nevertheless, Portouli et al. [61] reported that students use ASBs more frequently than employees, unemployed persons, or retirees do. This might be attributed to the impact of ageing.

Household income was found not to affect preference for ASBs over their traditional counterparts [50], or willingness of using ASBs [60]. Similarly, Salonen [19] reported an insignificant effect of income on concerns about safety on-board, in traffic or in an emergency, as did Dekker [53] regarding trust in ASBs. Dong et al. [45] argued that a person's greater income increases their intention to use ASBs, but only in the case of not considering the effect of AV knowledge.

Regarding residential location, some research stated that residents of densely populated regions have greater intentions to use ASBs at higher levels [47]. Rural and urban populations in Germany had equal intentions to use ASBs [60]. In contrast, US respondents were found to be more inclined to use ASBs than those in any of the other countries that were surveyed by Winter et al. [46]. Residents of areas with ASB services were shown to have more trust and intention to use ASBs than were residents of areas without ASB services in operation [53]. In a survey conducted on a German campus by Nordhoff et al. [17], campus workers regarded ASBs as being less efficient than their existing transit mode compared to non-campus workers. Contrary to parents in the US, parents in India were more open to the idea of their children riding in ASBs. However, residents and tourists in La Rochelle (France) and Lausanne (Switzerland) were equally open to the idea of using ASBs [58].

As noted, research findings differ concerning the influence of gender, age, education, employment, income and residential location on attitudes towards ADRT, and in particular ASBs. Such discrepancies might be due to variations in research "methodology (qualitative interview or an online survey; involving a shuttle trial or not), nature and size of study samples, usage contexts (campus, city centre or rural environment) or vehicle considered (shuttle, buses)" ([27], p. 268). Even though there are extensive detailed studies in this field, they have mostly focused on the US and European populations. The applicability of those findings to the Australian context, thus, is questionable. Empirical research is lacking for measuring public perceptions and attitudes towards ADRT in Australia, especially in the ASB context. Only a small number of individual characteristics have been explored, which restricts both the depth and breadth of our knowledge of the association between Australians' socio-demographics and their perceptions and attitudes towards ADRT. Cross-national differences may obscure individual differences in attitudes towards and adoption of ASBs according to Kyriakidis et al. (2015). Further, prior findings indicate that the public's perception towards AVs more generally varies between nations, namely between Australians [29] and others, highlighting the need for further study in the regional context.

The current research builds upon prior studies, not only by measuring perceptions and attitudes towards ADRT among adult residents of SEQ but also by carrying out an in-depth exploration of how those perceptions and attitudes are associated with particular socio-demographic characteristics.

3. Research Method

A stated preference survey was designed and implemented to investigate challenges and opportunities in the adoption of ADRT services by adult residents of the case study region. SEQ is a metropolitan region centred on Brisbane that has a land area of 35,248 km^2 and a population of 3,817,573 million (2021). The per capita gross state product of Queensland is AUD 71,037 (USD 53,280) [63]. It has 12 adjoining local government areas (LGAs), where a LGA is a municipality administered by the third and lowest tier of government.

The survey respondent recruitment methodology involved only individuals living within the urban and peri-urban areas of SEQ (see Figure 1, highlighted in red and purple, respectively) including a total of 250 postcodes. Rural areas were excluded from the study because the implementation of this survey was not cost-efficient due to low density.

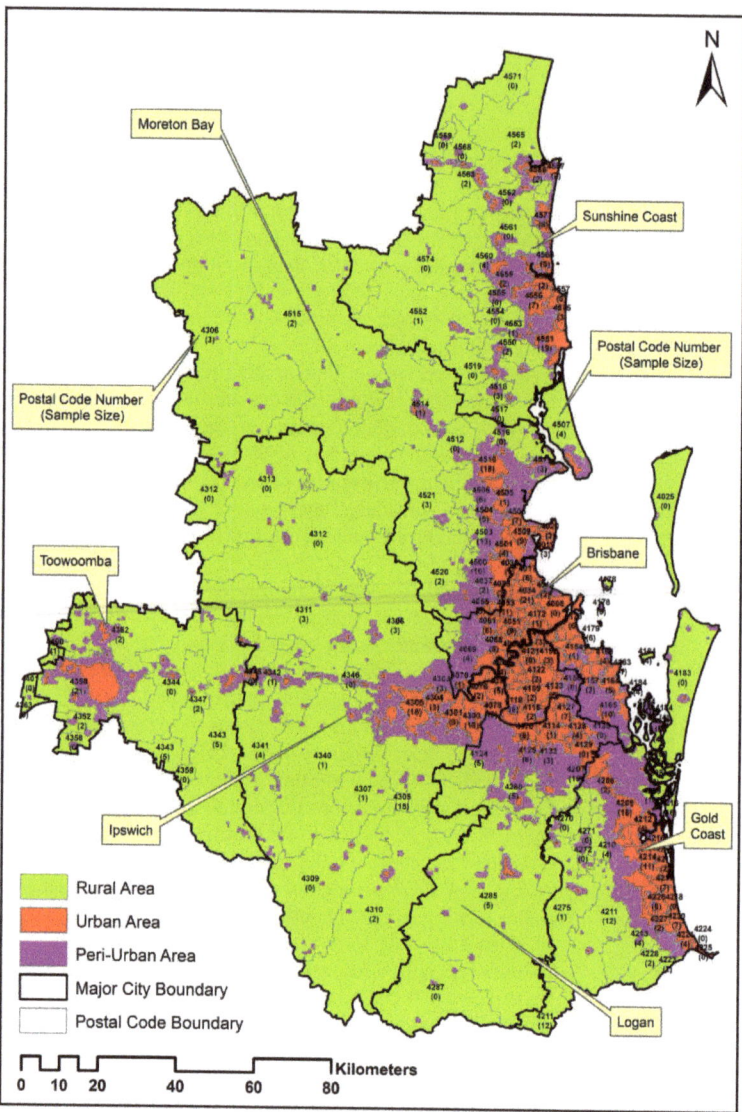

Figure 1. The map of the study area [64].

The questionnaire items were adapted and developed following a systematic literature review [14] to verify the content's validity. Preliminary testing was conducted by surveying a group of higher-degree research students and the staff of the university because these people usually have broader knowledge regarding the application of surveys for reliable results. Preliminary and main survey participation was entirely voluntary. The final questionnaire was revised following the feedback provided by an expert supervisory panel review representing views of key informants in the field, specifically civil engineering and built environment academics specialising in transport systems and autonomous vehicles. The questionnaire consisted of three sections: (1) questions about the respondent's socio-demographic characteristics, (2) questions relating to the respondent's existing travel habits—such factors being worth mentioning in understanding the attitudes towards ASBs, and (3) attitudinal indicators contained to assess perceptions that might affect the adoption of ASBs. The related indicators were measured by applying a 5-point Likert scale owing to its widespread usage in the literature and its ease of use in analysis. For a clearer interpretation of the typical usage of ASBs to deliver ADRT, an introductory paragraph was included stating that "Autonomous shuttle buses are fully automated electrically powered vehicles which are being trialled in Australia including SEQ as a new travel mode. They can serve potentially similar markets to conventional shuttles and have similar passenger-carrying capacities. However, they are not driven by a person, instead, they are controlled by smart technology that safely optimises travel times, vehicle kilometres travelled, and energy consumption. They are expected to be in public use with a surveillance system on board in place of a human driver." Two photos of ASB were also depicted at the beginning of the questionnaire (Figure 2).

Figure 2. Introductory photos of ASBs presented to the survey participants regarding ADRT.

The University Human Research Ethics Committee (UHREC RN: 2000000747) approved the final questionnaire, which was made available online for self-completion. To accommodate the limitations and risks posed by the COVID-19 pandemic, the researchers enlisted the services of Qualtrics, a professional web-based survey platform provider, to employ a convenient random sampling method in reaching the target respondents and gathering data for the study. Each potential respondent received an email containing the survey link to ensure broad public access during May 2021. The e-mail explicitly displayed a brief description of the academic purpose of the project and voluntary participation. The screening question ensured that only participants who were over 18 years old and residing in SEQ were asked to respond to the survey. Overall, 357 respondents finished the survey. Ultimately, after screening and cleaning the data, 300 responses with no missing values, invalid observations or outliers were deemed to be valid for further analysis. Based upon Krejcie and Morgan [65], a minimum sample size for a population above 1,000,000 (confidence = 95% and Margin of Error = 6%) is 300.

4. Descriptive Statistics

It is necessary to explore how the SEQ population is represented in our sample to fully understand both the background that yields the subsequent findings and the associated implications for the uptake of ADRT among Australians more broadly. The descriptive analysis was carried out using SPSS v.27 [66].

4.1. Socio-Demographic Characteristics

The analysis results identified a total of seven socio-demographic predictor variables associated with personal characteristics including gender, age, education, employment, household income, residential location, and household size. Figure 3 illustrates the distribution of each personal characteristic. The multicollinearity assessment results indicated that predictor variable inflation factors (VIFs) were all acceptable at a level of <2.50 [67].

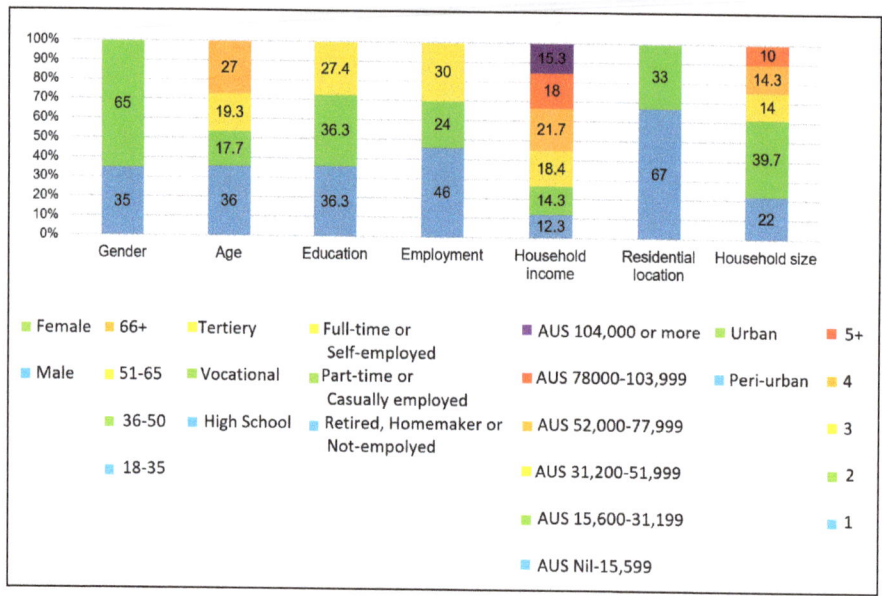

Figure 3. Demographic characteristics of SEQ respondents.

Out of the 300 survey participants, the age group between 18 and 35 years old constituted the largest proportion at 36%. Respondents aged 36 to 50 years old accounted for 17.7% of the participants, while those aged 51 to 65 and over 66 years old represented 19.3% and 27%, respectively. The number of female respondents was nearly twice that of males (65% compared to 35%). Regarding education, 27.4% of participants held tertiary degrees and almost the same portion of them completed high school (36.3%) or a vocational certificate (36.3%). The retired, homemaker or not employed group accounted for 46% of respondents while part-time or casual employees accounted for 24% and full-time or self-employed (30%) individuals accounted for the remainder. The median and mode annual income bracket was AUD 52,000– AUD 77,999. The survey also showed that two-thirds of respondents (67%) were living in peri-urban areas, and most of them were from 2-person households (39.7%).

The distributions of existing travel characteristic response variables including (a) travel mode/frequency, (b) travel purpose/frequency, (c) driver's license, (d) daily travel time, and (e) travel mode satisfaction are outlined in Figure 4. It can be seen that the most frequently used modes are walk, car, while the least frequently used modes are mobility scooter, motorcycle/moped, e-bike/e-scooter. The most popular transit modes are bus, train/tram, taxi, then ferry and conventional shuttle bus. Commercial vehicle and bicycle usages are similar. The majority of the survey participants hold a valid driver's license. Almost the same portion of them had less than 30 min or 30 min–1 h of travel time. Only a small portion of them was neutral towards or dissatisfied with their current travel mode, while the rest were satisfied or very satisfied with it.

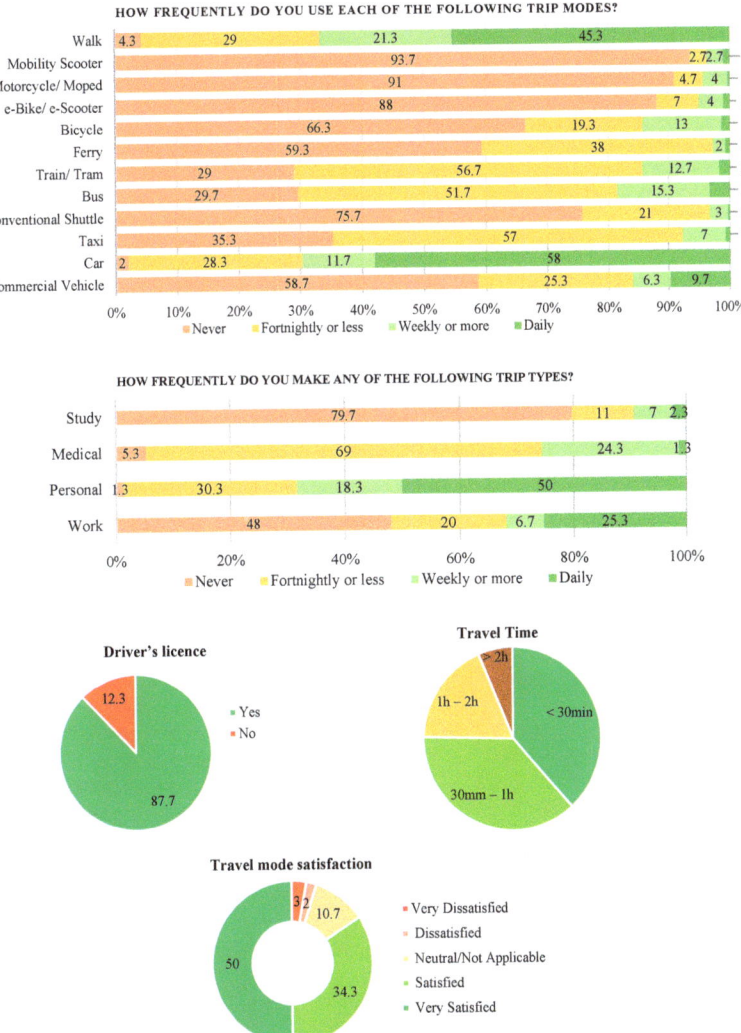

Figure 4. Summary of responses for travel characteristic variables.

The summary of responses regarding exposure to AVs comprising AV knowledge and experience variables is shown in Figure 5. The AV knowledge variable was ordered in the following categorical range on the survey: not familiar, somewhat familiar, and very familiar. Only 8 responses were recorded in the last category, so it was determined that the re-coding of categories was appropriate. As can be seen, a percentage of the survey respondents were aware of AVs but very few of them had already used them.

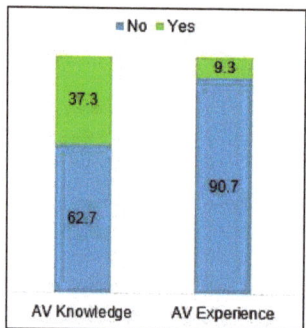

Figure 5. Summarized AV knowledge and experience response variables.

4.2. Attitudinal Characteristics

Public attitude towards ASBs is a key factor that will shape the demand and market for them [61]. Since perception and attitudes "represent an individual's latent beliefs and values and unlike observable variables cannot be directly measured. These latent constructs, however, influence an individual's decision-making process" ([68,69], p. 242). Psychometric indicators could be used to identify latent constructs [69]. Response variables in our study, which require respondents to rate certain statements on a scale, are psychometric indicators. In the literature response, variables are self-developed or modified effective statements. For each factor, the frequencies in each category were inspected and all were maintained for ordinal logistic regression. Reliability was checked by determining Cronbach's alpha (α) to assess the items' internal consistency. Each scale's Cronbach's α value should be greater than 0.7 [70]. The overall Cronbach's alpha was determined to equal 0.924 for perceived opportunities and 0.786 for perceived challenges, indicating strong consistency amongst all the response variables listed. The value of Cronbach's alpha for each item if deleted implies that the omission of none of the items could have substantively increased the reliability of this part of the survey [71]; however, 'Higher fare' is less consistent than the others.

Public perception and attitudes towards ASBs were tested regarding the perceived opportunities and challenges of using ASBs compared to those of using conventional shuttles. The survey participants were presented with a list of opportunities to be expected by using ASBs. Their opinions on the agreement with the listed opportunities on the 5-point Likert scale ranging from 'strongly disagree' to 'strongly agree' are shown in Figure 6. The majority of the survey respondents gave responses ranging from neutral to agree, with each of the eight perceived opportunities listed. Of the opportunities that were agreed upon, the most appealing ones were 'Less congestion/emissions' (41%), and this was followed by 'Easy to learn how to interact/travel' (39%), and 'Reduced fleet need' (38%). The least appealing ones were 'Safer' (18%) and 'More attractive' (23%).

The survey participants were presented with a list of challenges relating to the use of ASBs. Their opinions regarding the concerns about the listed challenges on the 5-point Likert scale ranging from 'very concerned' to 'not concerned' at all are shown in Figure 7. The majority of the survey respondents were concerned to very concerned with all listed challenges. Of the challenges, the most concerning was 'Unreliable technology' (51.3% were concerned and 24.7% were very concerned), followed by 'Malfunction' (43% were very concerned and 40% were concerned), 'Traffic accidents' (38% were very concerned and 39% were concerned), and 'Higher fare' (44% were concerned and 18.7% were very concerned).

Response Variable / Caregory	Strongly Disagree	Disagree	Neutral	Agree	Strongly Agree	Cronbach's α if item deleted
More efficient	10.3	16	38	28	7.7	0.909
Reduced fleet need	7	13.3	35.7	38	6	0.916
Less congestion/emissions	6.7	13.3	30.3	41	8.7	0.918
Fewer driver errors	8	15.3	39	28	9.7	0.913
Easy to Learn How to Travel	6	9.3	35	39	10.7	0.919
Safer	15	26	35.7	18	5.3	0.91
More Attractive	12.3	20	39	23.7	5	0.914
More Positive Attitude	11	15.7	34.7	32	6.7	0.911

Figure 6. Perceived opportunities of autonomous shuttle buses (ASBs) compared to conventional shuttles (%).

Response Variable/ Caregory	Very Concerned	Concerned	Neutral	Not Concerned	Not Concerned at All	Cronbach's α if item deleted
Higher fare	18.7	44	24.3	11	2	0.867
Unreliable technology	24.7	51.3	14	9	1	0.673
Traffic accidents	38	39	11	11	1	0.649
Malfunction	43	40.7	9.7	5.7	1	0.694

Figure 7. Perceived concerns of autonomous shuttle buses (ASBs) (%).

The survey participants' intention to use ASBs if they become available is shown in Figure 8. More than two-thirds (38%) of the respondents stated that they would be happy to ride in ASBs that operate for special purposes, and about one-fifth (19%) did not consider using ASBs at all. Of the rest of the potential users of ASBs, 25% preferred to ride in ASBs that operate on all roads/streets, 10% preferred to ride on private streets, and 8% preferred to ride on local streets.

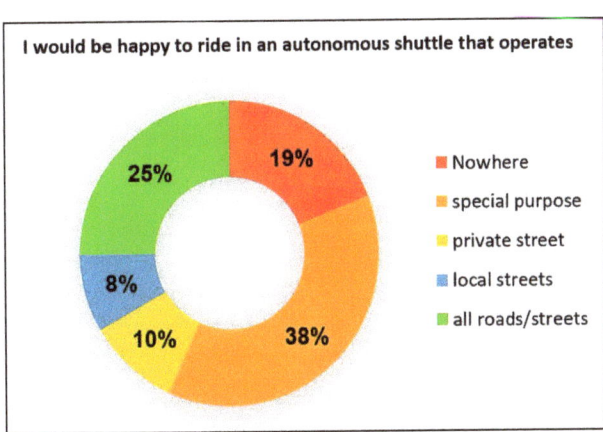

Figure 8. Autonomous shuttle bus (ASB) adoption choice.

5. Findings and Implications for Transition to ADRT

Following the descriptive analysis of the survey, an ordinal logistic regression was employed using SPSS v.27 to develop a model to understand associations of the socio-demographic predictor variables for each response variable within each tabulated grouping of existing travel characteristics and attitudinal variables. The link function that was used was Logit. For this exploratory study of each response variable, a backward elimination method was used to obtain the parsimonious model using only the predictor variables that pass the threshold significance of 0.05 [72].

The next section presents the results of this modelling. For ordinal logistic regression and binary logistic regression, the omnibus test, like the likelihood-ratio chi-square test, is used to test whether or not the current model outperforms the null model as evidenced by $p \leq 0.05$. For the ordinal logistic regression, the parallel lines test is used to test the null hypothesis that the slope coefficients in the model are the same across response categories, and therefore that the one-equation model is valid, as evidenced by $p > 0.05$, suggesting the model fits well [73–75].

In our evaluation, we characterise relatively the predictor variables' odds ratios for decreasing odds: extremely strong > 0.2, $0.2 \geq$ very strong > 0.4, $0.4 \geq$ strong > 0.6, $0.6 \geq$ moderate > 0.8, and $0.8 \geq$ mild > 1.0. We use the inverses of these values for increasing odds [76–78]. Here, we present findings from our ordinal/binary logistic regression analysis.

5.1. Associations between AV Exposure and Socio-Demographic Predictor Variables

The results of the goodness of fit tests and statistics of the binary logistic regression models for these response variables are listed in Table 1.

Table 1. Significant binary logistic models of AV exposure to socio-demographic predictor variables.

Response Variable Model	Omnibus Sig.	Predictor Variable	Std. Error	Wald Sig.	OR	OR 95% Wald C.I.	
						Lower	Upper
AV Knowledge	0.038	Employment	0.140	0.038	1.335	1.015	1.755
AV Experience	0.002	Gender (male)	0.408	0.018	2.635	1.184	5.860
		Household Inc.	0.142	0.015	1.411	1.069	1.861

Omnibus significance indicates that the AV knowledge model has a better fit than the intercept-only model. According to the odds ratio, evidence suggests that an increasing employment status across the scale from the retired, homemaker or not employed level to the full-time or self-employed level is strongly associated with an increase in the likelihood of having knowledge about AV.

The AV experience model has a superior fit to the intercept-only model. Evidence suggests the following effects in the likelihood of having experienced AVs of any kind. Being male is very strongly associated with an increase. Increasing household income across the scale from the Nil to the AUD 15,599 level to the AUD 104,000 or more level is extremely strongly associated with an increase.

5.2. Associations between Attitudinal Characteristics and Socio-Demographic Predictor Variables

The results of the goodness of fit tests and statistics of the ordinal logistic regression model for each remaining response variable are listed in Table 2. All the response variable models have a superior fit to the threshold-only models, while the proportional odds assumption appears to have held.

Regarding perceived opportunities and challenges, evidence suggests the following, discussed according to the response variable.

Overall, the information highlights the advantages of ASBs over conventional shuttles, including their efficiency, reduced traffic congestion and emissions, the presence of fewer driver errors, ease of learning, safety, attractiveness, and positive attitudes towards ASBs. For each of the following response variables, no model was found to be significant via regression using the socio-demographic predictor variables from Figure 6 of 'Reduced fleet Need', 'Unreliable technology', and 'Malfunction'.

Table 2. Significant OLM of attitudinal characteristics to socio-demographic predictor variables.

Response Variable Model	Omnibus Sig.	Parallel Lines Sig.	Predictor Variable	Std. Error	Wald Sig.	OR	OR 95% Wald C.I. Lower	OR 95% Wald C.I. Upper
Perceived opportunities of ASBs								
More efficient	0.000	0.541	Age	0.087	0.001	0.742	0.626	0.881
			Household Inc.	0.066	0.032	1.153	1.011	1.315
			Household Inc.	0.068	0.001	1.263	1.106	1.442
Less congestion and emissions	0.001	0.493	Age	0.088	0.001	0.757	0.637	0.899
Fewer driver errors	0.003	0.153	Age	0.087	0.004	0.780	0.658	0.924
Easy to learn how to interact/travel	0.000	0.783	Age	0.088	0.003	0.770	0.647	0.915
			Household Inc.	0.068	0.001	1.263	1.106	1.442
Safer	0.007	0.052	Age	0.086	0.008	0.796	0.674	0.939
More attractive	0.000	0.131	Age	0.098	0.000	0.709	0.584	0.861
			Employment	0.138	0.036	1.337	1.014	1.762
			Drivers Lic (yes)	0.331	0.009	0.423	0.221	0.809
			Age	0.098	0.000	0.690	0.570	0.834
			Household Inc.	0.068	0.024	1.165	1.020	1.331
More positive attitude	0.000	0.124	Gender (male)	0.247	0.040	1.660	1.018	2.708
			Drivers Lic (yes)	0.331	0.009	0.423	0.221	0.809
			Age	0.098	0.000	0.690	0.570	0.834
			Household Inc.	0.068	0.024	1.165	1.020	1.331
Perceived challenges of ASBs								
Higher fare	0.008	0.529	Res Location (peri-urban)	0.228	0.044	1.584	1.012	2.479
			Education	0.136	0.031	0.746	0.571	0.973
Traffic accidents	0.003	0.472	Gender (male)	0.227	0.028	1.647	1.055	2.570
			Drivers Lic (yes)	0.327	0.037	0.506	0.267	0.959

OLM: ordinal logistic models; ASBs: autonomous shuttle buses; OR: odds ratio; C.I.: confidence interval.

Individuals with lower employment levels tend to have less familiarity with autonomous vehicles (AVs). Therefore, it would be beneficial to explore ways to enhance their knowledge about AVs, especially if such an improvement can positively influence their willingness to adopt AVs when and where they are available. Additionally, females and individuals from lower-income households are less likely to have experienced riding in any type of AV. For these socio-demographic groups, it may be worthwhile to investigate methods of increasing exposure to autonomous shuttle buses (ASBs), such as through demonstrations, as increased exposure could potentially enhance their acceptance and the adoption of ASBs when and where they are deployed.

Male respondents exhibit a more favourable attitude towards ASBs, as do those who do not possess a driver's license. Furthermore, younger respondents also demonstrate a more positive attitude towards ASBs. They perceive ASBs as more appealing, efficient, safe, and less congesting, with fewer emissions and driver errors compared to conventional shuttles. Younger respondents also believe that learning how to travel in an ASB is relatively easy. On the other hand, respondents with higher employment levels perceive ASBs as more attractive than conventional shuttles. Similarly, individuals from higher-income households hold a more positive attitude towards ASBs, perceiving them as more efficient and easier to learn how to use. These socio-demographic groups should be targeted to encourage the adoption of ASBs when and where they become available. For the socio-demographic groups that exhibit the opposite characteristics, it may be worthwhile to explore approaches to improve agreement regarding the benefits and opportunities associated with ASBs, as such improvements could enhance their willingness to adopt the use of these.

Respondents residing in peri-urban areas tend to be more concerned about fares when using ASBs compared to conventional shuttles. This concern is also observed among respondents with lower education levels. For both socio-demographic groups, it would be valuable to investigate whether or not fare structures based on spatial zones, time periods, and concession categories contribute to their concerns. Addressing these concerns related to fare structures, specifically in the context of ASB deployment, could help alleviate the worries and increase acceptance among these groups. Additionally, male respondents, those without a driver's license, and individuals with higher employment levels are more concerned about traffic accidents when using ASBs compared to conventional shuttles. It is important to further explore how the automation of the driving task contributes to these perceived challenges and identify steps that can be taken to address these concerns specifically in the context of ASB deployment for these socio-demographic groups.

Addressing trust difficulties and worries about faulty technology can be carried out in several ways [79]:

- **Education and Awareness**: Policymakers should implement education campaigns that explain how ADRT works, its benefits, and the safety measures put in place. Transparency about technology can help alleviate fears.
- **Regulation and Standards**: Policymakers should establish stringent standards and regulations for ADRT systems. This would not only ensure safety but also promote public confidence in the technology.
- **Demonstrations and Trials**: Public demonstrations or pilot programs can also help to increase public trust in ADRT. By seeing the technology in action and understanding its benefits first-hand, people might be more likely to trust and adopt it.
- **Addressing Equity Concerns**: A significant subset of the population that might be sceptical about ADRT could be those who worry about access and equity, particularly if they live in underserved areas or have limited mobility. Policymakers need to assure these communities that ADRT will be accessible and affordable to all, not just a privileged few.
- **Stakeholder Involvement**: Involving different stakeholders in the policymaking process can also build trust. This could include public forums or consultations where citizens can express their views and contribute to decision-making about ADRT.
- **Data Privacy and Security Measures**: Given the digital nature of ADRT, data privacy and cybersecurity are crucial. Policymakers should define clear guidelines to protect user data and ensure that robust cybersecurity measures are in place.

The ultimate goal for policymakers should be to foster a favourable public opinion towards ADRT while ensuring safety, accessibility, and trust in the technology. They should continuously gauge public sentiment and address concerns proactively to promote widespread acceptance and adoption.

6. Conclusions

The implementation of autonomous demand-responsive transit (ADRT) as a feeder to regular public transit holds the potential to enhance the effectiveness of public transportation. While autonomous trains and trams are already widely integrated into public transit systems worldwide [57,80], the acceptability of pioneering ADRT services, such as autonomous shuttle buses (ASBs), raises questions and concerns. To address these issues, our study focused on understanding the social dynamics behind how different groups perceive ADRT mobility, specifically ASBs, in the SEQ region, Australia. By exploring the perceptions and attitudes of individuals based on factors such as gender, age, education, employment, income, household size, residential location, and the possession of a driver's license, we gained insights into the opportunities and challenges associated with these innovative transportation services in urban areas.

The findings from the present study provide valuable insights for alleviating concerns and increasing the adoption of automated driving and ride-sharing technologies (ADRT) in the Southeast Queensland (SEQ) region. These insights can serve as a useful guide for planners, suppliers, and policymakers, helping them cater to the demands and preferences of current and potential users, considering the variations in socio-demographic characteristics.

Our findings revealed the following key points: (i) the primary perceived opportunity of ASBs was the potential to reduce congestion and emissions, while the main anticipated challenge was related to concerns about the reliability of the technology; (ii) fully employed respondents showed greater familiarity with autonomous vehicles (AVs), while females and individuals from lower-income households had less experience riding in any form of AV; (iii) male respondents, younger individuals, those with higher employment and incomes, and individuals without a driver's license held a more favourable opinion of ASBs. Additionally, male respondents, those with higher employment and incomes, and those without a driver's license expressed greater concern about traffic accidents when using ASBs. Less-educated respondents and individuals living in peri-urban areas were more concerned about fares.

We employed a methodological approach utilizing binary and ordinal logistic regression modelling to understand the significance of socio-demographic variables in predicting changes in travel characteristics. This approach, supported by odds ratios, allowed us to analyse how variations in socio-demographic factors affected the likelihood of changes in travel characteristics. By identifying significant predictor variables and their odds ratios for each travel characteristic, our methodology provided valuable insights to inform policies and practices in order to address key issues (e.g., safety concerns) and target specific groups (particularly females) when planning public communication strategies to enhance receptiveness to ADRT.

To promote the adoption and future uptake of ADRT, policymakers should focus on fostering favourable attitudes (e.g., highlighting perceived opportunities) and addressing existing unfavourable attitudes (e.g., addressing perceived challenges). Our findings emphasize the importance of avoiding pilot operations that lead to negative experiences and fail to meet mobility demands. Providing reliable, effective, and convenient ADRT services is crucial for alleviating prospective users' concerns. Measures such as information screens and easy, obstacle-free access to vehicles can compensate for the absence of a driver, as suggested by Pigeon et al. [27]. In terms of deployment locations for ADRT, normal urban traffic conditions are currently perceived as less acceptable. Instead, deployment in secure contexts, such as dedicated routes, campuses, or areas with no existing public transport links such as peri-urban regions, is generally seen as desirable.

7. Limitations and Future Research

While conducting this research, certain simplifications were made, which may have resulted in limitations to the present study. Most survey respondents had no experience riding in an ASB, and thus some of our conclusions are based on prospective users' perceptions (stated preference) rather than actual users' opinions (revealed preference), which may limit their generalizability. Future research could include individuals who have used these services once they become available, as demonstrated by Dennis et al. [81] in their study on autonomous shuttles. Longitudinal studies exploring adoption attitudes over different time intervals could also provide valuable insights by recognizing patterns over time and identifying significant outcomes [28].

It is worth noting that our study, like most previous quantitative surveys, primed respondents by listing specific potential opportunities and challenges associated with ASBs before assessing their opinions. This approach may lead individuals to perceive these issues as potential problems, even if they have minimal influence on their decision to use ASBs. An alternative approach to enhance ASB adoption could prioritize communication on aspects of deployment that users consider more important, to alleviate existing concerns, rather than addressing perceived problems of low importance. To facilitate this, data collection procedures should allow respondents to proactively raise issues, rather than directing their attention to aspects of ASB deployment they may not have considered otherwise [38,39].

While the target respondents of our study were the public, it is important to acknowledge that the benefits of ADRT might be particularly significant for the transport-disadvantaged population. Further studies can focus on specific socio-demographic groups in more detail, such as elderly individuals and people with disabilities, to better understand their demands and challenges [27,44].

In future research, the methodology employed in this study can be replicated for the SEQ region. By comparing results between panel data, reasons for similarities and differences in travel characteristics over time can be investigated, particularly in response to geographical and socio-demographic shifts, as well as changes in policy and practice related to personal transport. This methodology is directly transferable to different regions, allowing for comparisons to identify similarities and differences in travel characteristics between different areas.

Further research will employ structural equation modelling with this dataset to gain deeper insights. Cross-referencing the results of this study will help determine the implications for each methodology and enable a comprehensive interpretation of findings. An extensive hypothesis testing approach is likely to benefit the analysis [82–84].

Author Contributions: Conceptualization, F.G., T.Y. and J.B.; methodology, F.G., T.Y. and J.B.; software, F.G.; validation, F.G. and J.B.; formal analysis, F.G.; data curation, F.G. and J.B.; writing—original draft preparation, F.G.; writing—review and editing, F.G., T.Y., A.P. and J.B.; supervision, F.G., T.Y., A.P. and J.B. All authors have read and agreed to the published version of the manuscript.

Funding: This research received no external funding.

Institutional Review Board Statement: The study was conducted in accordance with the Declaration of Helsinki, and approved by the QUT Human Research Ethics Committee (approval number 2000000747, Date 19 November 2020).

Informed Consent Statement: Informed consent was obtained from all subjects involved in the study.

Conflicts of Interest: The authors declare no conflict of interest.

References

1. Golbabaei, F.; Yigitcanlar, T.; Bunker, J. The role of shared autonomous vehicle systems in delivering smart urban mobility: A systematic review of the literature. *Int. J. Sustain. Transp.* **2021**, *15*, 731–748. [CrossRef]
2. Wadud, Z.; MacKenzie, D.; Leiby, P. Help or hindrance? The travel, energy and carbon impacts of highly automated vehicles. *Transp. Res. Part A Policy Pract.* **2016**, *86*, 1–18. [CrossRef]
3. Harb, M.; Xiao, Y.; Circella, G.; Mokhtarian, P.L.; Walker, J.L. Projecting travelers into a world of self-driving vehicles: Estimating travel behavior implications via a naturalistic experiment. *Transportation* **2018**, *45*, 1671–1685. [CrossRef]
4. Taiebat, M.; Brown, A.L.; Safford, H.R.; Qu, S.; Xu, M. A review on energy, environmental, and sustainability implications of connected and automated vehicles. *Environ. Sci. Technol.* **2018**, *52*, 11449–11465. [CrossRef] [PubMed]
5. Nunes, A.; Woodley, L.; Rossetti, P. Re-thinking procurement incentives for electric vehicles to achieve net-zero emissions. *Nat. Sustain.* **2022**, *5*, 527–532. [CrossRef]
6. Silva, Ó.; Cordera, R.; González-González, E.; Nogués, S. Environmental impacts of autonomous vehicles: A review of the scientific literature. *Sci. Total Environ.* **2022**, *830*, 154515. [CrossRef] [PubMed]
7. Wu, Y.; Zhang, L. Can the development of electric vehicles reduce the emission of air pollutants and greenhouse gases in developing countries? *Transp. Res. Part D Transp. Environ.* **2017**, *51*, 129–145. [CrossRef]
8. Vidhi, R.; Shrivastava, P. A review of electric vehicle lifecycle emissions and policy recommendations to increase EV penetration in India. *Energies* **2018**, *11*, 483.
9. Fagnant, D.J.; Kockelman, K. Preparing a nation for autonomous vehicles: Opportunities, barriers and policy recommendations. *Transp. Res. Part A Policy Pract.* **2015**, *77*, 167–181. [CrossRef]
10. Milakis, D.; van Arem, B.; van Wee, B. Policy and society related implications of automated driving: A review of literature and directions for future research. *J. Intell. Transp. Syst.* **2017**, *21*, 324–348. [CrossRef]
11. Soteropoulos, A.; Berger, M.; Ciari, F. Impacts of automated vehicles on travel behaviour and land use: An international review of modelling studies. *Transp. Rev.* **2019**, *39*, 29–49. [CrossRef]
12. Narayanan, S.; Chaniotakis, E.; Antoniou, C. Shared autonomous vehicle services: A comprehensive review. *Transp. Res. Part C Emerg. Technol.* **2020**, *111*, 255–293. [CrossRef]
13. Spurlock, C.A.; Sears, J.; Wong-Parodi, G.; Walker, V.; Jin, L.; Taylor, M.; Todd, A. Describing the users: Understanding adoption of and interest in shared, electrified, and automated transportation in the San Francisco Bay Area. *Transp. Res. Part D Transp. Environ.* **2019**, *71*, 283–301. [CrossRef]
14. Golbabaei, F.; Yigitcanlar, T.; Paz, A.; Bunker, J. Individual predictors of autonomous vehicle public acceptance and intention to use: A systematic review of the literature. *J. Open Innov.* **2020**, *6*, 106. [CrossRef]
15. Paddeu, D.; Parkhurst, G.; Shergold, I. Passenger comfort and trust on first-time use of a shared autonomous shuttle vehicle. *Transp. Res. Part C Emerg. Technol.* **2020**, *115*, 102604. [CrossRef]
16. Ainsalu, J.; Arffman, V.; Bellone, M.; Ellner, M.; Haapamäki, T.; Haavisto, N.; Åman, M. State of the Art of Automated Buses. *Sustainability* **2018**, *10*, 3118. [CrossRef]

17. Nordhoff, S.; de Winter, J.; Madigan, R.; Merat, N.; van Arem, B.; Happee, R. User acceptance of automated shuttles in Berlin-Schöneberg: A questionnaire study. *Transp. Res. Part F Traffic Psychol. Behav.* **2018**, *58*, 843–854. [CrossRef]
18. Rehrl, K.; Zankl, C. Digibus©: Results from the first self-driving shuttle trial on a public road in Austria. *Eur. Transp. Res. Rev.* **2018**, *10*, 51. [CrossRef]
19. Salonen, A.O. Passenger's subjective traffic safety, in-vehicle security and emergency management in the driverless shuttle bus in Finland. *Transp. Policy* **2018**, *61*, 106–110. [CrossRef]
20. Mouratidis, K.; Cobeña Serrano, V. Autonomous buses: Intentions to use, passenger experiences, and suggestions for improvement. *Transp. Res. Part F Traffic Psychol. Behav.* **2021**, *76*, 321–335. [CrossRef]
21. Millonig, A.; Fröhlich, P. Where Autonomous Buses Might and Might Not Bridge the Gaps in the 4 A's of Public Transport Passenger Needs: A Review. In Proceedings of the International Conference on Automotive User Interfaces and Interactive Vehicular Applications, Toronto, ON, Canada, 23–25 September 2018.
22. Nenseth, V.; Ciccone, A.; Kristensen, N.B. *Societal Consequences of Automated Vehicles–Norwegian Scenarios*; TØI Report (1700/2019); Institute of Transport Economics: Oslo, Norway, 2019.
23. Nordhoff, S.; Stapel, J.; van Arem, B.; Happee, R. Passenger opinions of the perceived safety and interaction with automated shuttles: A test ride study with 'hidden' safety steward. *Transp. Res. Part A Policy Pract.* **2020**, *138*, 508–524. [CrossRef]
24. Beiker, S.A. Deployment of automated driving as an example for the San Francisco Bay area. In *Road Vehicle Automation 5*; Springer: Cham, Switzerland, 2019; pp. 117–129.
25. Stocker, A.; Shaheen, S. Shared automated vehicle (SAV) pilots and automated vehicle policy in the US: Current and future developments. In *Road Vehicle Automation 5*; Springer: Cham, Switzerland, 2019; pp. 131–147.
26. Iclodean, C.; Cordos, N.; Varga, B.O. Autonomous shuttle bus for public transportation: A review. *Energies* **2020**, *13*, 2917. [CrossRef]
27. Pigeon, C.; Alauzet, A.; Paire-Ficout, L. Factors of acceptability, acceptance and usage for non-rail autonomous public transport vehicles: A systematic literature review. *Transp. Res. Part F Traffic Psychol. Behav.* **2021**, *81*, 251–270. [CrossRef]
28. Haboucha, C.J.; Ishaq, R.; Shiftan, Y. User preferences regarding autonomous vehicles. *Transp. Res. Part C Emerg. Technol.* **2017**, *78*, 37–49. [CrossRef]
29. Schoettle, B.; Sivak, M. *A Survey of Public Opinion about Autonomous and Self-Driving Vehicles in the US, the UK, and Australia*; University of Michigan, Transportation Research Institute: Ann Arbor, MI, USA, 2014.
30. Kyriakidis, M.; Happee, R.; de Winter, J.C.F. Public opinion on automated driving: Results of an international questionnaire among 5000 respondents. *Transp. Res. Part F Traffic Psychol. Behav.* **2015**, *32*, 127–140. [CrossRef]
31. Bansal, P.; Kockelman, K.M.; Singh, A. Assessing public opinions of and interest in new vehicle technologies: An Austin perspective. *Transp. Res. Part C Emerg. Technol.* **2016**, *67*, 1–14. [CrossRef]
32. König, M.; Neumayr, L. Users' resistance towards radical innovations: The case of the self-driving car. *Transp. Res. Part F Traffic Psychol. Behav.* **2017**, *44*, 42–52. [CrossRef]
33. Shabanpour, R.; Golshani, N.; Shamshiripour, A.; Mohammadian, A.K. Eliciting preferences for adoption of fully automated vehicles using best-worst analysis. *Transp. Res. Part C Emerg. Technol.* **2018**, *93*, 463–478. [CrossRef]
34. Gkartzonikas, C.; Gkritza, K. What have we learned? A review of stated preference and choice studies on autonomous vehicles. *Transp. Res. Part C Emerg. Technol.* **2019**, *98*, 323–337. [CrossRef]
35. Nastjuk, I.; Herrenkind, B.; Marrone, M.; Brendel, A.B.; Kolbe, L.M. What drives the acceptance of autonomous driving? An investigation of acceptance factors from an end-user's perspective. *Technol. Forecast. Soc. Chang.* **2020**, *161*, 120319. [CrossRef]
36. Regan, M.; Cunningham, M.; Dixit, V.; Horberry, T.; Bender, A.; Weeratunga, K.; Hassan, A. Preliminary Findings from the First Australian National Survey of Public Opinion about Automated and Driverless Vehicles. *Transportation* **2017**. [CrossRef]
37. Pettigrew, S.; Talati, Z.; Norman, R. The health benefits of autonomous vehicles: Public awareness and receptivity in Australia. *Aust. N. Z. J. Public Health* **2018**, *42*, 480–483. [CrossRef]
38. Pettigrew, S.; Dana, L.M.; Norman, R. Clusters of potential autonomous vehicles users according to propensity to use individual versus shared vehicles. *Transp. Policy* **2019**, *76*, 13–20. [CrossRef]
39. Pettigrew, S.; Worrall, C.; Talati, Z.; Fritschi, L.; Norman, R. Dimensions of attitudes to autonomous vehicles. *Urban Plan. Transp. Res.* **2019**, *7*, 19–33. [CrossRef]
40. Ledger, S.A.; Cunningham, M.L.; Regan, M.A. Public Opinion about Automated and Connected Vehicles in Australia and New Zealand: Results from the 2nd ADVI Public Opinion Survey. In ADVI Australia and New Zealand Driverless Vehicle Initiative Project; 2018. 28th ARRB International Conference—Next Generation Connectivity. Available online: https://trid.trb.org/view/1987511 (accessed on 18 November 2022).
41. Kaur, K.; Rampersad, G. Trust in driverless cars: Investigating key factors influencing the adoption of driverless cars. *J. Eng. Technol. Manag.* **2018**, *48*, 87–96. [CrossRef]
42. Cunningham, M.L.; Regan, M.A.; Horberry, T.; Weeratunga, K.; Dixit, V. Public opinion about automated vehicles in Australia: Results from a large-scale national survey. *Transp. Res. Part A Policy Pract.* **2019**, *129*, 1–18. [CrossRef]
43. Butler, L.; Yigitcanlar, T.; Paz, A. Factors influencing public awareness of autonomous vehicles: Empirical evidence from Brisbane. *Transp. Res. Part F Traffic Psychol. Behav.* **2021**, *82*, 256–267. [CrossRef]
44. Nordhoff, S.; Kyriakidis, M.; van Arem, B.; Happee, R. A multi-level model on automated vehicle acceptance (MAVA): A review-based study. *Theor. Issues Ergon. Sci.* **2019**, *20*, 682–710. [CrossRef]

45. Dong, X.; DiScenna, M.; Guerra, E. Transit user perceptions of driverless buses. *Transportation* **2017**, *46*, 35–50. [CrossRef]
46. Winter, K.; Cats, O.; Correia, G.; van Arem, B. Performance analysis and fleet requirements of automated demand-responsive transport systems as an urban public transport service. *Int. J. Transp. Sci. Technol.* **2018**, *7*, 151–167. [CrossRef]
47. Roche-Cerasi, I. Public acceptance of driverless shuttles in Norway. *Transp. Res. Part F Traffic Psychol. Behav.* **2019**, *66*, 162–183. [CrossRef]
48. Acheampong, R.A.; Cugurullo, F. Capturing the behavioural determinants behind the adoption of autonomous vehicles: Conceptual frameworks and measurement models to predict public transport, sharing and ownership trends of self-driving cars. *Transp. Res. Part F Traffic Psychol. Behav.* **2019**, *62*, 349–375. [CrossRef]
49. Alessandrini, A.; Alfonsi, R.; Site, P.D.; Stam, D. Users' Preferences towards Automated Road Public Transport: Results from European Surveys. *Transp. Res. Procedia* **2014**, *3*, 139–144. [CrossRef]
50. Alessandrini, A.; Delle Site, P.; Zhang, Q.; Marcucci, E.; Gatta, V. Investigating users' attitudes towards conventional and automated buses in twelve European cities. *Investig. Users' Attitudes Towards Conv. Autom. Buses Twelve Eur. Cities* **2016**, *43*, 413–436.
51. Wien, J. An Assessment of the Willingness to Choose a Self-Driving Bus for an Urban Trip: A Public Transport User's Perspective. Master's Thesis, Delft University of Technology, Delft, The Netherlands, 2019.
52. Winter, K.; Wien, J.; Molin, E.; Cats, O.; Morsink, P.; van Arem, B. Taking The Self-Driving Bus: A Passenger Choice Experiment. In Proceedings of the 2019 6th International Conference on Models and Technologies for Intelligent Transportation Systems (MT-ITS), Cracow, Poland, 5–7 June 2019.
53. Dekker, M. Riding a Self-Driving Bus to Work: Investigating How Travellers Perceive ADS-DVs on the Last Mile. Master's Thesis, Delft University of Technology, Delft, The Netherlands, 2017.
54. Anania, E.; Rice, S.; Walters, N.; Pierce, M.; Winter, S.; Milner, M. The effects of positive and negative information on consumers' willingness to ride in a driverless vehicle. *Transp. Policy* **2018**, *72*, 218–224. [CrossRef]
55. Madigan, R.; Louw, T.; Wilbrink, M.; Schieben, A.; Merat, N. What influences the decision to use automated public transport? Using UTAUT to understand public acceptance of automated road transport systems. *Transp. Res. Part F Traffic Psychol. Behav.* **2017**, *50*, 55–64. [CrossRef]
56. Nordhoff, S.; Van Arem, B.; Merat, N.; Madigan, R.; Ruhrort, L.; Knie, A.; Happee, R. User acceptance of driverless shuttles running in an open and mixed traffic environment. In Proceedings of the 12th ITS European Congress, Strasbourg, France, 19–22 June 2017.
57. Pakusch, C.; Bossauer, P. User Acceptance of Fully Autonomous Public Transport. In Proceedings of the 14th International Joint Conference on e-Business and Telecommunications (ICETE 2017), Madrid, Spain, 24–26 July 2017.
58. Madigan, R.; Louw, T.; Dziennus, M.; Graindorge, T.; Ortega, E.; Graindorge, M.; Merat, N. Acceptance of Automated Road Transport Systems (ARTS): An Adaptation of the UTAUT Model. *Transp. Res. Procedia* **2016**, *14*, 2217–2226. [CrossRef]
59. Moták, L.; Neuville, E.; Chambres, P.; Marmoiton, F.; Monéger, F.; Coutarel, F.; Izaute, M. Antecedent variables of intentions to use an autonomous shuttle: Moving beyond TAM and TPB? *Eur. Rev. Appl. Psychol.* **2017**, *67*, 269–278. [CrossRef]
60. Kostorz, N.; Hilgert, T.; Kagerbauer, M.; Vortisch, P. What do people think about autonomous minibuses in Germany. In Proceedings of the Symposium der European Association for Research in Transportation (hEART), Budapest, Hungary, 4–6 September 2019.
61. Portouli, E.; Karaseitanidis, G.; Lytrivis, P.; Amditis, A.; Raptis, O.; Karaberi, C. Public attitudes towards autonomous mini buses operating in real conditions in a Hellenic city. In Proceedings of the 2017 IEEE Intelligent Vehicles Symposium (IV), Los Angeles, CA, USA, 11–14 June 2017; pp. 571–576.
62. Alessandrini, A.; Delle Site, P.; Stam, D.; Gatta, V.; Marcucci, E.; Zhang, Q. Using Repeated-Measurement Stated Preference Data to Investigate Users' Attitudes Towards Automated Buses Within Major Facilities. In *Advances in Systems Science, Proceedings of the International Conference on Systems Science 2016 (ICSS 2016), Wroclaw, Poland, 7–9 September 2016*; Springer International Publishing: Berlin/Heidelberg, Germany, 2016; pp. 189–199.
63. Available online: https://www.abs.gov.au/statistics/economy/national-accounts/australian-national-accounts-state-accounts/latest-release (accessed on 18 November 2022).
64. Mortoja, M.G.; Yigitcanlar, T. Public perceptions of peri-urbanism triggered climate change: Survey evidence from South East Queensland, Australia. *Sustain. Cities Soc.* **2021**, *75*, 103407. [CrossRef]
65. Krejcie, R.V.; Morgan, D.W. Determining sample size for research activities. *Educ. Psychol. Meas.* **1970**, *30*, 607–610. [CrossRef]
66. George, D.; Mallery, P. *IBM SPSS Statistics 27 Step by Step: A Simple Guide and Reference*, 17th ed.; Routledge: New York, NY, USA, 2021.
67. Daoud, J.I. Multicollinearity and Regression Analysis. *J. Phys. Conf. Ser.* **2017**, *949*, 012009. [CrossRef]
68. Ben-Akiva, M.; McFadden, D.; Gärling, T.; Gopinath, D.; Walker, J.; Bolduc, D.; Rao, V. Extended Framework for Modeling Choice Behavior. *Mark. Lett.* **1999**, *10*, 187–203. [CrossRef]
69. Thapa, D.; Gabrhel, V.; Mishra, S. What are the factors determining user intentions to use AV while impaired? *Transp. Res. Part F Traffic Psychol. Behav.* **2021**, *82*, 238–255. [CrossRef]
70. Pallant, J. *SPSS Survival Manual: A Step by Step Guide to Data Analysis Using IBM SPSS*; Routledge: New York, NY, USA, 2020.
71. Briggs, S.R.; Cheek, J.M. The role of factor analysis in the development and evaluation of personality scales. *J. Personal.* **1986**, *54*, 106–148. [CrossRef]

72. Bursac, Z.; Gauss, C.H.; Williams, D.K.; Hosmer, D.W. Purposeful selection of variables in logistic regression. *Source Code Biol. Med.* **2008**, *3*, 17. [CrossRef]
73. Allison, P.D. *Logistic Regression Using SAS: Theory and Application*; SAS Institute: Singapore, 2012.
74. Brant, R. Assessing proportionality in the proportional odds model for ordinal logistic regression. *Biometrics* **1990**, *46*, 1171–1178. [CrossRef]
75. Liu, X. *Applied Ordinal Logistic Regression Using Stata: From Single-Level to Multilevel Modelling*; Sage Publications: Newbury Park, CA, USA, 2015.
76. McHugh, M.L. The odds ratio: Calculation, usage, and interpretation. *Biochem. Medica* **2009**, *19*, 120–126. [CrossRef]
77. Szumilas, M. Explaining odds ratios. *J. Can. Acad. Child Adolesc. Psychiatry = J. L'academie Can. Psychiatr. L'enfant L'adolescent* **2010**, *19*, 227–229.
78. Norton, E.C.; Dowd, B.E.; Maciejewski, M.L. Odds ratios—Current best practice and use. *JAMA* **2018**, *320*, 84–85. [CrossRef]
79. Golbabaei, F.; Yigitcanlar, T.; Paz, A.; Bunker, J. Navigating Autonomous Demand Responsive Transport: Stakeholder Perspectives on Deployment and Adoption Challenges. *Int. J. Digit. Earth*, 2023, in press.
80. Fraszczyk, A.; Mulley, C. Public Perception of and Attitude to Driverless Train: A Case Study of Sydney, Australia. *Urban Rail Transit* **2017**, *3*, 100–111. [CrossRef]
81. Dennis, S.; Paz, A.; Yigitcanlar, T. Perceptions and attitudes towards the deployment of autonomous and connected vehicles: Insights from Las Vegas, Nevada. *J. Urban Technol.* **2021**, *28*, 75–95. [CrossRef]
82. Paz, A.; Arteaga, C.; Cobos, C. Specification of mixed logit models assisted by an optimization framework. *J. Choice Model.* **2019**, *30*, 50–60. [CrossRef]
83. Golbabaei, F.; Yigitcanlar, T.; Paz, A.; Bunker, J. Understanding Autonomous Shuttle Adoption Intention: Predictive Power of Pre-Trial Perceptions and Attitudes. *Sensors* **2022**, *22*, 9193. [CrossRef] [PubMed]
84. Beeramoole, P.; Arteaga, C.; Haque, M.; Pinz, A.; Paz, A. Extensive hypothesis testing for estimation of mixed-Logit models. *J. Choice Model.* **2023**, *47*, 100409. [CrossRef]

Disclaimer/Publisher's Note: The statements, opinions and data contained in all publications are solely those of the individual author(s) and contributor(s) and not of MDPI and/or the editor(s). MDPI and/or the editor(s) disclaim responsibility for any injury to people or property resulting from any ideas, methods, instructions or products referred to in the content.

 *sustainability*

Article

An Economic Feasibility Model for Sustainable 5G Networks in Rural Dwellings of South Africa

Hloniphani Maluleke [1,*], Antoine Bagula [1], Olasupo Ajayi [1,*] and Luca Chiaraviglio [2]

[1] Department of Computer Science, University of the Western Cape, Cape Town 7535, South Africa
[2] Department of Electronic Engineering, University of Rome Tor Vergata, 00133 Rome, Italy
* Correspondence: hhmaluleke@uwc.ac.za (H.M.); ooajayi@uwc.ac.za (O.A.)

Abstract: Numerous factors have shown Internet-based technology to be a key enabler in achieving the sustainable development goals (SDG), as well as narrowing the divide between the global north and south. For instance, smart farming, remote/online learning, and smart grids can be used to, respectively, address SDGs 1 and 2 (ending poverty and hunger), 3 (quality education), and 7 and 9 (energy and infrastructure development). Though such Internet-based solutions are commonplace in the global north, they are missing or sparsely available in global south countries. This is due to several factors including underdevelopment, which dissuades service providers from investing heavily in infrastructure for providing capable Internet solutions such as 5G networks in these regions. This paper presents a study conducted to evaluate the feasibility of deploying 5G networks in the rural dwellings of South Africa at affordable rates, which would then serve as a pre-cursor for deploying solutions to improve lives and achieve the SDGs. The study evaluates the economic viability of a hybrid network model which combines terrestrial and aerial networks to provide 5G coverage in rural areas. The feasibility study reveals that such a network can be engineered at low monthly subscription fees to the end users and yield good returns to the service providers in rural areas; however, for large but sparsely populated suburban locations, the traditional terrestrial network with base stations is more suitable.

Keywords: 5G; economic feasibility; internal rate of return (IRR); sustainable development; unmanned aerial drones (UAV)

Citation: Maluleke, H.; Bagula, A.; Ajayi, O.; Chiaraviglio, L. An Economic Feasibility Model for Sustainable 5G Networks in Rural Dwellings of South Africa. *Sustainability* 2022, *14*, 12153. https://doi.org/10.3390/su 141912153

Academic Editors: Rashid Mehmood, Tan Yigitcanlar and Juan M. Corchado

Received: 30 July 2022
Accepted: 14 September 2022
Published: 26 September 2022

Copyright: © 2022 by the authors. Licensee MDPI, Basel, Switzerland. This article is an open access article distributed under the terms and conditions of the Creative Commons Attribution (CC BY) license (https:// creativecommons.org/licenses/by/ 4.0/).

1. Introduction

According to the United Nation's World Economic Situation and Prospect (WESP), globally, countries fall into one of three categories based on their economy: developed economy, economy in transition, and developing economies [1]. Most of the countries in Europe, North America, and Australia are classified as developed or in transition, while those in Africa, Asia, and South America are considered developing or "global south" nations. While the global north nations lead in terms of technological advancements and high standards of living, global south nations are in contrast characterized by a human development index lower than 0.8, gross national income per capita of USD 4100 or less, dilapidated infrastructures, and limited access to basic human needs. Narrowing the gap between the global north and south countries is one of the purposes of the sustainable development goals (SDG), specifically goals one to nine: ending poverty (1) and hunger (2), access to good health (3), quality education (4), equity (5), potable water (6), energy (7), economic growth (8), and infrastructure development (9) [2].

Recent evidence has shown that technology plays a pivotal role in achieving many of the SDGs, and its adequate deployment can help in narrowing the gap between the global north and south nations. For instance, by applying smart agricultural practices, crop yield can be improved to address world hunger [3], while wireless body sensors and the Internet of Things (IoT) can be used to monitor patients remotely [4,5]. Similarly, cloud collaboration can be used to improve infrastructure and economic growth [6], online and remote learning to provide quality education [7], and sensor networks to monitor water quality for drinking and irrigation [8]. A common factor among these technological solutions is a good communication network, which enables the interconnection of millions of access networks scattered across the world, as well as providing billions of global users with access to these networks via the Internet. Hence, both the Internet and next-generation mobile networks can be considered primary enablers of sustainable development.

The rapid proliferation of mobile devices and the corresponding growth in the volume of multimedia data traffic have necessitated the push to re-architect the current generation of cellular mobile communication and move into the fifth generation of cellular technology. The fifth generation (5G) is characterized by three unique features, viz., ubiquitous connectivity, extremely low latency, and ultra-high-speed data transfer [9]. The fifth generation has been introduced with the promise of unlimited bandwidth, lower latencies, and virtualization capabilities, enabling network operators to meet the expected capacity demand from a multitude of emerging bandwidth-hungry and real-time applications. On the other hand, in an emerging ICT sector aiming at tremendous increases in bandwidth, reduction in latency, and drastic emissions reduction to mitigate the impact of climate change, 5G will enable many industry sectors to align with different SDGs, including:

- SDG 3, related to "good health and well-being", by using smart wearables to increase the efficiency and effectiveness of medical treatments.
- SDG 4, related to "equitable quality education", by enabling quality education via online channels without the need for large-scale land and construction.
- SDG 8, related to "decent work and economic growth", by providing faster data access leading to improved human performance, increased skills, and inclusive growth.
- SDG 9, related to "industry, innovation and infrastructure", by relying on its underlying technologies to increase precision in manufacturing, can save materials and energy.
- SDG 11, related to "sustainable cities and communities", by using the integration of 5G and IoT to optimize transport, traffic, and city transformation by citizens.
- SDG 13, related to "climate action", by building around 5G to digitize a range of services and industries and therefore reducing greenhouse gas emissions and global warming, while simultaneously saving energy.

Though Internet penetration has improved significantly in the past few decades, many global south countries still lag their northern counterparts. Several factors are responsible for this lag, including inadequate electricity supply (goal 7), poor supporting infrastructure (goal 9), stunted economy (goal 8), and limited purchasing power of the population (goal 1). These factors discourage telecommunication service providers (TSPs) from building expensive network infrastructure in locations where the potential to recuperate returns on huge capital expenditure (CAPEX) and operational expenditure (OPEX) is limited.

Therefore, it is important to reduce the factors affecting the total cost of ownership (TCO) for mobile network operators and mobile service providers, especially as there might be a mismatch between the requirements of the market and capabilities provided by network equipment. Telecommunication base stations (BS) are extremely expensive, running into thousands of USD. Beyond the cost element, it also takes several months for the necessary licence(s) to be approved. Table 1 summarises the primary cost estimation of acquiring a spectrum licence in South Africa (ZA). The actual cost of the spectrum blocks is not included because these are often auctioned to the highest bidder.

As an alternative to this expensive outlay, several solutions have been proposed to provide 5G network coverage to developing nations. These include beaming down Internet from the sky using balloons, as was the case with Google's Project Loon [10], or using hybrid networks, which utilize a combination of air-based unmanned aerial vehicles (UAVs) or drones with terrestrial-based communication radios to provide Internet. One such hybrid network was proposed in [11,12]. This work focuses on the hybrid network illustrated in

Figure 1 and discusses the economic viability of such a network in a developing country such as South Africa (ZA).

Table 1. Spectrum cost matrix.

Feature	Prices
Individual Application	ZAR 500,000 (USD 32,000)
Class Application	ZAR 12,187 (USD 790)
Renewal	ZAR 6094 (USD 380)
Amendment	ZAR 60,940 (USD 3800)
Uni Price per MHz	ZAR 2344 (USD 160)
Price per Block	Auctioned
Auction Investment	ZAR 25 Bn (USD 1.5 Bn)
Satellite Hub Station	ZAR 58,596 (USD 3700)

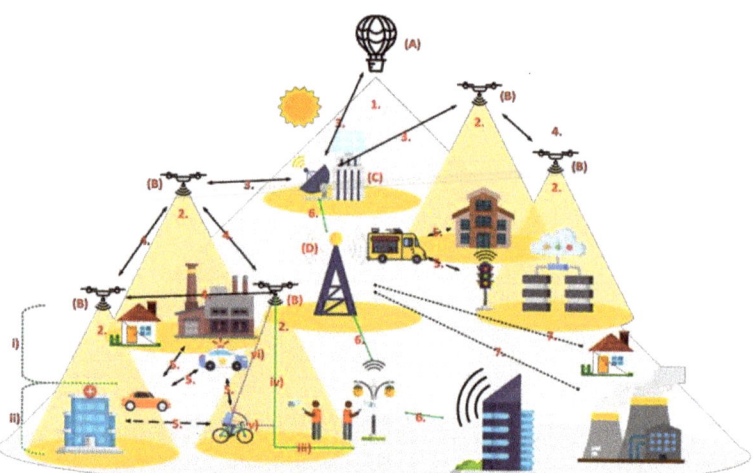

Figure 1. Hybrid 5G network. A = RRH-Balloon; B = RRH-UAV; 2 = UAV coverage area; C = terrestrial base station; D = cell tower; 1, 3, and 4 = backbone network; 5, 6, and 7 = wireless network [12].

In the hybrid network presented in Figure 1, three types of networks are considered to provide 5G coverage to rural areas. The first is by using UAVs, which relay Internet from terrestrial base stations over a coverage area. The second is through the use of cell towers, as is the case with mobile cellular networks; we refer to this as large cell (LC)-based. The third is by using wireless networks or Wi-Fi access points mounted in and around buildings; we refer to this as Hotspot.

The major contribution of this work is thus to determine if such a hybrid network is viable for providing 5G network access to rural dwelling areas of ZA. Thirteen locations were selected, viz., five district municipalities, four township areas, three rural residential areas, and one low-income town, with the expectation of:

- Determining the number of cell nodes required to effectively provide coverage in these locations as carried out in [13].
- Comparing the terrestrial networks (LC and Hotspot) to the aerial (UAV) network in terms of expenses and profitability for the TSP across all 13 locations.
- Revealing the optimal billing model (per gigabit or per minute) for users across the locations.

The remainder of this paper is as follows: Section 2 presents an overview of the economic model, including the description of the use cases. In Section 3, the economic feasibility analyses for both the capital and operation expenditures are presented, while the revenue analyses are conducted in Section 4. Section 5 then discusses the subscription fee required to sustain the model. Section 6 concludes the paper and gives some insights into future works.

2. Economic Model Foundation

Modern telecommunication systems have recently witnessed the convergence of cloud networking, fast connectivity, and high processing power taking place over the existing Internet model [14]. However, despite the gap between market requirements and network capabilities, there is still a significant absence of literature that caters to the rolling out of heterogeneous telecommunication technologies [14]. Frequently, researchers either concentrate solely on modelling the spatial viability aspect, as evidenced in the fixed broadband literature by [15], and/or on cost-effective radio network deployment such as in the work of [16]. It has been predicted that with the emerging heterogeneous 5G wireless network infrastructure, the administration of services and networks will be performed in an assembled way [17]. Hence, this works studies the total cost of ownership (CAPEX, OPEX, return on investment (ROI), internal rate of return (IRR), and the economic value added (EAV)) for deploying 5G basic wireless connections into rural and low-income areas of South Africa (ZA).

2.1. Assumptions and Scope

For this work, the following assumptions are made: (i). In computing the CAPEX, the costs of obtaining both the spectrum operating licence(s) and the Remote Operator's Certificate (ROC) for operating UAVs are not considered. This is due to the cumbersome process(es) involved, which cannot be directly modelled. (ii). For the aerial network, all UAVs are assumed to have autopilot functions, allowing them to hover over an area to supply coverage. Furthermore, they are equipped with energy-saving protocols for prolonged flight-times.

All cellular nodes have poor and limited connections to the public gateway base station. The economic framework considered in this study includes the cost of equipment and deployment scenarios that will enable the computation of CAPEX, OPEX, and the best monthly subscription fee. These financial and economic analyses are performed on 13 locations in ZA, which are split into five district municipalities, four townships, three rural residential areas, and one low-income town. For this work, we define a community as a cluster of individuals in the form of families living together, for a long time in a neighbourhood, while having mutual goals, interest, ways of life, and cultural norms. A rural community is thus an area under development and characterized as follows:

- Sparsely populated with clustered settlement.
- Residents are mostly involved in various forms of peasant agriculture with relatively low income. Recent statistics show that the average income of people living in rural areas is significantly lower than those in urban areas. For instance, in 2017, the average monthly income of a rural household in ZA was ZAR 2732 or USD 170 [18], while urban dwellers earned about ZAR 21,966 (USD 1442) [19].
- Rural communities experience slower development compared to urban areas because of the higher rate of illiteracy, smaller economy, and slower adaptation of modern technologies.
- Poor roads, mountainous landscapes, and few vehicles and transportation networks, all of which pose challenges to the installation and maintenance of cellular towers.
- Intermittent electricity supply from the grid makes it difficult to guarantee service quality in these areas, especially if the network equipment is powered by the grid.

2.2. Deployment Scenarios and Sites

As stated earlier, the economic analysis carried out in this study is performed to estimate the costs and possible revenue to be generated from deploying a hybrid 5G network architecture in certain areas of ZA, as well as the ideal monthly subscription fee for users in each location.

2.2.1. Demography

Table A1 gives a high-level description of the areas of interest in this work as extracted from the South African government's statistics website (Stats SA). It reveals that, on average, less than 10% of the young adult population has higher education and about 50% of them are unemployed. The table also reveals mining and agriculture as the prominent industries in these regions.

It is important to note that the values in Table A1 are simply used as a general guide and may not accurately reflect real-world conditions. For instance, in rural residential areas (such as Hlankomo and Gono'on'o), though the official statistics show that locations have an adequate electricity supply, physical visitation of the locations by the researcher reveals the complete opposite. There are no grid lines or electrical cables in these locations, and most homes have been without electricity for decades. A similar situation plays out in the Lulekani and Duduza township areas, with the exception being that most homes are visibly illegally connected to the electricity grid.

Municipalities

As stated earlier, five district municipalities are considered, namely Chris Hani in the Eastern Cape, Mopani, Vhembe, and Waterberg in Limpopo province, and Frances Baard in the Northern province. Figure 2 depicts the locations of these municipalities, as extracted from Google Maps. Chris Hani District Municipality is a Category C municipality situated in the north-eastern part of the Eastern Cape. It is the second-largest district, linking to all regions in the province. The municipality makes up six local municipalities, namely: Inxuba Yethemba, Intsika Yethu, Engcobo, Sakhisizwe, Enoch Mgijima, and Emalahleni. The Mopani District Municipality is found within the north-eastern quadrant of the Limpopo province. The district consists of five local municipalities: Ba-Phalaborwa, Greater Letaba, Greater Tzaneen, Maruleng, and Greater Giyani. Moreover, the Vhembe District Municipality is found in the northern part of the Limpopo province. It shares borders with Zimbabwe and Botswana in the north-west and Mozambique in the south-east through the Kruger National Park. It is made up of four local municipalities: Thulamela, Musina, Makhado, and Collins Chabane. The Waterberg District Municipality is a located in the western part of the Limpopo province. The municipality is the biggest district in the province, sharing its five-border control points with Botswana. It is comprised of five local municipalities: Bela-Bela, Modimolle-Mookgophong, Mogalakwena, Thabazimbi, and Lephalale. Another Category C municipality, Frances Baard District Municipality is a located in the far eastern part of the Northern Cape province. The municipality is the smallest district in the Northern Cape, accommodating the largest proportion of the province's population. It comprises the four local municipalities of Dikgatlong, Phokwane, Magareng, and Sol Plaatje.

Townships and Low-Income Areas

The four townships considered in this work are Soweto and Duduza (in Gauteng province), Khayelitsha (in Western Cape province), and Lulekani (in Limpopo province), while the low-income area was Zeerust (in North West province).

Soweto and Khayelitsha are low-income highly populated areas. Soweto has approximately 1,271,628 inhabitants and an average population density (user density) of 6400 people per square kilometre (users/km^2) [20]. Khayelitsha has a population of 391,749 inhabitants and an average of 10,000 people per square kilometre (users/km^2). The digital population statistics in ZA projects that about 80 of all Internet access will be through mobile phones in 2023 [21]; hence, for this study, we assume a modest 80% of the population in Soweto and Khayelitsha as active users of the Internet due to their proximity to Johannesburg and Cape Town, which are the two major economic hubs of ZA. Similarly, we propose an average downlink throughput of about 100 Mbps per user in these towns.

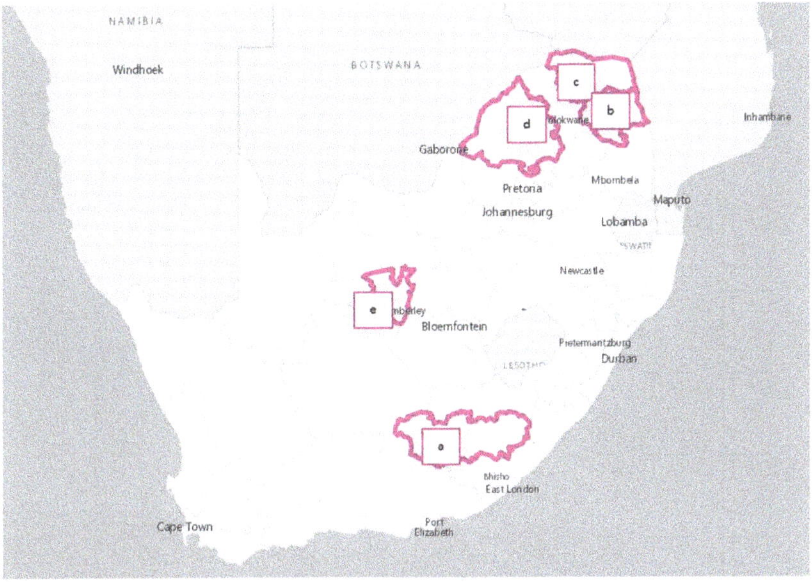

Figure 2. Map of District Municipality Areas: (**a**) Chris Hani; (**b**) Mopani; (**c**) Vhembe; (**d**) Waterberg; (**e**) Frances Baard.

Lulekani and Duduza are the two other township areas considered. Most areas within these towns do not have electricity, with only a few places illegally connected to the electricity grid. For these areas, the deployed network will have to rely mainly on solar power and batteries. We assume a download throughput of at least 50 Mbps for these areas, and about 60–80% of the population would have access to the Internet and use wireless communications. Zeerust is a small commercial town in North West province with approximately 9093 inhabitants. The main economy is based on cattle, wheat, maize, tobacco, and citrus fruit farming, as well as fluorite and chromite mining. It has an average user density of 160 users/km^2.

Rural Residential Areas

Hlankomo and Mandileni are rural residential areas in the Eastern Cape. Both have about 200 households and a population of approximately 1200 people each. Only 2% of these households have access to potable water within their dwellings. Gon'on'o is a village in Limpopo with similar characteristics to the two other areas. These three villages are not connected to the national electricity grids; hence, deployed 5G cells will have to be powered by solar panels and batteries.

2.2.2. Climate

Though there are numerous climatic conditions across ZA, and these climates can generally be grouped into three major categories, namely, arid, equatorial, and tropical [22]. Figure 3 shows a climate map, with the 13 locations of interest indicated. From the map, Frances Baard (F), Gon'on'o (G), Khayelitsha (K), Lulekani (L), Mopani (O), Vhembe (V), Waterberg (W), and Zeerust (Z) are in the arid regions, while Chris Hani (C), Duduza (D), Hlankomo (H), Mandileni (M), and Soweto (S) are in the tropical regions. Both the arid and tropical regions receive about 70% sunshine throughout the year, as shown in Figure 4. This makes them ideal locations for implementing the proposed hybrid 5G network.

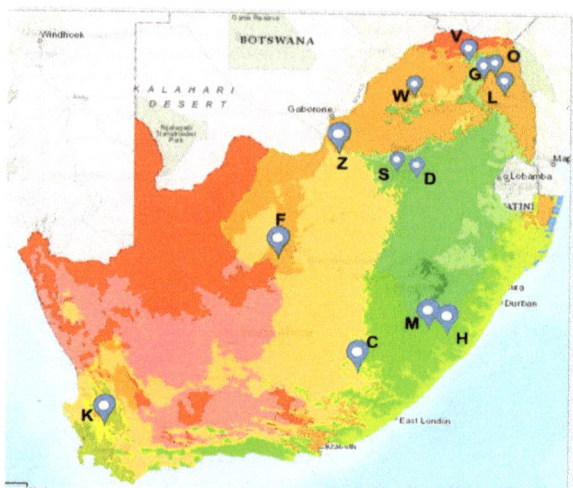

Figure 3. Climatic regions of ZA.

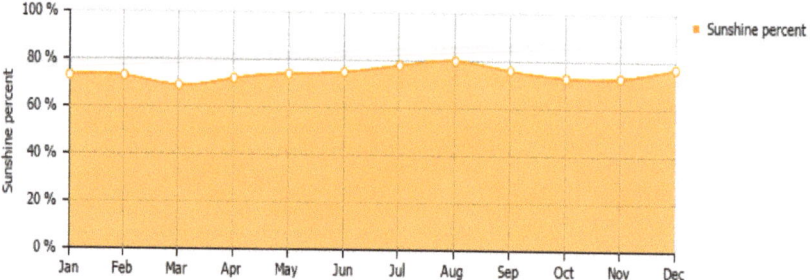

Figure 4. Average percentage of sunshine in specific regions of ZA [23].

2.2.3. Parameters Set over the Different Scenarios

Table A2 describes a detailed set of parameters for the different deployment scenarios. The lack of power grids in rural areas contributes to fewer people having devices that can access wireless networks. Hlankomo and Mandileni have a 30% active user ratio due to lack of electricity, while in sharp contrast, Duduza in Gauteng (an area also without legal connection to the electricity grid) has a higher active user ratio of 80%.

3. Economic Feasibility Objectives

The commercial feasibility analysis consists of determining the financial investments required for the implementation of the proposed network architecture in rural areas and if a sufficient return on investment can be obtained in the shortest period. Starting a new business can be extremely costly; hence, it is crucial to have a business plan that analyses the CAPEX needed to obtain necessities and implement the services to be offered. Likewise, to determine the IRR (internal rate of returns), the daily operational cost must be known. This section estimates both CAPEX and OPEX for deploying the proposed hybrid 5G network across 13 different locations in South Africa, as well as the computation of the minimum monthly subscription fees that will yield an ideal IRR for each deployment scenario.

Table 2 discusses the essential tangible and intangible requirements that form the basis of this analysis. The analysis excludes marketing and brand awareness expenses. Three network types (UAV, LC, and Hotspot) are considered for providing 5G as described in the introductory section. The goal of this analysis is mainly to provide information on the benefits that the initial expenditure will bring and prove to service providers that investing in a rural area can be beneficial. The computations of the CAPEX, OPEX, IRR, and subscription fees for all scenarios were performed using Microsoft Excel and the Python programming language.

Table 2. Fifth generation network node features [24].

Feature	Symbol	Description	UAV-Based	LC-Based	Hotspot-Based
Lifetime	L	Average time before disposal.	5 years	10 years	5 years
Cell Radius	R	Maximum cell range.	0.5 km	10 km	0.5 km
Peak Capacity	γ	Maximum capacity available to users. We assume a maximum downlink throughput T^{MAX} = 100 Mbps.	4.2 Gbps	12.6 Gbps	67.2 Gbps
Max. Power	p^{MAX}	Maximum power consumed when the maximum available capacity to users is being utilized.	1.4 kW	3.5 kW	5.6 kW
Min. Power	p^{MIN}	Minimum power consumed when the node does not serve any user (20% of the maximum node power).	0.28 kW	0.88 kW	0.28 kW
Battery Cost	C_B	Cost of a lead-acid battery with 12 V and 200 Ah generating 2.4 kWh.		R2.2 k/battery	
Solar Panel Cost	C_{SP}	Cost for a standard module type, size 1 kWp, system losses 14%, tilt 20, azimuth 180, DC to AC size ratio 1.1, inverter efficiency 96%, ground coverage ratio 0.4.		R11.55 k/battery	
Computing HW Cost	C_{CHW}	Cost of high-level computing hardware (HW) and networking of the virtual functionalities.	R144.4 k	R433 k	R 144.4 k
Radio HW Cost	C_{RHW}	Cost of the Remote Radio Head (RRH) and interconnection between them.	R144.4 k	R938.2 k	R 39.5 k
UAV Cost	C_{UAV}	Cost for rotary-wing quadcopter with 5kg payload.	R62.1 k	-	-
Site Acquisition Cost	C_{SA}	The total site acquisition cost mainly depends on the cell type, the cost to connect the site to the electricity network (if available), and the cost to build an access road up to the cell location.			
Spectrum Licence Cost	C_{SL}	Cost for spectrum licensing.			
Node Maintenance Cost	C_M	The yearly cost of inspection, solar panel cleaning, and software updates.	R5.1 k/year	R7.65 k/year	R 2.55 k/year

3.1. Capital Expenditure

The capital expenditure (CAPEX) is the foundational business cost that creates future benefits. This includes the cost of tangible assets concerning remote cell computing hardware, site acquisition, and UAVs. Additionally, analysis of the number of 5G nodes required for various deployment scenarios is considered. The possible number of base stations (BS) can be easily obtained using Equation (1), defined as:

$$N_{BS} = \frac{(1+m) * T^{MAX}}{c} \tag{1}$$

where T^{MAX} is the total peak throughput capacity per node, C is the average capacity supplied by microcell, and m is the ratio of connected margin to c. The number of 5G RRH-UAVs (N_c) required is obtained using Equation (2), defined as:

$$N_C = max(N_{C_{area}}, N_{C_{users}}) \tag{2}$$

where $N_{C_{area}}$ is based on the size of the area A of interest, defined by

$$N_{C_{area}} = \frac{2 \cdot A}{3\sqrt{3} \cdot R_c^2} \tag{3}$$

and $N_{C_{users}}$ is based on the number of active users N_u.

$$N_{C_{users}} = \frac{N_u \cdot \alpha \cdot T}{\gamma} \tag{4}$$

R_c is the radius of the hexagonal cell coverage area, A is the size of the prescribed area, N_U is the total number of users, α is the ratio of active users in the network, T is the average throughput per subscribed user, and γ is the peak capacity of the RRH network cell.

3.1.1. Nodes Comparison

Here, the number of nodes required for each scenario described in Table A2 for each network type is presented. The value is determined using three approaches, which are "Based on Max" (Equation (2)), "Based on Area" (Equation (3)), and "Based on Active Users" (Equation (4)). The number of cellular networks forms the basis of the entire CAPEX analysis. It also influences the OPEX because the cost of operation grows in proportion to the number of nodes required.

In Figure 5a,b, comparisons of the various deployment scenarios are shown. The figures show the possible number of 5G nodes required for all three network types, varied number of active users, area sizes (in square meters), and highest values. It can be seen from Figure 5a that covering each of the municipalities (Mopani, Vhembe, Waterberg, Chris Hani, and France Baard) requires a significantly higher number of nodes compared to the rural areas, as shown in Figure 5b.

For the five municipalities, the area-based approach yields a higher value. Note that the "Based on Max" approach simply selects the higher value between the area-based approach and users-based approach and hence and would have the same value as the higher of the two. Though Soweto and Khayelitsha townships are smaller than the municipalities in area size, they have denser populations. This causes the user-based approach to be higher than the area-based approach, as depicted in the figure. Moreover, the two townships have a higher number of literates with access to cellular phones, the Internet, and multimedia, which also influences the higher value for the user-based approach.

3.1.2. Expense Analysis for Remote Access Network (RAN)

This sub-section discusses the CAPEX of three network types (UAV, LC, and Hotspot) over the same scenarios in Table A2. The total number of cell nodes obtained in the previous subsection is used in this CAPEX analysis. Equation (5) gives the total CAPEX needed to deploy a RAN using any of the network types.

$$CAPEX = N_C(C_B N_B + C_{SP} P_{SP} + C_{CHW} + C_{RHW} + C_{UAV} + C_{SA}) \tag{5}$$

Here, C_B is the cost of a single battery, N_B is the number of batteries per site, C_{SP} is the cost for one (kWp) of the solar panels, P_{SP} is the power of the solar panels per site, C_{CHW} is the cost of computing hardware, C_{RHW} is the radio hardware cost, C_{UAV} is the UAV cost, and C_{SA} is the site acquisition cost [24].

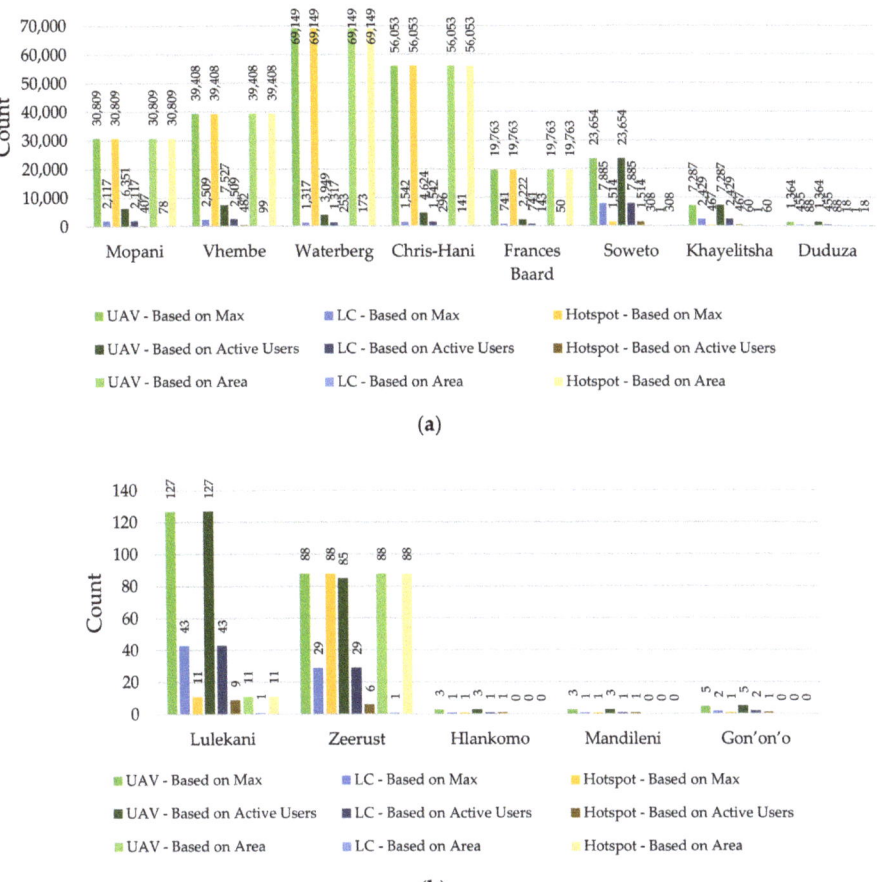

Figure 5. (a) Deployment for municipalities and township areas; (b) deployment for rural residential areas.

Based on the Number of End Users

Figure 6a–c depict the total CAPEX computed based on the number of users for the 13 locations. Each graph shows the cost of each parameter needed to deploy a network in South African rands. Interestingly, in each scenario, the UAV-based and Hotspot-based solutions consistently require more CAPEX than the LC-based solution. Across the board, the most substantial contributors to the costs are site acquisition and computing/radio hardware (HW) expenses, while the UAVs, solar panels, and batteries have a lower impact on the CAPEX. Of the municipalities, Vhembe has the highest number of users and hence the higher CAPEX; similarly, due to their dense populations, Soweto and Khayelitsha townships required much more CAPEX than the other township areas.

Based on Area Size

The CAPEX breakdown bar graphs in Figure 7 show the expenses of each scenario based on location size. Costs are directly proportional to the size of the targeted areas; hence, the five districts have significantly higher expenses compared to the other locations. The figures also show that due to the coverage area, the UAV-based and Hotspot-based solutions need greater CAPEX than the LC-based solution. This is because both models need more cell nodes to cover the entire area compared to LC, which only requires a few (possibly only one) nodes. Across the locations, site acquisition accounts for more than half of the entire CAPEX.

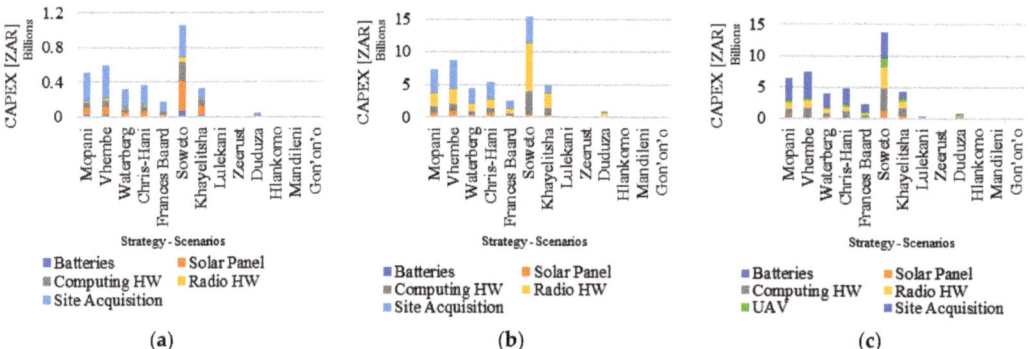

Figure 6. CAPEX breakdown based on the number of active users for each network type: (**a**) LC-based; (**b**) Hotspot-based; (**c**) UAV-based.

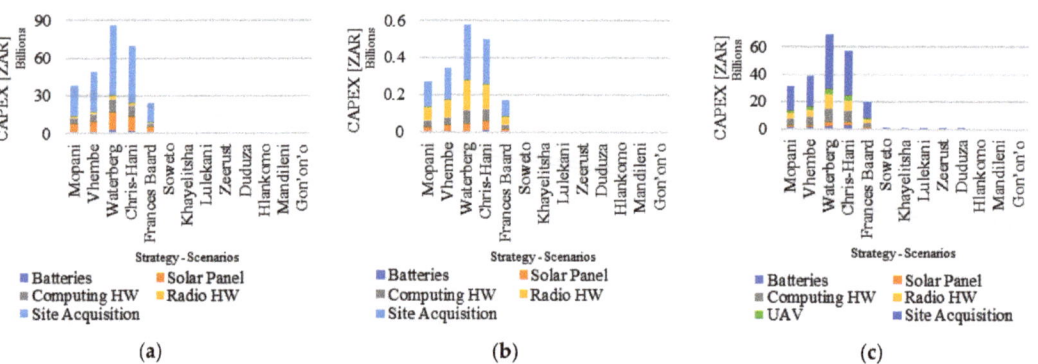

Figure 7. CAPEX breakdown based on area size for each network type: (**a**) LC-based; (**b**) Hotspot-based; (**c**) UAV-based.

Based on the Highest Number of Cells

Figure 8 presents the expenditures of each scenario by showing the analysis for RAN. Like the first two cases, the UAV-based and Hotspot-based solutions need greater CAPEX compared to the LC-based. However, in this analysis, the size of the scenario has a greater impact on the CAPEX, with the expenditure being significantly higher for the district municipalities.

For the rural residential areas, a single LC-based solution can supply basic network services over most of the considered areas. Looking closer at these zones, Gon'on'o requires five UAVs, two LCs, or a single Hotspot-based cellular node to provide full coverage to the village, while Mandileni and Hlankomo require either three UAVs, one LC, or one Hotspot-based cell. Though Gon'on'o is a small residential area, it needs more nodes than the other rural residential areas because there are more people who live there.

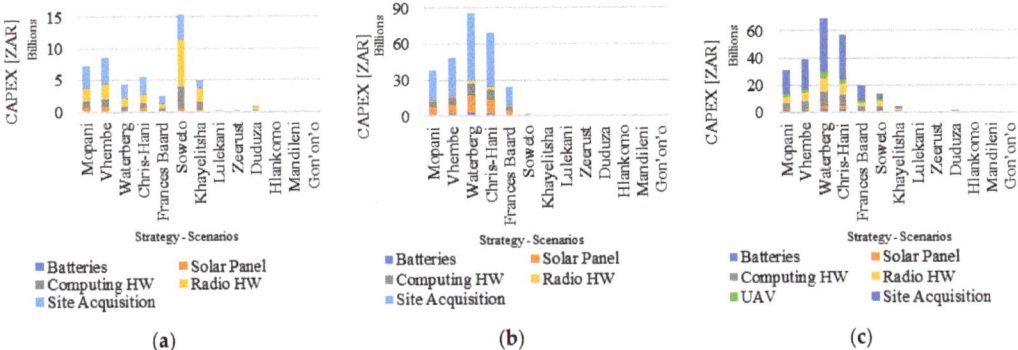

Figure 8. CAPEX breakdown based on highest number of cells: (**a**) LC-based; (**b**) Hotspot-based; (**c**) UAV-based.

For the townships, in the LC-based solution (Figure 8a), Soweto township has the highest CAPEX over all other scenarios because of its vast population density. Conversely, Mopani, Vhembe, Waterberg, Chris Hani, and Frances Baard municipalities have the highest CAPEX in the Hotspot-based (Figure 8b) and UAV-based (Figure 8c) solutions due to their immense area size. Despite the dense population of the townships, the UAV-based or Hotspot-based solution costs less. Computing and radio HW cost slightly more in the LC-based solution because the targeted scenarios have a vast area that requires many cells to have full coverage. Contrarily, they cost less in UAV-based and Hotspot-based solutions due to the coverage range of a single cellular unit. A considerably large area requires more cells, which in return contributes extensively to site acquisition expenses.

3.2. Operational Expenditure

Operational expenditure (OPEX) refers to costs incurred while operating the 5G network. It includes but is not limited to maintenance and administrative expenses. Other expenses, such as insurance, depreciation, and interest, are not considered in our OPEX calculation. For brevity, only the OPEX required to run the highest number of cells is shown, as this depicts the maximum expenditure. Equation (6) is used to compute the OPEX for an entire year:

$$OPEX_i = N_C \left[365 \cdot \left(\sum_h * P_h * C_E \right) + C_M \right] \quad (6)$$

where N_c is the number of deployed network cell nodes, which in this case refers to Equation (2), P_h is the power required from the electricity grid by the site at hour h, C_E is the cost for one kilowatt-hour (kWh) of energy, and C_M is the maintenance cost.

The line graph in Figure 9 depicts the expenses required to supply 5G network coverage for a year over the 13 selected locations using the three network types. In all scenarios, the LC-based network cost less than the others to operate. However, when using the LC network, Soweto township still required an OPEX of about ZAR 90 million (USD 5.7 m) annually, compared to the other locations with ZAR 30 million (USD 1.9 m) at most.

For the five municipalities, the Hotspot- and UAV-based systems cost significantly more to run than the LC-based model. Waterberg and Chris Hani have the largest area expanse and hence the priciest scenarios to run both network types. On the contrary, though Soweto has the smallest area compared to the district municipalities, it is expensive to run the UAV-based network there because of its huge population density. The low-income town and rural residential areas have the lowest OPEX of all network types due to their small area sizes and low population. These areas thus require fewer cells for coverage. The maximum OPEX for Lulekani, Zeerust, Duduza, Hlankomo, Mandileni, and Gon'on'o is ZAR 0.5 m (USD 0.32 m), irrespective of the cells deployed.

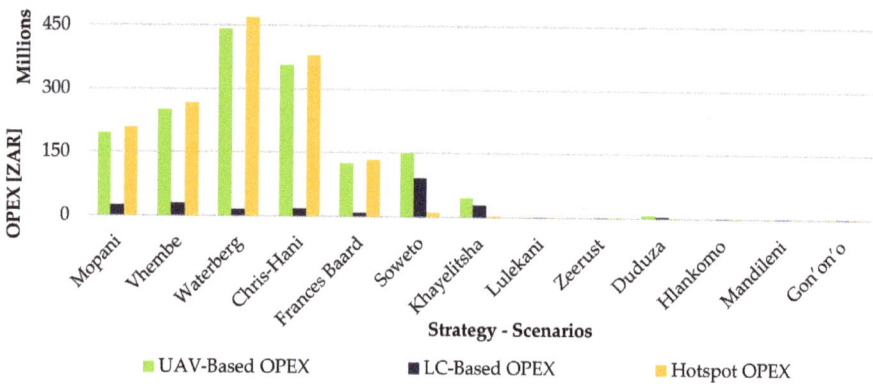

Figure 9. Operating expenditure over selected scenario.

4. Revenues over Time

This section analyses the return on investment (ROI) for deploying the proposed hybrid 5G network in some of the currently disadvantaged ZA areas. The standard statistical profitability ratio helps to determine the loss or profit obtained in each network type for the total CAPEX. Figure 10 depicts censors and generalized regional service charges for users over targeted scenarios. This revenue calculation assumes that the number of users remains relatively constant and that users pay their subscription fees monthly.

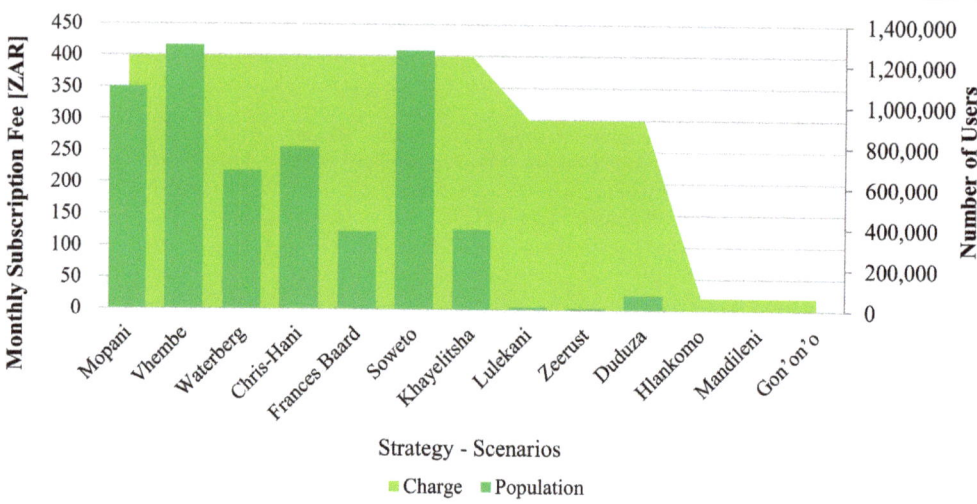

Figure 10. Population and service charge over scenarios.

The revenue (REV) is the income generated from network coverage service operations including discounts and network sharing, while cash flow (CF) is the net amount of money that moves into and out of a business. Furthermore, the IRR discount rate estimates the overall profitability of potential investments during CAPEX budgeting. It makes the net present value (NPV) of all CF from a network deployment project to be equal to zero. Moreover, IRR computations depend on the same formula as the NPV, with some slight adjustments.

4.1. Revenue Analysis

The yearly revenue (REV_i) forecasts profits to be made throughout the expected lifetime of the cell over the chosen areas, where i is the number of years, assuming each user pays a monthly subscription fee F to use the network. Equation (7) can thus be used to calculate income based on this constant monthly subscription.

$$REV_i = N_U \cdot 12 \cdot F \quad (7)$$

Figure 11 shows a line graph for the annual income of all network types. From a glance, all five district municipalities generate more revenue compared to rural residential areas and townships, while the France Baard region is the lowest producer, generating approximately ZAR 2b (USD 126 m) of income. Vhembe district municipality and Soweto township both have a vast population and as expected also have considerably higher revenue per year. Though Vhembe has the highest revenue, it is only marginally higher than Soweto, due to its lower average population density when compared to Soweto (see Table A2). Finally, for the rural residential areas, only about half a billion ZAR (USD 33 m) is attainable at most as revenue.

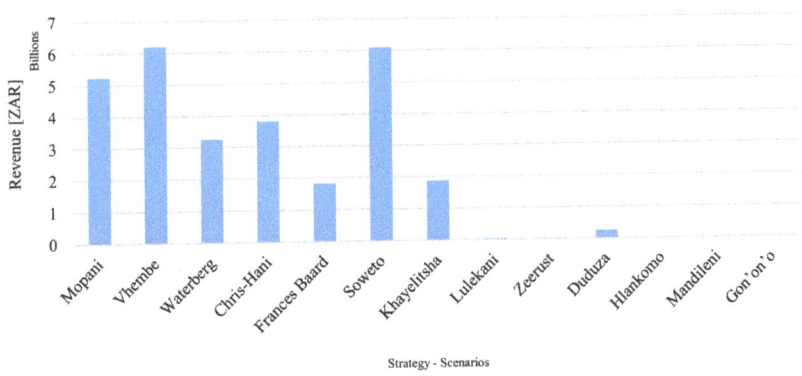

Figure 11. Revenue over selected scenario.

4.2. Cash Flows Analysis

With the revenue and expenditure obtained in the previous sections, the cash flow analysis can then be done. The expression in Equation (8) is for obtaining the operators' annual net cash flows (CF_i), where i is a specific year during the network operation, and l is the lifetime of the solution in years.

$$CF_i = \begin{array}{l} -OPEX \text{ for year } i = 0 \\ REV_i - OPEX_i \text{ for year } 0 < i < l \end{array} \quad (8)$$

At the inception (first year, where $i = 0$), we simply subtract the OPEX for that year. CF_i represents the profit or loss value of the network operator during a specific period.

Given the requisite knowledge of CF_i, it is important to first determine if the revenues can compensate the CAPEX and OPEX, by computing the net present value (NPV). Specifically, by definition, NPV is the summation of cash flows CF_i over the entire lifetime, each normalised by $(1 + \eta)$, where η is the discount rate, i.e., the return (in percentage), that could be earned with an ideal financial investment (such as bank funding, loans, etc.) [11]. Equation (9) adopted from [25] is used to calculate the NPV:

$$NPV = \sum_{i=1}^{L} \frac{CF_i}{(1+\eta)^i} - CF_0 \quad (9)$$

where CF_0 is the total first investment expense, and i is the period (in years).

The analysis starts with a current balance and produces a closing balance sheet after accounting for all cash inflows and outflows during the period. Using the monthly subscription fee (shown in Figure 10), the computed OPEX (using Equation (6)) and annual revenue (computed using Equation (7)), for the same scenario parameters on Table A2, the NPV can be calculated using Equation (9). The clustered column bar graph in Figure 12 depicts the NPV for the three network types.

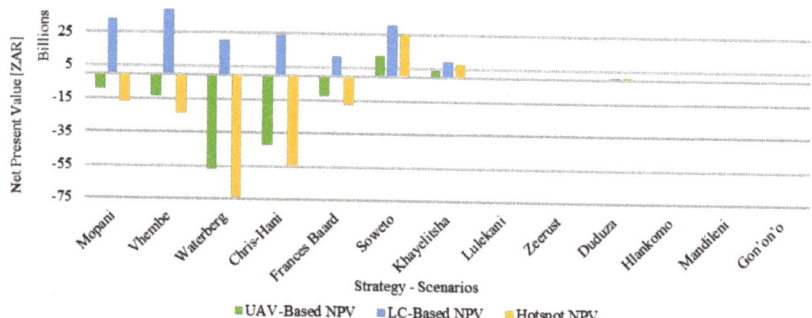

Figure 12. Net present value over selected scenario.

Interestingly, in each scenario, the LC-based solution with the proposed monthly subscription fee in Figure 10 yields a more profitable return than both the UAV- and Hotspot-based solutions. Hence, by using only UAV- and Hotspot-based solutions to supply 5G services to any district municipalities, the operator will not be able to recover the initial CAPEX. For instance, Waterberg region requires more than ZAR 55 B (USD 3.7 B) for both UAV- and Hotspot-based solutions to run until their lifetime expires, but it only generates about ZAR 3B (USD 200 m) (see Figure 11). In the case of Vhembe, due to its larger population compared to the other municipalities, it requires more SCs to fully supply coverage to the entire area and hence more expenditure. To this end, only the LC-based solution is more profitable in the district municipalities. On the contrary, the low-income and rural residential areas are profitable for all network type, with Soweto and Khayelitsha townships yielding the highest cash flows.

4.3. Internal Rate of Returns

The internal rate of return (IRR) is a measure of an investment's rate of return. The term "internal refers" to the fact that the calculation excludes external factors, such as the risk-free rate, inflation, the cost of capital, or various financial risks. To calculate the IRR, we set Equation (9) to zero and solved for the discount rate η (IRR) using the other values given.

The graphs in Figure 13 depict IRR for the three model solutions being considered over the 13 ZA locations. The LC-based solutions (Figure 13a) would require users to pay close to a ZAR 1,860 (USD 127) monthly subscription fee to obtain at least 10% IRR across all locations. When UAVs are used, Figure 13c reveals that with about ZAR 200 (USD 13), an IRR of 10% can be obtained across all locations. Finally, the Hotspot-based solution (Figure 13b) would require users to pay almost ZAR 1838 (USD 116) for a 10% IRR. In essence, by using UAVs, with a monthly subscription fee of just ZAR 30 (USD 2), a 50% IRR can be obtained in the rural areas or ZAR 200 (USD 13) for profitability across all locations.

$$F = \frac{NPV + NPO + C_0}{NPP_{N_u}} \qquad (10)$$

Here, NPO is the net present operational expenditure obtained using Equation (11), and NPP is the net present payment per user, calculated using Equation (12).

$$NPO = \sum_{i=1}^{L} \frac{OPEX_i}{(1+\eta)^i} \quad (11)$$

$$NPP = \sum_{i=1}^{L} \frac{N_U \cdot 12}{(1+\eta)^i} \quad (12)$$

Equation (12) yields the best monthly subscription fee, which is then used to obtain the IRR graph in Figure 14. A rate (η) of 30% was used to yield the subscription fee over the selected scenarios. The graph reveals that township areas such as Soweto, Khayelitsha, and Duduza have more potential for lucrative growth than any of the municipalities, while rural residential areas require less than ZAR 50 to yield a 100% IRR.

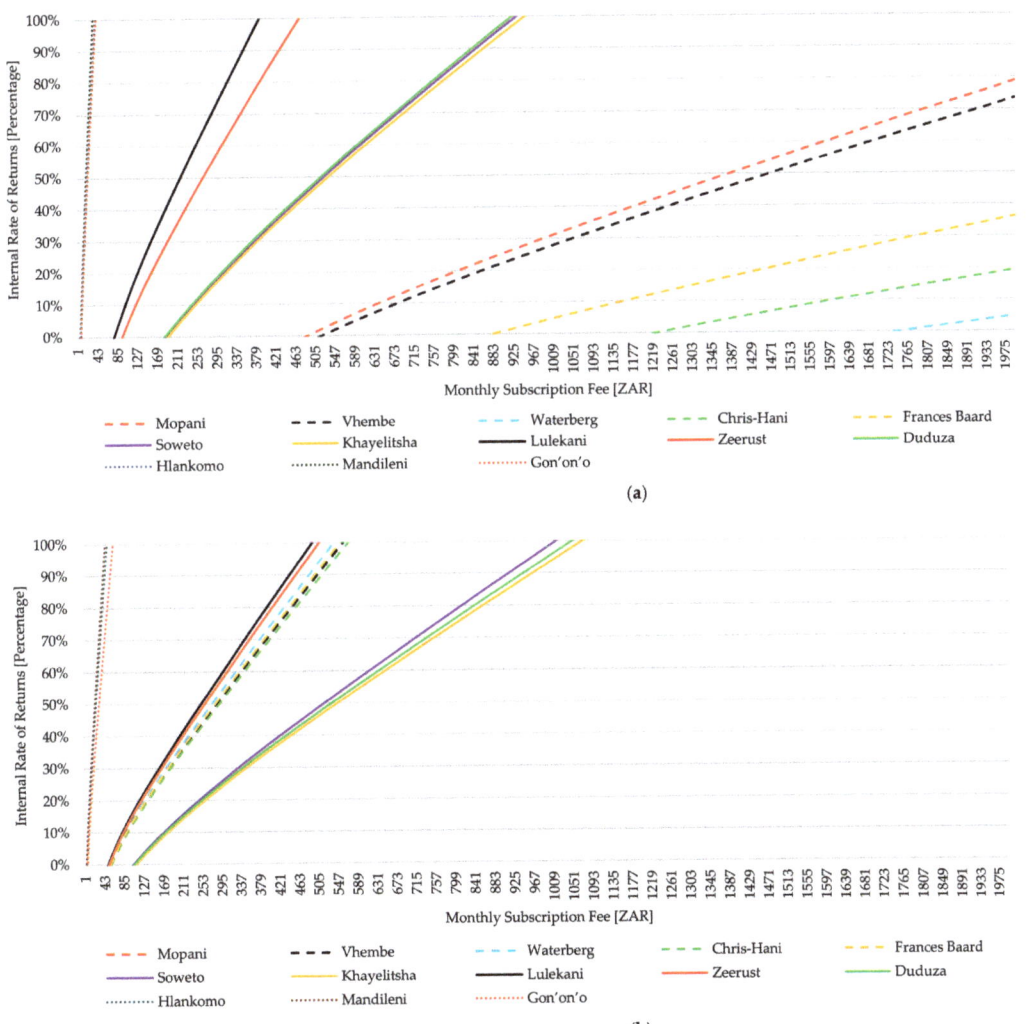

Figure 13. *Cont.*

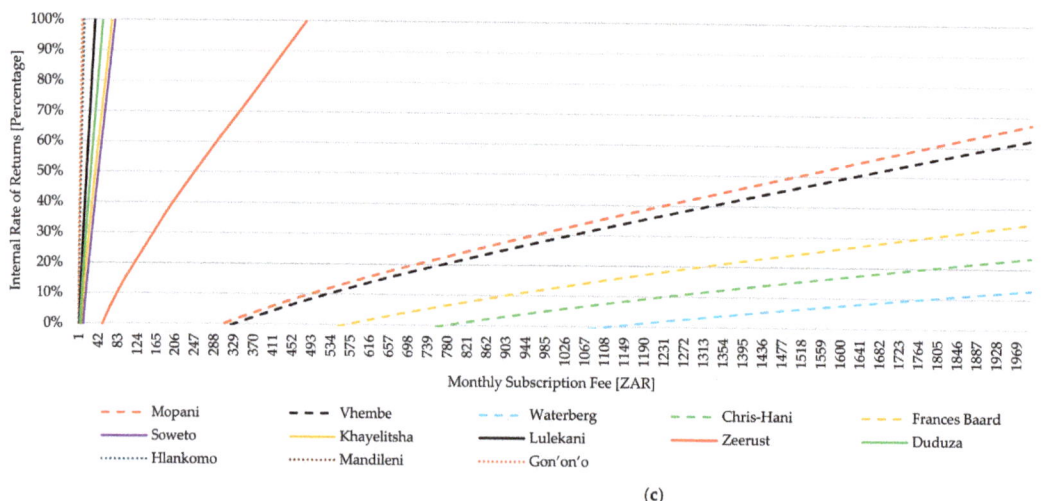

Figure 13. Internal rate of returns over the considered scenarios: (**a**) LC-based; (**b**) Hotspot-based; (**c**) UAV-based.

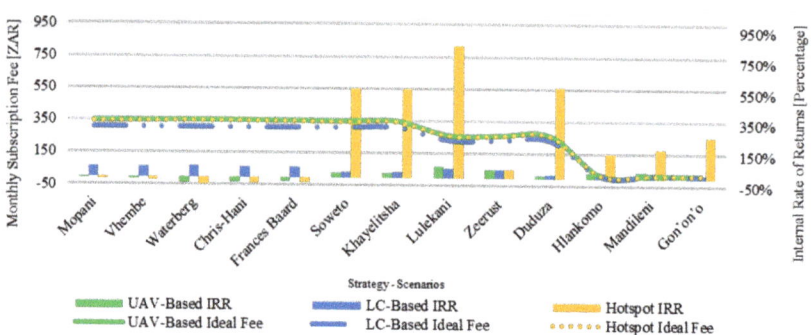

Figure 14. Internal rate of return based on monthly subscription fee over selected scenario.

5. End-User Subscription Fee

In an article published by Fin24, it was claimed that the South African telecommunication services providers MTN and Vodacom charged up to 2639% more for out-of-bundle data. It was also reported that while on contract, a Vodacom 20 GB data bundle costs ZAR 329 (USD 20.75) or ZAR 0.02 per megabyte, while for out-of-bundles the rate per megabyte was ZAR 0.44 (USD 0.03) [26]. This is an estimate of about 2630% higher for out-bundle than in-bundle. Similarly, MTN's 25 GB prepaid bundle costs ZAR 1250 (USD 79) or ZAR 0.05 per megabyte, while the out-of-bundle package cost ZAR 0.99 (USD 0.06) per megabyte. This represents a 1928% difference between in and out-of-bundle charges. Data bundle prices for major operators in ZA are compared in Table 3, with monthly data usage estimated from the Verizon Wireless website.

Table 3. Data bundle price comparison across ZA telecommunication service providers.

Usage	Size (GB/Month)		Price (ZAR)			
			Vodacom [1]	Telkom [2]	MTN [3]	Cell-C [4]
e-Mail (Text only)	7500 (e-Mail)	0.07		R29		
Web Access	7500 (pages)	10.99	R748	R598	R648	R748
Stream Music	60 (h)	3.52	R399	R275.25	R398	
Stream HD Video	15 (h)	30	R1 598	R1 398	R1 249	R899
Stream SD Video	30 (h)	19.04	R999	R899		R799
Upload and Download Photos	3000 (photos)	14.65	R999	R798	R899	R799
4G VoIP	60 (h)	2.64	R299	R199	R378	R299
4G VoIP with Video	60 (h)	15.23	R999	R837	R899	R799

[1] http://www.vodacom.co.za/vodacom/shopping/data/prepaid-data, (accessed on 18 September 2022);
[2] https://secure.telkom.co.za/today/shop/personal/plan/100-gb-data-bundles/, (accessed on 19 September 2022);
[3] https://www.mtn.co.za/Pages/MTNDataBundle.aspx (accessed on 18 September 2022); [4] https://www.cellc.co.za/cellc/bundles-contract-detail/DataBundles#/sku6850032, (accessed on 18 September 2022).

5.1. Monthly Subscription Fee

This section compares the average monthly subscription fees for uncapped data users (as at the time of writing) versus prepaid users. Figure 15 depicts uncapped subscription fees for five TSPs in ZA versus the proposed average monthly fee (ZAR 282 or USD 18) from the analysis of our hybrid 5G network.

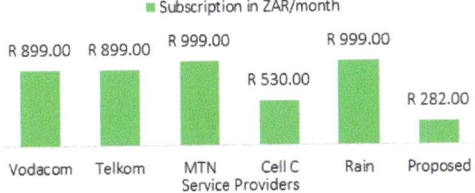

Figure 15. Monthly subscription fee comparison.

5.2. Capped Subscription Fee

A gigabit (Gb) is a unit measurement of digital storage that is based on binary multiples of bits, while a megabyte is based on binary multiples of bytes with MB being a standard symbol. There are 128 megabytes in a gigabit; hence, a transfer rate of 1 Gb/s is equal to 125 MB/s. Table 4 shows the estimated daily transfer capacity of different cells based on the sinusoidal function of power consumption given in Table 2. Equations (13) and (14) are used to obtain the prepaid subscription fees "per GB" and "per minute", respectively. These fees are inclusive of mandatory tax(es).

$$P_{GB} = \frac{N_c \cdot F}{\omega \cdot \alpha \cdot \beta} + Tax \quad (13)$$

$$P_t = \frac{N_c \cdot F}{t \cdot \alpha \cdot \beta} + Tax \quad (14)$$

The line graphs in Figure 16 depict the prepaid price for the three network types considered over the selected scenarios. The price modelling framework is based on Figure 14 and Equations (13) and (14), where t is time in minutes. Furthermore, the expression considers the probability of active users on the network and how long each user will be active. Both costs "per minute" and "per GB" graphs have different charge curves as shown in Figures 16 and 17. Overall, rates per GB are more expensive than per minute rates.

Table 4. Estimated daily data transfer.

	Symbol	UAV-Based	LC-Based	Hotspot
Peak Capacity	γ^{MAX}	15.12 Tb/h	45.36 Tb/h	241.92 Tb/h
Min. Capacity	γ^{MIN}	3.024 Tb/h	9.072 Tb/h	48.384 Tb/h
Mid. Capacity	m	6.048 Tb/h	18.144 Tb/h	96.768 Tb/h
Traffic per Day	ω	27.216 TB	81.648 TB	435.456 TB

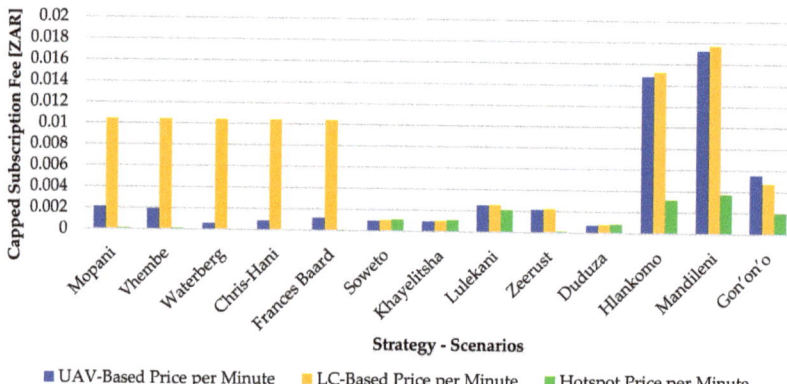

Figure 16. Capped User Subscription Fee—Per Minute.

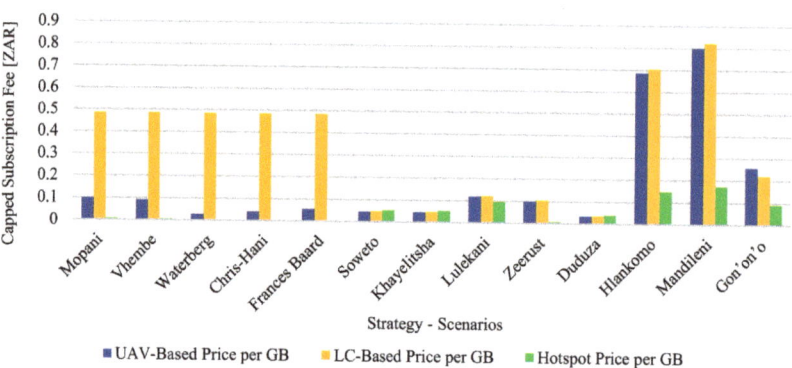

Figure 17. Capped user subscription fee (per GB).

The graphs reveal that the rural residential areas of Hlankomo and Mandileni would pay the most for all network types and significantly more for the LC- and UAV-based solutions. On the contrary, the users in the township areas pay the least across all network types, while the municipalities are charged about an average of the rural and township prices. Despite these values, it is important to note that our average proposed price for all three network types (UAV-, LC-, and Hotspot-based network) is ZAR 0.50 (USD 0.031) for 1 GB of data bundles. Even at a peak rate of ZAR 0.80 (USD 0.05), our proposed hybrid network is still extremely cheaper compared to other TSP rates, such as Telkom, which charges ZAR 60.00 (USD 3.8) or Cell C with a rate of ZAR 75.66 (USD 4.8) for 1 GB of data bundles.

6. Conclusions

The objective of this paper was to determine whether it is economically feasible to deploy a hybrid 5G network in rural areas, which uses cellular nodes (mounted on an unmanned aerial vehicle) to beam network coverage from the sky to users, while piggybacking on terrestrial cellular nodes. This network was to be deployed to serve as an enabler in achieving the sustainable development goals, including providing good health care, reducing poverty, and improving infrastructural development in less developed areas of the world. Thirteen locations were selected in South Africa, including five district municipalities, four township areas, three rural residential areas, and one low-income area. Three scenarios were considered per location, using three network types: UAV-based, Hotspot-based, and LC-based. In performing the analysis, the capital expenditure (CAPEX), operation expenditure (OPEX), internal rate of return (IRR), return on investment (ROI), and power requirements were considered. All of which were used to obtain the recommended monthly user subscription fees for Internet access per GB and per minute.

From the analysis, it can be concluded that it is more expensive to deploy the proposed hybrid 5G coverage in large but sparsely populated areas. For such areas, the traditional LC-based system is more profitable. On the contrary, implementing the hybrid architecture in rural residential areas costs less and yields higher revenue than low-income areas. The analysis also reveals that with the proposed model, the best monthly subscription fee will cost far less than the current data bundle prices being offered by telecommunications providers in South Africa.

It is important to note that this work did not consider several factors such as cost of acquiring the spectrum licence, cost of site constructions, electricity grid tariffs, staff salaries, depreciation, etc. These factors are vital and can impact the overall performance of the proposed network. Incorporating these factors might be one avenue of extending this work in future. In the same vein, various models for the optimal placement of UAVs to maximize network coverage could also be considered for future works.

Author Contributions: Conceptualization, A.B. and L.C.; methodology, H.M. and A.B.; software, H.M.; validation, A.B. and O.A.; formal analysis, O.A. and A.B.; investigation, H.M.; resources, L.C. and A.B.; data curation, H.M.; writing—original draft preparation, H.M.; writing—review and editing, O.A. and A.B.; visualization, H.M.; supervision, A.B. and O.A. All authors have read and agreed to the published version of the manuscript.

Funding: This research received no external funding.

Institutional Review Board Statement: Not applicable.

Informed Consent Statement: Not applicable.

Data Availability Statement: Not applicable.

Conflicts of Interest: The authors declare no conflict of interest.

Appendix A

Table A1. Demography of the 13 regions considered (adapted from [27]).

Parameters	Mopani	Vhembe	Waterberg	Chris Hani	Frances Baard	Soweto	Khayelitsha	Lulekani	Duduza	Zeerust	Hlankomo	Mandileni	Gon'on'o
	District	District	District	District	District	Township	Township	Township	Township	Low-Income	Rural Residential	Rural Residential	Rural Residential
Municipality						City of Johannesburg	City of Cape Town	Ba-Phalaborwa	City of Ekurhuleni	Ramotshere Moiloa	Ntabankulu		Greater Giyani
Main Economic Sectors	Mining (30.1%), Community Services (22.6%), Trade (14.6%), Finance (14.6%), Transport (8.2%), Agriculture (3.2%), Electricity (2.8%), Construction (2%)	Mining, Community services, Finance	Mining, Agriculture, Tourism	Community Services (52%), Trade (15%), Finance (14%), Transport (6%), Agriculture (4%), Manufacturing (4%), Electricity (2%)	Community services (28%), Finance (22%), Trade (15%), Transport (12%), Mining (10%), Agriculture (4%), Manufacturing (4%), Construction (3%), Electricity (2%)	Finance and business services, community services, manufacturing, trade (collectively 82%)	Finance and business services (36.1%), manufacturing (16.1%), trade and hospitality (15.6%), community services and general government (15.0%), transport, storage, and communication (11.2%), construction (4.1%), electricity (1.1%), agriculture (0.7%), mining (0.1%)	Mining, agriculture, manufacturing, tourism	Manufacturing (23%), finance and business services (21.3%), community services (20%), trade (15%), transport (11%), construction (4.1%), electricity (2.3%), mining (2.3%)		Agriculture, sand and quarry mining, forestry, tourism		Agriculture, tourism, retail, transport
Unemployment rate (Aged 15–34)	51.4%	~50.6% (Year 2011)		~60%	43.9% (Year 2011)	31.5 (Year 2011)	31.9 (Year 2011)	50.2%	28.8 (Year 2011)		53.7% (Year 2011)		61.2%
Higher Education (Aged 20+)	8.1%	9.6%	9%	6.5%	8.4%	14.7%	14.4%	9.2%	11.9%	5.8%	4.3%		8.5%
Piped water inside dwelling	12.8%	7.4%	24.4%	22.3%	48.4%	60%	76.7%	30.6%	56%	16.8%	1.1%		10.3%
Electricity	94.5%	94.6%	86.1%	89.9%	90.2%	90%	97.2%	98.1%	85.4%	88.6%	51%		92.5%
Sanitation	20.5%	20.9%		32.8%		86.2%	89.4%	20.5%	70.5%		2.0%		

Table A1. Cont.

Parameters	Scenario												
	Mopani	Vhembe	Waterberg	Chris Hani	Frances Baard	Soweto	Khayelitsha	Lulekani	Duduza	Zeerust	Hlankomo	Mandileni	Gon'on'o
	District	District	District	District	District	Township	Township	Township	Township	Low-Income	Rural Residential	Rural Residential	Rural Residential
Flush toilet connected to sewerage	14.1%	16%	43.8%	31.6%	78.4%	88.6%	91.0%	36.8%	88.4%	25.9%	0.5%	0.5%	11.4%
Solid Waste Services	No	No	No	No	No	Yes	Yes	Yes	Yes	Yes	No	No	No

Table A2. Parameters set over the different scenarios.

Parameter	Symbol	Scenario												
		Mopani	Vhembe	Waterberg	Chris Hani	Frances Baard	Soweto	Khayelitsha	Lulekani	Zeerust	Duduza	Hlankomo	Mandileni	Gon'on'o
Type	-	District	District	District	District	District	Township	Township	Township	Low-Income	Township	Rural Residential	Rural Residential	Rural Residential
Area Description	-	Category C Municipality located in Limpopo	Category C Municipality located in Limpopo	Category C Municipality located in Limpopo	Category C Municipality located in Eastern Cape	Category C Municipality located in Northern Cape	Next to Johannesburg	Next to Cape Town	Outside Phalaborwa in Limpopo	Commercial town situated in North West	A township west of Nigel on the East Rand	A village next to Qumbu and Mthatha in Eastern Cape	A village next to Mthatha in Eastern Cape	A village next to Giyani in Limpopo
Area Size	A	20,011 (km^2)	25,596 (km^2)	44,913 (km^2)	36,407 (km^2)	12,836 (km^2)	200.03 (km^2)	38.71 (km^2)	6.61 (km^2)	57.09 (km^2)	11.23 (km^2)	- (km^2)	- (km^2)	- (km^2)
Average Density	δ	55 (users/km^2)	51 (users/km^2)	15 (users/km^2)	22 (users/km^2)	30 (users/km^2)	6400 (users/km^2)	10,000 (users/km^2)	2200 (users/km^2)	160 (users/km^2)	6500 (users/km^2)	- (users/km^2)	- (users/km^2)	- (users/km^2)
Average Downlink Throughput	T	50 (Mbps/user)					100 (Mbps/user)		50 (Mbps/user)		100 (Mbps/user)		10 (Mbps/user)	
Number of Inhabitants	NU	1,092,507	1,294,722	679,336	795,461	382,086	1,271,628	391,749	14,464	9093	73,295	1111	~3500	~5000
Active Users Ratio	α		0.5	0.5	0.8	0.8	0.8	0.75	0.8	0.3	0.4			
Probability of Usage	β		0.3	0.3	0.6	0.6	0.6	04	0.6	0.1	0.2			
Electricity Grid Cost	CE	R 2.89 (/kWh)									No legal connection	No connection	No connection	No connection

Table A2. Cont.

Parameter		Symbol	Mopani	Vhembe	Waterberg	Chris Hani	Frances Baard	Soweto	Khayelitsha	Lulekani	Zeerust	Duduza	Hlankomo	Mandileni	Gon'on'o
Solar Panel Power	UAV-Based	PSP	4.5 (kWp/site)	3.5 (kWp/site)	4.1 (kWp/site)	3.8 (kWp/site)	3.1 (kWp/site)	4.8 (kWp/site)	4.6 (kWp/site)	2.6 (kWp/site)	3.2 (kWp/site)	3.4 (kWp/site)	1.8 (kWp/site)	1.9 (kWp/site)	2.1 (kWp/site)
	LC-Based		12.7 (kWp/site)	12.6 (kWp/site)	11.5 (kWp/site)	10.7 (kWp/site)	12 (kWp/site)	12.8 (kWp/site)	12.5 (kWp/site)	10.7 (kWp/site)	10.8 (kWp/site)	10.2 (kWp/site)	10.2 (kWp/site)	10.5 (kWp/site)	10.2 (kWp/site)
	Hotspot-Based		7.5 (kWp/site)	7.6 (kWp/site)	7.5 (kWp/site)	7.5 (kWp/site)	6.9 (kWp/site)	9 (kWp/site)	8.1 (kWp/site)	6.5 (kWp/site)	6.3 (kWp/site)	6.8 (kWp/site)	6.4 (kWp/site)	6.5 (kWp/site)	6.9 (kWp/site)
Number of Batteries	UAV-Based	NB	15 (units/site)	13 (units/site)	12 (units/site)	20 (units/site)	15 (units/site)		6 (units/site)	5 (units/site)		5 (units/site)	3 (units/site)	10 (units/site)	7 (units/site)
	LC-Based		26 (units/site)	27 (units/site)	18 (units/site)	32 (units/site)	24 (units/site)	5 (units/site)	13 (units/site)	10 (units/site)	2 (units/site)	10 (units/site)	7 (units/site)	17 (units/site)	11 (units/site)
	Hotspot-Based		18 (units/site)	18 (units/site)	18 (units/site)	18 (units/site)	18 (units/site)	20 (units/site)	20 (units/site)	15 (units/site)	15 (units/site)	9 (units/site)	7 (units/site)	7 (units/site)	7 (units/site)
Number of Deployed 5G-Nodes	UAV-Based	NC − Max	30,809	39,408	69,149	56,053	19,763	23,654	7287	127	88	1364	3	3	5
	LC-Based		2117	2509	1317	1542	741	7885	2429	43	29	455	1	1	2
	Hotspot-Based		30,809	39,408	69,149	56,053	19,763	1514	467	11	88	88	1	1	1
	UAV-Based	NC − User	6351	7527	3949	4624	2222	23,654	7287	127	85	1364	3	3	5
	LC-Based		2117	2509	1317	1542	741	7885	2429	43	29	455	1	1	2
	Hotspot-Based		407	482	253	296	143	1514	467	9	6	88	1	1	1
	UAV-Based	NC − Area	30,809	39,408	69,149	56,053	19,763	308	60	11	88	18			
	LC-Based		78	99	173	141	50	1	1	1	1	1			
	Hotspot-Based		30,809	39,408	69,149	56,053	19,763	308	60	11	88	18			
Site Acquisition Costs	UAV-Based	CSA			ZAR 577.3 (k/site)	ZAR 400		ZAR 173.3 (k/site)	ZAR 173.3 (k/site)		ZAR 120 (k/site)	.		ZAR 120 (k/site)	
	LC-Based				ZAR 1732 (k/site)			ZAR 519.6 (k/site)			ZAR 480.8 (k/site)			ZAR 480.8 (k/site)	
	Hotspot-Based				ZAR 812 (k/site)			ZAR 240 (k/site)			ZAR 160 (k/site)			ZAR 160 (k/site)	
Monthly Subscription Fee		F									ZAR 300			ZAR 20	

References

1. United Nations WESP. Country Classification. Available online: https://www.un.org/en/development/desa/policy/wesp/wesp_current/2014wesp_country_classification.pdf (accessed on 11 June 2022).
2. United Nations Sustainable Development Goals. Available online: https://sdgs.un.org/goals (accessed on 11 June 2022).
3. Yinka-Banjo, C.; Ajayi, O. Sky-farmers: Applications of unmanned aerial vehicles (UAV) in agriculture. In *Autonomous Vehicles*; IntechOpen: London, UK, 2019; pp. 107–128.
4. Celesti, A.; Fazio, M.; Galán Márquez, F.; Glikson, A.; Mauwa, H.; Bagula, A.B.; Celesti, F.; Villari, M. How to develop IoT cloud e-health systems based on FIWARE: A lesson learnt. *J. Sens. Actuator Netw.* **2019**, *8*, 7. [CrossRef]
5. Bagula, M.F.; Bagula, H.; Mandava, M.; Kakoko Lubamba, C.; Bagula, A. Cyber-healthcare kiosks for healthcare support in developing countries. In *e-Infrastructure and e-Services for Developing Countries*; Springer: Cham, Switzerland, 2019; pp. 185–198.
6. Ajayi, O.O.; Bagula, A.B.; Maluleke, H.C. Africa 3: A continental network model to enable the African fourth industrial revolution. *IEEE Access* **2020**, *8*, 196847–196864. [CrossRef]
7. Ajayi, O.; Maluleke, H.; Bagula, A. Least Cost Remote Learning for Under-Served Communities. In Proceedings of the International Conference on e-Infrastructure and e-Services for Developing Countries, Ebene City, Mauritius, 2–4 December 2020; Springer: Cham, Switzerland, 2020; pp. 219–233.
8. Ajayi, O.; Bagula, A.; Maluleke, H.; Gaffoor, Z.; Jovanovic, N.; Pietersen, K. WaterNet: A Network for Monitoring and Assessing Water Quality for Drinking and Irrigation Purposes. *IEEE Access* **2022**, *10*, 48318–48337. [CrossRef]
9. Panwar, N.; Sharma, S.; Singh, A.K. A survey on 5G: The next generation of mobile communication. *Phys. Commun.* **2016**, *18*, 64–84. [CrossRef]
10. Kaur, S.; Randhawa, S. Google loon: Balloon-powered internet for everyone. *AIP Conf. Proc.* **2018**, *2034*, 020006.
11. Chiaraviglio, L.; Blefari-Melzzi, N.; Liu, W.; Gutiérrez, J.; van de Beek, J.; Birke, R.; Chen, L.; Idzikowski, F.; Kliper, D.; Monti, P.; et al. Bringing 5G into rural and low-income areas: Is it feasible? *IEEE Commun. Stand. Mag.* **2017**, *1*, 50–57. [CrossRef]
12. Maluleke, H.; Bagula, A.; Ajayi, O. Efficient Airborne Network Clustering for 5G Backhauling and Fron-hauling. In Proceedings of the 16th International Conference on Wireless and Mobile Computing, Networking and Communications (WiMob'20), Thessaloniki, Greece, 12–14 October 2020; pp. 99–104.
13. Maluleke, H.; Bagula, A.; Ajayi, O. 5G for Sustainable Development. In Proceedings of the Southern Africa Telecommunication Networks and Applications Conference, Cape Town, South Africa, 28–30 August 2022.
14. Bouras, C.; Panagiotis, N.; Andreas, P. Cost modeling for SDN/NFV based mobile 5G networks. In Proceedings of the 2016 8th International Congress on Ultra Modern Telecommunications and Control Systems and Workshops (ICUMT), Lisbon, Portugal, 18–20 October 2016; pp. 56–61.
15. Oughton, E.; Zoraida, F. The cost, coverage and rollout implications of 5G infrastructure in Britain. *Telecommun. Policy* **2018**, *42*, 636–652. [CrossRef]
16. Nikolikj, V.; Janevski, T. A cost modeling of high-capacity LTE-advanced and IEEE 802.11 ac based heterogeneous networks, deployed in the 700 MHz, 2.6 GHz and 5 GHz Bands. *Procedia Comput. Sci.* **2014**, *40*, 49–56. [CrossRef]
17. Narang, M.; Xiang, S.; Liu, W.; Gutierrez, J.; Chiaraviglio, L.; Sathiaseelan, A.; Merwaday, A. UAV-assisted edge infrastructure for challenged networks. In Proceedings of the 2017 IEEE Conference on Computer Communications Workshops, INFOCOM WKSHPS, Atlanta, GA, USA, 1–4 May 2017.
18. Pienaar, L.; Lulama, T. Understanding the smallholder farmer in South Africa: Towards a sustainable livelihoods' classification (No. 1008-2016-79955). In Proceedings of the International Association of Agricultural Economists (IAAE) 2015 Conference, Milan, Italy, 9–14 August 2015.
19. Trading Economics. South Africa Average Monthly Gross Wage. Available online: https://tradingeconomics.com/south-africa/wages (accessed on 6 July 2022).
20. Stats SA. 2011 Census. Available online: https://www.statssa.gov.za/?page_id=3839 (accessed on 6 July 2022).
21. Statista. Mobile Internet User Penetration in South Africa from 2018 to 2027. 2022. Available online: https://www.statista.com/statistics/972866/south-africa-mobile-internet-penetration/ (accessed on 6 July 2022).
22. CSIR. Climate Indicators Koppen-Geiger Climate Classification. 2015. Available online: http://stepsa.org/climate_koppen_geiger.html (accessed on 10 June 2022).
23. Weather and Climate. Average Percent of Sunshine in Middelburg (Eastern Cape). n.d. Available online: https://weather-and-climate.com/average-monthly-percent-Sunshine,middelburg,South-Africa (accessed on 10 June 2022).
24. Chiaraviglio, L.; Liu, W.; Gutierrez, J.A.; Blefari-Melazzi, N. Optimal pricing strategy for 5G in rural areas with unmanned aerial vehicles and large cells. In Proceedings of the 27th International Telecommunication Networks and Applications Conference, ITNAC 2017, Melbourne, VIC, Australia, 22–24 November 2017; IEEE: Piscataway, NJ, USA, 2017; pp. 1–7.
25. Fernando, F. Internal Rate of Return (IRR). 2022. Available online: https://www.investopedia.com/terms/i/irr.asp (accessed on 7 March 2022).
26. Fin24. MTN, Vodacom Charging Up to 2 639% More for Out-of-Bundle Data—Report. 2018. Available online: https://www.news24.com/Fin24/mtn-vodacom-charging-up-to-2-639-more-for-out-of-bundle-data-report-20180312-2 (accessed on 28 June 2022).
27. Stats SA. Department of Statistics, South Africa. Available online: https://www.statssa.gov.za/ (accessed on 7 March 2022).

Article

Implementing Smart Sustainable Cities in Saudi Arabia: A Framework for Citizens' Participation towards SAUDI VISION 2030

Abood Khaled Alamoudi [1,2,*], Rotimi Boluwatife Abidoye [2] and Terence Y. M. Lam [3]

[1] Department of Architecture, College of Architecture and Planning, Imam Abdulrahman bin Faisal University, Dammam 31451, Saudi Arabia
[2] School of Built Environment, University of New South Wales, Kensington, Sydney, NSW 2052, Australia
[3] Department of Architecture and Built Environment, Northumbria University, Newcastle NE1 8ST, UK; terence.lam@northumbria.ac.uk
* Correspondence: a.alamoudi@unsw.edu.au

Abstract: Cities in Saudi Arabia need to expand rapidly due to the rapidly growing urban population. To develop smart sustainable cities (SSC), human, social, and environmental capital investments must be expanded beyond just focusing on technology. There have been several cities that have adopted smart city labels as recognition of the advantages of smart cities. Many countries acknowledge the value of citizens' involvement in public urban planning and decision making, but it is difficult to evaluate their impact and compare it to other factors. This study aims to develop a citizens' participation framework, identify any additional stakeholder's management measures (SMM) (in addition to the ones previously developed by the authors), and explain the relationship with citizens' participation level (CPL) for driving SSC. Three rounds of the Delphi method were conducted to structure and validate the framework by the decision maker in the field of urban planning and reach a consensus of understanding the drivers of SSC. The study group was limited to 25 participants because this study focuses on the perspective of decision makers toward CP. Mean score (MS) ranking and Kendall Coefficient were used to confirm the importance of these additional stakeholders' management measures. The results suggest three main component structures of the conceptual framework, which are SMM, CPL, and Citizens' Participation Recruitment (CPR), which are all necessary for smart sustainable city outcomes (SSCO) for achieving the Future Sustainable Cities Plan (FSCP) within the context of Vision 2030 and government policy in Saudi Arabia. Using the proposed framework will enable all the stakeholders to gain a deeper understanding of SSC and their complex natures from a conceptual and practical standpoint. The contribution to knowledge of this study is by developing a conceptual framework that can support the implementation of SSC, and by providing an understanding of the CPR standards and the involvement of citizens in urban development, which eliminates any debate regarding SSC.

Keywords: smart sustainable cities; citizens' participation framework; citizens' participation recruitment; citizens' participation level; stakeholder's management measures; Saudi Arabia

Citation: Alamoudi, A.K.; Abidoye, R.B.; Lam, T.Y.M. Implementing Smart Sustainable Cities in Saudi Arabia: A Framework for Citizens' Participation towards SAUDI VISION 2030. *Sustainability* **2023**, *15*, 6648. https://doi.org/10.3390/su15086648

Academic Editors: Rashid Mehmood, Tan Yigitcanlar and Juan M. Corchado

Received: 4 February 2023
Revised: 31 March 2023
Accepted: 7 April 2023
Published: 14 April 2023

Copyright: © 2023 by the authors. Licensee MDPI, Basel, Switzerland. This article is an open access article distributed under the terms and conditions of the Creative Commons Attribution (CC BY) license (https://creativecommons.org/licenses/by/4.0/).

1. Introduction

Smart sustainable cities (SSC) have been acknowledged globally in response to rapid urbanisation and enormous consumption which require attention and collaboration from diverse professions [1]. The United Nations [2] estimated that 90 per cent of the increased population would live in cities by 2050. Globally, urban areas consume about 70 per cent of the world's natural resources, which significantly contribute to greenhouse gas emissions [3]. Saudi Arabia has also witnessed an expanding in urban development, wherein the cities expand rapidly. As a result, several consequences of urban issues have occurred, such as traffic congestion, insufficient transportation facilities, resource depletion at an accelerated pace, and a certain issue that is not being addressed culturally [4]. Due to the lack of comprehensive planning frameworks, rapid population growth coupled with weak institutional structures has led to sprawling and lopsided development [5].

Gassmann, Böhm, and Palmié [6] and Ramaprasad, Sanchez Ortiz, and Syn [7] argue that advanced technology such as Artificial Intelligent (AI) and Internet of Things (IOT) play an important role in promoting SSC. Moreover, opportunities such as innovation, entrepreneurship, and job creation can be attracted by SSC, which leads to economic growth and flourish, as well as equitable and inclusive urban environment. However, Alamoudi, Abidoye, and Lam [8], Bibri [9], and Embarak [10] debate that cities that are driven by technology are most likely to exacerbate social inequalities, whereas cities that consider human involvement and participation in the SSC development are more likely to do so equitably, justly, and particpatorily. Human needs and interests are prioritised and promoted not only to privileged groups, but also marginalised communities. Ultimately, cities have been challenged to balance between utilising Information and Commination Technology (ICT) and ensuring that citizens' participation (CP) is applied.

In response to these rapid urbanisation challenges, many sustainability measurement models and frameworks have developed, including but not limited to the Leadership in Energy and Environmental Design (LEED), the Building Research Establishment Environmental Assessment Method (BREEAM), and the Comprehensive Assessment System for Built Environment Efficiency (CASBEE) [11]. Over the past few decades, several governments have adopted a variety of urban sustainability systems. Even though most of these systems were designed for buildings, the advantages of ICT have not been taken into consideration [9]. The complexity and sophistication of urban areas are incredible, and it requires a holistic framework such as the SSC concept to manage its complexity [12,13]. Smart cities have been viewed by various scholars as a new paradigm created to accommodate rapid urbanisation and economic development [10,12,14], while other spectators believe the smart cities concept is not new [1,15]. The phrase, smart cities concept, was introduced in 2007/2008 when ICT was introduced to businesses, institutions, and the public; on the other hand, the concept of smart growth originated in the late 1900s during the growth movement [1,12]. Based on academic expertise, smart cities can be viewed as a complex ecosystem that is supported by technological infrastructure and means of transforming the engagement, participation, and learning of citizens [16]. Although scholars acknowledge that SSC is primarily a techno-centric concept because it leverages ICT, they claim that social, cultural, economic, and environmental aspects are crucial [17–20].

SSC are those that have extensively integrated ICT with their urban systems [21]. In the past, urban governments have struggled to achieve sustainability goals through ICT [22]. ICT technology and community participation are absent from policies and strategies for sustainable urban development. By using a smart sustainability framework, urban development initiatives can be driven by technology and CP with positive environmental, economic and social outcomes [23]. Sustainable urban planning is considered one of the key outcomes of smart cities, which are open to embracing new technologies. Smart city initiatives, however, do not provide evidence of how sustainability outcomes are achieved [24]. It is possible to collect and analyse datasets for urban intelligence functions using ICT approaches. A framework can be used to formulate decision-making strategies to achieve SSC [3].

Urban planning and challenges can be addressed with ICT [16]. However, transitioning to SSC requires an understanding of urban governance [25]. In urban governance, there are two types: (1) traditional government that is characterised by centralisation, little or no public involvement, and private partnerships, namely, "traditional government", and (2) one that emphasises decentralisation, public participation, partnerships, and consensus building, referred to as "modern governance" [26]. Urban planning and governance are also interconnected and involve a variety of stakeholders [27]. Almughairy [28] suggests that planning, governance, and implementation must be coordinated for regional development to be successful. It is imperative that urban planning and its governance are linked in order for urban sustainability to be achieved [27]. According to Almughairy [28], by utilizing a region's uniqueness in planning and implementation, any community and its residents can be assured of a prosperous future. Other scholars such as Al-Hathloul [29] argue that Saudi Arabia's management system has a national and local focus and is centralised at the national level.

Understanding the six characteristics of smart cities is essential; these include: smart people, smart economy, smart mobility, smart living, smart governance, and smart environments [14]. Various technologies are used by SSC in order to achieve a sustainable lifestyle and steady, healthy quality of life (QoL). Sustainable development is primarily achieved by creating, deploying, and promoting ICT. As a result, it is referred to as a "new TechnoUrban phenomenon" [3]. It has been widely discussed that CP plays a significant role, but there has not been evaluation of its effects to compare its contribution to other influences [30–32]. Several studies have found that countries that empower CP perform significantly better in urban projects than countries that do not [33–35]. For example, in 2016 the Future Saudi Cities Program (FSCP) was established by the Minister of Municipal and Rural Affairs (MoMRA) in collaboration with UN-Habitat to capture the urban challenges in Saudi Arabia [36]. FSCP aims to promote spatial balance, reduce urban sprawl, and develop a decentralised planning framework in Saudi Arabia for a sustainable city. QoL, environmental protection, and economic competitiveness are all part of FSCP's business objectives. Boosting the productivity, equitability, social and ecological well-being of Saudi cities is the objective of FSCP. Smart Sustainable Cities Outcomes (SSCO) are seen in three-primary areas as business objectives: 'QoL', 'economic competitiveness', and 'environmental protection' [37]. QoL as a measure of social sustainability aims to have productive and prosperous cities through high-quality urban design that is equitable and socially inclusive, and which has an adequate and efficient infrastructure. Environmental protection considers reducing sprawl, enhancing spatial balance development, and promoting the environment. Economic competitiveness is distinguished by producing better financing, a greater degree of well-being, and better employment opportunities [38]. These outcomes rely heavily on ICT. An example is using sensors to collect air and water quality data, waste management data, and other environmental information. In addition, cities can boost their economic competitiveness by leveraging ICT to attract investment, promote entrepreneurship, create jobs, and grow their economies. Moreover, social inclusion, community engagement, cultural diversity, and public safety can all be enhanced through ICT in cities, as well as crime and violence reduction through ICT. UN-Habitat's objectives for SSCO leave CP untouched, creating gaps between ICT and CP as facilitators of urban sustainability and citizens engaging in the development of cities as stakeholders. To achieve the implementation goal, it is necessary to study and address these gaps. Therefore, there is a need to develop a comprehensive framework that can work together to bridge the gap between ICT and CP to achieve SSC.

Recently, the 12 Vision Realization Program of strategic importance for the government of Saudi Arabia was established and named VISION2030. Its objective is to improve the lifestyle of individuals by creating an ecosystem that boosts participation in cultural, entertainment, and sports activities, develop events for communities that enhance liveability, and enhance the ranking of Saudi cities [38]. According to UN-Habitat [37], the Saudi Government's aim is to make Saudi's cities considered one of the top 100 cities globally by 2030. Some Saudi cities may be able to improve their social, economic, and environmental conditions through this program [17].

There is a need to mitigate the undesirable consequences of rapid urbanisation by adapting the SSC framework. This study aims to develop a citizens' participation framework, identify any additional stakeholders' management measures as revealed by the stakeholders involved in the FSCP program, and explain the relationship with CPL for driving SSCO for FSCP and VISION2030. In particular, we raise the research question: How can the citizens' participation be enhanced to achieve the business objectives of FSCP, i.e., SSCO? Three rounds of the Delphi method were conducted to fulfill the study's aim. The paper contributes significantly to the literature on SSC by developing a framework that supports CP in the form of two-way communication with all urban development stakeholders. In other words, local governments and other stakeholders can better understand how smart cities operate through a practical framework.

The novelty of the proposed framework lies on the component of the framework. It contributes to understanding the issue conceptually and practically. The novelty of the framework introduces a new approach to archive and understand the involvement of CP in the development of SSC. In addition, its components, including SMM, CPL, SSCO, and Citizens' Participation Recruitment CPR, differentiate it from previous frameworks. Another advantage is the ability to identify the most appropriate SSC implementation measures for different cities, as well as the expectations of stakeholders, to assist the decision makers. Meaning, it aims to support the communication between the government and decision makers and identify what is expected from the citizen and vice versa to achieve SSCO. This novel framework contributes to advancing the field of urban planning and provide significant understanding for policymakers, practitioners, and researchers.

The structure of this study is as follows. Firstly, we present the current research problem. Subsequently, a literature review of various frameworks that support the SSC concept is presented. The research methodology is illustrated in the Section 3, and research questions are discussed in detail; in the Section 4, the results, discussions, and validation of the framework are presented. As a conclusion to the paper, the Section 5 discusses the study findings, implications, and limitations, and future studies will be proposed.

2. Literature Review

2.1. Review of Sustainability Frameworks

Previous studies show that many governments around the world have been implementing different approaches towards smart cities and sustainable urbanisation [3,24,39]. Globally, over 30 rating systems have been used to measure and monitor sustainability in environmental, economic, and social aspects [40]. Measurements (see Table 1), such as the Urban Management Program of UN-Habitat [41], Melbourne City Council's City plan [42], the government of Singapore's Green Plan [43], have been used to guide and monitor urban sustainability. Smartainability aims to include most of the urban sustainability indicators and allows the estimation of how smart cities promote sustainability [13]. The first introduced rating system was BREEAM, which was developed in 1990 [44]. Out of these rating systems, three are the most accredited and famous systems: LEED, the Estidama pearl rating system, and the Global Sustainability Assessment System (GSAS) [45]. However, GSAS is recognised to function in countries in the Middle East and North Africa (MENA) region, including the Gulf and Saudi Arabia [40]. Because of the range of explanations of SC and urban sustainability, many frameworks and ranking systems have been developed (see Table 1 for the sustainability frameworks) [22]. There are few studies that compared the impact of these frameworks and their related indicators [22]. However, there is very little or nothing in the literature about weighting these frameworks and their indicators in order to adopt the suitable one, nor about the integration of ICT with sustainable cities.

Table 1. Best Practices Frameworks for Urban Sustainability.

Name of the Framework	Description	Number of Category *	Number of Indicators *	Limitation
ISO 37120 *	Sustainable development and resilience are assessed holistically through an integrated and holistic approach to quality of life QoL and service delivery in cities [22]	17	100	Some of the indicators were eliminated due to space limitations [46]
RFSC *	The European Cities Toolkit is a free tool aimed at promoting and improving the integrated urban development actions of cities and urban territories [22]	4	24	It supports only local European Union authorities to restricted access
BREEAM	The purpose of an assessment method is to improve, measure, and certify the sustainability of large-scale development plans in terms of social, environmental, and economic factors [22]	9	62	Difficulties in controlling the quality assurance and high cost to obtain it [47]
LEED-ND for Neighbourhood Development	Using standards to distinguish whether the neighbourhood is environmentally improved; green certification is applied to the neighbourhood context [22]	5	53	The cost of earning such credits is high, while few points are earned for meeting their criteria [48]
CASBEE for Urban Development (CASBEE-UD)	Assessing the effects of a conglomeration of buildings on the environment at the urban scale [22]	6	76	Incorporates some of the issues in the main categories into the management side, instead of the main category of sustainable urbanisation itself [49]
STATUS *	Developing locally relevant tools to help establishing targets for urban sustainability through a joint initiative by researchers and practitioners [22]	8	46	It supports only local European Union authorities to restricted access
SustainLane	Ranking system of 50 of the country's largest cities to recognise the depths, challenges, and potential of each major city's management policies [22]	16	46	A description of how weights were assigned to individual initiatives or why certain initiatives were included in the city rankings is not provided [50]
UN-Habitat CPI	An extensive set of indicators that measure progress toward the Habitat Agenda and the Millennium Development Goals includes 20 key indicators, 8 checklists, and 16 extensive indicators [22]	5	42	The definition of prosperity does not address all kinds of urban typologies such as slums [51]
UN-Habitat SDG *	Analyses how countries are performing on SDGs on an average. High SDG rankings are strongly related to high natural resource demands per person [52]	17	169	Resource security is not well represented among the goals and targets, so a more complete and carefully constructed SDG will not have a significant impact on results [52]

* Category: the impact of indicators, * Indicators: A measure that captures information about a complex phenomenon, * ISO 37120: An indicator of the QoL and sustainable development of cities, * RFSC: An acronym for the Reference Framework for Sustainable Cities in Europe, * STATUS: Sustainability Tools and Targets for the Urban Thematic, * SDG: for Sustainable Development Goals, which was developed by UN-Habitat.

2.2. Review of Smart Cities Frameworks

Table 1 summarises the urban sustainability frameworks. Many researchers see urban sustainability from three pillars/dimensions, which are economic, environmental, and social [53,54], while Khogali [55] added a fourth pillar, which is the cultural pillar. Every pillar/dimension comprises measures based on a set of indicators and sub-indicators. On one hand, Table 2 shows the frameworks and indicators that are used to measure SSC in many countries. For example, the United States of America uses LEED, France uses RFSC, Japan uses CASBEE, and England uses BREEAM. On the other hand, Table 2 shows a wide range of frameworks designed for measuring smart cities, where each framework uses a number of categories and indicators.

According to Alamoudi, Abidoye, and Lam [14], SSC falls under six major domains. Each domain is measured using a set of indicators and sub-indicators. These domains are Smart Economics, Smart Environment, Smart Governance, Smart People, Smart Living, and Smart Mobility. Alamoudi, Abidoye, and Lam [56] assessed SSCO using three sets of measures. First: primary areas of urban sustainability proposed by FSCP. Second: urban indicators utilised by FSCP. Lastly: the most common indicators and sub-indicators revealed by literature review for measuring urban sustainability.

Alamoudi, Abidoye, and Lam [56] suggested the following indicators and sub-indicators for SSC, which are Smart Economics: innovative spirit, entrepreneurship, economic image, trademark, flexibility of labour market, and E-business; Smart Environment: attractivity of natural conditions, pollution, environmental protection, sustainable innovation, and safe transport systems; Smart Governance: participation in decision making, public and social services, transparent governance, and E-government; Smart People, level of qualification, inclination to lifelong learning, social and ethnic plurality, flexibility creativity, cosmopolitanism/open mindedness, and participation in public life; Smart Living: cultural facilities, health conditions, individual safety, housing quality, education facilities, touristic attractivity, and social cohesion; Smart Mobility: local accessibility, international accessibility availability of ICT-infrastructure, sustainable, and innovative and safe transport systems.

Table 2. Selection of Best Practice Frameworks for Smart Cities.

Name of the Framework	Description	Number of Category *	Number of Indicators *	Limitation
European Smart Cities Ranking	Ranking of European cities developed by the University of Technology Vienna [22]	6	64	It requires open data in order to function the best [57]
The Smart Cities Wheel	By examining all key components that make a smart city, Boyd Cohen developed an integrated framework to support them [22]	6	26	Especially in developing nations, limit the concept to smaller and emerging cities [57]
Smart city benchmarking in China	Developed as part of a Chinese project and used for evaluating 28 Chinese cities' smartness [22]	5	43	The model was built based on a comparison with other cities' strategies, planes [58]
Triple-helix network model for smart cities performance	For measuring the performance of smart cities, a model links the interrelationship between their components [22]	5	45	Its main focuses are on digital services only [59]
Smart City PROFILES	Five SC indicators, with a focus on energy efficiency and climate change [22]	5	21	It focuses on climate change and energy [60]
City Protocol	Creating city-centric approaches that benefit citizens is the goal of an international collaborative innovation that starts in Amsterdam [22]	9	190	This program ended in 2018 although all the insightful information is still accessible [61]
CITYkeys	Providing a holistic measurement framework (under the EU H2020 program) [22]	20	73	The data set and indicators are calculated based on the availability and reliability of the needed data [62]

* Category: the impact of indicators, * Indicators: A measure that captures information about a complex phenomenon.

There is a need to better understand how smartness and sustainability are related and interconnected [63]. As shown in Tables 1 and 2, a significant number of contradictions in theory and practice are rooted in the technological world, yet the definition of the SC concept is not unified [22,24,64–66]. As a result, its definition, character, and dimensions are shaped by the scholar's background and how it is applied [24,67]. Although the SSC concept has only recently been introduced to academic discourse as a means to promote sustainable urban development, it still remains an area of nascent empirical research [21].

As proposed by Alamoudi, Abidoye, and Lam [68], a strong smart sustainable city system relies on four factors: knowledge, awareness, citizen participation, and opinion about government policy. On the other hand, the relationship between stakeholders' management measure (SSM) and CPL has been tested and validated by Alamoudi, Abidoye, and Lam [8]. As suggested, Regulation, Collaboration, Legitimates, and Control are the most important stakeholder management variables that drive CPL. In additional, the impact of CPL on the SSCO has also been tested and validated by Alamoudi, Abidoye and Lam [56], which demonstrates the following CPL variables: Accountability and Responsibly Transparency, Participation, and Inclusion. This paper defines an additional SSM as revealed by the stakeholders involved in the FSCP program, which will be examined and determined by utilizing the Delphi method.

Figure 1 shows the relationship between CPL, SSM, CPR, and SSCO. This research hypothesises that E-government/ICT, engaging/empowerment, and socio-cultures factors are significant measures in the stakeholder management process and can influence CPL and SSCO.

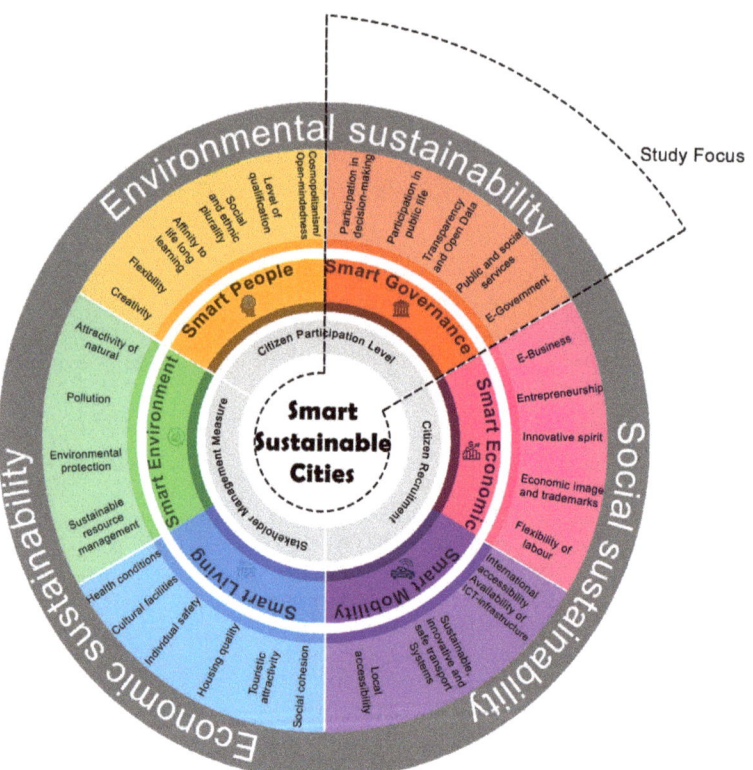

Figure 1. A framework for holistic Smart Sustainable Cities and the areas of study focus. Adapted from: Alamoudi, Abidoye, and Lam [56].

3. Methodology

To assess SSCO from adopting citizens' participation measures and stakeholder communication enhancement measures, and, hence, validate the stakeholder management framework for achieving smart sustainable cities outcomes, a Delphi method was adopted. It contributes to understanding the SSC by structuring and validating results from experts on built environments [69,70]. Three rounds of questionnaires were sent to experts for brainstorming, narrowing down, and ranking the most important components of the framework [71]. The first round aimed to express experts' opinions to confirm the framework and identify any additional measures and relationships for the citizens' participation framework for driving SSCO for FSCP, which will support better communication between the stakeholders involved in smart cities development. In the second round, the questionnaire was sent out with feedback from the first round for validation of the responses of the structure of the framework by comparing it with the consolidation of others' opinion. In the third round, the responses from the second round were presented to the participants to gain a consensus experts' opinion. Moreover, the participants were asked an open-ended question to confirm and identify the influencing measures and to explain the relationships between them. The first survey was structured into five sections: (1) general questions about the participants, (2) foundation of the Citizens' Participation framework (Recruitment), (3) foundation of the framework—E-government/ICT Factors, (4) foundation of the framework—Engaging/Empowerment Factors, and (5) foundation of the framework—Social-Cultural factors. The items were scored on a five-point Likert scale: "Least Important (1)", "Fairly Important", "Important", "Very Important", and "Extremely Important (5)", respectively [72]. The data were collected from a mix of participants groups, including government representatives who work at FSCP and/or (MoMRA), professionals, and academics. The participants were reached through the webpage of their companies or via their LinkedIn profiles, which contained their position, experience, and involvements. The research team made initial contact with potential participants by directly sending a recruitment invitation email. If no response was received, a friendly reminder was sent out to the participants. If no response was received after this reminder, this indicates no interest to participate, and the potential participant was then removed from the survey.

3.1. Data Collection for Delphi Method

To obtain a comprehensive view of stakeholders, an online questionnaire was distributed [73]. By mixing local practitioners and academics in Saudi Arabia, any misunderstanding, lack of knowledge, and lack of observational evidence are eliminated [74]. This study, therefore, collected opinions from stakeholders in the FSCP sector, from professionals (urban planners, architectural designers, real estate developers), as well as representatives from governments (FSCP officers from MOMRA). In addition to policymakers and UN-Habitat, academics also participated. To determine the importance of each performance predictor and outcome, a five-point Likert scale was used [75].

Table 3 shows that majority—24 (96.0%)—of the respondents are male, while only 1 (4.0%) is female. This revealed that males participated more than females in this study. According to the World Bank [76], it is no surprise that female response rates are low in Saudi Arabia as most urban professions are dominated by men. The Saudi Arabian government and the World Bank reported that the current total female workforce in Saudi Arbaia is 20.4%, and in the Built Environment field the percentage drops to 12%. This study captures 17.4% of women, which validates the work [76]. Nevertheless, the homogenous group and the study group size are limitations of this study, and it forms a separate area for further research. Moreover, 9 (36.0%) of the respondents are in the age group of 40–49, 8 (32.0%) are in the age group of 30–39, and the age group of 50 and above has a total number of 8 (32.0%) participants. As regards geographical area, more than half—14 (56.0%)—of the respondents are from the Riyadh region, 9 (36.0%) are from the Eastern region, while only 2 (8.0%) are from the Makkah region. The geographical area was limited to these three major cities due to the fact that all the decision makers are located in one of these cities.

Furthermore, as regards field of profession, 11 (44.0%) respondents specialise in urban planning, 7 (28.0%) specialise in Information Technology (IT), while only 4 (16.0%) are professionals in Management. More than half, i.e., 21 (84.0%), of the respondents practice in the public and private sector, while only 8 (16.0%) practice in the private sector and in academia. Four of the participants hold PhDs, which indicates that they are well educated and can contribute to the achievement of the goal of this current study. Capturing the perspective of experts who have good experience is essential. About 10 (40.0%) of the respondent indicated that they possess 16–20 years of experience in their field of practice, while 7 (28.0%) possess 10–15 years of experience, and 8 (32.0%) hold 21 years and more of experience. In addition, 6 (24.0%) of the respondents are CEOs, 5 (20.0%) are managers, and 4 (16.0%) are academics.

Table 3. Descriptive statistics of respondent demographics.

Characteristics		Frequency (N-25)	Percentage
Gender	Male	24	96.0
	Female	1	4.0
	Others	0	0
Age	30–39	8	32.0
	40–49	9	36.0
	50 and above	8	32.0
Region	Riyadh Region	14	56.0
	Makkah Region	2	8.0
	Eastern Region	9	36.0
Field of profession	Architecture	3	12.0
	Urban Planning	11	44.0
	Management	4	16.0
	IT	7	28.0
Sector of practice	Public Sector	17	68.0
	Private Sector	4	16.0
	Academia	4	16.0
Years of experience	10–15	7	28.0
	16–20	10	40.0
	21-more	8	32.0
Position in your firm	Partner/Founder	1	4.0
	Principal	4	16.0
	CEO	6	24.0
	Manager	5	20.0
	Supervisor	2	8.0
	Professor	2	8.0
	Associate Professor	1	4.0
	Assistant Professor	4	16.0

3.2. Data Analysis Techniques

The relationship between the categorical variables can be determined in several ways. Mean Score (MS) helps to determine the significance of a variable to the others in terms of the most important to the least important. In addition, data were analysed using Regression Analysis. The standardised coefficient represents the strength and direction of the relationship between a predictor variable and the response variable, with a positive coefficient indicating a positive relationship and a negative coefficient indicating a negative relationship [8]. The Statistical Package for the Social Sciences version 26.0 software (SPSS) (Chicago, IL, USA) was utilised, which is widely used in the fields of social science, business, and education.

The significance of the independent and dependent variables was evaluated using the MS technique [77]. Analysis of the collected data was conducted to determine if there were any additional stakeholder management measures (SMMs) that were associated with them. MS is widely used to evaluate the significance of variables in built environment studies [78–80]. The MS rankings of the variables were calculated using Equation (1) [79]. The data collected were analysed using SPSS software for cross-tabulations, relationships, and groupings.

$$M = \frac{\sum s}{n} \quad (1)$$

where M represents the mean score, s is the participants' score based on a Likert scale, and n is the total number of participants.

3.3. Data Reliability

In statistics, Cronbach's alpha represents an estimate of the data's reliability or consistency. A Cronbach's alpha value of 0 indicates that there is no consistency among the items in the test, while a value of 1 indicates perfect consistency [81]. In order for a scale to be considered reliable, it must have a Cronbach's alpha coefficient greater than 0.5 [82]. To calculate Cronbach's alpha, the following Equation (2) was adopted.

$$alpha = \frac{k}{(k-1)} * \left(1 - \frac{sum(vi)}{sum(ve)}\right) \quad (2)$$

where k is number of items in the test, vi is the variance of each item in the test, and ve is the variance of the test as a whole.

In terms of the CP and indicators of SSCO, all of the variables show higher reliability. Table 4 shows that the average response values are higher than 5. On average, the respondents were neutral about the following variables: Citizens' Participation Recruitment, E-government/ICT Factors, and Engaging/Empowerment Factors, while the respondents on average fairly achieved Social-Cultural factors.

Table 4. Reliability of data.

Factors	Number of Items	Cronbach's Alpha
Citizens' Participation Recruitment	4	0.733
E-government/ICT Factors	14	0.724
Engaging/Empowerment Factors	11	0.843
Social-Cultural factors	17	0.664

Additionally, considering the background of participants (public, private, and academic), Kendall's Coefficient of Concordance was utilised to determine the degree of consensus between the groups [83]. For the responses that were collected from the first round, all identical responses were removed and consolidated, then factors were grouped into categories to make it easier for panellists to compare when returned for the next round [70]. In terms of responses' validation, during the next round the experts were asked to verify that their responses have been interpreted correctly and to verify and refine the category. The second round narrowed down the factors based on different perspectives and backgrounds. The responses were validated, similar to the previous round. Moreover, the participants were requested to select the most important factors. The final round was the ranking round, where the participants were asked to rank the most important factors until the result reached a consensus. In addition, recommendations of the proposed framework for better communication were examined and validated. Kendall's Coefficient of Concordance ranges between 0 and 1, with values closer to 1 being the strongest indication of agreement and values closer to 0 being the weakest. [72]. Equation (3) was developed by Siegel, Castellan, and Me Graw-Hill [84] to calculate the Kendall's Coefficient.

$$W = 12 \frac{\sum_{i=1}^{n}(Ri - R)2}{P2(n3 - n) - pT} \quad (3)$$

where n = number of factors, Ri = ranks assigned to the i the factor, R = mean value of the Ri values, P = number of respondents, and T = correction factor for the tied ranks.

4. Results and Discussion

A qualitative and quantitative study was conducted to examine the framework's development and qualification, involving a number of participants who reported on their understanding of SSCs and different factors affecting its development. The study aims to develop a framework in Saudi Arabia through three rounds of the Delphi method. Data were categorised under different themes according to emerging contexts.

4.1. First Round of Delphi Method

Table 5 shows the frequency distribution of variables. The majority—24 (96.0%)—of the respondents, reported that the provision of SC vision is extremely significant, and it has an MS score of 3.8. It is believed that a smart city will decrease costs, improve QoL, and improve the efficiency of services. Some of the key aspects of an SC might include sustainable infrastructure and buildings, advanced transportation systems, energy efficiency, advanced communication systems, robust public safety systems, access to high-quality healthcare, and strong education systems [85]. Moreover, a little more than half—17 (68.0%)—of the respondents reported that random recruitment is extremely important, with a score of MS 3.7, while only 4 (16.0%) reported it as least important. As suggested by Carson and Martin [86], it is an effective way to reduce bias that may result from the participants, and it is a promising technique to promote participation in decision making. As regards decision makers' interaction level, 17 (68.0%) of the respondents reported that decision makers' interaction level is extremely important in smart cities development, and that has an MS score of 2.7, while only 1 (4.0%) reported this as important. Effective community depends heavily on the availability of data, yet maintaining the confidentiality of information depends on the authorised access level of the participant [87]. In addition, majority—23 (92.0%)—reported 'governments to promote monitoring and accountability to its citizens' as extremely important. Lindquist and Huse [88] argue that balance principles of citizen accountability have been debatable and operationalised. However, ICT and digital tools should be leveraged to achieve the balance of accountability of citizen participation. With respect to one-way stakeholders' interaction level, only 8 (32.0%) reported that one-way stakeholders' interaction level is an important factor, while 5 (20.0%) reported that this factor as extremely important, and it has an MS score of 2.2. According to Piqueiras, Canel, and Luoma-aho [89], the ability to communicate is essential to engage citizens in urban development. In addition, shift from one-way communication to two-way communication is essential to respond to the rapid urbanisation. Majority—24 (96.0%)—of the respondents reported that the provision of a smart cities vision is extremely important, and it has an MS of 2.19.

Table 5. MS Ranking of Performance Predictors.

	Level of Adoption					Mean Score	SD **
	LI *	FI *	I *	VI *	EI *		
Smart cities provide vision	1 (4.00)	00 (0.00)	00 (0.00)	00 (0.00)	24 (96.0)	3.8664	0.82927
Random recruitment	4 (16.0)	1 (4.0)	3 (12.0)	0 (0.00)	17 (68.0)	3.7627	0.90557
The existing decision makers' interaction level	00 (0.00)	00 (0.00))	1 (4.00)	7 (28.0)	17 (68.0)	2.7415	1.07433

Table 5. Cont.

	Level of Adoption					Mean Score	SD **
	LI *	FI *	I *	VI *	EI *		
Citizen-centric E-services	00 (0.00)	3 (12.00)	3 (12.00)	3 (12.00)	17 (68.0)	2.5193	1.06707
Governments to promote monitoring and accountability to its citizens	00 (0.00)	00 (0.00)	1 (4.00)	1 (4.00)	23 (92.00)	2.4873	1.02098
Development delivery	00 (0.00)	00 (0.00)	1 (4.00)	1 (4.00)	23 (92.00)	2.4492	0.9728
One-way stakeholders' interaction level	00 (0.00)	5 (20.00)	8 (32.00)	7 (28.00)	5 (20.00)	2.2032	0.8943
Two-way stakeholders' interaction level	1 (4.00)	00 (0.00)	00 (0.00)	00 (0.00)	24 (96.0)	2.1921	0.8821

* Least Important, Fairly Important, Important, Very Important, Extremely Important, ** Standard Deviation.

4.2. Second Round of Delphi Method

Table 6 shows the result from both the round one and round two Delphi study and the consensus reached regarding the associated factors by the experts. These 14 factors were proposed by the expert participants in the Delphi survey. Citizens' trust refers to the level of confidence and belief that members of a community have in their government and its institutions [90]. It is an important factor in the functioning of a healthy democracy, as it helps to ensure that citizens feel that their voices are being heard and that their needs are being addressed by those in positions of power. Citizens' knowledge refers to the understanding and awareness that members of a community have about their rights and responsibilities as citizens, as well as about the issues and challenges facing their community [91]. From the perspective of a citizen living in an SSC, they may experience a number of benefits such as: Increased efficiency, Improved public safety, Better QoL, and Greater access to information [92]. Cultural factors can influence the way that citizens in a city experience and perceive their environment, including their attitudes towards technology and the use of it in their city [93]. Some examples of cultural factors that may affect technology adoption include values and beliefs, social norms and expectations, and level of technological literacy. Citizens' visibility refers to the level of attention or exposure that an individual receives from the government. It is important for individuals to carefully consider the level of visibility [94]. It is important to recognise that everyone's experience is unique, and an individual's marital status does not necessarily define their ability to participate in their community or in public life. In general, all citizens have the right to participate fully in their communities and to have their voices heard, regardless of their marital status [95]. Gender can be a significant factor in an individual's ability to participate in their community [96]. To promote gender equality and inclusivity, it is important for communities and public institutions to recognise and challenge these barriers to participation and to create opportunities for the full and equal participation of all members of the community, regardless of their gender [97]. To summarise, Table 6 shows the result of the Delphi survey for both Round One and Round Two for CPR. The rankings of these factors have similar MS and ranking in both Delphi rounds. However, the citizens' gender has been de-escalated to be less important than citizens' age while the remaining CPR remain in the same sequence.

Table 6. Result of Delphi survey Round One and Round Two for citizens recruitment.

Associated Factors	Round 1		Round 2	
	Ranking	Mean Index	Ranking	Mean Index
Factors—Citizens' Trust	1	4.92	1	5
Factors—Citizens' Knowledge	2	4.91	2	4.96
Factors—Citizens' Perspectives	3	4.9	3	4.925
Factors—Citizens' Cultural factors	4	4.79	4	4.89
Factors—Citizens' Relevance	5	4.77	5	4.87
Factors—Citizens' Visibility/Publicity	6	4.76	6	4.86
Factors—Citizens' Marital Status	7	4.46	7	4.56
Factors—Citizens' Employment Status	8	4.14	8	4.26
Factors—Citizens' Spatial Behaviour	9	3.98	9	4.08
Factors—Citizens' Ethnicity	10	3.82	10	3.92
Factors—Citizens' Religion	11	3.79	11	3.72
Factors—Citizens' Income	12	3.11	12	3.05
Factors—Citizens' Gender	13	2.93	14	2.23
Factors—Citizens' Age	14	2.85	13	2.46
N		25		25
Kendall Coefficient		0.783		0.574
p-value		0.000		0.000

4.3. Third Round of Delphi Method

Common Theme 1: The Engagement, Management, and Adoption of ICT by Stakeholders in Smart City Planning

The result of this round reveals the consensus that the engagement of stakeholders is an imperative process in having the desired smart city of choice. Their involvement in the planning of smart cities will make a whole lot of difference as they will be from different professional backgrounds and levels. A participant opined that stakeholders should be fully engaged as they are important individuals in building an enabling and very active society. Similarly, one of the participants said that "*We can engage stakeholders by three aspects: The first aspect is the organizational aspect*"; "*The second aspect is physical organization. The third aspect is a good ICT infrastructure to achieve the goals of smart cities*". This further validates the position of participants that stakeholders should be empowered by giving them some autonomy to operate within their jurisdiction as far as the building of SSC is concerned. "*I think stakeholders are very important to be engaged in any development and I would like to see them very active in society*". Urban development must be filled with stakeholders from different backgrounds and different levels.

Furthermore, the knowledge and understanding of stakeholders about smart cities hold a significant responsibility in the organisation of time and other related resources for smart city building. A participant said that "*management is essential to measure the participants availability and measure their contribution and measure their inputs and measure their knowledge*". As much as the management of external stakeholders is important, the adoption of ICT leverage cannot also be overemphasised in the building of smart city. The majority of the participants were of the opinion that the ICT system should ensure the process of the type of information to share, when to share it, and how to share the information with the citizens. This will allow an effective and automatic process in communicating the ideas from policymakers down to the citizens. Moreover, communication technology should consider different variables in measuring the goals of stakeholders with respect to the available resources. A participant said that "*an effective and efficient way to collaborate, coordinate and communicate via ICT is to define the level of power and to know your participants*". Another respondent suggested that "*my thoughts in designing a system would be to take into consideration the who, what, where, and when to use the information*". The system must include variables that help achieve the goals such as governance of the data, creating the brain of the cities and assigning the task to the right people.

Common Theme 2: The Role of Citizens' Participation in the SSC as a Driver of Sustainable Cities

The SSC is dependent on the cooperation of citizens in almost every section of the development process. The survey results for round three show that the majority of the participants are in agreement that the citizens should participate fully in the urban development that will lead to sustainable cities. It is noteworthy that a participant suggested that the citizens should be empowered for decision making; however, their level of autonomy should be regulated by the relevant stakeholders. A participant said that *"The engagement of citizens participation should not be limited to just get their voices but also to be part of the development"*. The findings further reveal that citizens and policymakers must have a cordial relationship that will lead to bridging different forms of gaps that could lead to hold-up in development of some city areas. A participant also shared their thought about the participation of citizens in development of SSC, as they feel that citizens' participation must be properly prioritised in decision making in adopting SSC, in agreement to the respondent who claimed that *"I totally support the engagement of citizens participation, however, to an extent to have only a maximum of the partnership of power with the government"*. Further, *"the higher stakeholder's participation the better for urban development which leads to better outcomes"*.

Additionally, the participants highlighted some of the important roles of citizens in the development process of SSC. A participant revealed that citizens should have access to government data as well as a countable voice in the government bodies. However, data must be governed and encrypted for security and protection purposes [98]. Similarly, another participant opines that *"the role of citizen participation must be very high in the neighbourhood level while being very low at the national level"*.

4.4. Toward Smart Sustainable Cities Framework

SSC is regarded to be all-inclusive and is carried out to improve social sustainability, economic sustainability, and environmental sustainability. The three rounds of the Delphi survey focus on obtaining the opinions of experts on SSC with pre-defined questions used to identify and validate their responses. Round three of the survey reveals that citizens and stakeholders play an interrelated and dependent role in the development of SSC. The different categories of stakeholders will need the cooperation of citizens to accomplish the bigger picture of SSC. The majority of participants were of the opinion that citizens should be allowed to make certain decisions since they are mostly affected by the overall decisions of the government stakeholders. Hence, their voices should be acknowledged and considered in every decision process in order to ensure an all-inclusive decision making for the development of SC. The educational and demographic background of stakeholders should be considered before assigning them to project management. This will ensure that they are optimally performing since they have similar backgrounds in city building and project management. Moreover, data security and management should be given priority to maintain the safe identity of all citizens without violation of any sort in driving the smart sustainable cities.

A framework for developing SSC should be based on a comprehensive and participatory planning process that involves all stakeholders, including citizens, government, businesses, and community organisations. This study develops citizen participation for smart sustainable cities framework (CPSSCF) (see Figure 2). It is a combination of research domains and experts' experience used to verify the accuracy and quality of data, models, and systems. The structure of the CPSSCF consists of SSM, CPL, and CPR to effectively identify, engage, and communicate with stakeholders in order to manage their expectations and ensure that their interests are taken into account in decision making. Knowledge of SC and FSCP was examined. A consideration was made of the awareness from the perspective of both the government and the citizens. There is a desire on the part of the CP in this development. As a final point, some opinions were discussed regarding some urban agendas. Furthermore, an essential part of the framework is SMM. SMM consists of four critical factors, which are Regulation, Collaboration, Legitimates, and Control which are factors that support the increase of CPL [8]. Regulation refers to the act of controlling or directing something according to a set of rules or laws. Collaboration refers to the act of working together with others to achieve a common goal. Legitimates refer to something that is lawful, proper, or in accordance with the rules. Control refers to the ability to direct or manage something.

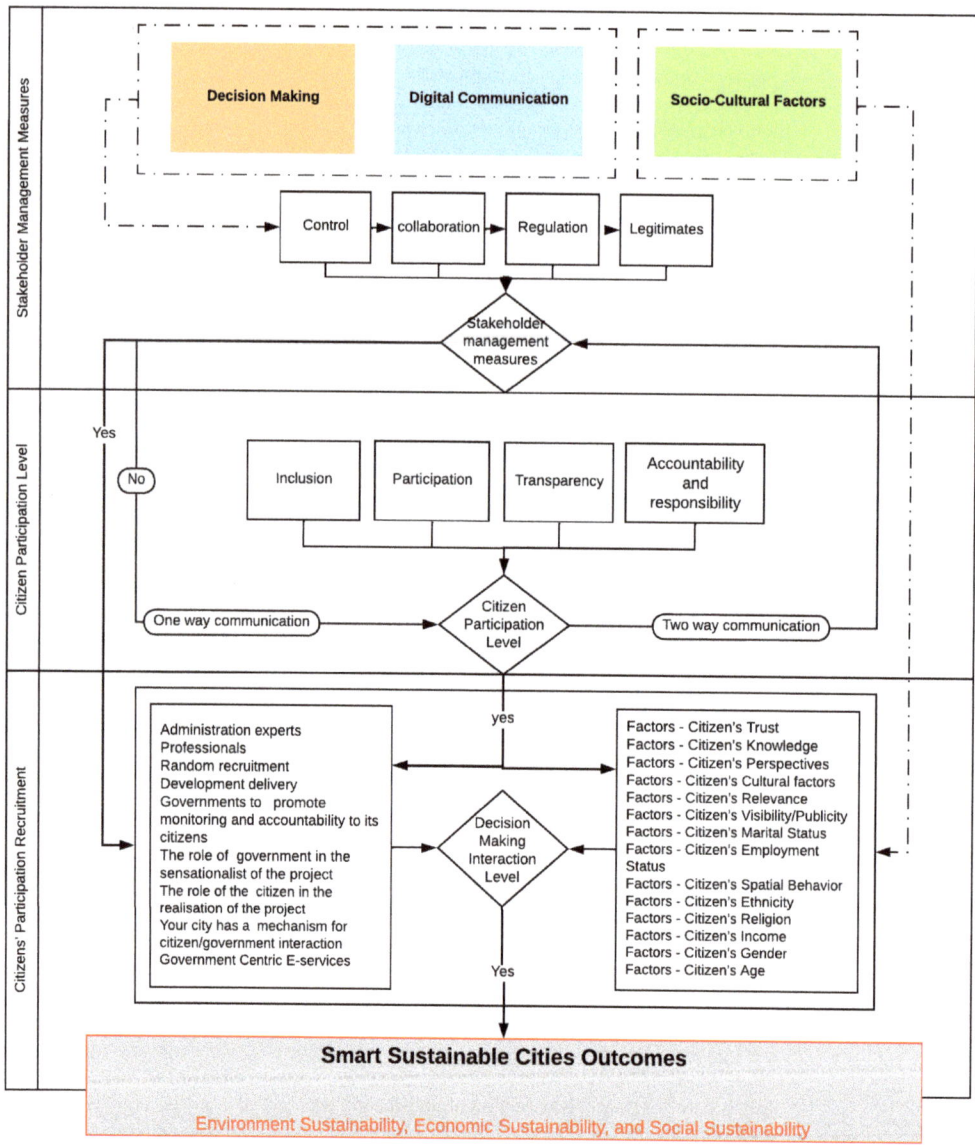

Figure 2. Citizen Participation for Smart Sustainable Cities Framework (CPSSCF).

On the other hand, CPL can help to ensure that the needs and perspectives of all members of the community are taken into account and that the resulting plan reflects the values and priorities of the community and drives SCCO. Four factors were considered in this framework [56]. Accountability and responsibility refer to the obligation of an individual or organisation to answer for their actions and decisions and to take ownership of their consequences. Transparency is the quality of being open and honest, providing access to information, and being easily understood. Participation refers to being actively engaged in a process, such as decision making or community engagement. Inclusion is the act of making sure that all individuals have an equal opportunity to participate and be heard, regardless of their background or identity. Together, these concepts promote good governance, democratic decision making, and social justice by ensuring that all voices are heard and all actions are accountable.

Lastly, CPR, an additional implementation measure identified by this study, is another important factor that sets the criteria to involve the most relevant participants. This recruitment can be achieved by involving two characteristics. First, the attributes of the participant are as follows: citizens' trust, knowledge, perspective, cultural factors, relevance, visibility publicity, marital factors, employment status, spatial behaviour, ethnicity, religion, income, gender, and age. Additionally, the quality of participants is crucial, such as in administration, random recruitment delivery, accountability, role of government, role of citizen in realisation of projects, and two-way interaction with government.

The expected outcomes are presented in Figure 2, which are Environmental Sustainability, Economic Sustainability, and Social Sustainability. It involves a holistic approach that addresses the interrelationship of these three areas. It also includes actions such as: developing policies and programs, implementing regulations and incentives, investing in the conservation and restoration of natural resources, fostering economic growth, advocating for social justice and protecting human rights, and encouraging community involvement and participation. It is a multi-stakeholder approach that involves government, business, and civil society working together to implement SSC solutions.

5. Conclusions

As determined through this study, SSC-related standards are being developed by various international scholars, organisations, and government entities within their specific domains, but little attention is given to citizens' participation. A framework for citizens' participation was developed with the objective of determining whether any additional stakeholder management measures are necessary, as well as explaining the relationship between SMM, CPL, and CPR. Three rounds of the Delphi method were conducted. The importance of these additional stakeholder management measures was confirmed by MS ranking and Kendall Coefficient. The results suggest three main component structures of the framework, which are SMM, CPL, and CPR. Essentially, CPR specifies the standards for recruiting suitable citizen participants, SMM motivates citizens to participate and raise CPL in the SCC development process, and all of these result in SSCO to achieve FSCP within the context of Vision2030 government policy.

The proposed framework is an essential contribution to understanding the issue conceptually and practically. This study is built upon theoretical foundations which can provide a solid foundation for understanding and addressing an issue of SSCO. Theoretical underpinnings can help explain why the Delphi method is being used. It can also provide a basis for evaluating the effectiveness of the framework. Developing a conceptual framework that can support the implementation of SSC will contribute to the body of knowledge by acknowledging the contribution of CP and understanding CPR standards.

The implication to knowledge is that the framework provides a structure for organizing and understanding existing knowledge, as well as for highlighting gaps in the current body of knowledge. This study proposes a framework where SMM is correlated to CPL, and CPL is also correlated to SSCO within the context of Saudi Arabia. Moreover, CPR is an essential foundation where it identifies the characteristics of participants. It can also be used as a tool to guide and inform future research, helping to expand and deepen knowledge in the SSC field to cover other related aspects, as presented in Figure 1. Additionally, the developed framework can serve as a common language or reference point for researchers and practitioners in involving and facilitating communication and collaboration for CP in SSC.

Another implication is in providing a conceptual and practical framework for understanding the urban challenges. Policy implications include facilitating the decision makers' implementation of SSC in other cities and understanding stakeholder expectations. In other words, SSCO supports communication between the authorities and decision makers and identifies what citizens are expected to do. Moreover, this study recommends that authorities raise the level of CP by involving stakeholders' participation in smart cities by providing them with the opportunity to participate in the development of SSC regulations and engaging them in the process, as well as providing them with a basis for improving strategic management, which involves their participation at every stage. Subsequently, this research develops inclusive communication through the CPSSCF framework. Consequently, SSC will be developed and implemented.

For future research, the proposed framework should be explored for its scalability so that it can be aligned with VISION 2030 and government objectives and strategies as well as broader regulations to provide sight between government policies, citizens' requirements, and infrastructure asset performance in the future. To improve the overall generalisation, additional research should be conducted when the FSCP is fully implemented in 17 pilot cities. It is, therefore, important to be cautious when generalising the findings of this study. Moreover, the survey's respondents were limited to Saudi Arabians and a small study group, indicating that a more diverse sample is needed. The study was conducted with the aim of including female respondents, despite the majority of urban professionals in Saudi Arabia being male. Moreover, a solid connection between urban development and ordinary citizens could have been improved. Therefore, once women have a greater presence in the industry, future studies will explore their views on citizen participation. Furthermore, future research could include qualitative approaches such as focus groups and interviews for a more in-depth understanding. It is important to consider these limitations when examining how the CPSSCF framework could be adopted in developing countries in order for SSC to achieve success.

Author Contributions: Conceptualisation, A.K.A., R.B.A. and T.Y.M.L.; methodology, A.K.A., R.B.A. and T.Y.M.L.; software, A.K.A.; validation, A.K.A., R.B.A. and T.Y.M.L.; formal analysis, A.K.A.; investigation, R.B.A. and T.Y.M.L.; resources, A.K.A., R.B.A. and T.Y.M.L.; data curation, A.K.A.; writing—original draft preparation, A.K.A.; writing—review and editing, R.B.A. and T.Y.M.L.; visualisation, A.K.A., R.B.A. and T.Y.M.L.; supervision, R.B.A. and T.Y.M.L.; project administration, A.K.A., R.B.A. and T.Y.M.L. All authors have read and agreed to the published version of the manuscript.

Funding: This research received no external funding.

Institutional Review Board Statement: Not applicable.

Informed Consent Statement: Not applicable.

Data Availability Statement: It can be made available upon request to the corresponding author.

Acknowledgments: This paper forms part of a larger research project which focuses on citizen participation to support the implementation of smart sustainable cities, from which other papers will be produced with a different objective/scope but sharing the same background and methodology. The Saudi Arabia government, represented by Imam Abdulrahman Bin Faisal University (IAU), is appreciated for their internal financial sponsorship and other support for this PhD study.

Conflicts of Interest: The authors declare no conflict of interest.

References

1. Harrison, C.; Donnelly, I.A. A Theory of Smart Cities. In Proceedings of the 55th Annual Meeting of the ISSS-2011, Hull, UK, 17–22 July 2011. [CrossRef]
2. United Nations. Revision of World Urbanization Prospects. Available online: https://www.un.org/development/desa/publications/2018-revision-of-world-urbanization-prospects.html (accessed on 5 October 2022).
3. Bibri, S.; Krogstie, J. Smart sustainable cities of the future: An extensive interdisciplinary literature review. *Sustain. Cities Soc.* **2017**, *31*, 183–212. [CrossRef]
4. Alshuwaikhat, H.M.; Aina, Y.A.; Binsaedan, L. Analysis of the implementation of urban computing in smart cities: A framework for the transformation of Saudi cities. *Heliyon* **2022**, *8*, e11138. [CrossRef]
5. Aina, Y.; Wafer, A.; Ahmed, F.; Alshuwaikhat, H. Top-down sustainable urban development? urban governance transformation in Saudi Arabia. *Cities* **2019**, *90*, 272–281. [CrossRef]
6. Gassmann, O.; Böhm, J.; Palmié, M. *Smart Cities: Introducing Digital Innovation to Cities*; Emerald Group Publishing: Bingley, UK, 2019.
7. Ramaprasad, A.; Sanchez Ortiz, A.; Syn, T. *A Unified Definition of a Smart City*; Springer: Cham, Switzerland, 2017; pp. 13–24.
8. Alamoudi, A.K.; Abidoye, R.B.; Lam, T.Y.M. The Impact of Stakeholders' Management Measures on Citizens' Participation Level in Implementing Smart Sustainable Cities. *Sustainability* **2022**, *14*, 16617. [CrossRef]
9. Bibri, S. A foundational framework for smart sustainable city development: Theoretical, disciplinary, and discursive dimensions and their synergies. *Sust. Cities Soc.* **2018**, *38*, 758–794. [CrossRef]
10. Embarak, O. Smart Cities New Paradigm Applications and Challenges. In *Immersive Technology in Smart Cities: Augmented and Virtual Reality in IoT*; Aurelia, S., Paiva, S., Eds.; Springer International Publishing: Cham, Switzerland, 2022; pp. 147–177. [CrossRef]
11. Kuster, C. A Real Time Urban Sustainability Assessment Framework for the Smart City Paradigm. Ph.D. Thesis, Cardiff University, Cardiff, UK, 2019.
12. Neirotti, P.; Marco, A.D.; Cagliano, A.C.; Mangano, G.; Scorrano, F. Current trends in Smart City initiatives: Some stylised facts. *Cities* **2014**, *38*, 25–36. [CrossRef]
13. Girardi, P.; Temporelli, A. Smartainability: A Methodology for Assessing the Sustainability of the Smart City. *Energy Procedia* **2016**, *111*, 810–816.
14. Alamoudi, A.K.; Abidoye, R.B.; Lam, T.Y. Critical Review of Citizens' Participation in Achieving Smart Sustainable Cities: The Case of Saudi Arabia. In *International Summit Smart City 360°*; Paiva, S., Li, X., Lopes, S.I., Gupta, N., Rawat, D.B., Patel, A., Karimi, H.R., Eds.; Springer: Berlin/Heidelberg, Germany, 2022; Volume 442, pp. 434–454. [CrossRef]
15. Damian, D.; Phan, T. *Introduction to Smart Cities in Asia: Regulations, Problems, and Development*, 1st ed.; Thanh Phan, D.D., Ed.; Springer: Singapore, 2022.
16. Andone, D.; Holotescu, C.; Grosseck, G. Learning Communities in Smart Cities. Case Studies. In Proceedings of the 2014 International Conference on Web and Open Access to Learning (ICWOAL), Dubai, United Arab Emirates, 25–27 November 2014; pp. 1–4. [CrossRef]
17. Aina, Y. Achieving smart sustainable cities with GeoICT support: The Saudi evolving smart cities. *Purinergic Signal* **2017**, *71*, 49–58. [CrossRef]
18. Mora, L.; Bolici, R.; Deakin, M. The first two decades of smart-city research: A bibliometric analysis. *J. Urban Technol.* **2017**, *24*, 3–27. [CrossRef]
19. Calixto, V.; Gu, N.; Celani, G. A Critical Framework of Smart Cities Development. In Proceedings of the 24th International Conference on Computer-Aided Architectural Design Research in Asia (CAADRIA 2019), Wellington, New Zealand, 15–18 April 2019.
20. Shah, M.; Nagargoje, S.; Shah, C. Assessment of Ahmedabad (India) and Shanghai (China) on smart city parameters applying the Boyd Cohen smart city wheel. In *Proceedings of the 20th International Symposium on Advancement of Construction Management and Real Estate*; Springer: Singapore, 2017; pp. 111–127. [CrossRef]
21. Martin, C.; Evans, J.; Karvonen, A.; Paskaleva, K.; Yang, D.; Linjordet, T. Smart-sustainability: A new urban fix? *Sustain. Cities Soc.* **2019**, *45*, 640–648.
22. Ahvenniemi, H.; Huovila, A.; Pinto-Seppä, I.; Airaksinen, M. What are the differences between sustainable and smart cities? *Cities* **2017**, *60*, 234–245. [CrossRef]
23. Silva, B.N.; Khan, M.; Han, K. Towards sustainable smart cities: A review of trends, architectures, components, and open challenges in smart cities. *Sustain. Cities Soc.* **2018**, *38*, 697–713. [CrossRef]
24. Yigitcanlar, T.; Kamruzzaman, M.; Foth, M.; Marques, J.; da Costa, E.; Ioppolo, G. Can cities become smart without being sustainable? a systematic review of the literature. *Sustain. Cities Soc.* **2018**, *45*, 348–365. [CrossRef]
25. Romero-Lankao, P.; Frantzeskaki, N.; Griffith, C. Sustainability transformation emerging from better governance. *Urban Planet. Knowl. Towards Sustain. Cities. Camb. Univ. Press Camb.* **2018**, 263–280. [CrossRef]
26. Evans, B.; Joas, M.; Sundback, S.; Theobald, K. Governing local sustainability. *J. Environ. Plan. Manag.* **2006**, *49*, 849–867. [CrossRef]
27. Allmendinger, P.; Tewdwr-Jones, M. New Labour, new planning? The trajectory of planning in Blair's Britain. *Urban Stud.* **2000**, *37*, 1379–1402. [CrossRef]

28. Almughairy, A.M. Rethinking Regional Development Strategies in Saudi Arabia: Planning Processes, Governance, and Implementation. *J. Sustain. Dev.* **2019**, *12*, 131. [CrossRef]
29. Al-Hathloul, S. Riyadh development plans in the past fifty years (1967–2016). *Curr. Urban Stud.* **2017**, *5*, 97. [CrossRef]
30. Erete, S.; Burrell, J.O. Empowered Participation: How Citizens Use Technology in Local Governance. In Proceedings of the 2017 CHI Conference on Human Factors in Computing Systems, Denver, CO, USA, 6–11 May 2017; pp. 2307–2319. [CrossRef]
31. Gaber, J. Building "A Ladder of Citizen Participation": Sherry Arnstein, Citizen Participation, and Model Cities. *J. Am. Plan. Assoc.* **2019**, *85*, 188–201. [CrossRef]
32. Sigwejo, A.; Pather, S. A citizen-centric framework for assessing e-government effectiveness. *Electron. J. Inf. Syst. Dev. Ctries* **2016**, *74*, 1–27. [CrossRef]
33. Sartori, G. *The Theory of Democracy Revisited*; Chatham House Pub: London, UK, 1987; Volume 1.
34. Dahl, R.A. *Democracy and Its Critics*; Yale University Press: New Haven, CT, USA, 2008.
35. Schumpeter, J.A. Capitalism, socialism and democracy (1942). *J. Econ. Lit.* **1976**, *20*, 1463. [CrossRef]
36. UN-Habitat, Jeddah CPI Profile 2018. 2018. 9. Available online: https://unhabitat.org/cpi-profile-jeddah (accessed on 6 April 2023).
37. UN-Habitat, Saudi Cities Report 2019. 2018. Available online: https://unhabitat.org/saudi-cities-report-2019 (accessed on 6 April 2023).
38. Saudi Arabia VISION2030. Vision 2030 Overview: An Ambitious Vision for an Ambitious Nation. Available online: https://www.vision2030.gov.sa/v2030/overview/ (accessed on 2 October 2022).
39. Caragliu, A.; Del Bo, C.; Nijkamp, P. Smart cities in Europe. *J. Urban Technol.* **2009**, *18*, 65–82. [CrossRef]
40. Khater, I. Certification Systems as a Tool for Sustainable Architecture and Urban Planning, Sase Study: Estidama, Abu Dhabi. Master's Thesis, HafenCity University, Hamburg, Germany, 2013.
41. UN-Habitat, Urban Management Programme (UMP). 2003. 2018. Available online: http://www.fukuoka.unhabitat.org/programmes/detail04_05_en.html (accessed on 1 April 2023).
42. Melbourne City Council, City Plan 2010: Towards a Thriving and Sustainable City. 2005. Available online: https://librarysearch.melbourne.vic.gov.au/cgi-bin/spydus.exe/FULL/OPAC/BIBENQ/1039536/20988041,2 (accessed on 3 April 2023).
43. Chua, L.H. *The Singapore Green Plan 2012: Beyond Clean and Green towards Environmental Sustainability*; Singapore Ministry of the Environment: Singapore, 2002.
44. Ling, W.; Wei, D.; Lian, F. The differences of typical assessment standard systems for green building and implications for China. *IOP Conf. Ser. Earth Environ. Sci.* **2018**, *186*, 012024. [CrossRef]
45. Umer, A.; Hewage, K.; Haider, H.; Sadiq, R. Sustainability assessment of roadway projects under uncertainty using Green Proforma: An index-based approach. *Int. J. Sustain. Built Environ.* **2016**, *5*, 604–619.
46. ISO 37120; Dahleh, D.; Fox, M.S. An Environmental Ontology for Global City Indicators. 2016. Available online: https://www.rd-alliance.org/system/files/documents/GCI%20Environmental%20Ontology%20Final%2017sep2016.pdf (accessed on 2 October 2022).
47. Aspinal, S.; Sertyesilisik, B.; Sourani, A.; Tunstall, A. How accurately does BREEAM measure sustainability? *Creat. Educ.* **2013**, *3*, 1.
48. Garde, A. Sustainable by design: Insights from U.S. LEED-ND pilot projects. *J. Am. Plan. Assoc.* **2009**, *75*, 424–440. [CrossRef]
49. AlQahtany, A.; Rezgui, Y.; Li, H. A proposed model for sustainable urban planning development for environmentally friendly communities. *Archit. Eng. Des. Manag.* **2013**, *9*, 176–194. [CrossRef]
50. Saha, D. Factors influencing local government sustainability efforts. *State Local Gov. Rev.* **2009**, *41*, 39–48.
51. Abubakar, A.; Romice, O.; Salama, A.M. Slums and prosperity: A complex, dynamic Pathway of intervention. *Archnet-IJAR Int. J. Archit. Res.* **2019**, *13*, 314–330.
52. Wackernagel, M.; Hanscom, L.; Lin, D. Making the sustainable development goals consistent with sustainability. *Front. Energy Res.* **2017**, *5*, 18.
53. Marsal Llacuna, M.L. City indicators on social sustainability as standardization technologies for smarter (Citizen-Centered) governance of cities. *Int. Interdiscip. J. Qual. Life Meas.* **2016**, *128*, 1193–1216. [CrossRef]
54. Wilson, D. *The Politics of the Urban Sustainability Concept*; University of Illinois: Urbana-Champaign, IL, USA, 2019.
55. Khogali, H. Comparison of four global sustainable building rating systems carried out with focus on hot and dry climate. *J. Sustain. Dev.* **2016**, *9*, 1–25. [CrossRef]
56. Alamoudi, A.K.; Abidoye, R.B.; Lam, T.Y.M. The Impact of Citizens' Participation Level on Smart Sustainable Cities Outcomes: Evidence from Saudi Arabia. *Buildings* **2023**, *13*, 343. [CrossRef]
57. Lekamge, S.; Marasinghe, A. Developing a Smart City Model that Ensures the Optimum Utilization of Existing Resources in Cities of All Sizes. In Proceedings of the Biometrics and Kansei Engineering (ICBAKE), Tokyo, Japan, 5–7 July 2013; pp. 202–207.
58. Lu, D.; Tian, Y.; Liu, V.; Zhang, Y. The performance of the smart cities in China—A comparative study by means of self-organizing maps and social networks analysis. *Sustainability* **2015**, *7*, 7604–7621. [CrossRef]
59. Lombardi, P.; Giordano, S.; Caragliu, A.; Del Bo, C.; Deakin, M.; Nijkamp, P.; Kourtit, K. An advanced Triple-Helix network model for smart cities performance. In *Green and Ecological Technologies for Urban Planning: Creating Smart Cities*; IGI Global: Hershey, PA, USA, 2011.

60. Storch, D.A. Smart City Profiles. Available online: https://smartcities.at/activities/smart-city-profiles-en-us/ (accessed on 30 March 2023).
61. City Protocal. Amsterdam Smart City. Available online: https://amsterdamsmartcity.com/projects/city-protocol (accessed on 25 March 2023).
62. Airaksinen, M.; Seppa, I.; Huovila, A.; Neumann, H.-M.; Iglár, B.; Bosch, P. Smart city performance measurement framework CITYkeys. In Proceedings of the 2017 International Conference on Engineering, Technology and Innovation (ICE/ITMC), Madeira, Portugal, 27–29 June 2017; pp. 718–723.
63. Albino, V.; Berardi, U.; Dangelico, R.M. Smart cities: Definitions, dimensions, performance, and initiatives. *J. Urban Technol.* **2015**, *22*, 3–21. [CrossRef]
64. Mahesa, R.; Yudoko, G.; Anggoro, Y. Dataset on the sustainable smart city development in Indonesia. *Data Brief* **2019**, *25*, 104098. [CrossRef]
65. Rajput, S.; Sharma, P. *Sustainable Smart Cities in India: Challenges and Future Perspectives*; Springer: Cham, Switzerland, 2017. [CrossRef]
66. Ringenson, T.; Eriksson, E.; Börjesson Rivera, M.; Wangel, J. The Limits of the Smart Sustainable City. In Proceedings of the 2017 Workshop on Computing Within Limits, Santa Barbara, CA, USA, 22–24 June 2017; pp. 3–9. [CrossRef]
67. Yigitcanlar, T.; Kamruzzaman, M. Planning, development and management of sustainable cities: A commentary from the guest editors. *Sustainability* **2015**, *7*, 14677–14688. [CrossRef]
68. Alamoudi, A.K.; Abidoye, R.B.; Lam, T.Y.M. An evaluation of stakeholders' participation process in developing smart sustainable cities in Saudi Arabia. *Smart Sustain. Built Environ.* **2022**; *ahead-of-print*. [CrossRef]
69. Toepoel, V.; Emerson, H. Using experts' consensus (the Delphi method) to evaluate weighting techniques in web surveys not based on probability schemes. *Math. Popul. Stud.* **2017**, *24*, 161–171. [CrossRef]
70. Okoli, C.; Pawlowski, S.D. The Delphi Method as a Research Tool: An Example, Design Considerations and Applications. *Inf. Manag.* **2004**, *42*, 15–29. [CrossRef]
71. Jang, S.-g.; Gim, T.-H.T. Considerations for Encouraging Citizen Participation by Information-Disadvantaged Groups in Smart Cities. *Sustain. Cities Soc.* **2022**, *76*, 103437. [CrossRef]
72. Osei-Kyei, R. A Best Practice Framework For Public Private Partnership Implementation For Infrastructure Development in Chana. Ph.D. Thesis, The Hong Kong Polytechnic University, Hong Kong, China, 2018.
73. Pratama, A.; Imawan, S. A Scale for Measuring Perceived Bureaucratic Readiness for Smart Cities. *Public Adm. Policy Asia-Pac. J.* **2019**, *22*, 25–39. [CrossRef]
74. Niezabitowska, E.D. *Research Methods and Techniques in Architecture*; Routledge: London, UK, 2018; pp. P138–P260.
75. Akins, R.; Tolson, H.; Cole, B. Stability of response characteristics of a Delphi panel: Application of bootstrap data expansion. *BMC Med. Res. Methodol.* **2005**, *5*, 37. [CrossRef]
76. The Work Bank. Labor force, female (% of total labor force)—Saudi Arabia. Available online: https://data.worldbank.org/indicator/SL.TLF.TOTL.FE.ZS?locations=SA (accessed on 22 November 2022).
77. Ke, F. A qualitative meta-analysis of computer games as learning tools. In *Gaming and Simulations: Concepts, Methodologies, Tools and Applications*; IGI Global: Hershey, PA, USA, 2011; pp. 1619–1665. [CrossRef]
78. Bangor, A.; Kortum, P.; Miller, J. Determining what individual SUS scores mean: Adding a subjective rating scale. *J. Usability Stud.* **2009**, *4*, 114–123. [CrossRef]
79. Cheung, E.; Chan, A.P. Risk factors of public-Private partnership projects in China: Comparison between the water, power, and transportation sectors. *J. Urban Plan. Dev.* **2011**, *137*, 409–415. [CrossRef]
80. Gliem, J.A.; Gliem, R.R. Calculating, Interpreting, and Reporting Cronbach's Alpha Reliability Coefficient for Likert-type Scales. 2003. Available online: https://scholarworks.iupui.edu/handle/1805/344 (accessed on 30 January 2023).
81. Zhu, W.; Yan, R.; Song, Y. Analysing the impact of smart city service quality on citizen engagement in a public emergency. *Cities* **2022**, *120*, 103439. [CrossRef]
82. Hayu, R.; Surachman, S.; Rofiq, A.; Rahayu, M. The effect of website quality and government regulations on online impulse buying behaviour. *Manag. Sci. Lett.* **2020**, *10*, 961–968. [CrossRef]
83. Sen, P.K. Estimates of the regression coefficient based on Kendall's tau. *J. Am. Stat. Assoc.* **1968**, *63*, 1379–1389. [CrossRef]
84. Siegel, S.; Castellan, N.; Me Graw-Hill, J. *Nonparametric Statistics for the Behavioral Sciences*; McGraw-Hill: New York, NY, USA, 1988; pp. 174–183.
85. Musambi, D.; Dirir, A.; Yaqoob, I.; Salah, K.; Jayaraman, R.; Puthal, D. NFTs in Smart Cities: Vision, Applications, and Challenges. *IEEE Consum. Electron. Mag.* **2022**, 1–14. [CrossRef]
86. Carson, L.; Martin, B. Random selection of citizens for technological decision making. *Sci. Public Policy* **2002**, *29*, 105–113. [CrossRef]
87. Asaro, P.V.; Land, G.H.; Hales, J.W. Making Public Health Data Available to Community-Level Decision Makers—Goals, Issues, and a Case Report. *J. Public Health Manag. Pract.* **2001**, *7*, 58–63. [PubMed]
88. Lindquist, E.A.; Huse, I. Accountability and monitoring government in the digital era: Promise, realism and research for digital-era governance. *Can. Public Adm.* **2017**, *60*, 627–656. [CrossRef]
89. Piqueiras, P.; Canel, M.-J.; Luoma-aho, V. Citizen Engagement and Public Sector Communication. In *The Handbook of Public Sector Communication*; John Wiley & Sons, Inc.: Hoboken, NJ, USA, 2020; pp. 277–287. [CrossRef]

90. Mansoor, M. Citizens' trust in government as a function of good governance and government agency's provision of quality information on social media during COVID-19. *Gov. Inf. Q.* **2021**, *38*, 101597. [CrossRef] [PubMed]
91. Mees, H.L.P.; Uittenbroek, C.J.; Hegger, D.L.T.; Driessen, P.P.J. From citizen participation to government participation: An exploration of the roles of local governments in community initiatives for climate change adaptation in the Netherlands. *Environ. Policy Gov.* **2019**, *29*, 198–208. [CrossRef]
92. Bozeman, B. Public values: Citizens' perspective. *Public Manag. Rev.* **2019**, *21*, 817–838. [CrossRef]
93. Masood, A.; Azfar Nisar, M. Administrative Capital and Citizens' Responses to Administrative Burden. *J. Public Adm. Res. Theory* **2021**, *31*, 56–72. [CrossRef]
94. Trottier, D. Digital Vigilantism as Weaponisation of Visibility. *Philos. Technol.* **2017**, *30*, 55–72. [CrossRef]
95. Bolzendahl, C.; Coffé, H. Are 'Good' Citizens 'Good' Participants? Testing Citizenship Norms and Political Participation across 25 Nations. *Political Stud.* **2013**, *61*, 45–65. [CrossRef]
96. Fraune, C. Gender matters: Women, renewable energy, and citizen participation in Germany. *Energy Res. Soc. Sci.* **2015**, *7*, 55–65. [CrossRef]
97. Schlozman, K.L.; Burns, N.; Verba, S.; Donahue, J. Gender and Citizen Participation: Is There a Different Voice? *Am. J. Political Sci.* **1995**, *39*, 267–293. [CrossRef]
98. Sun, L.; Zhang, H.; Fang, C. Data security governance in the era of big data: Status, challenges, and prospects. *Data Sci. Manag.* **2021**, *2*, 41–44. [CrossRef]

Disclaimer/Publisher's Note: The statements, opinions and data contained in all publications are solely those of the individual author(s) and contributor(s) and not of MDPI and/or the editor(s). MDPI and/or the editor(s) disclaim responsibility for any injury to people or property resulting from any ideas, methods, instructions or products referred to in the content.

Review

Understanding Local Government Digital Technology Adoption Strategies: A PRISMA Review

Anne David [1], Tan Yigitcanlar [1,*], Rita Yi Man Li [2], Juan M. Corchado [3], Pauline Hope Cheong [4], Karen Mossberger [5] and Rashid Mehmood [6]

1. City 4.0 Lab, School of Architecture and Built Environment, Queensland University of Technology, Brisbane, QLD 4000, Australia; annejeevana.david@hdr.qut.edu.au
2. Sustainable Real Estate Research Center, Department of Economics and Finance, Hong Kong Shue Yan University, Hong Kong 999077, China; ymli@hksyu.edu
3. Bisite Research Group, Department of Computer Science and Automation, University of Salamanca, 37007 Salamanca, Spain; corchado@usal.es
4. Hugh Downs School of Human Communication, Arizona State University, Phoenix, AZ 85287, USA; pauline.cheong@asu.edu
5. Center on Technology, Data & Society, School of Public Affairs, Arizona State University, Phoenix, AZ 85287, USA; karen.mossberger@asu.edu
6. High-Performance Computing Center, King Abdulaziz University, Jeddah 21589, Saudi Arabia; rmehmood@kau.edu.sa
* Correspondence: tan.yigitcanlar@qut.edu.au; Tel.: +61-7-3138-2418

Citation: David, A.; Yigitcanlar, T.; Li, R.Y.M.; Corchado, J.M.; Cheong, P.H.; Mossberger, K.; Mehmood, R. Understanding Local Government Digital Technology Adoption Strategies: A PRISMA Review. *Sustainability* 2023, *15*, 9645. https://doi.org/10.3390/su15129645

Academic Editor: Martin De Jong

Received: 20 May 2023
Revised: 6 June 2023
Accepted: 12 June 2023
Published: 15 June 2023

Copyright: © 2023 by the authors. Licensee MDPI, Basel, Switzerland. This article is an open access article distributed under the terms and conditions of the Creative Commons Attribution (CC BY) license (https://creativecommons.org/licenses/by/4.0/).

Abstract: Digital technologies are used in various local government activities. Adopting suitable digital technology strategies could enhance service efficiency, effectiveness, and accountability. The challenges of technology adoption among local governments, however, are also evident. One of the major challenges is capacity, including the lack of knowledge or awareness of how to balance the local government's resources and the strategies that need to be implemented. This challenge also forms a research gap. The study aims to consolidate the understanding of local government digital technology adoption strategies via the Preferred Reporting Items for Systematic Reviews and Meta-Analyses (PRISMA). It analyses the adoption opportunities, challenges, and strategies through the lens of people, processes, and technology frameworks. The results show that: (a) Strategies concerning the people aspects include building a platform for public participation, employees' skills, and decision-makers' positive mindset development. (b) Strategies concerning the process aspects include recognizing the players' roles, having a clear aim and procedure, proper regulation, and receiving user input. (c) Strategies considering the technology aspects include understanding the effect of the technology, technological preparedness, and convenience adoption. The findings inform local government policymakers in digital technology adoption and transformation endeavors.

Keywords: technology adoption; local government; digital transformation; technology policy; urban technology; urban policy; public policy; smart city; City 4.0

1. Introduction

Local governments play an important role as front-line service providers to citizens, providing clear benefits for cities to become smarter and more sustainable [1–3]. Citizen dependency on the local government is high, and therefore, quick responses from the local government are anticipated among citizens. To meet citizen demand, local governments are experimenting with adopting appropriate digital technology to deliver services more efficiently, effectively, and accountably [4]. These experiments are not just about adopting new technology; they are about embracing new practices, procedures, and strategies that can improve the capacity of the local government to provide services that cater to the citizens' needs [5]. Those service provisions are more comprehensive but not limited to paying bills and local taxes, checking transit schedules, issuing and renewing licenses, supporting business start-ups, posting complaints, offering subscription opportunities to receive real-time updates and alerts, providing online ticket booking and parking slot allocation, supporting emergency services, and so on.

The popularity of smart cities or City 4.0 urbanization brought digital transformation to the forefront of urban discourse [6–9]. Even though local governments have adopted various digital technologies, many smaller or less-resourced local governments lack the capacity to research and comprehend how new technologies might improve their operations or the lives of citizens [10]. This lack of understanding makes the adoption process challenging since investment failure is likely. Therefore, when local governments introduce digital technologies, they need a proper strategy to maintain their information technology (IT) capacity, comparative advantage, current organizational operations, managerial capabilities, and other factors influencing the decision of the government authority to adopt or reject the new technology [11].

Accordingly, it is important to understand the opportunities and challenges associated with adopting technologies so that effective strategies may be developed; because it is critical to not only be aware of the challenges posed by digital technologies but also to develop plans of action that minimize those challenges and seize the opportunities for local governments [12,13].

The combination of local government and digital technologies has been the subject of numerous studies; the literature spans from investigating the benefits and challenges associated with the adoption of a specific technology among local governments, such as information and communication technology (ICT) [14–16], artificial intelligence (AI) [17], cloud computing [18], Web 2.0 [19], the influencing factors that drove technology adoption in local governments [4,11,20], the adoption of the digital technology for the sustainability of the local government [21,22], and the employees, city managers, and chief technical officers' perception on adopting digital technology for local government functions [23–25].

Even though several reviews have been carried out, none of these comprehensively looked at digital technology adoption in local government. Accordingly, this paper aims to consolidate the understanding of the landscape of local government digital technology adoption through the following main elements: (a) types of technology utilized for local government services; (b) digital technology adoption opportunities; (c) digital technology adoption challenges; and (d) strategies derived from adopting the digital technology.

This study adopted the People–Process–Technology (PPT) framework. It is defined as "the methodology in which the balance of people, process, and technology drives action: People perform a specific type of work for an organization using technology to streamline and improve these processes" [26]. Corporate management specialist Harold Leavitt developed the PPT framework in the early 1960s and published his model for bringing about organizational change [27]. Nowadays, this model has been utilized by software companies to maintain the balance of their resources. It has been used in several research fields, such as knowledge management [28], the construction sector [29], and healthcare [30], due to its ability to improve resource utilization and operational efficiency. Therefore, the study adapts this framework to the local government context. The framework consists of the following three pillars:

- People: People are referred to as the stakeholders who are internally and externally involved in the local government function, such as city managers, employees, politicians, citizens, etc. Having the right people who clearly understand their roles and responsibilities is important. They must comprehend what they must do, why they must do it, and how the changes will impact them. Any new processes or technologies cannot be implemented without the people's full support;
- Process: The process refers to a series of procedures or actions carried out to achieve a specific outcome or how people and technology achieve a desired goal. The process is concerned with how work is done in local governments;
- Technology: Technology is the tool for carrying out the government's procedures. It concerns how technology supports the work done by local governments. New tech-

nologies impact the local government the most. The local government, however, must ensure that the technology works.

These three pillars of people, process, and technology work in concert. People and processes must adjust if digital technology changes. For instance, many local governments use advanced technologies and expensive equipment. Nonetheless, the efficiency of technology depends on how it is used and managed. People's activities will be inefficient if organizations do not implement them well. They will also waste a significant portion of the benefits that technology offers. Citizens will not be able to benefit from the technology if they do not know how to use it appropriately. If the new technology does not match the existing procedures, the results will be the same or may even worsen. On the other hand, if the organization becomes overly fixated on the process, it will produce a plan that looks nice on paper but lacks the personnel or the technological resources needed to make it work. A good balance between these three pillars is the key to the success of the local government [31].

Accordingly, this paper looks at local government digital technology adoption opportunities, challenges, and strategies through a PPT framework to understand the balance between these three pillars of local governments. Following this introduction, Section 2 introduces the materials and methods. Section 3 presents the results. Section 4 presents and discusses the key findings. Section 5 concludes the paper.

2. Materials and Methods

A systematic literature review has been carried out using the Preferred Reporting Items for Systematic Reviews and Meta-Analyses (PRISMA) protocol, and the following research questions were identified for the present study: How do local governments use strategies to adopt digital technologies? The literature search task was conducted in February 2023. To answer this research question, the literature was reviewed in four steps: (a) identification; (b) screening; (c) eligibility; and (d) inclusion.

2.1. Identification

The first phase of identification involves the research aim, question, keywords, and inclusion and exclusion criteria. The research aims to consolidate the understanding of local government digital adoption strategies. The university's library search engine and Google Scholar were used to search for the literature online, including Science Direct, Scopus, Web of Science, and Open Access journals. The investigation was carried out until 10 February 2023 by using the following Boolean operation ((("digital technology*" OR "digital transformation") AND ("local government" OR "local governance" OR "municipal" OR "municipality" OR "regional council" OR "city council") AND ("strategy*" OR "recommendation"))). The beginning date of the search was kept open. The search resulted in a total of 443 references.

2.2. Screening

In the second screening phase, this study set out specific inclusion and exclusion criteria, as shown in Table 1, to reduce the number and help screen articles effectively. The peer-reviewed English articles that suit the research aim and have the full text available online are included in the screening process. The articles that do not belong to the inclusionary criteria are eliminated. Accordingly, the records were reduced to 265. Then, the abstract was read, and the articles irrelevant to the aim were removed. Subsequently, the suitable articles were sent to phase three, which is the eligibility phase. A total of 107 articles were included in this stage.

Table 1. The literature selection criteria.

Inclusionary Criteria	Exclusionary Criteria
Peer-reviewed journal articles	Books, chapters, conference proceedings, editorials, reports
English language	Journal articles in a language other than English
Relevant to the research aim/question	Not peer-reviewed
Full-text articles	Not relevant to the research aim/question
Available online	
Published date: published before 10 February 2023	
Case study area: unspecified	
Research method: unspecified	

2.3. Eligibility and Inclusion

During the eligibility phase, the articles were fully read, their research aim was considered, and they were further narrowed down to 95, and the final round of full-text reading shortened the number of relevant papers to 60. Lastly, these 60 journal articles were categorized and analyzed (Figure 1). All 60 papers were related to a particular technology, 34 were about digital technology adoption opportunities, 34 were about digital technology adoption challenges, and 33 provided technology adoption strategies. The list of these papers is included in Appendix A.

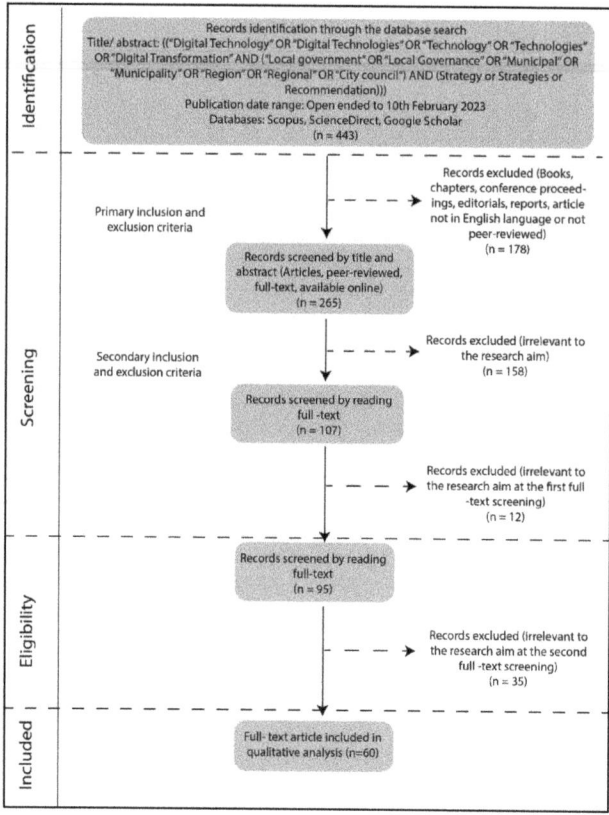

Figure 1. Summary of the PRISMA review.

Technologies offer different opportunities and challenges based on the adoption context. Strategies are considered a tool that helps capitalize on opportunities and prepare for the organization's challenges [32]. Considering the above and the aim of the study, the literature is categorized into four areas, i.e., technology types and application areas, adoption opportunities, challenges, and strategies and is further divided into the PPT framework dimensions.

3. Results

3.1. General Observation

Initially, the research papers were classified as per published year, with [33] the contribution of the oldest article included on this subject. Until 2019, the subject area had fluctuating growth in publications, but after that date, there was a drastic growth (Figure 2). The year 2020 records the largest number of journal articles published on the topic (13). This indicates that government-forced lockdowns during the COVID-19 pandemic, which started in 2019, led to an increase in the interest in this area. Social segregation and digital technologies have been utilized to bridge the gaps between local government and citizens [34]. Eventually, it became a research-focused area.

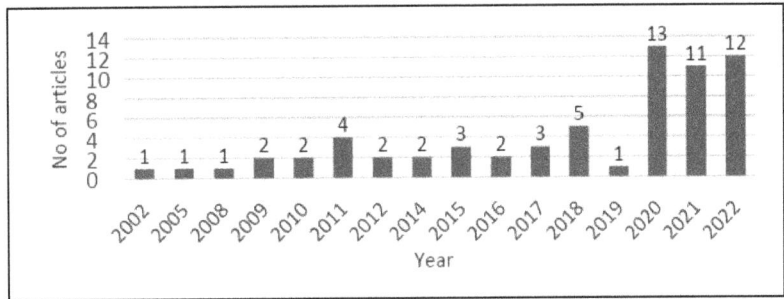

Figure 2. Publication distribution by year.

More than half of the papers ($n = 43$) used qualitative research methods, 18 presented the findings through quantitative methods, and only 3% followed a mixed method. Most journal articles ($n = 40$) were empirically tested, and 20 papers theoretically tested the subject. In total, 68% of the articles were based on surveys. Among them, 15 papers surveyed experts (managers, ICT coordinators, professors, heads of the departments, etc.), six articles were based on a staff (employees) survey, four papers were with Chief Administrative Officers (CAO), a couple of papers investigated Chief Information Officers (CIO), responsible officers, and all these papers reflected the policymakers and stakeholders' perspectives (Table 2).

Table 2. Characteristics of the reviewed articles.

Criteria	Category	No	%
Research Method	Qualitative	43	68%
	Quantitative	18	29%
	Mixed	2	3%
	Empirical	40	63%
	Theoretical	20	32%
	Mixed (empirical and theoretical)	3	5%

Table 2. Cont.

Criteria	Category	No	%
Case Study Area	Europe	23	33%
	Asia	19	27%
	North America	13	19%
	Oceania	7	10%
	Africa	6	9%
	South America	2	3%
Technology Type	ICT	28	47%
	Cloud Computing	11	18%
	AI	8	13%
	Web 2.0	5	8%
	Customer Relation Management (CRM)	3	5%
	Big data	2	3%
	IntTech	1	2%
	Internet-of-Things (IoT)	1	2%
	Master Data Management (MDM)	1	2%

The literature on this subject is featured in technology, government, and sustainability-orientated journals. Government Information Quarterly is a major outlet with 10 publications. In total, three articles were published in the International Journal of Information Management, and several were published by the International Journal of Cloud Application and Computing, the International Journal of Electronic Government Research, the International Review of Administrative Science, the Social Science Computing Review, and Sustainability. A total of 70 countries published articles in this field (meaning authors that have published articles in this field in diverse contexts, including 70 countries), and 63 articles conducted a single or comparative case study. European countries are the most frequently mentioned (33%), and South American countries are the least (3%).

As per Table 2, row 4, the results indicate that most articles mentioned ICT usage in local government ($n = 28$), cloud computing ($n = 11$), AI ($n = 8$), Web 2.0, CRM, and Big Data, IntTech, IOT, and MDM are some other technologies mentioned in the articles which are adopted for local government services. Some of these technologies have an interconnection. For example, MDM is a business and IT-related technology; but this paper looked at MDM separately to specify the technology type, which is applicable to other technologies mentioned in Table 2.

3.2. Local Government Digital Technologies

Technology adoption has a long history in the public sector, dating back to mainframe operations in the 70s and microcomputers in the 90s [15]. Local governments have also long used technologies to administer public services [35,36] as they are the frontline public service provider [1]. The extent of technology adoption capabilities, however, varies significantly between local governments [36]. It is becoming increasingly crucial to comprehend how various digital technologies influence local government operations and why certain governments adopt specific technologies over others [35].

Local governments use several digital technologies such as ICT, the Internet-of-Things (IoT), big data, AI, cloud computing, customer relation management (CRM), master data management (MDM), Web 2.0, Intech, etc., to provide their service [37]. It is evident from the literature that ICT is the dominant technology most local governments adopt. Past studies have shown that people who view technology favorably are more willing to use these technologies [38] due to the advantages associated with it, i.e., an accelerator for economic growth, generating new ideas, improving decision-making, boosting demand, cutting costs, fostering employment and regional development, and eliminating unsustainability [39].

A critical component of management in any organization is the efficient use of resources. A study [40] stated, "over the past decades, this notion has gradually expanded in the mainstream ICT sector with the emergence of resource-sharing concepts that include cloud computing". Cloud computing is "a mechanism or model for enabling easy, convenient, on-demand network access to a shared pool of devices such as server, network, storage services, application, service and other advanced computing devices which are configurable" [41]. Cloud-based delivery models are quickly grabbing the attention of IT government leaders due to limited budgets, a lack of adequate skills, and as part of the e-Government agenda [42].

For government organizations, cloud computing results in a significant cost reduction, a decrease in the infrastructure needs for ICT, an increase in organizational performance, and better customer service delivery [18]. Still, [43] finds that many local government organizations do not adopt cloud computing because (a) it is still in the initial stage and (b) it contains a high level of risk. Transparency and complexity have been widely discussed as the risk of cloud computing directly affecting citizens' trust [40]. Although cloud computing is identified as one of the best investments in technology, implementing these technologies in local governments is being done with caution because its long-term effects are unknown [44].

In recent times, many municipalities have begun using social media as an additional channel for online communication [45], which is known as Web 2.0, i.e., Facebook, Twitter, Instagram, LinkedIn, and other applications, in general, represent the most recent development in government Internet use [46]. These technologies empower citizens, accelerate transparency, and expand democracy through two-way communication methods [46]. According to [47], with two-way communication flows, citizens will no longer be positioned as just 'end users' but as partners and cocreators of information and services.

AI is a disruptive technology that profoundly affects communities and how local government services are organized and provided [48]. AI is defined as a group of interconnected technologies and systems that can make suggestions and judgments without or with little explicit human direction by performing perceptual, cognitive, and conversational functions typical of the human mind [48,49]. Different authors have acknowledged AI systems as a unique set of technological innovations that will make public services more efficient and effective. However, it changes public administration and management significantly and will shape the future of public organizations [50] by potentially improving the quality of public services, fostering citizen trust [17], enhancing efficiencies, tackling complexity, managing repetitive tasks, and automating routine decisions [51]. There are risks here as well if AI is built on misinformation or incomplete or biased information [52–54], but experimentation with these technologies is already underway at the local level.

Local governments have built digital technology infrastructure over the past few decades and created new applications for effective digital service delivery [55]. Although many local government services have made significant advancements, the full potential of digital technology adaptation has not yet been achieved. Hence, the subsections that follow elaborate on the digital technology adoption opportunities, challenges, and strategies to reach the full potential of local governments by maintaining a balance between the people, process, and technology.

3.3. Local Government Digital Technologies Adoption Opportunities

This subsection discusses the opportunities associated with adopting digital technologies in a local government function, i.e., the advantages that could be gained through adopting digital technologies through the subsections of (a) people, (b) process, and (c) technology.

3.3.1. People

The discussion in this subsection proceeds along three points, in accordance with the opportunities received by the actors: (a) increased citizen convenience and engagement, (b) perceived usefulness, and (c) increased accountability on the part of the decision-makers. These are elaborated below, and the summarized information is presented in Table 3.

- Increased Citizen Convenience and Engagement

Citizens expect the local government to provide convenient services [4]. Local government services have typically been provided in person, at various places, and usually using paper forms. However, nowadays, many local governments use smartphone applications, kiosks, chatbots, and user-friendly web platforms to simplify the service process and reduce customer waiting times. A study [24] underlined that due to these advancements, people do not need to visit the council in person to access the services.

Along with the growth of digital technologies, people have a greater interest in getting involved with their local government. This indicates that the conventional public service organization structure (one-way interaction meaning information provided to the public by the authority rather than two-way communication) is less acceptable in a digital age. Several studies [56,57] underlined that citizens should be a part of the planning process for developing new digital government initiatives. The public and the government interact positively when they have excellent relations, which results in more open and conducive governance [20].

Accordingly, several local governments have introduced Web 2.0 [58] to allow citizen participation in (a) gathering and disseminating feedback, and local knowledge, (b) collaboration and discussion via forums, comments, opinion maps, and surveys, (c) simulation software for 3D design and budget allocation, (d) idea gathering through voting and rating, and (e) tools for analyzing comments, votes, and user behavior across the platform [19]. Given the benefits of digital technologies and the fact that they enable collaborative participation, citizens are more likely to support their adoption [4].

- Perceived Usefulness

Perceived usefulness can be defined as the expected benefits that the employee can gain through the adopted digital technologies. This includes higher accuracy and faster processing, which in turn lead to reduced workload, pressure, and employee burden [24,59]. Milton Keynes Council (UK) adopted AI technology to strengthen services and boost effectiveness throughout its planning domain. Its initiative uses open source technology, including citizen self-service and customer-facing chatbots, to respond to real-time public inquiries. The number of calls has fallen since the project's introduction in 2018, while the number of chatbots has increased. This frees up considerable time for the planning officer [59]. Employees could use this time to build their capacity to improve their competence and become experts in digital technologies [24] or sharpen their skills and knowledge to provide a more satisfactory service. Article [24] argues that digital technologies enhance public employees' capabilities and allow them to concentrate on high-level and non-routine duties.

- Increased Accountability of Decision-Makers

Decision-makers are the most powerful in local governments, giving instructions, suggestions, and direction toward boundary development [20]. Accountability refers to an institution's dedication to its work, recognition of its unique organizational position, and transparency provided to the users or customers [57]. Digital technologies increase decision-makers' accountability specifically in three aspects: (a) knowledge enhancement, (b) innovativeness, and (c) capability and authority [60].

To meet citizen demands, guide employees, handle the pressure associated with the implementation of digital technologies, and support the local government, managers need to enhance their knowledge by understanding the advantages of digital technologies and allocate adequate funds and other resources for the implementation of the technology [61–63]. Innovativeness enhances the decision-makers' openness to implementing new technology, bringing fresh perspectives to the company, and cultivating innovative procedures that benefit the business and boost organizational performance [20]. A wide range of innovative and capable managers lower the dangers through a flexible ICT infrastructure design and the use of ICT skill-based resources [11], diversify the tasks assigned to employees, and reduce staffing restrictions. All these give more freedom to government officers to experiment with new technologies and enhance the effectiveness of the decision-makers [15].

Table 3. Local government digital technologies adoption opportunities—people.

Context	Attribute	Study
Increase citizen convenience and engagement	Citizen demand, expectation, involvement, participation, public pressure/expectation, socioeconomic attainment.	[1,4,11,20,24,39,56,57,60–62]
Perceived usefulness	Attitude, behavioral intention, ease of use, effort expectancy, knowledge management, motivated employees, performance expectancy, perceived availability, previous use, perceived usefulness, professionalization, staff request, social influence, and self-efficacy.	[15,56,57,62]
Increase the decision-makers' accountability	Efficiency changes and leadership, decision-making, managerial accountability, managerial innovations, managerial capability and authority, professional management, and support of top management.	[4,11,20,40,57,60–63]

3.3.2. Process

This subsection explains the opportunities digital technologies provide in the process under two aspects: (a) cost-effective finance management, and (b) enhanced service delivery. These are elaborated below, and the summarized information is presented in Table 4.

- Cost-Effective Finance Management

Previous research emphasized that cost-effective finance management is the primary opportunity that comes from adopting digital technologies as it is the local government's economic sustainability and primary function [40,56,61]. Local governments are trying to devise cost-efficient ways to restructure their IT infrastructure to cut expenses [42]. Electronic document delivery to the stakeholders and the adoption of energy-efficient technology are basic finance management methods adopted by most local governments [22]. Meanwhile, as an advanced method, local governments adopt cloud computing as it shares a common platform and networks, decreasing hardware expenditure, maintenance expenses, and energy consumption [42]. Additionally, [25] identified several benefits of utilizing AI in local governments. Among them is cost cutting. For example, the Blackpool City Council (UK) launched Project Amber in 2020. The council deployed AI-powered space satellite imagery and analysis to identify road deterioration and potholes. After that, the data were delivered back to the repair teams. Local government repaired over 5000 potholes while saving £1 million compared to conventional maintenance techniques.

- Enhance the Quality-of-Service Delivery

Quality is a crucial facilitator for enhancing various organizational capacities and determining the success of digital technologies [22,39]. The international standards of quality, as identified by [64], are composed of five characteristics, such as (a) effectiveness, (b) efficiency, (c) satisfaction—usefulness, trust, pleasure, and comfort, (d) freedom from risk—economic risk mitigation, health and safety risk mitigation, and environmental risk mitigation, and (e) context coverage—context completeness, flexibility [64].

Local governments benefit from using digital technology to understand their constituents better, acquire deep insights into what matters to them, and increase the accessibility of service delivery [4]. Local governments have access to social media platforms such as Facebook, where they openly ask the public for feedback to create a more customer-centric experience. Similarly, by automating repetitive tasks such as bookings and confirmation emails, digital technology has the potential to save governments and municipalities a significant amount of time and money. Effective deployment of features such as service automation will improve the client experience, expedite processes, and free up staff to concentrate on other crucial responsibilities [57].

Table 4. Local government digital technologies adoption opportunities—process.

Context	Attribute	Study
Cost-effective finance management	Budget and time, cost serving, expectation of reduced costs, funding, goal to improve service despite the increased cost, reduction in electricity and natural resource consumption.	[22,40,42,44,56,57,60]
Enhance the quality-of-service delivery	Anticipated benefits, appropriate system design, business operation, clear implementation plan, data governance, effort expectancy, goal clarity, improvement in government activity, organizational resource, organizational efficiency, performance measures, phased implementation, professional project management, strategic focus, transparency, and uncertainty.	[1,4,11,39,40,42,57,60–63]

3.3.3. Technology

This subsection discusses the opportunity associated with the adoption of technology as a tool from the perspective of (a) improved user-friendliness, and (b) reduced complexity. These are elaborated below, and the summarized information is presented in Table 5.

- Improve Usability

The adopted technology should have high-level usability or, in other words, should be user-friendly. The user interface should make the system simple to use, as services will be provided frequently [65]. Friendliness can be assessed through the language, users' culture, and accessibility for users with any disability [65,66], i.e., if the implemented digital technologies are simple to use and understand, the public will be much more likely to use them. This undoubtedly contributes to the simplification of numerous tasks that were previously carried out manually during face-to-face contact. This will save time and money when local governments streamline the procedures. User-friendliness lowers the digital gap, bringing the government and its citizens closer [65]. For example, Newham City Council (Australia) represents a population speaking more than 200 languages, and the council faces a communication problem between government employees and the local population. Then, the council introduced Futa—the multilingual chatbot which translates questions and answers, escalates complex chats to live chat operators, and supports many languages. Within six months, 10,491 inquiries were resolved automatically, 84 h less were spent on calls, and savings of £40,000 were achieved [67].

- Reduce Complexity

Complexity is the "degree of difficulty for a firm to implement the innovation" [20] (p.3). Complexity has been shown to play a significant role in the decision to adopt any new technology. The researchers looked at the complexity negatively [12,20]. Hence, it involves the determination of the organization and the employees to learn the adopted new technology. A study [61] (p.1) emphasized that "the easier an organization perceives a new technology to learn and use, the less complex the former perceive the latter to learn and use, and vice versa". Further, digital technologies can tackle the complexity associated with the traditional system, such as document maintenance, physical attendance for service consumption, repetitive tasks, and loss of data.

Table 5. Local government digital technologies adoption opportunities—technology.

Context	Attribute	Study
Improve user friendliness	Facilitating condition, integration able, interactivity, perceived ease of use, perceived benefits, relative advantage, scalable, user friendly, usability.	[1,59,65,66]
Reduce complexity	Complexity, technology interoperability, tracking complexity.	[20,40,48,59–61,66]

3.4. Local Government Digital Technologies Adoption Challenges

The continuous growth of digital technology creates direct and indirect challenges for local governments. Not only looking at an organization's opportunities but also understanding the challenges will assist in making optimal use of the resources. This subsection investigates the challenges associated with local governments' digital technology adoption under the subsections, i.e., the PPT framework.

3.4.1. People

This subsection looks at the challenges associated with digital technologies that have been faced by the actors of the local government under three aspects: (a) lack of technical staff and knowledge, (b) lack of decision-makers' support, and (c) acceleration of the inequalities in the society. These are elaborated below, and the summarized information is presented in Table 6.

- Lack of Technical Staff and Knowledge

Lack of technical staff and knowledge could impact the adoption of local government technology on employees (including decision-makers) and public aspects. Human resources with good technical knowledge can produce the best results for the local government function [20]. Meanwhile, the receivers with excellent technological understanding will be supportive of experimenting with new technology by the local government because the successful adoption of technology is based on citizen demand for the introduced technology. A study [68] indicated that most government employees are proficient in fundamental abilities such as word processing and web navigation. However, some government employees lack several specialized talents, such as programming, application development analysis, and software applications, and digital-based public services demand them. This digital knowledge deficit increases the complexity of the local government function [40].

Meanwhile, there is a general understanding that, compared to younger people, older people are less likely to use digital technology. Adopting new technologies such as AI could be difficult not only for local council staff but it could also be confusing for the general population, especially elderly people. Many authors highlighted that age and knowledge could hinder the adoption of advanced technologies [51].

- Lack of Decision-Makers' Support

Most of the literature indicated that decision-makers with positive attitudes towards adopting digital technology for local government service provision are more likely to provide/approve funding [4,20,40]. Hence, successful digital technology adoption depends on the fund secured by decision-makers and the support from decision-makers to achieve the goals. A study [69] identified three main challenges related to the lack of decision-makers' support, such as (a) no clear direction from the management, (b) lack of knowledge of technology adoption, and (c) the absence of a digital strategy. In the meantime, before they invest in new experimental technology, they demand larger rates of return [11]. Managers' attitudes are a challenge to adopting digital technology for local government functions.

- Accelerate the Inequalities of the Society

In general, local governments serve diverse local communities with different sociocultural, educational, and economic backgrounds. Each community has its level of digital technology adoption capacity. Higher-level educated stakeholders tend to be more perceptive of technology advancements in terms of affordability and knowledge to utilize. Nevertheless, lower-level income and education communities may be unable to afford and access digital technologies due to income and digital literacy constraints [70–73]. This means the community context matters for digital government adoption, whether people in the community will use it. This will be harder when local governments adopt advanced technologies such as AI [74,75].

Table 6. Local government digital technologies adoption challenges—people.

Context	Attribute	Study
Lack of technical staff and knowledge	Web staff, lack of technology staff, lack of technical expertise, lack of technical expertise on staff, skill challenges, interpretation challenges, human resources, lack of understanding of the cloud, unqualified or inappropriate staff, and lack of organizational resources or staff.	[15,17,19,33,56,57,72,73]
Lack of decision-makers' support	Poor planning and execution of local e-government adoption, application process involved in obtaining a 311 designation, attitude towards risk, organizational and managerial challenges, bureaucratic mentality of the policymakers, IT leadership, the influence of policymakers, lack of support from managers, and bureaucratic friction.	[11,15,17,46,57,72–75]
Accelerate the inequalities in society	Social and societal challenges, social elite concentration, political ideology of a community, political participation of citizens, civic environmental groups, and sociocultural disruption.	[17,71,73,75]

3.4.2. Process

This subsection discusses the challenges associated with the adoption of local government technology from the process perspective under the four aspects: (a) lack of planning, (b) lack of internal and external collaboration, and (c) lack of ethical framework and regulation. These are elaborated below, and the summarized information is presented in Table 7.

- Lack of Planning

The local government is expected to be ready, in terms of quality of planning, human resources, sufficient funds, proper policy and regulation, procedure, etc., to adopt a technology [20]. The reason behind the lack of formalization is due to (a) the lack of a benchmarking system, i.e., no standard model to compare and understand the requirement, (b) the lack of a self-assessment guide to understanding the available and non-available resource [69], and (c) inadequate time in the planning stage leading to an overly complex adoption process [57]. Moreover, decision-makers' ignorance of technology, poor communication among the local government institutes, and attitude towards risk contribute to their failure to recognize the uncertainty that might arise. Increased uncertainty makes planning and decision-making even more challenging [11].

- Lack of Internal and External Collaboration

The efficiency of the local government service distribution depends not only on internal collaboration but also on establishing effective connectivity among various organizations [11,68]. In practice, there is significantly less collaboration within and outside of the organization, which means it is necessary to adopt new means by which a local government is to function.

The power relation within the organization creates a gap between the decision-makers and the employees. A study [76] put forward the main characteristics of this power relation as follows: (a) Until a decision-maker authorizes, employees cannot use digital technologies. (b) In general, employees who desire to make their own decisions in the local government would be immediately discouraged. (c) For a final decision, even minor issues must be brought to the attention of a decision-maker. For example, even though the junior employee wishes to adopt new technology, the decision still depends on the senior's approval.

At the same time, considering the risk factor, council managers do not want to share data and information with other institutions, which constantly limits the organization's collaboration [68], resulting in a lack of intra-organization cooperation where similar tasks are repetitively run, causing budget duplications. In contrast, this budget can be effectively invested in facilitating technology adoption matters.

- Lack of Ethical Frameworks and Regulations

Structures, protocols, and policy mechanisms are required to ensure inclusive and equitable benefits in the new digital era. The local government's technology adoption would be hindered without effective procedures and documented data quality policies [61]. Other elements, such as privacy, security, and organizational trust, are intertwined with policies. It is difficult to gain users' trust, and it will be challenging to adopt technology for government services if it cannot ensure privacy protection and reduce the collection and storage of personal information. A study [74] mentioned that numerous policy problems exist, including government surveillance, privacy, security, and communications capacity. At the same time, adopted technology will be transformed together with the public demand and growth of the technology. Failure of flexible policy and regulation to adopt digital transformation also imposes challenges on the local government.

Table 7. Local government digital technologies adoption challenges—process.

Context	Attribute	Study
Lack of planning	Degree of formalization, uncertainty, government-based facilitation condition, difficulties in operational change management, administrative culture, project management and planning, poor communication, overly complex projects, insufficient benchmarking, and process-related challenges.	[11,12,19,20,42,48,50,57]
Lack of internal and external collaboration	Centralized and decentralized decision-making, lack of collaboration among departments, decision-making shared between politicians and senior executives, organizational centralization, egoistic and lack of collaborative efforts, intra-organizational culture, and nature of the decision.	[11,19,56,68,76]
Lack of ethical framework and regulation	Government law and policy, government regulation, lack of ethical frameworks, uncertainties around legal issues, security and privacy policies, ethical and legitimacy challenges, information assurance and governance, policies are considered too slow.	[12,17,19,40,42,48,50,61,68,71,74]

3.4.3. Technology

This subsection discusses the challenges associated with the adoption of local government technology from the perspectives of (a) lack of technical infrastructure readiness, (b) lack of security and privacy, and (c) data-related challenges. These are elaborated below, and the summarized information is presented in Table 8.

- Lack of Technical Infrastructure Readiness

Infrastructure readiness is a barrier identified from the perspective of technological challenges. It includes precise and detailed infrastructure requirements, the availability of qualified human resources to handle the infrastructure, and infrastructure budget support, for example, internet facilities, computer servers, data centers, and disaster recovery centers [77–79]. While the internet/online facilities and the disaster recovery center are the most critical infrastructure, the online facility is determined by accessibility, availability, and speed, whereas the disaster recovery center is a precautionary measure against potential threats that could eventually compromise system continuity [74]. The failure of one of these factors will be a challenge for the local government to adopt digital technologies.

- Lack of Security and Privacy

Data security involves preventing unauthorized entry, while privacy refers to who is permitted access to the data. These are critical issues for the local government [74]. Before choosing data-driven innovation, the organization must consider data security and privacy [61]. People are concerned about protecting the privacy of their confidential information because doing so is a basic human right [18]. For example, people do not know where their information is stored in Web 2.0—an open platform where citizens' privacy is at risk while providing sensitive information and cloud computing. Hence, adopting digital technologies would be challenging for the local government without proper security and safety protocols.

- Data-Related Challenges

The data-related challenges include data integration, data availability and acquisition, data quality, absence of structure and homogeneity, data bias, and resulting inaccuracies [80]. Advanced applications such as AI and predictive analytics depend on large quantities of data. A study [25] stated that eliminating bias in training data for machine learning is the biggest challenge. AI systems always have errors unless this barrier is eliminated. The risk is, therefore, significant for a public entity. Another study [81] identified four main data quality-related issues: (a) Complex data make the data integration part difficult. (b) A large data set consumes a lot of time. (c) Advanced technology is required to process big data. (d) There is not any benchmarking setting to understand the quality of data. Without a reliable and accurate data set, implementing digital technology could be challenging for the local government.

Table 8. Local government digital technologies adoption challenges—technology.

Context	Attribute	Study
Compatibility	Lack of data integration, interoperable integration, and lack of compatibility.	[20,74,79]
Lack of technical infrastructure readiness	ICT infrastructure, lack of technology, lack of technical upgrade, unaffordability of technological investment, need to upgrade technology, underutilization of technology, technological infrastructure, IT facilities and infrastructure, effective network, data storage location, backup of data, and internet connectivity.	[15,19,20,33,48,50,56,57,71,74,79]
Lack of security and privacy	Security and privacy concerns, data security, privacy, automation risks, trust, access authorization, and data leakage.	[12,18–20,33,42,50,56,61,68,70,74]
Data-related challenges	Data bias and resulting inaccuracies, data management, availability of data and information, data challenges, and system failure.	[17,18,51,71,74]

3.5. Local Government Digital Technologies Adoption Strategies and Recommendation

Strategies are defined as effective use of the available resources. They can also be viewed as a "pattern of decisions in an organization which formulates objectives, purposes, produces, policies and plans to achieve the goals" [82]. In the local government context, digital technology adoption strategies are investigated in this subsection concerning people, process, and technology aspects.

3.5.1. People

This subsection looks at how stakeholders strategically work to resolve the barriers and use the resources to adopt digital technology for local government services by: (a) Investing in interdisciplinary skill development among employees. (b) Utilizing power with responsibility. (c) Increasing open participation. These are elaborated below, and the summary is presented in Table 9.

- Invest in Interdisciplinary Skill Development for Employees

Regarding employee-related strategies, most of the literature emphasizes the importance of skill training and workshops with the aim of helping employees adopt digital technologies [1,15,73]. The installation, management, planning, and implementation of ICT infrastructure require technical expertise [1]. A study [40] argued that by helping staff with training and information when adopting digital technologies, local governments could benefit greatly, and the adoption rate would likely increase. Meanwhile, the adoption process would accelerate by recruiting staff familiar with the technologies [77]. The staff with good knowledge is likely to: (a) Lead the team. (b) Explain the benefits to the stakeholders and organize professional development programs. (c) Educate and network with the existing staff [40]. Simultaneously, employees should be aware that, as technology quickly advances, citizen expectations for the delivery of government services also rise. Hence, attending agencies or organizations for orientation, workshops, training, and exposure is essential. Another study [15] evidenced the discrepancy between the courses offered by academic programs and practitioners' requirements at work. Therefore, future research must investigate the pedagogical methods that schools and colleges use to emphasize digital technology competencies related to local governance in undergraduate and graduate curricula.

- Utilizing Power in a Responsible Manner

Decision-makers can use rewards or penalties to motivate government officials to adopt digital technologies. Accordingly, utilizing the power of correct direction would be the most effective strategy for adopting digital technologies. For example, organizing regular meetings with employees to understand the difficulties in using digital technologies and creating a step-by-step implementation schedule so that citizens and employees find it easier to adapt to the new process [73]. The decision-makers should ensure data privacy and security by formulating a proper procedure or policy document [20,45] and properly allocating organizational resources, such as staff time and budgetary costs [57].

- Increasing Open Participation

Citizens and communities must be involved in the local government's decision-making process. Local governments are practicing Web 2.0 to ensure equitable participation [19,20,58], specifically in policymaking. While the local government expects that having a Facebook page or Twitter account is enough to garner citizen feedback, they should create social media platforms that solicit and support active public engagement [38]. Most of the public is not motivated to voice their opinion due to privacy concerns and a lack of trust in the government system. However, the local government should be open to citizens' participation by introducing accessible and affordable digital technologies [83].

Table 9. Local government digital technologies adoption strategy—people.

Context	Attribute	Study
Invest in interdisciplinary skill development for employees	Regular orientation and workshop training, professional staffing, creating incentives by rewarding individuals, identifying a "champion", training and open communication with staff, personal mastery of employees, engaging employees in adopting ICT, appropriate staff training, training civil servant's knowledge and skills, project leaders need to engage municipal government employees across multiple departments, hiring an adequate number of motivated and qualified staff.	[1,4,15,22,40,57,73,77]

Table 9. *Cont.*

Context	Attribute	Study
Utilizing the power in a responsible manner	Improve information culture and align the technology with strategic objectives. Articulate a timeline and hold regular meetings. Managers could build on an existing culture of awareness of and sensitivity to information, awareness about potential opportunities and risks associated with technologies, recognized standing and interdisciplinary skills, methodological competence, and digital background, managed by qualified people, and focus on content management. Managers must also be held accountable for implementing their projects and exercising their authority to enhance performance.	[20–22,50,57,73,83]
Increasing open participation	Enabling the user to create and tailor content requires the commitment of more resources. Open participation, collaboration, and ubiquitous engagement should be a part of the planning process.	[38,57]

3.5.2. Process

This subsection looks at what processes relate to strategies that could assist in adopting digital technologies in three aspects: (a) introducing policies and regulations, (b) proper planning and goal setting, and (c) fostering cross-sectoral collaboration. These are elaborated below, and the summarized information is presented in Table 10.

- Introducing Policies and Regulation

The creation of formal policies and regulation by the local government is required to support the adoption procedure. While the government plans to use digital technologies, it must consider options outside of technology. It is essential to have written regulations that support change, provide instructions for execution, and give legal authority for the policy and regulation implementation [1,20,73]. In the meantime, policies should elaborate on how data are handled, gathered, preserved, analyzed, deliberated, and disclosed. The level of trust and security help minimize the associated risk and encourage the user to adopt the technology without reluctance [12,21].

- Proper Planning and Goal Setting

The second factor which aligns with policies and regulation is planning and goal setting. Goal setting is a process that identifies what the local government needs to accomplish and helps create a plan to achieve target results. Policies, regulations, planning, and goal setting should be aligned to maximize the outcome [20]. The planning includes (a) technology capacity in terms of technical and human capacity [15], (b) existing infrastructure compatibility assessment [4], (c) a budget proposal to address concerns about cost, and (d) discussion with internal and external parties to get advice on security issues, etc., [40]. At the same time, at the planning stage, identifying the challenge of local government to adopt digital technologies is equally important to reduce failures while setting goals.

- Fostering Cross-Sectoral Collaboration

Increasing inter- and intra-institutional collaboration would accelerate the adoption of digital technology [84]. It has several advantages, starting from: (a) Collaboration between citizens and employees would enhance the employees' understanding of their needs, that is, to what extent they understand the digital technologies, as per the requirement of adopting the technology and improving the employees' skills so that effective services may be provided to citizens [85,86]. (b) Collaboration between different local governments—each local government has unique methods and designs for adopting digital technologies, which increases the expenditure of state government. This limitation could be overcome by adopting a set of universal development standards [87]. (c) Collaboration with stakeholders and politicians—adopting and/or implementing digital technologies in local governments requires support from stakeholders and elected leaders. Local governments must establish channels for disseminating information about the advantages of digital innovation to gain support from politicians and stakeholders [34]. (d) Collaboration with academic institutions—local governments should collaborate with academic institutions to offer new executive education programs that can fill the knowledge gaps found in this study [88].

Table 10. Local government digital technologies adoption strategy—process.

Context	Attribute	Study
Introducing policies and regulation	There should be proper legislative and executive actions; with a rigid culture, the government needs to prepare formal regulations. Give legal status, clarify laws and regulations, and reform processes by simplifying regulations and procedures. Data protection policies should be regulated. Local governments need to establish desirable legal and policy guidelines. For security issues, proper risk assessment, information assurance, and governance, the legal system mandatorily requires e-disclosure through the municipalities' website. Legislation should regulate the use of social media by governments, and strengthen policies by compiling risk management guidelines.	[1,4,15,22,33]
Proper planning and goal setting	Equipping government agencies with relevant infrastructure, procuring external advice on security issues, developing a budget proposal to address concerns regarding costs, assessing compatibility, and building IT capacity.	[1,4,15,22,33]
Foster cross-sectoral collaborative strategies	More collaboration and interaction between local, regional, and national governments, adopting a common framework of standards for the development of e-gov websites, and creating avenues to provide information about the benefits of digital innovation. Strengthening the interactivity of websites. Community-based organizations should play active roles. Local governments should work with academic institutions. Process efficiency, effective coordination of the e-government by a coordination team, and sharing the results of the digital maturity evaluation between municipalities are very useful as they allow for comparisons with others.	[34,65,68,73,85,86,88]

3.5.3. Technology

This subsection looks at how technology relates to strategies that could assist in adopting digital technologies in two aspects: (a) building the technical infrastructure and (b) creating an enabling environment. These are elaborated below, and the summarized information is presented in Table 11.

- Building the Technical Infrastructure

The technical infrastructure is identified as a primary driver of the adoption of digital technologies by local government [4,89]. The adoption of digital technologies is made more accessible if the technical readiness level is higher. It allows government organizations to collaborate, communicate, and exchange work, making daily activities easier and utilizing technology to reduce staff time and effort. The technical infrastructure includes proper network, hardware, software, security, and privacy standards [57]. A study [89] detailed this strategy by notifying the important elements to be included, such as: (a) upgrading the equipment and ensuring consistency across all local government departments, including personal computers, servers, and desktop software, (b) creating shared information systems for the primary duties of local governments; (c) implementing appropriate security measures and technology. These include dependable firewalls, data encryption methods, and public key infrastructure (a collection of rules, policies, and processes required to create, manage, distribute, utilize, store, and revoke digital certificates), and (d) Evaluate the utilization of local government data centers with disaster recovery processes and tools.

- Creating an Enabling Environment

All stakeholders in the process of digital technology adoption should be able to provide and receive services equally. Accessibility includes cost-effective, language-friendly, and user-friendly (people can understand the procedure without training) devices that all users can afford. This could be achieved when the technology used to introduce new concepts must be created at a literacy and comprehension level open to all. Increased public Wi-Fi availability, technical literacy programs, computer lab resources, and dependable infrastructure boost trust in local government and increase the use of tools for managing citizen relationships [70]. A study [90,91] advocated that local governments should create mobile engagement tools within an organization to help cover a broader range of people's perceptions. The accessibility strategy increases the actors' trust and facilitates the adoption of digital technologies.

Table 11. Local government digital technologies adoption strategy—technology.

Context	Attribute	Study
Building the technical infrastructure	Providing solid technical support for digital, push strategy and data transparency, e-government initiatives need adequate infrastructure to meet the citizens' high expectations regarding privacy and security. Set technology standards and minimum requirements.	[4,39,57,84,91]
Creating an enabling environment	The system must provide a good user experience. Governments must ensure open access to public cloud services, and internet access should be available to mobile devices. Local governments should develop mobile orientation participation tools. The introduction of technology must be designed at a comprehensive level, and technology tools and training should be accessible to the neighborhood. Expand the public Wi-Fi, technical literacy training, and computer lab resources. Reliable infrastructure will not only increase citizen trust in government but should also increase engagement with citizen relationship management tools.	[12,20,68,70,88]

4. Findings and Discussion

Local government experiments with new digital technologies and methods for their service provision play a vital role in the effective and efficient service provision of the local government. These adoption processes are complicated by uncertainties. The involved government officials must adapt to the process and technology, the process must be continuously updated, and the technology must be properly integrated into the local government system. The local government must understand the balance between people, processes, and technology to gain its full potential. The key findings are discussed below and summarized in Table 12.

Table 12. Summary of the findings.

Domain	Opportunity	Challenge	Strategy
People	■ Increase citizen convenience and engagement–citizen demand and engagement in the process. ■ Perceived usefulness–employee support, skill development. ■ Increase the decision-makers' accountability–innovativeness, capability, and authority.	■ Lack of technical staff and knowledge–level of understanding. ■ Lack of decision-makers' support–no clear direction, lack of knowledge. ■ Accelerate the inequalities of society–social, economic, and educational.	■ Invest in interdisciplinary skill development among employees–skill development workshop. ■ Utilizing the power in a responsible manner–decision-makers authority. ■ Increasing open participation–accepting people's opinions.

Table 12. *Cont.*

Domain	Opportunity	Challenge	Strategy
Process	■ Cost-effective financial management–cost-effective solution. ■ Enhance the quality-of-service delivery–effectiveness, efficiency, satisfaction, freedom from risk, and context coverage.	■ Lack of planning–no benchmarking, no planning. ■ Lack of internal and external collaboration–collaboration with others. ■ Lack of ethical framework and regulation–No standard procedure, no flexibility.	■ Introducing policies and regulation–formulization. ■ Proper planning and goal-setting strategies–resource allocation, time frame, etc. ■ Foster cross-sectoral collaboration–employee–citizen, other local government, academic institution.
Technologies	■ Improve user friendliness–language, culture, and disability concerns. ■ Reduce complexity–employees adopt new technology, the complexity of the traditional method.	■ Lack of technical infrastructure readiness–internet, computer server, etc. ■ Lack of security and privacy–hacking and no understanding of the data storage. ■ Data-related challenges–integration, quality of data.	■ Building the technical infrastructure–software, hardware, standards. ■ Creating an enabling environment–devices, affordability, language.

4.1. Understanding the Actors

Internal actors, such as employees, decision-makers, and external key actors, such as citizen politicians, stakeholders, and so on, are connected to the local government system. Technology in local government cannot work without building the capacity of the actors first [4,57]. The difference between a successful and a poor local government is the presence of the right actors having the right attitude towards adopting digital technology. A stusy [22] stated that "improvement of information culture is fostered by constant improvement in digital and sociocultural competencies of employees and managers of the public administration as well as their personal mastery and creative attitudes".

Actors' social, cultural, economic, and educational backgrounds vary greatly. As a result, the decision-making style, working style, and adoption style will vary [75]. For example, citizens from low-income backgrounds cannot afford to pay for the hardware. Citizens with less digital literacy increase the workload for employees, employees with less digital literacy slow down service delivery, and citizens with higher educational backgrounds put more pressure on decision-makers. Decision-makers and employees with less digital literacy and strategy might lead to system malfunction.

- Nothing in an organization is more crucial than excellent communication, particularly when implementing solutions for technology and processes. So, citizens should speak up first by outlining their needs in detail [84]. In other words, citizens should be enthusiastic communicators and not hold back when sharing their thoughts with the local government. Accessible and organized communication leads to the flow of ideas, which inspires the local government to understand the requirement of the people and accordingly introduce digital technology. Meanwhile, the local government needs to open platforms where citizens can share their thoughts and ideas without affecting their privacy—it also needs to actively solicit input from residents through outreach, as just because a platform is there does not mean it will be used. A study [92] underlined that social media sites such as Facebook and Twitter engage the audience actively; it also goes beyond simply having an account there;
- Secondly, the local government needs employees with the appropriate talents and skills to handle digital technologies. It includes experience and attitude with skills, as these are equally crucial to ensuring a successful implementation of digital technology [1]. Additionally, the local government should offer skill-training workshops to hiring staff and current employees who are already familiar with the technology to keep up with the updates [73];
- Thirdly, these activities will be practically feasible if the decision-makers cultivate a constructive attitude towards the employees and citizens by accepting their needs and requirements [57].

4.2. Formulating the Process

Having the right processes in place aligned with the right employees helps to know what must be done to ensure that citizens receive the required services. Citizens require local governments to provide high-quality services. Describing how services are provided is more important than the types of services being offered [93]. Thus, when local governments design the process, the four matters described below should be considered for the effective implementation of digital technologies [31].

- The actors should understand how they fit in the process, what their role is in it, and what they need to achieve throughout the process. For example, decision-makers must be held responsible for carrying out the plan and use the authority and skill to allocate local government resources, such as employees' time and budgetary costs, responsibly [57];
- The local government should have a reasonable goal and a procedure to achieve the goal. Thus, improving these procedures will impact process efficiency the most [20];
- To improve the success of digital innovation, local governments must develop acceptable legal and regulatory standards rather than just adopting regulation out of isomorphic pressure [34];
- Getting feedback from the actors and constant improvement are important for the process to have the best effect [15].

4.3. Technology as a Tool

The actors should understand that technology does not address all the problems. It is a tool the actors use to implement the process and which aids in automating some of the steps. A study [19] argued that "identifying the main causes for limited or ineffective citizen engagement with local government activities requires us to look beyond the technology itself". Therefore, before implementing digital technology, local governments should have a proper understanding of:

- The effect of the equipping technology on the actors' productivity and ability to simplify employees' and citizens' lives, the challenges they might encounter, and the means to resolve them [1];
- The local government should adequately understand the level of digital readiness across service delivery, planning and development, and internal systems before implementing digital technology. Because the implementation of digital technology is more accessible, the technical readiness level is greater [4];
- Technology has far more reach than we could have imagined and knows no bounds. Therefore, rather than adopting complex technologies, technology should be easy to use, affordable, and comprehended. People should not feel overwhelmed by it [70].

Local governments' starting point may be chosen according to the resources, capacity, availability, and other factors. For instance, the local government can determine the citizens' needs and capabilities before creating the procedure and implementing the appropriate technology. In addition, decision-makers may decide to spend money on technology while also retraining their employees or developing processes for skill development. However, to minimize risk and maximize impact, the interaction between the three elements must be balanced correctly.

Despite challenges, the future of technology adoption in local government holds great promise. Edge computing, virtual reality, the sixth generation (6G) networks, multimodality machine learning models, and blockchain, among other emerging technologies, are actively transforming the landscape of local governance and citizen services. Edge computing [94,95] offers a range of benefits, including reduced latency, greater data privacy and security, increased accessibility, and increased resilience and durability. It not only reduces costs but also allows for the efficient deployment of IoT and the facilitation of effective disaster response and emergency management. Virtual reality (VR) [96,97] is gaining traction as a driver of citizen participation, accessibility, training, urban planning, remote collaboration, public safety, cultural heritage protection, and data analysis. Its impact will extend to encouraging inclusiveness and creative governance solutions.

The 6G network [94] integration will result in improved connection, higher capacity, easy access to cloud services, and seamless integration with VR and augmented reality (AR) technologies. These developments will enable data-driven decision-making, strengthen cybersecurity safeguards, and help IoT scale. As a result, they will improve service delivery, stimulate urban planning projects, and spark innovation. Multimodality machine learning models [98] will play a pivotal role in augmenting natural language understanding, citizen engagement, data analysis, accessibility, information processing, language translation, risk detection, and decision-making. Their adoption would enable comprehensive data analysis, facilitate effective communication, streamline processes, and empower inclusivity and informed governance. Blockchain technology [99,100] stands as a bulwark for data security, streamlined processes, smart contracts, citizen identity management, supply chain traceability, citizen engagement, data sharing, and improved financial transaction efficiency. Its incorporation will foster openness and trust and improve the government's efficiency [101,102].

4.4. Limitations and Further Research

There are some limitations to this study: (a) The number of local councils which developed their digital strategy reports, e.g., Northern Beaches Council Digital Transformation Strategy, Digital Strategy of the London Borough of Sutton and the Royal Borough of Kingston Upon Thames (2018–2021), Digital Transformation Strategy of Bayside (2018–2021), Digital Strategy of Croydon–UK (2019–2024), Digital Strategy of Logan City Council (2019–2022), Digital Strategy–Brent (2022–2026), Digital Unley, City of Palmerston Digital Strategy 2021, eMandurah (2012), and Whitehorse City Council Information Technology Strategy (2020–2025). Nonetheless, this study only reviewed journal articles. (b) Each digital technology has its opportunities, challenges, and strategies, but this study focused on the general idea of digital technology. Future studies will address these constraints, and we will continue our endeavors to contribute to these exciting developments.

Meanwhile, this research identifies the directions for future research on digital technology adoption in the public sector, more specifically for the local government administration: (a) Application of the PPT framework for the local government sector is a relatively new research approach, whereas it has been a proven framework for improving the operational efficiency in the private sector. Further research based on this framework in the public sector may be extended to the means to the adoption of technology on raising public sector operational efficiency. (b) Understanding the interconnectivity of these attributes through quantitative methods would assist the local government policymakers in developing the strategy more precisely and reducing resource overlap.

5. Conclusions

This research reviews the technology adoption opportunities, challenges, and strategies through the lens of the PPT framework. This framework provides an understanding of how the balance between the people, process, and technology aspects should be maintained to successfully implement digital technologies.

The findings indicate several opportunities and challenges in adopting digital technology for local government activities. The opportunities are increasing citizen convenience and engagement, perceived usefulness, increased accountability among decision-makers, cost-effective financial management, enhanced service delivery, improved user-friendliness, and reduced complexity. The challenges include the lack of technical staff and knowledge, the lack of decision-makers' support, accelerated societal inequalities, lack of planning, internal and external collaboration, ethical framework, technical infrastructure readiness, security, and challenges related to privacy and data.

At the same time, the opportunities and the strategies must be well aligned to resolve the challenges. Accordingly, the people-related strategies invest in interdisciplinary skill development among employees, utilizing the power responsibly and increasing open participation. The process-related strategies introduce policies and regulations, proper planning, and goal setting and foster cross-sectoral collaboration. Finally, the technology-related strategies build the technical infrastructure and create an enabling environment. These findings are useful for the policymakers to keep up the balance with the available resources and achieve the full potential of the adopted technology.

Author Contributions: A.D., Data collection, processing, investigation, analysis, and writing—original draft; T.Y., supervision, conceptualization, writing—review and editing; R.Y.M.L., J.M.C., P.H.C., K.M. and R.M., supervision, writing—review and editing. All authors have read and agreed to the published version of the manuscript.

Funding: This research was funded by the Australian Research Council Discovery Grant Scheme, grant number DP220101255.

Institutional Review Board Statement: Not applicable.

Informed Consent Statement: Not applicable.

Data Availability Statement: Data sources are listed in Appendix A.

Acknowledgments: The authors thank anonymous referees for their invaluable comments on an earlier version of the manuscript.

Conflicts of Interest: The authors declare no conflict of interest.

Appendix A

Table A1. Local government technology adoption opportunities.

Study	Journal	Title	Year	Framework Element	Description
[63]	Journal of Information Technology and Politics	The digital world of local government: a comparative analysis of the United States and Germany	2009	People	▪ Professional management; ▪ Demographic characteristics; ▪ Presence of chief administrator; ▪ Full-time employees working for city hall; ▪ Socioeconomic attainment among residents in terms of education and wealth;
				Process	▪ Organizational resources;
[66]	Online Information Review	E-government evolution in EU local governments: a comparative perspective	2009	Process	▪ Transparency;
				Technology	▪ Interactivity; ▪ Usability; ▪ Web site maturity;
[57]	Government Information Quarterly	The adoption of centralized customer service systems: a survey of local governments	2009	People	▪ Public pressure/ expectations for customer service; ▪ Elected official's pressure; ▪ Staff request;
				Process	▪ Goal to improve services despite increased cost; ▪ Expectation of reduced costs;

Table A1. Cont.

Study	Journal	Title	Year	Framework Element	Description
[58]	International Journal of Organization Theory and Behaviour	Digital governance success factors and barriers to success in Prague	2011	People	▪ User-friendliness; ▪ Motivated employees; ▪ Recruitment and retaining employees; ▪ Managerial support; ▪ Managerial accountability; ▪ Citizen involvement; ▪ Political support; ▪ Reputable and known technology;
				Process	▪ Budget and time; ▪ Performance measures; ▪ Appropriate system design; ▪ Clear implementation plan; ▪ Professional project management; ▪ Phased implementation; ▪ Goal clarity;
				Technology	▪ Effective communication; ▪ Adequate infrastructure;
[64]	Government Information Quarterly	Customer relationship management (CRM) technology and organizational change: evidence for the bureaucratic and e-Government paradigms	2011	People	▪ Efficiency changes and leadership; ▪ Management change;
				Process	▪ Organizational change;
[59]	International Journal of Electronic Government Research	Electronic transformation of local government: An exploratory study	2011	People	▪ Perceived usefulness; ▪ Perceived motivation;
				Process	▪ Compliance with local government organization's policy;
				Technology	▪ Perceived ease of use; ▪ Perceived compatibility; ▪ Complexity; ▪ Relative advantage; ▪ Trustworthiness;
[42]	International Journal of Cloud Applications and Computing	Cloud computing in local government	2012	Process	▪ Cost serving; ▪ Economic of scale; ▪ Strategic focus;
[80]	The Journal of Contemporary Issues in Business and Government	An investigation of the main factors to be considered in cloud computing adoption in Australian regional local councils	2015	Technology	▪ Cost;
[11]	Information and Management	Investigating factors influencing local government decision-makers while adopting integration technologies (IntTech)	2015	People	▪ Personality; ▪ Perceptions; ▪ Attitudes to risk; ▪ Ethics and values; ▪ Knowledge of integration technologies; ▪ Managerial capability and authority; ▪ Culture and climate; ▪ Politics; ▪ Management style;
				Process	▪ Nature of decision; ▪ Uncertainty; ▪ Centralized and decentralized decision-making; ▪ Organizational compatibility;
[45]	Government Information Quarterly	Factors influencing social media use in local governments: The case of Italy and Spain	2016	People	▪ Size of the population; ▪ Income level;

Table A1. Cont.

Study	Journal	Title	Year	Framework Element	Description
[1]	Transforming Government: People, Process, and Policy	Are government employees adopting local e-government transformation? The need for having the right attitude, facilitating conditions and performance expectations	2017	People	■ Performance expectancy; ■ Social influence; ■ Attitude;
				Process	■ Effort expectancy;
				Technology	■ Facilitating condition;
[15]	State and Local Government Review	Conceptualizing e-government from local government perspectives	2018	People	■ Political competition and citizen adoption; ■ Technical skill; ■ Professionalization; ■ Sheer size of the workforce;
[67]	IOP Conference Series: Materials Science and Engineering	A study of application and framework smart city in Bandung: a survey	2019	Technology	■ Reliable; ■ Interoperable; ■ Scalable; ■ User-friendly; ■ Integrable;
[62]	International Journal of Information Management	Determinants of master data management adoption by local government organizations: An empirical study	2019	People	■ Top management support; ■ Citizen demand;
				Process	■ Data governance; ■ Technological competence;
				Technology	■ Complexity; ■ Quality of master data;
[12]	Computer Law and Security Review	The role of government regulations in the adoption of cloud computing: A case study of local government	2020	Process	■ Quality of service; ■ Flexibility;
				Technology	■ Cost;
[43]	Government Information Quarterly	Assessing information security risks in the cloud: a case study of Australian local government authorities	2020	Technology	■ Data transmission; ■ Data storage; ■ Data privacy; ■ Risk management; ■ Security control; ■ Awareness; ■ Backup; ■ Encryption; ■ Trustworthiness; ■ Service level agreement;
[16]	Sustainability	Digital transformation and knowledge management in the public sector	2020	People	■ Quality of organization's knowledge management;
				Process	■ Complementing each other for significant improvement in the public sector;
[61]	Lecture Notes in Business Information Processing	Digital transformation in the public sector: identifying critical success factors	2020	People	■ Change management; ■ Leadership engagement; ■ Citizen participation;
				Process	■ Organizational culture; ■ Skill development program; ■ Funding; ■ Political stability; ■ Regulatory framework;
				Technology	■ Data security; ■ IT architecture; ■ Interoperability; ■ Data-driven agility; ■ Telecommunication service quality;

Table A1. Cont.

Study	Journal	Title	Year	Framework Element	Description
[23]	Journal of Accounting and Investment	Determining factors of cloud computing adoption: a study of Indonesian local government employees	2020	People	■ Performance expectancy; ■ Effort expectancy; ■ Perceived availability; ■ Behavioral intention;
[69]	Journal Komunikasi: Malaysian Journal of Communication	Digital transformation of the government: a case study in Indonesia	2021	Technology	■ Data transmission; ■ Data storage; ■ Data privacy; ■ Risk management; ■ Security control; ■ Awareness; ■ Backup; ■ Encryption; ■ Trustworthiness; ■ Service level agreement;
[20]	Sustainability	Citizens' or government's will? Exploration of why Indonesia's local governments adopt technologies for open government	2021	People	■ Organizational culture; ■ Support of top management; ■ Managerial innovativeness; ■ Strategic goal; ■ Citizen/Community demand; ■ Political influence;
				Process	■ Policy and regulation; ■ Legislation; ■ Bandwagon effect;
				Technology	■ Perceived benefits; ■ Compatibility; ■ Complexity; ■ ICT infrastructure;
[43]	Information Technology and People	Cloud computing technology adoption: an evaluation of key factors in local governments	2021	People	■ Top management support; ■ Organization size;
				Process	■ Cost; ■ Anticipated benefits;
				Technology	■ Compatibility; ■ Complexity; ■ Security concern;
[24]	Journal of Public Affairs and Development	Adoption of artificial intelligence (AI) in local governments: an exploratory study on the attitudes and perceptions of officials in a municipal government in the Philippines	2021	People	■ Previous use of AI; ■ Perceived usefulness; ■ Perceived ease of use; ■ Social influence; ■ Facilitating conditions; ■ Self-efficacy; ■ Attitude towards using AI; ■ Behavioral intention to use AI;
[22]	Information Systems Management	The contribution of ICT adoption by local governments to sustainability—empirical evidence from Poland	2021	People	■ Improvement in social and political life;
				Process	■ Reduction in electricity and natural resources consumption; ■ Improvement in governments activity; ■ Improvement in management and decision-making;
[40]	Information Systems Frontiers	Assessment of complexity in cloud computing adoption: a case study of local governments in Australia	2022	People	■ Knowledge management;
				Process	■ Business operations;
				Technology	■ Data processing capability; ■ Technology interoperability;

Table A1. Cont.

Study	Journal	Title	Year	Framework Element	Description
[89]	Government Information Quarterly	Determinants of digital innovation in the public sector	2022	People	▪ Age;
				Technology	▪ Electoral competition;
[34]	Information Technology and People	Assessing the drivers of the regional digital divide and their impact on eGovernment services: evidence from a South American country	2022	People	▪ Education; ▪ Income; ▪ ICT usage;
[4]	Sustainability	Exploring driving factors of digital transformation among local governments: foundations for smart city construction in China	2022	People	▪ Citizen's expectation; ▪ Superior pressure;
				Process	▪ Organizational efficiency; ▪ Public service delivery;
				Technology	▪ Technology readiness;
[48]	AI and Society	Artificial intelligence in local governments: perceptions of city managers on prospects, constraints, and choices	2023	Technology	▪ Creating efficiencies; ▪ Tackling complexity; ▪ Managing repetitive tasks; ▪ Processes and decisions; ▪ Automating routine decision; ▪ Minimizing errors and improving productivity.

Table A2. Local government technology adoption challenges.

Study	Journal	Title	Year	Framework Element	Description
[33]	Public Administration Review	The evolution of e-government among municipalities: Rhetoric or reality?	2002	People	▪ Lack of technology staff; ▪ Lack of technical expertise;
				Process	▪ Lack of financial resources;
				Technology	▪ Lack of technical upgrade; ▪ Security issues; ▪ Privacy issues;
[56]	International Journal of Electronic Government Research	Citizen-initiated contacts with Ontario local e-government: administrators' responses to contacts	2005	People	▪ Lack of technology/web staff; ▪ Lack of technology/web expertise; ▪ Staff resistance to change; ▪ Lack of support from elected officials; ▪ Lack of information about e-government applications;
				Process	▪ Lack of financial resources; ▪ Issues relating to convenience fees for online transactions; ▪ Lack of collaboration among departments;
				Technology	▪ Issues regarding security; ▪ Issues regarding privacy; ▪ Need to upgrade technology;

Table A2. Cont.

Study	Journal	Title	Year	Framework Element	Description
[57]	Government Information Quarterly	The adoption of centralized customer service systems: a survey of local governments	2009	People	<ul><li>Application process involved in obtaining a 311 designation;</li><li>Lack of support from elected officials;</li><li>Unfamiliar with the technology;</li><li>Lack of technical expertise among staff;</li></ul>
				Process	<ul><li>Too expensive;</li></ul>
[85]	Journal of E-Governance	Impact of citizen relationship management (CRM) on government: evidence from U.S. local governments	2010	Process	<ul><li>Lack of funding;</li><li>Difficulty for departments to give up control of their customer management;</li></ul>
				Technology	<ul><li>Contact channels such as Web, over-the-counter, and email lack alignment, which cause conflict and confusion;</li><li>Security and privacy concerns with customer data;</li><li>Underutilization of this technology;</li></ul>
[73]	Policy & Internet	Digital divides in urban e-government in South Korea: exploring differences in municipalities' use of the Internet for environmental governance	2010	People	<ul><li>IT leadership;</li><li>Human resource;</li><li>Social elite concentration;</li><li>Political ideology of a community;</li><li>Political participation of citizen;</li><li>Civic environmental group;</li></ul>
				Process	<ul><li>Financial resource;</li></ul>
[83]	International Journal of Organization Theory and Behavior	Digital governance success factors and barriers to success in Prague	2011	People	<ul><li>Lack of training or education;</li><li>Unqualified or inappropriate staff;</li><li>Lack of organizational resources or staff;</li><li>Lack of support from managers;</li><li>Poor support from elected officials;</li></ul>
				Process	<ul><li>Lack of planning;</li><li>Poor communication and overly complex projects;</li><li>Mission creep;</li></ul>
[79]	International Journal of Cloud Applications and Computing	A framework for analysing the impact of cloud computing on local government in the UK	2011	People	<ul><li>Choices of vendors;</li></ul>
				Process	<ul><li>Business process change;</li><li>Information assurance and governance;</li><li>Product and approach;</li></ul>
[42]	International Journal of Cloud Applications and Computing	Cloud computing in local government	2012	Process	<ul><li>Service level agreement;</li><li>Business process change;</li><li>Project management and planning;</li></ul>
				Technology	<ul><li>Security and reliability of data;</li><li>Privacy and access;</li></ul>
[11]	Information and Management	Investigating factors influencing local government decision-makers while adopting integration technologies (IntTech)	2015	People	<ul><li>Culture and climate;</li><li>Perception;</li><li>Attitude towards risk;</li></ul>
				Process	<ul><li>Organizational compatibility;</li><li>Nature of decision;</li><li>Uncertainty;</li><li>Centralized and decentralized decision-making;</li></ul>

Table A2. Cont.

Study	Journal	Title	Year	Framework Element	Description
[80]	The Journal of Contemporary Issues in Business and Government	An investigation of the main factors to be considered in cloud computing adoption in Australian regional local councils	2015	People	▪ Provider dependability; ▪ Employees' knowledge;
				Technology	▪ Internet connectivity; ▪ Data storage location (policy issues related to data storage); ▪ Integration; ▪ Data back-up; ▪ Transportability;
[75]	Journal of Information Security and Applications	An investigation of the challenges and issues influencing the adoption of cloud computing in Australian regional municipal governments	2016	People	▪ Availability of different providers; ▪ Influence of policymakers; ▪ Lack of understanding of the cloud;
				Process	▪ Cost;
				Technology	▪ Security and Privacy; ▪ Trust; ▪ Data management; ▪ Infrastructure; ▪ Effective network; ▪ Security and loss control over data; ▪ Data storage location; ▪ Backup of data; ▪ Integration;
[77]	American Review of Public Administration	Determinants of information and communication technology adoption in municipalities	2016	People	▪ Governmental stakeholder influence and non-governmental stakeholder influence; ▪ Work routines; ▪ Personal constraints;
				Process	▪ Organizational centralization;
[1]	Transforming Government: People, Process, and Policy	Are government employees adopting local e-government transformation? The need for having the right attitude, facilitating conditions and performance expectations	2017	People	▪ Age and length of work experience;
[46]	Social Science Computer Review	Governance models for the delivery of public services through the web 2.0 technologies: a political view in large Spanish municipalities	2017	People	▪ Bureaucratic mentality of the policymakers;
[15]	State and Local Government Review	Conceptualizing e-government from local government perspectives	2018	People	▪ Web staff; ▪ Lack of information about e-government application; ▪ Lack of support from elected officials; ▪ Poor planning and execution of local e-government adoption; ▪ Security and privacy;
				Process	▪ Lack of financial resource;
				Technology	▪ Lack of technology;

Table A2. Cont.

Study	Journal	Title	Year	Framework Element	Description
[19]	International Journal of Information Management	Beyond technology: identifying local government challenges for using digital platforms for citizen engagement	2018	People	▪ Digital illiteracy and digital divide; ▪ Availability of human resources;
				Process	▪ Institutional framework; ▪ Process related challenges; ▪ Intra-organizational culture;
				Technology	▪ Internet accessibility; ▪ Technological advancement; ▪ Data management;
[18]	Future Computing and Informatics Journal	A proposed hybrid model for adopting cloud computing in e-government	2018	Technology	▪ Lack of data control; ▪ Security and privacy control; ▪ System failure; ▪ Access authorization; ▪ Data leakage;
[62]	International Journal of Information Management	Determinants of master data management adoption by local government organizations: an empirical study	2019	Process	▪ Government policy;
				Technology	▪ Relative advantage; ▪ Data security;
[12]	Computer Law and Security Review	The role of government regulations in the adoption of cloud computing: a case study of local government	2020	People	▪ Competition; ▪ Public awareness; ▪ Management;
				Process	▪ Government-based facilitation condition; ▪ Firm-based facilitating condition;
				Technology	▪ Security; ▪ Privacy;
[76]	Journal of Information Technology Teaching Cases	Digital transformation: learning from Italy's public administration	2020	People	▪ Sociocultural disruption; ▪ Political upheaval; ▪ Digital literacy; ▪ Bureaucratic friction;
[17]	Government Information Quarterly	Implications of the use of artificial intelligence in public governance: a systematic literature review and a research agenda	2021	People	▪ Organizational and managerial challenges; ▪ Skill challenges; ▪ Interpretation challenges; ▪ Social and societal challenges;
				Process	▪ Ethical and legitimacy challenges; ▪ Political, legal, and policy challenges; ▪ Economic challenges;
				Technology	▪ Data challenges;
[20]	Sustainability	Citizens' or government's will? Exploration of why Indonesia's local governments adopt technologies for open government	2021	People	▪ Personal competence;
				Process	▪ Degree of formalization;
				Technology	▪ Compatibility; ▪ ICT Infrastructure; ▪ Security and Privacy concerns;

Table A2. Cont.

Study	Journal	Title	Year	Framework Element	Description
[43]	Information Technology and People	Cloud computing technology adoption: an evaluation of key factors in local governments	2021	People	■ Employees knowledge;
				Process	■ Government regulation; ■ Information intensity;
[69]	Journal Komunikasi: Malaysian Journal of Communication	Digital transformation of the government: a case study in Indonesia	2021	People	■ The competency of employees who are well-versed in ICT is minimal;
				Process	■ Policies are considered too slow; ■ Not having a working culture of electronics; ■ Egoistic and lack of collaborative efforts
				Technology	■ Lack of data integration;
[24]	Journal of Public Affairs and Development	Adoption of artificial intelligence (AI) in local governments: an exploratory study on the attitudes and perceptions of officials in a municipal government in the Philippines	2021	People	■ Anxiety;
[74]	Journal of Indonesian Legal Studies	Confronting e-government adoption in Indonesian local government	2021	People	■ Human resource–Human resources must be structured and managed with E-government goals in mind. A well-trained and motivated workforce is critical to E-government success;
				Process	■ Law and Policy–The application of Information Technology and Communication (ICT) to the government may encounter legal or policy barriers Legislatures must ensure that laws are updated to recognize electronic documents and transactions. Policymakers implementing E-government must consider the impact of law and public policy;
[72]	IOP Conference Series: Earth and Environmental Science	Smart city development innovation strategy and challenges for the government of Jember Regency	2021	People	■ Artificial intelligence of human resources; ■ Social adaptation of the community and development of application systems;
				Process	■ Security and privacy policies;
				Technology	■ Availability of data and information; ■ IT facilities and infrastructure;

Table A2. Cont.

Study	Journal	Title	Year	Framework Element	Description
[50]	Government Information Quarterly	Technological frames, CIOs, and artificial intelligence in public administration: a socio-cognitive exploratory study in Spanish local governments	2022	People	■ Inequality; ■ Citizen literacy; ■ Suppliers control; ■ Social unawareness;
				Process	■ Budget; ■ Governance framework; ■ Regulation; ■ Administrative culture;
				Technology	■ Digital divide; ■ Technological infrastructure; ■ Data privacy; ■ Data security; ■ Human labor elimination;
[78]	Technological Forecasting and Social Change	Smart territories and IoT adoption by local authorities: a question of trust, efficiency, and relationship with the citizen-user-taxpayer.	2022	People	■ Organizational and human experience in new technologies;
				Process	■ Decision-making shared between politicians and senior executives;
				Technology	■ Lack of needed infrastructure;
[34]	Information Technology and People	Assessing the drivers of the regional digital divide and their impact on eGovernment services: evidence from a South American country	2022	People	■ Age; ■ Rurality;
[71]	JSTOR	Trust, tech, and tension: digital citizen engagement and urban	2022	Technology	■ Communication; ■ Time; ■ Trust;
[24]	AI and Society	Artificial intelligence in local governments: perceptions of city managers on prospects, constraints, and choices	2023	People	■ Lack of trust and resistance from users–particularly senior citizens; ■ Limited local council personnel knowledge and experience;
				Process	■ Lack of ethical frameworks and regulations; ■ Limited in-house know-how and difficulties in validating autonomous decisions; ■ Limited funds for adoption and deployment; ■ Difficulties in operational change management; ■ Uncertainties around legal issues;
				Technology	■ Data bias and resulting inaccuracies; ■ Unaffordability of technological investment; ■ Automation risks;

Table A3. Local government technology adoption strategies.

Study	Journal	Title	Year	Framework Element	Description
[33]	Public Administration Review	The evolution of e-government among municipalities: rhetoric or reality?	2002	Process	■ To enhance the effectiveness of their e-government practices, many municipal governments will need to move towards a higher level of e-government development, which will require more technical, personal, and financial commitments; ■ Municipal governments also need to establish systematic and comprehensive e-government plans in which they assess available resources and address related legal issues such as privacy and security;
[66]	Online Information Review	E-government evolution in EU local governments: a comparative perspective	2009	Process	■ To increase the contribution of websites to promoting transparency, accountability, and openness and to alter the bureaucratic relationship between government and citizens, governments and policymakers will have to strengthen the interactivity of their websites soon;
[73]	Policy & Internet	Digital divides in urban e-government in South Korea: exploring differences in municipalities' use of the internet for environmental governance	2010	Process	■ Collaborative partnerships should be fostered between the different levels of government to resolve the digital divide; ■ Budget constraints and limited technical expertise found in local governments. To address this problem, the central government should develop programs that provide financial subsidies and technological assistance, enabling municipalities to adopt state-of art technologies for local governance innovations; ■ Community-based organizations should play active roles in helping cultivate social networks promoting civic interest in accessing public information online;
[58]	International Journal of Organization Theory & Behaviour	Digital governance success factors and barriers to success in Prague	2011	People	■ At the individual level–training and ensuring that employees have adequate access to continued professional development was identified as the most critical factor; ■ Before new programs are implemented, project leaders need to engage municipal government employees across multiple departments; ■ Hiring adequate number of motivated and qualified staff; ■ Managers must also be held accountable for implementing their projects and engage in professional project management that properly allocate organizational resources like staff time and budgetary costs; ■ Citizens should not only be engaged in digital governance, but they should also be a part of the planning process for developing new digital government initiatives;
				Process	■ New technology projects must not be overly complex, and adequate planning must be conducted to ensure proper implementation;
				Technology	■ E-government initiatives need adequate infrastructure to fulfill the high expectations for privacy and security by citizens;
[79]	International Journal of Cloud Applications and Computing	A framework for analyzing the impact of cloud computing on local government in the UK	2011	Process	■ For security issues proper risk assessment, information assurance and governance, service level agreements, and policies are areas that will require further investigation;

Table A3. *Cont.*

Study	Journal	Title	Year	Framework Element	Description
[86]	International Journal of Information Management	E-government and citizen's engagement with local affairs through e-websites: the case of Spanish municipalities	2012	People	■ Managers could build on an existing culture of awareness of and sensitivity to information and technologies to positively contribute to e-government success and use;
				Process	■ More collaboration and interaction can be developed within and across governments, and this can also positively contribute to relationships between local, regional, and national governments; ■ Since e-government results from the interaction between government employees and citizens, it is important to know how government employees perceive e-government and to what extent they are aware of all aspects related to the e-government projects to their viability and potential impacts;
[80]	The Journal of Contemporary Issues in Business and Government	An investigation of the main factors to be considered in cloud computing adoption in Australian regional local councils	2015	People	■ Cloud service providers may need to improve their interaction with regional councils that are involved in cloud computing, to create a healthy environment for cloud computing adoption and to remove any doubts surrounding this technology;
[45]	Government Information Quarterly	Factors influencing social media use in local governments: the case of Italy and Spain	2016	People	■ Qualified people should manage social media applications to prevent the misuse of these tools, so there is a need to identify new organizational roles in the municipality, such as social media manager; ■ Politicians should focus on content management on Facebook pages and on information provision that properly addresses different users' needs;
				Process	■ Legal system mandatorily requires e-disclosure through municipalities' websites, and legislation should regulate the of social media governments;
[93]	Government Information Quarterly	Are small cities online? Content, ranking, and variation of U.S. municipal websites	2017	People	■ While user orientation means more than just having a Facebook page or Twitter account, those tools may be used to fully engage the public. Enabling users to create and tailor content requires a higher commitment of resources and effort from the city and possibly input from a contractor;
[1]	Transforming Government: People, Process, and Policy	Are government employees adopting local e-government transformation? The need for having the right attitude, facilitating conditions and performance expectations	2017	People	■ Employees should understand technology is rapidly improving. At the same time, citizen expectations of government service delivery are also rising, and therefore regular orientation, workshops, training, and exposure to agencies or organizations are highly required;
				Process	■ The e-government transformation should be adoptable by considering financial, technical, political, and structural support; ■ There should be proper legislative and executive actions to ensure that the transformation efforts have legal bases;

Table A3. *Cont.*

Study	Journal	Title	Year	Framework Element	Description
[90]	Quality Management	Digital technologies and the modernization of public administration	2018	Process	■ Providing improved public services using e-government; ■ Promoting adoption of e-government services; ■ Optimizing the use of ICT in governmental operations;
[15]	State and Local Government Review	Conceptualizing e-government from local government perspectives	2018	People	■ Professional staffing-IT skills among local government employees;
				Process	■ Empirical testing of e-government models; ■ Best practices; continuous focus on the factors and determinants of success and, more importantly, identify challenges to e-government implementation and strategies to reduce IT failures; ■ IT capacity–IT capacity refers to both technical capacity and human capacity in an organization;
[21]	Ecological Economics	Digital transformation and localizing the sustainable development goals (SDGs)	2020	People	■ Public and administrative policymakers in developing countries should direct/encourage investment in the "The digital Network Architecture" (DNA) infrastructure;
				Process	■ Developing countries need to review their institutional competence in dealing with information data; collection, preservation, analysis, deliberation, disclosure, and standards of confidentiality as well as privacy protection along the lines of recent initiatives and legislation to reduce the risk of infringement of individual privacy;
[84]	Government Information Quarterly	Know-how to lead digital transformation: the case of local governments	2020	People	■ Local governments and IT service providers should establish a public–private partnership with the purpose of (I) transferring contact-related knowledge to IT service providers from local governments about their organizational processes and (ii) co-creating some of the requisite know-how to enact an integrated enterprise system to support a high level of cooperation among stakeholders with process management; ■ Recommendation 2. Local government managers should outsource to IT service providers for their competencies in enacting integrated enterprise systems, and then focus on developing the core competence to manage a selection of the most regarding innovations and the best plans for implementing these innovations in support of improved public service delivery; ■ Recommendation 3. Key stakeholders in public service delivery, such as policymakers in higher-tier governments, local governments chief administrative officers and the citizens and businesses served, should demand that managers of multiple local governments actively work in joint problem-solving teams to identify opportunities to exploit private sector know-how to manage digital transformation; ■ Recommendation 4. Policymakers in higher-tier governments should exercise their authority to promote performance evaluation and incentive pay schemes for local governments that are explicitly linked to exploring and exploiting private sector know-how to manage digital transformation;
				Process	■ Recommendation 5. Local governments should work with academic institutions to develop an integrated knowledge base specific to the local government contact, supplemented with additional in-depth case studies examining municipal governance that leverages private sector know-how to manage digital transformation; ■ Recommendation 6. Local governments should work with academic institutions to design executive education programs specifically to close the knowledge gaps identified in this research;

Table A3. Cont.

Study	Journal	Title	Year	Framework Element	Description
[12]	Computer Law and Security Review	The role of government regulations in the adoption of cloud computing: a case study of local government	2020	People	■ Cloud service providers must make a significant effort to assure users that their data are safe. Market forces may drive service providers to differentiate themselves regarding higher levels of security, and the government should play a role by proactively implementing cybercrime laws and data-breach legislation;
				Process	■ Government regulations must clarify the applications used in the delivery of cloud services—The government can encourage the availability and adoption of cloud computing through tax adjustments to service providers, subsidies to low-income people, and management of the wireless spectrum. Fostering data portability and the expansion of broadband capacity through market-led and technology-neutral regulations can help to ensure a wider diffusion of services; ■ Data protection policies regulated by the government could play a critical role in the adoption of cloud computing by Australian regional governments;
				Technology	■ Governments must ensure open access to public cloud services. Access to the fundamental infrastructure of cloud computing should not be driven by biased pricing and should not offer an unfair benefit to other users;
[39]	Procedia Computer Science	Exploring levels of ICT adoption and sustainability: the case of local governments from Poland	2020	People	■ Government units should focus on increasing the personal mastery of employees, employees' creativity, digital literacy, and the sociocultural competencies of employees; ■ Engage employees in adopting ICT and enhancing digital competencies by employing incentive systems;
				Process	■ The adoption of the latest management concepts and the alignment between information society strategy and ICT adoption by government units are needed;
[22]	Information Systems Management	The contribution of ICT adoption by local governments to sustainability—empirical evidence from Poland	2021	People	■ Improvement of information culture;
				Process	■ Improvement of ICT management;
				Technology	■ Improvement of ICT quality;
[92]	International Journal of Teaching and Case Studies	E-government and digital transformation in Libyan local authorities	2021	People	■ Set technology standards and minimum requirements; communication infrastructure be developed across the country; establish common information system; standards and technologies for website development; security measures and technologies need to be introduced; data centers with disaster recovery procedure and technology, partnership with local and national technology and service companies;
				Process	■ Provide appropriate training, exposure to successful e-government strategies and projects, attitude and adaptability, and a coordinated roadmap for transition; ■ Process efficiency. Task and process documentation, process improvement;

Table A3. Cont.

Study	Journal	Title	Year	Framework Element	Description
[69]	Journal Komunikasi: Malaysian Journal of Communication	Digital transformation of the government: a case study in Indonesia	2021	Process	■ Strengthen policies by compiling risk management guidelines, service management guidelines, and ICT audit management guidelines; ■ Effective collaboration of the e-government by a coordination team that involves related institutions; ■ To make effective use of the architecture and map of the e-government plan; ■ Accelerate the integration of e-government services to stop government agencies from building their applications and encourage shared applications. It is to prevent silos in central and regional government agencies; ■ Develop the apparatus' ICT competence, inculcating digital work culture in government organizations and developing partnerships both in government organizations and the other institutions that have adequate ICT capacity;
				Technology	■ Preparing digital infrastructure technology, specifically by building a shared e-government infrastructure, utilizing broadband networks for accessibility, utilizing cloud-based applications, and developing technology-based services 4.0 (cloud computing, artificial intelligence, big data, and the internet of things);
[43]	Information Technology and People	Cloud computing technology adoption: an evaluation of key factors in local governments	2021	People	■ Identify a "champion" for the adoption and eventual handover of the project;
				Process	■ Assess the compatibility of current IT infrastructure with cloud technology; ■ Develop a budget proposal to address concerns about costs; ■ Procure external advice on security issues;
[74]	Journal of Indonesian Legal Studies	Confronting e-government adoption in Indonesian local government	2021	People	■ Articulate a timeline for implementation in a step-by-step approach so the reforms will not seem overwhelming to the bureaucracy; ■ Hold regular meetings between e-government policy leaders and the involved workforce so employees are active participants; ■ Create incentives by rewarding individuals and agencies that apply the reforms rapidly;
				Process	■ Consult with stakeholders to assess how existing laws may impede the desired results; ■ Give legal status to the online publication of government information; ■ Clarify laws and regulations to allow electronic filings with government agencies; ■ Reform processes by simplifying regulations and procedures;
[87]	Smart Cities and Regional Development Journal	Smart government in local adoption-Authorities in strategic change through AI	2021	People	■ This also includes fast and binding communication, the use of digital technologies, and casual culture of ideas without hierarchical barriers in decision-making practice. To experience this, company ambassadors with recognized standing and interdisciplinary skills, methodological competence, and digital background are required in work processes that are critical to success;
				Process	■ It is agreed that barriers such as separate data silos within the authorities or access to public administration data for cooperation partners and service providers have a significant influence factor for the further development and development of the maturity of automated systems. In this respect, coming up with a phrased strategy with goals and principles of action is the first and necessary step for many authorities to deal with the concept of data usage and the associated ecosystem;

Table A3. Cont.

Study	Journal	Title	Year	Framework Element	Description
[20]	Sustainability	Citizens' or government's will? Exploration of why Indonesia's local governments adopt technologies for open government	2021	People	■ Top management support in terms of aligning the technology with the strategic objective is one of the steps that third-party vendors can consider, increasing the probability of adoption;
				Process	■ As an institution with a rigid culture, the government needs to prepare formal regulations to support the adoption process; ■ The government also needs to align the adoption initiative with the regional strategic goals;
				Technology	■ The system must provide a good user experience so that the government officers who use the system can operate it efficiently;
[83]	International Review of Administrative Sciences	Strategic alignment of open government initiatives in Andalusia	2022	People	■ Pull strategy–open participation; ■ Networking or Mingling strategy–Open collaboration and ubiquitous engagement;
				Technology	■ Push strategy–data transparency;
[40]	Information Systems Frontiers	Assessment of complexity in cloud computing adoption: a case study of local governments in Australia	2022	People	■ Training and open communication with staff are necessary to boost organizational knowledge;
[50]	Government Information Quarterly	Technological frames, CIOs, and artificial intelligence in public administration: a socio-cognitive exploratory study in Spanish local governments	2022	People	■ Awareness of potential opportunities, and risks, of AI technologies in public organizations, need to be widely (and wisely) fostered in governmental settings, including political appointees, general managers, and street-level bureaucrats in the recipe;
[91]	NISPAcee Journal of Public Administration and Policy	Digital transformation of Slovenian urban municipalities: a quantitative report on the impact of municipality population size on digital maturity	2022	Process	■ Municipalities must ensure that the e-government concept is not only aimed at providing a large number of services to increase efficiency and effectiveness, opting for a top-down approach according to the need of the municipal administration but that decisions are made on the needs of the citizens, a bottom-up approach; ■ Sharing the results of the digital maturity evaluation between municipalities is very useful as it allows for comparison with others, especially those who are more advanced in terms of digital transformation, and allows those seeking advice to become more aware of best practices, leading to fewer mistakes and better digital transformation outcomes;

Table A3. Cont.

Study	Journal	Title	Year	Framework Element	Description
[89]	Government Information Quarterly	Determinants of digital innovation in the public sector	2022	Process	▪ Support of such stakeholders and elected officials is essential to adopting and/or implementing digital innovation in local governments. To obtain such support from stakeholders and legislators, local governments must create avenues to provide information about the benefits of digital innovation; ▪ Local governments need to establish desirable legal and policy guidelines which are crucial for enhancing the effectiveness of digital innovation rather than just jumping on the bandwagon of adopting legitimate innovation due to isomorphic pressure;
[78]	Technological Forecasting and Social Change	Smart territories and IoT adoption by local authorities: a question of trust, efficiency, and relationship with the citizen-user-taxpayer	2022	People	▪ Appropriate staff training and recruiting personnel, who have already implemented technological innovation, can help develop the capacity for innovation implementation;
				Process	▪ The state's public communication policies towards local authorities and citizens can reduce the fears and reluctance of managers to adopt technological innovations. The state must encourage in its communication policy a kind of mimicry favorable to innovation between public agents, managers, and citizens;
[34]	Information Technology and People	Assessing the drivers of the regional digital divide and their impact on e-government services: evidence from a South American country	2022	Process	▪ Each local government e-websites followed different designs, which accelerated the cost of e-gov–this limitation could be mitigated by adopting a common framework of standards for the development of e-gov websites and the online services provided to citizens; ▪ Local government should include as a priority in their strategic planning the implementation of online services that require user authentication and, consequently, design data privacy and protection policies;
				Technology	▪ Internet access should be available for mobile devices to be adopted by a broader range of citizens; ▪ Local governments should develop mobile orientation participation tools;
[71]	JSTOR	Trust, tech, and tension: digital citizen engagement & urban	2022	People	▪ Expanding public Wi-Fi access, technical literacy training, computer lab resources, and reliable infrastructure will increase citizen trust in government and engagement with citizen relationship management tools;
				Technology	▪ The introduction technology must be designed at a reading and comprehension level that is accessible to all; ▪ Technology tools and training should be accessible to neighborhoods that have previously experienced disinvestment;
[4]	Sustainability	Exploring driving factors of digital transformation among local governments: foundations for smart city construction in China	2022	People	▪ Training civil servants' knowledge and skills;
				Process	▪ Equipping government agencies with relevant infrastructure;
				Technology	▪ Providing solid technical support for digital transformation.

References

1. Batara, E.; Nurmandi, A.; Warsito, T.; Pribadi, U. Are Government Employees Adopting Local E-Government Transformation? *Transform. Gov. People Process Policy* **2017**, *11*, 612–638. [CrossRef]

2. Perveen, S.; Kamruzzaman, M.; Yigitcanlar, T. Developing Policy Scenarios for Sustainable Urban Growth Management: A Delphi Approach. *Sustainability* **2017**, *9*, 1787. [CrossRef]
3. Clement, J.; Crutzen, N. How Local Policy Priorities Set the Smart City Agenda. *Technol. Forecast. Soc. Chang.* **2021**, *171*, 120985. [CrossRef]
4. Xiao, J.; Han, L.; Zhang, H. Exploring Driving Factors of Digital Transformation among Local Governments: Foundations for Smart City Construction in China. *Sustainability* **2022**, *14*, 14980. [CrossRef]
5. Silvia, B. Enhancing the Contribution of Digitalisation to the Smart Cities of The Future. 2019. Available online: http://www.oecd.org/regional/urban-development.htm (accessed on 13 March 2023).
6. Ziosi, M.; Hewitt, B.; Juneja, P.; Taddeo, M.; Floridi, L. Smart Cities: Reviewing the Debate about Their Ethical Implications. In *The 2022 Yearbook of the Digital Governance Research Group*; Springer Nature: Cham, Switzerland, 2023; pp. 11–38. [CrossRef]
7. Rosemann, M.; Becker, J.; Chasin, F. City 5.0. *Bus. Inf. Syst. Eng.* **2020**, *63*, 71–77. [CrossRef]
8. Hunter, M.; Soro, A.; Brown, R.; Harman, J.; Yigitcanlar, T. Augmenting Community Engagement in City 4.0: Considerations for Digital Agency in Urban Public Space. *Sustainability* **2022**, *14*, 9803. [CrossRef]
9. Becker, J.; Chasin, F.; Rosemann, M.; Beverungen, D.; Priefer, J.; vom Brocke, J.; Matzner, M.; del Rio Ortega, A.; Resinas, M.; Santoro, F.; et al. City 5.0: Citizen Involvement in the Design of Future Cities. *Electron. Mark.* **2023**, *33*, 10. [CrossRef]
10. Youens, K. The New Digital Future of Local Government: LinkedIn. 2021. Available online: https://www.linkedin.com/pulse/new-digital-future-local-government-keith-youens/ (accessed on 2 March 2023).
11. Kamal, M.; Bigdeli, A.; Themistocleous, M.; Morabito, V. Investigating Factors Influencing Local Government Decision Makers While Adopting Integration Technologies (IntTech). *Inf. Manag.* **2015**, *52*, 135–150. [CrossRef]
12. Ali, O.; Osmanaj, V. The Role of Government Regulations in the Adoption of Cloud Computing: A Case Study of Local Government. *Comput. Law Secur. Rev.* **2020**, *36*, 105396. [CrossRef]
13. Blazquez, C.; Laurent, J.; Nazif-Munoz, J. Differential Impacts of Ridesharing on Alcohol-Related Crashes by Socioeconomic Municipalities: Rate of Technology Adoption Matters. *BMC Public Health* **2021**, *21*, 2008. [CrossRef]
14. Kamal, M.; Alsudairi, M. Investigating the Importance of Factors Influencing Integration Technologies Adoption in Local Government Authorities. *Transform. Gov. People Process Policy* **2009**, *3*, 302–331. [CrossRef]
15. Manoharan, A.; Ingrams, A. Conceptualizing E-Government from Local Government Perspectives. *State Local Gov. Rev.* **2018**, *50*, 56–66. [CrossRef]
16. Alvarenga, A.; Matos, F.; Godina, R.; Matias, J. Digital Transformation and Knowledge Management in the Public Sector. *Sustainability* **2020**, *12*, 5824. [CrossRef]
17. Zuiderwijk, A.; Chen, Y.; Salem, F. Implications of the Use of Artificial Intelligence in Public Governance: A Systematic Literature Review and a Research Agenda. *Gov. Inf. Q.* **2021**, *38*, 101577. [CrossRef]
18. Ali, E.; Mazen, A.; Hassanein, E. A Proposed Hybrid Model for Adopting Cloud Computing in E-Government. *Future Comput. Inform. J.* **2018**, *3*, 286–295. [CrossRef]
19. Falco, E.; Kleinhans, R. Beyond Technology: Identifying Local Government Challenges for Using Digital Platforms for Citizen Engagement. *Int. J. Inf. Manag.* **2018**, *40*, 17–20. [CrossRef]
20. Adnan, H.; Hidayanto, A.; Kurnia, S. Citizens' or Government's Will? Exploration of Why Indonesia's Local Governments Adopt Technologies for Open Government. *Sustainability* **2021**, *13*, 11197. [CrossRef]
21. ElMassah, S.; Mohieldin, M. Digital Transformation and Localizing the Sustainable Development Goals (SDGs). *Ecol. Econ.* **2020**, *169*, 106490. [CrossRef]
22. Ziemba, E. The Contribution of ICT Adoption by Local Governments to Sustainability—Empirical Evidence from Poland. *Inf. Syst. Manag.* **2021**, *38*, 116–134. [CrossRef]
23. Salam, N.; Ali, S. Determining Factors of Cloud Computing Adoption: A Study of Indonesian Local Government Employees. *J. Account. Investig.* **2020**, *21*, 312–333. [CrossRef]
24. Distor, C.; Khaltar, O.; Moon, M. Adoption of Artificial Intelligence (AI) in Local Governments: An Exploratory Study on the Attitudes and Perceptions of Officials in a Municipal Government in the Philippines. *J. Public Aff. Dev.* **2023**, *8*, 33–65.
25. Yigitcanlar, T.; Degirmenci, K.; Inkinen, T. Drivers behind the public perception of artificial intelligence: Insights from major Australian cities. *AI Soc.* **2022**. [CrossRef]
26. Simon, B. Complete Guide to the PPT Framework | Smartsheet. Smartsheet 2021. Available online: https://www.smartsheet.com/content/people-process-technology (accessed on 1 June 2023).
27. Leavitt, H. Applied organization change in industry: Structural, technical and human approaches. In *Handbook of Organization*; Routledge: London, UK, 1965; pp. 1147–1170.
28. Hosseini, M. The Impact of People, Process and Technology on Knowledge Management. 2014. Available online: https://www.iiste.org/Journals/index.php/EJBM/article/view/16022 (accessed on 13 March 2023).
29. Dave, B.; Koskela, L.; Kagioglou, M.; Bertelsen, S. A critical look at integrating people, process and information systems within the construction sector. In Proceedings of the 16th Annual Conference of the International Group for Lean Construction, Manchester, UK, 16–18 July 2008; pp. 795–807. Available online: https://iglcstorage.blob.core.windows.net/papers/attachment-379f0ce2-a46e-40ac-92bd-f6935ffd1af5.pdf (accessed on 1 June 2023).
30. Husby, B. Integrating People, Process, and Technology in Lean Healthcare. 2012. Available online: https://deepblue.lib.umich.edu/handle/2027.42/94025 (accessed on 1 June 2023).

31. Khanduri, A. People, Process, Technology. 2022. Available online: https://www.plutora.com/blog/people-process-technology-ppt-framework-explained (accessed on 1 June 2023).
32. Lögdal, N.; Calissendorff, P. Digital Platforms Challenges and Opportunities: Evidence from a Traditional Market Sector. 2018. Available online: http://umu.diva-portal.org/smash/get/diva2:1222284/FULLTEXT01.pdf (accessed on 1 June 2023).
33. Moon, M. The Evolution of E-Government among Municipalities: Rhetoric or Reality? *Public Adm. Rev.* **2002**, *62*, 424–433. [CrossRef]
34. Sarango, M.; Naranjo-Zolotov, M.; Cruz-Jesus, F. Assessing the Drivers of the Regional Digital Divide and Their Impact on EGovernment Services: Evidence from a South American Country. *Inf. Technol. People* **2021**, *35*, 2002–2025. [CrossRef]
35. Li, M.; Feeney, M. Adoption of Electronic Technologies in Local U.S. Governments. *Am. Rev. Public Adm.* **2012**, *44*, 75–91. [CrossRef]
36. Kim, H.; Bretschneider, S. Local Government Information Technology Capacity: An Exploratory Theory. In Proceedings of the Hawaii International Conference on System Sciences, Big Island, HI, USA, 5–8 January 2004. [CrossRef]
37. Zachlod, C.; Samuel, O.; Ochsner, A.; Werthmüller, S. Analytics of Social Media Data – State of Characteristics and Application. *J. Bus. Res.* **2022**, *144*, 1064–1076. [CrossRef]
38. Feeney, M.; Fusi, F.; Camarena, L.; Zhang, F. Towards More Digital Cities? Change in Technology Use and Perceptions across Small and Medium-Sized US Cities. *Local Gov. Stud.* **2020**, *46*, 820–845. [CrossRef]
39. Ziemba, E. Exploring Levels of ICT Adoption and Sustainability—The Case of Local Governments from Poland. *Procedia Comput. Sci.* **2020**, *176*, 3067–3082. [CrossRef]
40. Ali, O.; Shrestha, A.; Ghasemaghaei, M.; Beydoun, G. Assessment of Complexity in Cloud Computing Adoption: A Case Study of Local Governments in Australia. *Inf. Syst. Front.* **2021**, 1–23. [CrossRef]
41. Kumar, P.; Ghose, M. Cloud Computing: Possibilities, Challenges and Opportunities with Special Reference to Its Emerging Need in the Academic and Working Area of Information Science. *Procedia Eng.* **2012**, *38*, 2222–2227. [CrossRef]
42. Chang, J.; Johnston, M. Cloud Computing in Local Government. *Int. J. Cloud Appl. Comput.* **2012**, *2*, 1–15. [CrossRef]
43. Ali, O.; Shrestha, A.; Osmanaj, V.; Muhammed, S. Cloud Computing Technology Adoption: An Evaluation of Key Factors in Local Governments. *Inf. Technol. People* **2021**, *34*, 666–703. [CrossRef]
44. Johnston, K.; Kervin, L.; Wyeth, P. Defining Digital Technology. Australian Research Council's Centre of Excellence for the Digital Child. 2022. Available online: https://www.digitalchild.org.au/blog/defining-digital-technology/#:~:text=Our%20statement%20defining%20digital%20technology (accessed on 1 June 2023).
45. Guillamón, M.; Ríos, A.; Gesuele, B.; Metallo, C. Factors Influencing Social Media Use in Local Governments: The Case of Italy and Spain. *Gov. Inf. Q.* **2016**, *33*, 460–471. [CrossRef]
46. Bolívar, M. Governance Models for the Delivery of Public Services through the Web 2.0 Technologies. *Soc. Sci. Comput. Rev.* **2016**, *35*, 203–225. [CrossRef]
47. Frissen, V.; Kool, L.; Kotterink, B.; Nielsen, M.; Millard, J. *Public Services 2.0: The Impact of Social Computing on Public Services*; Publications Office of the European Union: Luxembourg, 2009; Available online: https://doi.org/10.2791/31908 (accessed on 1 June 2023).
48. Yigitcanlar, T.; Agdas, D.; Degirmenci, K. Artificial Intelligence in Local Governments: Perceptions of City Managers on Prospects, Constraints and Choices. *AI Soc.* **2023**, *38*, 1135–1150. [CrossRef]
49. Collins, C.; Dennehy, D.; Conboy, K.; Mikalef, P. Artificial Intelligence in Information Systems Research: A Systematic Literature Review and Research Agenda. *Int. J. Inf. Manag.* **2021**, *60*, 102383. [CrossRef]
50. Criado, J.; Zarate-Alcarazo, L. Technological Frames, CIOs, and Artificial Intelligence in Public Administration: A Socio-Cognitive Exploratory Study in Spanish Local Governments. *Gov. Inf. Q.* **2022**, *39*, 101688. [CrossRef]
51. Yigitcanlar, T.; Li, R.Y.M.; Beeramoole, P.; Paz, A. Artificial Intelligence in Local Government Services: Public Perceptions from Australia and Hong Kong. *Gov. Inf. Q.* **2023**, *40*, 101833. [CrossRef]
52. Yeh, S.-C.; Wu, A.-W.; Yu, H.-C.; Wu, H.C.; Kuo, Y.-P.; Chen, P.-X. Public Perception of Artificial Intelligence and Its Connections to the Sustainable Development Goals. *Sustainability* **2021**, *13*, 9165. [CrossRef]
53. Bibri, S.E.; Alexandre, A.; Sharifi, A.; Krogstie, J. Environmentally Sustainable Smart Cities and Their Converging AI, IoT, and Big Data Technologies and Solutions: An Integrated Approach to an Extensive Literature Review. *Energy Inform.* **2023**, *6*, 9. [CrossRef] [PubMed]
54. Nili, A.; Desouza, K.; Yigitcanlar, T. What Can the Public Sector Teach Us about Deploying Artificial Intelligence Technologies? *IEEE Softw.* **2022**, *39*, 58–63. [CrossRef]
55. Vogl, T.; Seidelin, C.; Ganesh, B.; Bright, J. Smart Technology and the Emergence of Algorithmic Bureaucracy: Artificial Intelligence in UK Local Authorities. *Public Adm. Rev.* **2020**, *80*, 946–961. [CrossRef]
56. Reddick, C. Citizen-Initiated Contacts with Government. *J. E-Gov.* **2005**, *2*, 27–53. [CrossRef]
57. Reddick, C. The Adoption of Centralized Customer Service Systems: A Survey of Local Governments. *Gov. Inf. Q.* **2009**, *26*, 219–226. [CrossRef]
58. Melitski, J.; Carrizales, T.; Manoharan, A.; Holzer, M. Digital Governance Success Factors and Barriers to Success in Prague. *Int. J. Organ. Theory Behav.* **2011**, *14*, 451–472. [CrossRef]
59. Stamati, T.; Martakos, D. Electronic Transformation of Local Government. *Int. J. Electron. Gov. Res.* **2011**, *7*, 20–37. [CrossRef]
60. James, X. Local Authorities Achieving Results with AI Roll-Outs. 2021. Available online: https://www.government-transformation.com/data/local-authorities-achieving-results-with-ai-roll-outs, (accessed on 1 June 2023).

61. Jonathan, G. Digital transformation in the public sector: Identifying critical success factors. In Proceedings of the Information Systems: 16th European, Mediterranean, and Middle Eastern Conference, EMCIS 2019, Dubai, United Arab Emirates, 9–10 December 2019; Springer International Publishing: Cham, Switzerland, 2020; Volume 16, pp. 223–235. [CrossRef]
62. Haneem, F.; Kama, N.; Taskin, N.; Pauleen, D.; Abu Bakar, N. Determinants of Master Data Management Adoption by Local Government Organizations: An Empirical Study. *Int. J. Inf. Manag.* **2019**, *45*, 25–43. [CrossRef]
63. Wohlers, T. The Digital World of Local Government: A Comparative Analysis of the United States and Germany. *J. Inf. Technol. Politics* **2009**, *6*, 111–126. [CrossRef]
64. Reddick, C. Customer Relationship Management (CRM) Technology and Organizational Change: Evidence for the Bureaucratic and E-Government Paradigms. *Gov. Inf. Q.* **2011**, *28*, 346–353. [CrossRef]
65. ISO/IEC 25010:2011; Systems and Software Engineering. Systems and Software Quality Requirements and Evaluation (SQuaRE): Geneva, Switzerland, 2011. Available online: https://www.iso.org/standard/35733.html (accessed on 1 June 2023).
66. Pina, V.; Torres, L.; Royo, S. E-Government Evolution in EU Local Governments: A Comparative Perspective. *Online Inf. Rev.* **2009**, *33*, 1137–1168. [CrossRef]
67. Fadli, M.; Sumitra, I. A Study of Application and Framework Smart City in Bandung: A Survey. *IOP Conf. Ser. Mater. Sci. Eng.* **2019**, *662*, 022083. [CrossRef]
68. Futr. Examples of AI in Local Government. 2021. Available online: https://futr.ai/from-chatbots-to-automation-3-examples-of-ai-in-local-government (accessed on 1 June 2023).
69. Aminah, S.; Saksono, H. Digital Transformation of the Government: A Case Study in Indonesia. *J. Komun. Malays. J. Commun.* **2021**, *37*, 272–288. [CrossRef]
70. Danial, M.; Velasquez, D. Digital Transformation in Australian Local Government: A Systematic Literature Review. 2022. Available online: https://acis.aaisnet.org/wp-content/uploads/2022/11/ACIS_2022_paper_75.pdf (accessed on 1 June 2023).
71. Renz, E. Trust, Tech, and Tension: Digital Citizen Engagement & Urban. *JSTOR* **2022**, *59*, 91–106.
72. Maulana, A.; Haerah, K. Smart City Development Innovation Strategy and Challenges for the Government of Jember Regency. *IOP Conf. Ser. Earth Environ. Sci.* **2021**, *717*, 012008. [CrossRef]
73. Lim, J. Digital Divides in Urban E-Government in South Korea: Exploring Differences in Municipalities' Use of the Internet for Environmental Governance. *Policy Int.* **2010**, *2*, 29–66. [CrossRef]
74. Martitah, M.; Arifin, S.; Sumarto, S.; Widiyanto, W. Confronting E-Government Adoption in Indonesian Local Government. *J. Indones. Leg. Stud.* **2021**, *6*, 279–306. [CrossRef]
75. Ali, O.; Soar, J.; Yong, J. An Investigation of the Challenges and Issues Influencing the Adoption of Cloud Computing in Australian Regional Municipal Governments. *J. Inf. Secur. Appl.* **2016**, *27*, 19–34. [CrossRef]
76. Datta, P.; Walker, L.; Amarilli, F. Digital Transformation: Learning from Italy's Public Administration. *J. Inf. Technol. Teach. Cases* **2020**, *10*, 54–71. [CrossRef]
77. Wang, S.; Feeney, M. Determinants of Information and Communication Technology Adoption in Municipalities. *Am. Rev. Public Adm.* **2014**, *46*, 292–313. [CrossRef]
78. Leroux, E.; Pupion, P. Smart Territories and IoT Adoption by Local Authorities: A Question of Trust, Efficiency, and Relationship with the Citizen-User-Taxpayer. *Technol. Forecast. Soc. Chang.* **2022**, *174*, 121195. [CrossRef]
79. Chang, J. A Framework for Analysing the Impact of Cloud Computing on Local Government in the UK. *Int. J. Cloud Appl. Comput.* **2011**, *1*, 25–33. [CrossRef]
80. Ali, O.; Soar, J.; Yong, J. An Investigation of the Main Factors to Be Considered in Cloud Computing Adoption in Australian Regional Local Councils. *J. Contemp. Issues Bus. Gov.* **2015**, *21*, 72. [CrossRef]
81. Son, T.; Weedon, Z.; Yigitcanlar, T.; Sanchez, T.; Corchado, J.; Mehmood, R. Algorithmic Urban Planning for Smart and Sustainable Development: Systematic Review of the Literature. *Sustain. Cities Soc.* **2023**, *94*, 104562. [CrossRef]
82. Cai, L.; Zhu, Y. The Challenges of Data Quality and Data Quality Assessment in the Big Data Era. *Data Sci. J.* **2015**, *14*, 2. [CrossRef]
83. Alcaide Muñoz, C.; Alcaide Muñoz, L.; Rodríguez Bolívar, M. Strategic Alignment of Open Government Initiatives in Andalusia. *Int. Rev. Adm. Sci.* **2022**, 002085232210861. [CrossRef]
84. Pittaway, J.; Montazemi, A. Know-How to Lead Digital Transformation: The Case of Local Governments. *Gov. Inf. Q.* **2020**, *37*, 101474. [CrossRef]
85. Reddick, C. Impact of Citizen Relationship Management (CRM) on Government: Evidence from U.S. Local Governments. *J. E-Gov.* **2010**, *33*, 88–99. [CrossRef]
86. Cegarra-Navarro, J.; Pachón, J.; Cegarra, J. E-Government and Citizen's Engagement with Local Affairs through E-Websites: The Case of Spanish Municipalities. *Int. J. Inf. Manag.* **2012**, *32*, 469–478. [CrossRef]
87. Schachtner, C. Smart Government in Local Adoption—Authorities in Strategic Change through AI. *SCRD* **2021**, *5*, 53–62.
88. Athapaththu, H. An Overview of Strategic Management: An Analysis of the Concepts and the Importance of Strategic Management. *Int. J. Sci. Res. Publ.* **2016**, *6*, 2016.
89. Hong, S.; Kim, S.; Kwon, M. Determinants of Digital Innovation in the Public Sector. *Gov. Inf. Q.* **2022**, *39*, 101723. [CrossRef]
90. Todorut, A.; Tselentis, B. Digital Technologies and the Modernization of Public Administration. *Qual. Manag.* **2018**, *19*, 73–78.
91. Debeljak, A.; Dečman, M. Digital Transformation of Slovenian Urban Municipalities: A Quantitative Report on the Impact of Municipality Population Size on Digital Maturity. *J. Public Adm. Policy* **2022**, *15*, 25–51. [CrossRef]

92. Wynn, M.; Bakeer, A.; Forti, Y. E-Government and Digital Transformation in Libyan Local Authorities. *Int. J. Teach. Case Stud.* **2021**, *12*, 119. [CrossRef]
93. Feeney, M.; Brown, A. Are Small Cities Online? Content, Ranking, and Variation of U.S. Municipal Websites. *Gov. Inf. Q.* **2017**, *34*, 62–74. [CrossRef]
94. United Nations. E-Government Survey 2014 E-Government For The Future We Want. 2014. Available online: http://www.un.org/desa (accessed on 1 June 2023).
95. Janbi, N.; Katib, I.; Albeshri, A.; Mehmood, R. Distributed Artificial Intelligence-As-a-Service (DAIaaS) for Smarter IoE and 6G Environments. *Sensors* **2020**, *20*, 5796. [CrossRef] [PubMed]
96. Janbi, N.; Katib, I.; Mehmood, R. Distributed Artificial Intelligence: Review, Taxonomy, Framework, and Reference Architecture. *SSRN Electron. J.* **2023**. [CrossRef]
97. Shafiee, S.; Jahanyan, S.; Ghatari, A.R.; Hasanzadeh, A. Developing Sustainable Tourism Destinations through Smart Technologies: A System Dynamics Approach. *J. Simul.* **2022**, 1–22. [CrossRef]
98. Ashtari, N.; Bunt, A.; McGrenere, J.; Nebeling, M.; Chilana, P. Creating Augmented and Virtual Reality Applications: Current Practices, Challenges, and Opportunities. In Proceedings of the 2020 CHI Conference on Human Factors in Computing Systems, Honolulu, HI, USA, 25–30 April 2020. [CrossRef]
99. Ouyang, L.; Wu, J.; Jiang, X.; Almeida, D.; Wainwright, C.; Mishkin, P.; Zhang, C.; Agarwal, S.; Slama, K.; Ray, A.; et al. Training language models to follow instructions with human feedback. In Proceedings of the Advances in Neural Information Processing Systems, New Orleans, LA, USA, 28 November–9 December 2022; Koyejo, S., Mohamed, S., Agarwal, A., Belgrave, D., Cho, K., Oh, A., Eds.; Curran Associates, Inc.: New York, NY, USA, 2022; Volume 35, pp. 27730–27744.
100. Pournader, M.; Shi, Y.; Seuring, S.; Koh, S. Blockchain Applications in Supply Chains, Transport and Logistics: A Systematic Review of the Literature. *Int. J. Prod. Res.* **2019**, *58*, 2063–2081. [CrossRef]
101. Almalki, J.; Al Shehri, W.; Mehmood, R.; Alsaif, K.; Alshahrani, S.; Jannah, N.; Khan, N. Enabling Blockchain with IoMT Devices for Healthcare. *Information* **2022**, *13*, 448. [CrossRef]
102. Fan, L.; Gil-Garcia, J.; Song, Y.; Cronemberger, F.; Hua, G.; Werthmuller, D.; Burke, G.; Costello, J.; Meyers, B.; Hong, X. Sharing big data using blockchain technologies in local governments: Some technical, organizational and policy considerations. *Inf. Polity* **2019**, *24*, 419–435. [CrossRef]

Disclaimer/Publisher's Note: The statements, opinions and data contained in all publications are solely those of the individual author(s) and contributor(s) and not of MDPI and/or the editor(s). MDPI and/or the editor(s) disclaim responsibility for any injury to people or property resulting from any ideas, methods, instructions or products referred to in the content.

Article

Lifelong Learning as a Factor in the Country's Competitiveness and Innovative Potential within the Framework of Sustainable Development

Aleksandra Kuzior [1,2,*], Dariusz Krawczyk [1], Kateryna Onopriienko [3], Yuriy Petrushenko [3], Iryna Onopriienko [4] and Volodymyr Onopriienko [5]

1. Department of Applied Social Sciences, Faculty of Organization and Management, Silesian University of Technology, 41-800 Zabrze, Poland
2. Oleg Balatskyi Department of Management, Sumy State University, 40000 Sumy, Ukraine
3. Department of International Economic Relations, Education and Research Institute for Business, Economics, and Management, Sumy State University, 40007 Sumy, Ukraine
4. Department of Marketing and Logistics, Sumy National Agrarian University, 40007 Sumy, Ukraine
5. Department of Ecology and Botany, Sumy National Agrarian University, 40007 Sumy, Ukraine
* Correspondence: aleksandra.kuzior@polsl.pl

Abstract: The aim of this paper is to examine the interdependence between adult education and the competitiveness and innovative potential of the economy in the conditions of sustainable development. To examine the mentioned, we used a sample of data that includes European countries. The Global Competitiveness Index and its components were taken for research as a numerical display of the country's competitiveness. For indicators of lifelong learning, the share of persons aged 18–64 years involved in education was taken. The paper applies correlation and regression Pearson analysis of comparative data sections. The non-parametric Kruskal–Wallis test and the Wilcoxon–Mann–Whitney test were applied to verify the data, and Vosviewer software was used for bibliometric and graphical analysis. The research findings indicate a strong correlation between lifelong education and the competitiveness and innovative potential of the economy.

Keywords: lifelong learning; sustainable development; competitiveness; innovations

1. Introduction

General trends in the development of the global economy show that innovations and knowledge become the main factors that determine the competitiveness of the country. Therefore, in modern socio-economic conditions, the development of the country can only be ensured by creating an innovative economy based on scientific knowledge and achievements, and this, in turn, can be created only by a person who is engaged in lifelong education.

The question of interdependence between lifelong education and the competitiveness of the country is becoming more and more discussed and requires an increasingly thorough study to present measures that can be taken in the future to improve the country's economic indicators, that ensure the country's competitiveness. Therefore, the research asked the question: «Can adult education affect the country's competitiveness and its innovative potential»? To answer this question, we hypothesized that lifelong education has a positive effect on the country's competitiveness and is related to innovation potential.

2. Materials and Methods

The article uses two main methods—bibliometric analysis and Pearson correlation-regression methods.

Bibliometric analysis is a powerful tool to quantify scientific production, quality, and impact. This technique also provides readers with full information related to intellectual,

conceptual, and social structures of a certain area together with its evolution over time [1]. In general, bibliometrics can be described as a systematic review approach that allows the (scientific) literature to be analyzed statistically [2]. Analytics from the Scopus database and Vosviewer software were used for bibliometric analysis, which allows us to graphically see connections between keywords and their density. In the study, articles were taken for analysis by the keywords "competitiveness" and "learning", the database revealed 4957 (on the date of the study) documents that were taken for graphical analysis.

The Pearson correlation–regression method was chosen for the main study. The application of correlation–regression methods makes it possible to understand the deep essence of the processes of interrelationships. Correlations are found between two terms in this article—between The Global Competitiveness Index and the share of adults participating in education. In these relationships between cause and effect, there is no complete correspondence, but only a certain relationship in the form of a coefficient is observed. That is, when the dependent variable decreases or increases, the effective indicator will increase or decrease.

The Global Competitiveness Index and its components for 2012–2021 year were taken for research as numerical display of the country's competitiveness. For indicators of adult education, the share (%) of persons aged 18–64 years involved in education was taken from Eurostat database. For the study, 12 parameters of the Competitiveness Index for 36 European countries and indicators of the share of participation in adult education for 10 years were taken.

3. Literature Review

Many researchers agree that education and skills will be a key factor in increasing competitiveness, and one of the most important preconditions for achieving this goal is quality lifelong education. The economic component in education is described in the research of Tanjung, E.F. [3], Akpoviroro, K.S. [4]. About the impact of education on the country's competitiveness writes Chentukov Y. [5], Fojtíková L. [6], Mendez, S. [7]. Tanjung, E.F. points, that public wellness, government effectiveness, literacy rate, and population growth significantly impact the quality of education and country's competitiveness [3]. Fojtíková L notes, that in order to attain highly skilled human capital, economic entities should improve their competitiveness and increase investments in education, science, and technology [6]. Chentukov Y. claims, that the internationalization of curricula is considered to be a recognized tool for improving the quality of education and as the next step—increasing competitiveness [5].

Among others, Shmygol, N. et al. [8], Kuzior et al. [9,10], Vidic, F. [11], and Kharazishvili, Y. et al. [12] indicate innovation and education interdependence. Vidic, F. notes that knowledge assets—technological and human capital—have been recognized as key resources for sustainable competitive advantage in a dynamic turbulent environment. Existing knowledge is not enough to be competitive in the future market. Firms must collect, disseminate, and create innovative knowledge capital [11]. Analyzing the Scopus database using the keywords "competitiveness" and "learning", the number of scientific works for such keywords reached 4957 articles, while for the keywords "competitiveness" and "lifelong education" the system showed only 17 scientific works, which increases the relevance of this research. We see a rapid increase in the number of scientific works from 2016 and from 2019, that is, from the year when the world was gripped by a pandemic, which led to the emergence of new methods of education [13], new types of work [14] and as a consequence to innovation and additional education. This year, the number of scientific studies was twice as much as compared to 2012 (Figure 1).

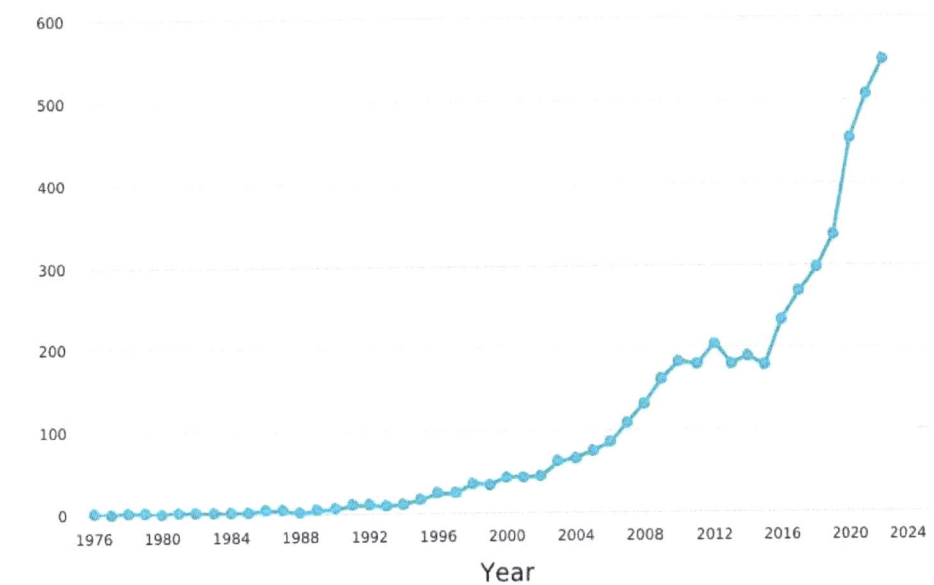

Figure 1. The trend of the number of scientific works by the keywords «competitiveness» and «learning». Source: Scopus database.

Using the Vosviewer software, the found scientific works from the Scopus database were analyzed for the density of connections between words such as "competitiveness", "innovation", and "education". We see that these concepts are closely related. Additionally, the infographic shows that innovation is quite close to competitiveness and education, and the sectors are large and close to each other. This means that many world scientists in their research paid attention to the relationship between competitiveness and education and more, to other concepts reflected in small circles (Figure 2).

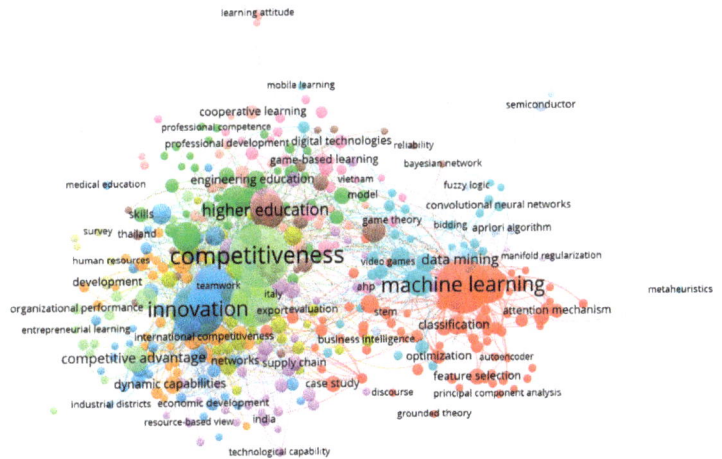

Figure 2. Networks map between the keywords of articles published on competitiveness. Source: Built by the author using Vosviewer software.

It is also clear from the infographic that competitiveness is connected not only with economic concepts, as was commonly believed, but also with education. Moreover, the large cluster on the right is occupied by the cluster of machine learning, that is, with the help of innovative tools and technologies. We believe that this will be the next level of education development and, as a result, its quality will affect the economic indicators of countries.

4. Results

The objective need for the competitive development of the country, the formation of an innovative economy put forward a new system of requirements for a person as a link in the economy. Gradually, the need is realized even for an established specialist to update knowledge and change the scope of professional activity several times throughout his life, constantly adapting to changing socio-economic conditions, to the situation on the labor market, and to changes in the knowledge-based economy [15].

It is important to note that back in the middle of the last century, knowledge doubled every 50 years, and this allowed a person who received an education to be satisfied with the professional education he received once throughout his working life [16]. At the beginning of the 21st century, experts argued for the need to update knowledge every six years. Today, experts say that the amount of knowledge is doubling every three years and will double every 11 days in the coming years [17,18].

In the specialized literature, there is even a special unit for measuring the obsolescence of a specialist's knowledge—the so-called "competence half-life" [16], which reflects the length of time after graduation from a professional educational institution, when, as a result of the obsolescence of the acquired knowledge, as new information becomes available, the competence of a specialist decreases by 50%. Accordingly, the competitiveness of the country is determined by how quickly a person can again meet the needs of the economy at a particular stage [19].

Today, population aging is observed in almost all countries. According to UN estimates, in the next 15 years, the number of elderly people (60 years and older) will increase by 56% on a global scale: from 901 million people in 2015 to more than 1.4 billion by 2030 [20]. If these predictions come true, by 2030, for the first time in history, the number of elderly people will exceed the number of children under the age of 9, and by 2050, teenagers and young people aged 10–24 [21].

At the same time, adults will be forced to work longer than previous generations. Finding ways to improve their skills and professional reorientation due to technological changes and globalization will become a vital necessity for them and for ensuring the country's competitiveness [22]. Adults will also look for new learning opportunities to continue their professional and personal development, and the country must look for ways to educate adults so that they can respond competently to the changing economy and ensure their competitiveness [23].

The most competitive economies in Europe are also the most innovative and those where the share of adults in education is high compared to other countries (Figure 3). Switzerland, Sweden, Denmark, Finland, the Netherlands, and Germany are leaders in innovation in the world, as well as examples of successfully functioning adult education systems.

What they all have in common is that they all have strong knowledge-based economies [24]. They are characterized by a strong research and development sector with good international connections and a broad and constantly renewed talent base. GDP per capita illustrates the level of economic development of the country, and the share of participation in adult education, in turn, has the same fluctuations as GDP, which gives reason to assert that the level of economic development of the country is related to adult education and vice versa (Figure 3).

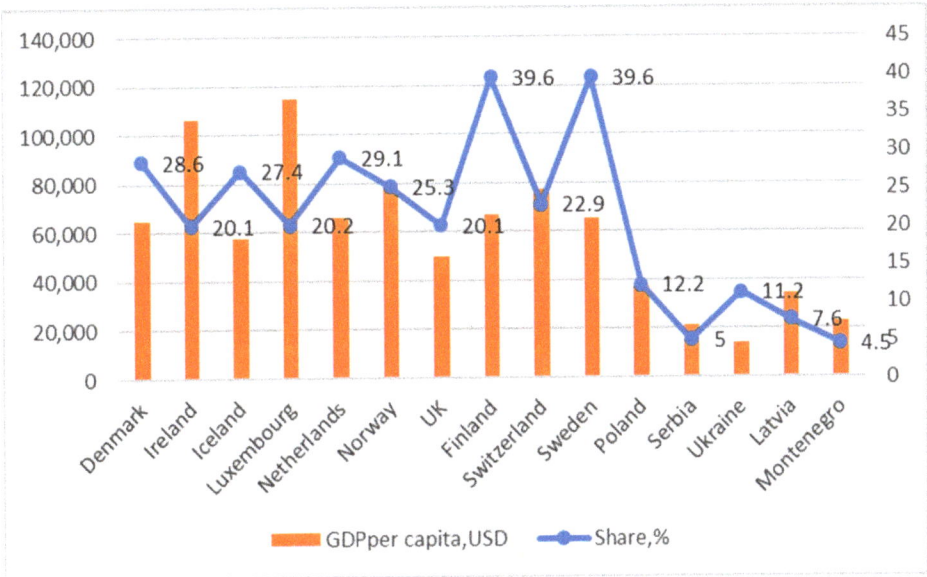

Figure 3. GDP per capita and the share of the population (18–64 y.o.) involved in lifelong learning in European countries in 2022. Source: Built by the authors.

The awareness of the importance of the implementation of lifelong education is prompted by numerous external factors [25], mostly documents and initiatives of the UN, UNESCO, initiatives of the International Labor Organization, the Council of Europe, and the European Commission, as well as resolutions, conventions, recommendations approved by many global and regional forums on lifelong education issues as a key element of lifelong learning [26]. The 2030 Agenda for Sustainable Development, adopted by all United Nations Member States in 2015, provides a shared blueprint for peace and prosperity for people and the planet, now and into the future. At its heart are the 17 Sustainable Development Goals, which are an urgent call for action by all countries—developed and developing—in a global partnership [27]. According to this strategy, it is necessary to achieve three forms of growth: sustainable growth, which implies promoting a resource-efficient, green, and competitive economy; smart growth, which means the development of a society based on knowledge and innovation; and inclusive growth, which implies a high-employment economy [28].

International institutions create indices based on which they measure and rank countries according to various aspects, including competitiveness. The methodology of measuring the competitiveness of the economy of the World Economic Forum is based on the Global Competitiveness Index [29]. The competitiveness of economies is monitored through the 12 pillars of competitiveness. The index is calculated for all economies in the same way, and the final value of the index is a simple average of the 12 components. Such indicators are:

1. Institutions;
2. Appropriate infrastructure;
3. Stable macroeconomic framework;
4. Good health and primary education;
5. Higher education and training;
6. Efficient goods markets;
7. Efficient labor markets;
8. Developed financial markets;

9. Ability to harness existing technology;
10. Market size—both domestic and international;
11. Production of new and different goods using the most sophisticated production processes;
12. Innovation [15,30].

As the Industrial Revolution 4.0 continues, all competitiveness factors are considered to equally affect the competitive position of an economy regardless of income level, so each pillar can be considered as a potential priority.

However, the analysis of the foundations of competitiveness in the WEF reports clearly shows that in many countries the main reasons for slow development and growth are the inability to use the new opportunities provided by the fourth industrial revolution in the form of modern information and innovative technologies, and the "old" problems of social development in the form of «poor» institutions, infrastructure, and skills available to workers [31].

5. Results

As already mentioned, information and innovative technologies and skills are the fundamental drivers of competitiveness. In addition, the quality of the institutional environment largely determines the level of innovation and the development of physical and human capital, which are the main sources of income inequality (GDP) in countries.

It is important to say that the prevailing view in science is that the education system, as a key factor in the competitiveness of the modern economy, plays an essential role in socio-economic development.

It should be noted that the fifth measure of the Global Competitiveness Index, called Higher Education and Training, has eight sub-pillars or dimensions of economic competitiveness:

5.01 Secondary education enrollment rate;
5.02 Tertiary education enrollment rate;
5.03 Quality of the education system;
5.04 Quality of math and science education;
5.05 Quality of management schools;
5.06 Internet access in school;
5.07 Local availability of specialized training services;
5.08 Extent of staff training [21,22].

Analyzing all eight, we did not see a mention of lifelong education, but it is the driver of a person as the main component of human capital and economic benefit for the country. This became the basis for the hypothesis: does participation in adult education affect the competitiveness of the country? The Global Competitiveness Index and its components for 2012–2021 year were taken for research as numerical display of the country's competitiveness. For indicators of adult education, the share of persons aged 18–64 years involved in education was taken from Eurostat database. For the study, 12 parameters of the Competitiveness Index for 36 European countries and indicators of the share of participation in adult education over 10 years were taken. The tools of Pearson's correlation–regression analysis became a mathematical method for proving or refuting a hypothesis.

In the process of calculations using the method of general regression, as well as regression clustered by years or countries, it was found that the general regression gives the most reliable data, namely, the coefficient = 0.0018. In our case, it means a positive change in the index by 0.0018 points when the share of participation increases by 1%.

Analyzing the countries further, they were divided according to the principle of "developed" and "developing", respectively, further group "1" and group "0". In addition, for the reliability of the distribution, the distribution of countries by GDP per capita was made, and the countries were divided into groups of GDP per capita more and less than 40,000 dollars. This distribution confirmed the distribution by parameters of development and the groups turned out to be the same (Table 1).

Table 1. Distribution of countries by GDP per capita.

Developing	Developed	
Ukraine	Spain	Austria
North Macedonia	Estonia	Belgium
Serbia	Cyprus	Sweden
Montenegro	Lithuania	Netherlands
Bulgaria	Slovenia	Denmark
Turkey	Czech Republic	Switzerland
Greece	Italy	Norway
Slovakia	Malta	Ireland
Croatia	UK	Luxembourg
Latvia	France	
Romania	Germany	
Portugal	Finland	
Hungary	Iceland	
Poland		

Conducting research using the general regression model revealed no significant data for both groups. However, the next stage of the research was clustering by years. As a result of the calculation, an interesting result was revealed: developing countries have a positive relationship between the index and the education of adults, i.e., coefficient = 0.0078. The coefficient in developing countries is higher than in developed countries. This is due to the fact that when the education system is already developed, the demand for it is not high, because at this stage the economy of the country is functioning efficiently. At the same time, in developing countries, the education sector is also developing, which means that it has a closer influence on economic indicators, and within the framework of our study, on indicators of the country's competitiveness (Table 2).

Table 2. The general results of all data sets between the share of the population (18–64 y.o.) involved in lifelong learning and competitiveness index.

Name of Parameter	General Regression	Clustering by the Years. Developed Countries	Clustering by the Years. Developing Countries
AE_Coef	0.0018	0.0043	0.0078
R^2	0.92	0.71	0.91
Number of studies	359	139	220
$P > |t|$	0.28	0.068	0.008
T	1.08	3.08	4.82

Given that the index for the study was taken on a scale of 1–7, the coefficient is quite high and influential on the overall picture of the relationship between adult education and the global competitiveness index. The non-parametric Kruskal–Wallis test and The Wilcoxon–Mann–Whitney test were chosen to verify the results. Both tests rejected the hypotheses that: developed and developing countries are the same, and that the population in both groups of countries is homogeneous, that is, the differences between the samples are statistically significant.

Considering that the study was actually divided into two groups, for more visible results, our next step was the analysis of two groups of countries using a graphical method (Figure 4). We were interested in the limits of the Global Competitiveness Index and the limits of the share of adult education for the two groups of countries, because we proved that the groups are different, and the data for the two groups also do not overlap.

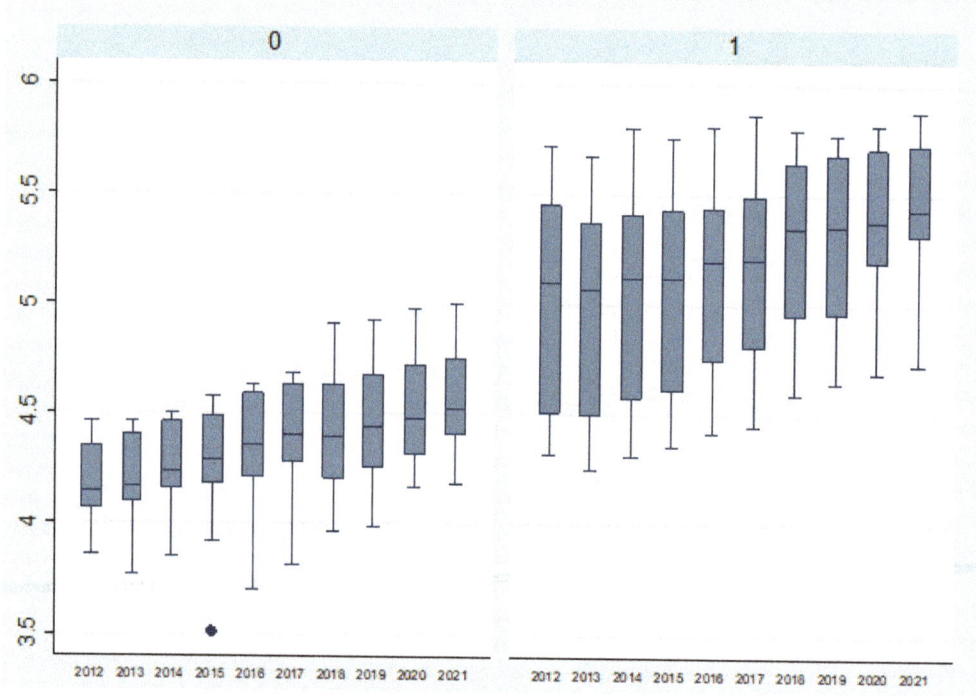

Figure 4. Dynamics of the Global Competitiveness Index in two groups of countries, developing (0) and developed (1). Source: Built by the authors.

Therefore, on this graph of the dynamics of the Global Competitiveness Index, we can see the situation for two groups of countries "0" and "1", where "0" is developing, and "1" is developed countries. The difference between the indicators immediately draws attention, where in the developed group the maximum is 6.4, and in the developing group, the maximum is 5 on a scale from 1 to 7. Observing the fluctuations over the years, we can see relatively not strong fluctuations in the "1" group and a constantly growing trajectory in group "0". In 2016, the "0" group experienced a downward "jump" for the minimum value of the index, but the same fluctuation is not observed for the value of adult education. Therefore, we can claim that adult education was not the factor behind such a minimal value of the index.

Graphically, we can see that the two groups of countries differ significantly in the indicators of participation in adult education (Figure 5). If in group "0", which is responsible for developing countries, the maximum indicator is 20, and the minimum is 3, then in the group of developed countries the maximum indicator is almost 40, which is twice as much as in the group of developing countries. Additionally, the graph shows that 90% of the sample is within the color box. The horizontal bar in the box itself represents the sample mean for each individual year.

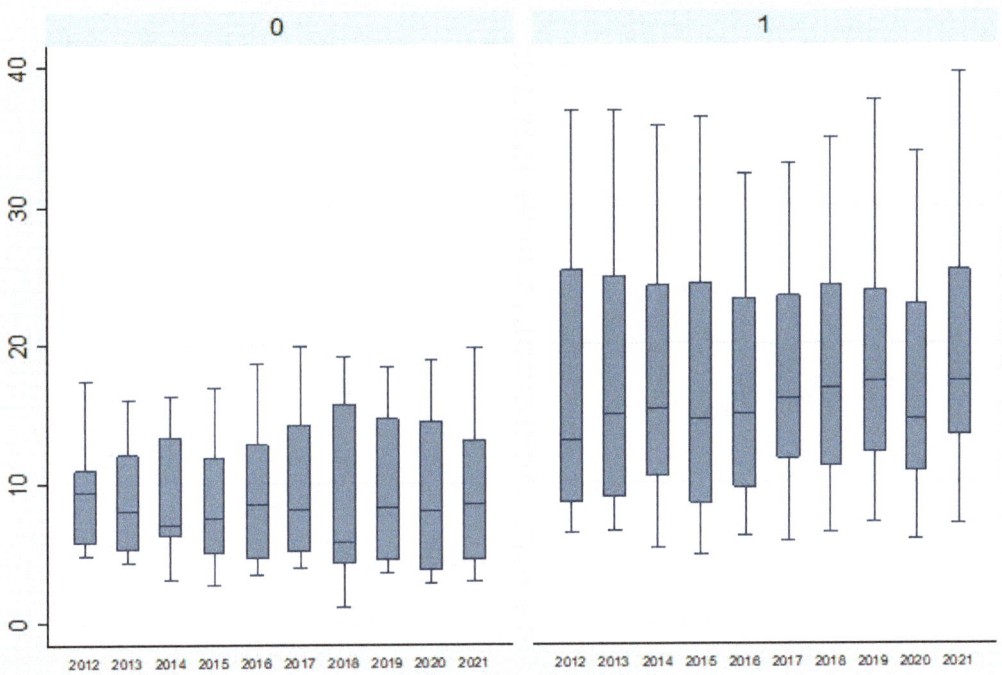

Figure 5. Dynamics of the share of the population (18–64 y.o.) involved in lifelong learning in two groups of countries, developing (0) and developed (1), %. Source: Built by the authors.

Analyzing by year, we see a different, interesting situation of fluctuations in 2016–2017 for two groups of countries. In the "0" group, 2017 became the peak year, and after that, the share of adults' participation decreased. For the "1" group, 2017 became the minimum year after 2016. That is, it was in 2016 that such events occurred that led to an increase in the education of adults in the "0" group and a decline in the "1" group. We see this as a basis for further research since the factors of such fluctuations can be not only economic, but also political, social, and financial.

6. Discussion

Another point of research is the innovation potential of the country and its connection with lifelong education. Choosing the Global Competitiveness Index for analysis and researching it, we found among the 12 indicators a sub-index of education and a sub-index of innovation. This, in turn, gives reason to assert that for the study of the global competitiveness index, and therefore of the country, indicators of both education and innovation are taken, and therefore they are related to each other. Developed countries have high indicators of education, as well as innovation. (Figure 6) The bibliometric analysis also showed a close connection between education, innovation, and competitiveness.

We see that developed countries have the highest indicators of innovation, namely those where a negative relationship between adult education and the competitiveness index was found.

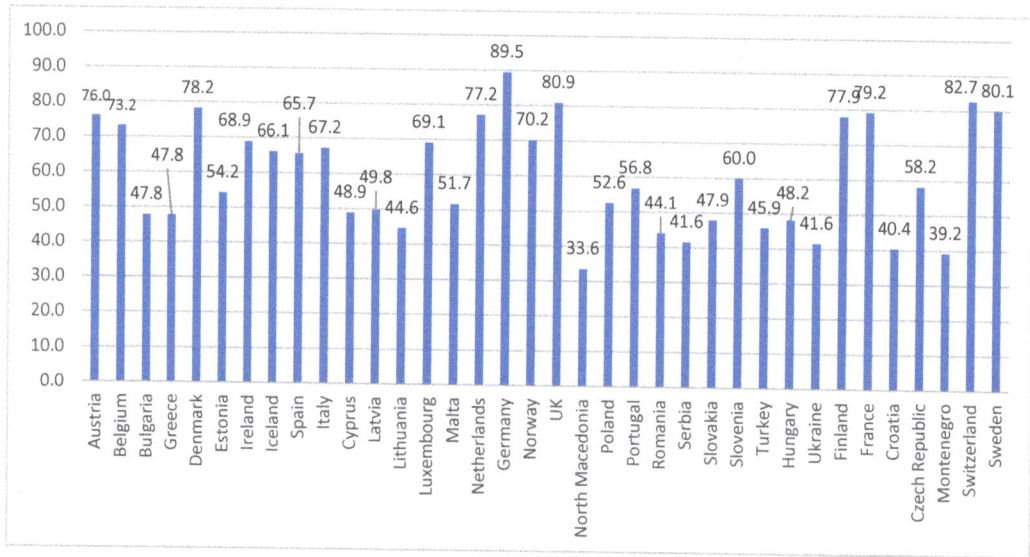

Figure 6. Indicator of the level of innovation in European countries for 2022. Source: Built by the authors.

It is too early to say what exactly influenced such a result, but we can say that innovation is one of the factors that directly shows: the more developed the country, the higher its innovation indicators. The graph shows countries such as Austria, Denmark, Germany, and Switzerland have the highest marks. Moreover, this trend was not only in 2021, as shown in the graph, but also throughout the 10 years studied.

The relationship between lifelong learning and innovative technology is an important factor in the development of countries in the modern era. The use of the latest technologies and their improvement is a factor in the development of countries in accordance with modern global standards of digitalization, as well as increasing their competitiveness in the international space [30]. Analysis of the impact of lifelong learning on the Global Competitiveness Index showed that increasing the number of adults engaged in education can contribute to increasing the competitiveness of the economy and, thus, achieving sustainable development.

In this sense, the corrective activity of the competent authorities should be aimed at developing the skills of an adult by organizing new internship programs, forming university business incubators, and ensuring an increase in financial incentives for the entry of as many companies and universities into the dual education system as possible, stimulating stronger ties between science and the economy by introducing tax and other benefits, motivating educated people to return to their homeland, etc. [19,31,32]. It is very important that the competent authorities in the analyzed states take into account the specifics of their own economy and the specifics of their own education systems when developing the above recommendations [33].

7. Conclusions

Lifelong education and learning is one of the most important tasks facing the countries under the Sustainable Development Goals 2030, since possession of innovative knowledge and qualification, the ability to study throughout life is one of the modern variables in the world [34].

Our research confirms the key role of lifelong education and shows that the global index of the country's competitiveness depends positively on the level of lifelong education.

A total of 65% of human capital has been accumulated in the world, while the accumulated material resources account for only 16% of social wealth. Human capital is 70–80% of national wealth in developed countries and about 30% in developing countries [35].

Therefore, lifelong learning is an important factor in increasing competitiveness, as well as the innovative development and potential of the country. Thus, the development and investment in lifelong education should be perceived rather than expenses, but as an investment in the future. In addition, it can be seen that the research will be useful for the process of lifelong education advocacy in the international arena.

Author Contributions: Conceptualization, A.K., D.K., K.O., Y.P., I.O. and V.O.; methodology, A.K., D.K., K.O., Y.P., I.O. and V.O.; formal analysis, A.K., D.K., K.O., Y.P., I.O. and V.O.; investigation, A.K., D.K., K.O., Y.P., I.O. and V.O.; writing—original draft preparation, A.K., D.K., K.O., Y.P., I.O. and V.O.; writing—review and editing, A.K., D.K., K.O., Y.P., I.O. and V.O.; visualization, A.K., D.K., K.O., Y.P., I.O. and V.O. All authors have read and agreed to the published version of the manuscript.

Funding: This research was funded by a grant from the Ministry of Education and Science of Ukraine "Modelling educational transformations in wartime to preserve the intellectual capital and innovative potential of Ukraine" (reg. n. 0123U100114). This research was funded under the research subsidy of the Faculty of Organization and Management of the Silesian University of Technology in Poland for the year 2023 (13/990/BK_23/0178).

Institutional Review Board Statement: Not applicable.

Informed Consent Statement: Not applicable.

Data Availability Statement: Not applicable.

Conflicts of Interest: The authors declare no conflict of interest.

References

1. Akin, M.; Eyduran, S.P.; Krauter, V. Food Packaging Related Research Trends in the Academic Discipline of Food Science and Technology: A Bibliometric Analysis. *Clean. Circ. Bioeconomy* **2023**, *5*, 100046. [CrossRef]
2. Akın, M.; Eyduran, S.P.; Rakszegi, M.; Yıldırım, K.; Rocha, J.M. Statistical modeling applications to mitigate the effects of climate change on quality traits of cereals: A bibliometric approach. In *Developing Sustainable and Health Promoting Cereals and Pseudocereals*; Academic Press: Cambridge, MA, USA, 2023; pp. 381–396.
3. Tanjung, E.F. Impact of Public Wellness, Competitiveness, and Government Effectiveness on Quality of Education in Asian Countries. *Cypriot J. Educ. Sci.* **2020**, *15*, 1720–1731. [CrossRef]
4. Akpoviroro, K.S.; Adeleke, O.A.O. Moderating Influence Of E-Learning On Employee Training And Development (A Study Of Kwara State University Nigeria). *SocioEconomic Chall.* **2022**, *6*, 83–93. [CrossRef]
5. Chentukov, Y.; Omelchenko, V.; Zakharova, O.; Nikolenko, T. Assessing the impact of higher education competitiveness on the level of socio-economic development of a country. *Probl. Perspect. Manag.* **2021**, *19*, 370–383. [CrossRef]
6. Fojtíková, L.; Staníčková, M.; Melecký, L. Modeling of human capital and impact on eu regional competitiveness. In *Modeling human Behavior: Individuals and Organizations*; Nova Science Publishers: Hauppauge, NY, USA, 2016; pp. 133–164.
7. Mendez, S.; Karaulova, A.D. Internationalization of higher education as a factor of competitiveness. In *Innovative Development of Regions: The Potential of Science and Modern Education*; eLibrary.Ru: Moscow, Russia, 2019; pp. 136–138.
8. Shmygol, N.; Galtsova, O.; Solovyov, O.; Koval, V.; Arsawan, I.W.E. Analysis of country's competitiveness factors based on inter-state rating comparisons. *E3S Web Conf.* **2020**, *153*, 03001. [CrossRef]
9. Kuzior, A.; Pidorycheva, I.; Liashenko, V.; Shevtsova, H.; Shvets, N. Assessment of National Innovation Ecosystems of the EU Countries and Ukraine in the Interests of Their Sustainable Development. *Sustainability* **2022**, *14*, 8487. [CrossRef]
10. Kuzior, A.; Arefieva, O.; Kovalchuk, A.; Brozek, P.; Tytykalo, V. Strategic Guidelines for the Intellectualization of Human Capital in the Context of Innovative Transformation. *Sustainability* **2022**, *14*, 11937. [CrossRef]
11. Vidic, F. Knowledge asset as competitive resource. *SocioEconomic Chall.* **2022**, *6*, 8–20. [CrossRef]
12. Kharazishvili, Y.; Kwilinski, A.; Dzwigol, H.; Liashenko, V.; Lukaszczyk, Z. Identification and Comparative Analysis of Ukrainian and Polish Scientific-Educational and Innovative Spaces of European Integration. In Proceedings of the 37th International Business Information Management Association (IBIMA), Cordoba, Spain, 30–31 May 2021; pp. 3707–3721.
13. Ober, J.; Kochmańska, A. Remote Learning in Higher Education: Evidence from Poland. *Int. J. Environ. Res. Public Health* **2022**, *19*, 14479. [CrossRef]
14. Kuzior, A.; Kettler, K.; Rąb, Ł. Digitalization of Work and Human Resources Processes as a Way to Create a Sustainable and Ethical Organization. *Energies* **2022**, *15*, 172. [CrossRef]
15. Novikov, V. Intercept of Financial, Economic and Educational Transformations: Bibliometric Analysis. *Financ. Mark. Inst. Risks* **2021**, *5*, 120–129. [CrossRef]

16. Koibichuk, V.; Samoilikova, A.; Herasymenko, V. Education and Business in Conditions of Coopetition: Bibliometrics. *Bus. Ethics Leadersh.* **2022**, *6*, 49–60. [CrossRef]
17. Antonyuk, N.; Plikus, I.; Jammal, M. Human Capital Quality Assurance under the Conditions of Digital Business Transformation and COVID-19 Impact. *Health Econ. Manag. Rev.* **2021**, *2*, 39–47. [CrossRef]
18. Onopriienko, K.; Onopriienko, V.; Petrushenko, Y.; Onopriienko, I. Environmental education for youth and adults: A bibliometric analysis of research. *E3S Web Conf.* **2021**, *234*, 00002. [CrossRef]
19. Okunevičiūtė Neverauskienė, L.; Danilevičienė, I.; Tvaronavičienė, M. Assessment of the factors influencing competitiveness fostering the country's sustainability. *Econ. Res.-Ekon. Istraživanja* **2020**, *33*, 1909–1924. [CrossRef]
20. Artyukhov, A.; Volk, I.; Vasylieva, T.; Lyeonov, S. The role of the university in achieving SDGs 4 and 7: A ukrainian case. *E3S Web Conf.* **2021**, *250*, 04006. [CrossRef]
21. Petrushenko, Y.; Onopriienko, K.; Onopriienko, I.; Onopriienko, V. Digital learning for adults in the context of education market development. In Proceedings of the 2021 11th International Conference on Advanced Computer Information Technologies (ACIT), Deggendorf, Germany,, 15–17 September 2021; IEEE:: Piscataway, NJ, USA; pp. 465–468.
22. Beyi, W.A. Visibility profession: Managing the position, communication or the public? *SocioEconomic Chall.* **2022**, *6*, 116–128. [CrossRef]
23. Isik, A. The Most Common Behavioural Biases among Young Adults in Bristol, UK and Istanbul. *Financ. Mark. Inst. Risks* **2022**, *6*, 27–39. [CrossRef]
24. Schwab, K. *The Global Competitiveness Report*; World Economic Forum: Cologny, Switzerland, 2021.
25. Kanaan-Jebna, J.M.A.; Alabdullah, T.T.Y.; Ahmed, E.R.; Ayyasamy, R.K. Firm Performance and the Impact of Entrepreneurial Education and Entrepreneurial Competencies. *Bus. Ethics Leadersh.* **2022**, *6*, 68–77. [CrossRef]
26. Khushk, A.; Ihsan Dacholfany, M.; Abdurohim, D.; Aman, N. Social Learning Theory in Clinical Setting: Connectivism, Constructivism, and Role Modeling Approach. *Health Econ. Manag. Rev.* **2022**, *3*, 40–50. [CrossRef]
27. Kyrychenko, K.; Laznenko, D.; Reshetniak, Y. Green University as an Element of Forming a Sustainable Public Health System. *Health Econ. Manag. Rev.* **2021**, *2*, 21–26. [CrossRef]
28. Moskovicz, A. Post-pandemic Scenario for University Startup Accelerators. *Financ. Mark. Inst. Risks* **2021**, *5*, 52–57. [CrossRef]
29. Nohut, F.; Balaban, O. Employee's innovative personality and self-efficacy. *Mark. Manag. Innov.* **2022**, *1*, 58–66. [CrossRef]
30. Artyukhov, A.; Dluhopolskyi, O.; Vasylieva, T.; Lyeonov, S.; Dluhopolska, T.; Tsikh, H. Local (university) rankings and quality of education: Identification of publication activity indicators. In Proceedings of the 2021 11th International Conference on Advanced Computer Information Technologies, Deggendorf, Germany, 15–17 September 2021; ACIT 2021—Proceedings. pp. 246–249. [CrossRef]
31. Nwaibe, C.I.; Ogbuefi, J.U.; Egbenta, I.R. Organizational Learning and Risk Management Maturity: Systematic and Meta-Analyses Approach. *Bus. Ethics Leadersh.* **2022**, *6*, 68–76. [CrossRef]
32. Pudryk, D.; Kwilinski, A.; Lyulyov, O.; Pimonenko, T. Towards Achieving Sustainable Development: Interactions between Migration and Education. *Forum Sci. Oeconomia* **2023**, *11*, 113–131. [CrossRef]
33. Raisiene, A.G.; Rapuano, V.; Raisys, S.J.; Lucinskaite-Sadovskiene, R. Teleworking Experience of Education Professionals vs. Management Staff: Challenges Following Job Innovation. *Mark. Manag. Innov.* **2022**, *2*, 171–183. [CrossRef]
34. Samoilikova, A.; Zhylinska, O.; Pal, Z.; Kuttor, D. «Business-Education-Science» Coopetition and Innovation Transfer for Sustainable Development. *Mark. Manag. Innov.* **2022**, *2*, 220–230. [CrossRef]
35. Vorontsova, A.; Vasylieva, T.; Lyeonov, S.; Artyukhov, A.; Mayboroda, T. Education expenditures as a factor in bridging the gap at the level of digitalization. In Proceedings of the 2021 11th International Conference on Advanced Computer Information Technologies, Deggendorf, Germany, 15–17 September 2021; ACIT 2021—Proceedings. pp. 242–245. [CrossRef]

Disclaimer/Publisher's Note: The statements, opinions and data contained in all publications are solely those of the individual author(s) and contributor(s) and not of MDPI and/or the editor(s). MDPI and/or the editor(s) disclaim responsibility for any injury to people or property resulting from any ideas, methods, instructions or products referred to in the content.

Article

Research on the Evolution of the Economic Spatial Pattern of Urban Agglomeration and Its Influencing Factors, Evidence from the Chengdu-Chongqing Urban Agglomeration of China

Rui Ding [1,2,†], Jun Fu [1,2,†], Yiling Zhang [1,2,*], Ting Zhang [1,2], Jian Yin [3], Yiming Du [1,2], Tao Zhou [1,2] and Linyu Du [1,2]

1. College of Big Data Application and Economics (Guiyang College of Big Data Finance), Guizhou University of Finance and Economics, Guiyang 550025, China
2. Key Laboratory of Green Fintech, Guizhou University of Finance and Economics, Guiyang 550025, China
3. School of Water Conservancy and Civil Engineering, Northeast Agricultural University, Xiangfang District, Harbin 150050, China
* Correspondence: evalinzyl@mail.gufe.edu.cn
† Co-first author.

Citation: Ding, R.; Fu, J.; Zhang, Y.; Zhang, T.; Yin, J.; Du, Y.; Zhou, T.; Du, L. Research on the Evolution of the Economic Spatial Pattern of Urban Agglomeration and Its Influencing Factors, Evidence from the Chengdu-Chongqing Urban Agglomeration of China. *Sustainability* 2022, 14, 10969. https://doi.org/10.3390/su141710969

Academic Editors: Rashid Mehmood, Tan Yigitcanlar and Juan M. Corchado

Received: 30 June 2022
Accepted: 25 August 2022
Published: 2 September 2022

Copyright: © 2022 by the authors. Licensee MDPI, Basel, Switzerland. This article is an open access article distributed under the terms and conditions of the Creative Commons Attribution (CC BY) license (https://creativecommons.org/licenses/by/4.0/).

Abstract: To investigate the spatial evolution process of economic development in the urban agglomeration and its influencing factors, the network construction method, modified gravity model, geographic detector and Geographically Weighted Regression (GWR) model are used to analyze the intensity of urban association; then, the evolution of economic, spatial pattern and its influencing factors are further discussed, and the Chengdu-Chongqing urban agglomeration of China from 2005 to 2020 is studied as an example. The results show that: (1) the economically developed zones of the Chengdu-Chongqing urban agglomeration mainly concentrated in the core cities of Chengdu and the central city of Chongqing, and the region shows an uneven spatial pattern of economic development distribution. (2) The share of economic linkages with the central city of Chengdu and Chongqing as the twin cities is significant, the intensity of Chengdu and its neighboring cities is gradually decreasing, while the central city of Chongqing has increased, but it still has an insufficient influence on the peripheral areas. (3) The intensities and directions of the factors influencing economic development in the Chengdu-Chongqing urban agglomeration are different. The total output value of the secondary industry, total social fixed asset investment, the number of beds in health institutions, and road freight turnover are significant factors with consistently strong explanatory ability for economic development. The promotion effect of these four significant factors on economic development is mainly concentrated in the eastern and western regions of Chengdu-Chongqing urban agglomeration, while the inhibiting effect is mainly on the cities in the south and north. Based on this study, relevant recommendations are made to promote the coordinated development of the Chengdu-Chongqing urban agglomeration.

Keywords: economic spatial pattern; gravity model; geographic detector; geographically weighted regression; Chengdu-Chongqing urban agglomeration

1. Introduction

As an advanced phenomenon of regional economic and spatial forms in the process of industrialization, urban agglomeration is a landmark product of a certain stage of urban development, and urban agglomeration planning has become an important strategic development deployment in China. In 2016, China issued the Chengdu-Chongqing Urban Agglomeration Development Plan, which states that the Chengdu-Chongqing urban agglomeration is an important platform for the development of the western region, strategic support for the Yangtze River Economic Belt, and an important demonstration area for China to promote a new type of urbanization. Due to the huge differences in education and health levels, trade and commerce service capacity, transport infrastructure construction and investment environment among the cities, there are enormous dissimilarities in the economic development levels of the cities in the urban agglomeration. Therefore, it is of great significance to scientifically grasp the economic development level of each city in the Chengdu-Chongqing urban agglomeration and analyze its influencing factors to promote the coordinated development of the urban agglomeration and optimize its spatial layout.

As for the spatial pattern of regional economies, the existing research is mainly carried out in the following two directions. The first direction is the structuralist narration based on the calculation of spatial differences and the description of the current situation of spatial layout. Some literature uses indicators such as urban resident population, per capita GDP, total retail sales of social consumer goods, the added value of the primary industry, added value of secondary industry and added value of the tertiary industry. ESDA [1–3], Gini coefficient [4–7], coefficient of variation [8], entropy method [9], Theil index [8], gravity model [10,11], social network analysis [12] and other methods are used to carry out the research. For example, Dong et al. [2] used the ESDA method to analyze the spatial pattern of county economies in the Chang-Zhu-Tan urban agglomeration of China, answering whether the county economies in the Chang-Zhu-Tan urban agglomeration developed according to the integration policy. Chen et al. [8] analyzed the spatial and temporal characteristics of the urban–rural income gap and its driving forces in the Yangtze River Economic Belt from 2000–2017 using the coefficient of variation and the Theil index and found that the spatial divergence pattern of the urban–rural income gap is influenced by both natural and socio-economic factors; of these, socio-economic factors predominate. The second direction is the relational narrative based on cities' connection and network construction. At present, there are three different perspectives: economic connection, transportation network, and information flow. For example, Ye et al. [13] used the urban flow intensity to modify the traditional gravity model to construct the economic connection matrix to analyze the evolution characteristics of the economic connection network structure of Guanzhong Plain urban agglomeration and its impact on economic growth. Guo et al. [14] used the complex network analysis method to further analyze the characteristics of urban connection networks in Northeast China from the changes of the "high-speed railway+" network in different periods, through the comparison between "high-speed railway+" networks and high-speed railway networks. Qiao et al. [15] analyzed the characteristics and influencing factors of an urban spatial connection and network structure of urban agglomeration in the Yangtze River Delta from the perspective of information flow. At the scale of urban agglomeration, the research on inter-city network structure based on economic spatial pattern and economic connection mainly focuses on Beijing-Tianjin-Hebei [16–18] and the Yangtze River Delta regions [16,19–21]. Some scholars have discussed the factors affecting economic development from different perspectives, such as Zhao et al. [22] from the perspective of the energy-economy, focused on the estimation of energy economic efficiency of the Yangtze River Urban Agglomeration (YRUA) and decomposed the energy-economic efficiency into pure technical efficiency and scale efficiency to better explore the restrictive factors for the improvement of energy-economic efficiency. Wei et al. [23] studied the evolution of marine industrial structures and analyzed their impact on the maritime economy's Green Total Factor Productivity (GTFP). Chen et al. [24] explored the drivers of the tourism economic network structure formation on the Qinghai-Tibet Plateau from 2015–2019, using the gravity model and social network analysis, and they have found that A-class attractions and star-rated hotels significantly contributed to spatial associations. From the spatial dimension, they used several indicators to comprehensively evaluate the development of regional tourism employment through horizontal and vertical comparison; their results show that the regional tourism economic growth is driven by investment.

The above-mentioned studies on the spatial pattern of the regional economy have all achieved fruitful results, but there is still some room for expansion. Firstly, there are more studies on the Beijing-Tianjin-Hebei and Yangtze River Delta regions, but there is a

14. Zhang, Y. Measuring and Applying Digital Literacy: Implications for Access for the Elderly in Rural China. *Educ. Inf. Technol.* **2022**, 1–20. [CrossRef]
15. Wang, C.-H.; Wu, C.-L. Bridging the Digital Divide: The Smart TV as a Platform for Digital Literacy among the Elderly. *Behav. Inf. Technol.* **2022**, *41*, 2546–2559. [CrossRef]
16. Zhang, X.; Nedospasova, O. Impact of Digital Literacy on the Labour Income of the <<Young>> Elderly: Evidence from China. *J. Wellbeing Technol.* **2022**, *2*, 105–122.
17. Jin, Y.; Jing, M.; Ma, X. Effects of Digital Device Ownership on Cognitive Decline in a Middle-Aged and Elderly Population: Longitudinal Observational Study. *J. Med. Internet Res.* **2019**, *21*, e14210. [CrossRef]
18. Zeng, F.; Chen, T.-L. A Study of the Acceptability of Smart Homes to the Future Elderly in China. *Univers. Access Inf. Soc.* **2022**, 1–19. [CrossRef]
19. Song, Y.; Yang, Y.; Cheng, P. The Investigation of Adoption of Voice-User Interface (VUI) in Smart Home Systems among Chinese Older Adults. *Sensors* **2022**, *22*, 1614. [CrossRef]
20. Wang, R.; Liu, Y.; Lu, Y.; Zhang, J.; Liu, P.; Yao, Y.; Grekousis, G. Perceptions of Built Environment and Health Outcomes for Older Chinese in Beijing: A Big Data Approach with Street View Images and Deep Learning Technoique. *Comput. Environ. Urban Syst.* **2019**, *78*, 101386. [CrossRef]
21. Fang, E.F.; Xie, C.; Schenkel, J.A.; Wu, C.; Long, Q.; Cui, H.; Aman, Y.; Frank, J.; Liao, J.; Zou, H.; et al. A Research Agenda for Ageing in China in the 21st Century (2nd Edition): Focusing on Basic and Translational Research, Long-Term Care, Policy and Soical Networks. *Ageing Res. Rev.* **2020**, *64*, 101174. [CrossRef]
22. Dou, J.; Qin, J.; Wang, Q.; Zhao, Q. Identification of Usability Problems and Requirements of Elderly Chinese Users for Smart TV Interactions. *Behav. Inf. Technol.* **2018**, *38*, 664–677. [CrossRef]
23. Zhang, H.; Wang, Y.; Wu, D.; Chen, J. Evolutionary Path of Factors Influencing Life Satisfaction among Chinese Elderly: A Perspective of Data Visualisation. *Data* **2018**, *3*, 35. [CrossRef]
24. Liu, S.X.; Shen, Q.; Hancock, J. Can a Social Robot Be Too Warm or Too Competent? Older Chinese Adults' Perceptions of Social Robots and Vulnerabilities. *Comput. Hum. Behav.* **2021**, *125*, 106942. [CrossRef]
25. Ke, C.; Lou, V.W.-Q.; Tan, K.C.-K.; Wai, M.Y.; Chan, L.L. Changes in Technology Acceptance among Older People with Dementia: The Role of Social Robot Engagement. *Int. J. Med. Inform.* **2020**, *141*, 104241. [CrossRef]
26. Chen, S.-C.; Jones, C.; Moyle, W. Health Professional and Workers Attitudes towards the Use of Social Robots for Older Adults in Long-Term Care. *Int. J. Soc. Robot.* **2020**, *12*, 1135–1147. [CrossRef]
27. Jianying, K.; Jiale, W. The Realistic Dilemma of Mutual Aid for the Aged in Rural Areas and Solutions. In Proceedings of the 2021 4th International Conference on Humanities Education and Social Sciences, Xishuangbanna, China, 29–31 October 2021. [CrossRef]
28. Sun, F. Caregiving Stress and Coping: A Thematic Analysis of Chinese Family Caregivers of Persons with Dementia. *Dementia* **2013**, *13*, 803–818. [CrossRef]
29. Hong, Y.A.; Zhou, Z.; Fang, Y.; Shi, L. The Digital Divide and Health Disparities in China: Evidence from a National Survey and Policy Implications. *J. Med. Internet Res.* **2017**, *19*, e317. [CrossRef]
30. Liu, G.; Li, S.; Kong, F. Association between Social Support, Smartphone Usage and Loneliness among the Migrant Elderly Following Children in Jinan, China: A Cross-Sectional Study. *BMJ Open* **2022**, *12*, e060510. [CrossRef]
31. Sun, X.; Yan, W.; Zhou, H.; Wang, Z.; Zhang, X.; Huang, S.; Li, L. Interent Use and Need for Digital Health Technology among the Elderly: A Cross-Sectional Survey in China. *BMC Public Health* **2020**, *20*, 1386. [CrossRef]
32. Zhang, X. The Application of Spatial Information Technology in the Rural Elderly Care Model under the Strategy of "Building a Country with a Strong Transportation Network" in China. *Transp. Res. Procedia* **2022**, *61*, 481–486. [CrossRef]
33. Shou, H.; Green, G. The Political Economy of Organisational Violence in Chinese Industry. *J. Curr. Chin. Aff.* **2016**, *45*, 201–230. [CrossRef]
34. Feng, Z.; Glinskaya, E.; Chen, H.; Gong, S.; Qiu, Y.; Xu, J.; Yip, W. Long-Term Care System for Older Adults in China: Policy Landscape, Challenges, and Future Prospects. *Lancet* **2020**, *396*, 1362–1372. [CrossRef] [PubMed]
35. Wang, Y.; Zhang, L. Status of Public-Private Partnership Recognition and Willingness to Pay for Private Health Care in China. *Int. J. Health Plan. Manag.* **2019**, *34*, 1188–1199. [CrossRef] [PubMed]

Disclaimer/Publisher's Note: The statements, opinions and data contained in all publications are solely those of the individual author(s) and contributor(s) and not of MDPI and/or the editor(s). MDPI and/or the editor(s) disclaim responsibility for any injury to people or property resulting from any ideas, methods, instructions or products referred to in the content.

still be experiencing the seed stage, the start-up stage or the development stage. The success of popularising the delivery of smart homes in upper-tier cities can accelerate the rate of innovative elderly caregiving development in lower-tier regions as the latter are able to witness the short- and long-term benefits technological advancement can contribute to the construction of sustainable and organised societies. As a result, insofar as local governments from lower-tier regions are motivated to build age-friendly, pro-elderly services, and when the presence of opportunities for introducing relevant public-private initiatives expands to less-developed locations, the development of smart homes will no longer restrictively concentrate in more urbanised, advanced areas.

For China to realise its policy focus of building a people-oriented urbanisation model, the mentioned policy gaps must be addressed insofar as possible. Challenges encompass opportunities, and vice versa. For example, the author mentioned that Chinese senior populations, especially those who are not city-based, might be digitally illiterate to some extent. However, many of them demonstrate curiosity in, and potential to, learn(ing) digital knowledge and skills. So long as China introduces a wider share of its senior citizens to a variety of smart home devices and makes such innovative products financially accessible, a growing number of its elderly populations will expectedly be showing an increased interest in building their digital repertoire. By then, China can better fulfil its policy focus on building a more sustainable urban and regional development. Not only will cities become more technologically advanced and inclusive but also villages and towns will become more urbanised and habitable too.

Funding: This research received no external funding.

Institutional Review Board Statement: Not applicable.

Informed Consent Statement: Not applicable.

Data Availability Statement: Not applicable.

Conflicts of Interest: The authors declare no conflict of interest.

References

1. Leung, J. Family Support for the Elderly in China. *J. Aging Soc. Policy* **1997**, *9*, 87–101. [CrossRef] [PubMed]
2. Wang, X.-Q.; Chen, P.-J. Population Aging Challenges Health Care in China. *Lancet* **2014**, *383*, 870. [CrossRef] [PubMed]
3. Wong, Y.C.; Leung, J. Long-Term Care in China: Issues and Prospects. *J. Gerontol. Soc. Work.* **2012**, *55*, 570–586. [CrossRef] [PubMed]
4. Zeng, Y.; Hu, X.; Li, Y.; Zhen, X.; Gu, Y.; Sun, X.; Dong, H. The Quality of Caregivers for the Elderly in Long-Term Care Institutions in Zhejiang Province, China. *Int. J. Environ. Res. Public Health* **2019**, *16*, 2164. [CrossRef] [PubMed]
5. Chen, Z.; Yu, J.; Song, Y.; Chui, D. Aging Beijing: Challenges and Strategies of Healthcare for the Elderly. *Ageing Res. Rev.* **2010**, *95*, 52–55. [CrossRef] [PubMed]
6. Qiu, Z.; Liu, Y.; Wang, Z.; Peng, S.; Wan, D.; Jiang, Y. Analysis on Long-Term Care and Influencing Factors of Empty-Nest Differently Abled Elderly People in China. *Open J. Prev. Med.* **2020**, *10*, 299–311. [CrossRef]
7. Zhang, Q.; Li, M.; Wu, Y. Smart Home for Elderly Care: Development and Challenges in China. *BMC Geriatr.* **2020**, *20*, 318. [CrossRef]
8. Zhang, L.; Shen, S.; Guo, Y.; Fang, Y. Forecasting Future Demand of Nursing Staff for the Oldest-Old in China by 2025 Based on Markov Model. *Int. J. Health Policy Manag.* **2022**, *11*, 1533–1541. [CrossRef]
9. Meng, Q.; Hong, Z.; Li, Z.; Hu, X.; Shi, W.; Wang, J.; Luo, K. Opportunities and Challenges for Chinese Elderly Care Industry in Smart Environment Based on Occupants' Needs and Preferences. *Front. Psychol.* **2020**, *11*, 1029. [CrossRef]
10. Li, M.; Woolrych, R. Experiences of Older People and Social Inclusion in Relation to Smart "Age-Friendly" Cities: A Case Study of Chongqing, China. *Front. Public Health* **2021**, *9*, 779913. [CrossRef]
11. Hu, Y.; Gong, R.; Peng, J.; Liu, X.; Wang, X.; Liu, Z.; Luo, J.; Lin, H. Rural Smart Elderly Care Model: China's Development and Challenge. In Proceedings of the IEEE 5th International Conference on Universal Village, Boston, MA, USA, 24–27 October 2020. [CrossRef]
12. Chen, M.; Gong, Y.; Lu, D.; Ye, C. Build A People-Oriented Urbanisation: China's New Type Urbanisation Dream and Anhui Model. *Land Use Policy* **2019**, *80*, 1–9. [CrossRef]
13. Yu, B.; Sun, F.; Chen, C.; Fu, G.; Hu, L. Power Demand Response in the Context of Smart Home Application. *Energy* **2022**, *240*, 122774. [CrossRef]

care services providers to participate in the market activities, regardless of whether they focus on delivering higher- or lower-end innovative services.

Public–private partnerships have been formed where local governments and commercial enterprises cooperate to deliver smart elderly care services. Here, governments avoid investing in building and running elderly care institutions, but play a role as a regulator [11,35]. Local governments encourage enterprises to develop and deliver smart elderly care services and assume public responsibilities but do not interfere in the latter's management and operation [11]. This demonstrates how local governments lacking financial resources can still regulate the operation of smart elderly care services within their administrative regions. However, even when private enterprises are given the right to enter the elderly care market to provide relevant services, local rural governments need to ensure their citizens have the financial resources to enjoy smart elderly care experiences. One of the possible solutions in relation to financing is to encourage the Central Government to distribute the financial resources for elderly care to rural and urban governments in a more equal manner, so as to prompt rural elderly populations to enjoy smart elderly care services in a similar fashion to their urban counterparts.

4. Conclusions

Despite being an upper-middle-income country, China has been facing entrenched sociospatial inequalities. Ample Chinese provinces, especially those in inner and northwest China, are underdeveloped and lack financing. It is necessary for the Central Government to draw a fairer share of policy focus on suburban and rural regions. Here, financing must be in place in order for city-level governments to develop human resources because low salaries and employment status both bar caregivers and nurses from showing an interest in working in elderly care. When smart home elderly care providers design mobile applications to match caregivers with elders who seek caregiving services, it is essential for the providers themselves to ensure the former is paid at a satisfactory, rewarding rate. Such delivery of caregiving services does not and should not need to be full-time jobs. The caregiving provision should complement caregivers' farming, and caregivers in the market should be compensated financially by the beneficiaries of the services and, more importantly, by local governments which subsidise caregiving per se. The inferior status caregivers are attached to, given the conventional social perception that caregivers are uneducated, unskilled and disdained, should be addressed. Here, more public advertising to present the importance, value and positive images of caregivers, especially when China attempts to build a more age-friendly sustainable future, should be arranged and delivered. Public education at family-, community-, and regional-levels should be encouraged where senior family members, community organisations, and local governments, for example, can give guidance or design freely-accessible workshops for the purpose of enhancing individuals' understanding of and respect for whoever undertaking the roles as caregivers.

Financing needs to be efficiently arranged among the public-private initiatives too. The private sector of elderly care in China is established to some extent. Richer individuals are able to take care of themselves as they can financially invest in obtaining elderly care services as private goods—where private services are inclined to be of better quality and more comprehensive. However, lower-tier, and rural, governments that entail the provision of basic, universal elderly care services to less advantaged Chinese citizens need better financing to offer affordable or free elderly care services. Public financing can be supported by state and public-private initiatives. Many of these initiatives have already been piloted and outcomes can unveil whether vertical and horizontal governance is clearly structured and organised as well as if the quality of innovative technologies available in the elderly care market is satisfactory. Relevant actors in China should take the western or Japanese models as references when designing and performing public-private initiatives, as these pro-elderly models are developed maturely and successfully.

While upper-tier Chinese cities have been undergoing the popularisation stage of building smart homes, villages and towns located in less-developed regions might plausibly service popularisation, technology research, construction of the industry standard, and the development of smart care platforms were employed [7]. While the Central Government has formulated national policies, lower-tier governments need to be able to translate these state guidelines into city-level policies. Facing the problems of bureaucracy, city-level governments may receive multiple orders from upper-level governments, so there could be confusion when lower-tier, city-level governments make their policies [33]. A clearer, more organised governance structure should be arranged to ensure city-level governments understand concretely and concisely what elderly care policies they can exploit. As a status quo, the insufficient top-level design and unified standards force some city-level governments to facilitate smart elderly care by themselves within their own administrative regions, resulting in unsatisfactory compatibility of smart elderly care data and severe duplication of the development of service platforms [11]. China follows a complicated governance structure. It is necessary for upper-tier governments to apply horizontal communications to avoid the delivery of different versions of policy guidelines to the same city-level governments. Otherwise, policy confusion will be significantly caused.

Home-based elderly care services used to be public goods exclusively in China. However, in 2010, the *Construction Plan of Social Elderly Care Service System* (2011–2015) was implemented by the General Office of the State Council where home-based elderly care services become quasi-public goods—sharing the dual characteristics of public and private goods [7]. To date, public long-term care financing is minimal and significantly restricted to supporting welfare recipients and subsidising the delivering of residential care beds and operating costs. Within the public sector, weak quality assurance in the long-term care system is concerning. In response, China has been witnessing an increasing involvement of the private sector in supporting the long-term care system [34]. As elderly care services can now be purchased in the market as private goods, it benefits richer individuals, especially urban natives, who can and are willing to spend financial resources on enjoying better-designed elderly care services. It is necessary for lower-tier governments to offer basic elderly care-related insurance to less advantaged urban natives or rural citizens. Otherwise, the socioeconomic inequalities in elderly care would remain profound. Hu et al. back up the suggestion of further integrating differentiated rural and urban elderly care systems and promoting the pooling of basic elderly care within China [11]. By providing a universal insurance system, Chinese citizens, especially those from poorer or rural origins, can benefit from elderly care services. Otherwise, disadvantaged elders are unable to afford expensive healthcare and elderly costs, particularly those that require innovative technologies to operate, barring the sustainability of the ageing society. Another financial challenge faced by elders in the elderly care sector is the lack of pension entitlement to rural elderly populations [25]. It is essential for local rural governments to provide elderly care services at a subsidised rate or as public goods, in order to ensure those living without pensions can enjoy basic elderly care services at the very least. Specifically, local rural governments should purchase smart elderly care services and distribute them to those in need for free or at a reduced rate. Therefore, the disadvantaged elderly populations can also gain access to innovative technologies in favour of their everyday life. However, rural China is unable to deliver free elderly care services completely with the restrictive fiscal revenues [7]. Therefore, part of the elderly care services has to be pragmatically offered as private goods. Smart elderly care services providers aim at making profits through the supply of innovative services, where such technological advanced services are inclined to be expensive [7]. Hence, only richer urban natives may demonstrate an interest in purchasing smart elderly care services as private goods. If local governments want to massify the exploitation of smart home care services, they should subsidise their citizens earning less than a certain level of wages or incomes to purchase common, simplistic smart home care services; otherwise, the smart home care market would shrink. When richer individuals spend their own financial resources to purchase more technological advanced elderly care services, China can ensure that both higher-end and lower-end smart elderly care markets have a certain degree of demand. Such a circumstance motivates smart elderly to understand the maturity and potential of technological advancement in the industry. Hong et al. found that while 83 percent of middle-aged and elderly Chinese respondents used mobile phones, only 6.5 percent of them had access to the Internet [29]. There is still a significant proportion of elderly populations without Internet access, so such a circumstance hints that there is a large potential for smart home care service providers to engage in the market insofar as local governments can continue to expand the coverage and provision of Internet services. Local governments can consider issuing vouchers for mobile phone and Internet access subscriptions to the elderly populations [29,30]. If local governments are willing to hand out vouchers to elders, poorer Chinese citizens should benefit from the suggested policy the most due to their significant financial limitations. Disadvantaged Chinese elders, in particular, can therefore purchase digital devices that allow their access to digital elderly care and healthcare services.

Zhang et al. argued that elders are sensitive to the price of innovative, intelligent devices. They have high expectations of the convenience of using such intelligent services [2]. Elders may be reluctant to learn about new technologies, especially when they are complicated to use. It is thus needed for local governments, especially rural governments, to marketise the importance and benefits of using elderly care technologies, alongside building elders' digital literacy necessary for the use of such intelligent devices. An interesting study was carried out by Sun et al. (2020) in 13 cities in the Heilongjiang Province of China between May and July 2018. The findings indicated that 38.6 percent of respondents aged at least 60 used the Internet. However, they mostly used the Internet for online dating (74.2 percent), dieting (63.1 percent) and exercising (47.1 percent). Sun et al. called for more endeavours delivered by equipment manufacturers and family members, along with local governments, to encourage Chinese senior adults' use of the Internet for elderly caregiving purposes [31]. Zhang also made a constructive, supporting point by highlighting that more conservative elders cannot accept the use of elderly care smart home services in lieu of caregiving delivered by family members [32]. Therefore, inviting elders to experience the use of smart home care services and carrying out more piloting experiments would be deemed necessary to change the narratives of the use of intelligent devices in more conservative, rural regions. While digital illiteracy maybe recognised as a significant barrier to Chinese senior populations' experience of using smart home devices, Li and Woolrych (2021) found that many urban Chinese elderly respondents reportedly were keen on widening their interests in learning digital knowledge and developing intellectual curiously by exploring the Internet in order to build a deeper sense of connectedness and benefit more from the growth of urbanisation and digitalisation in the long-term [10].

Smart elderly care experience centres should be established in rural communities, where elderly cohorts and their relatives or friends should be invited to experience the use of smart, innovative products [11]. Such a suggested policy is conducive to ensuring more individuals would accept the use of non-traditional services or devices in the long-term, raising the demand for smart home care services that ultimately expands the supply of such services in the market. Until elders experience the convenience of smart home elderly care services, they would be yet to know the comprehensiveness, precision, and alternative advantages of intelligent healthcare and elderly care services *per se* [11]. Therefore, allowing elders to experience intelligent services in person would facilitate their acceptance of new technologies.

China, to date, has built smart elderly care services platforms. However, due to the inadequate demand for such innovative services, ample smart home care platforms, funded by the state, are no longer available [7]. It is needed to raise the demand for smart home services if the Central Government plans to build a thriving, sustainable smart elderly care industry in China. Again, marketing and promoting should be the focal points and baby steps for local governments to expand the smart home care market, along with the demand for such services. China's Ministry of Civil Affairs issued an *Action Plan for the Development of Smart Health and Elderly Care Services* (2017–2020), marking a milestone in specialising national policies on smart home services in elderly care. Specific plans for more funding should be arranged and delivered by local governments, especially those in rural areas, in order to develop better quality social robots.

In addition, China lacks professional training for rural elderly care services staff. China also faces a shortage of labour services for part-time or professional mutual caregiving. The majority of caregivers are women, so such a circumstance causes inconvenience to meet the caregiving needs of male elders [27]. It is important to recruit more part-time caregivers where middle-aged mothers who have children can spend hours of daytime delivering caregiving when children go to school. Part-time caregiving jobs offer significant flexibility so the recruitment of caregivers should be deemed easier and more appealing. Mobile applications can also be developed that match caregivers and elderly cohorts for caregiving services. It is not a significant issue if rural elders lack digital literacy, because their significant others, such as family members, can act as the persons to coordinate and use the mobile applications to recruit part-time caregivers for them. This kind of bonding is coined "mutual assistance" for the elderly, which helps heighten the availability of social support resources within communities. The mutual assistance model for the elderly is an effective approach to solve the shortage of nursing staff and caregivers in rural areas and, meanwhile, enhance the social connections between members of the communities [27]. The use of Internet services allows individuals to match caregiving beneficiaries with caregivers easily, saving a lot of costs and time from paying agencies to search for suitable candidates who can offer caregiving. Amid the pandemic, with social distancing rules and home confinement rules that may occasionally apply, it is necessary to develop smart home care services where a certain level of social communications and interactions can be maintained. Distance communications also become conveniently available where left-behind elderly populations can use digital devices to easily carry out facetime with their family members. The smart home care providers should continue to better design the smart home care services in order to ensure the elderly cohorts can interact with peers within their communities and healthcare staff so the social bonding they enjoy can be strengthened.

Sun (2013) carried out semi-structured face-to-face interviews with 18 family caregivers of individuals with dementia in Shanghai. He found that role strains and family conflicts are salient stressors discouraging them from undertaking caregiving roles [28]. Findings suggest that the inferior status of caregiving roles often hinders potential job-takers from occupying the available positions. The Central Government and local governments should advertise the importance and required skillsets of caregiving, in order to reduce the general public's negative perceptions of caregiving jobs in the long term. Only by lowering the occupational discrimination against caregivers can China meet the needed supply of caregivers in order to respond to the growing ageing concerns of the country.

Smart devices should provide personalised interaction and services to reduce the loneliness suffered by elders who are left-behind. However, the satisfaction of personalisation of using such devices is yet to be desirable, especially in rural areas [9]. The design of smart devices should be human-centric. For example, when an emergency button is pressed by the smart device user and a caregiving staff is sent to the housing unit of the elder, the elder may be dissatisfied that a stranger comes visit their home. It would be more human-centric if the smart device providers can let the users enter the contact details of several trustworthy caregivers of their choice in the devices, so they will feel more comfortable when someone they know visits their home, when necessary. Moreover, local governments or elderly care institutions can also pay for younger-aged elderly cohorts to take care of older-aged elderly counterparts when the former still have yet to experience physical dysfunction or chronic illnesses that bar them from delivering caregiving. For example, a 65-year-old elder can be paid on an hourly basis to provide caregiving to an 85-year-old counterpart who loses, partial or in full, their physical function.

3. Policy Development

In addition to discussing the challenges and progress of innovative technologies in elderly care, it is necessary to discuss the relevant (suggested) policy development so as compatibility [11]. It is necessary for the Central Government to play a role to proactively centralise private smart home care services providers' collection of behaviour data and to share such data publicly with all private or potential services providers in order to ensure those working in the industry can optimise their opportunities to succeed in sustaining their businesses in innovative elderly care. Grounded in the analysis of the Chinese Longitudinal Healthy Longevity Survey 2002–2014 data, Zhang et al. (2018) found that the visualisation of physiological, demographic, psychological, economic, behavioural, and social data helps Chinese researchers and policymakers better evaluate health conditions of Chinese elderly and arrange pro-elderly health policies. This, again, demonstrates the importance of collecting sufficient, multi-faceted big data in Chinese contexts, in order for relevant actors to better arrange care support for the elderly [23]. The systematic, centralised publicisation of such data can also encourage more potential private services providers to join in the market, allowing for a higher degree of healthy competition in the market which helps keep the market prices down and the quality of services in a satisfactory fashion.

It is noteworthy that the concept of a social robot has been introduced in China in recent years. Here, social robots mean "robotic technologies that are designed to interact autonomously with people across a variety of different application domains in natural and intuitive ways, by using the same repertoire of social signals used by humans" [7]. Elders worry about the replacement of human caregiving by social robots. In order to minimise the replacement by social robots, French elders preferred small robots that resemble teapots, so their children or grandchildren would not be aware of such social robots. In doing so, children and grandchildren would maintain the responsibilities of family caregiving [24]. Liu et al.'s study shows that elders prefer caregiving from, human attachment to, and communications with their own family members [9]. It may be more sensible to view social robots as complementary pieces that help the elders to live their everyday life in a more convenient way rather than to deem social robots as caregiving being in replacement for family care. Chen et al. (2020) applied randomised control trials to analyse 103 Chinese residents who were clinically diagnosed with dementia with an average age of 87.2 years old. They discovered that the use of respondents being accompanied by a social robot over a timeframe of 32 weeks displayed lower levels of loneliness and agitation. However, they noted that the elderly respondents' acceptance rate of using social robots was dissatisfactorily low [25]. Due to the urgency of the ageing challenges China is facing, social robots have the potential to be used substantially in order to assist the everyday life of elders. It is concerning when elders express their anxiety and fear about social robots, given the circumstance that such an innovative technology may be widely applied in the coming years or even decades. Such a negative view faced by elders may be particularly common among rural Chinese elderly populations who are seemingly more conservative but perhaps less independent. It is, therefore, necessary for local government agencies to deliver community education, including arranging public seminars, to rural elders. Rural elders who are introduced to the benefits of befriending social robots may plausibly be more willing to accept such technologies. In Taiwan, Chen et al. (2020) applied the Chinese version of attitudes towards the use of social robot questionnaire to survey 416 Taiwanese health professionals between November 2017 and May 2018. Survey outputs indicated that elders in caregiving needs are more likely to accept the use of social robots if their attitudes towards such use are more positive. By using social robots elders display better psychosocial well-being [26]. Therefore, the outputs of this Taiwanese study further hint that Chinese government officials should actively change the senior adults' perceptions of social robots, in order to allow the integration of social robots into the local health and care services industry.

Another concerning problem is that the application of social robots is proven to be successful societally in Japan, the United States, and Western Europe [24]. As most research on social robots is deemed a success in advanced countries' contexts, it is uncertain if the social robot quality in China can be as satisfactory as in those advanced western countries due to the former's immature and limited capacity of research and development. Therefore, can apply VUI, a function that allows senior adults suffering from declined physical and cognitive abilities to conveniently interact with innovative products.

To facilitate the development and expansion of smart home elderly care services, alongside ensuring such services can be delivered in a user-friendly fashion, it is important to collect customers' behavioural data and analyse such collected big data by smart devices in order to assist the managers of elderly care institutions to make better elderly caregiving decisions [9]. Big data and deep learning technologies have proven value in China. Here, government authorities and local academic scholars use big data of street view images provided by, for example, Tencent Street View images—an alternative to Google Earth—to monitor Chinese neighbourhoods' safety and social organisations in Beijing [20]. Fang et al. (2020) that argue China should prioritise the use of big data, alongside machine learning techniques, to monitor disease patterns suffered by those who need the elderly and long-term care at the population level. They point out that the use of big data and machine learning techniques is increasingly necessary to transform China into a hub allowing for sufficient pro-elderly caregiving and medical support. These technological advancements help build more sustainable futures for Chinese communities in the next decades [21]. However, to date, most smart products offered by Chinese elderly care institutions fail to satisfy the personalised demands of elders themselves since the data collected are significantly insufficient [9,11]. Therefore, Chinese policymakers should create more pilot studies, allowing more elderly cohorts to experience the use of smart home elderly care services while enabling more elderly care institutions to collect customers' data to better personalise the elderly caregiving services in the long run.

Moreover, elderly care institutions should use wearable devices to collect the physiological data of the elders and to transfer such data to the health services institutions via the smart elderly care services platform. Medical professionals can therefore better understand the physical conditions of the elderly populations by analysing the collected physiological data. The availability of physiological data can also allow nursing staff to adjust their services, diet plans, and rehabilitation treatment for the elderly beneficiaries in order to enhance the user-friendliness and personalisation of medical and caregiving services for the elders [11]. This argument shows how behavioural data are the cornerstone to changing the healthcare provision in relation to elderly care. Local governments, guided by their central counterpart, should urge more smart home elderly care providers to collect behavioural data and to circulate such data within the medical and nursing departments or institutions. Therefore, both elderly care and healthcare services quality can be improved. An example of Chinese elders using physiological characteristics to instruct smart devices domestically is their popular employment of smart television interactions. It is difficult for Chinese senior populations to type *pinyin* on television with remote control. Dou et al. (2018) found that the elderly in China have the disposition to use smart televisions where they exercise voice search when instructing the television to perform. The study demonstrates that the collection of necessary physiological data is important in Chinese contexts, in order to enable the innovation of smart home devices to make Chinese seniors' lives more convenient [22]. To effectively understand the needs of the elderly population for smart elderly care, it is sensible to carry out in-depth interviews and questionnaire surveys with elderly interviewees. Questions asked can include their views on smart gadgets in entertainment and leisure, home cleaning, social interaction, and medical care, alongside their willingness to purchase and use such devices [11]. Established sociologists and sociodemographers can lead the research teams to work on collecting such in-depth data from the elderly populations as they are experienced in and have a deep understanding of surveying. Data collected should be organised, structured, and trimmed by these research teams, followed by being shared with the targeted parties or the public.

To date, smart home elderly care data are scattered among various organisations [11]. Hu et al. conclude the Central Government should focus on two streams: enhancing human resources training quality and implementing a standardised intelligent elderly care system, so as to ensure the provision of quality elderly care services personnel and data even rural natives to accept the use of such devices. Otherwise, the market for smart home elderly services will remain highly restricted, and services providers may not be able to sustain their businesses due to the lack of demand.

As noted, China is facing a significant problem of nursing staff shortage. Smart homes have the potential to make up for the challenge of the shortage of caregiving labour by reducing the costs of manpower and time and providing a more accurate, efficient, and high-quality service for elders. Zeng and Chen (2022) found that, aside from digital literacy, financial concerns are a primary factor hindering Chinese individuals' purchase of smart homes. While respondents mostly agreed that smart homes are convenient by easing their housework burdens and making elders' lives more independent, they could only purchase smart homes if financial circumstances allow. In order to popularise the use of smart homes in China, local governments need to subsidise their citizens who are financially in need to buy such properties. Otherwise, even if Chinese citizens, including those who are seniors, are willing to accept the use of innovative devices domestically, they are financially barred from purchasing smart homes. Such restrictions limit the lifestyle and caregiving transitions of the local Chinese communities and hamper the attainment of sustainable futures [18]. Li and Woolrych (2021) studied the experiences of Chinese urban senior populations on living in smart homes in Chongqing. They found that ample respondents expressed financial concerns about the access to smart home devices. While those respondents learned the importance of incorporating technology in support of their everyday ageing challenges, they believed that the adoption of such smart interventions, owing to the expensive costs, were only made available for the affluent Chinese senior cohorts [10]. Zhang et al. (2020) echoed by arguing that the Chinese elderly are very sensitive to the price of intelligent products. They, concurrently, have higher requirements for the convenience of innovative devices [7]. Unless such devices are affordable and user-friendly, otherwise local governments can hardly develop, not even popularise, the market for elderly-care smart homes.

As earlier as in 2014, the Ministry of Civil Affairs already implemented a national-level smart home for elderly care project in seven nursing institutions. Here, sleep monitoring and falling detection devices and self-service physical examination services have been installed and delivered in nursing institutions. Additionally, in 2014, Shanghai issued *Guiding Opinions on Promoting the Pilot Construction of Liveable Communities for the Elderly* and established smart care centres in 40 pilot communities, providing services such as emergency assistance, security monitoring, and everyday elderly care [7]. It is noteworthy that the digital literacy and financial security of urban elites are much higher than less privileged urban natives and rural citizens. Therefore, more pilot communities should be established in first-tier cities first. If positive outcomes (such as smart home elderly care users are willing to learn and are satisfied with the use of, such services) result, then pilot communities can be targeted and arranged in second- and third-tier cities, followed by villages. Piloting should, therefore, be implemented in phases. The progress and outcomes of delivering smart home elderly care services in first-tier cities can serve as a reference for lower-tier cities to take into account during piloting in order for the latter to make any adjustments in the provision of smart home elderly-care services, if needed.

Since different interface standards are used by manufacturers among industries, ample manufacturers of smart products encounter difficulties in data collection. It is necessary for the Central Government to form policies and require manufacturers in different industries to standardise the interface standards used [9]. Setting up pilot communities would allow Chinese policymakers to test which interface standard should be used in a standardised, efficient, and cost-effective manner. Pilot studies should, again, be focused on first-tier cities that house the majority of digitally literate elderly populations, so the operation of piloting could be run efficiently. Globally, voice-user interface (VUI) has gained popularity in recent years. Song et al. (2022) surveyed 420 Chinese senior adults and found that Chinese elders accept the use of VUI owing to the satisfactory levels of perceived usefulness, perceived ease of use, and trust [19]. They suggested that more smart devices in the Chinese market the disposition to use innovative devices infrequently, and the lack of practice further limits their development of fluent device use [15].

Relative to younger generations, elders are inclined to demonstrate a negative view of learning new things and possess a rather poor learning ability. Therefore, a highlighted challenge of technological advancement in elderly care is the elderly population's lack of willingness to accept smart elderly care products. Moreover, smart elderly care goods are costly while the consumption behaviour of the majority of the elderly cohorts is conservative, further compounding the elders' acceptance of using smart home care services [9]. Here, despite Zhang (2022)'s findings, younger family members with higher digital literacy and acceptance of new technologies can serve as the significant others to influence or encourage the elder family members to use smart home elderly care services. Beyond domestic settings, developing the Chinese elderly's digital literacy is beneficial to their household's financial, and societies' social, burdens in the long term. Zhang and Nedospasova (2022) analysed the Chinese Social Survey 2017 dataset and unveiled that younger Chines elderly—meaning those who just met the official retirement age (i.e., 60 years old)—who are digitally literate are more likely to stay active in labour markets and earn financial incomes for their households. Local societies housing more digitally literate individuals who reach the retirement age also benefit from the lower social burdens as the senior populations who are active in the labour markets depend less on social pensions [16]. Therefore, within and beyond domestic settings, building senior populations' digital literacy can enhance China's attainment of multi-faceted sustainable futures, implicating the need for local Chinese governments to introduce more digital learning programmes or information to Chinese citizens, especially those who are of senior status. Pilot smart elderly care communities should also be arranged by Chinese policymakers to "test the water" and to understand feedback given by the elderly beneficiaries who experience the use of smart home elderly care services. Only when smart gadgets are user-friendly, reliable, and safe would elders show a willingness to use such technologies because they do not want to spend an undue amount of time and effort to master the method of using these technologies *per se* [11]. User-friendliness enables the elderly populations with a lack, or an absence, of digital familiarity and literacy to learn how to use these smart services and devices.

For the elderly, cognitive decline is a major risk factor for disability and death and a primary barrier to their ability to use innovative products. Jin et al. (2019) analysed the Chinese Health and Retirement Longitudinal Studies and found that Chinese elderly using digital devices more frequently can be cognitively stimulated and slow their rate of cognitive decline down. As a result, findings show that major relevant actors, including the Central Government and local governments of China, should actively popularise the use of digital devices among all age groups, in order to enhance the cognitive ability of senior adults and those who are becoming senior adults [17]. The improvement in Chinese citizens' cognitive ability can sustainably facilitate more potential innovative device users to possess the ability to explore digital platforms in the long term. Such a circumstance propels more Chinese citizens, including those who are of senior status, to become active users of digital devices, especially when those devices *per se* are user-friendly.

Elderly care institutions in China usually give the elderly beneficiaries a "smart box," which offers multiple technological services, such as smart medical care and home services. For example, those pressing the "smart medical" button would be informed of the contact details of nearby hospitals; and those clicking the "housekeeping service" button would be given the home service telephone number. More advanced smart home elderly care devices would be incorporated with big data analysis technology and artificial intelligence technology, which help reduce any manual tedious operation [11]. The major barrier to the expansion of such technological advancement is not any technological limitations but the digital literacy of the users themselves. Rural elderly populations have low education levels and few opportunities to be introduced to technologies. Therefore, again, smart home care providers have to translate complicated, advanced technological programming into user-friendly technological devices, in order to allow less-educated urban natives and vulnerable also engenders the Central Government to accelerate the provision of smart home care services to the Chinese elderly population [7]. Here, smart home investment and delivery are necessary when building a sustainable elderly care system. The investment in smart home elderly care can lessen the long-term burden on China's healthcare system as more elders would be able to self-manage their everyday life and minor physical and psychological problems. Moreover, along with enhancing societies' sustainable futures and senior populations' lifestyles, the smart home application can improve the flexibility of the power load and reduce the investments in China's power supply by 1.13–1.19 trillion RMB (approximately 158–166 billion USD) per year [12]. In designing, building, and delivering digital innovations, smart cities have the disposition to better respond to the worldwide urbanisation and ageing trends that raise opportunities but also challenges for how policymakers create sustainable, inclusive, and equitable urban environments [10].

China issued the "National New-Type Urbanisation Plan (2014–2020)," emphasising that the country has been prioritising to practise a new form of urbanisation known as people-oriented urbanisation. Under China's recent priority, the expansion of the use of age-friendly smart home devices has been seen as one of the core policy focuses in order to facilitate the country's sustainable urbanisation [13]. In this article, the author critically analyses China's implementation of smart home elderly care services, particularly on the benefits and challenges of technological advancement in elderly care and the advantages and problems of relevant policy development. The author also highlights how the informationalisation and digitalisation in elderly care and policy development enhance the convenience of the elderly populations' everyday life when family care is limited or absent. Additionally, the author assesses what the gaps are in existing smart home elderly care technologies and policy development that need to be addressed by Chinese policymakers to further advance the safety and convenience of the elderly cohorts' living. Relevant policymaking or policy amendment would be pivotal for China to accelerate its urbanisation and develop more sustainable, inclusive, and prosperous smart, habitable environments designated for its ever-growing senior populations.

2. Technological Advancement

In contemporary China, most enterprises designing and delivering smart home services in elderly care can restrictively provide elders simple services, including emergency rescue, smart door locks, and basic online health advice. More complex services such as comprehensive assistance, health management, and home security are rarely available in the market due to technological limitations [7,11]. The lack of technological progression in the elderly care sector should be considered a minor concern in China, especially in villages and lower-tier cities, because the elderly population lack digital literacy to use complex, advanced technologies, so simple services should suffice when helping the elderly cohorts to live a more convenient and safer life. Enhancing senior populations' digital literacy can lower the cost of knowledge and effective information acquisition, improve the efficiency of resource endowment distribution, and achieve a better sense of access. Zhang (2022) analysed the 2018 China Elderly Social Tracking Survey and found that, compared to the eastern, more urbanised regions of China, senior populations' digital literacy in non-eastern areas has significant room for improvement [14]. Here, for Internet-connected rural elderly in China, senior populations' basic digital literacy is at moderate to low levels. Even with the presence of family members' digital guidance, the effect of digital literacy on the rural elderly's sense of access remains moderated [14]. These findings reveal that rural elderly are, to a large extent, digitally (semi-)illiterate in China and hint that such a population lacks the motivation or willingness to develop their digital literacy even with the help of their junior family members. To further demonstrate the elderly's reluctance to develop their digital literacy, Wang and Wu (2021) noted that seniors perceive innovative devices as "too complicated to use," where they intend to reject learning how to use them to avoid the experience of technological anxiety. They are demotivated to memorise complicated operating procedures given their declined working memory. The senior populations have populations often endure a wide range of diseases, dysfunctions and cognitive impairment, so the corresponding healthcare services needed for them are substantial [5]. The rise in the elderly population's life expectancy has compounded the burden of the healthcare system in China in the long-term [6].

The socioeconomic transformation, the increase in rural-to-urban migration, and the low fertility rates propel significant difficulties for the urban and especially rural Chinese elderly to receive family care. A shortage of nursing staff within the country fails to satisfy the growing demand for services in elderly care [7]. In China, there were 2.7 million senior populations aged 80 or above in 2020 and the figure will reach over 100 million in 2050. Analysing the Chinese Longitudinal Healthy Longevity Survey, 2011–2014 datasets, Zhang et al. forecasted that 1.2 million of those aged 80 or above will be severely disabled in 2025, and the demand for low-skilled and high-skilled nursing staff will hit 5.6 million and 11.5 million, respectively. There is an expandingly vast gap between the demand and supply of nursing staff, where the shortage of such elderly caregivers is alarming and puts the sustainability of the Chinese elderly care system significantly at stake [8]. It is noteworthy to highlight the conventional Chinese model in the domestic setting known as the Confucian values of filial piety—family members are obliged to help and take care of the elders and cross-generational connections should be tightly formed [9]. However, given the lack of family care and the shortage of nursing staff, the concepts of smart home care are introduced to ensure the elders can better manage their everyday life. Here, the provision of smart home care aims to deliver safety, low costs in health and assistance, and independence when the elders are dwelling at home by themselves [7]. Smart home care means "the application of Internet of things, information technology, big data, cloud computing and other technologies to elderly care in order to provide the elderly with smart care or smart home environment, meet their needs for healthy and independent life, and finally improve their physical and mental health and quality of life" [7]. Joining Japan, the United States, and Western European countries, China has been turning from an agricultural society to an informational society to advance modernisation [9]. China mushrooming its development as an informational society prompts the supply of smart home care services. When more individuals, including those who are disadvantaged, are given opportunities to acquire digital literacy, a larger share of the Chinese population shall become familiar with and accept the use of smart home care services.

The construction of smart cities is a relatively new urban development strategy aimed at arranging and delivering sustainable urban settings through the enhancement of digital connectivity. Smart cities are the environments with an effective integration of human, physical and digital systems within the settings to deliver a sustainable, inclusive and prosperous future for local citizens. [10]. In China, given the ageing challenges mentioned above, the design, establishment and delivery of smart homes are seen as an urgent and critical approach to build a sustainable and inclusive future that accommodate the needs of the growing populations of senior citizens. The emergence of smart homes for elderly care in China occurred in 2008, where such an innovation had undergone through four development stages, namely the seed stage (2008–2011), the start-up stage (2012–2014), the development stage (2015–2016), and the popularisation stage (2017–2019) [2]. In 2017, the State Council of China published an action plan for the construction of a smart and healthy elderly care industry (2017–2020). The information technologies featuring the Internet of things, big data, cloud computing, and mobile Internet represent comprehensiveness, efficiency, accuracy, and wisdom, aiming to facilitate the convenience and advancement of individuals' everyday life [11]. The action plan designed and implemented by the State Council of China demonstrates the Central Government's determination to informationalise and digitalise the Chinese society. Therefore, the market of smart home care services should expectedly mushroom in the coming decades, as the demand for smart home care shall raise. However, there are a range of barriers to achieving the massification of smart home care services, which will be discussed in the following sections. In addition to the shortage of family care and nursing services, elders being physically and psychologically

Review

Smart Elderly Care Services in China: Challenges, Progress, and Policy Development

Jason Hung

Department of Sociology, The University of Cambridge, Cambridge CB3 0SZ, UK; ysh26@cam.ac.uk; Tel.: +44-(0)-7478119080

Abstract: In 2017, the State Council of China published an action plan for the construction of a smart and healthy elderly care industry (2017–2020). The action plan designed and implemented by the State Council of China demonstrates the Central Government's determination to informationalise and digitalise the Chinese society. Therefore, the market of smart home care services should expectedly mushroom in the coming decades, as the demand for smart home care increase. However, there are a range of barriers to achieving the massification of smart home care services, which will be discussed in the following sections. In addition to the shortage of family care and nursing services, elders being physically and psychologically vulnerable also engenders the Central Government to accelerate the provision of smart home care services to the Chinese elderly population. Here, smart home investment and delivery are necessary when building a sustainable elderly care system. The investment in smart home elderly care can lessen the long-term burden on China's healthcare system as more elders would be able to self-manage their everyday life and minor physical and psychological problems. In this article, the author would critically analyses China's implementation of smart home elderly care services, particularly on the benefits and challenges of technological advancement in elderly care and the advantages and problems of relevant policy development. The author also highlights how the informationalisation and digitalisation in elderly care and policy development enhance the convenience of the elderly populations' everyday life when family care is limited or absent. Additionally, the author assesses what the gaps are in existing smart home elderly care technologies and policy development that need to be addressed by Chinese policymakers to further advance the safety and convenience of the elderly cohorts' living.

Keywords: sustainable development; ageing; technological development; policy development; China

Citation: Hung, J. Smart Elderly Care Services in China: Challenges, Progress, and Policy Development. *Sustainability* **2023**, *15*, 178. https://doi.org/10.3390/su15010178

Academic Editors: Rashid Mehmood, Tan Yigitcanlar and Juan M. Corchado

Received: 27 October 2022
Revised: 17 December 2022
Accepted: 20 December 2022
Published: 22 December 2022

Copyright: © 2022 by the author. Licensee MDPI, Basel, Switzerland. This article is an open access article distributed under the terms and conditions of the Creative Commons Attribution (CC BY) license (https:// creativecommons.org/licenses/by/ 4.0/).

1. Introduction

China has been concerned about the national growth rate of the elderly population aged 60 or above. The annual growth rate of the elderly population was 3.37 percent in the 1990s, a figure that was nearly three times the then overall population growth rate of the country [1]. According to the China Research Centre on Ageing, a sum of 202 million elderly individuals dwelled in China in 2013, with 23 million of them aged 80 or above [2]. Among the elderly population in 2013, 100 million and 37 million suffered from non-communicable diseases and disabilities, respectively [2]. The provision of accessible, affordable long-term care services to the elderly has therefore become an urgent task that the Chinese Government has encountered [3]. The ageing population is projected to reach 240 million in 2030 (accounting for 16 percent of the national population) and 450 million in 2050 (accounting for 33 percent of the national population) [4]. Such forecasts have alarmed Chinese policymakers, as China will be turning from an ageing to an aged population. An increase in life expectancy and the decline in fertility rate have been attributed to the sociodemographic transformation of the country. The rapid growth of the elderly population will significantly burden the Chinese healthcare system as they are at higher risk of suffering from chronic illnesses and functional disabilities [4]. In geriatrics, aged

59. Yao, G.; Miao, J. Service Value Co-Creation in Digital Platform Business: A Case of Xianyu Idle Trading Platform. *Sustainability* **2021**, *13*, 11296. [CrossRef]
60. Espelt, R. Agroecology prosumption: The role of CSA networks. *J. Rural Stud.* **2020**, *79*, 269–275. [CrossRef]
61. Hevner, A.R.; March, S.T.; Park, J.; Ram, S. Design science in information systems research. *MIS Q.* **2004**, *28*, 75–105. [CrossRef]
62. Padgham, L.; Winikoff, M. *Prometheus: A Methodology for Developing Intelligent Agents*; Springer: Berlin/Heidelberg, Germany, 2003; pp. 174–185.
63. Bryson, J.J. *The Behavior-Oriented Design of Modular Agent Intelligence*; Springer: Berlin/Heidelberg, Germany, 2003; pp. 61–76.
64. Masad, D.; Kazil, J. MESA: An agent-based modeling framework. In Proceedings of the 14th PYTHON in Science Conference, Austin, TX, USA, 6–12 July 2015; pp. 53–60.
65. Maghsudi, S.; Stańczak, S. Hybrid centralized–distributed resource allocation for device-to-device communication underlaying cellular networks. *IEEE Trans. Veh. Technol.* **2015**, *65*, 2481–2495. [CrossRef]
66. Consoli, A.; Tweedale, J.; Jain, L. The link between agent coordination and cooperation. In Proceedings of the International Conference on Intelligent Information Processing, Adelaide, Australia, 20–23 September 2006; pp. 11–19.
67. Saint-Andre, P. Extensible Messaging and Presence Protocol (XMPP; RFC 6122, RFC series (ISSN 2070-1721), CA, USA, March 2011. Available online: https://www.rfc-editor.org/rfc/rfc6122 (accessed on 30 March 2022).
68. Committee, I.F.S. *FIPA Communicative Act Library Specification*; Technical Report; Foundation for Intelligent Physical Agents: Geneva, Switzerland, 2000.
69. Birant, D. Data mining using RFM analysis. In *Knowledge-Oriented Applications in Data Mining*; IntechOpen: Rijeka, Croatia, 2011.
70. Bocklisch, T.; Faulkner, J.; Pawlowski, N.; Nichol, A. Rasa: Open source language understanding and dialogue management. *arXiv* **2017**, arXiv:1712.05181.
71. Virtanen, P.; Gommers, R.; Oliphant, T.E.; Haberland, M.; Reddy, T.; Cournapeau, D.; Burovski, E.; Peterson, P.; Weckesser, W.; Bright, J. SciPy 1.0: Fundamental algorithms for scientific computing in Python. *Nat. Methods* **2020**, *17*, 261–272. [CrossRef] [PubMed]
72. Hintze, J.L. *User's Guide III: Regression and Curve Fitting*; NCSS Statistical Software: Kaysville, UT, USA, 2007.
73. Explosion Inc. A. spaCy: Industrial-Strength Natural Language Processing in Python. Available online: https://github.com/explosion/spaCy (accessed on 30 March 2022).
74. Sun, J. Jieba: Chinese Text Segmentation. Available online: https://github.com/fxsjy/jieba (accessed on 30 March 2022).
75. Facebook Inc. Duckling: Haskell Library that Parses Text into Structured Data. Available online: https://github.com/facebook/duckling (accessed on 30 March 2022).

27. Woods, T.; Ernst, M.; Tropp, D. *Community Supported Agriculture: New Models for Changing Markets*; United States Department of Agriculture, Agricultural Marketing Service: Washington, DC, USA, 2017.
28. Freedman, M.R.; King, J.K. Examining a new "pay-as-you-go" community-supported agriculture (CSA) model: A case study. *J. Hunger. Environ. Nutr.* **2016**, *11*, 122–145. [CrossRef]
29. Gebre, T.; Gebremedhin, B. The mutual benefits of promoting rural-urban interdependence through linked ecosystem services. *Glob. Ecol. Conserv.* **2019**, *20*, e00707. [CrossRef]
30. Preiss, P.; Charão-Marques, F.; Wiskerke, J. Fostering Sustainable Urban-Rural Linkages through Local Food Supply: A Transnational Analysis of Collaborative Food Alliances. *Sustainability* **2017**, *9*, 1155. [CrossRef]
31. Akaka, M.A.; Vargo, S.L. Technology as an operant resource in service (eco) systems. *Inf. Syst. E-Bus. Manag.* **2014**, *12*, 367–384. [CrossRef]
32. Vargo, S.L.; Lusch, R.F. Service-dominant logic: What it is, what it is not, what it might be. In *The Service-Dominant Logic of Marketing*; Routledge: Abingdon-on-Thames, UK, 2015; pp. 43–56.
33. Vargo, S.L.; Lusch, R.F. It's all B2B . . . and beyond: Toward a systems perspective of the market. *Ind. Mark. Manag.* **2011**, *40*, 181–187. [CrossRef]
34. Lusch, R.F.; Vargo, S.L.; Tanniru, M. Service, value networks and learning. *J. Acad. Mark. Sci.* **2010**, *38*, 19–31. [CrossRef]
35. Głąbska, D.; Skolmowska, D.; Guzek, D. Food Preferences and Food Choice Determinants in a Polish Adolescents' COVID-19 Experience (PLACE-19) Study. *Nutrients* **2021**, *13*, 2491. [CrossRef]
36. Wadolowska, L.; Babicz-Zielinska, E.; Czarnocinska, J. Food choice models and their relation with food preferences and eating frequency in the Polish population: POFPRES study. *Food Policy* **2008**, *33*, 122–134. [CrossRef]
37. Köster, E.P. Diversity in the determinants of food choice: A psychological perspective. *Food Qual. Prefer.* **2009**, *20*, 70–82. [CrossRef]
38. Forouli, A.; Bakirtzis, E.A.; Papazoglou, G.; Oureilidis, K.; Gkountis, V.; Candido, L.; Ferrer, E.D.; Biskas, P. Assessment of Demand Side Flexibility in European Electricity Markets: A Country Level Review. *Energies* **2021**, *14*, 2324. [CrossRef]
39. Shapley, L.; Scarf, H. On cores and indivisibility. *J. Math. Econ.* **1974**, *1*, 23–37. [CrossRef]
40. Ma, J. Strategy-proofness and the strict core in a market with indivisibilities. *Int. J. Game Theory* **1994**, *23*, 75–83. [CrossRef]
41. Abdulkadiroğlu, A.; Sönmez, T. School choice: A mechanism design approach. *Am. Econ. Rev.* **2003**, *93*, 729–747. [CrossRef]
42. Su, X.; Zenios, S.A. Recipient choice can address the efficiency-equity trade-off in kidney transplantation: A mechanism design model. *Manag. Sci.* **2006**, *52*, 1647–1660. [CrossRef]
43. Kesten, O. Coalitional strategy-proofness and resource monotonicity for house allocation problems. *Int. J. Game Theory* **2009**, *38*, 17–21. [CrossRef]
44. Schummer, J.; Vohra, R.V. Assignment of arrival slots. *Am. Econ. J. Microecon.* **2013**, *5*, 164–185. [CrossRef]
45. Dur, U.; Ünver, M.U. Two-sided matching via balanced exchange: Tuition and worker exchanges. *J. Political Econ.* **2019**, *127*, 1156–1177. [CrossRef]
46. Wooldridge, M. *An Introduction to Multiagent Systems*; John Wiley & Sons Ltd.: Chichester, West Sussex, UK, 2009.
47. Davis, R. *Report on the Workshop on Distributed AI*; Massachusetts Institute of Technology, Artificial Intelligence Laboratory: Cambridge, MA, USA, 1980.
48. Knoeri, C.; Binder, C.R.; Althaus, H.-J. An agent operationalization approach for context specific agent-based modeling. *J. Artif. Soc. Soc. Simul.* **2011**, *14*, 1729. [CrossRef]
49. Niazi, M.; Hussain, A. Agent-based computing from multi-agent systems to agent-based models: A visual survey. *Scientometrics* **2011**, *89*, 479–499. [CrossRef]
50. Michel, F.; Ferber, J.; Drogoul, A. Multi-agent systems and simulation: A survey from the agent community's perspective. In *Multi-Agent Systems*; CRC Press: Boca Raton, FL, USA, 2009; pp. 17–66.
51. Chun, H.W.; Wong, R.Y. N*—An agent-based negotiation algorithm for dynamic scheduling and rescheduling. *Adv. Eng. Inform.* **2003**, *17*, 1–22. [CrossRef]
52. Palanca, J.; Terrasa, A.; Julian, V.; Carrascosa, C. SPADE 3: Supporting the New Generation of Multi-Agent Systems. *IEEE Access* **2020**, *8*, 182537–182549. [CrossRef]
53. Billhardt, H.; Julián, V.; Corchado, J.M.; Fernández, A. An architecture proposal for human-agent societies. In Proceedings of the International Conference on Practical Applications of Agents and Multi-Agent Systems, Salamanca, Spain, 4–6 June 2014; pp. 344–357.
54. González-Briones, A.; De La Prieta, F.; Mohamad, M.; Omatu, S.; Corchado, J. Multi-Agent Systems Applications in Energy Optimization Problems: A State-of-the-Art Review. *Energies* **2018**, *11*, 1928. [CrossRef]
55. Reis, I.F.G.; Gonçalves, I.; Lopes, M.A.R.; Antunes, C.H. A multi-agent system approach to exploit demand-side flexibility in an energy community. *Util. Policy* **2020**, *67*, 101114. [CrossRef]
56. Damacharla, P.; Dhakal, P.; Bandreddi, J.P.; Javaid, A.Y.; Gallimore, J.J.; Elkin, C.; Devabhaktuni, V.K. Novel Human-in-the-Loop (HIL) Simulation Method to Study Synthetic Agents and Standardize Human–Machine Teams (HMT). *Appl. Sci.* **2020**, *10*, 8390. [CrossRef]
57. Bosse, S.; Engel, U. Real-Time Human-In-The-Loop Simulation with Mobile Agents, Chat Bots, and Crowd Sensing for Smart Cities. *Sensors* **2019**, *19*, 4356. [CrossRef]
58. Lusch, R.F.; Nambisan, S. Service innovation: A service-dominant logic perspective. *MIS Q.* **2015**, *39*, 155–175. [CrossRef]

Funding: This research was funded by the Ministry of Science and Technology, Taiwan, Republic of China, grant number 109-2410-H-007-019-MY2.

Institutional Review Board Statement: Not applicable.

Informed Consent Statement: Not applicable.

Conflicts of Interest: The authors declare no conflict of interest.

References

1. Edwards, F. Alternative food networks. In *Encyclopedia of Food and Agricultural Ethics*; Springer: Dordrecht, The Netherlands, 2016; pp. 1–7. [CrossRef]
2. Forssell, S.; Lankoski, L. The sustainability promise of alternative food networks: An examination through "alternative" characteristics. *Agric. Hum. Values* **2015**, *32*, 63–75. [CrossRef]
3. Milestad, R.; Westberg, L.; Geber, U.; Björklund, J. Enhancing adaptive capacity in food systems: Learning at farmers markets in Sweden. *Ecol. Soc.* **2010**, *15*, 29. [CrossRef]
4. Goodman, D.; DuPuis, E.M.; Goodman, M.K. *Alternative Food Networks: Knowledge, Practice, and Politics*; Routledge: Abingdon-on-Thames, UK, 2012.
5. Arkko, J. The influence of internet architecture on centralised versus distributed internet services. *J. Cyber Policy* **2020**, *5*, 30–45. [CrossRef]
6. Khoshafian, S. Can the Real Web 3.0 Please Stand Up? Available online: https://www.rtinsights.com/can-the-real-web-3-0-please-stand-up/ (accessed on 2 December 2021).
7. Vargo, S.L.; Lusch, R.F. *The SAGE Handbook of Service-Dominant Logic*; SAGE Publications Limited: Thousand Oaks, CA, USA, 2018.
8. Lusch, R.F.; Vargo, S.L.; Wessels, G. Toward a conceptual foundation for service science: Contributions from service-dominant logic. *IBM Syst. J.* **2008**, *47*, 5–14. [CrossRef]
9. Morgan, K.; Marsden, T.; Murdoch, J. *Worlds of Food: Place, Power, and Provenance in the Food Chain*; Oxford University Press on Demand: Oxford, UK, 2008.
10. Renting, H.; Marsden, T.K.; Banks, J. Understanding alternative food networks: Exploring the role of short food supply chains in rural development. *Environ. Plan. A* **2003**, *35*, 393–411. [CrossRef]
11. Lee, R. Shelter from the storm? Geographies of regard in the worlds of horticultural consumption and production. *Geoforum* **2000**, *31*, 137–157. [CrossRef]
12. Feagan, R.; Henderson, A. Devon Acres CSA: Local struggles in a global food system. *Agric. Hum. Values* **2009**, *26*, 203–217. [CrossRef]
13. Marsden, T.; Banks, J.; Bristow, G. Food supply chain approaches: Exploring their role in rural development. *Sociol. Rural.* **2000**, *40*, 424–438. [CrossRef]
14. Guthman, J.; Morris, A.W.; Allen, P. Squaring farm security and food security in two types of alternative food institutions. *Rural Sociol.* **2006**, *71*, 662–684. [CrossRef]
15. Gomiero, T.; Pimentel, D.; Paoletti, M.G. Environmental impact of different agricultural management practices: Conventional vs. organic agriculture. *Crit. Rev. Plant Sci.* **2011**, *30*, 95–124. [CrossRef]
16. Schönhart, M.; Penker, M.; Schmid, E. Sustainable local food production and consumption: Challenges for implementation and research. *Outlook Agric.* **2009**, *38*, 175–182. [CrossRef]
17. Born, B.; Purcell, M. Avoiding the local trap: Scale and food systems in planning research. *J. Plan. Educ. Res.* **2006**, *26*, 195–207. [CrossRef]
18. Esquinas-Alcázar, J. Protecting crop genetic diversity for food security: Political, ethical and technical challenges. *Nat. Rev. Genet.* **2005**, *6*, 946–953. [CrossRef]
19. Reisch, L.; Eberle, U.; Lorek, S. Sustainable food consumption: An overview of contemporary issues and policies. *Sustain. Sci. Pract. Policy* **2013**, *9*, 7–25. [CrossRef]
20. Sundkvist, Å.; Milestad, R.; Jansson, A. On the importance of tightening feedback loops for sustainable development of food systems. *Food Policy* **2005**, *30*, 224–239. [CrossRef]
21. Kloppenburg, J.; Hendrickson, J.; Stevenson, G.W. Coming in to the foodshed. *Agric. Hum. Values* **1996**, *13*, 33–42. [CrossRef]
22. James, S.W. Beyond local food: How supermarkets and consumer choice affect the economic viability of small-scale family farms in Sydney, Australia. *Area* **2016**, *48*, 103–110. [CrossRef]
23. Coley, D.; Howard, M.; Winter, M. Local food, food miles and carbon emissions: A comparison of farm shop and mass distribution approaches. *Food Policy* **2009**, *34*, 150–155. [CrossRef]
24. Virtanen, Y.; Kurppa, S.; Saarinen, M.; Katajajuuri, J.-M.; Usva, K.; Mäenpää, I.; Mäkelä, J.; Grönroos, J.; Nissinen, A. Carbon footprint of food–approaches from national input–output statistics and a LCA of a food portion. *J. Clean. Prod.* **2011**, *19*, 1849–1856. [CrossRef]
25. Weber, C.L.; Matthews, H.S. Food-miles and the relative climate impacts of food choices in the United States. *Environ. Sci. Technol.* **2008**, *42*, 3508–3513. [CrossRef]
26. Adam, K.L. *Community Supported Agriculture*; ATTRA-National Sustainable Agriculture Information Service: Butte, MT, USA, 2006.

stream. *Third*, through the design, building, and evaluation process, this study contributes to service system design knowledge and evaluation methods by integrating ABM and MAS in multi-agent simulation.

This study was conducted in the context of Taiwan, which is affected by urbanization and rural decline, and the food system is oriented toward industrialized and globalized production. Therefore, the design of CHASS will make a practical contribution to generating new resources for expanding the AFNs model to reach a balance between AFNs and the conventional food system. Applying CHASS for cooperative AFNs can bring many benefits, such as reducing the cost of order processing, coordination, negotiation, and member communication, because many cooperatives in Taiwan still receive orders via a google form, ecommerce website, or Line chat and then process orders manually. Furthermore, by better food allocation and direct service exchange, CHASS can help strengthen human relationships and contribute to urban–rural linkage. In addition, CHASS is designed to be an open and distributed system to achieve economic and technical sustainability to ensure long-term benefits to the community.

8.3. Limitations and Future Research Directions

In this study's simulation, we assume that CHASS is applied in a small cooperative in AFNs, and prices are set at a reasonable level based on transparency, similar to the price-setting mechanism in the CSA model. Therefore, we ignore the influence of the price factor on customer choice and only focus on evaluating the allocation mechanism and customer demand flexibility. However, if CHASS is deployed in AFNs with many customers and producers, the price factor certainly affects supply and demand. Therefore, developing a price consensus mechanism between members and including price factors in the customer decision model is necessary for future work. Furthermore, in Phase 1 of the TTC-Negotiation mechanism of the simulation, product supply is allocated to demand based on demand time priority. In future research, the TTC-Negation mechanism can be evaluated based on combining other priority methods such as Recency, Frequently, Monetary (RFM) models [69].

The second limitation is related to the capacity of the assistant agent to decide on behalf of the human. In the first CHASS prototype, the assistant agent can only make decisions based on a preset utility function. The user needs to set the parameters for the utility function or decision model. This issue will significantly affect the feasibility of practical deployment. In the next version, an assistant agent can be developed to be able to self-adjust the decision-making model (e.g., self-adjust utility function parameters) or self-build the decision-making model through the reinforcement learning process.

Another limitation is the flexibility level of assistant agents in communication with humans. In this study, we only prepared limited scenarios to train the assistant agent to detect user intents (e.g., buy or sell). Therefore, if the user asks other questions, they are classified as "out of scope, " which will probably make the user uncomfortable. We plan to develop a shared knowledge base so that all agents can access and retrieve data to handle questions related to sustainability from users.

Although CHASS offers many advantages and promises to contribute much to sustainability, more research needs to be done regarding CHASS implementation for a specific AFN model. Due to limited resources, in this study, the assistant agent still has several limitations on communication and the decision-making model. The ability to communicate with humans in natural language and self-adjusted decision-making models through communication are two essential features of the assistant agent expected to be implemented in CHASS in the near future to realize the human–agent cooperative service system.

Author Contributions: Conceptualization, F.-R.L.; Data curation, V.-C.T.; Formal analysis, V.-C.T.; Methodology, F.-R.L.; Project administration, F.-R.L.; Resources, F.-R.L.; Software, V.-C.T.; Supervision, F.-R.L.; Validation, V.-C.T.; Visualization, V.-C.T.; Writing—original draft, V.-C.T.; Writing—review & editing, F.-R.L. All authors have read and agreed to the published version of the manuscript.

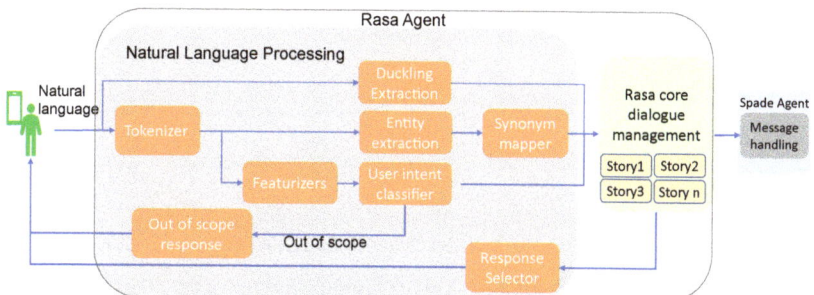

Figure 21. The natural language processing pipeline.

In parallel with the user-intent detection process, entities such as product names and locations will be extracted. We use the Duckling library [75] to detect and extract time, number, and weight units. Duckling supports multi-languages, so it can work for both English and Chinese. As a simple example, if a user inputs a sentence, " I want to buy 2 kg cabbage", the NLP module will detect the user's intent is "to buy", the product name "cabbage" is extracted, and Duckling will extract the number "2" and weight unit "kg". At the end of the process, the NLP converts natural language to structured data: ["intent" : "buy", "product" : "cabbage", "quantity" : 2, "unit" : "kg"]. Next, depending on user intent, the "Rasa core dialogue management" may respond in natural language to collect more information from human users. Finally, all structured data will be handled by SPADE cycle behavior, as mentioned in Figure 10.

8. Discussion and Conclusions

8.1. Summary

Concerned about the unsustainability of the conventional food systems, AFNs have emerged and are widely believed to be more sustainable. However, AFNs also face criticism for their limitations on economic sustainability. To increase economic efficiency, some AFNs formed an intermediary to aggregate products from producers and redistribute them to customers through a centralized digital platform to reduce transaction costs. However, such models will somewhat lose an essential feature of AFNs, which is the establishment of "strong relationships" between customers and producers, and a centralized platform is not technically sustainable.

This study develops a Cooperative Human–Agent Service System (CHASS) to overcome the limitations on the economic sustainability of AFNs and achieve technical sustainability based on decentralized technology. The outstanding features of CHASS are the human actor who has the agency for control and can be assisted by an assistant agent; a collaboration between humans, assistant agents, and coordination agents through the allocation and negotiation mechanism; and direct service exchange between actors.

8.2. Theoretical Contributions and Practical Implications

This research contributes to the existing literature in three aspects. *First*, this study proposes a two-phase TTC-Negotiation mechanism to facilitate food resource allocation and direct service exchange. In this study, we combine the "demand flexibility and resource allocation optimization" research stream that has proven to be economically beneficial and contributes to sustainable production and consumption in the energy field, and the research stream on "direct service exchange and value co-creation digital platform for sustainability" that contributes to the strengthening of human relationships and urban–rural linkages. The proposed two-phase TTC-Negotiation mechanism aims to balance the resource allocation optimization goal and human relationship establishment goal. *Second*, this study proposes a new approach to value co-creation through collaboration between humans and agents in a new generation of multi-agent systems that contribute to the human-in-the-loop research

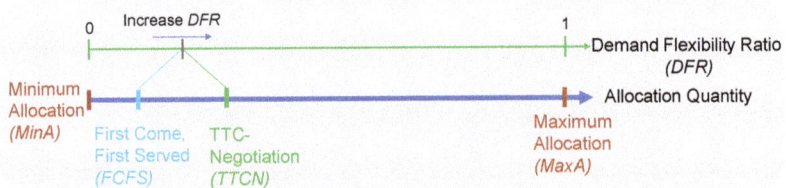

Figure 19. Formalizing the influence of demand flexibility on the order fulfillment performance.

7. Human–Agent Communication for CHASS Deployment

In Sections 5 and 6, we design the multi-agent simulation in which an ABM interacts with CHASS to evaluate the designed service system and formalize the learning. In this simulation, the simulated agents in ABM communicate to intelligent agents in CHASS through agent communication language (ACL). However, when implementing CHASS in practice, humans will communicate with assistant agents in CHASS through natural language. Human users will communicate with their assistants in CHASS in natural language via a chat application similar to interacting with commercial chatbots. The assistant agent can be installed on a personal computer or a cloud server. Users only need to install the chat application to be able to interact with their assistant agents. Furthermore, communication between human users and assistant agents is done through XMPP, an instant message protocol; therefore, users can also interact with other users on the same app by instant messages. The interaction between human–human, human–agent, and agent–agent is illustrated in Figure 20.

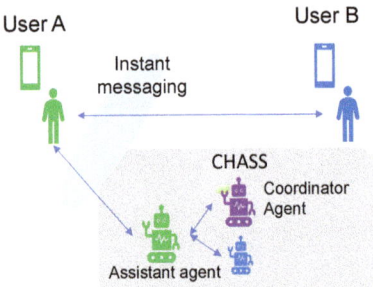

Figure 20. Human–agent communication.

To handle human–agent communication, the app needs to translate natural language to agent communication language and vice versa. To communicate with the assistant agent, users can use a mobile app that works as an XMPP client to send and receive instant messages. When the assistant agent receives a message in natural language, it will start the natural language processing (NLP) pipeline, as illustrated in Figure 21. The first step of natural language processing is tokenization. In this step, we use the spaCy library [73] for English and the Jieba library [74] for Chinese. Next, tokenized terms are passed through the feature process to convert them to vectors for user-intent classifier purposes. The user-intent classifier model was trained with a collection of human conversation data in pre-built scenarios. The classifier model will detect intent with a confidence score when receiving incoming messages. If the confidence score is less than the threshold set by users, that message will be classified as "out-of-scope", and the model will reply with an out-of-scope response.

Table 6. Illustration of the minimum allocation quantity and the maximum allocation quantity construct.

Product	Minimum Allocation Quantity			Maximum Allocation Quantity		
	Demand	Supply	Allocated	Demand	Supply	Allocated
Romaine	4	2	2	5	2	2
Iceberg	1	3	1	Romaine or iceberg	3	3
Cabbage	1	2	1	8	2	2
Cauliflower	5	2	2	Cabbage or cauliflower	2	2
	Total allocated quantity		6	Total allocated quantity		9

Since the moderation effect of *DFR* is opposite in different value ranges (Figure 17), we use the *piecewise-polynomial model* (also known as the *multiphase model*) to fit the data. The estimated model comprises two linear equations, each active over a different X range. The estimation equation has the form $Y = A + BX + C(X - D)SIGN(X - D)$, where D is the cut-off value that separates two linear equations. Using NCSS software from LLC, Kaysville, UT, USA, version 21.0.3 [72], we can estimate D = 0.31152 when the outcome performance is measured in percentage (Figure 17b). Based on this result, we use a cut-off value of *DFR*, 0.3, to separate the data into two groups and to run different regression models for each group. All standardized beta coefficients of the two regression models, as presented in Table 7, are significant at the 0.001 level. The interaction term between TTC-Negotiation and the *DFR* (Neg_x_DFR) is *0.732*, presenting the high positive moderation effect of the *DFR* in its range [0, 0.3], and *−0.678* presented the negative moderation effect of the *DFR* in its range [0.3, 1].

Table 7. Regression analysis results.

Data Group	Demand Flexibility Ratio ≤ 0.3			Demand Flexibility Ratio > 0.3		
	Standardized Beta Coefficients	t-Value	*p*-Value	Standardized Beta Coefficients	t-Value	*p*-Value
Neg	−0.189	−6.955	−0.189	0.839	53.292	0.000
Neg_x_MinA	−1.393	−23.614	−1.393	−5.404	−112.129	0.000
Neg_x_MaxA	1.707	30.276	1.707	5.693	122.146	0.000
Neg_x_DFR	0.732	62.966	0.732	−0.678	−63.758	0.000
	R^2 = 0.673			R^2 = 0.766		

6.5. Formalization of Learning

All simulation results can be illustrated briefly, as shown in Figure 19. With any supply and demand pattern, we can determine two thresholds: minimum allocation quantity *MinA* and maximum allocation quantity *MaxA* ($MinA \leq MaxA$). If the overdemand or oversupply situation happens, its equivalents $MinA = MaxA$ and any allocation methods give the same order fulfillment performance. On the contrary, in case $MinA < MaxA$, if increasing *DFR* from 0, the performance of both the *FCFS* method and the TTC-Negotiation (TTCN) mechanism will increase, but TTCN performance increases at a higher speed, and it gives a better performance than *FCFS*. When the *DFR* crosses the cut-off value of 0.3, the TTCN performance is very close to *MaxA*, so it can no longer increase, while *FCFS* performance continues to increase following the increase of the *DFR*. When *DFR* equals 1, both *FCFS* and TTCN reach the *MaxA* value.

tity) in Figure 17b. Here, we define a new variable: *"demand flexibility ratio"* (*DFR*), Which is measured by the quantity of flexible demand over the total demand. The *DFR* is affected by CFR. For example, if we set CFR to 10% in simulation, *DFR* will fluctuate around 0.1, since the demand quantity of each customer is different. From the scatterplot, we can see that, if the *DFR* is in the range [0, 0.3], the *DFR* positively moderates the allocation performance. In contrast, if the *DFR* is in the range [0.4, 1], the *DFR* negatively moderates the allocation performance.

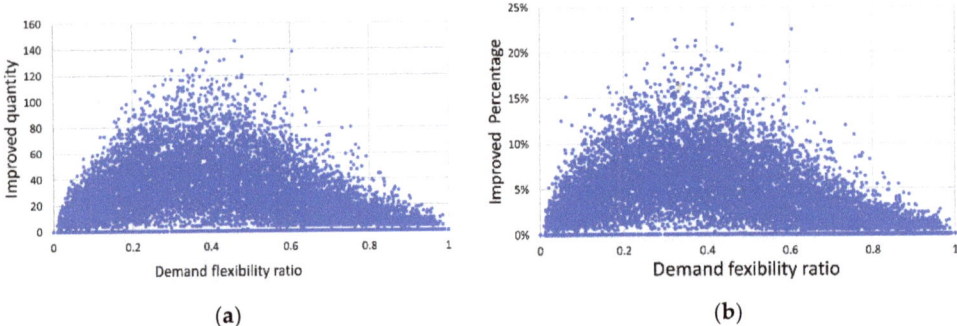

Figure 17. Order fulfillment performance of the TTC-Negotiation mechanism versus *FCFS*. (**a**) Performance in quantity. (**b**) Performance in percentage.

6.4. The Analysis of Experimental Results

To better understand the influence of the TTC-Negotiation mechanism on the order fulfillment performance under the moderation of supply, demand patterns, and demand flexibility, we conducted regression analysis for all the simulation data following the conceptual framework illustrated in Figure 18. The independent variable (TTC-Negotiation) is a dummy variable that equals 0 if using the *FCFS* allocation method and 1 if using the TTC-Negotiation method. The dependent variable is the "order fulfillment performance" measured by the improvement of fulfilled quantity in percentage when applying the TTC-Negotiation mechanism over the *FCFS* method. In addition to the moderating variable *DFR* mentioned above, we define two new moderating variables: *minimum allocation quantity* (MinA) and *maximum allocation quantity* (MaxA), to represent the supply and demand patterns. For any supply and demand patterns, there is always a high and low threshold of allocation quantity for any allocation methods. The MinA happens when the *DFR* equals 0 (100% of customers are inflexible), and the MaxA happens when the *DFR* equals 1. Table 6 illustrates the meaning of these two variables through a simple example. With the same supply and demand pattern, the MinA and MaxA are 6 and 9, respectively.

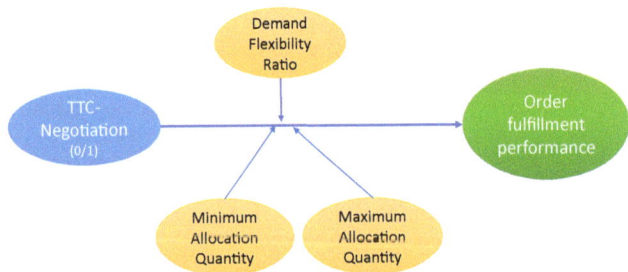

Figure 18. The conceptual framework of factors affects the order fulfillment performance.

Table 5. *FCFS* versus *TTC-Negotiation* mechanism.

Method	Time	Customer	Demand	Supply	Allocated
	0			X, Y, Z	
First Come, First Served	1	A	X (or Y, Z)	X̶, Y, Z	1
	2	B	X (or Y)	X̶, Y̶, Z	1
	3	C	X	X̶, Y̶, Z	0
			Total		2
TTC-Negotiation	4	A	X (or Y, Z)	X, Y̶, Z̶	1
	5	C	X	X̶, Y̶, Z̶	1
			Total		3

6.3. Performance Evaluation

We perform simulations with different supply and demand patterns and customer flexibility ratios to compare the allocated quantity between the *FCFS* method and the *TTC-Negotiation* mechanism. Two conclusions are drawn from the simulation:

1. Under the same condition of customer flexibility ratio, the allocation performance of the *TTC-Negotiation* mechanism is considerably moderated by the demand and supply pattern. This conclusion is clearly shown in Figure 16b. On some days, TTC-Negotiation performance is significantly higher than *FCFS* (e.g., day 95), while on other days, the difference is negligible (e.g., day 100).

2. The customer flexibility ratio (CFR) moderates the TTC-Negotiation mechanism performance. Figure 16 presents some simulation results at different scales of customer flexibility ratios. We started the simulation by setting CFR to 5% and found out that TTC-Negotiation obtained a slight improvement (Figure 16a) and continued to increase CFR. We saw significant improvement in the quantity made in transactions (Figure 16b); however, when the CFR is greater than 50%, we found that TTC-Negotiation no longer outperformed the *FCFS* method (Figure 16c,d).

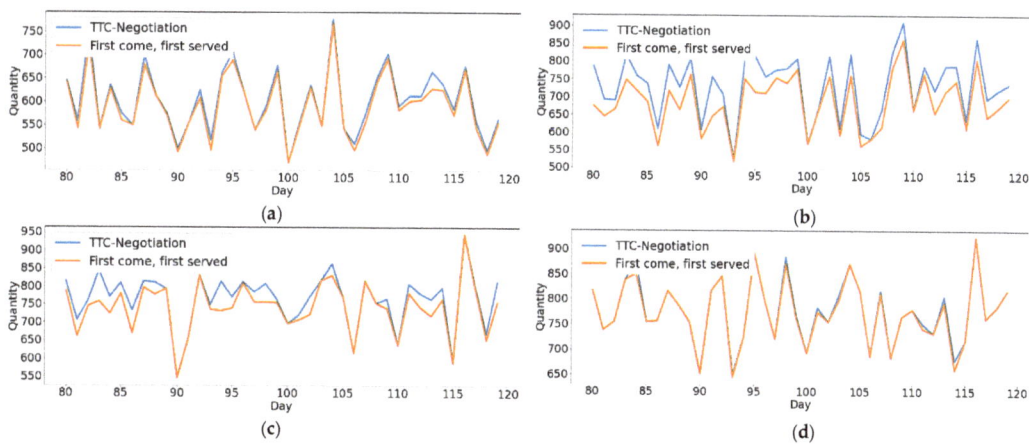

Figure 16. Evaluation of order fulfillment performance with different customer flexibility ratios. (**a**) Customer flexibility ratio CFR = 5%. (**b**) Customer flexibility ratio CFR = 30%. (**c**) Customer flexibility ratio CFR= 60%. (**d**) Customer flexibility ratio CFR = 90%.

To get a more general view of the effect of the customer flexibility ratio on allocation performance, we use a scatter plot to plot all cases with the Y-axis abbreviated as improvement in quantity (the difference of order fulfillment quantity) in Figure 17a and improvement in the percentage (improved quantity divided by the *FCFS* allocation quan-

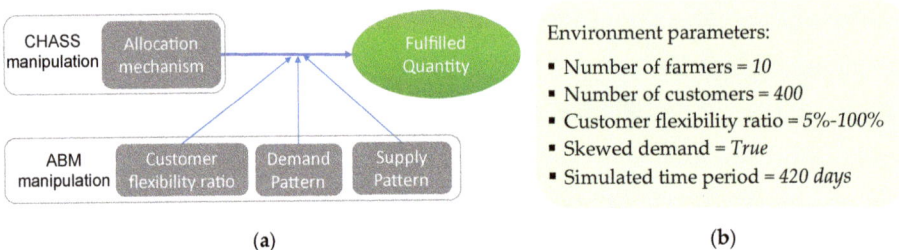

(a)   (b)

Figure 14. The illustration of parameters set for the simulation. (**a**) Simulation settings. (**b**) ABM environment parameters.

Figure 15a,b illustrate the supply pattern of the first 140 days. Depending on the farmer agent's decision on how many times to harvest, the supply can be as stable as Figure 15a or can show slight fluctuations as in Figure 15b. Figure 15c,d illustrate the demand pattern of the first simulation of 140 days. Demand has slight fluctuations as customers buy products one or two times on any day of the week. In addition, the demand for each product in the product group will be imbalanced since the "skewed demand" parameter is *True*.

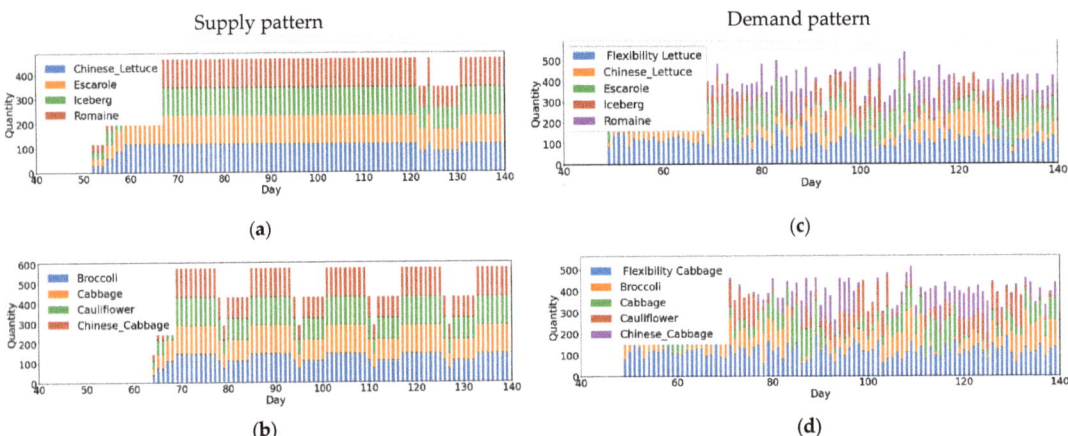

Figure 15. The illustration of demand and supply patterns generated by ABM. (**a**) supply pattern of the lettuce group. (**b**) supply pattern of the cabbage group. (**c**) demand pattern of the lettuce group. (**d**) demand patterns of the cabbage group.

6.2. First-Come-First-Served (FCFS) versus TTC-Negotiation Mechanism

Table 5 presents a simple example of the First-Come-First-Served (*FCFS*) method compared with the TTC-Negotiation mechanism. *FCFS* is a method of allocation based on time priority. As illustrated in Table 5, the demand of customers A, B, and C are allocated chronologically. A is allocated product X. The most preferred product of customer B is X, but X is out of stock, so B changed it to Y. Customer C is not allocated any products because he only wants to buy X. When using the TTC-Negotiation mechanism, the coordinator agent sends a negotiation message to ask A to switch to Z. If A agrees, the negotiation is successful. As a result, customer A will be allocated product Z, and C will be allocated product X.

measured by the number of flexible customers over the total of customers. For example, if we assume that the simulation model has 400 customers and the demand flexibility ratio is 0.2, then 80 flexible customers will accept negotiation and the rest will not. The flexible customers will provide their demand preference (e.g., [romaine, iceberg, Chinese lettuce, escarole]), while non-flexible customers only provide one product demand (e.g., romaine). The skewed demand parameter (True or False) creates an imbalance in the product demand of the non-flexible customer group. The SciPy library [71] is used to generate a skew-normal distribution for the demand. Figure 13b illustrates the total demand of all non-flexible customers when the skewed demand is *True*. If the skewed demand is set to *False*, products will be assigned randomly to every non-flexible customer. As a result, there is only a slight imbalance in demand for different products.

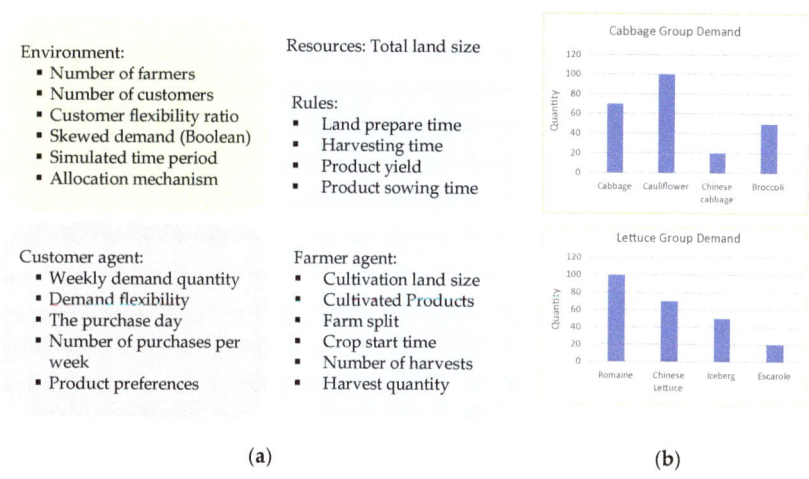

Figure 13. ABM simulation: (**a**) model parameters and (**b**) illustration of skewed demand.

6. Experimentation and Results

6.1. Experimental Setup

Multi-agent simulation is an integral part of the development of CHASS, in which the "design" and "evaluation through simulation" are integrated into a cyclic process. This subsection presents simulation results to evaluate the effect of the two-phase TTC-Negotiation mechanism mentioned in Section 4.4 on customer order fulfilled quantity. The "Fulfilled Quantity" is measured by the total quantity of all fulfilled orders after completing four stages of service flow in Figure 5 of simulation time steps.

In this simulation, we set up parameters for both CHASS and ABM to represent the real-world environment and the performance evaluation for CHASS (Figure 14a). First, we manipulate the resource allocation mechanism in CHASS: the two-phase TTC-Negotiation mechanism versus the first-come-first-served (*FCFS*) allocation method. Then, we generate demand and supply patterns in ABM by setting agent (customer, farmer) parameters, resources, rules, and environment (Tables 2–4 and Figure 14b). We set the food networks to have 10 farmers and 400 customers as the environmental parameters. The "skewed demand" parameter is set to *True* to simulate the imbalanced demand scenarios. The simulated period starts from time step 0 to 419 (420 days), in which the pre-harvest period is around 50 days, and harvesting is around 370 days, equivalent to one year of supply data. The "customer flexibility ratios" is set at 20 different levels (from 5% to 100%), with a 5% difference between the two adjacent levels. Simulation is performed two times for each "customer flexibility ratios" setting and each resource allocation mechanism. In summary, we performed 80 simulations, and each simulation included 369~370 data records (from day 50~51 to 419). The final simulation data consists of 29,560 records.

may accept negotiation to switch to another product in the same product group (lettuce or cabbage) according to the customer's product preferences in a shortage situation. The customer parameters used to generate demand data are described in Table 4.

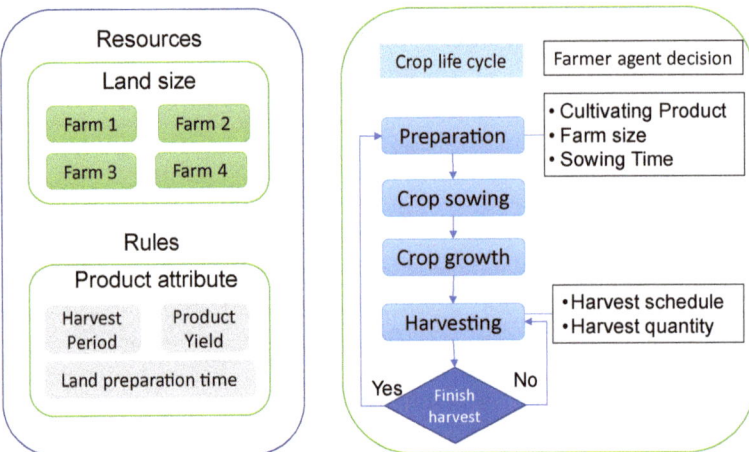

Figure 12. Resources, rules, and farmer agent decisions during the crop life cycle in the simulation.

Table 4. Customer agent parameters of ABM model.

Parameter	Value	Explain
Weekly demand quantity in unit weight	4~10	Depends on unit weight, e.g., lettuce (300 g/unit) or cabbage (500 g/unit) Random choice in the range 4~10, equivalent to 1.2–3 kg lettuce and 2–5 kg cabbage consumption per week
Purchases per week	1 or 2	The number of times customers purchase in a week
The purchase day	1~7	A choice of 1 or 2 days out of 7 days of the week
Demand flexibility (DF)	True/False	Customers agree or disagree with negotiation to switch to another product.
Product preferences (In case DF = False)	e.g., [cabbage]	Purchasing one product and not accepting a switch to another product
Product preferences (In case DF = True)	e.g., [Romaine, Iceberg, Chinese Lettuce, Escarole]	Purchasing one product in the product preferences lists in an orderly way and accepting negotiation to switch to another product

5.4. Simulation Model Parameters

Figure 13a provides an overview of all simulation parameters in ABM. These parameters can be divided into two groups: agent-level parameters (customers, farmers) and model-level parameters (environment, resources, and rules). The agent-level parameters can be set for each agent, and model-level parameters are set for the entire model. The supply data of each simulation step is generated based on land resources, crop rules, farmer's agent parameters, and the number of farmers. The demand data is generated based on the customer agent parameters, the demand flexibility ratio, and the skewed demand setting. Customer agents are classified into flexible customers, who accept negotiation, and non-flexible customers. The ratio of these two groups is set by the customer flexibility ratio,

Table 2. Product parameters of the ABM model.

Product Group	Product Name	Yield per Acre (Tonne)	Harvest Period (Day)	Unit Weight (kg)	Preparation Time (Day)
(1) Lettuce group	Romaine	3.5–3.8	50–80	0.3	7–10
	Chinese lettuce	3.5–3.8	50–80	0.3	7–10
	Iceberg	3.5–3.8	50–80	0.3	7–10
	Escarole	3.5–3.8	50–80	0.3	7–10
(2) Cabbage group	Cabbage	7.0–7.5	60–90	0.5	7–10
	Cauliflower	7.0–7.5	60–90	0.5	7–10
	Chinese cabbage	7.0–7.5	60–90	0.5	7–10
	Broccoli	7.0–7.5	60–90	0.5	7–10

Table 3. Farmer agent parameters of the ABM model.

Parameter	Value	Explain
Land size	0.5 acre	Farmer-owned land size
Cultivated product group	(1) or (2)	Either the lettuce group or the cabbage group is selected for cultivation. In the simulation, half of the farmers grow product group 1, and the others grow product group 2.
Land cultivation ratio	100%	The percentage of cultivated land on owned land
The first crop start time	1~80 days	Time to start the first crop, randomly chosen
Farm split factor	4	Split cultivated land to multi-farm
Maximum harvest period	14 days	The period of harvest time of a crop.
Quantity harvest	0~max	Quantity is each harvest time—the maximum value is the unharvested quantity that remains on the farm.

In the simulation model, each farm is a simulated object with a life cycle (crop sowing, growth, harvesting, and ending) similar to an actual crop life cycle, as presented in Figure 12. At the crop preparation stage, farmers decide the cultivating product, farm size, and sowing time. Then, when the farm reaches harvest time, farmers make a harvest schedule (e.g., the number of harvests and the quantity of each harvest). Because of the different growth rates of vegetables, farmers can harvest a crop multiple times on the same farm to ensure a stable supply in AFNs. In this simulation, the maximum harvest period is set to 14 days. The supply capacity of the cooperative AFNs in each simulation time step depends on farm capacity and the farmer's harvest decision. After harvesting, the farmer agent must wait a period for land preparation before starting the next crop (creating a new farm object).

5.3. Developing a Customer Agent for Demand Data Generation

The entire demand is created by aggregating individual customer agent demand. Referring to the actual vegetable needs of each member in the cooperative model, the weekly demand of each customer agent is set up randomly from 4 to 10 units for each product type, equivalent to 1.2~3 kg lettuce (300 g/unit) and 2~5 kg cabbage (500 g/unit) consumption per week. Then, each customer can buy these products once or twice weekly. These parameters are set based on the buying behavior of co-op members in Taiwan. An important attribute of a customer agent is "demand flexibility" with True/False value. If the "demand flexibility" is set to *False*, it means the customer agent only wants to buy the preferred product and does not agree to switch to another product even if that product is in shortage. On the contrary, if "demand flexibility" is set to *True*, it means the customer agent scheduled period. "Agent skills" are developed as a data processing function and can be reused for all three types of these behaviors. The output data of the "agent skills" is formed into FIPA agent communication language (ACL) [68] and sent out to other agents or transformed into natural language before being sent to humans. We built a "Rasa agent" using the Rasa framework [70] to convert from natural language to ACL and vice versa. The Rasa agent will be specified in more detail in Section 7.

5. Multi-Agent Simulation

This section describes a multi-agent simulation using the "Simulation for MAS" approach presented in Section 2.5.2. Firstly, we develop ABM using the Mesa framework [64], and ABM works as a design-supported tool to develop CHASS. The objective of the simulation is to evaluate the functions and applicability of CHASS in a cooperative model in AFNs to understand the mechanism of resource allocation and negotiation, thereby helping to create new requirements for the evolution of CHASS. ABM is a simulation tool that supports the development of CHASS. When implementing CHASS in practice, ABM will be eliminated. Instead, users will use the mobile application to directly interact with their assistant agents using natural language similar to interacting with chatbots.

5.1. Simulation Model

Multi-agent simulation is an integral process of the development and evolution of CHASS. The intelligent agent will be designed, tested, evaluated, and improved through simulation. We use the Mesa framework [64] to build an ABM, including simulated agents, social structure (resource, rules), and environment. The simulated agents, which represent humans in the real world, have different attributes and decision-making models to represent the heterogeneous population. Each simulated agent in ABM is assisted by an intelligent agent in CHASS, and the communications between simulated agents and intelligent agents are done through the XMPP protocol. The ABM generates supply and demand data over time, and all generated data are transferred to the CHASS platform in every time step of the simulation process, as shown in Figure 11. After receiving data from ABM, CHASS starts four stages of service flow, as illustrated in Figure 6. After completing the operations in Stage 4, CHASS sends back a finished notification to inform ABM to start a new simulation step. There are two types of simulated agents for AFNs in ABM: customer and farmer. The supply data is generated depending on the farm capacity and farmer agents' crop decisions, and the demand data is generated based on customer agents' attributes and decisions.

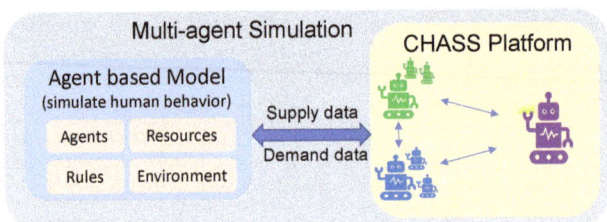

Figure 11. The illustration of the relationship between the ABM and the CHASS platform.

5.2. Develop Farmer Agent for Supply Data Generation

In ABM, each farmer agent owns a limited land size and chooses a group of products to grow. In practice, each farmer will have knowledge and experience for certain groups of products, and in the short term, they do not switch to other products. Therefore, in the simulation model, we assume that farmers will choose a group of products for the first crop and will not change to other products throughout the simulation. Each product type has land preparation time, harvest period, and product yield attributes. These parameters will remain constant during the simulation (Tables 2 and 3).

cooperative will be able to adjust the total supply to meet the total demands of members to avoid wasting food or not providing enough for members. When scenario 3 occurs, the negotiation process will be activated.

Table 1. The three scenarios of supply and demand pattern.

Scenario		Product X Quantity	Product Y Quantity	Allocated and Fulfilled	Unallocated & Unfulfilled	Status	Negotiation
1	Demand	1	1	X: 1, Y: 1	-	All demand is fulfilled.	No
	Supply	2	2	X: 1, Y: 1	X: 1, Y: 1		
2	Demand	2	2	X: 1, Y: 1	X: 1, Y: 1	All supply is allocated.	No
	Supply	1	1	X: 1, Y: 1	-		
3	Demand	2	1	X: 1, Y: 1	X:1	unallocated supply and unfulfilled demand	Yes
	Supply	1	2	X: 1, Y: 1	Y:1		

4.5. Intelligent Agent Design

The intelligent agent is designed based on the behavior-oriented design method [63] with a modular structure, as illustrated in Figure 10. Each agent can naturally act on its own. First, the functional requirements of the agent are formulated based on the scenario analysis. Then, these requirements are decomposed into simple behavior. We use the five behavior types of the SPADE [52]: cyclic, one-shot, periodic, timeout, and finite state machine. The cyclic behavior is used for handling messages from humans or other agents. In SPADE, a cyclic behavior works as a "while loop" to be always ready to process incoming messages. SPADE also supports storing data in an "agent knowledge", a type of in-memory key-value store. After the message is handled, it is converted to structured data and is passed to the state behavior module. Different decision-making models (e.g., utility function, trained models, etc.) can be used to process the data depending on the agent's current state and settings. The output of the decision-making model is the activation of one-shot, timeout, or periodic behavior.

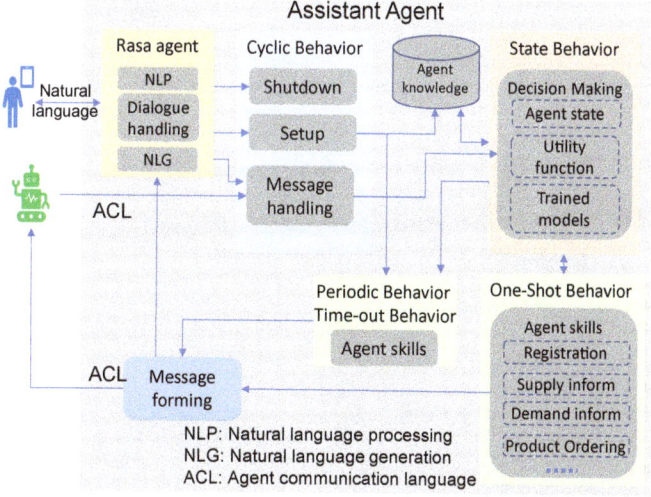

Figure 10. The illustration of the assistant agent component.

The structure of one-shot, periodic, and timeout behaviors are similar. The difference is that one-shot behavior can be run once at the activated time that, timeout behavior can be run once at a scheduled time, and that periodic behavior can be run many times in a

in the cycle is reduced accordingly. If this counter value reaches zero, the product node will be removed. If there exists a demand node that does not point to any product node, it will also be removed.
- Round k, k ≥ 2: Round k uses the same allocation and removing procedure as Round 1. This iteration will stop if no demand nodes or product nodes are left.

After the first TTC allocation, the negotiation condition is checked (Figure 9). If all demand is fulfilled or all supply is allocated, it means no more demand or supply can be allocated, and the best allocation has been reached; then, the allocation process is finished without negotiation. On the other hand, if there is still unfulfilled demand and unallocated supply after the first TTC allocation, the coordinator agent will send a negotiation invitation to the target assistant agents. Target agents are agents who belong to one of two groups: (1) agents who have unfulfilled demands or (2) agents who have fulfilled demands with products in shortage. The goal of the negotiation process is to convince agents in group 2 to switch to products that are not yet allocated so that the demands of agents in group 1 can be fulfilled. Next, all assistant agents who accept negotiation will be formed into a negotiation group; then, the second TTC allocation is run for this group. This process repeats in several rounds until the best allocation results are reached.

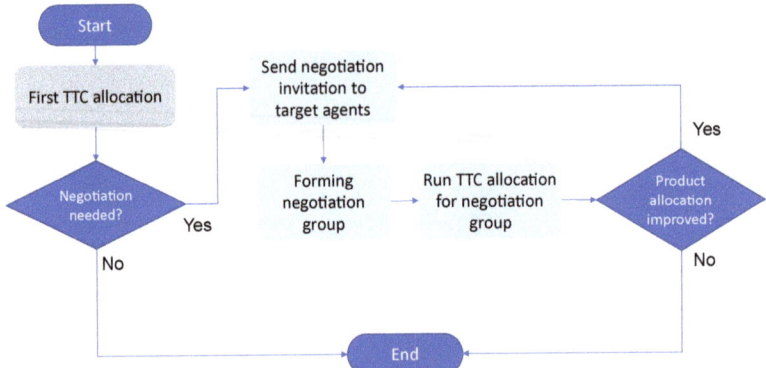

Figure 9. TTC allocation and negotiation flow. The negotiation process is carried out if there is unallocated supply and unfulfilled demand for substitute products.

Phase 2: Binding customer demand with provider

In phase 2, the customer demand and provider supply are bound based on priority provided by both sides (customers and providers). This phase aims to meet the design principles: (2) strengthening actors' relationships in the A2A network. The actor (customer or provider) has the autonomy to choose the exchange partners by providing a priority list. The assistant agent can be set up to compute other agents' priorities based on several criteria (e.g., product rating, trust level, etc.) on behalf of human users who set the priorities based on personal preference. If the assistant agent does not provide other actors priority, the coordinator agent will randomly generate the priority. Finally, the TTC mechanism is applied for each demand and supply group to bind each customer's demand to the corresponding providers based on the priority of both sides.

When is the negotiation needed?

The conditions for negotiation in Figure 9 are described more clearly through three scenarios presented in Table 1, in which X and Y are two interchangeable products. Scenario 1 is common in the CFS, where supply often exceeds demand and food waste occurs. Conversely, when events such as natural disasters occur, scenario 2 will occur. Scenario 3 is probably rare in CFS but possible in AFNs. In the cooperative AFN model, customers and producers are both members, and information is shared among members. Therefore, the

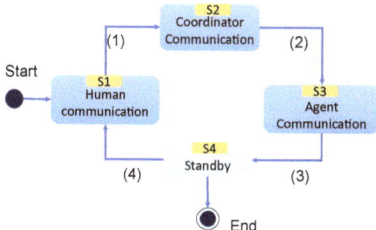

State Transition

(1) Finalize conversation with human user and get all demand/supply information.
(2) Receive the allocation result from coordinator agent.
(3) Finish all service exchange activity with other assistant agents.
(4) Receive message from human user.

Figure 7. State–transition diagrams of an assistant agent. (S1) Communicating to humans to obtain demand or supply data, (S2) communicating to the coordinator agent to inform supply or demand and negotiation, (S3) interacting with other assistant agents for service exchange, and (S4) standby.

4.4. Two-Phase TTC-Negotiation Resource Allocation Mechanism

As mentioned in Section 4.3, in Stage 1, the coordinator agent receives supply and demand information from assistant agents, and then the supply information is grouped by product and aggregated in quantity. After completing information acquisition, the coordinator agent starts the allocation and negotiation process in Stage 2. This subsection describes in detail the proposed two-phase TTC-Negotiation resource allocation mechanism (Figure 8). In phase 1, the product resource is allocated to each demand based on the product preferences and demand priority. In phase 2, the allocated demand and supply are grouped by product, and the TTC algorithm is applied for each product group to bind each customer's demand to corresponding providers based on the priority both sides provide (customer and provider).

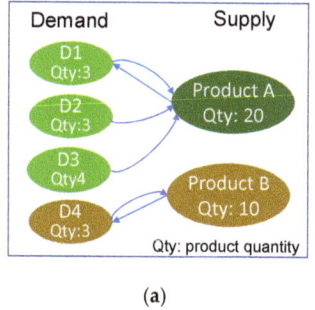
(a)

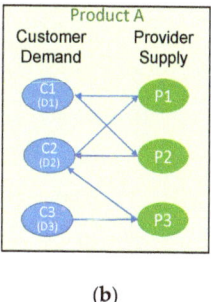
(b)

Figure 8. Two-phase TTC-Negotiation mechanism: (**a**) Phase 1—Product allocation and negotiation; (**b**) Phase 2—Binding customer demands with providers.

Phase 1: Product allocation and negotiation

This phase aims to meet the "efficient resource allocation" design principles. The TTC-Negotiation mechanism is used to allocate product supply to each demand based on customer demand priority and the product preferences of customers. Demand priority can be determined based on demand time or using priority models, such as the RFM (Recency, Frequency, Monetary) model [69]. Figure 8a illustrates the product allocation process, which is executed through several rounds of operations specified as follows:

- Round 1: Each product supply is presented as a supply node and is assigned a counter equal to the product supply quantity. Each customer demand is represented as a demand node and is assigned a counter equal to the demand quantity. The demand nodes point to their first preference of product node, and each product node points to the highest-priority demand node. Each demand node in a cycle is allocated the product it points to and is removed from the graph. The counter of each product node

4.3. Service Flow in CHASS

The service flow for resource allocation and value exchange in CHASS is divided into four stages, as presented in Figure 5. Stage 1, *information acquisition*, begins after the assistant agents receive the supply and demand information from customers and providers. In this stage, the coordinator agent receives demand and preferences for products and providers from the customer's assistant agents and supply and customer priority from the provider's assistant agents. Next, during Stage 2, *allocation and negotiation*, the coordinator agent interacts with the customer assistant agent for food resource allocation and negotiation. When the allocation and negotiation process is complete, the coordinator agent sends the allocation results to the corresponding customer and provider agents (Stage 3—*allocation result informing*). Finally, in Stage 4, *service exchange*, customer assistant agents make order requests to the matched providers based on the allocation information received. The service exchange process (e.g., ordering, additional service requests, order confirmation, payment) is done directly between the providers and the customers. In this stage, customers and providers have autonomy and freedom for service exchange to benefit each other. The service flow in Figure 5 will be further clarified through the agent state–transition diagram for a coordinator agent and an assistant agent (Figures 6 and 7).

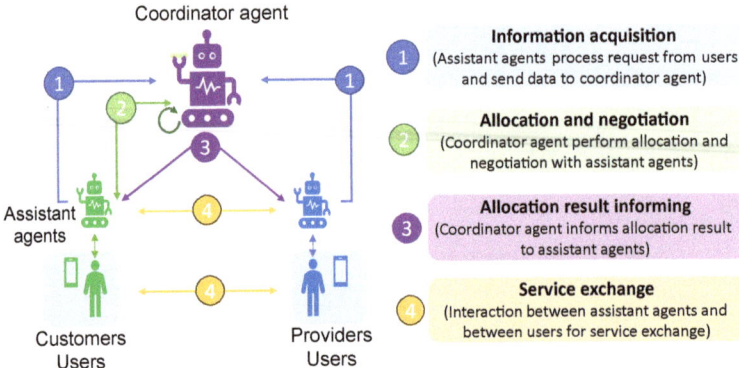

Figure 5. Resource allocation and service exchange flow in CHASS.

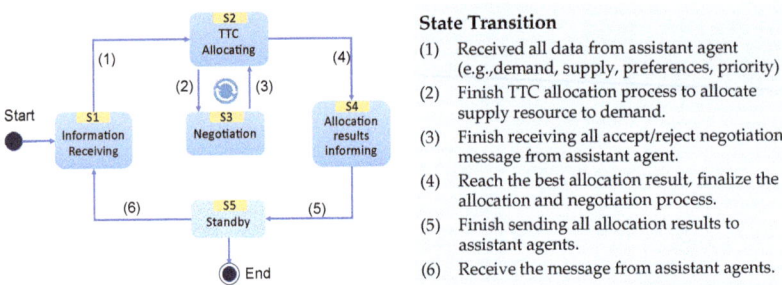

Figure 6. State–transition diagrams of a coordinator agent. (S1) Receiving demand/supply, (S2) running the TTC mechanism to allocate supply to demand, (S3) interacting with an assistant agent for negotiation, (S4) sending allocation results to all assistant agents, and (S5) standby.

agent computation power and communication costs. The more agents on the network, the more communication resources will be wasted on the allocation and negotiation process.

In this study, CHASS is designed based on a hybrid centralized–distributed architecture [65] for archiving economic and technical sustainability principles, as shown in (Figure 4a). This architecture has two types of agents: coordinator agent and assistant agent. The role of the coordinator agent is to coordinate the resource allocation and negotiation process, thereby minimizing the dense communication in a network. The assistant agent works as a personal virtual assistant carrying out some set of operations on behalf of humans with some degree of independence to generate value for its owner. Humans can communicate with their virtual assistants through a mobile app using natural language. From a service view, this architecture is designed based on the coordinative cooperation approach [66]: the coordinator agent invites the assistant agent to join in cooperation with other agents to achieve a common goal.

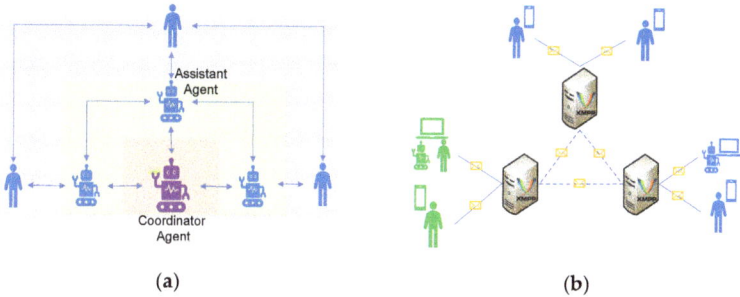

Figure 4. (a) The system architecture of CHASS and (b) decentralized communication in CHASS.

4.2.2. Decentralized Communication

In CHASS, the agent's communication is done over the XMPP (eXtensible Messaging and Presence Protocol), an open protocol for instant messaging that has been widely used in the industry (e.g., WhatsApp, Google Talk). In addition, XMPP uses a presence notification mechanism [67] that any entity may enact by providing a list of other entities as contacts and requesting to be notified when any contact changes their state.

XMPP supports a decentralized server architecture (Figure 4b) that supports agents and humans in directly communicating without a centralized authority. In addition, this decentralized architecture allows agents to be independent of the device's IP address where they are running. This feature makes a difference compared with many other MAS that rely on IP addresses to send and receive messages. In addition, agents are identified by the XMPP server where they are registered, not by the device where they are running; therefore, agents can migrate from one device to another transparently. Security is another crucial issue for MAS platforms deployed in the real world. XMPP protocol also provides security at different levels, such as certificates and Transport Layer Security (TLS), to encrypt communications and sign messages to ensure they are sent and received by reliable endpoints.

In CHASS, there are three types of interactions: agent to agent, agent to human, and human to human. All interactions are done through the XMPP protocol. The communication between agents is designed based on the FIPA Agent Communication Language Specifications (FIPA ACL) [68]. Human–agent interaction is performed in natural language. Human-to-human communication is also important because CHASS aims to establish a strong human relationship. In CHASS, humans can directly communicate with each other via mobile chat App, similar to human–agent communication.

collected and analyzed. For each simulation, the results are preliminarily evaluated and stored for later analysis.

3.4. Reflection and Formalization of Learning

Besides contributing to an innovative design artifact, this study contributes to service system design knowledge and evaluation methods. We synthesize the design knowledge through the process of designing and building the service system to solve a community problem. Furthermore, through intentional intervention and evaluation using multi-agent simulation, we can better understand under what circumstances the negotiation process will perform better. From then, a new requirement for the service system emerges. For example, by understanding the interaction mechanism of demand flexibility and the negotiation process on resource allocation performance, we know in which situation the system needs to provide incentives to encourage users to accept negotiation. Since then, the system requirements can be revised to develop the platform's next version.

In addition, we use regression analysis and a t-test to answer the research question: *How does a multiagent-enabled negotiation mechanism influence the service exchange?* The regression analysis results will shed light on the influencing mechanism of negotiation on the "resource allocation" and "order fulfillment" performance under the moderation of supply/demand patterns and the degree of customer demand flexibility. This step creates a clear understanding of the designed service system and generalizes the research outcomes.

4. Cooperative Human–Agent Service System (CHASS)

4.1. System Design Principle

A Cooperative Human–Agent Service System (CHASS) was designed based on three design principles: (1) efficient resource allocation, (2) strengthening actors' relationships in the A2A network, and (3) ensuring technical and economic sustainability.

The first and second design principles are the functional requirements to overcome the limitations of the current AFN forms. From the S-DL perspective, CHASS plays a role as a digital resource for integrating other resources through allocation, collaboration, and negotiation mechanisms. In addition, CHASS is designed to strengthen human relationships by giving human autonomy to select partners for service exchange. This is necessary to create a strong relationship between customers and producers and contribute to urban–rural sustainability.

The third design principle is a requirement to ensure the service system can maintain its capacity to sustain itself. A service system aiming to achieve sustainability goals needs to achieve economic and technical sustainability. To be technologically sustained, the service platform must be completely open, decentralized, and evolved based on community resources. In addition, the system platform must generate economic value higher than costs in terms of economic sustainability. Decentralized systems can contribute to economic sustainability since collectively supporting and contributing to the system operation could share the centralized operation and maintenance costs. This principle can be realized based on the following two requirements: (1) *distributed environment*, agents can operate anywhere on the public Internet and are flexibly deployable in differently resourced devices; (2) *decentralized control*, agents and humans can directly communicate for service exchange without a centralized authority.

4.2. System Architecture

4.2.1. Distributed Environment

To achieve the technical sustainability goal, CHASS is designed to be an open system deployed in a distributed environment where agents can be deployed on any device with an Internet connection. A distributed system will bring the advantages of data privacy, user autonomy, system scalability, and stability. However, the economic benefits of a distributed system are generally unclear and controversial. A distributed system has no centralized operating and maintenance costs but generates other hard-to-estimate costs:

AFNs [60]. This study develops MAS to work as a decentralized service value co-creation platform for sustainability.

3. Research Method

This study adopted the Design Science Research (DSR) method in information systems [61]. The DSR method focuses on the "design" process for building and evaluating the IT artifacts to solve problems. In design science, knowledge of the problem domain and its solution is achieved through the building and application of the designed artifact. Following the guidelines for design science in information systems research proposed by Hevner, March, Park and Ram [61], this study was conducted in four stages: (1) Problem formulation, (2) Design and building, (3) Design and evaluation, and (4) Reflection and formalization of learning.

3.1. Problem Formulation

The research problem is formed based on the author's experience, observation, and interview when participating in "university-community" projects in Taiwan, combined with a careful review of the limitations of the "regional revitalization" projects in Japan and Taiwan and a thorough review of AFN literature and other relevant studies. This stage follows the "problem relevance" guideline of the DSR method: the objective of design-science research is to develop technology-based solutions to important and relevant community problems [61].

3.2. Design and Building

This stage follows the guideline "design as an artifact" of the DSR method: design-science research must produce a viable artifact in the form of a construct, a model, a method, or an instantiation. We developed a MAS to solve the community problem.

In the design step, we combine the Prometheus method [62] and the Behavior-Oriented Design (BOD) method [63] to develop intelligent agents. The Prometheus method consists of three phases: (1) system specification, (2) architectural design, and (3) detailed design. We follow the first two phases of the Prometheus method: system specification focuses on identifying the basic functionalities of the system and architectural design to determine which agents the system will contain and how they will interact. We then design the agent in detail based on the BOD approach. The BOD is a development method for designing a complex agent, an agent that can function naturally on its own [63]. The BOD approach helps decompose the complex agent into simple behavior, so we can rapidly develop system prototyping using MAS middleware.

Based on the agent behavior design, we use SPADE [52], a middleware for multi-agent systems, to build the platform. SPADE supports five behavior types: cyclic, one-shot, periodic, time-out, and finite state machine, which can support the development of rapid system prototyping.

3.3. Design and Evaluation

This stage follows the "design evaluation" and "design as a search process" guidelines of the DSR method. The "design" and "evaluation" activities are integrated into a cyclic process to discover an effective solution. We use the multi-agent simulation method to conduct an intervention and evaluation. The intervention can lead to both "intended" and "unintended" outcomes. These "unintended" outcomes are essential factors for reshaping the design process.

We built a simulation by integrating the ABM with MAS. First, we designed and built an ABM using the Mesa framework [64] to model the real-world environment. Next, the ABM is set up to generate data similar to the data created by human users during interaction with the designed MAS. Then, we perform the intervention by setting different simulation parameters (environment, resources, rules, and decision model of simulated agent) in ABM to generate input data for the MAS, and then the output data of MAS is emerge [52]. Although MAS has been studied for many years, the progression in real applications in which agents can interact and assist humans in daily life has not yet reached the expected levels. Integrating humans and intelligent agents in the same system will be one key challenge in the next generation of MAS. Therefore, the next generation of MAS technology needs to support the development of applications wherein agents and humans can jointly provide services to other humans or agents in a "human–agent society." [53].

Human–agent societies can be developed based on the next generation of MAS that supports a natural interface for interaction between humans and agents. At the agent level, humans are integrated into the system in such a way that they appear as agents to other agents. While at the human level, the human can interact with agents using natural language. In addition, transparently communicating humans with agents will be vital in developing fully open systems wherein entities (humans, agents, or third-party elements) can dynamically enter or exit the system transparently [52]. This open system feature has traditionally been a challenge to be realized for real-world applications. However, it has become possible based on the development of natural language processing technology that allows human–agent interaction through natural language combined with the availability of an appropriate communication protocol and infrastructure.

2.7. Previous Related Studies:

This section will present three recent research directions related to this research, including the research direction of demand flexibility and MAS in the energy field, the human-in-the-loop in MAS, and the service value co-creation digital platform for sustainability.

2.7.1. Demand Flexibility and MAS for Resource Allocation Optimization

In the energy field, demand flexibility is the capacity to shift electricity consumption over time or to switch to renewable energy such as solar power and wind power locally to obtain economic benefits and achieve sustainable production and consumption goals. The research stream on MAS to solve the energy optimization problem has also been interested by many researchers and practitioners in recent years [54]. Under the MAS approach, each family will install an intelligent device acting as an autonomous agent to communicate, coordinate, and cooperate with other agents to reach demand flexibility [55]. In this study, we bring the concept of "demand flexibility" from the energy sector to the food sector and develop a MAS to achieve food-demand flexibility.

2.7.2. Human-in-the-Loop in MAS

The difference between MAS in the energy sector and the food sector is the involvement of a human actor. Each individual has a different food preference, which also changes over time. Therefore, the MAS in the food sector must be designed to allow humans to collaborate with the agent in the food choice decision-making process. Recent achievements in natural language processing have allowed the design of human–machine interaction systems through natural language. Some research directions related to the human-in-the-hoop stream can be mentioned, such as improving collaboration between humans and machines [56] and the interaction between humans and agents in the context of a smart city [57].

2.7.3. Service Value Co-Creation in a Digital Platform for Sustainability

A digital platform can play the role of an operand resource that can help hold together diverse actors and enable collaboration in the ecosystem. From the S-DL perspective, the service platform comprises tangible and intangible components that facilitate the interaction of actors and resources, leveraging resource liquefaction and enhancing resource density [58]. Two types of service value co-creation contribute to the sustainability mentioned in recent studies: second-hand trading platforms that enable sustainable consumption [59] and CSA digital platforms that support collaboration between members in the CSA model in to the intersection between MAS and simulation, which is separated into two approaches: (1) *Simulation for MAS* and (2) *MAS for Simulation*.

The first approach, *Simulation for MAS*, refers to projects wherein computer simulation is used to design, experiment, study, and run a MAS architecture. Simulation is generally recognized as one of the best design support technologies when designing a complex, dynamic, and stochastic system. This approach is similar to the software-in-the-loop approach in the software development field. The simulation method allows developers to experiment with MAS in a controlled and cost-effective manner, using simulation-run contexts instead of the actual run. In addition, the developers can gain extensive empirical experience with the essential issues in designing distributed problem-solving systems through the simulation process. Following this approach, the self-organizing MAS will be developed independently of the simulation tools.

The second approach, *MAS for Simulation*, is related to simulation experiments that use MAS as a modeling paradigm to build artificial laboratories. This approach is well-known as ABM. An agent-based simulation is a bottom-up approach wherein humans could explicitly define a simulated agent's decision processes at the micro-level in a multi-agent simulation model. Structures emerge at the macro level due to the agents' actions and interactions with other agents and the environment. The ABM helps us to understand how real systems' dynamics arises from individuals' characteristics and environments. Furthermore, it allows modeling a heterogeneous population in which each actor can have individual motivations and incentives while at the same time representing groups and group interactions.

2.5.3. Agents Negotiation

In MAS, the negotiation mechanism allows agents to negotiate to reach an optimal solution despite this lack of the complete knowledge of the environment [51]. The primary purpose of the negotiation algorithm is to find an optimal solution to a negotiation problem. The negotiation process is triggered by an autonomous coordinator agent, as shown in Figure 3. The coordinator agent initiates the negotiation event and manages the whole negotiation process. Besides the coordinator agent, there are several or more collaborating agents. This collaborating agent is named as the assistant agent in this study because it assists human users. The assistant agent is a semi-autonomous agent who can make a decision on behalf of human users. Assistant agents participate in the negotiation process to maximize utility based on their principals' preferences. Meanwhile, the coordinator agent will operate the negotiation process to maximize resource allocation. The negotiation process ends when the maximum resource allocation is reached.

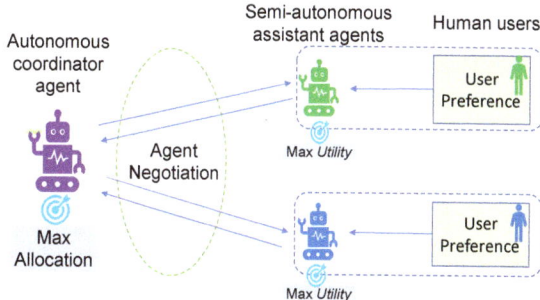

Figure 3. The MAS negotiation mechanism.

2.6. *The Next MAS Generation for Human–Agent Societies*

MAS technology allows the development of autonomous agents that are naturally designed to communicate with each other. This communication enables complex interactions, from which higher-level social activities such as cooperation or collaboration may

This section will describe a Multi-Agent System (MAS), an Agent-Based Model (ABM), multi-agent simulation, and agent negotiation.

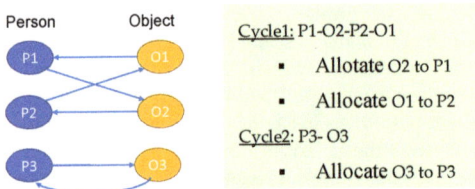

Figure 1. A simple illustration of the TTC algorithm.

2.5.1. Multi-Agent System (MAS) and Agent-Based Model (ABM)

A Multi-Agent System (MAS), as shown in Figure 2a, is a self-organized system composed of multiple agents interacting to reach goals that are difficult or impossible for an individual agent to achieve. MAS is mainly studied in the field of computer engineering to solve practical or engineering problems, and as a distributed system, agents in MAS can deploy and operate in different physical devices. A significant milestone in developing multi-agent systems is the "Distributed Artificial Intelligence" workshop, held at MIT in June 1980 [47]. Then this field gained widespread recognition in the mid-1990s and has grown enormously since then.

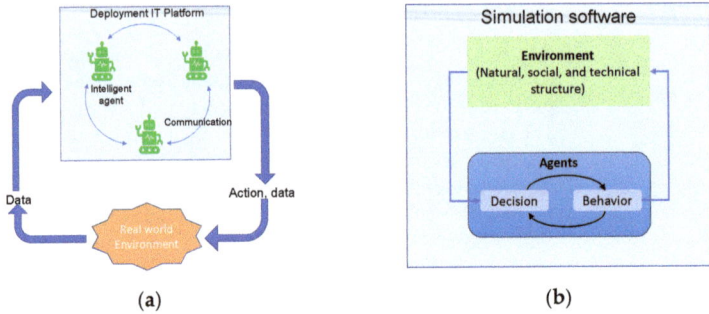

Figure 2. (**a**) A Multi-agent system, (**b**) an Agent-based model.

Although there is considerable overlap with the MAS, the goal of an ABM is different. The ABM (Figure 2b) is a computational model for simulating the actions and interactions of autonomous agents to understand a system's behavior and what governs its outcomes. ABM helps to understand collective behavior's effects by representing the rules governing agent decisions and the influence of these decisions in a real-world environment. ABM components, including agents and environment (natural, social, and technical structure), are simulated by computer software [48]. The outcome of the agent decision-making process can be directly affected by past individual behavior and the behavior of other agents. In addition, the agent's decision-making can be influenced by the environment. The ABM is used in many scientific domains, such as biology, medicine and health, ecology, and social science [49]. In summary, the ABM aims to explore insight into the agent and system behavior through simulation, while MAS is an IT system that was developed to solve practical problems.

2.5.2. Multi-Agent Simulation

The simulation is considered a computational tool to achieve two major goals: understanding a real system and developing a real operational system. According to the survey of Michel et al. [50], a large number of research works and software applications belong and value co-creation, through two concepts: resource liquefaction and resource density. Resource liquefaction refers to the possibility of decoupling information from its physical form to share it with others and become more valuable. The resource density is the level at which resources are quickly mobilized for a time/space/actor. Maximum density occurs when the best combination of resources is mobilized for a particular situation [34].

2.3. Food Preferences, Food Choice, and Demand Flexibility

Consumer preferences are the subjective (individual) tastes of various bundles of goods. It can be considered common knowledge that people have different food preferences. Some people like a variety of foods, while others may be picky eaters. Biological, psychological, and sociocultural factors influence food preferences [35]. The process of connecting food preferences and choices is not straightforward. According to Wadolowska, et al. [36], food preferences interact with different food choice factors (e.g., advertising, functional value, health, and price) and consumer socio-demographics (e.g., age, economic condition, education, gender). It might seem that we often make food choices based on intuitive thinking that are not consciously monitored, resulting in effortless and fast decisions [37].

Demand flexibility refers to the consumer demand that can be reduced, increased, or shifted to substitute products within a specific time. Demand flexibility is an essential concept in the energy field in the context of climate change because renewable energy is only generated for a particular time [38]. Under the S-DL perspective, the consumer can play a role as a value co-creator if they are flexible enough to adjust their consumption for the common good between themselves and service providers. "Demand flexibility" in this study refers to customers' flexibility to switch from a product to another substitute product in AFNs. The "food choice" factors (e.g., advertising or health) mentioned above are similar for different products within the same AFNs. Therefore, food preferences are the main factor affecting product switching acceptance. Demand flexibility can be viewed as a resource in a food system because it helps reduce food storage and spoilage costs.

2.4. Priority-Based Resource Allocation Algorithm

The priority-based resource allocation is a commonly observed problem in real-life. In this problem, the resources are allocated based on the participants' preferences and priorities. This section will review the top trading cycles (TTC), initially proposed by Shapley and Scarf [39], a popular algorithm to deal with the priority-based allocation problem. TTC is a unique core matching, Pareto efficiency, strategy-proof, and individually rational algorithm [40].

In the TTC algorithm, each person or object is presented by a node in a directed graph (Note: The graph in this context is made up of vertices (nodes), which are connected by edges (links) in graph theory). A person node points to its most preferred object node, and an object node points to its highest-priority person node, as shown in Figure 1. The allocation process starts with determining cycles in the graph. There is at least one cycle in the graph. Then, the nodes belonging to a cycle are allocated and removed from the graph. Finally, the same procedure is applied to reduce the market participant (nodes in the graph). If the object has multi-units, a counter is assigned to each object to denote available units at each allocation step. Many studies have developed TTC-based mechanisms to solve practical problems such as the school choice problem [41], kidney allocation [42], house allocation [43], landing slots assignment among flights [44], and tuition and worker exchanges [45].

2.5. Agent Systems

There is no strict definition of "agent" due to the rapid growth of the diversity and functionality of agents in different disciplines. In general, an agent can be defined as an entity with two important capabilities: (1) the capability to act with a certain degree of autonomy and (2) the capability to interact with other agents to engage in analogs of the kind of human social activity: cooperation, coordination, negotiation, and the like [46].

the physical distance and supply chain, but there are still many limitations in reducing the information distance.

2.1.3. Community Supported Agriculture (CSA) Model

The CSA is probably the best model to achieve the "strong relationship" goal among the many forms of AFNs. Initially, the CSA model consists of a community of individuals who pledge support to a farm operation where the growers and consumers provide mutual support, sharing the risks and benefits of food production [26]. The core value of the traditional CSA is the "support" and "cooperation" of the community. However, over time, the definition of CSA has changed significantly, and most CSA business models today operate in a very different way from the early CSA model. CSA models have shifted from emphasizing the farmer (community supports farmers) to focusing on the customer (how CSA works better for customers) [27].

Although the modern CSA models are also very diverse and different, product quality commitment and a close distance between customers and producers are standard features. However, the modern CSA models have gradually lost the original feature: community cooperation. That is a shift from the long-term commitment (e.g., annual subscription) to a shorter commitment (e.g., weekly subscription) and the emergence of the no-commitment model, the "pay-as-you-go" CSA [28]. The positive in the evolution of CSA models is that it has reached more customers, bringing more value to customers and producers. However, the "strong relationship" goal between the consumer and the producer has been traded off. In the modern CSA models, customers view the CSA as an organization from which they can buy products rather than cooperate with the producer.

2.1.4. Alternative Food Networks and Urban–Rural Linkage

In the ecosystem view based on "rural–urban linkage", food provision is an essential service in the relationship between urban and rural areas [29]. Therefore, strengthening food service is considered the most effective solution among existing solutions to strengthen rural–urban linkage. Over the last century, the food supply chain has become more industrialized and globalized, and these significant changes directly impact the urban–rural relationship. As a result, urban and rural areas have become less interdependent on food service systems. To react against the standardization, globalization, and unethical nature of the industrial food service system, "Alternative Food Networks" (AFNs) emerged. Therefore, developing AFNs is an approach to strengthen the linkage between urban and surrounding rural areas [30]. Furthermore, AFNs also play a crucial role in food security for urban and rural populations.

2.2. Service-Dominant Logic (S-DL)

The S-DL is a research stream that has emanated over the last 20 years from a concern about the traditional understanding of service(s). The S-DL identifies service –the process of using one's resources for the benefit of another actor—rather than goods as the fundamental basis of economic (and social) exchange [7]. In S-DL, the role of resources is central to the process of value creation, which occurs 'when a potential resource is turned into a specific benefit [8]. Moreover, the S-DL emphasizes the role of operant (intangible) resources that are capable of acting on operand (tangible) resources and even other operant resources to create value [8]. Technology is both an operand resource (e.g., system platform) and an operant resource, a combination of practices, processes, and symbols that fulfill the human purpose [31].

This study approaches the relationship between customers and producers in AFNs under the S-DL perspective: customers as a co-production and co-creation value rather than the receiver of value [32]. In S-DL, all participants with different roles (e.g., producers, customers) are viewed as actors in networks of other actors (A2A network) and co-creating value through resource integration and service provision [33]. The S-DL emphasizes information technology, which is an essential resource in the process of resource integration

2.1.1. The Promise of AFNs on Sustainability

The AFN initiative promises to contribute to all economic, environmental, and social sustainability aspects. In the *economic aspect*, AFNs improve producers' income by adding value through differentiated production methods [10], and social embeddedness enables the customer to accept a higher price [11]. Arrangements such as CSA are built on sharing the economic risk between producers and consumers [12], while the key ideas of another arrangement (e.g., producer cooperatives) create more negotiating power and resources for producers, thus better market possibilities and income. The reduction of supply chain distance allows a higher share of value to be captured by the producer [13]. Selling directly through the market is an excellent way for some small producers to get to the market [14]. Furthermore, the reduced physical distance in AFNs means more money is spent on local food and contributes more to the local economy.

In the *environmental aspect*, environmentally benign production choices can positively contribute to sustainability [15]. The reduced physical distance in AFNs reduces food transportation distances, equaling less fuel use and emissions to the air [16]. In the *social aspect*, food quality and production contribute to consumer health. "Natural" foods are believed to be healthier than highly processed foods. The reduced physical distance keeps food fresher and retains more nutrients [17]. Environmentally benign production methods can contribute to producer and consumer health and safety. Organic farming, for example, restricts the use of chemicals, thus addressing product and producer safety, health impacts, and biodiversity. Local and diverse production is considered critical for food security [16,18,19] and positively affects food culture. Traditional production methods can contribute to the preservation of traditional food cultures and diversity [16].

AFNs may also create indirect sustainability impacts related to learning and participation. For example, the reduced informational distance contributes to increasing participants' learning about and awareness of sustainability-related issues in the food system. Increased learning and awareness, in turn, are believed to lead to more sustainable practices [20,21]. In addition, these indirect impacts can reinforce participant choices about preferred production methods, the form and length of food supply chains, and governance arrangements [2].

2.1.2. Limitations of AFNs

Although the AFN initiative contributes much to sustainability, it also faces criticism. In terms of *economic aspect*, the reduced value chain distance raises the question of how value is being redistributed and what the net benefit to producers is. Many studies suggest that direct selling to consumers may require more resources, time, and energy from producers, and the net benefit may not live up to the theory [3]. For example, from an empirical study on the farmer's market, James [22] raised the question: Have farmers received enough income from farmers' markets? If there is a lack of customers, farmers may suffer losses, including financial loss and an accompanying loss of working time on the farm. Therefore, the farmers could not economically sustain attendance at the market, and farmers' markets could not provide a viable alternative for small-scale producers.

In terms of the *environment aspect*, reduced "food miles" may not be as significant as reducing transport-related emissions, and small-scale food distribution may be inefficient in the means of transport [23]. Transportation also generally causes only a tiny part of the life-cycle greenhouse gas emissions of food [24,25]. In terms of *social aspect*, fresher and more nutritious food due to shorter physical distance has been challenged by considering the time, not just distance in transport [17]. "Value-added" products with a higher price may benefit the producer but be out of the reach of lower-income consumers [4].

While AFNs represent a broad group of alternative agricultural relationships and practices, an important goal is to establish a "strong relationship" and trust between consumers and producers. However, the practical AFN forms nowadays do not establish "strong relationship" as expected due to the lack of regular interaction between producer and consumer. In general, most AFN models in practice can achieve the goal of reducing probably not technically sustainable. With the recent rise of decentralized Web 3.0 [6], it is evident that alternative, decentralized systems can be technologically and economically sustained. From a Service-Dominant Logic (S-DL) perspective, value is co-created by involved actors through service exchange; that is, one actor's service exchanges for other one's service [7,8]. Therefore, a decentralized information system can become an essential digital service for resource integration and value co-creation, on which consumers can play a role in value co-creation through information sharing and collaborative decision-making.

The objective of the study is to develop a decentralized service system as an innovative IT resource to help overcome the limitations of the AFN models and achieve technical sustainability. To achieve this goal, in this study, we propose a decentralized Cooperative Human-Agent Service System (CHASS), which supports service exchange in which the human actor has the agency to control and is assisted by an intelligent agent. CHASS is designed to achieve two goals: *(1) to improve food resource allocation performance through an multiagent-enabled negotiation mechanism* and *(2) to strengthen human relationships through service exchange*. Through designing, building, and evaluating the CHASS, this study will answer the research question *"How does a multiagent-enabled negotiation mechanism influence the service exchange under the moderation of different supply-demand patterns and customer's collaborative decision-making."*

This study was conducted in the context of Taiwan, which is affected by urbanization and rural decline. Since the late 2000s, the Taiwan government has been promoting many "rural revitalization" programs in response to this problem. However, although the impact of these government funding projects has claimed some success, some projects are no longer effective after the government funding ends. Moreover, taking a lesson from severe rural decline and urban–rural imbalance in Japan, using only financial resources seems insufficient to prevent rural decline and promote urban and rural linkage. Developing AFNs is an approach to strengthen the linkage between urban and surrounding rural areas and contribute to rural sustainability. This motivates this research to develop CHASS to contribute to the creation of an economically sustainable AFN model, which promises to create more value for rural areas and strengthen urban–rural linkages in Taiwan. Besides the contribution to the design artifact, design knowledge, and evaluation methods, this study has developed CHASS as a practical service system that can be used for performing actor-to-actor communication and coordination to achieve the sustainability of the service ecosystems. With the spirit of "engaged scholarship", CHASS will be further developed to contribute to sustainability in various domains, such as cooperatives, the circular economy, and community of practice in knowledge sharing and collaboration.

2. Literature Review

2.1. Alternative Food Networks (AFNs)

The term "Alternative Food Networks" (AFNs) has emerged both in practice and in academic works since the 1990s as a reaction against the standardization, globalization, and unethical nature of the "conventional food system" [1]. AFNs promote food consumption closer to the producer and change consumer culture and behavior. The three core characteristics of AFNs are: (1) the requirement for products and production, (2) the closer distance between producers and consumers, and (3) new forms of food market governance [2]. The products in AFNs are often characterized as fresh, natural, organic, quality, and "slow", while the production is described as environmentally benign using traditional production methods [9]. The distance between producers and consumers is measured in three dimensions: physical distance, supply chain distance (the number of intermediaries), and informational distance (the availability of information in the network). AFNs also generate new forms of food markets such as Community Supported Agriculture (CSA), farmer market, and consumer and producer cooperatives.

Article

The Development of a Service System for Facilitating Food Resource Allocation and Service Exchange

Viet-Cuong Trieu and Fu-Ren Lin *

Institute of Service Science, National Tsing Hua University, Hsinchu 30013, Taiwan
* Correspondence: frlin@iss.nthu.edu.tw

Abstract: To address the current limitation of Alternative Food Networks (AFNs) in tackling urban–rural sustainability issues, this study proposes a Cooperative Human-Agent Service System (CHASS) by leveraging the decentralized communication and coordination capability of a multi-agent system. The unique feature of CHASS is the collaboration between humans and agents for real-world deployment. From the perspective of Service-Dominant Logic (S-DL), value is co-created by involved actors through service exchange; that is, one actor's service exchanges for other one's service. With S-DL, technology is treated as an essential actant for resource integration, and the customer is a value co-creator. In this study, we propose a two-phase top trading cycle (TTC) negotiation mechanism to facilitate food resource allocation and service exchange. An agent-based model is developed to simulate the real-world environment and is integrated with CHASS to form a multi-agent simulation for system evaluation. In addition, to generalize the research outcomes, we use regression analysis to clarify the interaction mechanism between the algorithms applied by the platform and human decisions under the moderation of environmental factors. The results show the effectiveness of TTC-Negotiation mechanism to support resource allocation between customers and providers on CHASS. It shows the applicability of CHASS to the cooperative AFNs model.

Keywords: service system design; value co-creation; food resource allocation; cooperative food systems; alternative food networks; multi-agent system; multi-agent simulation; agent-based model; Service-Dominant Logic (S-DL)

1. Introduction

The Conventional Food System (CFS) has become industrialized and globalized, significantly impacting food and nutrition security. In reaction to the industrialization and globalization of the CFS, the Alternative Food Networks (AFNs) initiative emerged in the 1990s. AFNs seek to diversify and transform modern food provision by connecting ethical producers and consumers in more local, direct ways [1] and creating a trusting relationship in the food network. Although the AFN initiative aims to contribute to sustainability, there are also many criticisms regarding its unsustainability [2]. The most critical criticism concerns economic sustainability. For example, while removing intermediaries in the supply chain promises to redistribute more value to producers, selling directly to customers on a small scale may require more resources from producers, and the net benefit may not live up to the theory [3]. In addition, "value-added" products with a higher price may benefit the producer but be out of the reach of lower-income customers [4]. To increase economic efficiency, some AFNs have evolved towards forming an intermediary organization and using centralized digital platforms for serving more customers in busy modern life. However, such models will somewhat lose an essential feature of AFNs, which is the establishment of "strong relationship" between customers and producers.

Today's digital services are highly centralized. The dominant client–server architecture favors the centralized ownership of servers [5], causing a lack of interoperability, which leads to centralizing economic control and data. Furthermore, a centralized IT platform is

11. Ding, R.; Zhang, T.; Yin, J.; Zhang, Y.L.; Li, T.F. Study on the characteristics and toughness of the Urban Network structure of the New Land-Sea Corridor in West China. *J. Beijing Norm. Univ.* **2021**, *8*, 794–802. [CrossRef]
12. Yang, Z.K.; Hua, Y.X.; Cao, Y.B.; Zhao, X.K.; Chen, M.J. Network Patterns of Zhongyuan Urban Agglomeration in China Based on Baidu Migration Data. *ISPRS Int. J. Geo-Inf.* **2022**, *11*, 62. [CrossRef]
13. Ye, S.S.; Cao, M.M.; Hu, S. Study on the evolution of economic connection network structure of urban agglomeration in Guanzhong Plain and its impact on economic growth. *ARID Land Geogr.* **2022**, *45*, 277–286.
14. Guo, J.K.; Wang, Y.; Wang, Y.; Gao, H.H.; Li, F.X. Research on urban connection network structure in Northeast China based on "High-Speed Rail +" network. *Geogr. Geo-Inf. Sci.* **2021**, *37*, 51–56. [CrossRef]
15. Lin, Q.W.; Xiang, M.Y.; Zhang, L.; Yao, J.J.; Wei, C.; Ye, S.; Shao, H.M. Research on Urban Spatial Connection and Network Structure of Urban Agglomeration in Yangtze River Delta-Based on the Perspective of Information Flow. *Int. J. Environ. Res. Public Health* **2021**, *18*, 288. [CrossRef]
16. Li, H.L.; Dai, H.W. Comparison of dynamic changes of economic ties between Beijing Tianjin Hebei and Yangtze River Delta Urban Agglomeration—From the perspective of urban flow intensity. *Econ. Manag.* **2016**, *30*, 9–16.
17. Ren, H.; Li, Z.K. Influencing factors and spatial effects of economic growth in China's three major urban agglomerations. *Urban Issues* **2019**, *10*, 63–68. [CrossRef]
18. Tang, Z.Z.; Zhang, Z.X.; Zuo, L.J.; Wang, X.; Hu, S.G.; Zhu, Z.J. Spatial Econometric Analysis of the Relationship between Urban Land and Regional Economic Development in the Beijing–Tianjin–Hebei Coordinated Development Region. *Sustainability* **2020**, *12*, 8451. [CrossRef]
19. Fu, Y.; Zhong, Y.X.; Feng, X.H. Evolution of regional structure in the Economic Belt of the Yangtze River. *World Reg. Stud.* **2018**, *27*, 65–75. [CrossRef]
20. Wu, C.Y.; Huang, X.J.; Chen, B.W.; Li, J.B.; Xu, J. Spatial pattern of economic ties and trend of economic integration in the Yangtze River Economic Belt. *Econ. Geogr.* **2017**, *37*, 71–78. [CrossRef]
21. Wang, J.T.; Liu, H.B.; Peng, D.; Lv, Q.; Sun, Y.; Huang, H.; Liu, H. The County-Scale Economic Spatial Pattern and Influencing Factors of Seven Urban Agglomerations in the Yellow River Basin—A Study Based on the Integrated Nighttime Light Data. *Sustainability* **2021**, *13*, 4220. [CrossRef]
22. Zhong, Z.Q.; Peng, B.H.; Xu, L.; Andrews, A.; Elahi, E. Analysis of regional energy economic efficiency and its influencing factors: A case study of Yangtze river urban agglomeration. *Sustain. Energy Technol. Assess.* **2020**, *41*, 100784. [CrossRef]
23. Wei, X.Y.; Hu, Q.G.; Shen, W.T.; Ma, J. Influence of the Evolution of Marine Industry Structure on the Green Total Factor Productivity of Marine Economy. *Water* **2021**, *13*, 1108. [CrossRef]
24. Chen, X.D.; Wang, T.; Zheng, X.; Han, F.; Yang, Z.P. The Structure and Evolution of the Tourism Economic Network of the Tibetan Plateau and Its Driving Factors. *Land* **2022**, *11*, 241. [CrossRef]
25. Wang, J.F.; Xu, C.D. Geographic detector: Principle and prospect. *Acta Geogr. Sin.* **2017**, *72*, 19. [CrossRef]

play to the strategic supporting role of the Yangtze River Economic Belt and expand new space for development. Increase the economic ties between the northeastern and southwestern cities of the Chengdu-Chongqing urban agglomeration and Chengdu and Chongqing. At the same time, attention should be paid to the economic collapse of the central part of the Chengdu-Chongqing urban agglomeration to prevent severe regional differences in development.

(2) Enhance the radiation effects of the two core cities of Chengdu and Chongqing. Strengthen the important functions of production and employment, business services, education and health, and transportation hubs in the Chengdu-Chongqing urban agglomeration. Give full play to the core driving ability of Chengdu and speed up the process of urbanization in surrounding cities such as Deyang, Ya'an, Meishan, and Ziyang. Strengthen the strategic support of the western development of Chongqing Metropolis and the carrier function of the central hub in the west part of the Yangtze River Economic Belt. Take the central urban area of Chongqing as the core, link the urban belt along the river and the adjacent cities in Sichuan, and promote regional coordinated development.

(3) Pay attention to the role of significant driving factors. Improve the core competitiveness of industrial enterprises, mobilize the enthusiasm of private investment, enhance the service capabilities of primary health care institutions, and speed up the construction of road transport infrastructure. Strengthen the supporting role of production, commerce, health, and transportation networks for the economic development of the Chengdu-Chongqing urban agglomeration.

Author Contributions: Conceptualization, R.D.; methodology, R.D. and J.F.; validation, J.F., Y.Z. and T.Z. (Tao Zhou); formal analysis, J.F. and T.Z. (Tao Zhou); investigation, J.F.; resources, J.Y., T.Z. (Ting Zhang) and Y.D.; data curation, L.D.; writing—original draft preparation, R.D. and J.F.; writing—review and editing, R.D.; visualization, R.D. and J.F. All authors have read and agreed to the published version of the manuscript.

Funding: This work was supported by the National Natural Science Foundation of China (No. 72001053).

Data Availability Statement: The data presented in this study are available on request from the corresponding author.

Acknowledgments: We thank the editors and the anonymous reviewers for their valuable comments and suggestions.

Conflicts of Interest: The authors declare no conflict of interest.

References

1. Chen, Y.; Miao, Q.; Zhou, Q. Spatiotemporal Differentiation and Driving Force Analysis of the High-Quality Development of Urban Agglomerations along the Yellow River Basin. *Int. J. Environ. Res. Public Health* **2022**, *19*, 2484. [CrossRef] [PubMed]
2. Yu, S.; Kim, D. Changes in Regional Economic Resilience after the 2008 Global Economic Crisis: The Case of Korea. *Sustainability* **2021**, *13*, 11392. [CrossRef]
3. Hua, X.Y.; Lv, H.P.; Jin, X.R. Research on High-Quality Development Efficiency and Total Factor Productivity of Regional Economies in China. *Sustainability* **2021**, *13*, 8287. [CrossRef]
4. Li, Y.; Shao, H.; Jiang, N.; Shi, G.; Cheng, X. The Evolution of the Urban Spatial Pattern in the Yangtze River Economic Belt: Based on Multi-Source Remote Sensing Data. *Sustainability* **2018**, *10*, 2733. [CrossRef]
5. Panzera, D.; Postiglione, P. Measuring the Spatial Dimension of Regional Inequality: An Approach Based on the Gini Correlation Measure. *Soc. Indic. Res.* **2019**, *148*, 379–394. [CrossRef]
6. Panzera, D.; Postiglione, P. The impact of regional inequality on economic growth: A spatial econometric approach. *Reg. Stud.* **2021**, *56*, 687–702. [CrossRef]
7. Zhang, B.; Wang, M.M. How Will the Improvements of Electricity Supply Quality in Poor Regions Reduce the Regional Economic Gaps? A Case Study of China. *Energies* **2021**, *14*, 3456. [CrossRef]
8. Chen, L.; Shen, W. Spatiotemporal differentiation of urban-rural income disparity and its driving force in the Yangtze River Economic Belt during 2000–2017. *PLoS ONE* **2021**, *16*, e0245601. [CrossRef]
9. Zhang, M.; Xiao, H.; Sun, D.Q.; Li, Y. Spatial Differences in and Influences upon the Sustainable Development Level of the Yangtze River Delta Urban Agglomeration in China. *Sustainability* **2018**, *10*, 411. [CrossRef]
10. Lan, F.; Da, H.; Wen, H.; Wang, Y. Spatial Structure Evolution of Urban Agglomerations and Its Driving Factors in Mainland China: From the Monocentric to the Polycentric Dimension. *Sustainability* **2019**, *11*, 610. [CrossRef]

areas is not perfect, and the role of transportation in promoting the economy has not been brought into full play.

In general, the promoting effect of the above four factors on economic development is mainly concentrated in the eastern and western regions of the Chongqing-urban agglomeration. It mainly inhibits the cities in the north and south. The most significant difference in the spatial effect of road freight turnover indicates that the uneven development of the transportation network in the Chengdu-Chongqing urban agglomeration is significant. In the relevant construction affecting economic development, attention should be paid to the supporting role of the transportation network.

6. Conclusions and Recommendations

6.1. Main Conclusions

This paper constructs 14 evaluation index systems based on four subsystems of production and employment, trade and commerce services, education and health, and transportation in 36 cities of the Chengdu-Chongqing urban agglomeration. Using GDP per capita to represent the level of economic development, the evolution characteristics of the economic spatial pattern of the Chengdu-Chongqing urban agglomeration and its influencing factors are explored based on the performance of feedback effects in four time sections from 2005 to 2020, with the help of gravity models, geographic detector, geographically weighted regression, and other methods. The following main conclusions were drawn.

(1) From the evolution of the integrated centrality of Chengdu-Chongqing urban agglomeration, the high-value area of integrated centrality is a spatial pattern dominated by Chengdu and Chongqing central cities, with a significant agglomeration effect. The overall centrality of the Chengdu urban agglomeration is higher than that of the Chongqing urban agglomeration, and the uneven development between regions is still relatively obvious.

(2) The economically developed areas of the Chengdu-Chongqing urban agglomeration are mainly concentrated in Chengdu and Chongqing central cities and their surrounding areas. The economic development level of the neighboring districts and counties in the Chongqing central city is higher than that of the surrounding areas of Chengdu, indicating that the central city of Chongqing has a strong economic drive and significant radiation capacity to the neighboring regions.

(3) In terms of the urban economic linkages volume, the Chengdu urban agglomeration and the Chongqing urban agglomeration account for a significant proportion of the economic linkages, while economic links between other cities are weaker, especially in the central region where the collapse situation is obvious. On the whole, a "dual-core" pattern has been formed, with the central cities of Chengdu and Chongqing as the leading cities.

(4) In terms of the driving factors affecting economic development, the total output value of the secondary industry, total social fixed asset investment, number of beds in health institutions, and road freight turnover have consistently strong explanatory abilities for economic development. The four significant factors mostly promote the economic development of most cities in Chengdu-Chongqing urban agglomeration and inhibit a small number of cities. The promotion effect is mostly concentrated in the eastern and western cities of Chengdu-Chongqing urban agglomeration, and the inhibition effect is mostly concentrated in the southern and northern cities of Chengdu-Chongqing urban agglomeration.

6.2. Recommendations

Based on the above findings, the following recommendations are made to promote the collaborative economic development of the Chengdu-Chongqing urban agglomeration.

(1) Establish an open, competitive, and orderly market system for the city cluster. Break down administrative barriers between the cities in the Chengdu-Chongqing urban agglomeration. Promote the formation of a pattern of complementary resource advantages, rational division of functions, and infrastructure interconnection among cities. Give full

Table 2. Statistical test results.

Year	2005	2010	2015	2020
Model goodness of fit	0.730	0.733	0.795	0.793
Calibration model goodness of fit	0.666	0.651	0.760	0.766
Partial R^2	0.566~0.793	0.617~0.841	0.759~0.792	0.792~0.793
Conditions	14.869~29.993	21.268~29.990	25.982~29.997	23.803~23.829

(1) The total output value of the secondary industry is positively correlated with the dependent variable in all units of analysis except for 2010. During 2005–2020, the positively correlated areas are mainly located in the eastern and western regions of Chengdu-Chongqing urban agglomeration, while the negatively correlated areas are located primarily in the northern and southern regions. The overall regression coefficient shows the characteristics of "high in the east and west, low in the north and south," and the absolute value of the regression coefficient of the positive correlation areas decreases. It shows that the promotion effect of the output value of the secondary industry on economic development decreases, the negative correlation area increases, the absolute value of the regression coefficient increases, and the inhibition effect increases. From the time-space evolution process of the output value of the secondary industry, after 15 years of development, the cities in the east and west of the Chengdu-Chongqing urban agglomeration promote economic development, but the promotion effect is weakened. The output value of the secondary industry in the cities of the north and south is negatively correlated with the dependent variable, and the inhibition effect is strengthened.

(2) The regression coefficients on total social fixed asset investment are much less volatile than the other three variables. The effects of the regression coefficients vary less spatially, with a positive correlation with the dependent variable in 2010 and 2015, a slightly weaker correlation for the east and west regions of Chengdu-Chongqing urban agglomeration, and a slightly stronger correlation for the central north and south regions. In 2005, the center of the high value of the regression coefficient was concentrated in the northeastern parts of Chengdu-Chongqing urban agglomeration, with a greater dependence on the amount of fixed asset investment, resulting in a higher regression coefficient. By 2020, with the increase in total social fixed asset investment, the high-value area of the regression coefficient tends to shift to the west, and the value of the coefficient decreases, but is still positive, reflecting the driving effect of Chengdu on the surrounding cities. The regression coefficient of the cities in the north and south of Chengdu-Chongqing urban agglomeration is negative, indicating that the increase in the amount of fixed asset investment will instead inhibit the economic growth of these areas.

(3) The regression coefficient for the number of beds in health institutions is positive in all units of analysis only in 2010, with a significant suppressive effect on Nanchong and Yibin in 2005 and a positive promotional effect on all other cities. By 2020, the positive values of the regression coefficient are distributed in the eastern and western regions of the Chengdu-Chongqing urban agglomeration, and the negative values are distributed in the northeastern and southwestern axial zones. As the number of beds in health institutions increases, their contribution to the economically backward regions of the eastern part of the Chengdu-Chongqing urban agglomeration is obvious, and their economic contribution to the Chengdu urban agglomeration with Chengdu at its core is gradually becoming significant.

(4) The regression coefficient of road freight turnover fluctuates slightly in the first three years. In 2020, the spatial difference of its effect was significant, and the regression coefficient is around −0.899~0.469, but it is a mainly positive correlation. The positive area is concentrated in the west of Chengdu-Chongqing urban agglomeration and the Chongqing-urban agglomeration, with the central urban area of Chongqing as the core. At the same time, its effect is negative in the cities in the north and south of the Chengdu-Chongqing urban agglomeration. It shows that the transportation infrastructure in these

respectively, indicating that the fitting effect of the model is good. The condition number is greater than 0 and less than 30 in four time periods, indicating that the model has passed the multicollinearity test, the calculation result of the model is reliable, and the result of the factor detector is also reliable. The effects of each variable are spatially non-stationary, but the degree of difference and characteristics is different (Figure 7).

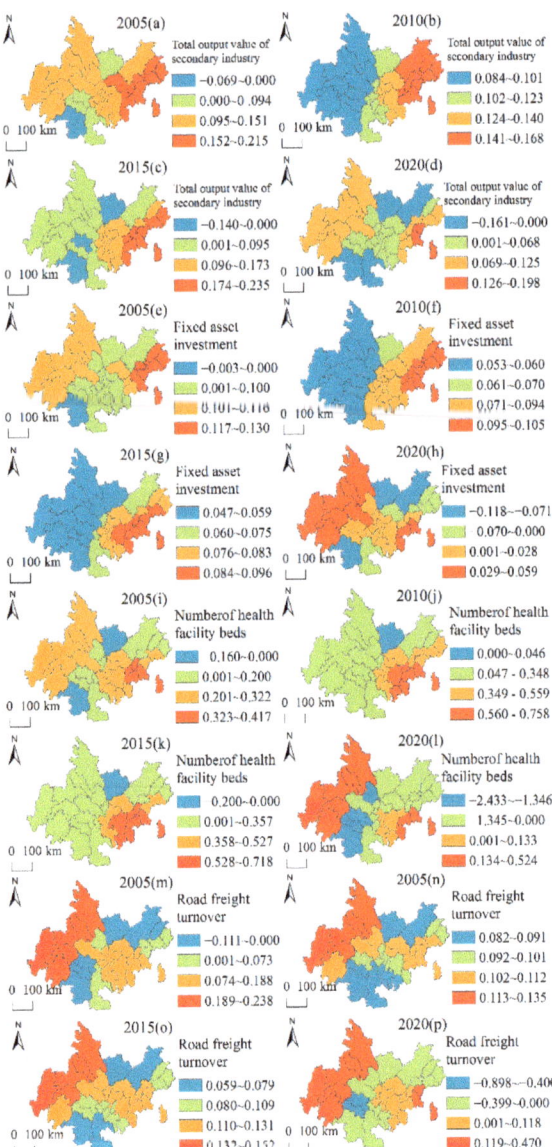

Figure 7. Four-year comparison of regression coefficients for significant impact factors. Pictures (**a–d**) represent the regression coefficient of total output value of secondary industry, (**e–h**) represent the regression coefficient of fixed asset investment, (**i–l**) represent the regression coefficient of number of health facility beds, (**m–p**) represent the regression coefficient of road freight turnover.

closer during this period. Road freight turnover has the most significant explanatory ability for economic development in 2010 and 2015, with q-values of about 0.6992 and 0.7316, respectively. By 2020, education level has become a significant factor affecting economic development. The number of ordinary primary and secondary schools has the strongest explanatory ability among all detection factors, with a q-value of 0.5896.

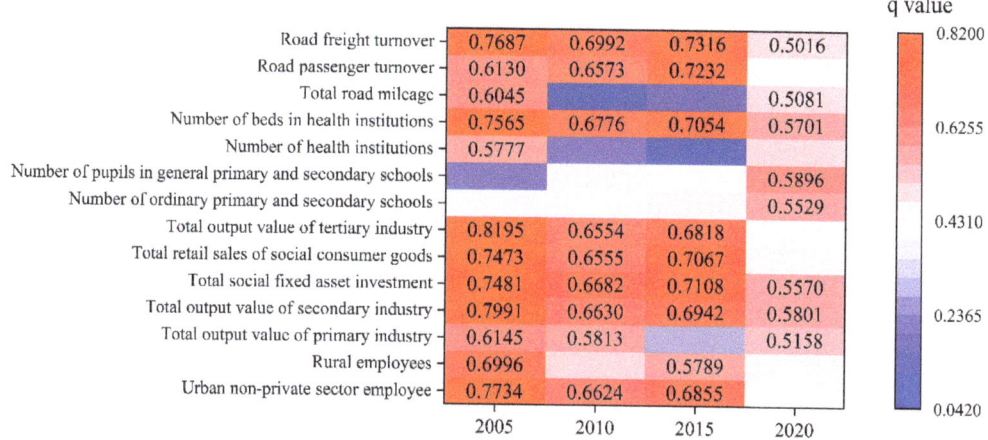

Figure 6. Heatmap of q-values for each factor in different years.

The total output value of the secondary industry, total social fixed asset investment, number of beds in health institutions, and road freight turnover are the indicators with consistently strong explanatory ability for economic development, while the q-values of the other indicators are all less than 0.5 in the period 2005–2020, with relatively unstable explanatory ability.

5.2. Analysis of Spatial Variation in the Role of Influencing Factors

The Moran's I values and statistical test Z values were calculated for 2005, 2010, 2015, and 2020 (as shown in Table 1), separately. Further, 2005 and 2020 Moran's I and Z values passed the 1% statistical test. The Moran's I and Z values for 2010 and 2015 passed the 10% statistical test, indicating the existence of a positive spatial autocorrelation, and the Moran's I values for the four years were in the interval of [0.1192, 0.4198], with apparent clustering effects.

Table 1. Moran's I, Z-value, and p-value test results.

Year	Moran's I	Z-Value	p-Value
2005	0.2825	3.8256	0.0001
2010	0.1192	1.7846	0.0743
2015	0.1210	1.8131	0.0698
2020	0.4198	5.2504	0.0000

According to the analysis of geographical detector results, the factors with q-values greater than 0.5 in the four years are the total output value of the secondary industry, total social fixed asset investment, number of beds in health institutions, and road freight turnover, which have strong and sustainable explanatory ability for the economic development of Chengdu-Chongqing urban agglomeration. Therefore, these four significant influencing factors are selected for GWR local spatial regression analysis to explore the spatial differences of the action direction and intensity of the four significant factors in different research units in the four time periods. The results in Table 2 show that the corrected R^2 of the model is 0.666, 0.651, 0.760, and 0.766 in 2005, 2010, 2015, and 2020

The changes in the pattern of linkages intensity among cities in the Chengdu-Chongqing urban agglomeration from 2005 to 2020 are as follows: (1) The area with the strongest economic interconnection among cities is in the Chengdu urban agglomeration with Chengdu as the core, followed by the area with stronger interconnection among cities in the Chongqing urban agglomeration with the central city of Chongqing as the core, while the linkages intensity among other cities is weaker, especially in the central region where the interconnection intensity values among cities are at low values, and the economic collapse is obvious. (2) The number of city pairs closely related to each other in the Chengdu urban agglomeration has decreased significantly, mainly concentrated in Chengdu and its surrounding cities, while the number of city pairs closely related to each other in the Chongqing urban agglomeration has increased, highlighting the "double core" structure led by Chengdu, and Chongqing central city, but with a weak external radiation effect.

5. Analysis of the Factors Influencing the Economic Development of the Chengdu-Chongqing Urban Agglomeration

5.1. Analysis of Impact Factor Geographic Detector Results

The economic development of the Chengdu-Chongqing urban agglomeration is affected and restricted by many factors. This paper uses per capita GDP to represent the explained variables to explore the influencing factors of economic development of Chengdu-Chongqing urban agglomeration from four aspects: production and employment, business services, education and health, and transportation. Taking into account the availability of data, select employees in urban non-private, rural employees, the total output value of the primary industry, the total output value of the secondary industry, total social fixed asset investment, total retail sales of social consumer goods, the total output value of the tertiary industry, number of ordinary primary and secondary schools, number of pupils in general primary and secondary schools, number of health institutions, number of beds in health institutions, total road mileage, road passenger turnover, and road freight turnover—a total of 14 indicators.

Using the geographic detector to detect the factors affecting the economic development of the Chengdu-Chongqing urban agglomeration from 2005 to 2020, the q-value was obtained. According to the factor detection results, the p-values of the 14 indicators have passed the 1% significance test in four time periods, indicating that the selected relevant influencing factors have a strong and significant impact on the development of the Chengdu-Chongqing urban agglomeration.

The heat map (Figure 6) shows the change of q value of different impact factors from 2005 to 2020, and the q value greater than 0.5 is marked in the figure. The intensity of the effects of different influencing factors on the economic development of the Chengdu-Chongqing urban agglomeration varies from year to year, but the q-values of the total output value of the secondary industry, total social fixed asset investment, number of beds in health institutions, and road freight turnover are all greater than 0.5 in all four years, with consistently strong explanatory ability. From 2005 to 2020, the explanatory ability of production and employment factors, business and trade service factors, and transportation factors for economic development showed a steady decline trend. Among them, urban non-private sector employees, total retail sales of social consumer goods, the total output value of the tertiary industry, and road passenger turnover in 2020 have q-values less than 0.5, and the influence is relatively weak compared with previous years. Among the factors of education and health, the explanatory ability of health level to economic development also shows a downward trend, while the level of education shows a steady increase trend, indicating that the impact of education on economic development is becoming more and more important. In 2005, the effect of business and trade services on economic development was more significant than other factors. Among them, the output value of the tertiary industry had the most significant impact, with a q-value around 0.8195. From 2010 to 2015, the effect of traffic factors on economic development exceeded other factors, which indicates that the relationship between traffic development and economic development is the linkages intensity between Chongqing Central City and the surrounding counties and districts is mostly in the range of 30 to 71. In 2010, the intensity of association between all cities decreased, with Chengdu and the central city of Chongqing as a whole being the two poles with the greatest intensity of association with their neighboring cities, with weaker interaction between cities in central and northeastern Chengdu and Chongqing, and weaker interaction between the Chongqing urban agglomeration and other cities in Sichuan province, with significant imbalances in development between regions. In 2015, the intensity of association between cities had increased to varying degrees, and a network development pattern with Chengdu and Chongqing central urban areas as the core has taken shape. However, the intensity of association between the Chengdu city cluster and the Chongqing city cluster is still weak, and the phenomenon of unbalanced regional development has not been greatly improved. By 2020, the number of cities closely related to each other in Chengdu and Chongqing will be significantly reduced, and the "double core" pattern, with Chengdu and Chongqing's central urban areas as the core, and Meishan, Deyang, and Mianyang as nodes in Sichuan, and Chongqing, with its central urban areas as the core, and Hechuan and Bishan as nodes in Chongqing, will be radiating. The intensity of association between cities in the central Chengdu-Chongqing region is weak, with the intensity of association mainly in the range of 0.01–30, showing a collapse of the economy in the central part of the country and an increase in the imbalance of development between regions.

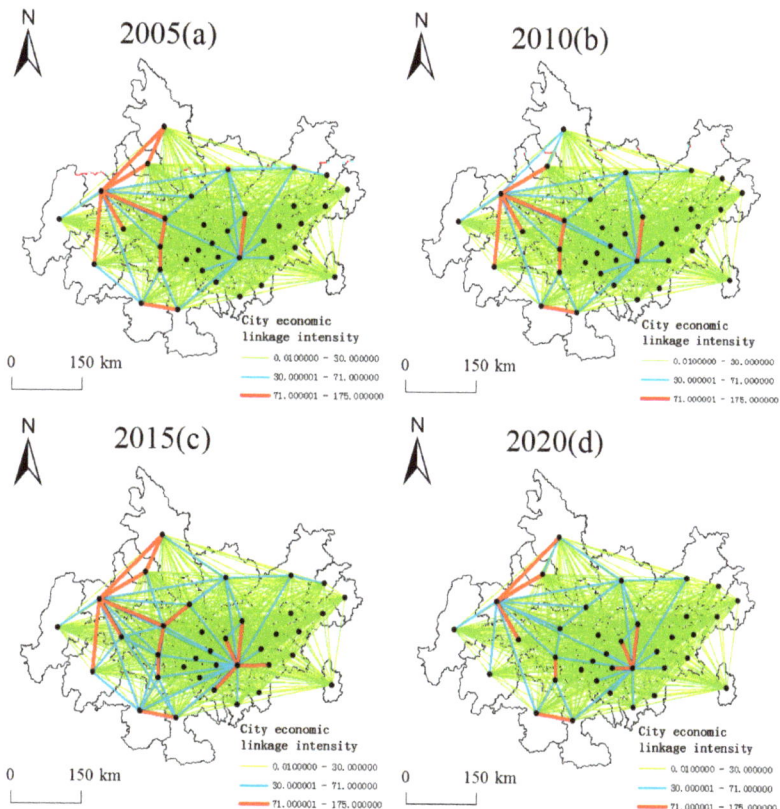

Figure 5. Economic linkages intensity of the Chengdu-Chongqing urban agglomeration in 2005 (**a**), 2010 (**b**), 2015 (**c**), and 2020 (**d**).

on the whole, the imbalance in economic development within the Chengdu-Chongqing urban agglomeration is still increasing.

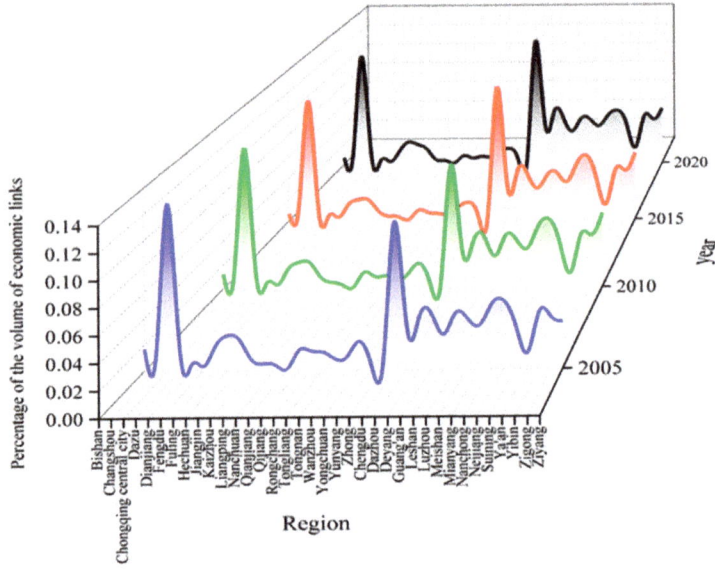

Figure 4. The percentage of the volume of economic links in each district in different years.

From 2005 to 2020, the evolution trend of the total economic connection of the Chengdu-Chongqing urban agglomeration is as follows: (1) The economic connection between Chengdu and the central urban area of Chongqing is the largest, and the spatial distribution of economic development is uneven; (2) The total economic connection of the Chongqing urban agglomeration with the central urban area of Chongqing as the core generally shows an upward trend, and the total economic connection of the Chengdu urban agglomeration with Chengdu as the core generally shows a downward trend. (3) The spatial change of the total urban economic connection. The characteristics are: From 2005 to 2020, the imbalance between Chengdu and surrounding cities intensified, and the imbalance between Chongqing and surrounding cities eased, but in general, the imbalance of regional economic development was still significant.

4.2. Analysis on the Spatial-Temporal Pattern of Linkages Intensity of Cities in Chengdu-Chongqing Urban Agglomeration

Using ArcGIS10.7 software to visualize the correlation intensity data in four time periods of 2005, 2010, 2015, and 2020, the spatial pattern map of the economic linkage of Chengdu-Chongqing urban agglomeration was obtained, and the cities' economic linkages intensity values were roughly divided into three intervals of 0.01~30, 30~71 and 71~175 according to the Natural breakpoint method, which can be combined with Figure 5. It is found that the linkages intensity of cities in the Chengdu-Chongqing urban agglomeration is weak during the period 2005–2020, and the gravitational value of each city is small, mainly concentrated in the interval of 0.01–30. In 2005, cities with high economic linkages intensity were Chengdu-Leshan, Chengdu-Meishan, Chengdu-Ziyang, Chengdu-Deyang, Chengdu-Mianyang, Deyang-Mianyang, Neijiang-Ziyang, Neijiang-Zigong, Yibin-Luzhou, and Chongqing Central City-Guang'an, with linkages intensity values in the range of 71 to 175. It can be seen that the linkages intensity between cities in the Chengdu city circle is high and dense, and several cities closer to Chengdu have relatively large gravitational values, while the economic linkages intensity between Chongqing city groups is weaker compared with that between Chengdu city groups, and

Wanzhou District, and Qianjiang District rising from a lower-value area to a higher-value area, Fuling District rising from a higher-value area to a high-value area, and Hechuan District rising from a higher-value area to a high-value area. In 2015, the overall development level of the Chengdu-Chongqing urban agglomeration declined, with low-value areas mainly in northeastern Chengdu-Chongqing, lower-value areas mainly in southwestern and central Chengdu-Chongqing, and high-value areas in central Chengdu, Chongqing and Fuling. In 2020, in the Chengdu urban agglomeration, the core position of Chengdu became more prominent, and the lower-value areas of economic development level increased significantly, mainly distributed in the northeast and central part of Chengdu and Chongqing. In the Chongqing urban agglomeration, the central urban area, Bishan District, Changshou District, Tongliang District, Rongchang District, and Fuling District are within the high-value areas. Liangping District, Dazu District, Yongchuan District, Hechuan District, and Jiangjin District are within the higher-value areas. From an overall perspective, the Chongqing urban agglomeration has a more advanced level of economic development than the Chengdu urban agglomeration. The Chengdu-Chongqing urban agglomeration still has a relatively obvious problem of economic development differences. Therefore, the cities of the Chengdu-Chongqing urban agglomeration should break down administrative barriers and deepen inter-governmental cooperation and exchanges. At the same time, it is necessary for Chengdu and Chongqing to strengthen policy exchanges in the core functional areas of the urban agglomeration to promote the economic development of the peripheral cities of the Chengdu-Chongqing urban agglomeration and the cities bordering Chengdu and Chongqing. Also, give full play to the role of a nuclear city, radiate farther, and promote the coordinated development of cities in the Chengdu-Chongqing urban agglomeration.

4. Analysis of the Intensity of Economic Linkages of Chengdu-Chongqing Urban Agglomeration

4.1. Analysis of the Linkages Volume and the Proportion of the Linkages Volume in the Chengdu-Chongqing Urban Agglomeration

Using the gravity model, the total economic linkages of cities within the Chengdu-Chongqing urban agglomeration in 2005, 2010, 2015, and 2020 were calculated.

From the economic linkages of cities in the four years (Figure 4), we can find that, during 2005–2020, the economic linkages of cities in the Chongqing urban agglomeration showed an overall trend of growth, with substantial growth in the central city of Chongqing, while the economic linkages of cities in the Chengdu urban agglomeration showed an overall trend of decline, with a larger decline in Ziyang, and smaller change in the economic linkages and the ratio of each city to the whole region. In 2005, the most closely linked cities in the Chengdu-Chongqing urban agglomeration were the Chengdu urban agglomeration, with Chengdu as its core. The cities most closely related to Chengdu were Leshan, Meishan, Ziyang, Deyang, and Mianyang, with these five cities accounting for 34.35% of the total economy, followed by the Chongqing urban agglomeration, with the central urban area of Chongqing as its core, including a total of 21 surrounding districts and counties, accounting for 28.04% of the economic ties. In 2010, the total economic linkages of the Chengdu city cluster, with Chengdu as the core, accounted for 30.39% of the region, a decrease compared to 2005, while the Chongqing city cluster accounted for 28.71%, a slight increase. In 2015, the total economic linkages accounted from the Chongqing city cluster was 32.80%, with the largest increase in economic linkages being in the central city of Chongqing, from 822.03 to 1228.67. The value of Chengdu city cluster was 30.53%, with little alteration. By 2020, the share of economic linkages between Chengdu and its neighboring cities tends to decrease, shrinking to 22.65%, leaving only Meishan, Deyang, and Mianyang as the three cities with the closest ties Chengdu. The uneven economic development within the Chengdu city cluster, with Chengdu as its core, has further intensified. The share of total economic linkages in the Chongqing city cluster has further increased, reaching 36.07%, and the unbalanced economic development within the city cluster has improved. However, the country with 834,900 undergraduates. The scientific and technological innovation ability and talent-saving capacity of the dual core cities occupy great advantages. The imbalance of regional development level is significant. Therefore, it is necessary to enhance the core driving role of polar cities, fully demonstrate the polarization effect, and achieve coordinated development.

3.2. Analysis of the Economic Development Level of Each City in the Chengdu-Chongqing Urban Agglomeration

In this paper, GDP per capita represents the economic development level of the Chengdu-Chongqing urban agglomeration and the spatial evolution characteristics of the economic development level of the Chengdu-Chongqing urban agglomeration illustrated by the changes in GDP per capita in four different years. The GDP per capita of each city/region in the Chengdu-Chongqing urban agglomeration from 2005 to 2020 is visualized in ArcGIS 10.7 using the Natural breakpoint method, as shown in Figure 3.

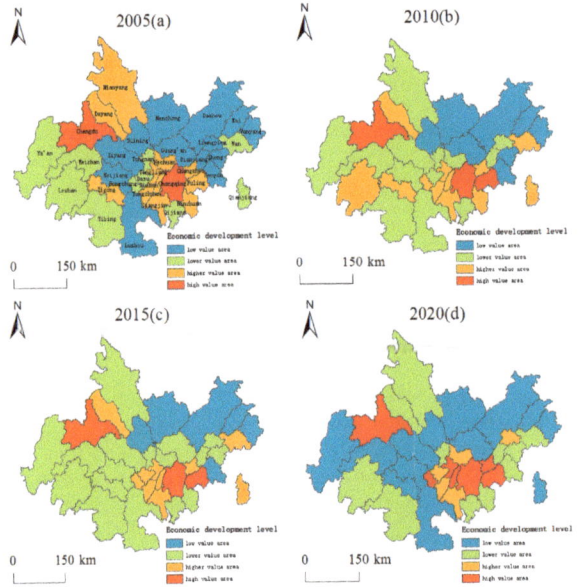

Figure 3. Spatial pattern of economic development levels in the Chengdu-Chongqing urban agglomeration in 2005 (**a**), 2010 (**b**), 2015 (**c**), and 2020 (**d**).

In 2005, among the 36 research units in the Chengdu-Chongqing urban agglomeration, the high-value areas of economic development were mainly located in the central urban areas of Chengdu and Chongqing, while the low-value areas were mainly located in the eastern part of the Chengdu urban agglomeration and the northern part of the Chongqing urban agglomeration. The economic development level of the Chongqing urban agglomeration shows a "circling" structure with the central urban area of Chongqing as the main focus, which shows that the regional development level of the Chengdu-Chongqing urban agglomeration is unbalanced, with Chengdu, Deyang, Mianyang, Zigong and the cities around the central urban area of Chongqing being relatively economically developed, while the southwest and northeast areas of Chengdu-Chongqing urban agglomeration are lagging behind and relatively economically backward. In 2010, the overall development level of the Chengdu-Chongqing urban agglomeration improved. The number of low-value areas decreased, with Mianyang City dropping from a higher-value area to a lower-value area, Leshan City rising from a lower-value area to a higher-value area, Ziyang, Neijiang, and Luzhou all rising from a low-value area to a lower-value area, Rongchang District, of Chengdu-Chongqing urban agglomeration has formed a spatial pattern with Chengdu and Chongqing as the leading cities and Nanchong as the deputy center. Therefore, it is necessary to expand basic public education and health services, co-ordinate the layout of educational and medical resources, break the boundaries between cities, and take the lead in realizing co-urbanization in Chongqing metropolitan area and Chengdu metropolitan area. The number of licensed doctors and the number of beds in health institutions in the central urban areas of Chengdu and Chongqing accounted for 38.67% and 31.11% of the entire urban agglomeration, and the number of full-time teachers in ordinary middle schools accounted for 22.84%. Both the levels of medical and health services and education and culture are much higher than other cities. Therefore, optimizing the allocation of public resources and promoting the equalization of the supply of basic public service resources are the keys to narrowing the development gap of the Chengdu-Chongqing urban agglomeration.

As can be seen from Figure 2m–p, in 2005, the high-value area of traffic centrality of the Chengdu-Chongqing urban agglomeration was distributed in Chengdu, the sub-high-value area was distributed in the central city of Chongqing and Luzhou, the higher-value area was distributed in Nanchong and Dazhou, and the overall traffic centrality of the Chengdu-Chongqing urban agglomeration was mainly in the lower-value area, while the low-value area and the sub-low-value area were mainly distributed in the Chongqing urban agglomeration. The unevenness of traffic development was remarkable. In 2020, the traffic centrality of the Chengdu-Chongqing urban agglomeration will still be dominated by sub-low-value areas, and the traffic centrality structure of Nanchong and Dazhou will also be prominent. Low-value and sub-low-value areas are still distributed around the central urban area of Chongqing. The transportation centrality of the Cheng-du-Chongqing urban agglomeration has formed a spatial pattern with Chengdu leading and the central urban area of Chongqing as the sub-center. The total road mileage in the main urban areas of Chengdu and Chongqing accounts for 22.05% of the total, with strong accessibility and significant transportation advantages. Relying on the main trunk lines of Chengdu and Chongqing, building the "backbone" supporting the development of the Chengdu-Chongqing urban agglomeration is an important measure to radiate and drive the development of cities along the line.

As can be seen from Figure 2q–t, in 2005, the high-value areas of integrated centrality of the Chengdu-Chongqing urban agglomeration were mainly located in the central cities of Chengdu and Chongqing, followed by the sub-high and higher-value areas in the Chengdu urban agglomeration, while the low-value areas, the sub-low-value areas and the lower-value areas were mainly in the Chongqing urban agglomeration, with the urban agglomeration of Chengdu being more central than the Chongqing urban agglomeration. In 2015, the integrated centrality of the Chengdu-Chongqing urban agglomeration increased, with the integrated centrality of Meishan and Suining rising from the higher- to the sub-high-values, and the lower-value areas of the Chongqing urban agglomeration decreasing. The urban agglomeration of Chongqing has decreased in the lower-value areas. By 2020, the integrated centrality of the Chengdu-Chengdu urban agglomeration decreases, with the integrated centrality of Suining, Ziyang and Meishan dropping from high-value area to a higher-value area, the integrated centrality of Yongchuan, Fuling and Kaizhou Districts dropping from a lower-value area to a sub-low-value area, and Dianjiang District county dropping from a sub-low-value area to a low-value area. The high-value areas are still distributed in the central urban areas of Chengdu and Chongqing. The comprehensive centrality of the Chengdu-Chongqing urban agglomeration is still dominated by the spatial pattern of the central urban areas of Chengdu and Chongqing. Chengdu is a vice-provincial national central city, Chongqing is a municipality directly under the Central Government of China, and the main urban area of Chongqing is the core functional area of Chongqing. The regional GDPs of the two cities are among the top 10 in the country and have strong economic strength. In terms of talent reserve, Chengdu has 879,300 undergraduate students in 2020, ranking fourth in the country. Chongqing's main urban area ranks seventh in

3.1. Analysis of the Centrality of Chengdu-Chongqing Urban Agglomeration

As can be seen from Figure 2a–d, in 2005, the production and employment centers of the Chengdu-Chongqing urban agglomeration were dominated by the central urban areas of Chengdu and Chongqing, which were within the high-value zone. The overall production and employment centrality of the Chengdu urban agglomeration was higher than that of the Chongqing urban agglomeration; most of the centrality of the cities around Chengdu was located in sub-high-value areas and high-value areas, and the distribution centered on Nanchong and Dazhou was also more prominent, ranking only second to the central urban areas of Chengdu and Chongqing, while four cities—Ya'an, Meishan, Neijiang and Zigong—are in the lower-value area. The production and employment centrality of the cities around the central city of Chongqing is mainly in the low-value area, the sub-low-value area and the lower-value area. Taking the central urban area of Chongqing as the core, it decreases in a "circle-layer" manner. By 2020, the only high-value area for production and employment will be Chengdu. The central urban area of Chongqing has dropped from a high-value area to a sub-high-value area. The lower-value areas of the Chengdu urban agglomeration increased. The imbalance of production and employment has increased. The centrality of production and employment in the Chengdu-Chongqing urban agglomeration has formed a spatial pattern dominated by Chengdu and the central urban area of the Chongqing sub-center. Chengdu mainly develops the primary industry and the secondary industry and has a comparative advantage in these two industries. Due to the high urbanization rate in the central city of Chongqing, it has a comparative advantage in the tertiary industry. Therefore, we can focus on the development of primary industries such as agriculture, forestry, animal husbandry and fishery and secondary industries such as industry in Chengdu and focus on the development of tertiary industries such as tourism and catering in Chongqing, so as to strengthen the dual core advantages of Chengdu and Chongqing.

As can be seen from Figure 2e–h, in 2005, the commercial service center of the Chengdu-Chongqing urban agglomeration was dominated by the central urban areas of Chengdu and Chongqing, which were in the high-value area. The overall commercial service center of the Chengdu urban agglomeration was higher than that of the Chongqing urban agglomeration, with more high-value areas in the south and north and mostly lower and lower-value areas in the center. By 2020, the high-value areas of trade service centrality are still dominated by the central urban areas of Chengdu and Chongqing, showing a good concentration effect of trade services; the central urban areas are dominated by lower-value areas, sub-low-value areas, as well as low-value areas; the cities in the north and south are dominated by higher-value areas; the east is mainly dominated by low-value areas; the trade service centrality of the Chengdu-Chongqing urban agglomeration has formed a pattern dominated by the twin cores of the central urban areas of Chengdu and Chongqing. Chengdu and Chongqing are both important commercial and financial centers in Southwest China and have great resource endowment advantages. In the future, it is necessary to continue to promote the development of business services, high-tech services and scientific and technological services, strengthen service capabilities, enhance the radiation force of the two core cities, and promote the common development of the Chengdu-Chongqing urban agglomeration.

As can be seen from Figure 2i–l, in 2005, high-value areas of education and health centrality in the Chengdu-Chongqing urban agglomeration were dominated by Chengdu City. The sub-high-value area was distributed in the central cities of Chongqing and Dazhou. The higher-value areas of education and health centrality were mainly distributed in the Chengdu urban agglomeration. The low-value areas, the second low-value areas, and the lower-value areas were mainly distributed in the Chongqing urban agglomeration. In 2020, the central cities of Chongqing and Chengdu are in the high-value area, but the center of the surrounding cities is still dominated by low-value areas and sub-low-value areas, and the imbalance of education and health level among regions has intensified. Nanchong City has replaced Dazhou City as the only sub-high-value area. The education and health center can clearly show the dominant areas and the differences between regions. As shown in Figure 2a–t.

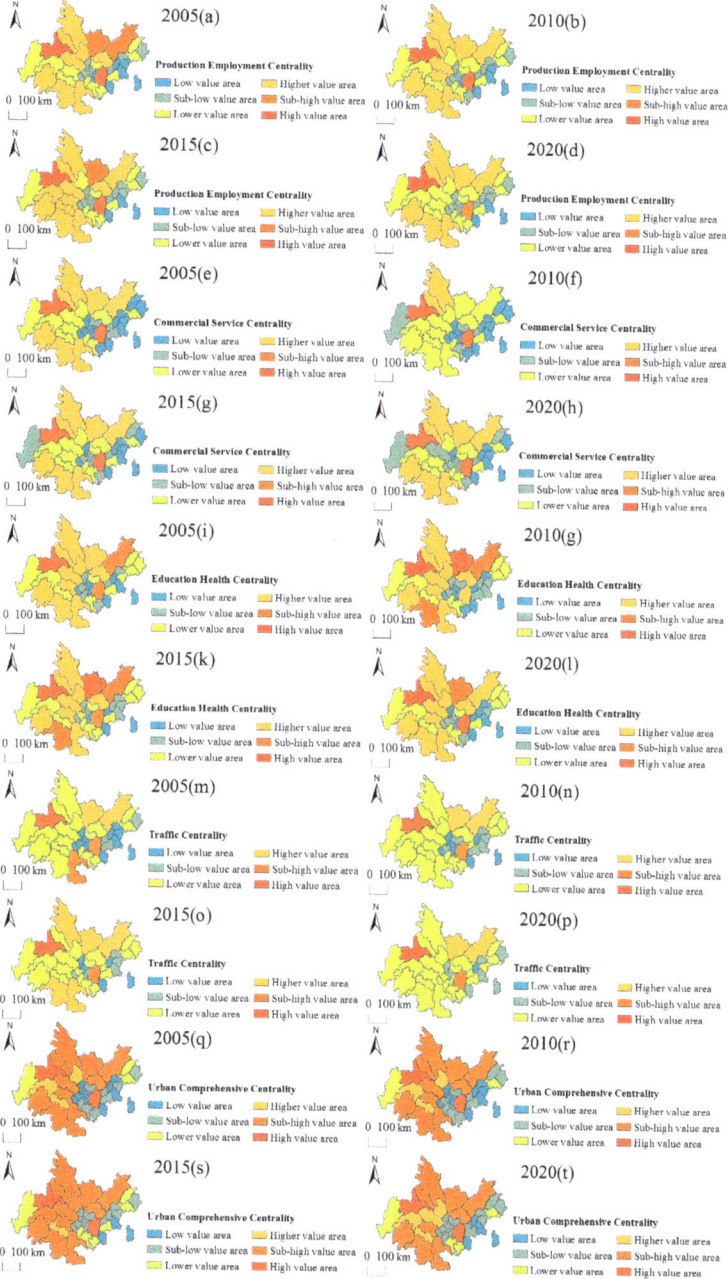

Figure 2. The centrality of the Chengdu-Chongqing urban agglomeration in different years. Pictures (**a–d**) represent the centrality of production employment, (**e–h**) represent the centrality of commercial service, (**i–l**) represent the centrality of education health, (**m–p**) represent the centrality of traffic, (**q–t**) represent the centrality of urban comprehensive.

$$w_j = \frac{g_j}{\sum g_j}. \tag{6}$$

Step 4, to calculate the index c_{ij} of the j-th indicator for the i-th city based on the weight w_j of each indicator and the standardization matrix $y = \{y_{ij}\}36 \times 14$. The formula is as follows:

$$c_{ij} = w_j \times x'_{ij}. \tag{7}$$

Step 5, to add each index to get the central comprehensive index c_i of each city, which can be expressed as:

$$c_i = \sum c_{ij}. \tag{8}$$

2.3.2. Gravitational Model

The study of applying the gravity model to the scope of urban economic influence is called the urban gravity model. The inter-city distance d_{ij} and the combined city centrality score was chosen to calculate the city correlation intensity R, which is calculated as:

$$R = p \times \frac{c_i^a \times c_j^b}{d_{ij}^r} \tag{9}$$

where R denotes the economic correlation between two cities, c_i and c_j represent the combined centrality scores of city i and city j respectively; as only one city size indicator of city centrality has been chosen, it can be assumed that $a = b = 1$. This model is mainly used to measure the gravitational force between two cities, here p is constant 1; r is the distance decay coefficient, regarding other related studies, r is taken as 2; d_{ij} represents the distance between city i and city j, where d_{ij} can be measured according to the "point distance" tool in ArcGIS.

2.3.3. Geo-Detectors

The geographic detector is a spatial statistical method to reveal the spatial differentiation of geographical elements and the driving forces. To explore the factors affecting the economic development of the Chengdu-Chongqing urban agglomeration, the factor_detector is used for analysis to clarify the statistically significant independent variables and their explanatory strength of the dependent variables, measured by q-values, calculated by the formula [25]:

$$q = 1 - \frac{\sum_{h=1}^{L} N_h \sigma_h^2}{N \sigma^2} \tag{10}$$

where $h = 1, 2, 3, \ldots, L$ is the stratification of variable Y or factor X, that is, classification or partition; N_h, N is the number of cells in stratum h and the whole region respectively; σ_h^2, σ^2 are the variances of variable Y in stratum h and the whole area respectively.

2.3.4. Geographically Weighted Regression (GWR)

GWR is a spatial regression model based on the idea of local smoothing, which can not only effectively estimate the data with spatial autocorrelation, but also reflect the spatial heterogeneity of parameters in different regions. The model formula is:

$$y(u) = \beta_0(u) + \sum_{k=1}^{p} \beta_k(u) \times x_k(u) + \varepsilon(u) \tag{11}$$

where $\beta_0(u)$ is the intercept term; $\beta_k(u)$ is the regression coefficient of the k-th covariate; $x_k(u)$ is the value of the k-th covariate at position u; p is the number of regression terms; $\varepsilon(u)$ is the random error term at position u.

3. Analysis of the Spatial Pattern of the Chengdu-Chongqing Urban Agglomeration

In the ArcGIS10.7 software, using the Natural breakpoint method, each centrality is divided into six levels, namely Low-value area, Sub-low-value area, Lower-value area, Higher-value area, Sub-high-value area, High-value area. Through map visualization, it

2.2. Selection of Indicators and Data Sources

This paper selects four time periods from 2005 to 2020 to analyze the evolution of the economic spatial pattern of the Chengdu-Chongqing urban agglomeration, explore the action intensity of factors affecting economic development and analyze the spatial heterogeneity of significant factors. The urban comprehensive central system is divided into four subsystems: production and employment, business services, education and health, and transportation. Due to the availability and accuracy of the data, the production and employment center selects urban non-private sector employees (10,000), rural employees (10,000), the total output value of primary industry (100 million yuan) and the total output value of secondary industry (100 million yuan) for calculation. The business services center selects total social fixed asset investment (100 million yuan), total retail sales of social consumer goods (100 million yuan) and the total output value of tertiary industry (100 million yuan) are selected for calculation. The number of ordinary primary and secondary schools, number of pupils in general primary and secondary schools, the number of health institutions and the number of beds in health institutions are selected by the education and health center for calculation. Total road mileage (km), road passenger turnover (10,000 km) and road freight turnover (million ton kilometers) are selected for traffic center calculation. Through these 14 evaluation indexes, the urban centrality of the Chengdu-Chongqing urban agglomeration is comprehensively evaluated.

The centrality of the four subsystems is obtained by calculating these 14 comprehensive evaluation indicators, and the urban comprehensive centrality score is obtained by summing them up. Then the urban economic correlation intensity is further calculated based on the urban comprehensive centrality score and the geographical distance between cities. The indicators in four years are from Sichuan statistical yearbook, Chongqing statistical yearbook, and Chongqing traffic Yearbook; the missing values of some index data shall be replaced by similar years.

2.3. Research Methodology

The comprehensive centrality of the city and the improved gravity model is used to calculate the strength of urban economic correlation. At the same time, combined with the geographic detector and GWR model, this paper explores the significant driving factors affecting the economic development level of the Chengdu-Chongqing urban agglomeration.

2.3.1. Network Construction Methods

Step 1, to establish the initial matrix. The research object is the 36 cities/districts and counties in the Chengdu-Chongqing urban agglomeration; each research object uniformly selects 14 indicators, the initial matrix can be set as $x = \{x_{ij}\} 36 \times 14$ ($1 \leq i \leq 36$, $1 \leq j \leq 14$), x_{ij} represents the j-th indicator of the i-th city.

Step 2, to normalize the data. The standard matrix can be set as $y = \{y_{ij}\} 36 \times 14$, with an ideal value set as x'_{ij} and y_{ij} calculated as:

$$x_{ij} = \frac{x - x_{min}}{x_{max} - x_{min}}, \tag{1}$$

$$y_{ij} = \frac{x'_{ij}}{\sum x'_{ij}}. \tag{2}$$

Step 3, to calculate the entropy value e_j, the variability index g_i and the weight w_j for each indicator, calculated by the formula:

$$e_j = -k \sum y_{ij} ln y_{ij}, \tag{3}$$

$$k = \frac{1}{lnm}, \tag{4}$$

$$g_j = 1 - e_j, \tag{5}$$

lack of studies on the Chengdu-Chongqing urban agglomeration. Secondly, most studies have mainly explored the evolution of economic spatial patterns on a spatial scale, with relatively few studies combining temporal and spatial scales, and there is a lack of analysis of the direction and effects of the drivers affecting the level of economic development. Based on this, this paper uses the modified gravity model to take the 36 cities/counties of the Chengdu-Chongqing urban agglomeration as the research object, and selects four time periods, which are 2005, 2010, 2015, and 2020. Combined with the time and spatial scale, this paper explores the evolution characteristics of the economic spatial pattern of the Chengdu-Chongqing urban agglomeration. It uses the method of geographic detector combined with the GWR model to analyze the impact direction and effect of its driving factors on economic development, to provide some suggestions for the collaborative economic development of Chengdu-Chongqing urban agglomeration.

2. Data and Methods

2.1. Overview of the Study Area

This paper takes the Chengdu-Chongqing urban agglomeration as the research object. It adopts the scope stipulated in the Chengdu-Chongqing Urban Agglomeration Development Plan jointly issued by the National Development and Reform Commission and the Ministry of Housing and Construction in 2016, with 15 prefecture-level cities in Sichuan and 21 districts and counties in Chongqing as the research objects (Figure 1). As the names of administrative units in Chongqing differ slightly between 2005 and 2020, the latest administrative unit names from the 2021 Chongqing Statistical Yearbook are used in this paper. The central urban area of Chongqing includes Yuzhong District, Dadukou District, Jiangbei District, Shapingba District, Jiulongpo District, Nan'an District, Beibei District, Yubei District, and Banan District, which are combined into one zone. Chengdu-Chongqing urban agglomeration is located in southwest China, with a total area of about 185,000 km^2, with a resident population of 100.7 million in 2020, accounting for 6.9% of the country. The regional GDP is 6.8 trillion, accounting for 6.7% of the country. It is one of the regions with the best economic foundations and the strongest economic strength intensity in the west. It has the regional advantage of connecting the east and the west and connecting the north and the south. At the same time, it has an excellent endowment of natural resources, strong comprehensive carrying capacity, strong foundation of manufacturing business, finance, and other industries, high degree of openness, rich human resources, and a good innovation and entrepreneurship environment. It is a typical region with national economic importance and strong network connection characteristics.

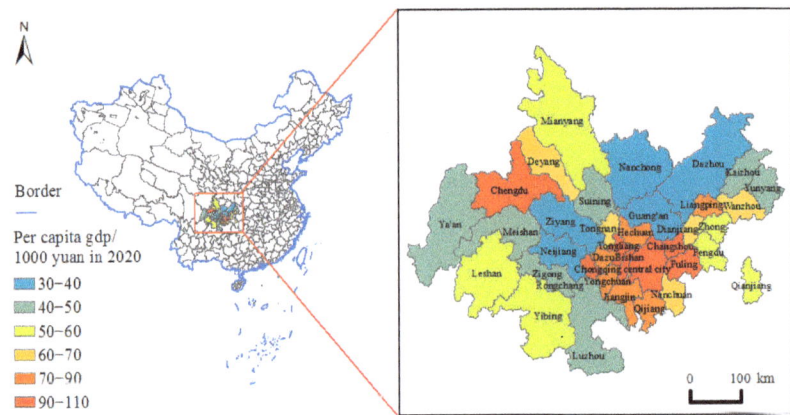

Figure 1. Research area and GDP per capita distribution.

MDPI
St. Alban-Anlage 66
4052 Basel
Switzerland
www.mdpi.com

Sustainability Editorial Office
E-mail: sustainability@mdpi.com
www.mdpi.com/journal/sustainability

Disclaimer/Publisher's Note: The statements, opinions and data contained in all publications are solely those of the individual author(s) and contributor(s) and not of MDPI and/or the editor(s). MDPI and/or the editor(s) disclaim responsibility for any injury to people or property resulting from any ideas, methods, instructions or products referred to in the content.